City of Wisdom: A Christian
Vision of the American University

City of Wisdom: A Christian Vision of the American University

David J. Hassel, S.J.

A Campion Book

Loyola University Press

Chicago   60657

DEDICATION

To the men and women

of St. Margaret Mary Parish School
(Rogers Park, Chicago)

of Loyola Academy (Chicago)

of St. Louis University

of Xavier University (Cincinnati)

of Loyola University of Chicago

whose generous lives of wisdom have made life bountiful
for so many of us, their students.

Contents

Preface

By subtitling this book *A Christian Vision*, the author wished to make it clear that other Christian visions of the university were quite possible. He had no illusory hope of producing *The* idea of a university, nor of penetrating into the very essence of university. But he did see the need to try to focus all the clichés about the university into a single vision of the university. Such a vision might well turn tired clichés into a practical wisdom. For this reason, readers of this book will not be surprised by individual sentences or paragraphs, but they may well be startled at what happens when these clichés are interrelated. Could it be that one might even reach a speculative wisdom?

The individual chapters eventually sketch a vast canvas with spare, quick strokes—strokes more suggestive than structural. But occasionally one must try to sketch the grand scene, however cursorily, in order to see the complex reality of the scene more clearly and deeply. Thus, the basic aim of this venture is to offer a common conceptual language with which university people can dialog more effectively and inventively. Even if people profoundly disagree about the accuracy of the concepts and the logic of the derived conclusions, they will know more clearly why they disagree and where the logic is weak. The hope of the writer, therefore, is that he is forming a framework for discussion. Naturally a framework must be adjustable and even finally dismantled when it has served its purpose. But setting the parameters for discussion is always the beginning of civilized understanding and cooperation by which a situation, even the university, may be bettered.

This book, since it is a sketch of the structure and activities of the Christian university, has not been footnoted. Because this essay is extensive, however, and since its author feels indebted to many people for its content, a series of end notes has been gathered at the back of the book to acknowledge debts of gratitude.

Also, at this point, I would like to express my thanks to the people who saw me through this book: to the late Vincent Horrigan, S.J., and Daniel Flaherty, S.J., Directors of Loyola University Press who never gave up

1

on me or this book; to Michael McCauley, who has painstakingly edited the book with a graciousness that is his very self; to my Jesuit community at Loyola University, who have, as always, supported me in every way during a sabbatical of eight months, and then had to endure my constant talk about this book; to William Byron, S.J., who took time off from his work, when he was President of Scranton University, to give a detailed and encouraging critique of the manuscript; to Dr. Gerald Gutek who, though he had just been appointed Dean of the School of Education at Loyola University, nevertheless took much time to give me astute advice on my project; to Robert Harvanek, S.J., the chairman of my philosophy department, who seems always willing to read and discuss whatever I write even as he tries to find time for his own writing; to John Donohue, S.J., who set aside work from his editorial desk at *America* magazine to go through this manuscript; to Walter Krolikowski, S.J., who pointed out to me many a pitfall in the manuscript and many a way to avoid them; to Mary Ellen Hayes, who added to her expert and patient typing and retyping of the manuscript many words of encouragement; to Arlene Ranalli, who flawlessly typed portions of this manuscript for emergency deadlines—and never missed one; to Joseph Appleyard, S.J., for a particularly acute and detailed critique of chapters 17 and 18, though I could not follow all his suggestions; to Dr. Julia Lane and Robert Bireley, S.J., for their artful critique and encouragement; to John Kilgallen, S.J., James Pirrie, Jerome Overbeck, S.J., and Anne Wente, R.S.C.J., for their reading and critique of a particular chapter; to all those unmentioned friends who, in their good fortune, never saw a page of the manuscript but whose friendship is my strength for whatever I attempt.

David J. Hassel, S.J.
August 15, 1982
Loyola University of Chicago

Introduction: A Christian Philosophy of the University Is Not Enough

A Bit of Personal History

The desire to write this book was first ignited at a brunch that had been arranged by a midwestern university in order to discuss with some of its leaders how faith and justice could be made more vibrant within the university. One leader, representing the viewpoint of despair, lamented that the university was so mammoth, so divided in both its knowledge-pursuits and its values, so resistant to any initiatives not generated from within the faculties, that there was no hope of ever moving the university, as a whole, to a higher quality of life. It could only happen piecemeal, according to this person, as each department developed in its own way. A second leader, representing the attitude of cynicism, noted wryly that, in his twenty-five years at the university, this was the third attempt to launch a universitywide improvement program. He predicted that this latest fever, like the previous two, would subside, but only after it had irritated the university community. Other leaders espoused positions that ranged somewhere between these two extremes in advocating a program for the university. They managed to use many of the usual clichés about university life: the need for the full perspective of Christian liberal education, the beauty of developing Christian wisdom, the duty to bring justice to the world, the blighting effect of secularism, and the call to service of the civic and ecclesial communities. All these clichés took for granted that the university, despite the pessimism and cynicism that had been voiced, did have a single vision guiding its planned future, and that this vision needed a new articulation to meet the new ideas and needs of the late twentieth century.

As I drove home from this brunch meeting, I wondered whether I should try my hand at painting such a vision to guide the university's future—if only for my own use, if only to meet, personally, the challenges of pessimism and cynicism. Why not find out whether or not the modern university is merely a scattered multiversity. As the months, and then years, went by as I formulated this single vision, I saw more and more clearly that it was only one of numerous possible Christian visions of the university. Yet someone, I thought, had to submit one such vision, no matter how flawed, in order to encourage others to produce their own visions. From the beginning, it was evident to me that I was not going to write a "mechanical manual" for an administrative retooling of a university. Nor was I intending to do a statistics-laden analysis of present behavioral patterns among American universities. Nor was I building a history of the Christian university that would yield perspective and insights into its future growth. Rather, I was attempting to sort out and to define the basic elements that constitute any and every university and then hoping to show how Christian life transformed these elements into a Christian university. I was doing this in the following ways: (1) by taking up, one by one, the basic problems facing the Christian university; (2) by gathering up the understandings of Christian university life that reflection on these problems has yielded; and (3) by correlating, painstakingly, these understandings until a Christian vision of the university began to emerge.

The resultant book is a complex sketch of an *ideal* Christian university, not a scientifically etched profile of the present American Christian university. It is a sketch because each chapter could readily be expanded into a book; it is complex because each chapter contains four or five basic principles that must be seen as connected with all the other principles discovered in the other chapters. Because it is a sketch, this book will naturally appear idealistic rather than down-to-earth. There are no concrete, detailed descriptions of problems and their provisional solutions contained in what follows; likewise, the book fails to meet the nitty-gritty objections of "university trench warfare." Because it is nevertheless complex, this book will naturally be abstract as it tries to mesh the basic principles of Christian university life out of which emerges a Christian vision of the university.

The Problematic

I am not, however, attempting a pious panegyric of the Christian university. Far from it. Instead, this Christian vision that I propose, while not meant to be a nightmare, contains quite a few disturbing insights for university people as it surveys the following, sometimes harrowing, problems.

1   Is the Western university a focal point for mirroring all the world's problems? If so, does not the university itself become an insoluble problem because of its highly complex operations, its mammoth size, and its never-ending ferment?

2 How can the university, as it rises out of its constituencies (i.e., government, church, mercantile and professional interests, students-parents-alumni), retain its autonomy and thus escape the dominance of these groups? In other words, how is the university's academic freedom achieved and kept whole?

3 How can the university escape a schizoid existence if it is both an institution of specialized knowledges-skills-arts and yet a community of wisdom that serves its various constituencies?

4 Is not a rampant pluralism fragmenting the university and the human race as the university proliferates, in a seemingly unending stream, new knowledges, skills, arts, and value systems?

5 Is ideology, with its repressive measures, the only way to achieve unity both within the pluralistic university and within its relativistic society?

6 Can strong discipline, which is needed for the orderly pursuit of truth and for community endeavors that promote justice, become a partner with unpredictable liberty, which is needed for inventive discovery and for community well-being?

7 Can philosophy, seemingly splintered by pluralism and shadowed by accusations of ideological thinking, reflect sufficient unity to the university as it seeks to reorganize its efforts and reconstitute its wisdom community?

8 Can Christian philosophy, possibly an artificial hybrid of contradiction, do more than pitch the university into warring camps with its seeming pietism and ghetto-mindedness? Or must it be dominant if the Christian university is to be Christian?

9 Is theology needed to give both a unifying purpose and a concrete destiny to any university. Is Christian theology essential to the Christian university?

10 Is the university the prime agent of secularization when it develops specialized knowledges-skills-arts and tries to integrate them for a total explanation of the world? Is this simply a secularistic *Weltanschauung?* What would "desecularization" be and do?

11 Must the vocational emphasis on a specialized major study in the undergraduate curriculum weaken the integrative core of liberal studies and rule out the freeing fun of elective courses?

12 Can the university community's radical contemplation (play) and its decisive actions (work) for the civic community be isolated from worship? What role, if any, is there for pastoral ministry within the university proper?

13 According to what models of the university (systems of ideals or values) should administrative decisions be guided? Is there a super-

    model for selecting, modifying, and hierarchizing these models in accordance with changing situations?

14   Is the university's pursuit of uniqueness merely an expensive delusion? Does the homogenization of all universities make them more useful to students, more cooperative with other universities, and more economical in their running?

15   If Christian wisdom should be the distinctive (unique) characteristic of the Christian university, what mysterious quality enables this wisdom to enter and modify each part of the university institution and community?

16   What are the odds of a Christian university remaining Christian if it fails to use Christian wisdom as its ultimate source of unity?

17   Should the Religious Founding Group (RFG) of a Christian university play the role of dominative patriarch, impartial umpire, encouraging friend; or should the RFG remove itself altogether from the university, lest it narrow the university's vision and embrace?

18   Can the RFG make a unique contribution to the university not only as a Christian university but precisely as a *university?*

19   Can the analysis of these eighteen problems and the fashioning of provisional solutions provide us with at least one example of a Christian vision for directing a university? Or are we faced with an uncontrollable behemoth, which we ride at our own risk?

    Clearly, the complexity and vast range of these problems indicate (1) that this book can be only a sketch and (2) that its usefulness is primarily that it attempts to correlate these problems and the probable principles for their solutions into a single vision centered within the Christ-life.

    But why speak of a Christian *vision*—instead of Christian philosophy and Christian theology—as the primary unifying principle of this book? The answer to this question must be blunt: Neither Christian philosophy, nor Christian theology, nor any combination of the two is adequate for describing the unity and distinctiveness of the Christian university— though they happen to be essential causes of this vision. A brief explanation of this response must be given here (and then greatly expanded in later chapters on philosophy and theology within the university). At this point, let us consider briefly (1) the reasons why Christian philosophy alone cannot sketch the constitution and dynamic operational unity of the Christian university; (2) the reasons why Christian theology is also insufficient for this task; and (3) the ways in which a Christian vision, arising out of both, is much more adequate.

The Inadequacy of Christian Philosophy

Since the term *Christian philosophy* is easily misunderstood, it would be wise to succinctly indicate what is meant by *philosophy* itself and then to quickly sketch how a relationship with Christian faith and theology will not muddle philosophy but rather will support and enrich it. It will be possible, then, to show why Christian philosophy cannot adequately explain the meaning of the Christian university.

Despite its limitations, philosophy is strategically important for evaluating the university because it alone offers both an ultimate overview and an ultimate "underview" of how knowledges-skills-arts are gained and then transmitted to others. The overview develops when philosophy studies, describes, and prescribes the ways in which various knowledges-skills-arts converge into some type of unity. The more so-called interdisciplinary courses and cooperative endeavors come into vogue, the more a philosophy of integrating them will be needed, not merely to preside over the conflicts of interest and opinion, but also to give the student a fair chance at accurate comprehension.

In addition, only philosophy deals competently with its own presuppositions and those of all other knowledges-skills-arts—including theology; this is the "underview" of gaining and transmitting knowledges-skills-arts. For no one element of this triad can, by itself without philosophy, search out its own implicit foundations. It is philosophy's peculiar competence to be able to judge the presuppositions on which the knowledges-skills-arts triad operates, and to see how the triad's findings can converge upon a single situation for unified action (e.g., the removal of pollution from the atmosphere or the improvement of the U.S. penal system).

Philosophy, however, grows in its overview and underview only if it lives closely with and feeds upon the other knowledges-skills-arts. How could it give credible criticism and support to the university process of gaining and transmitting knowledges-skills-arts unless it knows and respects deeply the psychology of learning, the sociology of knowledges-skills-arts, the methodic insights and theories of the physical sciences, the hermeneutics of secular and sacred literature, the dignity and limits of common-sense knowing, the unique generality of historical knowledge, the profundity of faith-knowledge, the creativity of skills, and the emotional imagination of the arts. Thus, the "imperial generalities" of philosophy are quite weak and rather limited without the concreteness of the social and physical sciences, the skills and the arts, common-sense knowing and theology.

Such a philosophy is named "Christian philosophy" if, by way of Christian theology, a Christian faith has challenged, supported, and enriched

7

it. The Christian revelation of a three-personed God has challenged philosophy to distinguish nature and person; the Christian revelation of a lawful universe has supported modern science and philosophy in their search for the intelligibility of the universe; and the Christian revelation of creation has enabled philosophy to enrich itself with the conception of linear history. Nor does this turn Christian philosophy into philosophical theology, since Christian philosophy retains its autonomous method of using only rational-sensible evidence for drawing its conclusions. Yet Christian philosophy is more than merely compatible with the basic Christian tenets; it is at home in Christian living. Nevertheless, without its autonomous structure, without its clear distinctness from theology and faith, it could not do its job of providing an overview and an underview of the other knowledges-skills-arts that are developing in the university. Indeed, both philosophy and theology, like mutually compatible and respectful marriage partners, can grow in distinct autonomy precisely by challenging, supporting, and leading each other more deeply into understanding mankind, the world, and God.

What, then, are the reasons why a strong Christian philosophy, in union with a Christian theology and with the university's knowledges-skills-arts, cannot be a sufficient guide for unifying the university? The first basic reason is that Christian philosophy, like any philosophy, is, of its nature, pluralistic. It is always exploring various ways of arriving at an ultimate explanation of the universe, e.g., by Malebranche's God who alone is capable of causation, by Spinoza's solitary divine substance, by Hume's passive stream of sensations, by Kant's projective human consciousness, by Hegel's universal dialectic beyond even contradiction, or by Whitehead's processing actual entities. Furthermore, each one of these philosophical explorations is offered as the *best* way to understand the universe, for each of these philosophers has seen his own philosophy as a single basic pattern arising out of the universe he has experienced. So, philosophy, taken as the various systematic efforts of philosophers to understand the universe, is plural; but philosophy, taken by any individual philosopher to mean the most adequate way to explain the universe, becomes single. This natural ambivalence of philosophy renders it less likely to provide a unified understanding of the university.

Philosophy suffers a second deficiency in attempting to provide a unified understanding of the university, which can be explained as follows: Although its power and competency is to include in its embrace the whole universe according to the universe's deepest (ultimate) principles, still its embrace of these concrete principles is only by way of intricately abstract concepts. For example, essence, existence, conditions of causality, providence and chance, qualitative change, calibration of nonqualita-

8

tive results by quantitative measurement, and so on, are concrete realities arrived at by existential judgments. But who can explain them without intricate conceptual analysis of direct experiences that, in this analysis, are found to be highly complex? As a result, philosophy can delineate deep realities and far-sighted goals, such as justice, civic peace, and a free community, but the concrete steps, the day-to-day procedures toward these goals are laid out by some other discipline (with the guidance, be it granted, of philosophic concepts and judgments). Here, again, philosophy is helpful to university planning but not sufficiently so.

A third deficiency arises, paradoxically, out of the strength of philosophy—its rationalist, systematic view of reality. This thoroughly systematic view makes it very difficult for philosophy to deal with the surds of life, such as physical evil, the misuses of human freedom, and chance events. Indeed, its rational approach renders it ill at ease with the role of love in the universe, e.g., God's providence, his cooperation in human freedom, and his infinite being. Moreover, natural mysteries such as heroism, the unity of the universe, human destiny and origin, the radical novelty of new beings, and the future of community amid atomic warfare make philosophy sharply aware of its limitations. Because the rational method of philosophy is simply not equipped to deal with mystery, other than to recognize it, it finds itself inadequate to the needs of university life, which cannot avoid these surds and mysteries of life. Thus, a dominant Christian philosophy, like any other philosophic system, is too narrow to span a university and too general to suggest specific university structures and operations. For even a particular Christian philosophy, dominant within a particular university, is simply one among a number of other Christian philosophies. It, too, is pluralistic, abstract, heavily rational, and unable to deal with the mysteries with which it may well be compatible. This is true, even though any Christian vision of the university will be dependent on a Christian philosophy for its clarity, wide scope, and intimacy with all other modes of knowledge-skills-arts in the university.

Christian Theology Is Not Enough

How is it that Christian theology, even in league with Christian philosophy, must be supplemented by something called "Christian vision"? Is it not true that Christian theology is the most concrete of knowledges in that it focuses itself totally on one historical person, Jesus of Nazareth, the Risen Christ? Are not Christ's applications of his teachings embarrassingly concrete for all Christians—for example, the final judgment scene in Matthew 25, with Christ's powerful reminder that whatever we do to the least of our brothers and sisters (the sick, the imprisoned, the hungry, the homeless, and so on) we do to Him? This would seem to take care of the charge that Christian philosophy is inadequate because it it too general. And yet, the theologian must admit that, even though Christ's applications are concrete, still the translation of His principles into twentieth-century situations depends on very complicated moral theology. For theology must work, under faith, by focusing philosophical ethics upon revelation. This is difficult enough in itself, but theologians must also discover the source of their philosophic ethics as they use the latest discoveries in the social and life sciences, in art and in history. Again, like philosophy, theology can certainly give guidance to the university as it takes concrete steps towards its concrete goals; but, like philosophy, it needs the help of other disciplines to lay the steps. Theology, alas, is very general and complicated exactly where the university needs simple and concrete understandings.

There is a second deficiency that Christian theology cannot escape, even though it is linked with a Christian philosophy: the dominant theology of any university is still only one theology despite its constant challenge by other theologies that are represented in the theology faculty and in the sponsoring group. This theology, because its systematized understandings have been influenced by a particular dominant Christian philosophy, naturally renders its practitioners less open to some areas of insight.

A third deficiency is endemic to theology. Like Christian philosophy, which deals rather vaguely with day-to-day means of pursuing its clearly conceived ultimates, Christian theology finds it difficult to make its grasp of life's mysteries relevant to the day-to-day operations of a university. It can be quite clear about what constitutes an injustice to a wage-earner or what is destructive of peace in the university or what is the essential value of teaching spiritual values to students; likewise, it is quite vocal about negative practices. But when it comes to giving positive guidance on the precise steps needed to ensure the just wage, to restore peace among warring faculty members, to construct and implement a program for teaching spiritual values throughout the university system, it is quite rightly more quiet. Theology does not have the competence to offer more than guidance to those who must build the specific programs that produce just wages, faculty peace, and effective teaching of spiritual values.

The Something More that Is Needed: Christian Vision

From the deficiencies noted in Christian philosophy and Christian theology, one can begin to construct what a concrete realistic Christian vision must be. It will be *Christian* insofar as it is guided by the principles of Christian philosophy and theology and implemented by men and women whose lives are infused with Christian charity. It will be a *realistic* vision insofar as it tries to see these principles operating within the current resources of the university and according to the present needs and realistic hopes of the people served by the university. It will be a *vision* insofar as it is not satisfied with the *status quo* but is stretching out to a better future for the university and for the people served by the university. It will be a *concrete* vision insofar as it draws upon literature, history, skills, the fine arts, and all the sciences. Admittedly, this is a rather vague sketch of what this vision is. To illustrate somewhat more concretely what is meant, let us consider briefly the grand vision of Teilhard de Chardin.

When, in *The Phenomenon of Man*, Teilhard popularized his total vision of the world's advance under Christ's leadership, he spoke to the minds and hearts of thousands and thousands of people. Yet he displeased philosophers because he failed to establish his principles with sufficient analysis of method and of concepts (e.g., his theory of matter). Scientists were angry because he suffused their principles of explanation with what they viewed as unwarranted additions and extended these principles against present evidence (e.g., the principle of orthogenesis). Theologians were aghast at his failure to give sin and evil sufficient attention. The criticism most bitter to Teilhard, however, was the charge that his vision was simply a Catholic dogmatist's ideology cleverly disguised in pseudo-philosophic and pseudo-scientific terminology.

These criticisms came despite the fact that, in *The Phenomenon of Man*, Teilhard explicitly disclaimed any attempt to do philosophy or to create a theology or to sketch new scientific hypotheses. He did want to give his vision of the universe—a vision that arose out of the convergence of paleontology, anthropology, philosophy, theology, biology, and art. This convergence, however, had not yet occurred except in Teilhard's own mental vision of the future. To talk about this converging future, he had to use the vocabulary and concepts offered by all these disciplines so that he could construct a recognizable bridge of understanding into the future. But because the future is different from the present, the concepts Teilhard employed had to be adapted to the future (e.g., "radial energy" and "tangential energy"), and new terms and concepts had to be invented (e.g., the "Omega-point," "noösphere," and "planetization"). If this vision is to exist, it must simultaneously live off of the present and yet modify the present so that it can express a possible future. Clearly, the modification of the present in terms of the future is done according to a single purpose, e.g., in Teilhard's work, the purpose is to show how the whole universe is evolving toward more beautiful living through the incarnate Christ's personal lure and the effective power of resurrected life.

In bringing together "all knowledge," as it were, in focusing all this according to a single theme, in making this theme as concrete as possible so that it could be "seen," Teilhard was bound to both offend the experts and charm the inexpert. Yet could he have done otherwise if he was to give a single vision, and if this vision was to concern palpably concrete matters? There are two other alternatives: (1) never to offer a vision since no scientist, no philosopher, no theologian—precisely as experts—could fully accept the vision; or (2) to offer a vision so abstract or fanciful that no one could deny it since no one could know exactly what its nebulous generalities mean (e.g., the writings of Kahlil Gibran).

Is is possible that the vision is a working hypothesis that every practical person necessarily uses, whether this person is a novelist writing out of a sketched plot, a housewife planning a budget, an architect working toward blueprints, a chemist developing an experiment to confirm an hypothesis, a philosopher attempting to challenge a newly developing philosophy, a theologian trying to integrate a new problem into his or her perspective, or a university president looking toward the reorganization of his or her university?

Could this rationale for Teilhard's grand vision of the universe be narrowed to the lesser vision of the university? Like Teilhard's vision, a Christian vision of the university will emerge out of Christian philosophy and theology, in accordance with the findings of the sciences, arts, and history. It will attempt, however, to fill, at least partially, the already cited deficiencies in concreteness and in breadth of view. Thus, a Christian vision of the university will attempt to embrace more than one theology or one Christian philosophy (much as Teilhard's vision has been claimed by both substance philosophers and process philosophers, by both liberal theologians and conservative theologians). Its concreteness will be such that it can accommodate both the current resources of the university and the present needs of the people it serves, and yet be elastic enough to stretch into the future by anticipating the future resources of the university to meet the newly developing needs of the community it serves. Finally, its depth will be such that, like myth, it can embrace mystery.

This vision of the university must be able to lure the whole university into the future with practical effectiveness. To accomplish this, the vision must offer room for experimentation and for the inventive planning of new options. At the same time, it must be able to inspire the university community to make the sacrifices that are necessary for a better future. Such self-sacrificing loyalty, once generated, provides the will to discover and to accept the opportunities and dangers uncovered by a five-year plan or ten-year plan for university development. The vision is, thus, not merely a brilliantly intelligent outlook, but truly a *possible dream* that arouses the emotions to give strength for the long haul.

This vision will shatter into bits, however, if it is not held together by a singleness of purpose that is painstakingly defined by the leaders of the university community. But, first, this singleness of purpose must arise from within the community and enter into its vision if and when all feel a sense of the university's unique vocation to serve its civic communities. Thus, the university's vocation is found and developed out of the many authorities that vouch for the university—the government chartering the university, the administration directing the university's service, the community of scholars pooling and transmitting its skills-knowledges-wisdom, the community of students and parents and alumni supporting the university, and the religious group founding and nuturing the university. The singleness of purpose that arises out of the sense of the university's vocation reciprocally projects this vocation into the future. For example, it may have been that a particular urban Catholic university's vocation had previously been to fit for business management and the professions the area's immigrant Catholics of the early twentieth century; now, however, the university's vocation is to equip for American life a new wave of immigrants into U.S. culture: the blacks, the Hispanics, those in their fifties and sixties who can now, for the first time, afford an education, and those coming from the Third and Fourth Worlds. Out of this immediate past and the presently developing scene could come the singleness of purpose that not only will unify the Christian vision of the university, but also will heal the faction-wounds in the university body. On this basis, the reorganization of the university becomes possible, for the university is focusing all its academic resources on the needs of the larger communities it serves. Moreover, it does this according to a Christian vision that arises out of the university's unique historical sense of its vocation and appeals, in its singleness of purpose, to the deepest feelings, values, and convictions of its faculty, students, and administrators so that they can unite as a Christian community of service.

All that has been said in defining and clarifying what is meant by a Christian vision of the university can be "proved" only by the ensuing chapters. Do they constitute a vision? Is this vision Christian, practical, inventive, attractive, and wise? Have the problems that are examined and the solutions that are sketched eventually developed a single Christian vision? The author, of course, would answer: "Yes, but it was necessary to choose from among various solutions and emphases. Thus, the vision advanced here is only one vision among other possible visions, even though it is unified out of many solid elements and made dynamic out of the experience of some years of university life. Naturally, it will appear idealistic. What vision does not?"

Nevertheless, this particular Christian vision is offered with the hope that the careful reader may enjoy (1) a rather comprehensive picture of the main struts and dynamics in the university apparatus; (2) a grasp of the basic problems facing the university; (3) rather full definitions of the realities behind the clichés used so often in baccalaureate talks (e.g., academic freedom, Christian wisdom, secularization, and so on); (4) strong hope in the university and particularly in the Christian university; (5) the conviction that a single Christian vision is possible, despite the size and complexity of the university, and that other Christian visions should be etched.

With these hopes declared, it is time to survey the historical development of the American university so that its elegant structures, its sharp uniqueness, and its vast problems can be somewhat assessed. Only then can one begin to discover what a Christian vision of the university can offer to the already complex, vastly accomplished, and unique American university.

Part I: The University Takes Stock of Itself

1 The University: Focal Point for the World's Problems

The university is a marvelous human invention. It does not simply mirror the world's problems as do literature and drama. It ingests them, to discover why they happened, and then it promotes their solution within its own being and into the world surrounding it. The thirteenth century struggle between church and state was internalized within the medieval university and the theories for balance between the two authorities were propounded and then lived out. The university of today also invents the future when, for example, it develops cybernetics to make possible the sorting, storage, and retrieval of data that are changing one-hundred-year-old procedures of business, military ordinance, and scholarship. Such progress, of course, causes in turn many problems that the university again tries to predict, mirror, ingest, and solve. No wonder, then, that the university has its own problems as well as those of the world. How minister to other's problems without contracting them and without developing one's own problems?

One partially comprehends the importance of university problems for nonuniversity people when one looks at contemporary society. The more complex a society becomes, the more specialized are the skills needed to supply its needs. A look at the console of instruments facing an airline pilot (or the driver of a five-axle, interstate transport truck), or one glance at the computerized accounting system of a major league baseball club, convinces us of this. And, the more specialized the skills become, the more educated must be the ordinary man or woman who performs them.

Furthermore, behind these complex skills are professional knowledges far more complex than the skills they direct. The airline pilot's instrumentation is the focal point of vast knowledges called, e.g., aerodynamics, physical chemistry, meteorology, flight engineering, and applied mathematics. These knowledges in turn are subsections of even vaster knowledges existing only in the minds of communities of scholars. Since these scholars reside in universities—or work in government and industrial research centers that depend upon university publications, staff, and professors—the university is deeply influential within Western civilization and culture. On the other hand, it is only to be expected that the university's own internal problems and tensions will affect its diagnosis of, and prescription for, the world's problems.

Thus, to note how the western university originated and grew into its present structure is to see more clearly the problems causing tension within the contemporary university and the community it serves. So let us now proceed to quickly scan the history of the American university in its roots and branches, to compare the five great university models (British, French, German, Soviet, and American), and to outline the problems of the university—especially in its Christian variety. All this could give us some insight into the Christian influence on university life, even as we witness this influence fading during the last century of the American university's history and even as we note, across the world, the steadily increasing influence of governments in all five major models of the university.

A Short History of the American University

Although the idea of grouping scholars and students in one place where they can undertake an orderly pursuit of wisdom is as old as Plato's Academy and Isocrates' School, the American university of the 1980s is even more closely rooted in the medieval universities of Bologna, Paris, Oxford, and Cambridge. This is not to deny, of course, the relevance of the Eastern universities: the National University of 30,000 students during China's Han dynasty, for example, or Alexandria's Museum of the Ptolemies; or Theodosius II's Constantinople University with its thirty-one endowed chairs; or Persia's Academy of Gondeshapur with its plurality of philosophies and theologies and its faculties of medicine, law, and mathematics; or the Islamic Universities of Cordoba, Seville, and Baghdad with their vast curricula of vocational and advanced studies. Rather, these earlier centers of learning indicate how the university is a natural outgrowth—at least partially—of sophisticated civilization. Some of them, too, have indirectly influenced the American university through their influence on medieval universities. The direct line of parentage for the American university, however, issues from the British college, particularly Emmanuel College at Cambridge on whose administrative structure, curriculum, and degrees Harvard was modeled. Cambridge also furnished more of the educational leaders for Puritan Harvard, to which John Harvard, an alumnus of Emmanuel College, had left his library of 300 volumes and half his property. Oxford scholars likewise influenced Harvard, but Cambridge dons brought an atmosphere more congenial to New England Puritanism.

This was a fortunate heritage in both autonomy and curriculum that Harvard received from Cambridge—a heritage first handed on by the University of Paris. The latter had arisen out of schools that were attached to the Cathedral of Notre Dame and governed by the cathedral's chancellor. In 1208, a unifying charter had been granted to the university so that it enjoyed much autonomy through self-governance—an all-important factor that has since characterized all the great European universities. Further, Pope Gregory IX's bull *Parens scientiarum* in 1231 gave recognition to the faculties to modify the constitution of the university.

This tradition of autonomy was not lost on Oxford University, which first came into existence, it would seem, when a group of students migrated across the English channel from the University of Paris to set up shop at the town of Oxford in 1167. In 1209 a second migration, this time from Oxford to the town of Cambridge, probably gave us the early roots of Cambridge University. Both English universities based their stability on the colleges that grouped around them and on an autonomous structure that the University of Paris—with its faculties of theology, canon law, medicine, and the arts—had wrested for itself from church and state and that now served as the model for other European universities.

Harvard College inherited that model of autonomy and put it into her life-structure when, in 1650, she added to the nonresident board of overseers (appointed by the general court at Boston in 1637 with full administrative powers) a resident corporation—composed of the president, five fellows, and the treasurer—whose decisions were reviewed by the nonresident board. This bicameral form of government, protective of the university's autonomy, became the model for almost all later American universities except Yale. That autonomy was to be seriously threatened only once, in the so-called Dartmouth College case, when the New Hampshire Legislature, taking advantage of a dispute between the president of Dartmouth and its board of trustees, tried to make the institution over into a state university. Chief Justice John Marshall in 1819 upheld the charter of Dartmouth as a private college, with the result that private and denominational interests were encouraged to found within the next 20 years almost twice the number of colleges established during the previous 180 years.

The tradition of autonomy that had been received from the medieval universities was not the only heritage of the first triad (Harvard, William and Mary, and Yale) of American universities. Their curriculum was astonishingly like that of the University of Paris and was ideally suited for training clergymen. It consisted of the *trivium* of grammar, rhetoric, and logic, and the *quadrivium* of geometry, arithmetic, music, and astronomy—enriched by ethics, ancient history, Greek, and Hebrew. After

19

four years, students received a Bachelor of Arts that could then be built into a Master of Arts if they wished to study for three more years. Peter Ramus' scholastic brand of philosophy, together with the experimental methods of physics and chemistry, became available to this first triad of colleges when professors from the Scottish Universities visited them and when Dissenters who had been barred from Oxford and Cambridge by the Act of Conformity (1662) took posts on their faculties.

But a striking curricular change occurred with the second triad of American colleges (Princeton, Columbia, and Pennsylvania). In 1751, under Benjamin Franklin's influence, Pennsylvania opened the curriculum to the "mechanic profession" and "useful learning," namely, English literature, modern languages, geography, chronology, navigation, surveying, history, agricultural chemistry, mathematics, natural and applied science. This did not mean that the Philadelphians abandoned the earlier ideal of the gentleman scholar who knows the best thought of the world. Rather, they simply introduced into the more contemplative curriculum a pragmatic and vocational factor, a distinctive feature of the American college.

A second factor entered into the American scene to widen further the American college's curriculum. Out of dissatisfaction with the somewhat haphazard apprenticeship "education" given to lawyers, doctors, engineers, and theologians, professional schools began to organize separately from the colleges—even as Harvard and Yale established chairs of theology; William and Mary, Columbia, and the University of Pennsylvania set up chairs of law; and the College of Philadelphia (later the University of Pennsylvania) created a chair of medicine. Gradually, in the nineteenth century, professional schools were absorbed one by one into the colleges and universities. Judge Tapping Reeve's law school at Litchfield became part of Yale, for example, and the College of Physicians and Surgeons in New York City was affiliated to Columbia. Professional schools of theology, however, such as Union Theological of New York, remained separate. But the initial success of separately organized professional schools demanded that colleges and universities such as Yale, Harvard, and Dartmouth establish schools of science and technology. Clearly this was quite a departure from the European university of the nineteenth century, outside whose walls most of the significant scientific research was being done by Faraday, Helmholtz, Joule, Darwin, Lister, Wundt, Pasteur, and Koch because the European university's curriculum remained fundamentally nontechnical and nonprofessional.

Developments such as these naturally brought the American college to a much more secular intent than it had at its beginnings. The first triad of colleges (Harvard, Yale, and William and Mary) had enjoyed not only a common language and origin, a similar New England milieu, and identical civil constitutions, but also a vigorous religious affiliation. Their twin aims of advancing learning and of training clergymen were quite attainable, for their curriculum had always offered more than mere divinity studies lest their clergymen be narrow-minded or their lay students receive an education impractical for the "business" of life.

The second triad of colleges (Princeton, Columbia, and Pennsylvania) enjoyed little of this unity. Their clientele had many diverse ethnic origins, religious affiliations, and geographical regions. Consequently, the second triad could not have the same close religious ties with a particular denomination; indeed, Kings College-Columbia had a board of trustees that was totally civil, although the majority of the board professed the Anglican faith. Nor could this triad be satisfied with a narrower curriculum emphasizing divinity studies since their faculty and student body were so much more diverse.

The third triad of American colleges (Brown, with its charter of religious freedom for all denominations but a requirement of Baptist affiliation for its president and for twenty-two of its thirty-six trustees; Rutgers, with its turbulent early history of conflict between conservatives and progressives in the Dutch Reformed Church; Dartmouth College, with its totally nonsectarian nature) pointed to the impossibility of maintaining strictly denominational auspices. And the secular aspect of these colleges was continually expanded through a growing concern for the practical, through the alluring rationalist approach of the enlightenment, and through the needs of the merchant classes. This trend is dramatically exemplified by the University of Virginia where, in 1779, under Thomas Jefferson's leadership, the trustees reorganized the school with chairs in medicine, mathematics, physics, moral philosophy, economics, law, and politics, while at the same time abolishing the chair of divinity as incompatible with the Republic's freedom. And again, although 70 percent of Harvard's early graduating classes were clergymen, by 1810 only 10 percent were so destined. What the founders of Yale University once had feared for Harvard now was fact: secular studies were dominant.

Another important thrust toward the secular occurred when the ideal of the German graduate school became incarnate at Johns Hopkins (1867), Clark (1887), and Catholic (1889) universities. These three colleges were founded to be graduate schools and to do only research for the advancement of learning. Already established colleges were likewise developing graduate schools based on the German model and granting doctoral research degrees: e.g., Yale (as early as 1861), Columbia, Harvard, Michigan, Wisconsin, Minnesota, and California. Thus, the American university came into existence for the first time as an unique amalgam of the British college and the German university, the latter, in its primary research-orientation, being an ideal embodiment of the national mind.

Even universities founded solely as graduate schools eventually developed undergraduate colleges because of the long tradition of college liberal arts, because of the need to educate undergraduates for graduate studies, and because of the sheer financial necessity of supporting expensive graduate schools. Moreover, the incorporation of professional schools of law, medicine, and divinity stimulated the parallel development of both graduate and undergraduate schools; while the schools of engineering, forestry, music, agriculture, and, later, social work ran parallel to the rich expansion of the undergraduate curriculum. Clearly, emphasis on the secular was a natural result of such rapid and diversified growth on both the undergraduate and graduate levels amid such widely differing religious communities.

This accelerating expansion of the American university in size and diversity could, however, also be interpreted as its fragmentation. Had the university not become, more quickly than it knew or planned, a multiversity? Daring as the maneuvers were, it was not entirely surprising that in the latter part of the nineteenth century Harvard's President Eliot introduced the elective system of courses into his university, nor that the University of Michigan adopted the credit-point system for degree achievement. For it was no longer clear just what the educated man should know, or how the liberal arts program could be integrated with preparation for the professional school, or what were the rights of the student to choose his own education. To balance this cafeteria-style education, the practice of majoring in a specific knowledge area during the undergraduate years became necessary. The German university's *Lernfreiheit* (freedom of the student to choose his or her own program) and *Lehrfreiheit* (freedom of the professor to develop a subject in his or her own way and to pursue research with this in mind) were being as neatly balanced as the late nineteenth-century American academic mind could do. Thomas Jefferson's spirit was walking delightedly through the fields of academe.

The democratization of the curriculum was not without parallel in other aspects of the university: in the opening of the university to other than the monied classes, for example, or in the support of private as well as state institutions, in the education of women alongside men, in the almost universal requirement of the high school, in the invention of the two-year junior college, and in the admission of a need to provide continuing education for all those requesting it. But in 1850 all these future events would have seemed the mere dreams of ideologists far removed from the real world of America.

Nevertheless, the Land-Grant College Act of 1862 sponsored by Justin S. Morrill did much to fund this democratization of higher education. The Act granted each state 30,000 acres of land per Senator and Representative in Congress, in order to support at least one college whose principal goal was to offer courses in "agriculture" and the "mechanic arts"—along with "other scientific and classical studies" and military training. In "founding" these A & M colleges, some states simply broadened the program of already existing public colleges (e. g., Georgia, Minnesota, Wisconsin); others apportioned money to private institutions (e.g., Cornell, which operates the New York State College of Agriculture and its Veterinary College); still others set up a new college (e.g., University of Massachusetts) and gave other funds to a private university (Massachusetts Institute of Technology). On the other hand, A & M colleges as such were separately established in twenty-seven states. In any case, after some initial mistakes, a number of long-lasting effects were introduced into American higher education: (1) academic recognition was given to disciplines hitherto isolated in separate professional schools (e. g., journalism, home economics, veterinary science, agricultural science); (2) farmers and industrial workers could now afford to send their children to college, once the privilege of only the wealthy; (3) schools of education, or so-called normal schools, were given a place within the university system; and (4) in seventeen southern states separate land-grant colleges were established for blacks (e.g., Dover, Tallahassee, and Petersburg).

By 1900 the land-grant colleges were beginning to expand their enrollments and by 1940 they were viewed as necessities, despite their initial difficulties: e. g., dilatory state legislatures suspicious of federal interference, ill-defined programs, teachers of the classics sometimes pressed into agricultural science, the contempt of many farmers for formal learning of farming, and the matriculation of poorly schooled rural students. No matter how weak their early practical influence was, the land-grant colleges did establish a mighty principle of American education: the university should be a service agency for the whole community. Ezra Cornell described the American university well, in its democratization of curriculum and of student opportunity, as "an institution where any person can find instruction in any study." Where else but in wealthy and generous America could such a principle be more than an ideological fancy?

Thus, public universities eventually changed the collegiate scene from one of selectivity to one of mass education. The strongest of these, of course, were the state universities, which took as their organizational model the pioneer University of Virginia. According to Thomas Jefferson's plans in 1819, this university would try to lay out a rich variety of courses and yet allow for specialized interests; it would be publicly controlled by a board of visitors named by the governor and appointed by the legislature; it would sponsor no school of theology since it was non-denominational; it would be supported principally by the State of Virginia but, through the reinforcing Morrill Act of 1890, would be eligible to receive sizeable federal appropriations. Later, state schools like the University of Michigan would become mammoth in size, international in reputation, and influential in specific areas of competence.

Strange to say, however, it would be private colleges and universities that would protect the state universities from undue government control. The early private institutions such as Harvard, Yale, William and Mary, Princeton, Brown, Rutgers, and Dartmouth had accepted some public funding but had nevertheless resisted any encroachments on academic freedom. Dartmouth, in a precedent-setting decision of Chief Justice Marshall noted earlier, successfully resisted a takeover by New Hampshire's Governor Plummer. And because most early American colleges were denominational in origin, they strongly resisted any state restrictions that might eventually render them nonsectarian and violate their original founders' purpose. A pattern of freedom was reinforced when the Johns Hopkins University arose out of the private endowments of Cornelius Vanderbilt and John Hopkins, Stanford University out of the estate of Leland Stanford, and the University of Chicago out of the fortune of John D. Rockefeller, Sr. These prestigious graduate schools, with their financial independence, could set high standards of university achievement and attain strong autonomy even while accepting some public funds. Thus, the state schools (e.g., California, Michigan, Wisconsin, Minnesota) could point to the American tradition of autonomous universities and protect their freedoms from undue restraint at the very time that they were becoming heavily dependent on state and federal monies for their expansion to university status. As a result, by 1900 twenty-six American universities had been founded in freedom from undue restriction.

The public universities, together with some of the newer private universities (e.g., those pioneers of coeducation, Oberlin [1833] and Antioch [1853] Colleges in Ohio), again took the lead in democratization of American education when they more easily accepted women alongside men into their programs. Beyond the Mississippi, every state university except Missouri was coeducational from its first beginnings. It was not until 1900, however, that the majority of graduate schools welcomed women. Opposition to coeducation came not merely from traditional public opinion but, perhaps not altogether unexpectedly, from separate independent women's colleges such as Mount Holyoke, Smith, Wellesley, Vassar, and Bryn Mawr, as well as from the nine men's colleges founded in colonial times. The latter preferred the coordinate women's college: e.g., Radcliffe for Harvard, Barnard for Columbia. In the acceptance of coeducation, Catholic institutions, at every level, lagged behind. True, Catholic men's colleges and universities were often reluctant to accept women lest nearby Catholic women's colleges be depopulated, but there was also operative an implicit philosophy of separatism. By 1960, however, the majority of Catholic schools admitted both men and women into graduate departments and had become coeducational—even though in 1964 the greater number of colleges exclusively for women were still under Catholic direction. In the 1970s, an unprecedented upsurge of women enrolled in colleges and graduate schools—particularly in the professions—that surprised the whole world and not merely the United States. In the U.S.S.R., for example, between 1960 and 1970 the proportion of women in both full-time and part-time higher education increased from 40 percent to 50 percent; indeed, in some nonscientific institutions it rose to 80 percent.

Another important factor in the democratizing of education for both men and women has been the spread of high school education to all classes of society—with sometimes paradoxical results. In 1827, the Massachusetts legislature demanded that all towns of 500 families provide public education not only in reading, writing, and arithmetic but also in American history, algebra, geometry, and bookkeeping; and that all towns of 4,000 furnish courses in history, logic, rhetoric, Latin, and Greek. Admittedly, public apathy greeted this legislation; nevertheless, it set the tone for the future and in the 1870s, the Michigan Supreme Court found for the city of Kalamazoo in declaring that the high school is an essential part of the state's public instruction. From that point on, the rapidly expanding enrollment of American high schools was little short of shocking. By 1900, 500,000 elementary school pupils went on to high school each year and some 75 percent of them entered college.

Naturally, American higher education would again be significantly affected by this democratization of pre-college education. So long as the college drew its students solely from the Latin academies or prep schools, and so long as the high schools were considered terminal in their training for life-situations (hence the courses in home nursing, home economics, cookery, carpentry, plumbing, and so on), the universities did not have to worry about entrance examinations. It was only in the 1870s that colleges and universities began to have to confront the highly utilitarian high schools with an inspection of their curricula (later to evolve into accrediting agencies), with standard regional examinations, and finally with national college board examinations. Clearly, high school democratization of curriculum and of student body was another factor pushing the universities to modify themselves from selective to mass education. Then, too, they had to struggle once again, at a different level from that of the professional schools, with the problem of vocational versus liberal education.

The successful proliferation of high schools in turn led naturally into the one distinctive educational feature invented in the twentieth century: the junior (or community) college, supposedly an extension of the high school conceived by William Rainey Harper, first President of the University of Chicago. Actually, the community college has evolved, with its very broad curriculum, into a dual schooling. One is terminal and imparts skills to chefs, automobile mechanics, carpenters, and so on; the other is strictly collegiate and enables students to complete their schooling later at a four-year college.

One wonders whether the community college is based on the assumption that every American should have the opportunity for at least two years of college. Since these tax-supported community colleges now provide "continuing education" across a broad spectrum of citizens, from eighteen-year-olds to sixty-year-olds and from housewives to business executives, democratization has taken a further step. Americans are now faced with the fact that an ever more complex education is being given for a longer time to ever more students at a rapidly escalating expense. Yet this seems to be necessary. For skills and knowledges become swiftly obsolescent in today's world, and to neglect their refurbishment is to neglect the economic and cultural future of the United States. Democratization of education would seem to be a worldwide wave of the future, an inevitable accompaniment of growth.

Five Great University Models

To sharpen the outline of the American university, it may be helpful to briefly compare it with French, British, German, and Russian universities, and then to see how these models are used to plan new universities in the Third World. Note has already been taken of the democratization of curriculum and of student-opportunity within American higher education; mass education now overshadows selective development. A second American characteristic is the reciprocity achieved between private and public education. This assures the autonomy of both structures, even though at times administrators of public institutions, in their scramble for tax-produced funds, seem to deprecate the contribution of private institutions. But the federal government assists (albeit unevenly) both types, through the states and through allotments to the individual student. Furthermore, the seemingly growing assumption in the United States that

26

the universal right to education should expand to include the community-college level seems correlative with a second assumption that the university should be a service agency for the whole community—not merely in the classroom, but in the business market, in judicial and legislative chambers, and in the arenas of social problems. Surely, as a result, the Board of Trustees for each autonomous American university carries back-breaking responsibilities. And those same trustees must also adjudicate the balance of liberal and vocational/professional elements in the university and determine how secular education allows emphasis of definite life-values. All these characteristics of American higher education offer points of contrast with the other four university models.

The French university system, for example, had been highly central-ized (though, since 1968, it is being diffused) around the University of Paris according to a Napoleonic pattern. All France and its overseas pos-sessions are geographically divided into *académies*, each of which is com-posed of three to eight *départements*. The centralization becomes clear when one finds that the academic head of each *académie* (a total educa-tional system) is also the rector of its major university and the representa-tive of the central Ministry of National Education, an appointee of the president of France. Within each faculty (law, science, letters, medicine, and pharmacy), the dean, appointed for three years at the recom-mendation of the faculty and the university council, is responsible for finances and administration. Thus, university teachers are unburdened of self-governing administration.

France's higher education is open and free to any student who has passed the *baccalauréat* examination given at the end of secondary studies. The first year of higher studies ends with a single examination, on the basis of which 30 to 40 percent of those who take the examination are selected for further studies; the rest undertake another year of study and eventually receive a certificate or diploma. Outside the universities, *grandes écoles* give advanced professional and technological training to *baccalauréat* holders selected by competitive examination (for which stu-dents may prepare for as long as two years). French universities also have a strong regional cast, because only limited state financial aid is given to students and they must therefore remain close to home. Finally, unlike the American model, French normal schools, or teachers colleges, are not considered to be part of higher education.

In almost direct contrast to the French system, each German princi-pality orginally aimed at strong government control of its local university. As a result, at the time of the unification of these German states no single center of power controlled the whole university system. Still, the univer-sity was considered to embody the national mind—especially through its research orientation. Although the local government exercises tight control over the university by permanently appointing the *Kurator* as head of the university's administration and finances, the university senate (composed of professors and of representatives from both staff and students) is still the main instigator of policy through its annually elected *Rektor* who is also the curricular and faculty chairman. The method of recruiting most university teachers from among the large number of assistants surrounding patron-professors, who recommend them for study beyond the first degree of doctorate, assures a great deal of mobility among these teachers that is matched by that of the students, who attend multiple universities in search of the best teachers. Consequently, there is remarkable freedom in the student's plan of study, in the organization of postgraduate courses, and in the style of awarding degrees. Unlike France, this mobility naturally requires complex student housing arrangements which must and do provide a large amount of social and cultural activity.

Despite the fact that English universities receive as much as 90 percent of their funding from the state, they nevertheless answer to no ministry, unlike the French and German universities, seat no government officials on their authoritative councils, and are free to recruit their own staff. Two reasons for this are the heavy endowments received from private individuals and corporations and the private founding of every university (until 1969 and the Open University). The premier universities of Oxford and Cambridge are simply federations of autonomous colleges, each governed by a group of fellows who, being involved in teaching and research and often living at the college, are elected for life. In the other universities of England, a senate, composed only of academic people and headed by a vice-chancellor, makes all the academic decisions. It is complemented by a council made up of academic representatives and lay representatives of local and regional interests. This council appoints the vice-chancellor for life, controls financial matters, makes decisions about issues where university policy affects regional and national interests, and routinely approves the academic decisions of the senate.

The strong autonomy of the English university is matched by its rigorous selection of students and its deeply influential tutorial system. Though the procedures for entrance to the university have been simplified by a central admissions bureau, the General Certificate of Education (received at the end of secondary studies) must still indicate a minimum of two "advanced passes" and three ordinary "passes" in five separate subjects if the student is even to be considered for entrance. If accepted, the student undergoes very close individual supervision by his tutor. As a result, most English undergraduates complete their first higher degree in three years, have already achieved a marked specialization of interest and competence, have been tested by "external examiners" from other colleges (to assure some uniform quality), and have been socialized in residences where "home qualities" are emphasized by resident scholars, common rooms, dining halls, and unifying athletic and social activities. And all this is supported extensively by public funds.

Into this atmosphere, colleges of education have been integrated as constituents within Institutes of Education administered by the universities. Technical colleges funded under the Fisher Act of 1918 were not so readily integrated into the university system. They have four levels of competence: local, area, regional, and colleges of advanced technology. The latter have the right to issue a graduate degree, the Diploma of Technology. Britain's new civic universities (e.g., London, Manchester, Birmingham) challenged the dominance of Oxford and Cambridge precisely by their excellence in technological studies, which then became matched by an equivalent quality of education in the fine and liberal arts. Now a new type of technical college, the polytechnic, offers mainly university-level technological courses along with general arts and sciences. The fact that student numbers at British universities rose from 50,000 in 1938 to 300,000 by 1970 has not made the solution to educational problems easier.

In contrast to the early autonomous rise of the four other university models mentioned so far, no Russian university came into being until the Empress Elizabeth founded the University of Moscow in 1755. Within the next fifty years, though, there followed the universities of Wilno, Kharkov, Karan, and St. Petersburg. All of them were creatures of the state, with no medieval tradition of autonomous institutions receiving protection in order to seek truth unswervingly. Later German influences nudged the Russian institutions towards the mainstream of European higher education—until the Revolution of 1917. Then the new Soviet government immediately applied its social-reconstructionist theory of education to abolish religious instruction in the interests of atheistic indoctrination, to institute total coeducation, to introduce self-government by students, to suppress all marks and examinations, to demand "productive labor" simultaneously with university study, and to create special workers' faculties for the new "intellectuals of the proletariat" at institutions of higher studies. By 1931, however, the last four goals of this new Soviet theory of education had to be reversed or greatly modified.

Fortunately, Lenin, with shrewd pragmatism, also directed a campaign against illiteracy and on behalf of widespread technical education so that there could be a foundation for the new industrial society. In accord with Marxist economic theory and with the vast needs of the U.S.S.R., a central committee for higher education (whose authority also ranged over universities) established two paramount goals: to provide specialized professional education within the limits of available manpower and of economic plans, and to keep strict control of students' programs with a heavy emphasis on evening and correspondence instruction. The success of this latter hope is attested to by the fact that 56.3 percent of students in higher education in 1970 were part-time students following broadcast, television, and correspondence courses, with academic meetings at local study centers. At the same time, they usually held full-time jobs. Significantly, they took only one year longer on the average than full-time students to complete their studies, even though they had been encouraged to work full-time for two years before starting their higher studies in order that the economic needs of Russia be clearly perceived. On the other hand, the rise of academic standards has been accompanied by a decline in the number of students from the peasant and blue-collar classes.

The strictly utilitarian essence of Soviet education becomes clear in the organization of its higher studies. Universities, except in the smaller Republics, limit themselves to the humanities and the pure sciences. Institutes—by far the largest in number—train specialists in a single field such as law, medicine, education, agriculture, technology, art, drama, economics. The "Polytekniks" work in the same areas as the institutes but group several of these fields together on a broad connecting scientific basis. During the Khrushchev reforms of 1958, an attempt was made to adapt the polyteknik approach to secondary schools, so that students could do specialized vocational work in industry and agriculture at 16 years of age and still get a general education. Yet in 1964 these reforms had to be undone, in order that secondary school pupils might get a firmer knowledge of basic subjects and develop a curiosity for further learning.

The centralization of Soviet education is unbelievably tight. All higher education is both financed and directed by the Ministry of Higher and Specialized Secondary Education, according to the formulated policies of the State Institute of Planning for Higher Education. The state gives a lifetime appointment to the rector of each institution, who is assisted by three pro-rectors working respectively in teaching, research, and administration. The rector is also chairman of the academic board composed of the pro-rectors, the deans of faculties, heads of departments, and representatives of public bodies. Most institutions of higher learning are established by the government; the rest are developed by trade unions, cooperatives, and the Communist Party. This gives the government the ability to make sudden revolutionary changes affecting the whole education apparatus. Amazingly, this Soviet system of education has managed to survive the dislocating changes of 1919, 1921, 1931, 1958, and 1964 brought about by social-reconstructionist principles: to wit, (1) by its complete control of education, the political party strives to conform society to the party's basic ideals, not vice versa; (2) in the curriculum, stress must be placed on science as theory of production, on mathematics as the language of science, and on manual work as symbol of man's cooperative growth. Clearly, two dominant factors in Soviet educational decisions are Marx's elevation of work over contemplation and his highly pragmatic use of economics as the imperial knowledge and the economic limit as the final determinant for every decision.

All these five great models of education have been exported. The French model has been used in the overseas territories of France (e.g., the University of Tunis) and in Latin America (e.g., the Federal University of Rio de Janeiro, itself a model for all future Brazilian universities). The German model was employed for the Russian University of Dorpat and the Johns Hopkins University in the U.S.A. The English model (especially in its London University form) has been dominant in all the former Dominions, such as Australia, India, Canada. The American model can be seen in the Philippines, Japan, and the American College of Beirut. The Russian model operates in countries with a Communist government but particularly in China where, since 1968, the Chinese government seems intent on repeating the mistakes of early Soviet education. What is more heartening, however, is that Third World countries now seem more ready and able to use the best elements from all five models to construct their universities: the French and British emphasis on quality scholarship, the German commitment to research, the American sense of flexibility and social consciousness, and the Russian pragmatism of part-time education and full-time work out of economic necessity. As these models are used in contrasting ways and as international education of students becomes a reality, the five major models are mutually modifying each other in a type of homogenization.

Problems Infiltrating the University Whether Christian or Secular

Given this brief history of American higher education as contrasted with four other models and noting the structures constituting the university, we can begin to formulate the problems that not only face the university but also enter into its very body. Each of these problems will receive the attention of a chapter unto itself. Because of their interlacing effects, however, each will also resurface in other chapters as an element in a new knot.

Clearly, the autonomy of the university is in jeopardy, if not lost, in the Russian model of the university. Just as clearly, this autonomy runs the danger of being used for fiscal and academic irresponsibility in the American and English models. But if each university is in fact a self-justifying being, if it has a unique and essential task to perform within the larger community, then what are the sources of its being and precisely what are the functions of its irreplaceable task? And how does one protect the university's work from the meddling of government, big business, false ideologies, and domineering groups? In other words, what is the authority of the university by which it preserves its identity and carries out its mission?

The authority of the university, indeed, has been attacked most bitterly by the charge that its proliferation of new knowledges and of novel departments of learning has rendered it, along with our contemporary culture, nearly impossible to understand and to unify. The university is said to have made modern man an unfeeling thinker, a computerized robot, a rationalist who can no longer decide for values against mere expediency. The university, in short, is accused of being the prime agent of secularization. No longer is it considered a city of wisdom or a bastion of moral strength. Rather, it is called at once a factory for opinions and a spawning place for all value systems.

This means, of course, that the university is guilty of spreading the disease called pluralism. In its inventiveness it continually offers more and more alternatives to the confused modern mind: many new knowledges and technologies, multiple theories of personality development, diverse theologies, seemingly contradictory explanations of man-society-universe, multiple political systems, and so on. Not only is the human mind fragmenting under the weight of this diversity, but the university itself is becoming impossible to unify. A chaos of opinions and theories is making the idea of a perduring wisdom laughable. The word *uni-versity* is self-contradictory. Such is the accusation.

As a result, even some university people are today beginning to think that unity can be achieved only through the use of an ideology like Marxism or a particular religious sectarianism or capitalism or liberalism-conservatism or participatory democratism. One must go beyond the scientific concepts, it is argued, beyond the present administrative apparatus, to enlist the passions so that a unity seemingly denied by a rampant pluralism can be attained. Perhaps university leadership will even have to use repressive measures in the name of an ideology in order to save the university (and the universe) from dissipation of its energies.

But would not the use of ideology in this manner attack the very meaning and being of the university? Should not the university's main

32

function be the reinterpretation of traditional knowledge for a changing world so that a fuller truth is attained? If this be the university's function, then the restrictive use of ideology would gradually paralyze this function. On the other hand, if the university is merely the producer of knowledge (or of synthesis) how does it differ, in its present mammoth size, from big business? And how does its merely functional thrust (its relativism) ever allow it to recognize and employ permanent values (absolutes) to guide itself and to offer guidance to others? The university, seemingly, cannot just pompously declare itself to be the seat of wisdom, since its main aim is to consistently reinterpret past knowledge for present and future use, with a view to making life better. Such reinterpretation would seem to make it clear that all truth is relative; yet the university is supposed to be the center of wise stability as well as revolutionary inventiveness. How achieve stability without absolutes? How live absolutes amid relativity without a community convinced of permanent values? Yet the university, it would seem, is much more an institution than a community of knowledge.

This dimension of community for the university takes on added mystery when one reflects that neither knowledge nor wisdom is gathered, held, and developed without discipline. But discipline is more than clenched jaws; it involves love, patience, prudence, a sense of justice, courage, and—above all—liberty. Can the university teach discipline to its students and develop it in its faculty, administration, and staff? Discipline, if it be a unity of virtues or good attitudes, is intelligible without itself being ideas and judgments. The cliché has it that the family teaches values; the university merely reflects on them. Not many families with college-age children, though, will agree with this. And the faculty will ask, in rebuttal to the parents, whether it is expected to teach *or* give homilies—since it cannot do both and remain a university faculty.

To turn to philosophy at this point seems fruitless because philosophy, though it abhors an ideological pursuit of unity, is itself undergoing an advanced case of pluralism. Not a few philosophers, of course, apart from the analytic school, accept philosophy as an "integrating" knowledge because of its simultaneous search for underlying presuppositions and for overarching systems of universal explanation. Still, those same philosophers offer many systems of thought, some of them contradictory. If that be the case, how could a community possibly unite around a certain set of values to form the wisdom community needed to run a universe appropriately? And even if philosophy did offer a unified view of the universe and, therefore, of the universe-mirroring university, the view would be too abstract for everyday decisions. Besides, some say: "Ask a philosopher what philosophy is and listen to his ideology."

33

Faith and theology, therefore, are needed to give concreteness to the ultimate aim of the university and thus to university decisions. Could Christian faith offer the unity denied to philosophy? Perhaps; but Christian faith has *de facto* been splintered by the sects, and theology has been pluralized by the philosophies which it must employ in order to live and grow. Moreover, if theology is going to mediate between contemporary culture and faith, it must draw competently upon the social and physical sciences, history, the fine arts, and communication skills, according to various philosophies of science and art, not just one. Then it must be able to communicate this splintered mirror to the students, as well as to the faculty teaching the students. How is such a mammoth unifying perspective possible?

But without some such perspective from philosophy, theology, and the other knowledges, how can one arrange a balanced program of studies for the students—and in what terms could one explain this program to them, so that they can gain a balanced competence for work and a superior outlook on life? To be specific, how does one fit together the culturally necessary specialization of the undergraduate major with the general integrative view of the core curriculum and then meld both of these with the freedom and fun of electives? To put this another way, how does one help the student balance the vocational with the liberal, the functional with the personal, the work-attitude with the play-contemplation? Admittedly, the faculty and administration should be living syntheses of these seemingly polar extremes. But then how does the faculty achieve this blend so that it charms the students into some imitation?

All the above problems, however, are unworthy of our attention if the university is administered by people whose model for decision (i.e., whose constellation of values that guide choices) is merely "good business" or "high quality education," or "stabilizing the students' Christian faith" or "fitting students for their jobs" or "passing on the Western tradition of learning." No one of these models for decision making, taken singly, is sufficient to keep a university from dying quickly. All of them (and more) must converge in each university decision—and the convergence within each decision differs according to the object of the decision, according to the present resources of the university, and according to the present needs of the larger community. The question then arises: how does the administrator or faculty member know the way to facilitate a convergence of these complex models or constellations of values upon a particular situation? Is there a super model for this convergence? Is this latter necessarily an ideology?

The problem is particularly acute since the university gets much of its meaning (to say nothing of its unity) from its sense of vocation: "No other university is working so well at fulfilling the particular needs of the community surrounding this university." This sense of uniqueness from its past tradition, its present competency, and its future hopes gives the university community passion for its work and contentment in its achievements. But is this sense of uniqueness merely an illusion? Is not everything done at this university duplicable at another university? Should not a university be busy copying the strengths of other universities? How to resist the uniformity imposed by government controls, by accrediting agencies, by the need to meet the competition of other local universities? When does uniqueness become an expensively false lure or a merely ancient routine or a bundle of quaint eccentricities?

This problem of uniqueness is especially pertinent to Christian universities, since they give as their unique *raison d'être* the development of Christian wisdom for both the university community and civic community. For, if Christian wisdom is simply secular wisdom that has been suffused with the life of Christian faith and, therefore, has been filled with mystery, then is not this secular wisdom narrowed in scope and darkened in insight? Would not the aims of the university be clouded with mystery and would not its procedures become sticky with hot piety? Indeed, would not Christian wisdom tend to polarize, rather than unify, the segments of the university?

The cutting edge of this suspicion about uniqueness and about Christian wisdom is sharpened when one looks at a university that is sponsored by a religious group, be it Presbyterian or Jesuit. Indeed, there are those who call the name *Christian university* an implicit contradiction, since university implies an unlimited spectrum of knowledges and values, while religious sponsorship explicitly means the narrowing of this spectrum by a particular faith viewpoint. Uniqueness is gained at the expense of the existence of the university. Thus, the sponsoring group runs the danger of being seen as an alien substance poisoning the life of the university. That individual Christians teach in the university is admirable, since this widens the spectrum of university knowledge and community experience; any attempt to introduce the Christian message into the university structure, however, would appear to be an attack on its very being.

Conclusion

From this survey, clearly, university problems are so tightly interrelated that no one of them can be adequately understood without all the others being simultaneously held in consciousness. Looked at from one perspective, this can be a discouraging complexity; from another perspective, though, their tight correlation points to a unified reality underlying

35

them. There truly is a *uni*-versity, a single reality. The aim of this book—
to survey the elements of a university and their dynamic interrelations—
is not just a fond hope. Given such a survey, administrators, faculty
members, or students can then hope to make reasonable decisions about
their present work, their career planning, and their future living. For
they will possess an intelligent framework within which to arrange their
values, assess their resources, estimate the needs of the situation, and
then make their decision. The discovery of such a framework is the "simple" aim of this book. No attempt will be made here to solve the thousand
other problems of finance, specific curricula, long-term goals, interdisciplinary studies, faculty unions, women's studies, student representation on
university committees, and so on. These more immediate problems
plague us all; individually and collectively, they can be disasters rather
than opportunities for growth when one tries to handle them outside an
intelligent framework for understanding what a university is and what it
can do. Even if the reader should disagree strongly with the so-called
intelligent framework discovered in this book, he or she will at least have
the major elements laid out so that this framework can be modified or the
reader can erect his or her own framework for future decisions.

2 By What Authority Does the University Constitute Itself Autonomous?

Perhaps the most precious part of the American university's inheritance from its medieval forebearers, particularly Oxford and Cambridge, is the tradition of university autonomy. Like the Church, the university may achieve a certain short-term efficiency through close ties with the contemporary government, as in the case of the dramatic, though erratic, advances of Soviet higher education. Universities can die suddenly alongside an embattled government, and they can also be stunted by a long-lived oppressive political dynasty (e.g., the Russian universities under the czars and the commissars). Thus, the very existence and growth of the university depends on its autonomy, its ability to control its own inner life through its own proper authority. In other words, the university appears to be a self-justifying reality with its own unique calling and with its own proper contribution to society.

This is not to imply that the university is totally independent of society, owing it nothing. The university rightfully answers to the authority of the multiple constituencies who have given it existence and sustenance. For the university has become not merely an integral, but an essential, part of the modern nation's life. A Third-World nation cannot avoid sinking into the Fourth World if it neglects higher education, the capstone of its future elementary and secondary school-systems—to say nothing of its agriculture and its light industries. It is beneficial, then, to consider briefly the various constituencies that empower and nourish the university so that we can assess the roots of the university's autonomy, explore its constitution in aims and structure, note its extrinsic authorization and its intrinsic authority, and, finally, mention the means of maintaining its academic freedom.

In this way, we can explore the root system and the trunk of the university in order to comprehend its many branchings and leafings. In fact, we may even discover its main branches and distinguish them from those distracting twigs.

The Constituencies of the University's Autonomous Life

It may be surprising to realize that the autonomous university issues out of, and is sustained by, at least eight different constituencies. The largest of these constituencies is the nation itself, all the peoples represented by the federal government. In seeking to promote the common good (i.e., the organized goodness) of the nation amid the worldwide scientific and technological civilization, the federal government is deeply dependent on the university for analysis, calibration, promotion, and control of the accelerating revolution called "progress." Only universities that have been in the vanguard of this revolution can understand it sufficiently to give the government hope of partially controlling the revolution. To see how true this is, one has only to scan the problems of ecological pollution, monetary inflation, population control, disarmament, insufficient world-food supplies, and a host of other unbelievably complex changes in international living.

Because the federal government has the responsibility for dealing efficiently with these problems, and yet cannot do so without pooling the resources of all its universities, it has every right to expect each university to focus its knowledges, arts, and skills on these problems. In addition, the federal government supplies American universities with large sums of money to conduct research, to house students, and even to support the fine arts. Furthermore, through the state governments, it makes loans and scholarships available to students. Therefore, on behalf of its citizens it monitors the use of this money and ensures a fair share of its benefits for its "citizen-students." If the government were not at all times to give careful attention to universities, it would be grossly failing its citizens for it would be heavily mortgaging the nation's future by allowing it to sink into mediocrity. Consequently, the government has no choice but to promote the university and to demand an accounting of the latter, thus establishing a facet of the problem of academic freedom.

Naturally, the second largest constituency of the American university is the state government which deals most directly with the university through its state laws regulating the establishment of colleges, the housing of students, the requisite training criteria for teachers, the number of class-hours or days required for accrediting courses, and so on. In most states, even private universities receive subsidies through the granting of state scholarships to students. Because the state government is responsible for the commonweal of the people within its boundaries, it, too, must not only monitor the funds given to universities, but also muster the resources of the universities within its boundaries to deal with such local problems as health, unemployment, agriculture, industrial development, and the education of state personnel (e.g., social workers, police, finance officers, physical education directors, inspectors, water conservationists, and so forth). Because each state has such diverse resources to be developed (e.g., mining, engineering, recreational areas, forestry, international finance, fisheries, electrical power, communication arts, and so forth), its universities must offer a vast array of services. Likewise, because the development of these resources demands highly sophisticated technology and science, the state cannot fittingly support its people without abundant university assistance. Again, the problem arises: how balance the university's academic freedom against the pressing needs of the state and its government?

The third constituency of the university is one that is not often considered, namely, the national community of scholars. Because this community develops the very disciplines that are to be passed on to the students for the intellectual and practical benefit of both local and national communities, these men and women rightly determine the criteria for the hiring of university personnel, the content of the courses to be taught, the procedures for protecting the rights of students and professors, and the description of administrative functions in guiding the university toward its goals. These criteria are often expressed through the regional accrediting agency, but they are also expressed in scholarly reviews, convention addresses, consultative visits, the American Association of University Professors, and the casual conversations that spark new ideas. As with the first two constituencies, however, a question arises: how does the individual university freely preserve its own identity under such pressures for uniformity?

The fourth constituency of the university is the faculty that assembles within the university to structure its courses, departments, and schools so that (1) knowledge is gathered, reinterpreted, and then generated in the students and (2) wisdom has a home in the collective mind of the university. The best wisdom of the faculty shapes the university academic program, offering students systematic introductions to new knowledges and skills so that they can provide for their families and can serve the needs of society. What is more, faculty members look beyond the particular program of the university to national and international programs of research, thus offering an expanding horizon to their university and its students. If the faculty's competence merits attention, other countries will seek the services of faculty members. Here one touches the central nerve of the university's authority—the competence of its faculty, which is the basic limiting and expanding factor of the university's autonomy and dignity. For the amount of life and creativity that the other constituencies can pour into the university is no larger or smaller than the competent activity

39

of the resident faculty. (*How* this interplay takes place, after one integrates academic freedom with demands for competence in specialized areas helpful to the civic community and to the students, is a problem that will be dealt with later.)

This is not to deny the importance of the fifth constituency, the student body of the university. Quality students increase the pleasure, and thus the concentration, of teaching, give critical honing to the professor's ideas, and offer cooperative enhancement to the professor's research. In fact, if the faculty constituency gives structure to the university, the student constituency makes this structure pulse with creative life. If you doubt this, see what vacations do to a university. There is no denying that the student tuition fees give economic life to the university, but it is the students' confidence in the faculty and administration and their as-yet-unbridled curiosity that ministers to the inmost life of the university. The students' high expectations of the faculty fuel the professors' ambitions and give fresh vibrancy to routines and to knowledge-schemes that may have previously been ready for entombment. There is nothing like this resurrection for exhausted professors and worried-to-death administrators.

If you wonder "whence comes this enthusiasm and ambition," look to the sixth constituency, namely, the parents of these students, many of whom are themselves former students of the university. The life-sacrifices of the parents have given birth to these children, nurtured them through childhood diseases and traumas, acculturated them with music and conversation, borne their expensive ingratitudes and wearying melancholy, and survived their hobbies and joys. And, when the time comes, parents (with the older brothers and sisters) will endure the crowning event of their daughters' and sons' young lives—collegiate growing pains. For parents' confidence in a particular university, as well as their flaming enthusiasm for learning, have started a small flame in the breast of their student sons and daughters. Likewise, the parents have breathed life into the university through both their day-to-day sacrifices for these students and their financial donations to the university. Their trusting expectancy of the university, again, elicits new hope and plans from the faculty. In so many ways, these families are the gnarled but nourishing roots of the university. Rightfully, they are canonized and glorified on graduation day. Rightfully, too, their voices must be heard even when their demands seem to endanger academic freedom.

Also within this sixth constituency are the alumni, who frequently become the parents of the next generation of college students. In many ways, their relationship to the university is one of parenting. Out of gratitude, they often support their *alma mater* by recruiting students

40

(directly, by soliciting them, and indirectly, by living their professional and family lives with integrity); by endowing the university with financial gifts; by returning to the university to instruct in their specialties; by helping other alumni with friendship, business contacts, and social life; and by their encouragement of faculty, staff, and administration through their efforts for the university. Most especially, alumni support the university through their enriching lives.

If the guidance of federal and local government is the matrix of the university, if the community of scholars is the origin of the university, if the faculty forms the very structure of the university, and if the students and their parents put the university into creative action, then the administrators and staff of the university form the constituency that gives direction to the institution. To see how chaotic the university would be without competent administrators, one has only to listen to discussions of administrative procedures at faculty committee meetings. It is not that faculty members lack brilliant ideas, nor that they cannot understand administrative problems. After all, the administrators often come from among them. However, many have not yet developed (some never will) the special prudence and shrewdness of the good administrator, nor do they have the overview of the university that is needed for drawing balanced judgments. To listen to them for an hour is to experience the faculty's dire need for administrative direction.

From this negative viewpoint, one can begin to appreciate the skill needed to balance multimillion-dollar budgets so that faculty paychecks arrive on time, blackboards are cleaned and rooms mopped, faculty grants are processed expeditiously, new experimental programs can begin, sabbaticals are regularly granted, and so on. More than this, however, the good administrator grasps the ideals incarnated in academic programs by the faculty, hones them to practical implementation, approves or disapproves or modifies procedures for hiring new faculty members and granting tenure after careful discussion with the faculty—all this in terms of the goals of the institution. The administrator has no choice but to be like Plato's philosopher-king. He or she must peer through all the university apparatus to see its ultimate struts, its basic reasons for existence, its finest hopes; and then the administrator must help the faculty incarnate their programs in precise detail with all the finesse of a skilled cabinetmaker. Somehow, in this process, the administrator must balance the ultimate with the most proximate while, at the same time, being an almost-Marxist economist. Unless an administration's skill is thus finely honed, great universities will stumble about like dying elephants.

Thus, the administrative constituency guides the university into the always more perilous future, ever seeking to adapt its resourceful faculty

41

to the needs of the students and to the hopes of the larger civic communities. Yet, competent administrators are always aware that such guidance and adaptation are possible only if truth is pursued for itself, and only if a priceless wisdom is being generated by the marvelous balance of playful contemplation and purposeful work in the community. What more could be asked of administrators than this role of philosopher-king? Yet, does this admittedly dominant role endanger academic freedom?

In religious-oriented, private universities, there is still another constituency of strategic importance, namely, the religious or churchly founding group. Parents often commit their children to a church-sponsored university and pay at least twice as much tuition as at a secular university because they give paramount value to this religious orientation. They do this on the assumption that this university has worked out a liveable synthesis of traditional religious faith with the contemporary culture so that when students graduate, they will not only feel at home in their own culture but also find their faith enriching their life with meaning and hope. Moreover, parents expect that the university faculty and administration will be living symbols of this Christian synthesis, quite capable of expressing it in their courses—not by fervent homilies but by their competence in a special area of knowledge, by their joy in their work, by their interest in the students, by their sense of justice for communities larger than the university, and by the natural ease with which their faith gives orientation and exuberance to their specialized work. In other words, parents have high hope that the faculty member will be a whole person who is deepened rather than narrowed by his or her specialized skills—a person faithful in all the so-called secular activities.

But such orientation is hard to sustain unless the supporting church group, the religious founders, live intimately within the university community as teachers, administrators, students, and parents of students. The Presbyterian or Catholic faith tradition will vibrantly direct the growth of the university only insofar as individuals bear that faith with them into classrooms, dormitory discussion groups, academic committee meetings, administrative planning sessions, and the school's liturgical prayer gatherings. But it is not sufficient to carry that faith individually; there must be a corporate presence wherein each faith-bearer knows that he or she shares values commonly held by others working in the university setting. What is more, each faith-bearer must feel that these values are growing within him or her and within the others as they together meet and partially solve daily university problems. Thus, the more deeply the individual faith-bearers are dedicated as a group to the university life, the stronger and more unitive their faith can become for them.

This faith, if it is genuinely Christian, does not seal off the believing community from those faculty members who do not share all their values. For genuine Christian faith, while sharpening the Christian's appreciation for his or her own deepest values, also makes each believer more aware and more respectful of the values espoused by others—even those values that Christians cannot accept for themselves, e.g., art is for art's sake alone, science will eventually find all the answers; hope dies at the graveside. Christian faith should make university persons more sensitive both to what unites them to fellow faculty members and to what necessarily distinguishes them from one another. Without a sharp awareness of what unites individual faculty members to one another, Christian members have difficulty in expressing why and how they hope to enrich the religious-oriented university's life. Without a deepened realization of what distinguishes Christian faculty members from those who do not hold their faith-value, these believers cannot explain why they do not teach at a secular university where the opportunities for research are richer and where the pay is higher. Nor do they know clearly how they can live more fully with those faculty members who share their values, in order to make the communal university life more dynamic. How this corporate presence of the founding faith group expresses itself concretely will be discussed later in detail. For the present, it is worth noting that this last constituency has the power not only to enrich the life and purpose of the university but also to curtail its academic freedom.

Clearly, eight constituencies contribute to the existence of the Christian university. They define to what degree its dynamic structure has autonomous authority, that is to say, to what degree the university is self-justifying. The full significance of this autonomy will be seen when we explore the Christian university as institution and wisdom-community, as "disciplined liberty", as agent of secularization, as unique reality, as a partnership with the risen Christ. For the time being, we can only describe that autonomy of the university to which the eight constituencies contribute and with which they dare not tamper lest they smother the university's academic freedom.

The Autonomy of the University Is Its Constitution (or Make-up)

Although the constituencies establish the university, they are neither its constitution nor, to use a metaphor, its dynamic body. Although they cause the constitution, the very autonomy of the university, they are distinct from it. This becomes clear when one notes how the constitution comes into being and then becomes the university's autonomy. To catch the shadow of the university's constitution, one should note its aims, then quickly outline its procedural structures for achieving those aims, and finally try to trap in words the elusive reality of its academic freedom.

The university appears to have dual independent missions. The more evident one is to reinterpret traditional truths that have been received from the various speculative disciplines (e.g., the physical and social sciences, history, philosophy, literature, theology), from the practical disciplines (e.g., nursing, medicine, communications, engineering, computer technology, criminology, dramatics), and from the fine arts (e.g., music, painting, sculpture, dance, and so forth). To interpret means to see old reality in a *new* way because one has previously understood the old way, in depth, but is now impressed with "something more" that demands a fuller, more detailed understanding. In other words, knowledge is growing from within, as does the budding flower, adjusting all its parts, and not from without, as when one adds a roof to a house, by simple external addition. This fuller knowledge is frequently somewhat shocking at first (e.g., Einstein's theory of relativity, which showed Newton's theory to be true of only a corner of physical reality); but then, on further examination, one sees how important it is (e.g., Einstein's discovery made accurate space-and-acceleration computation possible both in outer space and within the atom).

In a university setting, the discovery of fuller truth in one discipline is momentous for all other disciplines, jostling them into new discoveries within their own spheres of competence (e.g., note how Freud's theory of personality has changed the face of historical biography writing, anthropology, and philosophy). This jostling is quite disturbing at first because it shatters, or at least demands readjustments of, previous unified ways of looking at the world. But, in the long run, a fuller truth in one discipline leads not only to fuller truths in other disciplines, but also to a new overview of all reality. For example, Darwin's biology has remade philosophy and theology, as well as the sciences on which they draw.

This fuller view of man and his world eventually filters into classrooms, into communication systems such as TV, into board rooms of businesses, or into strategy sessions at the Pentagon. A particular reinterpretation may even begin to modify the very structure of the university, as when a theological revival of ecumenism opened the theology departments of Catholic universities to rabbis and Protestant ministers. Thus, the reinterpretation of traditional truth by the university is a powerful influence in our daily lives, no matter how many years it takes for the new view to filter down to us.

The second part of the university's dual mission is the accumulation of wisdom within the university community. When wisdom is defined as the supreme knowledge and evaluation of the ultimate principles of reality—a frequently encountered definition—one can feel either overwhelmed or underwhelmed. But actually, this wisdom is a concrete knowledge as well as a "feel" for what is really happening in the everyday world, for what are the deepest values or most intelligent principles in everyday life, and for what will work well to preserve these values and principles in life-and-death decisions about the future of humanity. University wisdom is distilled slowly out of both specialized knowledges and the experience and discipline of living these ideas; the result is an overview that arises out of these knowledges and experiences. This wisdom is, as it were, a by-product of many people pooling their special knowledges and experiences to see the world more integrally, and then moving to solve contemporary problems. It is simultaneously a contemplative and practical knowledge that gathers slowly and requires hard work and shrewd observations. Although this wisdom is worthwhile in itself for the richness of life it offers, it is also essential to the development of the specialized knowledges and skills that lead to the reinterpretation of traditional truth. For wisdom is essential to generate an overview of reality, to recognize when a specialized knowledge is truly advancing, to position one's work in a narrow field so that its real value is evident, to devise a method for successfully staging an experiment and for recognizing the true significance of the results, to admit the limits of one's science and the presuppositions controlling its advance, to sustain hope for the future amid personal failure or social disaster.

This wisdom has a second function within the university, namely, to conceive, implement, test, and promote (if good) new procedures, departments, and aims for the university. For example, American universities, unlike the other major models discussed earlier, very early learned to incorporate professional schools, blend the English college with the German graduate school, invent the community college, and develop the principle that the university could be the servant of all classes of society in many of their academic needs. These remarkable characteristics of the American university have helped the United States to support a democracy of education and opportunity never before seen in the world's history. In this way, the American university made its type of wisdom available to wider and wider circles, which eventually included large numbers of women—perhaps the most significant revolution in centuries.

Once these dual aims of the university are understood in their reciprocal influence on each other—reinterpretation of traditional truth causes

45

new wisdom that, in turn, directs (1) the development of newer interpretations, (2) the resultant modifications of university structure, and (3) the societal evolution of a nation and even of a world—it becomes clear how important to these aims are the procedures and structures that achieve the aims. For both the aims and the means to their achievement are the very constitution of the university. As earlier noted in the brief history of American higher education, graduate education, with its emphasis on research, makes the reinterpretation of traditional truth inevitable and enables the undergraduate colleges to be alert to the latest discoveries in content and method. Furthermore, while the undergraduate school prepares students for the professions, the graduate school challenges the professional school faculty who, reciprocally, place their detailed experience at the disposal of the theoreticians. Here the liberal and vocational aspects of education dialectically work on each other at both the undergraduate and graduate levels. In addition, the students challenge the faculty to make their studies relevant, while, at the same time, the faculty tries to open the narrow gaze of students to the full stretch and depth of what is truly relevant. The faculty attempts this as follows: (1) through the specialization of knowledge in various major studies, (2) through the integration of knowledges in the core curriculum and senior integrative seminar, and (3) through the spontaneity of surprising joy in the electives.

Meanwhile, the administration is absorbing the new ideas of the faculty for changes in curriculum, in university procedures, and in medium-range and long-range goals. Momentous decisions, after percolating up from lower administrative levels where they have already been criticized and discussed with the faculty, are presented to the Board of Trustees by the president and his vice presidents. The Board, mindful of both preserving the unique character of the university and determining the financial feasibility of the changes to be made, approves, modifies, or disapproves these proposals. Approvals by the Board of Trustees, with their mandatory qualifications, are then filtered back down to the deans, schools, heads of departments, and proposing committees so that plans can be put into operation. In this scheme, wisdom is operating when the best thoughts and most practical plans are carefully etched out by the faculty committees, ingested and criticized by administrators who are noted for their prudence and their overview of the university, tested and put into context by experts from all strata of society (the Board of Trustees and the president), then remitted down through the administrative structure to the original conceivers and implementers so that their ideas might be realized in curriculum, in equipment, in trained teachers, in advertising for students, in library purchases, in the successful pursuit of government and industry grants, and so on.

Later, the new interpretations of traditional truth generated by these innovations will be made available in the students' minds and hearts, in scholarly articles, in seminars for scientists-businessmen-government officials, and in procedures for university administrators. Still later, the wisdom, slowly accumulating from the convergence of other innovations and new interpretations, will surface in new attacks on old problems, in a new tentative overview of the world, in stronger patience and deeper hope about humanity's future. Such a wisdom is very tough in its roots of traditional, specialized knowledges, arts, and skills and in its perduring values stubbornly held. It is very sensitive, however, to hurt, especially as it makes its first budding attempts at overview, at new attacks on old problems, and at expressing hope.

All these remarks about wisdom point to the fact that the constitution of the university is at once remarkably sturdy and surprisingly sensitive and, therefore, does not suffer meddling very well. Over the last eight centuries, the Western university has evolved, through trial and error, a structure that has produced truth and wisdom. But this university structure has become as complex as the knowledge it reinterprets and as mysteriously effective as the wisdom it generates. Non-university people who tamper with this structure risk turning truth into error and wisdom into silliness. Academic freedom is much more than allowing professors to speak out on dangerous topics or allowing university facilities to be used for mounting rhetorical attacks on the U.S. government. Academic freedom is the liberty of a university to live and grow according to its own constitution, and thus to be its own authority in its particular areas of competence. It is the liberty of the university to be its unique self and not merely the suppliant servant of government, church, business, or any other institution. For any of these institutions to attempt to put undue control on the university is to cripple university operations and eventually undermine the very constitution of the university. (Obviously, the university as a part of the nation must have a qualified, or restricted, freedom like any other part of the nation.) Attempts of this kind ultimately render the university incapable of serving the nation well.

To see this more clearly, it might be helpful to try to describe the mysterious reality of the university. On the surface, it would seem that the university is not a natural community in the manner of the family and the nation. Yet, it is natural in the sense that the university is the exteriorization of humankind's collective personality, i.e., of the faculty, students, staff, and administration taken as a group. This means simply that as the individual human personality grows by acquiring one knowledge after the other, so also the university grows by incorporating departments that each stand for a distinct knowledge or distinct skill. Similarly, as the human personality becomes aware of subdivisions within each knowledge, so, too, the university department hires experts in various subfields of a particular science. Further, just as the human personality cannot endure separated distinct knowledges, but must find their underlying unity through philosophy of science and metaphysics, so also the university develops departments to teach these knowledges and establishes schools to unite these knowledges into integrated sets for the sake of an overview, or wisdom. Likewise, just as the human mind has been challenged and lured by revelation into a faith and theology that offer a concrete account of humankind's origin, life, and future destiny, so, too, the university risks loss of direction and meaning for its life if it does not have a department of theology—an ultimate wisdom—for challenging and enlivening this possible overview, or wisdom. Thus, the intellectual side of humanity's collective personality finds its exteriorization in the institutional side of the university, which promotes the differentiation or specialization of knowledges-arts-skills.

The volitional side of humanity's collective personality finds its exteriorization in the communal side of the university, in the side that promotes the unification of all these knowledges-arts-skills in wisdom. Wisdom arises out of the values recognized in a person's knowledge and experienced in practical decisions. Wisdom is a person's wholeness of knowledge, action, and life within a community of friends and acquaintances. This is exteriorized in the university when the faculty, students, and administration form a community (and not merely a work force in some huge assembly-line factory). This community begins to take shape when each department chairperson unites his or her department members not only in cooperative pursuit of truth within a particular discipline but also in awareness of the contributions of other departments to his or her own particular department. (For example, the philosophy department cannot seriously study evolution without the help of the anthropology, biology, theology, and paleontology departments.) In addition, the forming of friendships within each department and with members from other departments makes the pursuit of wisdom possible since, without friendship, wisdom withers under the scorn of rivalry, jealousy, one-upmanship, ambitious anger, and other acids. What is more, this incipient wisdom community is not limited to the faculty; it is called forth by the students whose needs, questions, and affections require a quasi-familial wisdom of value as well as knowledge. Although some may hold that the university cannot be *in loco parentis*, the faculty-community is not without obligations to father and to mother the adulthood of the students with the eloquent presentation of truth and goodness.

The growth of a wisdom community cannot happen merely by chance; it must be promoted by the administrators, that is to say, they must provide economic stability for the gathering place in which people can pursue wisdom. The administrator's effective grasp of the faculty's ideals and institutional aims enables university life to expand in all of its departments and, at the same time, achieve a unity of purpose in its many interlocking activities. In other words, the administrator enables the community's wisdom to be expressed in practical actions that build the institutional side of the university, enliven the student body with knowledge, skills, values, and some wisdom, and serve the needs of the larger civic and ecclesial communities. Here, the administrators are helping to form both the university community and the communities which have given the university life. Both the departmental specialization of knowledges-arts-skills and the forming of a wisdom community within a university setting explain what is meant by the sentence: the university is the natural exteriorization of the collective personality of humanity.

This statement, however, does not deny the fact that an element of the university is merely the fortuitous convergence of circumstances. The brief historical survey and comparison of five model universities in chapter 1 indicate how national history and chance events have entered into the very structure of the university. For example, Napoleon's autocratic conception of the French university dictated a highly centralized system organized around the University of Paris; the Russian system of part-time education combined with hugely complex correspondence courses is a result of tight economic straits and the pressing need for a vast cadre of educated industrial laborers and technicians. But, on the other hand, it should be noted that, as national university systems get to know one another better and as they pool their efforts to establish Third-World universities, the universities around the world become more homogenized, i.e., more internationalized, just like the great cities of the world. Certainly, university education is rapidly becoming more and more necessary to the average person if he or she is to exist decently in a scientific, technological civilization.

To summarize, therefore, the proper aims of the university (to reinterpret traditional truth and to develop a contemporary communal wisdom), as well as the proper procedures and structures used to effect these aims, and the view of the university as a living exteriorization of the collective personality of humanity indicate what constitutes the university and explain why this constitution is the very autonomy of the university.

The question of *how* this autonomy is to be exercised, however, raises a problem: From where does the university get its authority?

The Extrinsic Authorization and Intrinsic Authority of the University

The basis for the university's free and unique development is clarified by the claim that the university's constitution is its autonomy. But when one speaks of putting this constitution into operation, one is talking about power and authority. One can say that the university's authority to grant degrees is extrinsic, i.e., it is received from the state government. But this means little since the average state legislature is not very demanding lest it should appear to interfere with the university's freedom. Its requirements are general guidelines, except for the demand that a course have a certain number of hours or that the public officers of a university or college not be felons.

A second authorizer of the university, namely, the regional accrediting agency, is more stringent. In the last few years, however, its stringency has been centered squarely on the question of whether or not a particular university's aims are being fulfilled or can be fulfilled, given its present library, faculty education, economic status, and so forth. This approach leaves the university free to increase its resources or scale down its aims so that they more accurately conform to its present means.

A third extrinsic authorization comes from the founding group, e.g., a Presbyterian Synod whose experience as educators or as hirers of educators warrants calling the institution a university. Thus, the Synod, if it is not part of the university that it finances, extrinsically confers authority on the administrators of the university. A fourth authorizer is the community of scholars who vouch for the competency of doctoral graduates. But perhaps the most powerful extrinsic authorizers are the benefactors of the university, a group that includes the parents who send their sons and daughters, the wealthy who bestow their millions, the local community that gives its cheerful cooperation and loyal support to all university events, and the federal government that supplements state financial support with research grants and mortgage loans. All this extrinsic authorization, however, merely sets the stage for the university play; it is not the power by which the university intrinsically lives and grows, even though the removal of the extrinsic authorization would quickly bring the university to its knees and eventually to its death for lack of sustenance.

What, then, is the intrinsic authority of the university? Structurally (or formally) it is, (1) the competent knowledge possessed by each professor and shared with other professors; (2) each professor's ability to effectively communicate this knowledge to the students (after all, why else call him or her a professor?); (3) the faculty's shared vision of the university's stated aims and the faculty's passion for accomplishing these aims; (4) the fac-

50

ulty's cooperation in concretely planning and carrying out in meticulous detail the procedures that will achieve these shared aims; and (5) the *traditio* of the university, its past accomplishments still living on in the minds and hearts of the faculty, administration, and students. This tradition serves not only to enlighten the mind but also to warm the heart; it is freighted with the wisdom so necessary to the university's immediate aim of reinterpreting traditional truth for present times. (In this context, the committee work that is often denigrated by casual faculty conversations is seen in its full dignity—an exercise of wisdom in democratic freedom.) Without these five structural, that is formal, elements of authority, the university slowly atrophies. No one of the five can be omitted without serious harm.

If, however, the power of the university is considered administratively (or efficiently), it may be seen as the prudence and decisiveness of the Board of Trustees, the president, and his subordinate administrators when they carry out the aims of the university according to the procedures designed by the faculty. The administrators make the five elements of structural authority effective in the day-to-day operation of the university. But the administrators also foresee; along with the faculty, they devise five-year plans so that the university can grow or cut back in a balanced way, so that the institution can adapt to swiftly changing circumstances and grasp at unexpected opportunities, and so that the higher learning of the university can be readily available to the various civic communities it serves. This last item reveals a sometimes forgotten dignity of the university administrator. He or she is not just a technician whose job is to solve major institutional problems. When the administrator is operating at his or her best, he or she is a builder of community— not totally unlike the pastor of a congregation. For, if there is to be a wisdom community, it must have a prime promoter who, as Christ has hinted, must be the servant of all. The administrator is simultaneously a facilitator of institutional aims and the promoter-servant of a wisdom community that is composed of faculty, students, and staff. Without the administrator's deft use of authority, the institution begins to lurch about and the wisdom community starts to split into "cold-warring" factions. Then the university ceases to be a *multi*versity and becomes instead a *per*versity, since the resultant politics (to use a nice name) leave little time for reinterpreting traditional truth and no time for the contemplative gathering of wisdom in peace.

Once the administrators have a wisdom community growing, they can direct this community's skills to the needs of the larger civic and ecclesial communities so that the university becomes a healing agency amid the nation's problems. The university is thereby able to respond in gratitude

51

for all that it has received from its eight constituencies. Of course, the administrators, to say nothing of the faculty members, would have one hand tied behind their backs if they were without their staffs who perform the hidden, often split-second maneuvers, that rescue a seminar, a university-based convention, an important official speech, a research project, an outraged parent's dignity, a complicated curricular catalog, the lost humor of a faculty member, and the footnote-packed article that only a veteran secretary could read for typing. The staff members of the administration are not just the university's sinews for articulating its limbs; they are also its nerve ends for alerting the body to its needs and for enabling the limbs to work smoothly without the spasmodic jerks that create nagging headaches and occasional heartaches.

In addition to the structural (formal) and administrative (efficient) aspects of the intrinsic authority of the university, there is a dispositive (material) aspect, i.e., the academic, psychological, and financial cooperation of the students. The essential quality of this aspect of authority can be dramatized by a brief review of the 1969–70 winter of discontent that settled over the American universities. At one private university, a brilliant graduate student, who had lived on scholarships and university grants through all his schooling, pleaded in the university newspaper that the students band together and refuse to pay their tuition so that the university could be brought to heel for student demands that would have emasculated the curriculum.

To take a more positive tack, every professor has experienced a psychological affinity with a particular class that enlivens and even coruscates lectures. Moreover, class discussions with this class intelligently explore issues instead of aimlessly droning in circles, and tardy term papers show inventiveness and even compelling interest. But such economic and psychological cooperation of students gets its importance from the academic cooperation. For here the cooperation in seeking a reinterpretation of truth, even at the undergraduate level, is precisely that which builds the *traditio* of a university, which equips the student for a vocation of service to his blood family, his married family, and the larger communities, and which enables a wisdom community to take root. Such student cooperation breeds that marvelous loyalty which the philosopher Josiah Royce considers to be the virtue most characteristic of the mature man or woman since it forms the heart of any community. Is there anything more authoritative, more powerful in its gentility, than loyalty?

The last aspect of intrinsic authority of the university to be considered is its purposeful (or final) quality. If the university has arisen out of the previously mentioned constituencies to meet their academic needs, then it must continue to fulfill those academic needs or forfeit its right to exist.

When the university starts to become a political party or a church or an entertainment industry or an arm of the government or an army training camp or a nice club for cultural pursuits or a clever combination of any or all of these, then it has lost sight of the original aims for which it was given life. It is proving to be a rather ungrateful child to its parents. These extravagant examples of abusing the university's constitution graphically illustrate how the three other aspects of intrinsic authority depend on this last, purposeful aspect for their meaning and existence. Thus, the common good that is achieved by the university through the fulfillment of its dual intrinsic aims is the last aspect of the university's intrinsic authority. For the common good resides in the university itself insofar as it is reinterpreting traditional truth and building a communal wisdom within its faculty, students, administrators, and staff members.

Yet, the common good is not limited to the university, since it is exportable to the immediate neighborhood that surrounds the university, to the larger city or rural areas that adjoin it, to the local and federal governments, to the business centers, to the churches—in short, to all its constituencies. In this way, the university fits into the larger common good of the nation and is accountable, therefore, to its constituencies; they can withdraw their support freely just as they once gave it freely. Like every other autonomy and authority, those of the university are responsible and limited. For this reason, the university's academic freedom is not total, which raises the question: what are the limits to university autonomy and authority; how wide is university freedom? Without the previous description of the university's autonomy as its very constitution of aims and proper procedures, and without this recent distinction between extrinsic constituency-authorizations and intrinsic university authority in its four aspects, it would be hard to answer this question.

The Uses and Perils of Academic Freedom

The various constituencies that give life to the university may, in times of confusion, attempt to put a crimp in that life by nibbling at its autonomy (its very constitution) and hampering its intrinsic authority. The reason for this can be seen more clearly if one notes how the intrinsic authority of the university is used within its autonomous constitution and, consequently, is vulnerable to the meddling of its best friends.

Protection of academic freedom continually confronts faculty and administration with choices between the better and the less good (and often enough between the worse and the less evil) because growth and life are at stake. Faculty and administration alone have the requisite knowledge, wisdom, and experience to make the necessary evaluations and decisions concerning what is better or worse for the constitution of the university. The problem, however, is that these decisions do not stay within the university; they ripple out into the public common good for better or for worse. For example, if the universities, in an effort to escape vicious manipulation, refuse all cooperation with the Central Intelligence Agency (CIA), they will undoubtedly render the CIA less effective not simply for espionage but, more important, for the gathering of information needed to make diplomatic decisions and to protect national secrets. If, in the interest of peace, the universities refuse to do any basic research that could later be applied to weapons-systems (e.g. in aerospace projects), are they ensuring peace or are they precipitating an enemy take-over or loss of technological advances (with consequent heavy economic loss to American industry)? There seems to be no way to separate the university common good from the larger common good of the civic community.

A less obvious implication of the ripple effect of the university's common good is the fact that every decision within the university eventually sets off indirect reverberations within the larger community that enwombs the university. In the theoretical realm of the university, for example, an administrator faces the following questions: how can the university advance theoretic knowledge so that practical knowledge stays healthy (e.g., how scientific should the nursing program be?), and how can the university challenge theoretical knowledge with practice (e.g., how soon can medical students be safely introduced to patient care in the university hospital?). In the institutional area, administrators and faculty must ask how they can provide courses, books, expensive experimental equipment, visiting professors of renown, expanded library facilities, new buildings, small class seminars, computer services, teaching aids, and other services without gradually becoming so dependent on government funds that sudden cutbacks derange whole programs and necessitate the firing of young professors, staff, and even administrators. In the area of attitudes, how can administrators and faculty respect the students' freedom by admitting more of them to key university committees, by allowing them more electives, a greater number of class cuts, and a less discriminating marking system, by offering them more extensive and increasingly more expensive facilities for various types of counseling, and by giving them more protection from propagandizing professors, without dismantling precious procedures that have effectively protected the university's tradition? Such dismantling can, at times, depreciate the quality of the skills and knowledges that prepare students to provide service to the civic communities—a problem with which a number of South American universities have struggled.

Regarding personal concerns, how can administrators and faculty insist on the dual aims of the university through more humane (more free) university procedures, criteria, regulations, incentives, and job descriptions? For example, is it not necessary to insist that university professors who have reached sixty-five years of age retire lest, in the possibly diminished university enrollment of the late 1980s, young professors be sealed out of the university? Or, again, how can student evaluations of teachers be set up so that the student is protected and the teacher is not intimidated; or how can professors be rewarded for putting all their efforts into teaching excellence rather than be penalized for failing to publish? All of these problems deeply affect the creativity and quality of teaching which, in turn, determines the student's quality of skill and learning when he or she begins to serve the public as a social worker or a dentist or a high school teacher.

Considering the realm of faith, how can faith-values and faith-knowledge (theology) be incorporated into the academic program, the campus lives of the students, and the aims of the university while, at the same time, that most intimate freedom for faith-commitment in students, staff, administration, and faculty is respected? Parents of faith make substantial economic sacrifices to send their sons and daughters to religiously oriented universities with the expectation that their children's faith will mature, not disappear or go into cold storage. But what is to prevent a tenured professor from losing his or her faith so that (scandalously for the student) he or she gives no support to the student's faith? How can administrators and faculty help students avoid intellectualizing their faith into a vapor that not only contains no thought of justice for the poor but also feels no need for community? When these problems become multiplied because of cultural disenchantment with religion, the private, religiously oriented university is faced with seemingly insurmountable problems; yet, the Christian university is rightfully expected by its founding religious group to use all its considerable resources for developing the faith of its faculty, staff, and student body, without, of course, compromising their freedom. This is no small expectation, and yet the continued life of the religiously oriented university—precisely as it is religiously oriented—is at stake. It may survive as a secular university but not as a religiously oriented one; its *traditio* will have been jettisoned.

All these problems indicate that even the most intimate decisions of the university spill over its confines to cause large waves in the surrounding communities and among its constituencies. The latter cannot be indifferent to these decisions and therefore cannot avoid the temptation to interfere in them. The problem is that the complexity of the university makes it vulnerable to meddling persons who are rather ignorant of the university's constitution (its autonomy) and authority. The university's respect for its constituencies and the wise use of its intrinsic authority to cause the least harm and the most good for the commonweal of its constituencies should give the university an authoritative autonomy sufficient to stand up to the pressures applied by outside communities and institutions. But because the university happens to be one of the most influential institutions in the nation, whose decisions inevitably and deeply affect society at large, it must continually resist those who attempt to own it by manipulating it to enhance the interests of a particular business, government, church group, or other constituency.

Academic freedom, then, is mainly a matter of maintaining a delicate balance between two factors: on the one side is any constituency that may want the best for the university but wants it precisely from its own "advantage point"; on the other side is the university itself, which certainly wants the best for its constituencies but not to the diminishment of its own constitution (its aims and proper procedures) and intrinsic authority. For example, the state and federal governments must monitor the use of taxpayers' money and look to the needs of the citizens. Consequently, these two government bodies will rightfully push hard for affirmative action employment and for special programs for disadvantaged students; but the push can be so hard that the university staff is weakened and the quality of education is depressed enough to debilitate the university. The business community can move into a university, almost imperceptibly, in a variety of ways: through membership on the Board of Trustees, through benefactions (which give a quiet but effective voice in regions other than the business school), through short-term loans (especially when given to a financially strapped university), through business school students whose tuition is often paid by various business concerns, through the membership of its officers on various university fund-raising committees, and so on. Gradually the business model for thinking, planning, and deciding replaces the university models, and the university is on its way to being just another big business. The pragmatic engulfs the theoretical with soley practical concerns.

Likewise, the church community is not loath to control the university if it operates on the assumption that, having founded the university, it is, therefore, the sole owner. As founder, the church-community may still conceive the university as its small seminary-like college. The church-community has failed to note the moment in 1946 when, because of the GI Bill of Rights, this dependent college grew into an autonomous univer-

56

sity with a life and a growth pattern all its own. It may wish to control the university through economic and administrative power when actually it should limit its involvement to influencing the university's Christian spirit through devoted service. The church community is often tempted to get its way in the hiring of professors (e.g., for the theology and philosophy faculties) through power politics rather than through the normal university channels of influence. The same strategy may well be tried in structuring new curricula, legislating dormitory regulations, censoring student publications, appointing key administrators, narrowing the theology taught at the university to the dominant one of the religious founding group and disallowing other theologies in the theological faculty.

Because each pressure group wants the best for the university according to its particular needs (the government wants civic common good; business wants well-trained personnel; the church group wants the faith to be protected and given growth), and because the university is greatly in debt to these groups, some balance must be achieved between the aims and procedures of the university and the needs and expectations of the group. In addition, this delicate balance, this complexly reasonable compromising on both sides of each tension, is dependent on a further delicate balance: the contemporary wisdom of the university community itself which, in turn, accumulates out of the lived reinterpretations of traditional truth occurring in all the disciplines that structure the university. Only the university can know with certainty what reasonable compromises it can sustain without seriously hampering the pursuit of its dual aims. The pressuring groups must, therefore, trust the university community's decisions in these matters, just as the university community must trust the good faith and use the intelligent insights of the pressuring groups. Both sides have no alternative but to allow and to exercise academic freedom. The university, if it is to serve its country, must get deeply involved in political, social, ecclesial, and economic problems and yet must also retain a certain detached attitude. The university must be above these problems, not in order to avoid them, but in order to see them clearly as it attempts to find solutions. The university's academic freedom must be such that it is free to criticize national institutions (e.g., the labor unions and the National Association of Manufacturers) and, at the same time, free to work for the needs of these same institutions when asked to do so. On the other hand, state, church, business, labor organizations, and the entertainment world cannot afford to cripple the university's pursuit of truth and widsom; for in doing so, they will lose high-quality recruits for their work, strategic guidance for their growth, objective perspectives on their problems, and strong hope for the future.

Conclusion

If one were to compare the university to a great tree, then perhaps one could say that its eight constituencies form the roots. The taproot, of course, would be made up of the nation, the state, and the international community of scholars who give origin, basic sustenance, and dignity to the university through their *traditio* and criteria of achievement. The faculty, student body, and parents each offer, respectively, competent knowledge-art-skill-wisdom, vibrantly responsive life, and enthusiastic sacrifice. Meanwhile, the administrators and staff conserve and direct these exuberant energies while the churchly founding group offers the orientation of a faith seeking to understand, to support, and, if necessary, to criticize the resultant cultural growth. The eight constituencies, as the roots of the university, contribute to the trunk and branchings of the university's constitution. In other words, these "radical" constituencies help to define the autonomous structure of the university (the aims, the procedures to achieve the aims, and the university's collective personality) and, at the same time, set limits on the inner sap of intrinsic authority exercised within the university's autonomy or constitution. But they dare not try to own the university by modifying it to their own needs and advantages lest, in unduly restricting its autonomy (its ability to control its own life through its own proper authority), they cripple its dual intrinsic aims of (1) constantly reinterpreting the truth of specialized knowledges-arts-skills and (2) forming a wisdom-community. The constituencies, thus, extrinsically authorize the university; however, they are not its constitution nor do they exercise authority that is intrinsic to the university. This intrinsic authority is, structurally, the very competence of the faculty in specialized knowledge, shared vision, teaching, passion, and *traditio;* while administratively, it is the prudent decisiveness of university officials in effectively carrying out the aims of the university, in building a wisdom community, and in directing the dual intrinsic aims of the university toward extrinsic service to the larger civic community. In turn, this intrinsic authority is, dispositively, the intelligent and loyal cooperation of students, and it is, purposefully, the total university living up to its aims in order to achieve the university's commonweal and, ultimately, the commonweal of the nation.

Once the independent being, or autonomy, of the university is seen to be its constitution of proper aims and procedures, and once the extrinsic authorization of the constituencies is gratefully recognized by the university as it exercises its own proper authority within this constitution, then academic freedom becomes more understandable and liveable. For academic freedom can then be seen as a compound of three factors: (1) the

58

university's respect for its constituencies, (2) its wise use of its intrinsic authority to cause the least harm and the most good for the commonweal of its many constituencies, and (3) its resistance to those pressure groups attempting to mold the university to their needs and uses against its very constitution and authority. Academic freedom is, consequently, a delicate balance between two benevolent influences: (1) the constituency that wants the best for the university, but is governed by its own self-interests, and yet trusts the wisdom of the university community's considered decision to resist a particular pressure; (2) the university that wants the best for its constituencies, but is also governed by its constitutional aims and procedures, and yet trusts the good faith of the constituency and integrates their intelligent critiques. Academic freedom thus becomes the measure of health for both the university and its constituencies. It is the salubrious weather in which the university, like a tree, can grow and produce good fruit.

The following chapter will provide greater clarity by considering in more detail the dual aims of the university and how they point toward service of the civic community. In this way, one can appreciate the delicacy and the magnificence of the university's contribution to the nation's life and culture.

3 The University as Institution and as Wisdom Community: A Schizoid Being?

Although the university is a single reality distinguishable from other realities, still, like a coin, it has two sides. It is both institutional and communal. (Its latter side, however, is often obscured and misunderstood.) And those who fail to distinguish these two aspects of the one reality run the risk of making some costly errors. First of all, the same people who run the institutional aspect of the university are members of its communal aspect; they act in different ways, though, when functioning for the institution and when relating in the university community. Faculty members, for example, at work in a specialized field, are considered colleagues of the members of their team or department with whom they relate according to professional norms dictated by the functions they perform. A student writing a doctoral dissertation consults with these professors according to their special knowledge and skills, makes appointments to see them in their offices, observes the eight departmental steps for drawing up, researching, writing, and presenting the dissertation, and arranges for an examining board according to the six graduate school regulations. Meanwhile, the professors are observing the same careful protocol that, over the years, has proved helpful for avoiding last-minute disasters and prolonged agonies. This is how specialized knowledge, method, and skill is developed best.

Yet these some professors, so deferential amid protocol, turn out to be friends when, "after hours," they chat about their families, their research, crazy incidents in a seminar, the potential of a particular student, or repairing the refrigerator. And the student, having sweated anxiously through a three-hour oral examination only hours before, may feel included in this friendship. This is where wisdom happens, as official colleagues become personal acquaintances in the friendly exchange of ideas and hopes and laughs. But woe to the student who does not know how to distinguish between colleague-time and friend-time, between the institutional aspect and the communal aspect, between the properly scientific routine of building knowledge and the casual spontaneity of acquiring wisdom.

Failure to note the differences between the institutional and communal aspects of the university induces a second type of confusion: qualities and products may be asked of the institution that can only be given by the community—and vice versa. Only the institutional side of the university offers a highly specialized knowledge (e.g., a course in advanced topology), consistent training in specific skills (e.g., charcoal etching or #1042 computer programming), the protection of security officers when one is working late in the laboratory, guidance in writing government grants, scholarships for students, secretarial services for scholarly articles, free academic and psychological guidance—to name but a few institutional contributions. Only the communal side, on the other hand, offers the guidance of values, widsom for planning university expansion, loyalty to students and to the university (beyond the department), and hope for the future—again, to name but a few communal contributions. Frustration results when a person tries to pick apricots from the grapevine, when the institutional aspect is asked for wisdom and the communal aspect is requested to provide secretarial service or dormitory prefecting.

Many an administrator, in confusing the communal and the institutional aspects, has met such frustration: "I gave that department permission for every piece of equipment they wanted, I approved their wage increases without a whimper, I gave them funds for more graduate student scholarships, and still they are not happy, still they won't cooperate with the other departments, still they snarl at each other and at me." Such frustrations will not disappear simply because the administrator attends to the difference between the two sides of the university, but the frustration will at least become understandable. Even higher values than the mere avoidance of frustration are at stake in making this distinction between *Gemeinschaft* and *Gesellschaft* in the university setting. We would do well to explore it more fully.

University as Institution Organized for Truth

One has only to page through university catalogs to become aware of how beautifully expressive the institution is in listing university officers, trustees, deans, staff, and committees; in providing detailed descriptions of its various schools, correspondence and extension divisions, library facilities, summer-winter-spring sessions, various pre-professional programs, admission requirements, financial procedures, academic standards and special regulations, grading and credit-point systems, academic standing procedures, campus ministry, student services and housing, financial aid, and various degree programs. Finally, the catalogs painstakingly lead us through each department of each school in the university, from anthropology to zoology, listing its faculty, stating its specific objectives, and describing its courses, one by one. Nor is the catalog all there is to the "institutional" side of the university. There is still the faculty handbook, with diagrams of administrative authority-lines and descriptions of their responsibilities, the history and stated objectives of the university, a list of the various councils (or senate) and committees that administer the university, procedures and criteria for faculty ranking and promotion (to say nothing of dismissal proceedings), faculty rights and duties, retirement and protective benefits, and faculty-student relations.

There is still even more to the institutional side of the university; in the files of each department head are the faculty's approved criteria and procedures for hiring and for salary scales; in the files of administrators are job descriptions, by-laws for adjudicating issues, and guidelines for forming their staffs; and in the files of the faculty senate or council are the histories of previous decisions and outlines of procedures. Not to be forgotten are the buildings, maintenance cadres, laboratory equipment, warehouse for teaching aids, computer center for retrieving information, and the whole financial apparatus of the university. The mere listing of the institutional parts of the university is overwhelming; yet assembling them into the dynamic being that produces knowledgeable and technically skilled people is far more overpowering.

The institutional side of the university is a remarkable creature: it survives the death of its founders and builders; it grows even as it sends its best-trained students into the world; it develops a staff of administrators and assistants whose minute attention to important operational detail and planning frees students and faculty to pursue truth for itself; it guards carefully and promotes strongly the aims of the university as defined by the faculty and then develops faculty-invented-and-approved procedures to make these aims achievable.

To see the way this institutional facet is rendered dynamic, however, one must note precisely how its aims are different from the communal side of the university. Further, one must consider three levels of the university: (1) the undergraduate level, (2) the graduate level, and (3) the professorial research level. For the same ultimate aim of the institutional—namely, reinterpretation of traditional truth—is implemented differently, and yet reciprocally, at each of these levels. Thus, the undergraduate aims to achieve some competency in one specialized knowledge that he or she calls a "major." This is usually the vocational side of undergraduate education, since it equips the student with an incipient skill for a particular job market. But there is also the liberal or general side, which, concretely, is a core curriculum that is aimed at opening the student's eyes (perhaps even his or her heart) to all the ways mankind has devised for knowing himself and his world. This core curriculum gives a humane context for the student's specialized knowledge. Lastly, the undergraduate has room in his or her program for electives, in which the student may discover the spontaneity and fun of learning—for transfer to other studies; the student may even achieve a sneaking admiration for knowledge.

The undergraduate has to learn, above all, to reinterpret traditional truth, i.e., to discover a new world beyond that of high school learning, to reappropriate everything he or she has ever learned, to be as up-to-date as possible for the job he or she must win and the world he or she must live in. Naturally, this is a time of confusion and anger as well as a time of wonder and attempts to overthrow values. As a result, the thinking-suffering student will challenge the teacher to new depths of thought, new ways of expression, so that not only the undergraduate is forced to reinterpret traditional truth. At the same time, the challenged professor is also being deepened by his or her graduate students who, in learning to teach undergraduates and to research their special knowledge, have likewise been forced into deeper questioning of their discoveries and into wider integration of these discoveries within the discipline taught and with other relevant disciplines. (For example, teaching the philosophy of medical law requires venturing into biology, supreme court decisions, pharmacy, and sociology of the hospital.) The questions of these students, especially if they are close to the professor's own research area, demand that the professor constantly reinterpret his or her most cherished traditional stands.

Thus, the undergraduate is seeking to reinterpret traditional truth within his or her specialized knowledge in order to be well-stocked with knowledge for the job he or she seeks. The graduate student, on the other hand, undertakes this reinterpretation in order to develop his or her skill or methodic approach within the particular discipline. The professor, too, is occasionally delighting in the stimulating questions of undergraduates, in the discoveries of graduate students, and in his or her own research as this lights up his or her teaching of the undergraduates, his or her direction of the graduate students, and his or her own field of learning. All three levels are cooperatively developing, in different ways, the single institutional aim of reinterpreting traditional truth for the contemporary world. Although the researcher-professor attains this aim most fully, he or she nevertheless needs the spirited undergraduate questions in all their concrete practicality and naïveté. In addition, he or she needs the new knowledge discovered by the graduate students, together with their strong curiosity and their pressing desire to reintegrate this specialized knowledge.

But to appreciate the full significance of the institutional aim, it must be contrasted with its counterpart, the communal.

University as Wisdom Community—A Humbling Arrogance

The very complexity of the university organization, which mirrors the unbelievable complications involved in reinterpreting traditional truth, dramatizes the fact that only wisdom could direct the intricate university as it works toward its first aim. But where is this wisdom to be found? In the president of the university? In his or her councils or vice-presidents or Board of Trustees? In the other administrators and their staffs taken as a group? In the faculty, which initiates and implements changes of aims? In the student body, which challenges the wisdom it tries to absorb? Or does the wisdom lie in all these persons taken collectively? Perhaps such wisdom is beyond any collectivity and can be found, therefore, only in the total community of the university, a group of friendly, knowledgeable people whose love of the truth and of other people has united them in common pursuit of wisdom and in service of the civic community.

It would seem that only such a community arising out of loyalty can appreciate traditional wisdom, develop it, and pass it on to others. For wisdom is more than techniques, more than specialized knowledges, more than routines; wisdom is interpersonal knowledge and deeply felt values. Why? Because wisdom includes basic attitudes, i.e, intelligent virtues, that are incarnated in the simplest actions toward goals of great worth. Wisdom is a total vision of the world and, at the same time, a full embrace of the world—a world made up primarily of persons but secondarily of things that are both beautiful in themselves and handsome in their service of others. As a total vision and a basic stance, wisdom is the central source of community life and growth. And yet wisdom is as concrete as the day-to-day decisions which it infuses with shrewdness, as warm as the love for a particular friend which it fills with both tenderness and steely courage. At the other end of the spectrum, wisdom is meant to give us sight of far distant harbors just when we are battening down the hatches under the heavy weight of flooding waves and hurricane skies.

But what precisely *is* this wisdom in the university community? Basically, it is that single mysterious *esprit de corps* that inspires all university procedures, from teaching to sport events, from researching to leisure, from praying to examinations, so that students are humanely educated, professors advance in their fields, and the larger communities are well served by the university. More concretely, the first element of this wisdom is the integration of knowledges and values within each professor and administrator, then within each department and staff, next inside each

64

school, and finally throughout the university itself. It is a cumulative vision that surfaces in the balanced judgments and prudent decisions of individuals and groups during interdisciplinary courses, in faculty symposia concerning world problems, during committee meetings on university needs, processes, and hopes, or within advisory sessions for civic groups, but above all in the genial exchanges before, during, and after class with students and with fellow faculty members and administrators.

A second concrete element of this university wisdom consists in the willing ability of university people to cooperate out of mutual respect and even friendship. For wisdom is generated only in an atmosphere of relaxed truth-seeking and love-giving, since it demands the leisure of contemplation, the absence of fear and rivalry, the willingness to be proved wrong, the hope of finding beatific truth, the presence of playful humor. Although the intense and concentrated atmosphere of fellow professionals testing the new discovery of a colleague is both necessary to the university and to the reinterpretation of truth within a specialized knowledge, it usually does not generate wisdom. This often comes later, in a different atmosphere, when colleagues take out pipes and cigarettes, start to joke with each other, and, in the relaxed process of seeing truth together, forget about supper. This is not to deny the sudden wisdom-insight during an event of unexpected joy or sorrow, nor the discovery of wise agreement that underlies a turbulent committee meeting. It simply says that although wisdom includes science or knowledge, it is indeed something more that happens quite differently. University wisdom, then, includes the intelligently discovered and shared values that transform colleagues into friends, disparate knowledges into the appreciation of a single world vision, despair of the present into hope for the future. These two principles of university wisdom, then, reveal its more speculative side.

University wisdom has a third element within it, namely, the potential of the community to fulfill the complex needs of the individual student (e.g., "I've told you all I know as a psychologist about schizophrenia; why don't you consult Professor Jones on the biochemistry of it and Dr. Willoughby on schizophrenia in his psychiatric practice"). It also has the communal potential for composing the rationale behind the new undergraduate core curriculum, for restating university goals in light of the latest visit of the accreditation team, for saving the neighborhood surrounding the university, and so on. Thus university wisdom may have its head high in the theoretical sky, but it is also able to sink gnarled roots into deeply practical and uniquely difficult needs and problems of the total university rather than merely addressing the problems of a single department.

In its attempts to serve the larger civic community, university wisdom reveals its fourth constituent. For the university, as the home of the world's problems, imbibes, studies, and cooperatively prescribes for these problems out of its peculiarly elevated vantage point whereby it can correlate the knowledges and experiences of many experts. Because of this international experience, university wisdom is well equipped to deal with the needs of the local civic community. For example, since the university is the creator and user of new knowledges and skills for the Third World, it should know something about the unemployment problem of the inner city; since the university may be sending economic experts to advise the Congress of the United States on the effect of certain proposed taxes, it should have some inkling of how the use of state funds to support small businesses would change certain neighborhoods of the city. But university wisdom is not only a servant; it is also a herald of the future when it predicts how computer technology will affect industry in the next ten years. It is even a prophet, similar to those of the Old Testament, when it warns about the side effects of secularization—which it should know well, since it is the prime agent of this cultural phenomenon. Thus, there are four principles to university wisdom (the second of the university's dual aims): (1) integration of knowledges, (2) shared ultimate values, (3) resultant potential to run the university humanely, and (4) practical ability to deal with complex civic problems and needs. The last two principles of university wisdom reveal, of course, its practical side just as the first two principles uncover its more speculative side.

In order to see university wisdom more clearly (lest we confuse it with the university's first aim of reinterpreting traditional truth), it would be helpful to briefly explore its three gross levels, in each of which, the four above principles are operative. The highest, or speculative, level of university wisdom is the integration of all the physical and social sciences, along with history, literature, and the fine arts, by way of philosophy of science and philosophy proper, and according to theological understanding. Only a community of scholars in close communication with each other could achieve such an integration; no single person could do more than primitively approach this unity. Yet, without such an integration, the university grows haphazardly and risks exploding into hostile parts.

University wisdom must be more clearly a communal holding at its second level, the level of so-called middle principles. This crucial level is where the top-level theoretical principles become more concrete as they are applied toward a unique situation. To take an illustration from a practical science, let us suppose an artist sketches out a possible development of Cincinnati's riverfront sports complex and recreational center; it is beautiful and highly theoretical. An architect, however, must

66

now translate this envisioned beauty into floating round stadiums that seat thousands and provide each spectator a perfect view, into ribbons of concrete that will transport those thousands quickly to parking lots that are hidden from view by indirect lighting and waterfalls, into old-fashioned brick promenades equipped with newfangled rippling and cascading floodwalls that can be used not only for seating small concert audiences but also for mooring pleasure craft. What is required at this second level is not just a slide rule; there must also be a "feel" for how people recreate and for what pleases or distresses them.

At a third level, contractors and their construction crews will transform the plans into bulldozed mounds of dirt, steel pilings, poured concrete, tension cables, riveted I-beams, laid bricks, electric lines, sewer conduits, and four-letter words. The "truth" of the plans now emerges as the envisioned good called the sports complex.

Perhaps a more apt, though complex, example of these wisdom levels would show the application of the highly theoretical principle of the U.S. Constitution proclaiming that all men are created equal and that, therefore, they have a right to equal opportunity. The translation of this first-level principle of wisdom to the second level involved a practical decision that black children should have educational facilities equal to those enjoyed by white children. In turn, this middle principle was translated at the third level into a number of strategies: busing children from one school district to another, using special bonuses to attract experienced expert teachers to inner-city schools, developing magnet schools for drawing the better students from all districts, and experimenting with new teaching methods and with summer schools for improving reading and mathematics techniques. Again, compassion for people's feelings and respect for their dignity were as much needed as intelligence and technique.

When it comes to giving an example of how the university community is able to bring its total integration of knowledges through the middle principles of the second level into the concrete situation of the third level, an excellent example is the university itself. For it is the wisdom of the university community that has slowly built and made dynamic the whole institutional side of the university. At first glance, the institutional seems to have arisen first, as the various departments and schools of the university were developed or when an already existing professional school was gradually integrated into the university in order to fill the emerging needs of students. At second glance, however, one sees that wisdom usually anticipated, planned, and adapted this growth of the institutional.

Thus, at the topmost level, wisdom principles—such as "truth liberates humans for fuller personhood" or "truth leads to the goodness of virtue" or "truth must be freely explored" or "justice must be preserved as the very structure of the university" or "truth united to goodness produces wisdom" or "beauty is the splendor of truth" or "truth is ultimately one amid its diversities"—controlled university growth at the second level, or middle level, of their implementation. There the principles worked out courses to reinterpret truth for each discipline at the undergraduate school, the graduate school, and the professional school; they developed laboratories for testing hypotheses for truth; they offered criteria of competence and of success for university personnel and students; they established means for integrating (a) one knowledge with another knowledge, (b) knowledge with skill and art, and (c) faculty with faculty, for the sake of the students' integration; they invented a flexible core curriculum as a liberal context for each student's vocational specialization; and so on. Meanwhile, at the third level of wisdom, the first and second levels suggested the down-to-earth procedures that guide and guard the pursuit of truth in the courses; that promote the hiring of competent teachers and efficient administrators for directing the second and third levels, by way of the first level wisdom principles; that set up committees to devise solutions for procedural academic problems; that keep the university economically solvent, that provide academic and personal counseling; that produce job descriptions of interlocking responsibilities for staff, faculty, administration, and student body; that develop laws to protect the academic freedom of the above four groups; that construct various tests to stimulate and monitor intellectual integration of students, and so on. In this way, wisdom expands truth with goodness and offers happiness as well as intelligence.

The best example, perhaps, of three levels of university wisdom in action occurs when specialists from many universities gather with the President of the United States and his cabinet to present a task-force plan for, let us say, slowing the inflation rate or mediating a treaty between Israel and Egypt or conserving U.S. natural energy resources. The international scope of these problems and their fundamental importance for human survival require that the first-level principles of wisdom be seen and used in new ways (thus the need for constant reinterpretation of traditional truth). Then, second-level practical implementation requires much more minute knowledge, much more compassion for people's feelings and hopes, much more shrewdness in predicting problems and in meeting them adequately. Finally, the third level must be adaptable to the widely varying competencies of other countries and their universities. One wonders whether such a wisdom can exist. Yet health problems such as malaria and small pox have yielded to similar planning, and the beginning of the "green revolution" is due to just such scientific prudence.

More and more in our times, this wisdom can be seen as the *raison d'être* not only of the university, but also of worldwide human culture, no matter how many principles compose it and how many levels it may have. For the complex problems of the world yield only to wisdom, and wisdom is not only the architect of the university, but also the university's essential contribution to itself and to its constituencies.

For this reason, it would be good to note some of the characteristics of university wisdom, since they quietly point to the importance of certain university structures and alert us to recurring problems. These characteristics come into view when one notes that wisdom, if it is to be practical, must meet the unique situation, the historical moment, with both an acute perception of the singular and a wide comprehension of the universal. Consequently, one of the first characteristics of university wisdom is historical instinct—a sense of cumulative development in a nation or an individual, a feel for the uniqueness of an event. Such an appreciation demands the ability to recognize how this new situation is similar to previous events yet has characteristics never before witnessed. Without this double appreciation, intelligent accumulation of experience does not occur in the observer, nor can he or she ever recognize the significance of history. Rather, all events are seen as connected merely by time-sequence or space-sequence; the same level of perception occurs in the more intelligent animals.

The instinct for history makes possible the second characteristic of wisdom: recognition of continuities (similarities) between systems of thought, cultures, knowledges, and skill-procedures. Such continuities are absolutes, for they enable us to measure similar events and cultural analogies so that the individuality or uniqueness of each is also recognizable. In fact, absolutes make all science possible; without them, nothing is comparable or intelligible; everything is chaotically disconnected.

Actually, these absolutes, when treasured, become the values found in wisdom, its third characteristic. Such values include liberty, justice, intelligence, virtue, family life, religion, artistic beauty, education (the opportunity for seizing truth), creativity, other-centered love (or loyalty), economic development principles, and so on. In time, these values call forth commitment or love, the four characteristic of wisdom. But the love must be intelligent because, according to the shifting situation and the condition of the wise person, these values take on different priorities in his or her decisions. As a consequence, the discipline composed of intelligence, of free choice, and of willingness to suffer for these values, becomes the fifth characteristic of wisdom. Finally, wisdom engenders the confidence of intelligent hope because wisdom recognizes providence in the world, namely, the fact that no evil event happens without some

69

consequent good also occurring. Indeed, evil, taken as the absence of adequate goodness in an event, can exist only in the goodness of that event; evil has no existence of its own but only a quasi-existence, or parasitical existence, in the good. No situation, therefore, is impossibly difficult, nor totally defies intelligence, for there is a convergence of good even amid the fiercest evil. Otherwise, evolutionary theory is a false vaporizing and the growth of culture is a delusion.

Here, then, is a description of that university wisdom, which is the second of the dual aims of the university, the first being the reinterpretation of traditional truth. If it is accepted that the first aim is that of the institution and the second aim is that of the university community, then how do they fit together?

Dual Aim of the University—Chance for Schizoid Life?

The duality of the university is found within the daily life of university persons and can be quite disturbing if it is not recognized for what it is, namely, the normal conflict between *Gemeinschaft* (the personal or communal) and *Gesellschaft* (the institutional or organizational). For example, when a university faculty member is driving home with two colleagues to take dinner with them, the spirit is *fraternal*, whereas an hour earlier in the laboratory the motif was *teamwork*. In the first instance, one is living in trust with friends, according to primary relationships; in the second instance, one works under contract with functionaries, according to secondary relationships. The unity shared by the three professors around the dinner table derives from the value that each places on the others' person and companionship; the unity that is shared by the same three professors around the spectroscope derives from their common work and career.

To further illustrate the normal conflict between *Gemeinschaft* and *Gesellschaft*, let us consider two professors from the same department, Ralph and John, who are discussing John's failure to be appointed vice president for academic affairs. As a friend, Ralph finds himself comforting John; at the end of the evening, however, he cannot help wondering whether his own chances for the position are not greatly enhanced. Ralph feels somewhat ashamed of this last ambitious thought, but he should not; he is simply experiencing the two sides of the university, *Gemeinschaft* and *Gesellschaft*, twisting within him. Three weeks later, when Ralph is made vice president for academic affairs, John comes to him to ask for special consideration about a sabbatical. Ralph's sense of gratitude to John for their long friendship is tortured by his realization that justice toward other faculty members could be injured if he gives John preferential treatment. In addition, Ralph has noticed that some people who were once a bit truculent toward him, are now rather deferential; he is feeling how distinct institutional power is from the influence of comradeship. He is also aware that he had put more confidence in people before his appointment, but he now feels a need to protect himself from their failures. He should not feel guilty, however. The ambivalence he experiences is not necessarily a self-deterioration; rather, it is the sharpened struggle between the institutional and the communal within him. To attain peace, he must more sharply define for himself what the particular situation requires—friendliness or official demeanor—and act accordingly. This is no easy matter, especially when friends, who are unaware of this ambivalence, expect him to play, simultaneously, both the institutional and the communal sides of the university.

But the dual aim of the university presents more than psychological difficulty for the faculty member or administrator. It can confuse the whole meaning of the university and lead to poor administrative decisions. To illustrate, let us consider an admittedly outlandish example: Suppose the university required, as some businesses require, that each professor fill out at the end of each day a timecard and a work sheet that would indicate in detail how many students had been counseled, how many pages had been read for a research project, how often and for how many minutes and to whom he or she had spoken on academic affairs or on strictly personal matters, and so forth. This heavy emphasis on the institutional would, it seems, undermine the communal. Similarly, one of the perils of unionizing university professors is that they might well become assembly-line workers in the information business. In such a situation, the institutional aspect would be smothering the wisdom community and then be puzzled at its own growing derangement.

The distinction, therefore, between the dual aims of the university and the discovery of how they refer to each other is of major importance. There are a number of justifications for saying that the first aim of the university is the institutional one, namely, reinterpretation of traditional knowledge within each discipline for fuller truth. Actual practices of the university seem to imply this. When hiring to fill a faculty position, for example, the two prime criteria confronting the department chairperson are as follows: (1) Does the candidate possess a specialized knowledge at the doctoral level that combines with the methodological skill to further develop this knowledge? and (2) does the candidate have the ability to transmit this knowledge and skill to students and colleagues? Likewise, in hiring an administrator, the two prime criteria are (1) whether or not the candidate has an advanced degree in a specialized knowledge and (2) whether or not the candidate has demonstrated prudence in assisting faculty members to cooperate in advancing each other's specialized knowledge. The criteria for student admissions also stress the institutional aim of the university: (1) Does the student's high school scholastic achievement demonstrate that he or she is ready to begin an undergraduate major? (or does the student's undergraduate proficiency in a specialized knowledge demonstrate that he or she is ready to commence graduate work?); (2) does the student show the requisite discipline to complete a program of specialized knowledge or skill?

Beyond these practices of the university, there are intelligible principles that would seem to give priority to the institutional aim of the university. Unless solid reinterpretation of traditional truth is offered to undergraduate or graduate students, for example, they cannot keep up with the current trends of society and, consequently, the knowledge or skill that they do receive will seem purely informational and rather uninteresting. For the university does not merely prepare students to take their places in professional society as lawyers, doctors, social workers, computer technologists, sales managers, or teachers. This "vocational" approach to education would kill ambition and severely restrict the accumulation of wisdom. What is more, under these conditions, the specialized knowledge and the skill of reinterpreting it would gradually wither in the professor and never be seeded in the student. For the discovery of new aspects of truth in a specialized knowledge demands reinterpretation of its totality, since knowledge is tightly unified. A failure to reinterpret means that nothing new has been discovered or that laziness has won out. Besides, reinterpretation is the way by which the student and the professor appropriate knowledge as their own and by which mere information becomes truth. If reinterpretation is not occurring, then university research is at a standstill—so, too, its faculty and student body—and the university is slowly slipping into oblivion. It, therefore, has nothing to say or do for itself, for the student, or for the civic community. Its wisdom is evaporating, since only through the constant challenging and precious enriching of traditional knowledges can a living wisdom come into existence and operate in the individual student or faculty member, in the department, in the school, and in the university.

Thus, it seems evident that the institutional aim of the university must be first. Indeed, university wisdom must be preceded by a previous dialectic among the specialized knowledges—a dialectic that is occasioned when these knowledges are focused together upon the solution of a problem such as industrial pollution of the atmosphere or the planning of a model city. Of course, this dialectic requires, first, that each member of the team is competent in his or her specialized knowledge and, secondly, that each specialist is aware of the need to complement his or her knowledge with the other specialized knowledges, by way of an underlying philosophy of knowledge. The resultant wisdom, however, merely focuses the specialized knowledges cooperatively on the problem; the specialized knowledges and skills do the job. Biochemistry shows the effect of a water pollutant on the digestive tract; industrial chemistry demonstrates a new process whereby the chemicals that contaminate the water can be eliminated; theology and ethics provide the moral motivations for expending money to introduce this new process; law interprets the public responsibility of the company before the court; social psychology explains the effect of the company's irresponsibility on its own executives, its employees, and the general public. It would seem, therefore, that the second aim of the university—the accumulation of wisdom—is secondary to and derivative of the first aim, i.e., the reinterpretation of traditional truth in the specialized disciplines.

There is an inconvenience, though, attached to accepting this statement about the primary and secondary aims of the university. In so thoroughly subordinating wisdom to specialized knowledges, how does one keep the university from becoming merely a big business for developing mercantile or ecclesial personnel, merely a great and busy bureaucracy of the mind without much inner unity or peace, merely a merchandizer of highly sophisticated information available to any high-paying customer such as an oil-rich sultan, merely a functional operations-system for government research and planning? Will wisdom values become obscured in the temptation to huckster knowledge? Perhaps there are reasons for suggesting that, to the contrary, reinterpretation of specialized knowledge is a university aim that is secondary to and derivative of the primary university aim of accumulating wisdom.

First, wisdom goes deep within truth to reveal its goodness. This is to say that wisdom reveals values and enables us to live these values concretely in our decisions, so that *community* comes into existence. The separative loneliness of specialized knowledge is given the companionship of wisdom. Wisdom, thus, incarnates the perduring values that give a civilization warmth and stability. In other words, wisdom directs contemporary secularization to the commonweal of humanity—a matter to be discussed later, in more detail. But let us take these generalities and specify them within the university.

To put it compactly, wisdom makes possible solid development of the specialized knowledge, effective teaching of it, and competent use of it to fulfill the needs of the civic community. If the individual student or professor pursues a specialized discipline without much reference to other disciplines, to personal living, and to the needs of society, he or she risks monomaniacal tendencies that alienate cooperators, tend to miss the significant fact amid the myriad details, lose the stimulation to insight that comes from other disciplines and from daily living, and tempt one to value everything from the myopia of a single viewpoint. In other words, this individual is being less humane and, as a result, has begun to diminish the value of his or her work in the specialized knowledge. Similarly, what can be said of the narrow individual can become multiplied, with unfortunate results, when a whole department, or an entire school, or a total university becomes myopic. Wisdom, thus, turns out to be an important guiding factor in the expansion of each specialized knowledge.

A second consideration is that European universities have always regarded the wisdom community to be the best atmosphere for the learning and using of a specialized knowledge; they commonly accept the liberal communal attitude as the strongest basis for scientific growth and, thus, place heavy emphasis on the fine arts, on early training in the liberal arts before attempting specialization, and on small community living for students. It should also be noted that the most valuable product that the university can offer the civic and ecclesial communities is its collective wisdom; from this wisdom, the university offers guidance in such areas as government planning, business techniques, military ordnance, communications-industry expansion, and ecclesial updating. Only this collective university wisdom can keep faculty members and students aware of the hundred currents swirling around each of these societal institutions. If those in the university limit themselves to their own specialized knowledges, they may well offer short-term relief but ultimate disaster.

But let us go beyond the development of an individual specialized knowledge or skill, beyond its potential use for the community, and beyond the atmosphere in which it is best taught. Let us look to the university as a totality. Then we may perhaps glimpse the most important reason for saying that the accumulation of wisdom is the primary aim of the university's dual aims. The earliest American colleges—those that later became the great universities of Harvard, Yale, William and Mary, Brown, and Rutgers—did not start as narrow seminaries. At Harvard, for example, even those who were later to become Congregational ministers were schooled in the full range of liberal studies. In other words, wisdom, from the earliest days, directed the embryonic universities in their institutional growth as they later incorporated professional schools and still later added graduate schools. Though new specialized departments, such as urban studies, may be added somewhat extrinsically to meet new civic needs, they are gradually incorporated into the full university as they better and better meet its dual aims. Further, the very structure of the undergraduate program, as we shall see later, is meant to minister to an incipient student wisdom. Its specialized major is balanced by an integrative core curriculum that is designed to give a wisdom context and by

74

electives that are proportioned to stimulate the sighting of new values within that incipient wisdom. The whole university, then, is the creation of wisdom, and it therefore must live and grow by a wisdom resident in its faculty, administration, and students. In summary, then, it would seem that the aim of cumulative wisdom is primary and that the aim of reinterpretation of specialized knowledge is rather secondary and derivative.

University Aims Are Truly Dual

How can one resolve this seeming conflict over which university aim has priority unless one notes that they are *reciprocal?* They do minister to each other, and one aim cannot well exist, if at all, without the other. Of course, one could respond: "Why attempt to set up any priority between them? Just accept their co-presence." Such an attitude would be acceptable if it were possible. But university people have a way of emphasizing one aim over the other, when it serves their purposes; in fact, they do make one aim subservient to the other. To not understand the type of priority being used is, therefore, to be unable to come to a reasonable decision. Those who wish to remake the university into a social reform mechanism, for example, will emphasize the accumulation of wisdom and the need to put its values into revolutionary action upon society. Others, who prefer a university that is purely contemplative and not responsible for adjudicating social evils, will stress the reinterpretation of truth as the primary aim of the university. Hiring criteria and promotion guidelines would have to be readjusted according to these two dichotomizing conceptions of the university. Thus, either group could destroy the university; on the other hand, if both groups are understood and controlled they could provide the ferment that stimulates university growth. Such control, however, demands an understanding of how the dual aims of the university relate to each other beyond mere reciprocity.

It could be that the first aim, reinterpreting the traditional truth of a specialized discipline, has a priority of efficacy and of elemental being. Priority of efficacy means that university wisdom can only work *through* the specialized disciplines to discover values, to build the university community (one's membership card in the university is some specialized discipline), to erect the university institutional structure (the specialized knowledges, arts, and skills are the "building blocks"), and to serve the larger civic community. Reinterpreting the traditional truth of a specialized discipline also has a priority of elemental being, since wisdom comes into existence through the interplay of specialized disciplines as they try to discover how to relate to one another in order to work cooperatively on a single world problem.

75

The second university aim, cumulative wisdom, has a priority of finality and of mature being. The priority of finality means that the accumulated wisdom in the university community is not only the directive force within the growth of each specialized knowledge or skill, but also the unifier of all the specialized disciplines into a single vision (what is the world? where is it going? why is it going there?), and the focusing or contextual agent in their action on civic problems and needs. The priority of maturity in being indicates that the unification of the university into a dynamic totality (rather than into an arena for competing knowledges) is accomplished by cumulative wisdom, which is therefore the mature *esprit* of the university. If the university has a collective personality (a unified sum total of all the interrelating individual personalities that make up the university community), it is this *esprit*—a unique focusing of many minds and a pulsing union of many hearts in one magnificent enterprise of knowledge and wisdom in the service of humanity.

How, exactly, do these distinctions help? They clarify the reciprocity that exists between the dual aims of the university so that neither aim is allowed to dominate the other. Each aim must cede to the other, as the situation demands, according to the special contribution that each one brings to the situation. No one specialized knowledge and its department, for example, can be allowed to dominate the building of a university structure by way of wisdom. Thus, committees must include wide representation from as many schools and departments as the structure warrants. In addition, the team of administrators ideally should represent a wide variety of specialized disciplines in their pre-administrative preparation. On the other hand, it should be clear that each specialized knowledge and its department ordinarily should provide its own evaluation of credentials for membership, its own program for improving the department, as well as its own specific criteria (in addition to the general administrative criteria) for hiring, for not renewing a contract, and for promotion. At the same time, each department must be open to that surveillance which wisdom from other cooperating departments brings to it. For this reason, both internal teams of reviewers (from within the university) and external teams (from, for example, accrediting agencies) should be welcomed by a department. Naturally, the more ingrown and narrow a department becomes, the more resistant it will be to such accountability, maintaining that it alone knows its needs, resources, and goals.

Again, an understanding of how the dual aims reciprocally develop each other also enables one to see more clearly why people, rather than disciplines, discover the values that motivate a nation to greatness. Only in the university community where respect for persons dominates can lived values be discovered, so that wisdom occurs—so that, as a result, the specialized knowledges are directed more wisely and so that, consequently, the university matures in such a way that it serves the civic community more responsibly. Such a discovery of values, however, is contingent on the previous reinterpretation of traditional truth within particular specialized knowledges and skills. For university values are, above all, intelligently discovered, conceived, and expressed. Thus, the contemporary valuing of man, within the university community and its wisdom, has been intelligently prepared by genetics with its biological evolution of man, by social anthropology with its psychological evolution of man, by psychology with its evolving value-personality, by history with its developing cultures, and by philosophy with its expanding appreciation of person.

The importance of these distinctions regarding the ways in which the dual aims of the university cooperate becomes more evident when one notes that operating implicitly within these dual aims is a third aim, namely, service to the larger civic community. The dual aims previously discussed are concerned with the development of the university itself, while this third aim takes into account the fact that the university has been brought into existence by the larger community in order to serve the latter's needs. Thus, as a part of the larger society and community, the university has obligations to minister to the other societal parts or institutions.

One might remonstrate that the inclusion of a third aim is an unnecessary complication. It might be argued, for example, that the successful attainment of the first of the dual aims (reinterpretation of traditional truth within a particular discipline) will automatically result in students being fully prepared with the skills and specialized knowledge they require for taking jobs in the various institutions of business, government, church, entertainment, military, communications, and so on. Furthermore, when the professors act in an advisory capacity for these institutions, they are already using the second of the dual aims of the university (accumulation of wisdom) and are further developing this wisdom as they meet the challenging problems presented by civic society.

Despite these objections against too many distinctions, it is necessary to be aware of this third aim as distinct from the dual aims of the university, if only to protect the autonomy of the university. For, without wanting to hurt the university, other institutions that benefit from its services tend to try to make it over into their own images because of their own strong needs. Unwittingly, the government would like to use university research resources as its own bureaucratic arm; without realizing it, business would like to streamline university programs for producing trained personnel according to mercantile efficiency; without full awareness, the church would like to make the university over into a preacher of the Word; implicitly, socialistic reformers would change the university into a mechanism for political action. Somehow the university must, even while serving these constituencies, retain its own identity if only to serve them better.

The dual aims of the university do establish clearly the distinct structure of the university. But the third aim (serving the larger community) communicates clearly that the university, having received its existence from the larger community (from the eight constituencies), must in justice minister to the needs of this community. It can do this well, however, only according to the dual aims that structure the university. For example, the reinterpretation of traditional truth must be done, first of all, for the sake of each specialized knowledge or skill in itself and then, derivatively, for the sake of serving the various constituencies by offering them trained personnel. If the priorities are reversed, the needs of the constituencies will eventually determine *what, how much,* and *when* truth is to be discovered. This would effectively cripple the discovery of truth, which is the first of the dual aims of the university and the aim that best equips the student to meet the changing needs of society. Thus, to answer the first objection, the first university aim produces trained personnel for society indirectly, not automatically and directly. It is only insofar as truth is wholly accepted for itself in a specialized discipline that a student can be trusted to apply that truth integrally and accurately to a changing situation.

An example may help to deal with the second objection, which denies the need to assert a third aim for the university. It is true that the wisdom of a professor who is also an advisor to a civic institution will be challenged to a greater growth by that institution's problems. But the advisor is useless to the civic institution unless he or she brings to it a type of collective wisdom that can be challenged into growth, and not be confused into paralysis, by the sight of monster problems. In addition, the wisdom he or she brings must be wholesome wisdom, that is, a wisdom not previously warped by political, ecclesial, business, or military pressures of the moment, yet a wisdom that is well aware of the needs that cause these sometimes unbearable pressures. In that wisdom, there must be a serenity arising from long-time contemplation of all the problematic facets that have been revealed by the convergence of many specialized disciplines seen in their respective historical tradition. Clearly, this is the second of the university's dual aims; it must precede service to the civic community if this service is to be worthy of the university community and if it is to be truly of service to the civic community. Thus, one must distinguish carefully the dual aims of the university from the third aim of community service, lest the university lose its distinct identity and, thus, lose its ability to serve the community well.

Seeing this third aim more clearly also clarifies the university's dual aims. For, in serving the community, the second of the dual aims—cumulative wisdom—acts as the context that gives direction to the specialized knowledges; the first of the dual aims—improved specialized knowledges—enables the university specialist to work out a more effective practical solution to particular civic problems. In partially solving those problems, whether they be the energy crisis or labor-management disputes or inflation or Mideast diplomacy, the university is not only expressing its gratitude for its very existence, which is given by the larger civic community; it is, moreover, doing its duty and using its competency gladly.

More specifically, the university is making its specialized knowledges and skills available in a way that cannot be duplicated by any other institution, since no government technical institute and no industrial research complex, because of its very pragmatic nature, can match the wisdom with which university experts apply their specialized knowledges and skills. Paradoxically, it is university wisdom that enables the practical specialized knowledges to be more practical and more effective, since its contextual knowledge makes the specialist more aware of all the revelant elements to the problem, more sensitive to all the possible obstacles to success, more cognizant of the rich history of the problem. For the "reinterpretation of traditional truth" is actually a *reintegration* of this truth in terms of modern discoveries, not only in the particular specialized knowledge but also in adjacent scientific fields. Such reintegration is precisely what is needed to solve a complex civic problem; the more such reintegration is enriched with the collective wisdom of the whole university spectrum of studies the more effective and long-lasting it will be. What the university does best and uniquely for the world—i.e., serving the world's problems with scientific precision out of wisdom—it does out of its very being, namely, its dual aim.

For the religiously oriented university, the distinction of this third aim of the university is of particular moment. Such a university, if it is filled with the spirit of a Christian theology, will be especially sensitive to the needs of the civic community and alertly anxious to serve these needs. Central to the Judaeo-Christian message is care of the *anawim*, the dispossessed poor, who make up the bulk of the civic community in most nations, if not in the United States. For *religiously oriented* universities, it is important to note why this service of the poor will be in direct proportion to the successful implementation of the university's dual aims.

79

To begin with, justice within the university becomes exportable to the civic community only in the measure and quality with which the dual aims of the university are fulfilled. That is to say, justice in the university itself is measured simply by how well the particular university lives up to its true identity (its autonomy or constitution). Having accomplished this, the religiously oriented university can speak fairly to the injustices of its civic society, can act effectively to cure them, and can demand the assistance of other institutions. If the dual aims of the university are weakly pursued, then, in seeking its third aim, the religiously oriented university can expect to speak and act weakly and to receive little help from others.

Conclusion

It is rather unsettling to find that a university has three major goals. What university can survive such complications and escape a schizoid state? The situation is not simplified when one states that the first aim of the university is the reinterpretation of traditional truth within each specialized knowledge-skill-art. Reinterpretation entails at least a small revolution in each specialized department, and it occurs at all three levels of the department: faculty, graduate, and undergraduate. And yet, how can a knowledge-skill-art and its department grow unless there is constant reassessment of the field and unless this reassessment is allowed to filter down from faculty to graduate and undergraduate levels with consequent upset? Here we face the institutional side of the university—a side that is quite distinct from, yet intimately united with, the communal side.

As if all this were not bad enough, the second major aim of the university is made out to be the accumulation of wisdom within the university community. Wisdom is a notoriously difficult reality to describe—so infamous, in fact, that not a few consider it a chimera. This chapter has described four of its constituents (reintegration of disciplines and values into a total vision for prudently balanced judgments within individuals and groups, a willing ability to cooperate out of intelligently shared values, a potential for fulfilling the complex intellectual needs of university members, a correlation of international expertise for service of the constituencies) and, then, has noted that these four elements of wisdom move through three levels of principles: the highest, speculative level, wherein all the specialized disciplines are integrated; the middle level, wherein this integration is applied according to an integrated value system; and the lowest level, which is the unique historical situation that requires remedy or additional strengthening. Furthermore, in this process of application, six wisdom characteristics come to view: an ability to meet the unique historical moment because of a sense of tradition; the recognition, in this tradition and moment, of continuities (absolutes, values) between systems of thought and cultures; the treasuring of these absolutes so that intelligent commitment can occur and intelligent confidence be engendered; the willingness (discipline) to intelligently and freely suffer for these truths and values. Granted the mysterious complexity of wisdom, one must nevertheless ask; If wisdom is not directing the university (and, incidentally, the movement of civilization), what keeps the university somewhat unified, growing intelligently, and capable of wisely meeting the monstrous problems of inflation, disarmament, pollution, diminishing food supply for exploding populations, and so on?

The reciprocity of the dual institutional and communal aims would seem to partially solve the problem of schizoid existence for the university (1) because wisdom must do its work *through* the specialized disciplines and takes its sustenance for growth out of their dialectical interchanges and (2) because wisdom does furnish meaningful context and motivational drive for fruitful work within a specialized discipline and does so accomplish the unification of the university that wisdom is well called the *esprit* of the university (that remarkable focusing of many minds and uniting of many hearts in the service of specialized truth, integral wisdom, and world needs).

But then, there is still the third aim of the university, namely the service of the university's eight constituencies. The other two aims are intrinsic to the university; they are its very structure. Is not this third aim a mere distraction at best and a risky huckstering at worst? A possible response to this is that service to those who have given birth and continuous nurturing to the university is only a matter of justice. What is more, university services can not be duplicated by any other institution and are critically needed by the nation. Furthermore, the resultant interchange with the constituencies weaves the university into the very fabric of society, keeps the university from becoming a snobbish ivory tower, enriches the university's specialized departments with fresh insights, and protects the university from the pressures of other institutions. Indeed, for a Christian university, this third aim introduces the pastoral element into its decisions.

But a word of caution is necessary. In stressing that the university is both institutional and communal, that the university must develop as its first aim the distinct specialized knowledges to their fullest, and that the wisdom community of the university develops as its second dual aim a total context of value and knowledge both for directing the development of specialized knowledges and for serving the civic community, we have walked into several booby traps. First of all, the whole presentation takes for granted that the specialized knowledges can be related to each other, that they are integral to wisdom, and that a university community can have commonly shared values. This seems to deny the whole problem of pluralism in knowledges and value systems that is presently torturing every institution of modern society. There is also a second, allied problem. If a wisdom community must have unity of values, how can this be attained except through the use of an ideology? Lastly, the university wisdom community cannot expect wisdom to occur in the students or be well applied to civic problems unless the members of the university community undertake a deeply sacrificial lifestyle over a long time. More is needed than a passionate commitment that might come from an ideology. A remarkably strong discipline is being asked of the university community. What is this discipline, what are its sources, how does it work? The next three chapters will try to deal with the three problems—pluralism, ideological unity, and disciplined sacrifice—that seem to underlie the university aims.

4 Pluralism: Endemic to University Life or Epidemic?

Some cynics consider the term *university*, when applied to what they would call our present "knowledge factories," the largest irony of language. They contend that the term *multiversity* should be used, especially when, as in California, the state university has many branches at diverse locations. But the diversity within the single organization called "university" is not simply a matter of geography. It would seem that the very nature of a university is to *pluralize* knowledges and skills. A quick comparison of university catalogs for 1928 and 1978 shows an extensive explosion of knowledges and skills into such new departments as cybernetics and ecology, or into an array of subdivisions within a department, such as, for example, physiology, genetics, biophysics, and anatomy within biology.

Each "knowledge," of course, implies a new skill. As the School of Social Work expands, for example, into custodial care of juvenile delinquents, emergency aid for the aged, education for the unemployable, and support for unwed mothers, professional skills become more finely differentiated. Outside the university, the explosion of skills is also evident when one notices, among other things, the rapid differentiation of labor unions according to skills and the complexly technical job descriptions used by industry for hiring specialists. Here, too, the university is once again mirroring the complication of society itself. Yet the university does more than this; she promotes the explosion of knowledges and the consequent explosion of skills. Her reinterpretations of traditional truth within the specialized knowledges and within their skills result in ever more subdivisions of knowledge and skill. The university helps society to see more deeply into reality by way of new knowledges and, then, to construct new controls on reality by way of new skills. Without the university, the focusing of immense knowledge and of specialized skills, such as those produced by the U. S. space program with its new knowledges, techniques, skills, apparatus, and industries, might never have occurred.

In functioning as a principal agent of pluralism, therefore, the university is fostering the multiplication of new organizations grouped around a particular knowledge (around marine biology, for example, are gathered marine medical technology, sea-harvesting technology, and marine military technology) or around a particular skill (around computer programming, for example, are gathered the telecommunication and data-processing industries). Similarly, pluralism of the body politic enters into the life of the individual person so that each one finds his or her consciousness intersected by multiple community memberships. To cite but one example, the professional ballplayer is not just a member of a specific team; he and his family enter the *community* called the Pittsburgh Pirates baseball organization. In addition, he might also be an officer in the Professional Baseball Players Union, a deacon of the Second Baptist Church, a cosponsor of an investment group, a part-time student in a law school, and a member of the business community through his ownership of a chain of pizza parlors. The pluralism originally started by the university, and now maximized by society, has infiltrated the mind and heart of the individual person.

This pluralism becomes intensified when philosophies are multiplied both inside and outside the university. Since a person's philosophy deals with basic values and insights—such as the meaning and worth of life and death, of God and man, of work and play, and of hope and despair—the variety of philosophies eventually generates distinct communities of quite different lifestyles. Any community formed out of philosophic affinity cuts across all the knowledge and skill communities that constitute the particular nation. In the United States, for example, these philosophies have surfaced as the Republican party, the Democratic party, the Socialist party, the Communist party, and the Agrarian party as well as other less formally organized groups, such as flower children, monetary or tax reformers, ecology-minded protectionists, Pro-Life members, and so on.

A second intensifying factor of pluralism is religion, for a variety of theologies, or explanatory ways to God, are influenced by the variety of philosophies that sustain various lifestyles. This is not to say that the average person is an expert in philosophy and theology, but rather to imply that everyone has to take some position about life's basic values and insights if he or she is to stay sane while making everyday decisions. But no one takes such a position without the influence of the communications media and friends and family, all of whom are eventually affected by the philosophies and theologies developed in the universities. Once again, although the universities of the Western world are far from being the only and total cause of pluralism, they are nevertheless its prime promoters.

At this point, one has the duty to ask some poignant questions: Is pluralism good? Where is it propelling the world? Pluralism seems to be fragmenting the world if one looks at the following examples: the rapidly lengthening roll call of the United Nations; the unbelievably intricate sets of committees and subcommittees that make up the Congress of the United States; the mushrooming of the U.S. Department of Health and Human Services (within 25 years, it had created 400 programs, staffed by over 1 million people who spent $182 billion during 1978); and the monstrous cafeteria of courses offered by the average American university.

This seeming fragmentation of the outer world naturally thrusts itself into the inner world, or consciousness, of anyone attempting to survive in this outer world. Josiah Royce, the Harvard educator and philosopher, has noted that, within a highly complex civilization, specialization can push a person into isolation and can force cooperation at the expense of community interest. In other words, the social pressures and laws used to motivate a person to do his or her job, can prevent that person from internalizing his or her work or making the job truly his or her own. Thus, an individual learns to hate, rather than to love, his or her work; persons tend to become mechanical not only on the job, but also in their family life. In these circumstances, persons feel themselves crushed by the complexity of everyday living and often resort to drugs, thrills, alcohol, violent entertainment—anything to escape the now meaningless and minutely demanding routines of life, which are akin to the endless pumping of water by coolies into distance rice fields that they never see. A self-centeredness that both throttles love for others and isolates the individual seems to be the inevitable result of rampant pluralism.

Even the optimistic Teilhard de Chardin was aware of this possibility when he acknowledged the possible exhaustion of physical resources and the "ecstasy of discord" that could result from the "complexification of life" in the "noösphere." Is the university, then, unwittingly, even violently, fragmenting both society and the human being as she promotes pluralism through her constant reinterpretation (and further differentiation) of traditional truth within specialized knowledges and skills? Is the university propelling the world toward a moment of universal explosive violence?

These surreptitious charges against the university can promote a popular anti-intellectualism of vicious consequences. By trying to answer them, we may come to understand better the unique contribution of the university to contemporary living. Such an answer should (1) indicate the causes of pluralism, (2) note the course of convergent pluralism in world history, (3) distinguish convergent pluralism from divergent pluralism in order to calibrate their goodness, and (4) sketch the meaning of pluralism for the university.

The Inevitability of Pluralism

The inevitability of pluralism is best seen in the richness of the beings that mankind comes to know. Because every single thing in the universe is related to all other things, chemists are fond of saying that the total analysis of a grain of sand should reveal the total meaning of the universe. They know that their knowledge of the earth granule leads to knowledge of the grass that feeds on it, and to knowledge of the sheep that feed on the grass. In turn, the philosopher, taking the data of the chemist, the botanist, and the nutritionist, begins to discover the dynamic structure that characterizes granule, grass, and sheep so that these structures eventually reveal the structure of a supreme cause. Each being is not only rich in its individual self, but also, according to evolution theory, functionally related to every other being of the universe, past and present. Furthermore, these revealing functional relationships are multiplying with greater and greater complexity as the world evolves. For this reason, no single insight of mankind can encompass or exhaust any single being, much less the whole universe—in fact no million insights can do this.

Consequently, mankind must use a variety of insights that converge from many different angles to begin to understand the granule of sand or the blade of grass or the single sheep. As a result, one finds that many distinct sciences have developed over the centuries out of the diverse approaches (methods) to the single reality of granule, grass, sheep, and mankind. Similarly, many political parties spring up out of diverse approaches to a nation's single commonweal, and many professional groups come into existence to serve the diverse needs of the single nation. The very complexity of the universe, therefore, when compared to mankind's simple insight, seems to demand plural methods and disciplines. There is no escape from this—unless one claims that he or she is the God who causes and, therefore, knows all reality with one thought.

There is a second and reciprocal reason for pluralism: Not only is the reality that is known very complex; the mind of the knower is also remarkably unique. Each person sees the world from a different perspective that combines family, ethnic background, education, work interest, personal ambition, social milieu, and health of body. Thus, the artist, the landscaper, the botanist, the logger, the philosopher, and the paraplegic will see the same tulip tree differently, even though all will agree on why it is a tree and not a rose bush or a rabbit. Because this unreproducible individuality develops out of the unique experiences of each person, no one can ever totally agree on anything with any other person. Only with God can one achieve total intellectual compatibility. The fact that two

86

sane persons can communicate about a particular being indicates that total disagreement is just as impossible as total agreement. This is why pluralism of itself is never anti-communitarian, and yet is always differentiating persons and communities with its richness.

A third reason for pluralism, unfortunately, is mankind's prejudice, erroneous judgments, and misuse of common-sense knowledge. The prejudiced understanding of Aristotle's distinction between mathematics and physics, for example, brought the sixteenth century Aristotelians to condemn the new physics of Galileo and to retain their own discredited variety; so, too, the erroneous judgment of the Cartesians led them to set up a physics contrary to that of Newton. Furthermore the misuse of common sense can result in people depreciating scientific learning in order to establish, without much evidence, an imaginary alternative. Out of such a milieu come fantastic philosophies, extremist political parties, artistic fads, pseudo-psychology, simplified economics for the masses, quack pharmaceutics, and fundamentalist theologies. Josiah Royce has attributed this discordance to humanity's failure to love others enough to want only the truth for them. Such discord, seen in all its social consequences, is original sin—a profound cultural propensity of the human race to cause itself evil. But this dark aspect of pluralism should not obscure the bright side, namely, that pluralism is a mark of the world's rich being and of each person's unique insight into this ontic wealth.

Yet another source of humanity's blindness to this positive aspect of pluralism is the tendency to romanticize the past as "more simple and more livable." We humans have a tendency to forget that, although hospitals and medical techniques were less complex, less impersonal in the nineteenth century, the death rate of newborn babies was much higher than it is today. The simplicity of economic life in the 1930s, without social security payments, made a long depression quite possible.

Still another source of humanity's blindness to pluralism is the tendency to simplify the complex past. Even as far back as the "golden" Medieval period, for example, philosophic pluralism was so rampant that Professor De Wulf spent most of his scholarly life and two volumes of history to show that one could not find a universal definition of scholasticism among the various schools of Thomism, Scotism, and Nominalism with all their subspecies. Even supposedly monolithic Thomism, singled out for special approbation by Leo XIII's *Aeterni Patris* (1879) and given heavy ecclesial support in American Catholic colleges, developed at least four varieties in order to promote a tight unity for Catholic thought: they were classical Maritain, scientific Louvain, historical Gilson-Fabro, and transcendental Maréchal.

87

It would seem, then, that pluralism is more endemic to an understanding of reality than epidemic. Consequently, it might well be a compliment to call the university a prime promoter of pluralism. Yet, it is not quite so simple, for there are at least two ways to interpret this natural pluralism, which is not to be confused with the myriad fantasies caused by prejudice, error, sin, and failure to love truth. Natural pluralism can be interpreted as convergent or divergent, as issuing from a single underlying unity or as expressing many independent underlying unities.

Convergent Pluralism: Basis for the Work of a University?

The interpretation of pluralism that Josiah Royce espoused and called *convergent pluralism* uses the working assumption that diverse philosphic and scientific starting points do not preclude an ultimate meeting of their paths on the way to full truth. In other words, all the specialized knowledges and skills of the university, together with common-sense knowledge, will eventually converge to form a single vision of the world because a hidden unity within reality underlies the development of all these knowledges. On the other hand, the interpretation that William James offered and called *divergent pluralism* contends that there may well be more than one order underlying the phenomena of the universe and, therefore, there may be more than one system of truth. These orders of truth and reality may even contradict one another without being false, so long as each order allows a person to live successfully in this multiverse. Thus, Hume's, Kant's, and Merleau-Ponty's diverse interpretations of the world are all true in James' pluralism, even though Hume contradicts directly Kant's evidence that, in addition to sensation, mankind also enjoys thinking, and even though Hume denies implicitly Merleau-Ponty's evidence that sensation is not merely passive but is also active. The approach of James clearly jeopardizes the principle of contradiction, as well as a person's ability to know reality with some assurance of truth.

There is strong evidence *for* convergent pluralism and *against* divergent pluralism. Convergent pluralism can occur only if the universe develops according to a single purpose, or finality. If two or more totally independent finalities are operative, then our universe is actually a "multiverse," and conflict between the overlapping universes would be impossible to resolve since the ultimate purpose of each universe would be totally independent. Indeed, conflict would be necessary since the multiple universes could be competing within the same arena of beings, namely, ourselves and our things. If, on the other hand, the universes were reciprocally dependent on each other, and thus capable of cooperating toward a common goal, they would then constitute a single universe of common action toward this common goal and all would be governed by mutually shared laws of reciprocation and congruence. The opposite of this view, of course, is a divergent plurality of contradicting worlds operating within the same being and thus rendering that being divided in its very essence.

Perhaps this can be seen more graphically from the fact of biological evolution. Although biologists are hard pressed to define, unmistakably, "the better" among various evolving specimens, their science has little internal unity unless it is imaged as the evolving "tree of life"—a single tree despite its many twisted and interlacing branches. To be sure, evolution is generally defined as a one-way, irreversible, temporal process that, during its course, generates novelty, diversity, and higher levels of organization. These higher levels of organization are precisely the convergence of the multiple parts of the lower levels into a new being—a convergence enjoying novelty and spontaneity. Indeed, the fact of evolution is literally a convergence of evidence from paleontology, genetics, taxonomy, embryology, comparative anatomy, and biogeography.

Furthermore, the four basic biological theories (Lamarchian, Darwinian, Synthetic or Neo-Darwinian, and Saltation or Catastrophic) used to explore this fact have gradually coalesced into the single theory of the Neo-Darwinian Synthetic School. A number of philosophies, such as those of Bergson and Whitehead, have attempted to use biological evolution as a model for understanding the whole universe of phenomena. But the pluralism of both philosophies of evolution and biological theories must find their single source in the fact of evolution, the evolving tree of life. Evidently biologists look at a *universe,* not a *multiverse.* Despite Thomas Kuhn's theory of discontinuous scientific revolutions, most scientists and philosophers of science follow Wittgenstein and affirm a strong thread of continuity between the basic concepts that have historically shaped modern sciences. Each scientific revolution does not discover a different universe, but rather, sees the old universe in a new way. Thus, Einstein's "universe" includes and corrects Newton's. In addition, Ian Barbour's *Issues in Science and Religion* shows how all the knowledges, from the physical sciences to literature and religion, fit into a unified spectrum of human knowing, and how this spectrum can be focused to yield a single theology of nature that points to a single universe.

If one enters the inner world of the human personality, one rediscovers a *universe,* not a multiverse, mirrored there. For if the world were composed of multiple, independent universes, the human person would have to deal with each universe according to a different set of ideas, values, attitudes (or virtues), and fundamental options. In other words, the human person would have to develop a different personality for each universe. The biologist would have to work out of at least two different sciences of biology, two different modes of friendship with his or her colleagues, two different "parenthoods" and "spousehoods" with his or her family (and the family would appear to be at least two sets of children and two spouses). Existence for the biologist, consequently, would be at least schizoid. Because the multiple universes are independent, the biologist would rightly wonder whether any two events were connected causally; if the biologist could connect two events causally (e.g., passing a football to a child), he or she would always risk being under illusion. Thus, if there is no convergent pluralism, there would seem to be no possible unity for mankind's personality and life. No one doubts that Freud, Adler, Jung, and Rank disagree in their understandings of who man is. But, clearly, each assumes that the other is not entirely wrong and that all can communicate with one another about a common subject, namely, John Jones or Mary Smith. There is not a total discontinuity between their theories of man and between the various personality aspects of a John or a Mary. If divergent plurality were the truth, however, every person would be schizophrenic, including the diagnosing psychiatrist.

One also finds a convergent pluralism by exploring the meaning of secularization or contemporary social growth. For secularization may be seen as the gradual expansion of both the individual person and the collective personality of a community. Regarding the latter case, expansion occurs through the specialized development and integration of knowledges and skills within and between communities that are using these knowledges and skills to serve the nation. The rapid pluralization of knowledges, skills, and their serving communities is matched by the discovery of plural value systems called "secularities," since they are often derived from, and then directive of, the whole secularization process. Just as secularization brings men and women to penetrate, through specialized knowledges and skills, more deeply into the world of persons, animals, plants, and things and become more responsible for them (i.e., secularization brings men and women to marry the world), so secularity is the value system that animates human love for this world. This is true for both the individual personality and for its collective counterpart, the community.

Secularization regresses into the triviality of a narrowed mind and heart, however, if its specialization of knowledges and skills is not matched by integration or socialization. Unless the individual integrates his or her knowledges, skills, values, and role actions according to a supreme value or purpose for living that has been freely chosen, his or her personality tends to dissipate itself in erratic behavior and distract itself with trivial interests. The collective personality—whether it is a plumbers' union or a sporting team or a nation or even an international civilization—must also converge its plural knowledges, skills, values, interests, and activities or else suffer the pain of divisive quarreling and ever diminishing cooperation in organizing the good things of life. Somehow, within the process of ensuring the commonweal, a single finality must be discovered—a finality whose mystery is never completely grasped, whose fullness is never achieved, whose opportunities for inventive free choice are ever surprising, whose hopes are remarkably clear in their allure but terribly demanding in their experimental fulfillment. This is convergent pluralism experienced in its social dimension. Without such pluralism is human progress even thinkable?

Even philosophy, the pluralistic scandal in the eyes of university people, seems to find, within world-process, an underlying unity to which all philosophers respond. In his *Unity of Philosophical Experience,* Étienne Gilson has traced, from Abélard to Hegel and Marx, the historical dialectic of philosophy. He has found that the history of philosophy is not the biography of multiple philosophers, nor the literary history of their many philosophical writings, nor the plural philosophies created by individual philosophers. Rather, he has discovered that philosophical ideas, though intimately connected with philosophers and their philosophies, are somewhat independent of philosophers. Somehow, once philosophical ideas are discovered and described, they enjoy a life of their own. This life reveals itself in at least seven laws of development, which cannot be accounted for merely by historical, economic, and sociological factors. Instead, as philosophy flows through history, gathering momentum and ever richer content in its sweeps through reality, it develops according to a single inner dynamism, which no single philosophy can hope to capture but to which every major philosophy gives witness. In fact, as Josiah Royce has noted, every outstanding philosopher has proposed his own philosophy as *the* single explanation for the universe and, thus, has revealed his basic assumption that the world's pluralism is finally convergent.

Additional evidence for convergent pluralism occurs in the dual facts that people are able to communicate with each other and that this communication can be steadily improved over the years. If, as some have suggested, multiple, independent universes were to intersect within a person, it would be impossible for anyone to predict his or her own behavior or the behavior of a colleague, a friend, or a relative. For the act of one universe within a person (e.g., one person asks a colleague a question about mortgage financing) would be totally disconnected from a second act of a second universe within the same person (e.g., the first person hits the colleague in the mouth). If the colleague were in a different universe at the time of the question, he or she might begin to shine the shoes of the questioner. Even if, under these difficult circumstances, the two could communicate by waiting for the same universe to happen simultaneously in both, it might be a long wait and the individuals would have less and less in common as the basis for their communication. Under these circumstances, friendships would rupture, contracts would be broken, cooperation would diminish. Communication is difficult enough in a universe of convergent pluralism, a universe in which it is possible to accumulate common experiences as the basis for exchanging ideas, for building common ventures, and for committing to marriage and family. All this may become clearer if one examines the ordinary objections to convergent pluralism that have brought people to espouse divergent pluralism.

Divergent Pluralism: Does It Save Freedom, Faith, and Subjectivity?

Some feel that a cryptodeterminism lurks within convergent pluralism—something akin to Marxist or Freudian determinism—because a single finality is said to be unfolding within world process. They also fear that such convergence would attack faith and smother subjectivity. In response, it should be noted that freedom of choice expands as one's knowledge of diverse options increases. Thus, the aim of academic and vocational counseling (to say nothing of the university itself) is to increase, through information and encouragement, the number of options open to the person being counseled. But expanding the "cafeteria" of options is not enough; there is also a need to strengthen an individual's ability to choose the best possible option. This ability is his or her liberty, the fruit of disciplined free decisions of the past. Such liberty, taken concretely, is precisely the human personality, which is made up of a balance of virtues and knowledges. For this reason, the human personality is capable of choosing and carrying out effectively the more demanding, more difficult option because it is actually the better one. What is more, this liberty is increased through the accumulation of good decisions that are made according to a long-term, fundamental life-purpose.

As we shall see later, divergent pluralism does not permit a single life-purpose but demands, at best, two; it therefore prevents a person from accumulating good decisions by rendering that person ambivalent in all his or her actions—*necessarily* ambivalent because the individual is stretched between at least two life-purposes. The single life-purpose of convergent pluralism does not eliminate an individual's freedom since all the means by which one achieves this purpose can be chosen freely and the life-purpose itself can always be freely changed for another life-aim or drastically modified. Nor does the single underlying world-finality demand a deterministic world in which life-purposes are delusions. The finality, for example, of the biologist's tree of life or of Maslow's personality development is hardly without novelty, surprise, and probability of outcome. Not every finality is a Marxist straight line or a Skinnerian mechanistic response; there is also the finality of a portrait that the artist never stops improving or the finality of a kindergarten class that the children, in their spontaneity, and the teacher, in his or her inventiveness, never stop modifying. Convergent pluralism, therefore, not only allows for freedom but also, unlike divergent pluralism, makes liberty (the growth of freedom into adulthood) possible.

A second objection to convergent pluralism comes, perhaps unexpectedly, from neo-orthodox theologians. Karl Barth, for example, deplored the way in which liberal theologians proclaimed the rationalistic "continuities," or "integrations," between the sciences and revelation. He himself declared that theology was radically discontinuous and unintegrable with the sciences. God is "the wholly other," known only when He chooses to reveal Himself and never known by reason alone, that is, by simply reflecting on the activity of created things. Thus, even Scripture is a purely human record; it records, but is not, the revelation, which is the dynamic person of Christ. By refusing to admit the convergence of revelation and theology with any human knowledge, Barth hoped to keep faith free from human delusion and from any attack that uses science as its weapon. This dichotomy was strangely paralleled by the existentialists who irreparably separated knowledge of personal existence from knowledge of impersonal objects, and by the linguistic analysts who divorced forever religious and scientific language.

Such safe isolation of revelation and its theology from the sciences and from human frailty, such divergent pluralism, has some disadvantages. It tends to lift faith and theology out of everyday life; it fails to give theology any role within the university life of knowledge and wisdom; and it is based on an implicit metaphysics that, in allowing revelation and theology no communication with the sciences and other human knowledges, turns the world into a mere stage for the dramatization of revelation. Thus, the risk of cosmic artificiality is not small, for the world becomes rather meaningless in itself, and human life becomes simply a staging of witness to God. For this reason alone, the Christian university would certainly be wise not to endorse divergent pluralism, lest the university's very name carry within it a baffling contradiction.

It should also be noted that divergent pluralism offers the religious person a second, similar temptation to attribute goodness to one underlying order of the universe and evil to a second underlying order. In this way, God and the "good person" can never be accused of the sin that tears this world asunder. This temptation, once it is yielded to, inevitably leads to the formation of a sinless intellectual elite who eventually discover that they must separate themselves from the sinful nonintellectuals lest they be contaminated. The wisdom community of the university is hardly allowed, in this view, to grapple with the nasty, brutal, and dirty problems of the world.

A third objection to convergent pluralism charges that it leaves no place for the contingent, the pragmatic, the relative, and the subjective. Since these qualities are evident in any decision that a person makes, so the argument goes, only divergent pluralism is a realistic explanation of world process; convergent pluralism, in rendering decisions totally objective, kills subjectivity. Again, this objection seems to imply that convergent pluralism is a rigid, totally objective determinism that is unable to account for the contingent and the subjective factors that make the pragmatic and the relative possible. Clearly, if convergent pluralism has room for liberty, it also has room for all these qualities—in addition to the presence of evil. It is important, however, that this objection be faced in terms of those absolutes from which these four qualities derive their existence and meaning. One good way to do this is to see the part that absolutes play in the growth of human subjectivity and in the evolution of history.

To begin, let us state a definition: Subjectivity is generically the inner presence of one person to another person. This inner presence is expressed through the personality, an integrated complex of knowledges, feelings, attitudes, virtues, and imaginative habits. The personality, therefore, contains the total acquired history of the human being, as interpreted by him or her through relationships with other persons. Thus, the presence of one person to another is the focusing of this one personality, with all its experiential riches, upon the other person. Subjectivity, then, is basically interpersonal, or communal, although it is also infrapersonal, that is, focused on animals, plants, and things.

Subjectivity is enriched as daily experiences are gradually integrated into the whole of the personality, thereby expressing better the inner being of the person. Such integration depends on at least four factors: continuity of life (personal history), absolutes for establishing continuity, loyal and steady commitment to others, and liberty (a developing wholesomeness of personality). These four factors, in making possible the cumulation and focusing of experience, enable subjectivity to be enriched

94

continually in the midst of the relative, the pragmatic, and the contingent. In other words, they honor mankind's finite nature without letting it be dissolved by cynical relativism.

One quickly notes how dependent is the enrichment of subjectivity on the continuity of experience when one observes the effect of shock (discontinuity) on a young child. Shock causes the young child to retreat into the self, to refuse new experiences by entering into a dream world where shocks never occur. But usually, and fortunately, a child's pouting withdrawal ends when something exciting happens. The adult, on the other hand, moons in quiet bitterness over a lost job or anguishes in a daze over a lost love or slips into dulling lethargy at the death of favorite child. These sufferers from discontinuity are urged to "pick up the pieces" and "to rebuild their lives," if not for themselves, at least for others. For without continuity, life first comes to a standstill and then gradually disintegrates. Often, however, discontinuity shocks a person into entering a deeper, richer level of living. The continuity of subjectivity must, therefore, reassert itself and deepen itself against discontinuities so that it can go on cumulatively integrating life experiences and thus shaping a stronger personality.

This continuity is not just physical endurance, however. It is centered around understandings and consequent evaluations that prove lasting, that enable a person to link events together in a meaningful pattern and find a similar value in these events. These are the absolutes that establish commitment. A child, for example, links the pleasurable experiences of eating and cuddling with the warm presence of his or her mother, who gradually takes on "supreme value". The young insurance salesman, to cite another example, gets a good grasp of the insurance business and eventually learns to type people and to employ selling techniques accordingly. Gradually, he experiences the sustaining value of success: being considered a good salesman, earning a decent commission, and being helpful to people. Somewhere, amid all the relative changings of people, of sales gimmicks, of company procedures, and of insurance policies, the salesman has discovered perduring techniques (though they are applied differently to each customer), perduring types of people (though each person resists total typing), perduring understandings of the insurance business (though policy terms and premiums keep changing every six months because of inflation and new statistical surveys), and the perduring values of "doing one's job well" (though he may return to high school teaching two years from now) and of "putting the family before one's career" (though occasionally the family has to be asked to sacrifice present security in order that he may provide better for them in the future—the gamble of a second career).

These perduring understandings—supplemented by many others concerning leisure, God, the fine arts, and politics—and perduring values render the insurance salesman capable of commitment; that is to say, he can give sustained, loyal service and love to his family, his insurance company, his clientele, his church community, and his friends. For amid discontinuity and relative changes, he has also found continuity of family and business life with the perduring understandings and values called *absolutes*. He has discovered, and learned to appreciate, those living continuities, or absolutes, that are called "fellow human beings" through the wholesome living of the perduring understandings and values accumulated in his childhood, education, marriage, and business life.

In this way, he has developed, almost unknowingly, his *liberty*, namely, his ability to converge all his powers to choose intelligently and lovingly the more difficult alternative because it is the better one for himself and for those he loves. To achieve this unified life, he had first to see through the contingent changings to the perduring absolutes of meaning; he then had to be willing to suffer persistently for the perduring values he had discovered; and, finally, he had to live out these meanings and values in practical decisions that could, of course, never do justice to his understandings and values but were, pragmatically, the best he could muster under the circumstances. Thus, in this last step, he was cultivating the practical wisdom called *prudence*, which pragmatically focuses the contemplative understandings and values on a present event, such as a new job or a family illness or a sudden large inheritance.

Out of the salesman's enriched subjectivity comes a new awareness of his own powers, of other people, and of the world. Through his own interior growth, he sees others as historically developing toward a destiny of great importance. In other words, the unifying subjectivity of his own personal history has enabled him to recognize the convergent unity of mankind's history. In exploring the contingent events of his life, relative to his perduring insights and values, he has made pragmatic decisions that have loyally preserved his own values and those of his community. This is a subjectivity enriched by history.

Convergent Pluralism as Basis for History and Morality

Not only personal history, however, depends upon a convergent pluralism; so, too, do national history and culture. First, without persons, history cannot exist. As Augustine has shown so neatly in his *Confessions*, only mankind's spiritual powers enable men and women to remember the past, to be aware of the present, and to project the future in one compenetrating act so that the impact of the past on the present can be calibrated, and the planning of the future can be made in view of past and present moments. Only mankind intelligently converges events into his own history; only mankind, therefore, can understand what history is. Also, because mankind is able to see the perduring quality of understanding or of value in an event, men and women are able to appreciate the uniqueness of an event, in contrast with the universal perdurance that it has in common with other similar events. Isaac Newton, in the famous legend, is literally hit by the unique event of the falling apple and sees within that one event the law of gravity present in every other similar event of a free falling body. Because Arnold Toynbee—and, indeed, all competent historians—is so aware of the contingent relativity, or uniqueness, of each historical event, he is able to see the general patterns (the intelligibility or continuity) among events, so that he has been able to compare the unique cultural histories of various nations and civilizations in order to determine common patterns. Contingency, relativity, and uniqueness have meaning only if contrasted with the absolute and the universal; they have being only because of the perduring.

Thus, to say that history has no absolutes is to deny meaning and being to both individual history and social history. For one cannot fairly compare the Renaissance with the Enlightenment if one uses the principles and values peculiar to either one in order to judge the other; one must employ principles and values that are found in both. Such principles would even enable one to introduce a third era (the Victorian period, for example) for fair comparison. In this way, perduring values and understandings would eventually be seen to link all the eras of Western history. In addition they could be used to highlight, by contrast, the differences of each era so that a sense of evolving (or spiraling, as Toynbee would have it) history is evoked.

In achieving this overview, no one, least of all the historian, would deny that the absolute values and perduring understandings would be known only partially, that they would be discovered in contingent events, and that they would be applied with some degree of relativity because of their contingency and the partial way in which they are known. Still, no historian could write history without using universal terms to express the common themes that have been discovered when he or she has compared events, personages, stratas of society, centuries, eras, and civilizations. What is more, these universal terms and common themes would point directly to the perduring values and understandings that are used as the measuring rod of comparison. Consequently, though such comparison cannot escape the relative and contingent, it cannot even exist without absolutes such as these perduring values and understandings. Furthermore, without comparison, there can be no means of appreciating the accumulation of events into trends, the gathering of many minute details into a lifestyle, the assembling of personages into a movement, the marshalling of national trends-lifestyles-movements into a culture. To put it bluntly, unless historians compare events by way of absolutes, they can see no direction in life's events; this means, consequently, that there is no history—either individual history or social history.

This direction is precisely what is meant by the underlying finality that is characteristic of convergent pluralism. There are not two directions underlying world events as divergent pluralism would have it. Though there are certainly multiple interpretations of the single underlying finality, each historian, nevertheless, is always referring to the same one set of events with all their surprises, novelties, and pragmatic free decisions. For contingent events, of themselves, are meaningless in their discontinuous uniqueness, until historians perceive the absolute that is threading them into sets of meaning that have direction. Once human beings, so-called historical animals, see the meaningful direction of their own lives and that of their communities, they are freer to avoid the mistakes of the past and to plan a better future for others. This is the maturity of human subjectivity as men and women live out the convergent plurality of their world.

The objections brought against convergent pluralism by those who, like William James, advocate divergent pluralism have done us a service. They have clarified how convergent pluralism is actually a basis for mankind's freedom, faith response, developing subjectivity, and history. Convergent pluralism is also the basis for personal moral actions. This becomes clear when divergent pluralism, its opposite, is shown to undermine a person's moral nature. First, if the truth of a particular event is merely the sure prediction of its result, and if this truth is reached with close to equal accuracy by two or more contradictory philosophical interpretations, then it is only a calculus of interpretation-probabilities that guides us, not a perduring value that is found in the event itself. If the event is a person, then one places his or her trust not in the valuable person as faithful, but in one's calculus of probability about the person's loyalty. One's trust is placed in one's calculating self rather than in the person. Because divergent plurality offers more than one truth system, a word, gesture, or a moral action can mean one thing on one occasion and the exact opposite on another occasion. Depth and perseverance in love are difficult, at best, in these circumstances. Thus, one is discovering not absolutes or perduring values and understandings in another person, but probabilities in one's diverse understandings of that person according to the divergent underlying unities in the person and in his or her history. Because of this, the dominant human expression of insight is not "eureka" but a slight shrug; similarly, the deepest expression of human affection is not "I love you" but "maybe we can get along."

Divergent pluralism poses two further difficulties in living morally. Divergent pluralism tends to bifurcate human moral energies into divergent paths that offer no sure hope of ever reaching a supreme reality, for dual finalities tend to cancel each other out in distraction and in schizoid diffusion of energy that result in frustration becoming the supreme reality. Indeed, without a single finality, there is no ideology, no *Weltanschauung*, no vision to provide a context and give direction to one's decisions. One is, as it were, cut adrift on a swirling sea of events during a dark night of high winds. Thus, divergent pluralism, which frustrates the individual person into fatal confusion, is also capable of destroying the community of confused persons.

Ironically, those who espouse divergent pluralism usually base their actions on an implicit convergent pluralism of absolutes. It is necessary to stress that if divergent pluralism is true, there are no absolutes for guiding one's life; consequently, no two events can be linked by a common understanding of value because the first event might be happening according to underlying world unity "A" while the second event might be happening according to underlying world unity "B" or "C" or "D." Since each underlying world unity is totally independent of the other, there is no connection between the first event and the second event. If both the first and second event should occur according to the same underlying world unity, then the common value or understanding would be an absolute linking them; a third event, however, might be from another totally different underlying world unity. Because of the discontinuities between underlying world unities and between events that come from different world unities, there are no absolutes on which to base a person's certitude about outside events or even about internal events.

Under these circumstances, it is radically impossible to make comparisons and, hence, to find continuity in one's own life or in another's life; consequently, the individual history of a person evaporates as does the social history that surrounds him or her. Everyone and everything become atomized by discontinuities, by breaks in both consciousness and being. High probability becomes, at best, very low probability of pragmatic success because a person can never be sure what system of truth ("A" or "B" or "C" or "D") to apply in estimating his or her action toward a particular event, which may be issuing from world unity "A" or "B" or "C" or "D". In this way, no value that is intrinsic to a decision can be challenged for validity because all that counts is the practical success of the action that is extrinsic to the decision. Yet even this practical success cannot be truly measured since repetition of this decision in an apparently similar second event may be disastrous because the second event may actually be from a world unity that is radically unlike the first event. Life is turned into a lottery moving toward chaos.

Such probability of discontinuity makes permanent commitment to another person close to impossible since the series of events that constitute a person may be discontinuous at a number of crucial junctures—at the time of engagement, during the marriage ceremony, at the conception of a child, during an illness, while taking out a mortgage on a house. In other words, how many persons does one marry? This uncertainty rapidly multiplies when one tries to found a community that is larger than two people. Under these circumstances the aims of the university become hilarious rather than possible. How, for example, could the traditional truth of a specialized knowledge or skill be reinterpreted when the tradition might be atomized into a thousand parts and, furthermore, any reinterpretation would simply add one more part to the confusion. For reintegration demands a single truth system that develops from a single underlying world unity, not two or a thousand truth systems that have developed from two or a thousand underlying world unities. (Once divergent pluralism is accepted, there is no way of limiting how many world unities underlie the multiverse).

Moreover, if a community of two is hardly possible, then a university community of wisdom, composed of a thousand members, would be totally impossible. In other words, if the universe is a multiverse, then the university is a multiversity—or worse. For all practical purposes, then, divergent pluralism, in promoting the idea that there are multiple truth systems that correspond to the multiple underlying world unities, has made it clear that no truth systems exist. Divergent pluralism makes it impossible for any person to be sure what event corresponded to what underlying unity until *after* the event had taken place; only then would a person find out whether his or her decision had been successful. But if the decision had failed, the person would never be able to know whether it had failed because the wrong truth system had been chosen in making a response or because, by luck, the right truth system had been chosen but the person had failed to use it well. Thus, past experiences of mistakes would count for almost as little as past experiences of success.

In addition, since truth rises mainly, if not exclusively, from community experience, and since community is hardly possible under divergent pluralism, this philosophy, practically speaking, leaves one to operate with no truth system. The university also becomes an impossibility if divergent pluralism is the true understanding of the universe. Even the term *multiversity* is a misnomer since it implies some unities grouped under some great canopy. Taken to its roots, divergent pluralism is actualy seen to be the denial of all truth systems, and of all perceivable unities.

Concluding Unity

We now have some answers to the questions with which this chapter opened. Is pluralism endemic to the university? Yes, if by pluralism, one means convergent pluralism, since convergent pluralism makes possible teaching, researching, and the accumulating of wisdom. Teaching is possible because each student has an individual personal history into which he or she can integrate new knowledges and skills. Researching can happen because specialized truth can be reinterpreted or reintegrated according to a single underlying unity. Wisdom can be accumulated because each learning community has a social history that allows wisdom to be gathered over the years.

Is pluralism epidemic for the community? Yes, if it is divergent pluralism, for this understanding of pluralism virtually negates the existence of the university since it makes the reinterpretation of truth impossible according to any single truth system and since it undermines the beginnings of even the simplest community, not to mention the complex community of university wisdom. Divergent pluralism would make even a multiversity impossible. Without a community of truth and wisdom, the single person could hardly advance in truth, all the specialized knowledges could not converge toward a single vision of knowledge, the past could not be reassessed by present new knowledge in order that the future might be met intelligently, the smaller university community could not focus its wisdom in order to serve the larger civic community and/or the commonwealth of nations, nor could wisdom be focused to discover that supreme intelligence and love that is operative not only at the center of the universe, but also in the heart of every living person.

Despite all that recommends convergent pluralism, however, there is a *caveat;* convergent pluralism fails to tell a person how or where or when its elements converge into a meaningful vision. Convergent pluralism only establishes the fact that these specialized knowledges can be reinterpreted, that the specialized skills can be further refined for better cooperation, and that all of this can be integrated into a wisdom for the times. What does the university do while the plural elements are converging? How can the university exist as a university, as a center of unified knowledge and skills, until the great vision is attained? What, in short, keeps the university together? An answer: The university exists by fostering the convergence of knowledges and skills through its reinterpretation of traditional truth in specialized knowledges and skills and through its gathering of wisdom within its community. But how does it achieve the provisional unity needed to promote the convergence of plural knowledges and skills and to assure the accumulation of wisdom? It would seem that the final unity (the great whole) that the university seeks must be enjoyed before the search (the "wholing" process) can begin and move along its course. Yet, how could the university know its goal before reaching it?

The university does have something more than the fact of convergent pluralism to aid its unity; it has the successful work of the past 800 years to give it a sense of unity. And yet, this work must gain direction from something other than itself. What is this source of unity? Could it be the Christian faith? Christianity certainly gives the university a glimpse of the future when, in the letters to the Colossians and to the Ephesians, Paul speaks of all things leading to Christ and being recapitulated in Him: all knowledges lead to a living Wisdom of the great community of tomorrow. Still, Christianity provides only a glimpse, but it is a glimpse that could be the basis of a vision that could unite the university community in all its works—if this vision is developed according to a disciplined faith that is interpreted by a Christian philosophy (using all the data of the university's knowledges and skills) and a Christian theology (using philosophy to help it draw upon all these same knowledges and skills). This vision could enable the university community to *see* the unity; the discipline of faith could then enable this community to *live* the unity freely; the Christian philosophy and theology (aided by all the other knowledges and skills) could next enable the university community to *test* this unity wisely for its continuous growth.

The next three chapters will take up these three approaches to the unity of the university community in all its works.

5 Source of Commitment to a University's Purpose: Vision or Ideology?

One of the large anomalies of the university is the unity that its name implies. The notion of convergent pluralism establishes that unity is possible for a university, no matter how large it is, but it does not describe *how* this unity is to be attained amid the vast variety of knowledges and skills, the wide spectrum of communities that practice these knowledges and skills, and the great assortment of lifestyles that emerge from these communities according to various philosophies, theologies, and faiths.

To make the problem of unity more acute, the university is continually exploring *mystery*. All its rational approaches are actually roads of exploration into mystery. To cite a few examples: Physics, in entering deeply into the atom and its multiplying subatomic parts, uses two contrary theories of wave and particles to forge a "wavicle" with which to explore the mystery of energy and matter; biochemistry uses its knowledge of nonvital chemical processes to enter, ironically, into the vital genetic processes of deoxyribonucleic acid (DNA), the shadow of life; sociology studies the momentary relational procedures that structure an institution, such as a banking system, a neighborhood, a church, or a government, and wonders how this rickety being can persist over centuries; psychology tries out seventeen theories to explain human memory and smiles at its own bafflement. During the decades that have followed the two world wars—and have virtually promised a third—philosophy has been particularly fascinated by the problem of death and human destiny; yet even those who declare that death is a brutal cliffside or an unexplainable fact, nevertheless return to the scene of this crime against humanity to attempt to explain why it is unexplainable. Historians, whose trade depends totally on the cumulative aspect of events, argue whether culture is cumulative and civilization progressive. Theologians, whose work has no meaning unless their sacred scriptures are truly revealed by God, squabble over whether revelation is possible or, if it is possible, preservable from substantial error. Two agronomists point to the remarkable amount of food grown per acre in Belgium—one claims that such a yield can be duplicated in Third World nations, the other flatly denies this.

Nor is mystery dissolved by these careful, rational advances of the sciences into its domain. Rather, as scientists become wiser in their areas of specialization, they become paradoxically aware of their own growing ignorance; they begin to feel that each scientific step into mystery is disclosing two further steps that need to be taken. Mystery is outdistancing them even as they advance, and yet, each advance is yielding unexpected treasures of knowledge. If Einstein felt that his mathematical equations brought his mind to the "rim of mystery," what must be the collective experience of the university wisdom community as it endeavors to make scientific advances into mystery? Where is the distant point of understanding, to say nothing of love, that will give converging direction to all the university's rational paths that enter into mystery? Without such a point how does the university get, retain, and enhance its unity? Mystery lures university people into painstaking action, promising them joy beyond their comprehension, but attracting them into seemingly very different paths. Can the university long continue to support these seemingly divergent depth experiences?—especially as the language of each discipline becomes more arcane and, ironically, less communicative with other disciplines.

In order to more dramatically sketch the problematic dimensions of the university's unity, let us suppose that a genius-philosopher, or a group of amazingly like-minded metaphysicians, had succeeded in gathering (1) all the findings of the social, physical, and mathematical sciences; (2) all the discoveries of the literary, historical, and theological knowledges; and (3) all the evidences of common-sense knowledge. Then, let us suppose that, despite the narrowness of their own personal histories and peculiar vantage points, they had successfully found, *per impossibile*, within all of this data a metaphysics, the outlines of which permeated and integrated all the evidence into one great understanding of the world. This would be *the* metaphysics, *the* ultimate understanding of that single basic underlying unity of world process to which all knowledges converge and toward which all philosophers, throughout the centuries, have lunged with all their life energies.

Let us take a second, apparently impossible leap and suppose that a like-minded group of theologians was present at this momentous discovery of *the* metaphysics, *the* perennial philosophy. The theologians then take possession of not only this metaphysics, but also all the scientific, literary, and common-sense evidence on which it has been based. Again, *per impossibile*, beyond their peculiar life vantage points, they now grasp fully, in faith, the inner meaning of salvation history and then go on to express it in *the* Christian theology. Given *the* metaphysics and *the* Christian theology, both the philosophers and the theologians, to

104

our surprise, would not have completed their task. For this "wholesome" metaphysics must itself be further developed in all its branches; it is still a bare outline, magnificent and fruitful though it may be. But such development can only occur gradually, as history unfolds its novel challenges to bring forth the intricate growth of *the* metaphysics. In turn, *the* Christian theology will develop as it is challenged by this evolving "wholesome" metaphysics and as it meets the new evidences that are generated by history in all the university knowledges and in commonsense knowledge (which is the ultimate root and test of the university knowledges). Of course, during this history, we must postulate that mankind's willfulness will not set up rival, pseudo-wholesome systems of either metaphysics or Christian theology to distract from, or to contaminate, *the* true one. We must further postulate that, in each generation, groups of like-minded geniuses may be found to accept, reassess, and further develop *the* metaphysics and *the* Christian theology.

Now, during the centuries-long development herein described, university people will need some provisional means of keeping united in this task—something beyond *the* metaphysics and *the* Christian theology. Even these men of preternatural intelligence, of remarkable sanctity, and of unbelievably erudite scientific knowledge will be dependent on an extrapolation from their singular and hard-won metaphysics and Christian theology—an extrapolation to fill out the picture of reality for the sake of unity. What will the extrapolation be? An ideology? A vision of the type that Teilhard de Chardin painted? A *Weltanschauung?*

Possible Misunderstandings of 'Vision'

Clearly, the "extrapolation" that goes beyond Christian philosophy and Christian theology is not simply a passionate utterance. If this extrapolation is mainly imaginative rhetoric, cloaking its emptiness in philosophic clothing and yet demanding unquestioning and passionate allegiance, then we have Nazi demagoguery. Rather, the extrapolation intended here is a vision of the type exemplified by Teilhard de Chardin's *Phenomenon of Man,* but much more modest in scope and hope. As noted in the *Introduction,* a Christian vision of the university should be extrapolated from a Christian philosophy and a Christian theology, both of which are in close touch with all the university disciplines. Furthermore, it should be developed out of the "lived experience" of university men and women whose lives are suffused with Christian charity. Lastly, it should be proportioned to the current resources of the university and colored by the present needs and future hopes of the people who are served by the university.

As an extrapolation, this vision is only one way of merging and converging the evidence at hand; it, therefore, will not please those who are developing another vision in a different way from much the same evidence. Yet these diverse visions, if issuing from similar evidence, will have some large areas of agreement. Similarly, because each vision is an attempt to converge evidence beyond its present convergence in order to fill in "gaps," the chance of exaggeration or omission or downright mistake is always present. Then, too, new vocabulary must be used or old vocabulary must be stretched to introduce new meanings so that, for the sake of a unified vision, those gaps in understanding might be filled. Furthermore, this vision is more than a working hypothesis, a detailed intellectual scheme; it also contains imaginative elements to touch the heart of mankind and to elicit emotional commitment for the task of the university. Here it risks becoming an ideology; consequently, it must be carefully distinguished from an ideology—any unique system of ideas to be used passionately as weapons for social change.

It quickly becomes apparent that a Christian vision is not an ideology when one compares its characteristics with those of any ideology. Lewis S. Feuer, in his *Ideology and the Ideologists*, finds three basic ingredients in every ideology; (1) the Mosaic revolutionary myth, (2) an historically determined decision to redeem a particular exploited class of society, and (3) a compound of philosophical doctrines that alternate cyclically within the history of ideology. An ideology tries to demonstrate, by way of basic philosophical and scientific premises, the truth of its myth and the value of its commitment to the liberation of a particular group. Patrick Corbett, in his *Ideologies*, would underline two additional characteristics of ideology (which may well be implied in the previous three): ideology (1) demands a particular way of life and (2) is a means of securing and maintaining power. Let us contrast these five characteristics of ideology with those of Christian vision in order to more clearly see both these phenomena.

Feuer submits a remarkable sketch of how the Mosaic revolutionary myth, the first characteristic, runs through various ideologies like Marxism, Americanism, African Negritude, and Nationalism. Indeed, it is evident that Christianity is a revolutionary way of life that contains the Mosaic myth within the historical resurrection of Christ. Further, the university itself, be it Christian or secular, is among the strongest influences for revolutionary societal change. Yet, against this thesis that a Christian vision of the university is an ideology, one must note that both Christianity and the university cannot exist without *traditio*, a continuous linkage with the past. To advance, both need the bread of peace; on a propaganda diet, both quickly bloat and die. Moreover, both Christianity and the university have a pluralistic structure; neither could long survive on a single myth (no matter how rich) nor on a single knowledge or philosophy or theology or political doctrine. In fact, the documents of the Second Vatican Council not only counsel plural theological approaches to God but truly exemplify them. A Christian vision of the university, consequently, could hardly be realistic if it were controlled by a monomaniacal revolutionary caste.

Feuer notes, in his second characteristic, that ideologists are bent on liberating or redeeming a particular class, usually one considered lower than their own class. Again, this would seem to fit Christianity, since Christians have tried to live out Christ's criterion for vitality: "The poor have the Gospel preached to them" and "Whatever you do to the least of these, you do to Me." The *anawim* have always had the special concern of Christ and Christianity. As for the university, it has become, more and more, the path that the poor must take to escape economic slavery. Some other facts, however, contradict the statement that a Christian vision is ideology. Christianity and the university liberate other classes as well as the *anawim;* no one is excluded from the university or the Church because he or she lacks the credentials of the *anawim*. The university trains public servants for the civic jobs and professions that serve all classes; the Church tries to motivate public servants to serve all societal classes. There is no attempt to funnel all energies and projects exclusively to one class, no matter how needy that class is. Instead, both the university and Christianity tend to create new classes by supporting all the new knowledges and skills that develop new strata and classes of society. (Support of trade unions is one example of this attitude.) A Christian vision is more likely to promote the differentiation of society and to support the resultant new classes.

Feuer's third element of ideology, its use of philosophical principles to give itself a scientific façade for its secret evangelism, would seem to be, above all, a characteristic of a Christian vision as we have already described it; there is, however, a serious difference. Ideology attempts to show that its basic tenets are derived from, and supported by, philosophic and scientific principles; a Christian vision, on the other hand, uses philosophy, theology, and scientific disciplines to structure, render more concrete, illuminate, and guide itself, rather than to demonstrate its singular validity. Nor does a single philosophy or a single theology structure a Christian vision, since the single dominant philosophy and single dominant theology needed for a single vision are nevertheless challenged and modified by other philosophies and theologies that are represented at the university. Furthermore, all these philosophies and theologies, especially the dominant ones, are under the influence of all the disciplines represented in the university. In the presence of this critical challenge from every side, it would be difficult, indeed, for a Christian vision to be so monolithic as to manipulate and coerce the autonomous disciplines into forming a single facade for a hidden ideology. Moreover, of itself, a Christian vision for the university is temporary, disposable, and alternate. It is *temporary* because its power comes from being able to serve the always-changing needs of the larger civic community according to the always-changing resources of the smaller university community. It is *disposable* because all the disciplines, as well as philosophy and theology, advance beyond any particular Christian vision and demand its constant revision. It is *alternate* because it knows itself as temporary and disposable, i.e., as one alternative among several possible Christian visions. For this reason, the present book is subtitled *A* (not *The*) *Christian Vision of the American University*.

A fourth characteristic of ideology is that it demands a singular way of life, e.g., the Nazi, the Marxist, the Capitalist, the Flower Child, or the Reformist. There is no denying that a Christian vision of the university arises out of that university community's vocation—*a way of life*. But the very structure of the university is pluralistic, not only in its multiple skills and knowledges, but in the diversity of the philosophies and theologies represented in its faculty members who live their own different lifestyles. Besides, the structure of the university is, in itself, highly inventive (consider, for example, the explosion of knowledges in a university catalog) and experimental (consider, also, the constant use of hypotheses, and the experiments that are tailored to test them, as well as the current spate of "interdisciplinary studies"). Such a structure clearly does not cater to a single style of life that symbolizes a particular type of thought and action. Finally, a Christian vision is developed not to foreclose the future in an armored suit of the present structure, but rather to promote responsible planning (discover new options, resources, needs) and to support the freedom and creativity needed for such planning. In other words, the Christian vision is meant to stimulate reorganization by making it more possible and more reasonable; and reorganization involves new styles of life, not the preservation of old ones. Besides, the history of Christianity is a story of adaptations to many cultures and lifestyles—a story imaged in all the various liturgies of Christianity. Every church council is a rainbow of lifestyles and an orchestra of diverse languages. "Inculturation" is a new word, but it is an old story for the Christian faith's worldwide embrace.

For all of the above reasons, it should be clear that a Christian vision does not fulfill, nor was it meant to fulfill, the fifth characteristic of an ideology—to secure and maintain power for the university administration. It is also clear that a Christian vision is the creature of the faculty and of the students—a gift to the administration to enable that administration to make strong decisions for the healthy growth of the university. Indeed, a Christian vision is actually a means to help the university avoid being caught in ideological narrow-mindedness and to remind the university, and its administration, that they are servants rather than masters.

Such a distinction between a Christian vision and an ideology aids one in understanding that a Christian vision, though always allied to a *Weltanschauung*, is not itself such a world vision. As Peter Berger notes in his *Sacred Canopy*, a *Weltanschauung* is a highly theoretical and all-embracing legitimation for all mankind's activities within a societal nomos. But a Christian vision of the university refers to one institution of this society and, though it has theoretical moments, is finally concerned with the practical principles that go into concrete university decisions about goals, structures, and procedures within the institution and its community. Naturally, since the university is an integral, if not essential, part of modern society, a Christian vision of the university is guided by at least an implicit *Weltanschauung*. After all, the university does mirror the world's problems, and some university professors do offer one or another *Weltanschauung* to their students. A Christian vision, however, is much more modest and much more practically oriented. Consequently, it is much more open to misuse—a matter that needs immediate discussion.

The Misuse of Vision

Every thinking and sensitive person has gone through a period of ideology in his or her life. The young professor, fresh from doctoral studies and somewhat impatiently looking for a practical life-ideal, is at least strongly tempted to an ideology. There is a need to set one's course, and so, a star is sought. To tell the young professor who has espoused Marxism or Reformism or Capitalism or Liberalism or Democratism or any other "ism", that he or she has married a spouse who will emotionally exhaust one, will make narrowing demands upon one's mind, will prove false to one's ideals of fairness, and will rob one of freedom, is foolish. For romance has filled the young professor's heart and no one else exists except the spouse. The warning will be heard only after the day-to-day harshness of life's realities has soured the romance and made divorce thinkable. At that point, the young professor, now older in experience, knows what ideology is. A second marriage to another ideology will build the conviction that what he or she needs is a vision that does not claim to be more than provisional, that arises freely out of evidence rather than coercing evidence into preconceived patterns, that, therefore, opens one's eyes to broader horizons and newer fields, that is not confused with a *Weltanschauung* or with the union of philosophy and theology. Thus, ideology, as described by Feuer, can be seen as the substitute for a vision that every person needs in order to unify life. Ideology can be, therefore, the misuse of vision, the narrowing of vision to a single pattern, the glazing of vision with highly emotional demands, the warping of vision with unfairness. And so, the first type of misuse of vision is the attempt to substitute a more easily-gained-and-maintained ideology for a more hard-to-win-and-keep vision.

A second type of misuse of vision occurs when vision is transformed into an ideology. A dean may theoretically agree that the world is naturally plural and that human knowledge of this world will, therefore, be pluralistic. But, in a moment of despair over the open conflict in his or her psychology department between Jungians, Freudians, and Adlerians, he or she may order the department chairman to "get unity at any cost." If the Freudians outnumber the other two parties, it is easy to foresee whose contracts will not be renewed in the spring. This may well be the only solution available, but it should be recognized that this pragmatic ideological unity is being bought at a high price—the loss of convergent unity. A vision becomes an ideology when pluralism is denied existence.

A third, more blatant use of ideology instead of vision occurs when political unity is achieved in the name of unchanging ideology. The Marxist classless society is not the only utopian ideology that excludes other political parties leading along other roads into the future. The utopian ideology has everything its own way; it cannot be refuted with evidence because it speaks of a future event not yet existent; it cannot be displaced by another ideology or by a vision because it speaks with certainty about a single convergent point in the future. To reach this heavenly point, no other road is allowable. A university president, for example, might be faced with a faculty request that a department of theology be instituted in his or her university. The secularists might fight this proposal by arguing that the establishment of a department of theology gives credibility to a knowledge that is not scientific and that, because of its early future demise, will be misleading to students. The secularist utopia, wherein all scientific knowledge is living and all so-called superstition—theology, poetry, and common-sense knowledge—is dead, is ruling the university if the university president does not at least honor the request for a theology department with a hearing. A forced political unity is achieved by destroying any opposition to an unquestionable single future.

A fourth misuse of vision is to embalm it, much like an Egyptian mummy, and not let it grow by modification. In this instance, university people fail to understand that a vision rests on evidence from all the

110

university arts and knowledges, even as it searches beyond this evidence for a stage of unity not yet present in the evidence. Thus, a vision is a projection from the evidence to a point "beyond the evidence." To refuse to modify this vision, as the evidence supporting modification grows at its base, is to put the vision into a state of *rigor mortis* and, once again, to transform it into an ideology. Or worse; the vision may eventually become a fantasy that needs no evidence for its subsistence. Thus, "pure liberal education" of undergraduates, with no preparation for any particular area of skilled work, may have been a fine vision in 1830 for the independently wealthy landowners of the South. By the 1860s, however, it was becoming an ideology and, after the Civil War, it turned into a fantasy that was unaffected by contrary evidences. Clearly, these four misuses of a vision will inevitably cripple academic freedom because each is an attack on the institutional and communal aims of the university.

The Unavoidable Need for a Vision

The four misuses of vision stress the fragility of vision. Yet a vision is a necessity of life. The man or woman who has only a vague personal vision is risking the takeover of drab routine and the gradual narrowing of liberty. If one wants to reinvigorate a deteriorating business or a discouraged athletic team or a defeated nation, one must employ a sharp new vision. There must be some final, attractive scene toward which all the procedures, gatherings, structures, and hopes are moving so that the organization attains unity of operation. This vision generates the group's *esprit*, or *mystique*, so that, thus inspired, sacrifices are seen as a matter of course, rather than as an occasion for grumblings and even counter-demonstrations. The attempt to unite a group without using a vision implies an ideology in which mankind is conceived of as a kind of unfeeling machine to be run automatically, or as an irrational brute to be herded, or as a schizoid being to be galvanized only by the shocks of divergent pluralism.

Admittedly, for a newly minted vision to achieve a new unity, this vision must dominate the other visions that are always operative in any complex organization. Because a dominant vision is not an ideology brooking no opposition, it must achieve its superior strength through (1) a better use of the evidence from which it is projected ahead, (2) a dramatic imagery more elicitive of deep emotions, (3) a clarity of single-minded purpose, (4) a willingness to adapt quickly to changing needs and to evolving values, and (5) an openness to the substantive criticisms of either the other competing visions or the always present challenging ideologies.

111

These five qualities ensure that a vision will perduringly dominate so that, for example, a university can be stable amid both its constant reinterpretations of specialized knowledges and its steady accumulation of wisdom. Without such a dominating vision, the university will experience divisive factions that have unlimited power for distracting the university from its purposes. The university then becomes a large "mischief factory."

All this is rather general however. Let us now consider what concrete facts of university life demand a dominant vision. Four situations seem to require such a vision: (1) the insufficiency of all university knowledges, taken together, to give a concrete sense of unity; (2) the inability of these knowledges to keep up with new cultural problems; (3) the abstractness of these knowledges when they are compared with the concretely unique situation to which they are applied; and (4) the need of these knowledges to be challenged into creativity. If one looks at each of these situations, one can estimate how a vision operates in a university and why a university has built-in protections against the misuse of a vision.

First, the converging of all the university knowledges toward a synthesis that induces singleness of purpose is a complicated process. Few faculty members have the ability to confect such a process, even if they should have the remarkable intellectual gifts that are needed for recognizing such a synthesis; it requires more than a modicum of philosophy of science and more than ordinary familiarity with theology—along with an extensive knowledge of the sciences, literature, and the fine arts. And even this synthesis is always in need of reassessment and modification in accord with new findings in all these areas of knowledge. Consequently, the average faculty member (perhaps 95 percent of the faculty?) needs a vision in which he or she can cooperatively situate his or her own specialized knowledge alongside the other knowledges. This vision can then be grounded in the individual faculty member's common-sense knowledge of the university situation. Finally, the faculty member's intimate acquaintance with his or her own specialized knowledge enables each faculty member to challenge the vision for authenticity. Thus, the wisdom vision of the university enables a sociologist to estimate more accurately his or her need of statistics, social psychology, history, epistemology, and anthropology without having mastered those other sciences; the sociologist's own gritty, day-to-day knowledge of colleagues in these departments lets him or her know whether the others and the wisdom vision of the university can be trusted; and the sociologist's own expertness in sociology offers clear insight into the workings of the university as both an institution (is it striving heartily and honestly for truth?) and a community (does it generously share its findings with others?), so that the believability of this vision can be challenged.

Yet, even if the entire faculty and the administrators could truly appreciate the massive convergence of all university knowledges into a single synthesis, would such an intricate convergence have sufficient clarity to give the strength of definiteness to the decisions of administrators? Would not the simplicity of a vision that is based on this synthesis be much more usable in making the swift, tough, day-to-day decisions that both describe and instill the *esprit* or *mystique* of a university? Besides, a vision tends to elicit the emotional commitment that is needed for long endurance because it offers more concrete images than does any grand synthesis of specialized knowledges. Pluralism is taking place not only inside each discipline, but also between the disciplines as they multiply in subspecies. Thus, as specialized knowledges become more precise, their terminology becomes proportionately more complicated and the images expressed in their scientific terms become more abstract. Physics could once use the image of a planetary system to describe the Bohr atom; now, however, this system has been negated and the image has almost been obliterated. The graphs of economics have become three-dimensional and four-dimensional, so that now the science of topology must be applied if one hopes to read them with some accuracy.

There is no scientific image to bridge scientific schools with a single science, much less a non-scientific image to link the sciences. Consequently, a vision employs multiple images poetically (i.e., to express a truth and not merely fantasy) much in the style of Teilhard de Chardin. For, as Johannes Lindworsky noted in his famous studies of freedom of the will (*Experimental Psychology*. New York: Macmillan, 1931), the more realistically colorful and dynamically detailed is the image of a man's ambition, the more strength he has to suffer for it and the more certainty he has of its attainment. Thus, a vision of the university can instill (1) the clear unity of purpose, (2) the decisive strength of definiteness, and (3) the joyous *élan* of emotions into university life.

There is a second situation that requires the university to have a vision: Because university knowledges cannot keep pace with the swiftly developing problems of contemporary Western society, a vision is needed to signal that new needs of both students and the civic community are not being met. A vision of the university community as servant, for example, enables it to become alert to the rapidly expanding population and explosive needs of the Puerto Rican community in New York or Chicago. Once alerted by its vision, the university community can begin to sound out the problems of the Puerto Rican community before university knowledges can be focused for long-term solutions. Indeed, both the resources of the university and its vision determine what problems can be met scientifically and in what order of precedence. If, for example, a university is *Catholic* in its vision, it sees more clearly its obligation to the traditionally Catholic Puerto Rican community and hears more distinctly the call to minister to the spiritual needs as well as the material needs of this people.

In a third situation that demands wisdom—a situation in which abstract university knowledges are being applied, through "middle principles," to the practical operational level of a unique situation—a vision is a strategic guiding element. A vision of the university as servant, for example, will make university people more sensitive to the pleas of the people whose children are being bused to other school districts; a vision of the university as mediator for justice will enable university people to be more evenhanded in adjudicating between electrical power companies and environmentalists.

Finally, a vision of and for the university lures both philosophers and theologians into clarifying university aims and into better service of the community. Moreover, this vision does the same for all the other knowledges upon which the first two knowledges depend for their sustenance. Thus, a vision of the university as prophet warning the nation of its energy extravagances can lead a university into (1) the passionate discovery of truth and (2) the confident accumulation of wisdom for alleviating such injustices. (This point will receive more detailed treatment in the ensuing chapters.)

If such an empowering university vision can be misused, it is time that something was said about the university's natural protections against the abuses of turning a vision into an ideology or a fantasy. First, it is the very nature of the university to increase pluralism so that the singleness of a dominant vision is always in jeopardy, as it should be. Second, the constant reinterpretation of the specialized knowledges is forever introducing new ideas and skills, which demand the modification of a vision. Third, the wisdom of the university community, as it accumulates, introduces a genial cynicism about the absoluteness of any vision and keeps administrators alert to the temporal and doctrinal limits of any single vision by indicating other visions that are also operative under the dominant vision. Fourth, the changing needs of the students, faculty, and surrounding civic community constantly demand the refocusing of a vision. Fifth, administrators and faculty who are sensitive to both the severe shortcomings of ideologies and the dangers of transforming a vision into an ideology, are equally sensitive to the other visions challenging the dominant vision.

There are, then, abundant protective mechanisms within the very being of the university to protect her liberty against undue attachment to one or another dominant vision. This is why those who strenuously object to a Christian vision of the university may well be barking at the moon. For a Christian vision could be shedding a silver light on the university rather than casting a dangerous magical spell on her. This is a matter requiring further consideration.

Apologia and Need for a Christian Vision of the University

The university, like any other organized group, cannot escape having a dominant vision. The crucial question it faces, therefore, is not whether it will have a vision, but rather what will be the dominant vision among the competing visions that are present within its organization. The university will usually employ that vision which (a) is most compatible with the university's life-giving constituencies, (b) best enlists the enthusiasm of the university's academic leaders, and (c) is most agreeable with the other competing visions and ideologies. These three criteria, taken together, indicate that a dominant vision must arise freely from within the organizing group if it is to produce internal cohesion. This, of course, does not preclude the presence of judicious persuasion and compromise, the humane means of achieving cooperation.

Is there a Christian vision that can give unity to the university? The very existence of Christian universities proves the existence of Christian visions—though Christian visions have been seriously challenged by those secularists who appear to think that a university should be run by a pragmatic common denominator (ideology) that excludes all mention of religious values. What would such a Christian vision be? As an extrapolation of Christian philosophy and Christian theology, it must be plural since there are multiple Christian philosophies and Christian theologies. For this reason, Lutheran universities, Baptist universities, Benedictine universities, Franciscan universities, and Jesuit universities all have a different *esprit* or *mystique* according to their own diverse Christian visions. Yet, these different visions will have much in common, for each Christian vision is centered around Jesus Christ, whose person is considered, in faith, to be wisdom itself and whose actions are revelation itself. This faith is a unity of Christian experience that refers to the historical facts of Christ, His people, His teachings, and His sacraments, and it rises out of a communal experience of Jesus within a French or German or American or African or Vietnamese culture.

This faith-unity is not to be confused with its various theological and philosophical interpretations, nor with its various national inculturations, even though both of these elements deeply influence the living of the Christian faith. The Christian vision, then, radiates out from this faith-center according to the interpretations of various Christian theologies that

115

are influenced, in turn, by various Christian philosophies and national cultures. In this way, each Christian vision of the university takes life from this common faith-center in the same way that each flower takes life from the sun. But each vision, like each flower, gets its distinctive shape and hue from a particular Christian philosophy and theology and is interpreted according to a particular national culture. Consequently, the presence of Christ, admitted and enjoyed by each community that forms a Christian university, is the ultimate basis of unity for each university, because Christ is the illuminating and central cause of each Christian vision.

At the present time, the downgrading of Christian philosophies (even at Christian universities), the confusion among the Christian faithful due to cultural upheavals, and the consequent confusion among Christian theologies (e.g., the attempt to integrate Whiteheadian process philosophy with the Christian doctrine of immortality and continuity of the human person, with the incarnation of the God-man, and with creation-out-of-nothing), has put the unity and the quality of the Christian university in jeopardy. And so, if the Christian university is to remain Christian, it must have a dominant Christian vision. Admittedly, this Christian vision will only be as good as its center, the faith of its university community, and as intelligent and livable as the Christian theology that interprets it and as the Christian philosophy that supports that theology— matters to be discussed more fully later in this book.

Each Christian vision contains a number of qualities that are particularly helpful for enhancing the life of the university. Because each Christian vision is Christ-centered, for example, it emphasizes the personal in all university procedures as a balance to the institutional. Because the Christ is considered the Word, Wisdom Itself, the Christian vision sees the intellectual life as the highest of values; however, because this Christ declared that love of God and neighbor summed up all of life at its best, the intellectual life is seen as an expression of love and not of pride, of service and not of power. Thus, in the Christian vision, as distinguished from the Marxist vision, the love that is found in communal wisdom is ultimately more important than all the specialized works and expert accomplishments that fail to be expressions of love.

Because this resurrected Christ, who is at the center of the vision, is now living and working to liberate men and women from ignorance, from the constricting fears of prejudice, and from past sins and mistakes, the Christian university finds itself called to enhance the liberty of mankind. The Christian university does this with a combined sense of humor and tragedy because the Christian vision makes it aware that men and women have a propensity (original sin), which has been rendered compulsive by

116

centuries of injustice, to wound fellow men and women, even when, under the impulse of Christ's graceful presence, one person is trying to help another. The humility gained from such a frank admission of ignobility amid nobility enables the Christian university to see that the great pyramid of knowledges, which she is erecting, basically rests on the common-sense knowledge of the so-called masses, and that the university *intelligentia*, who lead the human procession up the pyramid of culture, live off the sweaty labors of the so-called common man.

A sense of destiny and history is also found within the Christian vision of the university. For Christ entered into history to lead it, through the centuries and amid the most variegated (pluralistic) communities and cultures, to that great moment when all nations will gather into the Great Community of the Great Tomorrow to celebrate the fullness of manhood and godhood—the divinization of man and the humanization of God in the incarnation. This is not accomplished, however, by a unilateral act of God. Yahweh asked mankind to co-create the world with Him; Christ asks mankind to form the people of God by slowly, over many centuries of trial and error, building the city of God. Patience and continuity, therefore, are more important than revolt and discontinuity. For liberty is built gradually and delicately out of many free decisions for the greater good of others, out of self-sacrifice done with devotion—the characteristic of the feminine, which renders power humane with tenderness. After all, the mother of Christ is also the mother of the people of God.

Clearly, then, the Christian vision is remarkably concrete; it includes the tragic-humorous, the humble, the historical-traditional, the adaptive, the communal-personal, the loving, the freeing, the feminine. But this vision has mystery at its very center in the Christ who cannot be captured by converging on Him all human knowledges and skills. Yet the Christ of this vision lures these knowledges-skills-arts into the deeper penetration of all the natural and more-than-natural mysteries that are eventually to be found centered in Him. Such mystery gives the Christian vision an unlimited openness to human developments; it cannot afford to be merely another closed ideology that claims to be open to all reality.

Because Christians, like other men and women, are quite finite-minded, they will unconsciously attempt to limit a Christian vision to their own horizons. This means that ghetto-mindedness will inevitably be operating in the Christian university on the premise that only the ghetto approach will enable the threatened group to form a close survival community. Thus, a form of Peter Berger's "plausibility structure" is erected, and the university's Christian vision is somewhat compromised. This peril of every Christian university should not distract us from the magnificence of the Christian vision, yet it should warn us of the discipline that is needed to remain open to the full Christian vision of the university—a vision whose characteristics reveal great riches to be used for the growth of the university. What this discipline might be and how it might be cultivated are questions that cannot be postponed. For if the Christian vision is slowly brought to term because it emerges only gradually out of the delicate discussions of the complex university community, then there must be something to sustain the university during this period of vision-incubation. The nature of this dynamic "something" will become clear in the next chapter.

6 The University Community is Disciplined Liberty or Else a Travesty

It is easy to find the "university as a travesty" in the popular stereotypes of the university professor sketched in film, novel, and joke. Unfortunately, these extreme examples of the university community are all too often drawn from flesh-and-blood people. Both the stereotypes and the subjects of these grotesque portraits are dramatically warning the university community that lack of integrity is especially destructive of university life and the ideals that it professes. It would be profitable to take a glance at these portraits in order to see the problem graphically.

At one time or another, each of us has had to listen to the "idea man." He is a veritable factory of ideas and opinions—a talk-machine. New insights on love, honor, liberty, creativity, world trade, pacifism, and the despair poets gush from his mind and flood his conversation. He has a remarkable ability to outline solutions for most world problems, though his own family difficulties appear to be insoluble. After long hours of listening, you have the suspicion that his feelings are frozen deep down within him—especially as he batters you with new ideas despite your attempts to make an escape with muttered apologies about being tired and having a hard day ahead. Compassion seems to be missing; however, opinionated pride is very much present.

Unlike the "idea man," who is trying to dedicate himself to world problems, the "professorial snob" has built around himself or herself a world of serene gentility in which, apart from the turbulent life of everyman, he or she can pursue private interests, such as restoring tapestries and studying the literature of courtly love. He or she is meticulous, even prissy, in class preparation and in scholastic procedures, and seldom leaves a circle of carefully chosen friends, habitats, and routines. Within the safe castle of the self, this professor quickly lifts the drawbridge if someone should attempt to intrude with a personal problem. A more lovable subspecies of the "professorial snob" is the "absent-minded professor"—an amiable person who is helpless when he or she is away from books and bookish people. He or she is forever surprised at the problems of students, and attempts to help students result in much fumbling and

119

failure. Both the "absent-minded professor" and the "professorial snob" have successfully escaped the real world; for the former, escape has been unwitting, but for the latter, escape has all too often been witting.

But if the previous professors have lost a feel for the everyday world and everyday persons, the "red-hot revolutionary professor" is absolutely sure that he or she not only knows the deepest aspirations of average people, but has discovered the message that will lift them out of their malaise to a new confidence in vigorous action for curing societal ills. Social-mindedness is so strong in the revolutionary that, at times, one wonders whether revolutionary zeal would move him or her to smash the individual who, by not accepting the "great message," obstructed social action. This revolutionary is electric with concern for the community, self-sacrificing for a single purpose in life, somewhat deaf to other alternatives, and always in a hurry.

A strange bedfellow of the "professor-revolutionary" is the "emotional aesthete," though their styles appear to be quite different. The aesthete's strong emotions lead him or her into sudden, deep concern for a student, fellow faculty member, or chance seat-partner on a flight to New York. A torrent of energy is expended in a short time to reassure the troubled person, to advance the career of a colleague, or to assist a beleaguered administrator. Then comes exhaustion, the need for relief from the heavy burden, withdrawal, and finally, loss of interest. Perduring patience with self and with the other is not the "emotional aesthete's" strongest characteristic.

The common feature of these caricatures is a basic lack of integrity or wholesomeness. Something is missing to balance the powerful talents, to ballast the soaring ambition, to stabilize the energetic flight. Could it be that self-discipline is the major missing element? The answer to this question is of great importance, for, if a Christian vision of the university is not sufficient for discovering the unity of the university, and if philosophy and theology are also inadequate for this task, then the unity of the professor's personal life, and the consequent unity of the university community's life, could be very important for discovering the unity of the university itself. At least this approach would be another converging approach toward this mysterious unity. For the practical living of university life yields to the individual, and hence to the community, wisdom-insights that may well reveal aspects of the very unity of the university.

In other words, if the university mirrors mankind as well as the universe, then human decisions about university life could contain implicit principles that might be usable for understanding the university itself. For the personal, professional, and communal aspects of a university person's life are not so carefully segregated that they cannot mutually reveal each other to the reflective person. Thus, in the psychology department, the sensitive wife and mother may, by that very sensitivity, be more aware of her volunteers in a psychological experiment and, consequently, render them "more accurate" subjects within the experiment. She may also be an especially valuable member of the core-curriculum committee because of her sensitive openness to new viewpoints. Could it be that the discipline of compassion, which she has learned from family living, has enabled her to be a more competent researcher and committee member and then, through this expeience, has given her insight into the unifying heart of the university? She may see, for example, that this heart is composed of human relationships honed sharp by professional activities, yet warmly intensified by amicable wisdom and common, strong concern for the world's needs.

Let us put this into more definite university terms. Does the university's problem of unity deeply involve the human will? Could it be that reinterpreted knowledge (the institutional aim of the university) and accumulated wisdom (its communal aim) cannot be *well* acquired, nor be *long* held, nor be *more fully* developed unless self-discipline is constantly operative in the university? If so, then such discipline would consequently improve the university's service to the larger civic community. Thus, reflection on the nature of discipline may well reveal something of the university's intimate unity.

There are, however, some difficulties with such a thesis. First, it is not easy to precisely define what discipline is. Discipline is often used as a "circus-tent term" under which anything can lurk and one that can, therefore, be employed to diagnose just about any problem. To change the metaphor, discipline turns out to be the "all-purpose elixir" of the medicine show. But there is an even greater difficulty. The rallying cry of *discipline* might be used to clamp down on the intelligent inventiveness that is needed for reinterpreting specialized truth: "Further funding of this research project has been terminated because the results do not seem commensurate with the expenses incurred. The original project has been extended beyond the described goals—apparently without the due notice of our stringent criteria for such expansion." Or discipline might be the excuse used to thwart the university's communal aim of accumulated wisdom: "The Tenure Committee is aware of your excellent undergraduate teaching and of your generous promotion of faculty seminars; however, it finds few scholarly articles in your dossier, though it notes your contributions to several university committees and your presence on a civic advisory board. Therefore, with regret. . . ."

In addition, the term *discipline* might be used as a synonym for self-sacrifice, which, in turn, stands for getting lost in community endeavors

121

and never finding one's own person. It might also mean a certain bracing of the personality so that one becomes noted for being "hardnosed," "wooden," "unable to adapt," "afraid of emotions," "repressed in affections," "insensitively rationalistic." Moreover, the accusation is sometimes made that discipline securely locks one within department activities or within university life so that the larger dimensions of familial and civic life are not experienced deeply. In this context, it is often taken to mean "putting one's nose to the grindstone and being afraid to look up lest precious time be lost."

Such misuses of the idea of discipline twist it into pejorative meanings, many of them implying undue restraint. Consequently, discipline is conceived of as destroying the liberty that is needed for healthy university life and as offering insight into constraint rather than into the true unity of the university. If lack of integrity, however, is the tragic flaw that cripples the individual professor and, hence, his or her university community, and if true discipline could possibly be an integrative healer of the university person and his or her community, then it would be wise to reflect on the true nature of discipline and how it works within university living. To do this, one would need, first, to analyze the meanings of liberty, since all the previous objections issue from a position that considers discipline to be a vise slowly tightening around human liberty. Second, because so much injustice has been done in the names of liberty and discipline, one would need to discover the role of justice in discipline and describe it. Indeed, since disciplined justice can be accused of throttling the love that is necessary to a university community, the influence of love in discipline would be the third element to consider in studying disciplined liberty. In light of these three characteristics, discipline does seem, does it not, to be a rather large "circus-tent." Or could it be that disciplined liberty just happens to be the heart of the university's unity?

Freedom Is Not Liberty

Some claim that freedom is paradoxically united with "the clamp of discipline," since one can freely choose to live or not to live in a disciplined way. They point to the person who stays with the difficult job of being a high-school director of athletics through twenty years and then contrast this person with someone who drifts from job to job. But is it possible that freedom and discipline are actually made for each other rather than only mysteriously united? To answer this question, let us discover, first, what freedom is and, secondly, what constitutes discipline.

Freedom is certainly more than a childish whim whereby a person decides, at a moment's notice, to buy a red polka dot raincoat. The purchase is called a childish decision precisely because it is more compulsive than free. Nor is freedom to be confused with a passionate gust of feeling when anger at a surly busdriver leads one to stuff the evening paper into the coin box so that no fares can be registered. Most law courts judge that passion reduces freedom and is not itself freedom. Nor is freedom to be limited to choosing between action and inaction when a person is invited to "come along to the movie." Freedom seems much more present as one agonizingly deliberates over whether or not to take out a particular type of mortgage during a business recession. The deliberation dramatizes the choice between options; the sense of accomplishment, which follows upon the decision, indicates the resolute decisiveness of one's freedom.

Some estimate the amount of freedom one enjoys according to the range of options that are available to one's decision. Consequently, they are tempted to say that modern persons are more free since they have a wider array of (a) weapons for hunting, (b) clothing for diverse occasions, (c) foods for satisfying hunger, (d) entertainments for enjoying leisure, (e) jobs for earning a living, and (f) men or women for marriage. Such observers evidently have not watched the "poor little rich kid" who is bewildered at the assortment of toys that are suddenly thrust upon him or her at Christmastime. Experiencing *ennui,* he or she plays with none of them or tries all of them, playing with each one for just a few moments. This child can be forty years old, twirling the television dial or even watching three TV sets simultaneously or jumping from job to job or spouse to spouse, and finally sinking into quiet apathy. Abundance of options can paralyze, rather than galvanize, one's ability to choose. Perhaps to better understand freedom, it is necessary to sketch out its stages of growth in a person. This procedure may even require that we distinguish freedom from liberty.

There would seem to be three stages in the child's growth toward freedom. The first stage occurs when the child elects to postpone an immediate pleasure. The giving of a favorite candy to a close friend may well be a preparation for that day in the future when the friend has the only bag of candy on the block. The postponement of pleasure not only allows time for new options to appear in the child's consciousness, but also makes possible the second stage of growth toward freedom—the devising and choosing of strategies to acquire a future option. Monica, for example, wants to play with the new doll house of the girl next door. So, Monica allows the girl next door to play with Monica's puppy, invites her to eat some of Monica's cookies, tells her how pretty her mother is, and, finally, asks whether or not she has ever shown her doll house to anyone. To the first stage—postponement of immediate pleasure—the child has now added the second stage—free choice among various strategies for reaching a distant goal. The third stage is freely choosing to cooperate with others in attaining a good that is attainable by oneself alone. The building of a tree house with the gang, for example, or the forming of a Little League baseball team will demand more than self-centered strategy. Both of these activities also demand the sacrifice of one's role as tree-house owner or as veteran third baseman.

The fourth stage actually is incipient liberty, a human state that is continuous with freedom but enjoys great qualitative difference from it, for liberty is more than freedom, more than the ability to choose or not to choose, to choose this option or another one without thinking of whether the options are good or evil. Liberty is the ability to habitually choose the good option over the evil one. Thus, to move from mere freedom to liberty is to leap from the amoral world to the moral world, and it is to courageously struggle along the path of goodness in that new moral world. At this point of growth, the child turns into the adolescent—the young man or woman of uncompromising ideals, of tortured conscience, of alternate moods of exultant hope and sobbing despair, of passionate and demanding loyalties. To intelligently persevere in pursuit of *the good*, that is, to enjoy liberty, implies balanced intelligence and much experience, combined with tested courage, cultivated thirst for justice, and patient endurance—qualities not yet developed in the adolescent, though need of them is nevertheless excruciatingly felt.

The fifth stage occurs when the adolescent perseveringly chooses not only the good, but the better among several good options, despite the severe suffering that might be involved. When, for example, a figure-skating coach says to a fourteen-year-old girl, "I think you are Olympic caliber; do you want to try for it in four years?" her decisive "yes" will cost her plenty of suffering to establish her career. Her resolute and habitual choice of the better over the good is a life attitude that is called maturing liberty. But it is the sixth stage in the individual's growth toward full liberty that underlines the social dimension of such a career decision. This adult phase of liberty includes a fuller wisdom that is composed of knowledges and virtues that have been honed by experiences of love and sacrifice. When a young man and woman begin to seriously think of marriage, loyal dedication to the other's good, at one's own expense, becomes a way of life. The coming of children only reinforces this loyalty as the man and woman systematically plan out the sacrifices necessary to pay off a mortgage, start an educational annuity for the children, and take out insurance policies against possibly disastrous expenses.

This mature loyalty to the family often enables parents to feel something of God's providence and affection for them. Consequently, loyalty to God—the seventh stage of maturing liberty—can arise as naturally as the joys and troubles of their family life. At this point, parents find their gaze penetrating beyond this world to the great community of the great tomorrow that will make all the joys and troubles of the past seem entirely worthwhile. In thus stepping back from the world, as it were, they discover new beauties in it: brotherhood and sisterhood with all in Christ, justice as an expression of love and not simply as something to be protected by civil law, and love of God and of neighbor interpenetrating in the same action. This fullness of liberty goes far beyond freedom; at the same time, however, it includes freedom. All that these adults have suffered and accomplished has produced in each one of them a wholesome personality, a full integrity that is ready for further growth. In fact, this mature person literally *is* liberty, for the personality of such a person enjoys a singleness of purpose, a balanced judgment, a strong network of virtues, an inventive imagination, hearty emotions, and good health. Indeed, this is the truly educated person.

No Liberty without Discipline

Is such freedom and liberty compatible with discipline? Yes, if discipline can be described as the sustained willingness to suffer for the truth, taken precisely as the good. Bernard Lonergan has noted in *Insight* that the fourth, fifth, and sixth volumes of Arnold Toynbee's *Study of History* document how cultures and civilizations gradually disintegrate when they slowly lose the capacity for sustained development because of schism in both the individual soul and the social body. Consequently, the integrity of mature and inventive liberty is needed for sustained cultural development in both the individual and the nation. But such liberty is never without its pain. Thus, the definition of discipline previously offered can be stated colloquially: "a nitty-gritty love of truth." But can such definitions be proved viable and can the life of discipline be composed with liberty? The answers to these questions are clearly crucial to the understanding and promotion of unity in the university since they describe the integrity of both the university person and the community.

Would it be wrong to consider discipline as the power to pursue truth rigorously and to seek the good decisively? Naturally, rigor and decisiveness would include a willingness to suffer that is not masochism but is simply the toughness needed to achieve the integrity and mature liberty previously described. More precisely, discipline would consist of five basic elements: (1) meticulous use of all the necessary means toward the

125

attainment of truth and the good—a professional attitude; (2) eagerness to cooperate with others in the use of these means—teamwork above a personal career; (3) strong desire to do things fairly with and for others—justice; (4) singleness of life-purpose—a personal and communal vision; and (5) channeling the emotions toward this purpose—the joy of passionate purpose. Let us briefly examine each of these elements to see how they work together within discipline.

Every professional feels the twinge of pain—even irritation, at times—when he or she meticulously uses *all* the necessary means to attain truth and the good. The trial lawyer reluctantly gives up a Saturday round of golf to make sure that he has mastered all the medical evidence for a personal injury suit on Monday morning. The chief surgeon, carefully going over the X rays and the brain-scan results for the sixth time, knows that such minute preparation removes some of the tension in the operating theater and makes for more sureness in the whole team. The historian, patiently plodding through the state archives in Madrid in search of an elusive letter from the Viceroy, hears the joyful sounds of the fiesta outside, but keeps pulling down the folios and carefully turning the ancient pages. Professionals are ascetics, whether they like it or not. They are never without the temptation of not using *all* the necessary means to the truth, of not suffering (as far as they are able) the whole truth and the total good for those dependent on their work.

Of course, such wholeness and totality require the cooperation of others, the second element in personal discipline. Unless today's professional is eager to cooperate with other professionals, he or she risks cheating the client. Our complex world does not easily tolerate the solitary genius. And yet, teamwork—i.e., the subordination of individual effort (and glory) to group effort—threatens the ambitious person with anonymity. There can be a deep-seated conviction that there is no room for a "grandstander" among the twenty-three experts composing a kidney-transplant team, or among the eight physicists studying the lattice structure of a rare chemical crystal. Thus, one reflects that selflessness is becoming almost a necessity of modern professional life as one observes the teams of experts deciphering for decades the Qumran *papyri* and collectively publishing their findings in the scriptural journals. There is a need to constantly defer to the opinions of others and yet, at the same time, to politely challenge others' views, to modify one's own hypothesis about the best way to reach a goal and yet, at times, to resist changes that one judges to be incompatible with the goal. Tension can be so tight that one finds it hard to breathe. Still, without the team there is no hope of attaining the truth and the good.

It is no surprise, then, that a desire to do things fairly, so that the cooperative work of the team reaches the truth and the good, is a necessity of professional work. A strong sense of justice, the third element of discipline, must be working in each member of the professional team so that they all treat each other fairly and so that they do not cheat the community of the truth and the good, which they are pursuing. The medical scientist, for example, who works for the prestigious research institute and fakes cancer-test results on mice, not only causes havoc within the institute; indeed, the explosive injustice done to his or her colleagues sends concussions beyond the institute to shatter people's confidence throughout the medical community and its various publics.

So, for reasons of professional attitude, teamwork, and justice, it becomes clear that honest singleness of purpose is critical to the disciplined pursuit of the truth and the good. Problems of consequence cannot be solved by people who are living double lives, guided by double truth-systems and double standards of value. The hypocrisy of such divergent pluralism becomes evident when truth is "managed" and the good is "staged." University administrators whose baccalaureate pronouncements on values seldom enter into their day-to-day decisions and their long-range plans have substituted easy expediency for the toughness of discipline. The family sociologist or the child psychologist whose scientific understandings leave his or her family unaffected is not suffering the truth nor accepting the pain of achieving the good. The difficulty with honest singleness of purpose is that it causes continual suffering since it involves ongoing conversion of mind, heart, and lifestyle. The firm choice of a new single life-aim or the firm acceptance of a new grasp of an old life-aim changes all one's safe and neat routines. This is more than irritating— unless the change comes from a new vision, personal and communal, of the worthwhileness of one's life-work.

Out of this vision of honest, single life-purpose, the fourth element of discipline can come a new commitment to oneself, to others, and to God. When, in this vision, a person sees the worthwhileness of his or her work, and when he or she experiences the respect of colleagues and family, not merely for the work but more particularly for his or her selfless integrity, then that person discovers within himself or herself a new depth of self-respect and a new self-confidence. From this solid base, this person becomes more decisive, more able to return love and affection, more sure of his or her loyalty to others, more precise in focusing and more generous in giving personal energies to a project, more consistent and perduring in following out his or her decisions with strong actions. Ironically, this growth in humaneness, if it is caused by the vision that directs a person's discipline, demonstrates that discipline is more a source of deep satisfaction than a cause of constant pain.

Moreover, this personal vision of honest singleness of purpose includes commitment to family, to a group of colleagues, to institutions such as the university and the church, and to the nation. The cooperation involved in this social commitment expands a person beyond his or her usual limitations of skill-knowledge-opportunity, balances off the stength of others against one's weakness, educates one to be "other-centered," and forms a community of truth. When the Broadway actress states to a TV interviewer that her superb performance in a recent play was drawn out of her by the two skillful co-actors who taught her the inner meaning of the play and who, then, through their performances, made her weaknesses look almost like strengths, she may not be overstating the case out of false modesty. She may just possibly have caught their contagious vision and selflessness. Such a vision of purpose may lead a person to integrate her values into a system of priorities (a "secularity") and then to discover within herself a devotion to something higher than her own acting career.

In a university, such teamwork binds administrators together so that they might carry out a new program in women's studies, for example; likewise, this teamwork enables an experimentation team to complete a three-year project or helps feuding factions in a political science department to heal their own wounds as well as those inflicted on the hapless students. In any case, this social commitment does make possible the first aim of the university—the reinterpretation of traditional truth. And, surprisingly, if this commitment within the vision is structuring one's personal discipline, then that discipline truly becomes a source of joy and not merely an instrument of suffering.

Lastly, the commitment contained in this personal vision of life-purpose may reach up to God who, according to the Book of Genesis, intends that men and women complete His creative act with their own inventivensss. Here the many single purposes of men and women converge within the single, grand, divine purpose to build the great community of the "great tomorrow." Already, according to Paul's letters to the Ephesians and to the Colossians, this community is forming in the convergence of many individual life-purposes. The Christian God, like the Marxist theoretician, asks that no one be arbitrarily excluded from this community and requires that each contribute to the community according to each one's unique set of gifts-opportunities-strengths-weaknesses. This vision of single life-purpose now reveals itself to be a wisdom-vision that could blend neatly into the wisdom community of a university and lead that community in its accumulation of wisdom. For, in luring each person into using his or her unique gift (e.g., a specialized knowledge or skill) for the community, according to the community's wisdom, this wisdom-vision builds the knowledge and skill communities into the larger com-munities of university, city, and nation. Thus, both the dual intrinsic aims and the single extrinsic aim of the university are achieved through the blending of many life-purposes into a larger single purpose (really recip-rocally dual purpose) of the university, and then, into the still larger purpose of the city-nation. All of this is made emotionally effective by the suffering and the joy of discipline.

This brings us to the fifth, and sometimes neglected, element of disci-pline—the channeling of emotions such as fear and joy. For, the intense pursuit of truth and the wonder of its discovery generate, at times, power-ful emotions. To read Galileo's works is to experience the high elation and the rich exuberance of his new vision of the world. His disciplined work on dynamics and the telescope brought values and joys into his life that could not be repressed. But how does discipline channel rather than suppress emotions? First, the emotions give strength to a person's sin-gleness of life-purpose, and that singleness of life-purpose then directs the emotion toward the truth to be found and the good to be revealed. Second, a person's attitudes or virtues can be made inventive beyond repetitive routine by the uniqueness of emotional experience. Yet, at the very same time, these same attitudes, having been flooded with this feeling, adapt the emotional experience to the life-purpose. The impel-ling power of Dante's deep devotion to Beatrice did not deflect him from his life-purpose but, rather, filled it with a tender wisdom and a wise tenderness of enduring strength. Third, emotional experience renders a person's imagination lively, ("I still laugh whenever I see the pointed beard of Henderson"), unforgettably historical ("Will you ever forget the day we burnt the mortgage"), and inventive ("Well, I saw this old reliable wheel leaning against the bright-red barn and remembered, to my cha-grin, how a roulette wheel sends the silver ball ricocheting around the black container, and then, with half-regret and half-elation, I . . .").

This emotion-tripped creativity of the imagination, once it has been introduced into a person's single life-purpose, can simultaneously pro-duce the joy of inventiveness, the frustration of directing creativity down the path of limiting circumstances, and the satisfaction of accomplish-ment. One sees this in the artist who must work swiftly under the limita-tions of water colors, failing light, and gusty winds that bend trees and send clouds scudding. The simultaneous joy and suffering of discipline shows most expressively in dance, painting, drama, and sporting events. But it is also present in the professor's tired face lighting up with a student's witticism or insight, in the relieved laughter of committee mem-bers as they reach the successfully compromised end of a meeting, in the

129

satisfied look of a team of experts as they hear their report finally being read and as they note their colleagues' acceptance of a job well done. Discipline does carry within it a sense of mastery over knowledge-situation-self and a sense of worthwhileness in one's endeavors. It is not all suffering, though, at times, it would appear to be merely a packet of pains.

Thus, discipline turns out to be passionate purpose arising within the vision of one's life-purpose; it is also a network of lived attitudes, which have been woven according to this purpose—a purpose now pursued with courageous joy, with the balance of temperate views and prudent actions, and with justice. Discipline turns out to be a deep, intelligent patience—much like St. Paul's *hupomone*, an active holding together of the community enterprise despite the storms.

If one admits that discipline is not all blood, sweat, and tears, then it is somewhat easier to see how it can be composed with the freedom and liberty described earlier—especially if one were to note how the seven-stage development of freedom becoming liberty is paralleled by a seven-stage growth of discipline in each person. For example, during the three stages of childish freedom, when the youngster learns to (a) postpone immediate pleasure, (b) plan strategy for acquiring something good, and (c) cooperate with others toward a goal that is unattainable by one person, the child builds in himself or herself a discipline that allows time for deliberation about options, that uses intelligence to attain a relatively distant goal, and that subordinates the self to a team effort toward some good that is desired and shared by all.

It must be granted that the child's discipline is heavily individualistic and self-centered; yet this discipline offers a solid base for the adolescent stages of liberty wherein the young person learns to distinguish the evil option and to perseveringly choose the good option. Later, the youngster learns to consistently elect the better option. At these two latter stages, this continuity of life-growth is bought with much suffering and loneliness that can be endured only if the adolescent develops an incipient vision of life-purpose and a beginning network of virtues, of good attitudes. Again, this adolescent discipline, though much more sophisticated and sturdy than that of the child, is still individualistic and career-oriented. But the sixth and seventh stages of liberty socialize personal discipline and render it other-centered. For, this discipline is now suffused with the love of dear ones and with a fuller vision that demands and makes worthwhile the adult sacrifices required by family, work-group, civic community, church, and nation. Because mature liberty is God-centered and, therefore, vibrant with a sense of justice, the liberated man or woman knows when and where to sacrifice prudently. He or she has definite priorities, a definite system of values to honor, and holds these with loving affection.

So it would seem, then, that, far from clamping freedom and liberty, discipline is an important contributing cause of full liberty, full human integrity, or wholesomeness. Such discipline, too, requires a liberating vision much more than an enchaining, "mono-minded" ideology. Clearly, this type of discipline is precisely the dynamism needed to deal with Original Sin—the cumulative drift of reaffirmed evil (within every generation and every culture) that tests contemporary human liberty to its roots. Finally, is it not discipline that enables the liberated person to go beyond being "kind and nice" and ultimately be *just and loving* amid the injustice and hatred that permeates many modern situations? If it is true that there is no liberty without discipline, could it be that there is no discipline without justice and love? Perhaps these last two questions deserve exploration since they may contain further insights into the integrity or unity of both the university person and the university community. This may put us at the heart of university *unity*.

What Is Discipline in the University without Justice?

The hugeness of the university apparatus can sometimes disguise its delicacy from us. An airline mechanic is well aware of how one small defective part in a Boeing 747 jet engine could cause a flameout that would result in the explosion of the wing gas tanks, sending the huge plane plummeting earthward in a flaming mass of twisted steel and screaming passengers. The university is just a little larger than an airliner—and a little more delicate. One has only to note how justice enters into the key operations of a university to see how failures in justice can vitiate, then cripple, and finally destroy university life because they undermine liberty and paralyze discipline. Justice, to be factual, is the delicate attuning of all the university procedures so that the melody of truth and wisdom sounds out in all its beauty. Injustice is the static that blurs this song and deafens people to its beauty. Let us escape the metaphor with some dissonant examples of what is meant.

Once student cheating becomes an "accepted fact of life," like pilferage at a supermarket, the level of trust among students themselves and between students and faculty becomes extremely low. Rivalry between students is sharpened with bitterness; hostility toward the faculty becomes the usual mode of address. A basic distrust about behavior spreads into the faculty's efforts to offer truth and the student's efforts to appreciate truth. The student strategy in this situation is rather straightforward: sequester important library books from the other students, suggest gang-tactics for whittling down the professor's standards of achievement, offer ways of studying less while achieving high marks (e.g., stealing examinations, doctoring experimental reports, slightly mutilating a commonly used specimen during a biology test, secretly studying with intensity while publicly organizing "no study," and so on). How can one attain, in this atmosphere, the institutional aim of reinterpreting traditional truth for contemporary society? Even the amount of mere information is considerably lessened—to say nothing of the truth that can only be possessed as personal appropriation.

Such a disease, if it has not already been promoted by a significant number of faculty members who fail to prepare their classes, will eventually attack the vitals of the professors who have been responsibly trying to teach their students. A malaise will enter the classroom procedures of the discouraged professors. The professors' perfunctory actions will take the excitement out of learning a specialized knowledge, and their hostility and anger will make the truth of the discipline seem to be merely information that is needed for bare survival. The professors then hate their own sloppiness, which, in turn, threatens to sour even their love for the discipline, which they now find somewhat disgusting to teach. Now, both the professors' specialized knowledge and the communal wisdom, which the professors' university community has so carefully accumulated, are in jeopardy. Each professor wonders (as he or she lackadaisically prepares classes, thinks seriously of pursuing a career in either industry or business, and dreads initiating new research) whether the agony of developing a wisdom is worthwhile or whether wisdom is any longer possible amid the seeming hypocrisy of university life. The hostility between professors and students eventually moves between departments and even between professors; distemper is everywhere. The communal aim of university wisdom clearly is in jeopardy.

Administrators and their staffs can hardly escape the contagion. The enforcement of university procedures that safeguard justice becomes sluggish not merely because the administration is experiencing failure of nerve, but because faculty and students are dispirited and uncooperative. In desperation, administrators may begin to threaten—at first subtly and later brutally. Although even brutal threats may initially bring cooperation, soon sullen stalling sets in. How can administrators plan ahead when present operations are bumping along slowly and demanding all their concentration? As a result, emergencies that should have been foreseen, crop up more and more frequently and require more and more energy and time. The university is grinding to a standstill and the world is starting to pass it by. For the world needs and supports a university only so long as the university reinterprets traditional truth for it and, out of this truth, generates a wisdom that is applicable to current world problems.

The total breakdown just described is due to the fact that justice *is* the very order of the university. If professors are failing to share truth with each other and with their students, then justice is not happening in the classroom, the department, the school, and the university. For the sharing of reinterpreted truth is the *raison d'être* of the university and all its parts; it is the reason why the university's constituencies have conceived and given birth to the university and continue to breathe life into it. Every institutional procedure, without exception, is structured to make truth "sharable"; no institutional procedure can escape being warped and inducing fallacy if it deviates from this aim. But if justice is the very order of the university, and if injustice is the destruction of this order which is meant solely for sharing truth, then injustice is the destroyer of wisdom in the community. For, how can values be discovered if the means of their discovery, namely, the specialized knowledges, are warped and turned vicious? And if the distrust engendered by injustice is dividing the community into factions that are suspicious of one another, if not warring with one another, how can communal wisdom long survive?

Of course, the blunting of the dual intrinsic aims of the university makes less efficient its service to the larger civic community, which is the extrinsic aim of the university. How can the university and her personnel dare to speak of justice or offer advice for just programs when the fever of injustice is racing through the university body and rendering it delirious? The patient can only feel sorry for the sick doctor and prudently refuse any ministrations.

It is to be expected that the individual member of the university will not escape this virus. The administrator, the student, and the professor will find their individual wisdom dying; wisdom without justice is the embezzling Pharisee who attempts to instruct Jesus about love for the poor. Wisdom must be expressed, if it is to continue to live; and among its chief expressions are acts of justice. Thus, any member of a university that is dying of injustice must abandon the university if he or she is to preserve minimal sanity or some personal wisdom.

It is equally clear, moreover, that this person's liberty and discipline are threatened. For if all university procedures are necessarily being filled with injustice, then the cooperator in such procedures, though he or she may abhor them, eventually becomes their promoter—a truth distilled out of the Gulag Archipelago experience of Aleksandr Solzhenitsyn, if not out of our own bitter experience. If mature liberty is the ability to perseveringly choose the greater good, then the direct opposite is occurring in the dying university that has been described. If discipline is the sustained willingness to suffer for the truth taken precisely as the good, then there is no reason to suffer since injustice in university procedures is making truth (and thus the good) increasingly less attainable. Besides, the hidden joy of discipline that is found in the mastery of a specialized knowledge and in the sense of worthwhileness of one's work is denied the professor, the administrator, and the student in the dying university. At this point, the member of the dying university is especially vulnerable to that ideology which claims to offer an efficient, quick way to restore order (justice) to the university. But the price would be high—diminishment of liberty and the use of a discipline that operates more out of fear than out of love. Can a university afford this?

What Is Disciplined Justice in the University without Love?

Just as discipline without justice eventually becomes inoperative, so also justice without love becomes impersonal, then mechanically restrictive, next joyless, and finally visionless. For these four reasons, the discipline of justice cannot operate well or long without love. Consider the first reason, for example; it is love that transforms impersonal routine into virtue. It may be that the eloquence of diction and of teaching technique does light up the possibility of virtue and call attention to this already-present structure in a person's behavior. But this is only the understanding of virtue, not virtue itself. Only exemplary love alluringly evokes virtue itself from the beloved. How is one to evoke the virtue of trust without first giving it; but how can one give trust without first loving the person trusted? The fifth of six children in a family learns what justice is when he or she observes the evenhandedness of parents who refuse to play favorites among their children. Later, when this child is a parent, raising his or her own children, he or she discovers that only a love that goes beyond momentary likes and dislikes makes such justice among his or her children possible. The young lawyer watches like a hawk the maneuvers of the senior partners in his or her firm and then closely observes one of them, promoted to the bench, begin to dispense justice. If this judge lacks a deep respect for defendants and a deeper respect for the workings of civil justice, the young lawyer quickly learns to appreciate the judge's maneuvers, which quickly get money and slowly undermine the judicial system. On the other hand, if the young lawyer sees the judge acting out of respect, and experiences in himself or herself the beauty of giving respect amid all the tearing tensions of law office and court, then this lawyer will do justice out of respect, that is to say, out of love.

In this way, justice remains a personal act rather than a mechanical routine for extracting money and exercising power. For justice, of itself, simply establishes rights, duties, and obligations so that people can segregate their possessions from one another, so that services can be exchanged according to definite specifications. All this is necessary so that clear relationships can be established and definite expectations can be trusted to be fulfilled. How can one run a supermarket unless the expected deliveries of salable, reasonably priced goods are made; unless the clerks and cashiers and other employees, all of whom have certain expected skills and have agreed to work for specified salaries, arrive at expected times to fulfill the expected needs of customers, who, then, pay the advertised prices; and unless the management plans its purchasing and hiring according to the guidelines (expectations) of the supermarket owners, with the justifiable expectation that superior skill will receive commensurate superior wages? Not only the single store, but also each company and the entire city runs on expectations fulfilled by the virtue of justice operative in each participant.

But once justice becomes vindictive or loveless ("I have *my* rights" might characterize this condition), and therefore separative of people (as in the ever-increasing supermarket scenes when everybody is leaping up and down, shouting for his or her rights), the cooperation that everyone expects gradually disappears and fighting soon begins. At this time, the unitive factor of love within justice has disappeared, and there is need to use forceful persuasion to restore the order of justice. Fear then becomes the chief promoter of cooperation and justice must be applied rigorously. Whereas love provides a certain give-and-take that allows for individual differences (e.g., "he's always late, but when he arrives, he works like a demon"), the absence of love necessitates that each person be treated with the same rigid criteria. The joy of humaneness has gone out of justice. This atmosphere generates wider separation not only between management and those who are managed, but also among those people who are managed. Either love works in justice as its soul, or justice becomes possessed by the twin demons, fear and coercion. Then justice is reduced, in a third inevitable step, to joyless, mechanical restrictions that lack humaneness. This condition perdures until love or mutual respect is, once again, gradually restored.

On the other hand, justice reciprocates by making love possible. Just actions are the expression of love; without justice, so-called loving actions are lethal. The child who is unjustly spoiled by overly lavish affection becomes a demanding monster to the once "loving" parents. Love that is structured by justice repays the whole debt with a sense of gratitude to the lender, not part of the debt with a sense of rancor at being a humiliated borrower. In the university, love can only work through justice. For, unless the professor is present for the contracted classes, offers good content within the particular course, demands adequate accounting of the students' work, works hard to elicit a usable skill that will enhance

135

the students' future, he or she will lack respect or love for the students—and, incidentally, for his or her colleagues, whose cooperative work and reputation the professor is endangering. Institutionally, love works through the specialized university knowledges to give competent, discriminating service to student, department, school, and civic community. Of course, this discriminating service is justice, the very order of the university itself.

It is clear, therefore, that justice proves to be impersonally mechanical, restrictive, and joyless if love is absent; at the same time love becomes destructive, ungrateful, and disrespectful if justice is absent. Justice can remove causes of social conflict, but it can never unite the minds and hearts of people as love can. On the other hand, love cannot long unite people whose expressions of love are unjustly incompetent. Men and women simply cannot exercise their liberty in a disciplined way without honoring both justice and love.

In a fourth step, love may be said to complete justice since love calls forth a wider, deeper vision of life than justice does. Indeed, without love, justice becomes tired over the years, satisfied with a gradually narrowing vision of life. It is a love-vision that keeps the husband-father tirelessly striving for the best for his family: decent housing, strong education for the youngsters, times of fun with children and wife, the security of solid investments. This love-vision is the source of his disciplined pursuit of business success, the source of his joy in hard work. In this way, love, which is free from a purely rationalistic vision of life, lends liberty to justice. It would seem that the openheartedness of love makes for more openmindedness and, thus, for more inventiveness in one's life. The teacher who loves to teach is always discovering and/or developing new ways to teach old principles and, incidentally, finding new principles in the process. Love tends to go beyond the traditional categories of duty and right ("If you can't see me right after class, why don't you stop at my house this evening after your last class and we'll go over your term paper"), beyond the strictly juridical ("All right, the contract was quite clear on this point, but I guess we can stretch it to accommodate you without demanding a penalty payment"), yet it relies on the duties, rights, and obligations of justice to hold the business and the school together.

There is, then, a warm expansiveness in a justice that is directed by love. Yet such justice remains realistic since one does not love a person or a group abstractly but very concretely, according to the uniqueness of the situation in which justice is working. Love is quite sensitive to the weaknesses of the person or situation loved. The management representative and the labor leader can be deeply respectful of each other and of each other's union and company; but they hammer out a carefully provisioned labor contract because the labor leader knows that some of the company officers are tricky and the management representative knows that the labor pool is fiesty with newly won power and has unruly elements in it. Both the union person and the management person have a common vision of a successful business and of a happy work crew; but the disparity between the vision and the reality makes both of them chuckle occasionally and work harder for a clean-cut and just contract, even as the vision nevertheless gives them a wide and deep perspective on themselves and on the future—a perspective based solidly on mutual respect and justice.

Because the union person and the management person share a common vision, their love enables them to identify together the values of the situation (increased worker-benefits have actually increased production, despite longer vacations and more assembly line coffee breaks), correlate values with each other (sharing profits has decreased absenteeism and brought suggestions for saving money and time), and set up value priorities (workers appreciate respect that is shown to them in awards and in better working conditions rather than in wage increases). Thus, justice ensouled with love brings openheartedness of values and openmindedness of vision to the situation.

A university person can immediately see parallels between university life and labor-management life. Faculty, students, and administration need a common, wide-ranging vision, not a narrowing ideology, to inspire a love that will unite them and energize just actions so that their work is personal and inventive rather than mechanical and restrictive as well as, humor-filled and humane rather than joyless and visionless. In this way, traditional truth can be reinterpreted in an atmosphere of trust so that inventiveness is stimulated and impersonal fear of injustice is muted. In this trusting and respectful atmosphere, people can form community and their wisdom can be joyfully accumulated. For the discipline of justice is tempered by a love inspired with vision. Thus, when the university enters into mystery, as it must, it proceeds with reverence and humility, not with mechanical brashness and arrogant rationalism. When the university tries to serve the larger civic community, it does so with humor, self-sacrifice, expert intelligence, and wisdom. In fact, one might be tempted to call the university a "disciplined liberty," since its loyalty to itself and to the civic community contains a sustained willingness to suffer for the truth as good. Indeed, its collective personality is steadily pursuing the better option for itself and for the civic community. It does this out of its specialized knowledges and by way of its communal wisdom. This is all possible because the university is doing justice out of love; and therefore its creative liberty is disciplined.

To all of this, the Christian community of a Christian university adds *caritas*, namely, love graced by Jesus Christ. The Christian believes that natural human love and justice is strengthened, rendered tender, expanded, and deepened by the acceptance of Christ and His word into a person's life. The Christian community believes that all its members are more intimately and closely united because each of them shares this one same Christ who came to render men and women just by means of His, the Father's, and the Spirit's love for them. In Augustine's eyes, this grace, or *caritas*, is precisely what turns human freedom into *libertas* and enables men and women to suffer creatively for their fellows in their everyday work and in the formation of a wisdom community. The vision that inspires this *caritas* is the beatific vision as it is interpreted to the Christian by scripture, by the Christian community or church, and by his or her own inner experience of the Trinity. Thus, the disciplined liberty of the university is quite "natural" to the Christian mind and heart. It is very clear to the Christian that there is no lasting justice without love, no personal discipline without justice and love, no mature liberty without discipline. But, like anyone else, the Christian university man or woman is puzzled. For how can a university teach love, justice, virtue, and liberty? How can a university achieve disciplined liberty?

How Can a University Act as Disciplined Liberty?

According to its institutional aim, the university teaches *about* justice, love, liberty, discipline, and the virtues (attitudinal values). In other words, the university uses conceptual understandings that are issuing out of an experience that has been clarified by the reflections of a specialized knowledge. When a specialized university group (e.g., psychologists or philosophers or anthropologists) enters into human mystery, this team paints a temporary vision to lure itself on and to test its own insights. This group builds up understandings of justice, love, liberty, discipline, and the virtues, within its own specialized discipline, in order to guide the researcher or the student toward these items; it cannot evoke them in the researcher or the student. Thus, institutionally, the university works rather abstractly and very indirectly with these items.

As a wisdom community, however, the university operates much more concretely and directly. It teaches justice, love, liberty, self-sacrifice, and virtue by literally *being* these values and *living* them out in its actions. If the university community's just actions are directed by love, then all these values are incarnate in the lives of administrators, professors, and students. This is the most effective teaching possible because it is done by "moral osmosis" insofar as the community puts the search for truth into an

138

atmosphere of affection. If this should be the Christian community of a Christian university, then it is following a Christian vision that is based on the beatific vision insofar as it is living out *caritas*. Indeed, its disciplined liberty is best summed up in its Eucharistic liturgy, where the Christ is present as both the suffering God-man of the cross and the fully liberated and liberating God-man of the triumphant resurrection.

From these descriptions of liberty and discipline, it is readily seen that the university's liberty is much more than academic freedom. Institutionally, this university liberty is, at the very least, the academic freedom to do justice to the students' hopes and needs. In practice, this is the individual professor, administrator, or student living out his or her personal dedication to a specialized knowledge, and it is the members of each individual department of the university collectively advancing a specialized knowledge. Communally, the university's liberty is the accumulated wisdom of the community, structured by the order of justice but directed by love (by *caritas* in the Christian university). Thus, this communal liberty is ideally other-centered, joyfully self-sacrificing, justly competent, capable of great vision, and expansive of humanity. No wonder, then, that the university community can best teach virtue by its presence. Of course, the institutional and the communal aspects of university liberty, like the university's dual intrinsic aims, reciprocally produce and modify each other. Further, the eight constituencies of the university that give it existence also give it liberty; likewise, from the university the constituencies receive the requisites for liberty: specialized knowledges and skills, wise guidance, vision of love and justice, presence of freedom, and discipline.

Consequently, if the person is liberty, to modify Sartre's phrase, then the collective personality of the university is, all the more so, liberty—and, more specifically, it is disciplined liberty.

Disciplined liberty, however, merely points out the road to the aims of the university. What are the steps along the way? How are they to be taken? How do knowledges get specialized and how do they become integrated to give wisdom, vision, and integrated personality? How do value systems arise and how do they become integrated to give a single purpose to life? If philosophy provides some help in answering these questions, would we still not have to consult theology to learn the destiny of all this specialization and integration? To put this another way, if one supposes that disciplined liberty gives a personal unity to the university, this personal unity nevertheless has to become better known in order to be better lived. Is this what philosophy and theology have to offer us in the university—a dynamic mapping of how the university is unified?

7 Philosophy: Indispensable Guide of the University

Philosophy is rather often accused of being insufferably snobbish—and with good evidence. What other knowledge has the nerve to claim the following: (1) that it deals with the ultimate reality of the world; (2) that it is seeking the basic unity of the universe, of mankind, and of all mankind's knowledges and loves; and (3) that, although other knowledges are not the final judges of their own unity, philosophy nevertheless defines its own unity and, finally, judges the unity of other knowledges? Is philosophy not aware that the pluralism rampant within it makes it appear more like the perennial madcap rather than the wise weaver of the many-stranded unity of the world? The one problem facing the critics of philosophy is that the more effective they are in criticizing, the more apt they are to fashion a new philosophy. Indeed, criticisms of philosophy show how really indispensable any philosophy is to civilized discourse. And who is to say that one critic's particular philosophy is better than all the rest?

Perhaps this is a captious retort to critical problems. For if philosophy is pluralistic of its very nature (as our consideration of pluralism in chapter 4 indicated), then is it not a contradiction for philosophy to promise a unified view of the universe? Actually, does not philosophy put up to the universe a splintered mirror composed of conflicting philosophic views of both the universe and mankind? How, then, can philosophy be of much service to the unity of the university, which also supposedly mirrors the universe and mankind? If philosophy is multiminded and multipurposed, can it do any more than further fragment the university? In reply to these questions, no philosopher can deny that the pluralism of philosophy is very humiliating at times; but the philosopher might add that this pluralism is also the glory and liberty of philosophy. Such is the mystery of philosophy and the philosopher.

The objections just presented are literally terrible—not only in their impact on the pursuit of philosophy, but also in their implications about university life. They would seem to say that the university is doomed to more and more fragmentation. As a result, the conflicting views of university experts will paradoxically splinter the society that they are trying to

140

better. To deal with these objections, it will be necessary to consider (1) how philosophy comes into existence, (2) what functions philosophy is supposed to perform, (3) how pluralistic philosophy can still be a unified knowledge, and (4) how philosophy can integrate the various knowledges and, thus, help to unify the university. This is a tall order for a book, much less for a chapter.

The Irrepressible Drive to Philosophize

Philosophy, far from being a luxury, is a necessity of human life. Human beings happen to be "philosophic animals." They can never be satisfied with a piecemeal knowledge of the world. Humans want, in one vision, to see the totality of the universe—not merely its parts as they are disclosed by the specialized knowledges and arts. The attempt to construct a total mosaic out of these parts is philosophizing, and its success is philosophy. Nor is mankind satisfied with the murkiness and disorder of common-sense knowledge, although this day-to-day knowledge always remains important, since it is the root and test of all scientific knowledge and of all the arts. Men and women want clarity and order even if they must endure the abstract expression and complex precision of philosophy. For in the human mind there runs a fervent ambition to illuminate the darkest depths of a being, its very existence—an ambition springing out of the murky depths of every human being's own act of existence. Mankind alone becomes mesmerized in contemplating the sheer mystery of being.

Powering this drive for a deep philosophic vision of all reality is the expansive human heart. Basically, men and women have a ravenous hunger to embrace the "totally loveable" with a total love. Out of these drives for total vision and love gradually issue a person's basic set of values, those for which he or she is willing to die and according to which he or she lives life's best moments. If a person's philosophic vision is shattered and if, consequently, his or her set of values breaks up into clashing bits, then this person's "wholeness" begins to disintegrate, his or her world becomes less and less sane, and his or her loves turn sour. To express vision and love, a person literally has to make sense out of the world. Otherwise, men and women learn to think of themselves as idiots and are shaken by self-disgust and some hatred of others.

Human beings are philosophic animals for pragmatic reasons, too; humans want to know where they and the universe are going and whether they can control the path that is to be taken. After all, through cunning, a person must wrest food from the earth, wrestle the sea and the seasons, learn to love and to sorrow, and become deeply acquainted with death and the ultimate. Human beings cannot avoid these mysteries; men and

141

women either dominate the mysteries or the mysteries crush them. For their very life's sake, they must get to the bottom of the world, to its ultimate dynamisms. The intensity of these struggles uncover in the person his or her own knowledges, drives, strengths, and weaknesses. The more wholesome is a person's experience of the world, the more integrity he or she finds within himself or herself. Thus, a person's philosophic vision and love of the world significantly color his or her happiness.

Because of these unavoidable dual drives for total vision and total love, men and women cannot fail to philosophize about life's ultimates. The question, however, is how *well* will humans philosophize, since their early knowledge of these ultimates is merely rudimentary or prescientific? Furthermore, this rudimentary philosophy can be poisoned by error when it is taken beyond the more primitive principles of life. A series of harmful mischances, for example, can undermine a person's belief in divine providence and gradually change his or her vision of the world from one of friendliness to one of hostility. It is, therefore, advantageous to develop one's rudimentary philosophy into a more scientific approach in order to protect against such poisoning. This is particularly important when one is living in a sophisticated scientific culture that can misuse science to attack rudimentary philosophy as, for example, the theory that alleges that the whole world is merely a cloud of atoms coalescing by chance and, so, human history is considered simply a string of chance atomic events. Nor, at this point, can a person substitute theology for philosophy since theology must use philosophy to help the person reflect upon and unify disparate historical revelatory events into a meaningful vision of salvation history. Besides, philosophy helps theology to recognize its own autonomy (proper sphere of competence) and to employ the other sciences for its reflection. In doing this, philosophy is rescuing theology from the imperialism of the currently dominant science, whether it is biology or sociology or psychology.

However, only the collective reflection of the community, led by the masterful insights of the rare philosophic genius, can, through the centuries, gradually distill a scientific philosophy out of rudimentary prescientific philosophy in order to protect the latter. This process of purification from error and of positive enrichment involves a continual reflective checking of the community's experience in meeting life's changing problems. It is also the adding of *proviso* after *proviso* to once starkly simple generalizations concerning this experience. Gradually, then, out of this prescientific philosophy there emerges a scientific body of knowledge about ultimate reality. This scientific philosophy, because of its newfound rigor and clarity, can now be efficiently imparted to those who have the time and the courage to master it. What took centuries to gradually accumulate, now can be acquired within a person's lifetime, if he or she rediscovers the philosophic truths within his or her own experience by using the purified method that has been distilled by his or her predecessors.

The importance of this accomplishment is seen when one notes how a culture is formed. If one roughly distinguishes "civilization" from "culture" by assigning the technological and mercantile aspects of a nation to its civilization, then culture becomes, in the gross, those commanding, emotionally charged ideals that control the aspirations, institutional processes, and activities of a society. These later three dynamisms would be embodied in society's religion, literature, legal tradition, science, foreign policy, mercantile endeavor, government apparatus, charitable organizations, sports, and entertainment. Culture, then, is the communal mind and heart expressing itself in all—and in each—of the community's endeavors.

Now, although the community's culture is always more than the sum of each individual member's culture, still the community culture, for better or for worse, ultimately is rooted in the mind and heart of each citizen. The ideals that each person holds in common with the majority of his or her fellow citizens form the ground of the community's culture. But these ideals, present in each individual, are necessarily suffused with, at the very least, a prescientific, or rudimentary, philosophy, that is, an "everyman's or "everywoman's" view of life's ultimates. Otherwise, the person has no overall vision in which to locate the various, already mentioned elements of the culture and within which he or she can see and appreciate his or her own societal role. Without such a rudimentary vision, the individual remains a child who not only is easily manipulated by shrewdly applied pressures, but also considers himself or herself to be merely a cog in the great societal machine. Such childishness breaks down the communal loyalties that hold a culture together. In this breakdown, we are already facing the need for the unifying function of philosophy.

The Five Functions of Philosophy

Philosophy, then, exposes the universal structure that runs through all the elements of a culture and then presents this unity to the minds of community members for their actions. This universal structure, in its prescientific and scientific modes, is the public philosophy that Walter Lippmann and John Courtney Murray feared was collapsing in America.

143

Whoever understands the philosophy that energizes a culture, therefore, also comprehensively grasps the culture itself, knows its people, loves them, and sees where the nation is heading. This is the first function of philosophy: to offer the student, the professor, the administrator, and the university a basic orientation for their work and life.

In a nation dominated by biology, psychology, and sociology, however, a very sophisticated philosophy is needed to understand and appreciate this country's culture and to map its path. Educated citizens should enjoy a philosophy that is somewhat commensurate with the sophistication of the dominant sciences lest they lose their cultural perspective, find their vision narrowed to one specialized knowledge or skill, and become the inmate of an imprisoning ideology. But a sophisticated scientific philosophy with such aspirations can appear to be absurdly pompous if one is not delicately aware that its aims, functions, and accomplishments are dictated by the very nature of the human mind and heart. For example, philosophy looks to *all* existents rather than to such specialized knowledges as mathematics, which deals only with quantifiable relationships, or such as anthropology, which is concerned only with physical, social, and cultural growth in human beings.

Philosophy not only touches upon all existent reality—in contrast to the highly specialized knowledges and arts—but also goes underneath each discipline to explore its specific foundations. Each discipline, because it is unequipped to investigate its own basic presuppositions, must take those presuppositions for granted in order to get on with its own work. Philosophy, for example, goes underneath the quantifiable relation that is studied by mathematics in order to determine (a) what a relation is, (b) what quantity is, (c) how relation and quantity come to be and affect each other, (d) what basis there is for their correlation, and (e) what they do for the things in which they arise. Mathematics is not equipped to do this for herself. Nor is philosophy satisfied with anthropology's mapping of human cultural development. Philosophy wants to find out why men and women, alone among the animals, have developed culture, why they feel the need to build and pyramid symbols of their interior life, and how insight produces cultural advances and oversight causes regressions. Anthropology cannot do this for herself.

Again, philosophy not only probes the symbolic factors of dance, art, and literature but also asks *what* symbol is, *how* a symbol changes meaning, and *why* its meaning can never be frozen. Moreover, philosophy wants to know what is happening when the historian generalizes on unique events to produce an historical account of a unique series of unique events; how the historian can generalize unique events without vaporizing them; and how the historian can escape implying that there are

144

no connecting threads, no absolutes, in history but that all history consists of relative, disconnected events.

In this way, philosophy finds itse.f asking the terrible questions that threaten the work of centuries. Indeed, even as philosophy acts like a prime agent of pluralism, it proceeds to reflect on whether pluralism is convergent or divergent. But, in stretching itself horizontally to all beings and in plunging vertically underneath all the specialized knowledges and arts with these terrible questions, philosophy constitutes itself a distinct and autonomous knowledge—a knowledge capable both of embracing the universe and of exploring the presuppositions which underlie all the specialized knowledges and arts as the latter report the universe, in piecemeal fashion, within the university.

Certainly this refusal of philosophy to be contained within any specialized knowledge or to be satisfied with the depth of insight given by any particular science seems excessively prideful, unless one comes to see that philosophy is simply mankind's legitimate attempt to fulfill a most basic drive—namely, the desire for the ultimate. Human "animals" cannot retain their mental growth, to say nothing of their physical existence, if they do not pursue their various knowledges into an ultimate view of self, world, and destiny. These ultimate findings, which are between and beyond the various sciences, are impossible unless men and women escape imprisonment within a single science, such as physics, or within all the sciences taken together, and unless they delve more deeply into reality than an individual science, such as sociology, allows, or more widely than the totality of the physical and social sciences can provide. These very explorations beyond the specialized knowledges and arts constitute a philosophy of the ultimate.

This is not to say that philosophy is merely a generalization of the various sciences. Mankind and philosophy, then, would still be imprisoned within the arts and sciences and would not be delving more deeply than these. Instead, philosophy would simply be a cloudy musing about matters that these arts and sciences have presented sharply and concretely in clear, realistic concepts. On the contrary, just as the various sciences complement one another—e.g., sociology, biology, meteorology, agronomy, and so on, in the study of ecology—so, also philosophy complements each and every specialized art and knowledge. Thus, although the physical and social sciences generally take for granted that the reality under study is something other than mankind's consciousness which is doing the study, philosophy explores this assumption. Similarly, although all the sciences assume that reality has intelligible patterns operating within its dynamic process, philosophy questions the very possibility of such patterns. In distinguishing the various knowledges and in probing their assumptions, philosophy performs the second of her proper functions. Thus, philosophy offers the student and the university a quasi-chart of the power, aims, and proper sphere of competency of each special art and knowledge so that the organization of the university may be clarified.

Philosophy, as it is investigating these assumptions, soon finds herself performing her third proper function—the correlation of all the specialized arts and knowledges. In order to understand the limits and foundations of a specialized art or knowledge, philosophy must explore the basic intelligible patterns discovered by this knowledge. Philosophy, for example, would have to study (a) energy and matter together with the various atomic models and laws employed by physics, (b) the DNA molecule and statistical population-models in genetics, (c) adaptation-patterns in biology, (d) community models in social anthropology, (e) institutional groupings in sociology, (f) historical trends and categories, (g) artistic explanatory schemes, and so on. By analyzing these intelligible patterns peculiar to each specialized knowledge and art, and by uncovering their latent presuppositions, philosophy begins to see how these knowledges range along a spectrum of increasing subjectivity and decreasing objectivity as one moves from the physical sciences to the social, thence to the humanities, next to religious studies, and finally to the arts. Yet philosophy finds each and all of these knowledges and arts to be selective of experience, abstractive in expression, interactive between experience and interpretation, employing community-developed paradigms, creating networks of explanatory concepts validated by similar criteria.

Philosophy thus begins to correlate the specialized arts and knowledges. To do this, it must first see what each intelligible unity of each knowledge or art has in common with other intelligible patterns in the other specialized arts and knowledges and simultaneously note the uniqueness of each intelligible pattern. This, in turn, requires that philosophy be discovering what intelligibility itself is and what the ground, or source, of all intelligibility is. At this juncture, philosophy has contacted the ultimate as ultimate, the reality of all realities, the final object of all philosophic search. Yet, at the same time, philosophy must keep observing all the individual intelligible patterns peculiar to each specialized knowledge, never leaving them for a moment. Without constant reflection on the concrete data and intelligible patterns of the specialized knowledges and arts to challenge its findings, philosophy could drift away into vaporous generalities.

Philosophy, then, does not supplant the sciences but supplements them. It furnishes them with a common background of understanding that includes the common cognitional structure of each knowledge (expe-

146

rience, understanding, and judgment), the common assumptions of all specialized knowledges, the continuous spectrum of knowledges and arts offered by the various disciplines, the similar laws of method, and so on. In this way, each specialized knowledge and art offers its detailed cameo of a specific section of reality that can then be fitted into a total vision of the universe.

Of course, the converging of arts and knowledges into a vision of the universe by way of their intelligible patterns, and the consequent ability to see how a particular culture is unified, enable philosophy to warn a particular specialized knowledge that an assumption of its procedure may vitiate its data or that an interpretation of its data lacks justification. Occasionally, for example, ethologists and psychologists appear to be applying data that has been gathered from studying pigeons and chimpanzees directly to men and women, as though the differences between animals and humans were simply quantitative differences of complexity in the central nervous system and not qualitative differences throughout the being. Or a biochemist might make an interpretation of data on the assumption that the universe is only a constant reshuffling of old atoms in new motions and be unaware that this interpretation makes radical novelty impossible and turns evolution into a scientific delusion. So, the philosophic activity of correlating the various specialized knowledges offers extrinsic guidance, or at least challenge, to the assumptions of scientists. The resultant conversation leads to deeper correlation of the sciences with one another and with philosophy. This is the third function of philosophy: to integrate all the specialized knowledges and arts into a speculative wisdom.

Now, in discovering the public philosophy that underlies a culture, in exploring the presuppositions of all the special knowledges in order to distinguish those knowledges from one another, and in correlating these knowledges into a total understanding of the universe, philosophy is indirectly performing its fourth function: discovering its own unity, the oneness of mankind, and the single ultimate presence that permeates the universe. For philosophy is a *triangular dialectic* between universe, humanity, and God. The unity of philosophy is no better than the unity it discovers in these three. For men and women find it quite impossible to become deeply interested in things and persons outside themselves without, at the same time, becoming more deeply aware of themselves. This is the self-consciousness that makes men and women so vastly different from the other animals. One speaks of "my boat," "my farm," "my spouse," "my understanding of archeology," "my duty to correct my children." Besides, as men and women protect their loved ones and themselves, they must constantly measure themselves against mastadons, flooding rivers, atom bombs, political rivals, religion, disease, and their own basic drives. Men and women tend to know and evaluate themselves to the same depth to which they intellectually penetrate and value the reality outside themselves. In a constant dialectic, this inner self, which is known, is used as a model to learn about outside reality, and the new knowledge about outer reality is, in turn, employed to reinterpret the inner world.

But this constant tension between mankind and universe always includes a third element in a triangular dialectic of mutual influence: a unifying presence between mankind and universe, namely, the mysterious *divine*. For men and women find within themselves a strong lure to mold the universe to greater beauty through personally costly decisions that are already reaching out into a barely controllable future. Such risky self-sacrifice for tribe or city brings into human awareness the awful presence of someone or something that is far greater than an individual, who calls a person to such sacrifice. This someone or something, in other words, promises a good future for the individual and his or her people and must, consequently, have some control over the universe. It may be Aristotle's First Mover, or Plotinus' One, or Aquinas' First Act, or Hegel's *Geist*, or Whitehead's Process God.

How men and women conceive of and act toward this great someone or something is determined by how they look at themselves and at the universe. The more explicit a person's worldview and "self-view" become, the more fully aware that person becomes of this great someone or something. But the more deeply a person knows the great someone or something, the more deeply he or she penetrates into himself or herself and into the universe. If a person sees the universe as a big machine, then God becomes the mighty mechanic and men and women become His most complicated chemical machines. If a person sees himself or herself as personal mystery, so, too, does he or she see the universe and God. If a person perceives God as an avenging judge, then the universe becomes an instrument of divine justice and men and women are the terrified convicts. In this way, philosophy of God is intimately connected with philosophy of the universe and philosophy of mankind. No one of these parts of philosophy can grow—or deteriorate—without producing a like effect in the other two parts.

There is at least a dialectical, functional unity within philosophy as it strives to find the unity between universe, humanity, and God. In the next section we will try to discover whether, beneath its functional unity, there is a deeper fundamental unity within philosophy itself as it strives to deal with the pluralism of the world. In any case, the unity of philosophy, functional or fundamental, will mirror how the unity of the university

148

exists and can be enhanced. For the university does mirror the world which philosophy contemplates and acts upon.

Once philosophy has elaborated its own speculative aspect through the four previous functions, it can begin to work at its practical aspect in its fifth function: the use of its speculative findings to control human and worldly destiny. After a person's philosophic understanding tells him or her where the national culture and the world are going and what this person's powers are to coordinate all these specialized arts and knowledges, he or she naturally begins to converge the specialized knowledges and arts for the bettering of the world. Thus, in order to understand the problems of the inner-city ghetto, a person must employ history and anthropology to investigate the multiple roots out of which the gnarled ghetto has twisted up into its many-branched existence. Then, sociology is used to check into the intertwined relations of people and institutions; economics is focused on the financial crisis that is eating away at the business life of the ghetto. Meanwhile, theological contemplation takes on the task of explaining how God respects and works with the dispossessed as His special concern; realistic motivation is needed to give courage.

In all this, philosophy guides the focusing of the various knowledges by indicating their diverse areas of competence, their diverse use of similar terminology, their limitations of method, and their common groundings for cooperation. This type of work with community problems constantly reminds the philosopher of his or her own internal problems with values. Are other problems, now neglected in order to work on the inner-city problems, more important? How does one measure the importance of problems without, at the same time, weighing the goods to be attained by solving the various problems? How does one measure these goods or values without knowing what is valuable for one's life? How does one figure out the value of humanity and of various human activities without knowing humanity's destiny? Should a person subordinate his or her own happiness to the welfare of the community? If so, are there any limits to self-sacrifice?

It is true that men and women know something of the unity and meaning of life from the first four speculative functions of philosophy. But only when a man or a woman tries to string his or her decisions into a meaningful, directed history, does he or she begin to shape a practical philosophic ethics. The more deeply a person penetrates into the communal problems surrounding him or her, the more aware the person becomes of the problematic values within his or her own interior world. It is always tempting to take the quick and simple decision of making a personal commitment to an ideology; however, a person's grasp of philosophy, with its wide horizons and deep plunges into mystery, warns him or her away from the narrow passion and superficial insight of an ideology. A person must always be projecting a vision beyond the present findings of his or her philosophy; he or she must always be readjusting this vision to new evidences—sometimes drastically. This means that philosophy is forever challenging the prevailing national or international ideology as it enters universities, political parties, religions, and scientific and artistic groups. Philosophy tries to free men and women from any false unity—without itself espousing one ideology in order to fight a second one. Consequently, the sufferings of its own pluralistic nature can be a disguised blessing in this constant struggle. The fifth function of philosophy, therefore, may well be to help the individual person and his or her community to achieve a true unity of life, a reasonable path to individual and communal destiny. Thus, there is a need for a vision of the present-future that arises out of a sophisticated philosophy.

If this seems a prideful description of the five functions of philosophy, consider the following humiliations of the so-called queen of the arts and knowledges. In her first function, philosophy may give insight into the drift of national culture, yet she is the child of everyday common-sense knowledge and faith experience, both of which have given life to men and women long before philosophy has taken shape in their lives. For this reason, even the philosopher must admit that, if forced to choose between philosophy and common sense and faith, he or she would have to prefer the last two over philosophy. Secondly, even though in her second function, philosophy may locate, differentiate, and give direction to the specialized knowledges and arts, still the specialized knowledges and arts give specific detail to the general philosophic schemes and put these schemes to the test of living.

In her third function of converging the specialized knowledges, skills, and arts within a single understanding of the universe (and, incidentally, of the university), philosophy must correlate the specialized intelligible patterns according to their common significance *and* unique differences. This is a way of looking at reality that is peculiar to philosophy: simultaneously seeing sameness and difference, universal and unique, within each phenomenon but without omitting or confusing these elements. This is the non-univocal, or analogical, knowing that enables philosophy to converge the specialized knowledges, skills, and arts, toward a total understanding of the evolving universe. It is also the reason why philosophy is wide-open to the charge that it is nothing more than vague generalizations about quite specific scientific and artistic data and theories. In carrying out her fourth function of setting up a dialectical unity between humanity-universe-God, philosophy reveals her own pluralistic tensions as she struggles with her many interpretations of what the ultimate is.

Her final humiliation occurs when philosophy helps the specialized knowledges and arts to converge upon a communal problem and then offers them values that they alone can successfully incarnate. She is further humiliated when these efforts uncover within the philosopher his or her own interior struggle to discover, reflect upon, and then incarnate personal values into his or her own life without succumbing to an easy ideology. Philosophy is deeply dependent upon the other knowledges and the arts; yet this dialectical dependence also indicates her pivotal importance for stimulating deep devotion to the specialized knowledges and arts as she attempts to unite them in the university and in everyday living.

Philosophy is rightfully humiliated by her many shortcomings. But she does offer a natural wisdom that arises directly out of human dissatisfaction with anything less than total vision and total love of the universe. Because her influence is often indirect and taken for granted, she must continually justify herself while, at the same time, she is being surreptitiously used to rule the secular world of communism, fascism, and capitalistic democratism. Is this ambivalence of philosophy also due to the fact that she seems to have failed to find her own internal fundamental unity?

Does Philosophy Enjoy a Fundamental Unity?

Would it be an overstatement to say that the unity of the university is rooted in the fundamental unity of philosophy? The functional unity of philosophy, which was discussed in the preceding section, would seem to be a strong justification for this statement, for it does much to explain how a university is systematized and how its systems are integrally articulated. And yet, how could this functional unity occur unless it were issuing from a fundamental unity within philosophy itself? A person glimpses the interior structure of something on the basis of what it does and then he or she names it. The five proper functions by which philosophy is uniquely distinguished from any other knowledge or art presume an interior fundamental unity of philosophy, namely, a unified set of understandings and values that form a total understanding and total love of the universe, God, and humanity. This is to name philosophy for what it is. Otherwise, wisdom would not exist, the university community of wisdom would be a rabble, and the unity of the university would be splintered into a thousand specialized knowledges and unrelated values.

Thus, if philosophy has no fundamental unity, then the human mind, the university, and the universe will be progressively atomized by the rapidly multiplying specialized knowledges-arts-skills. Nor would there be the slightest hope of assembling these specialized knowledges-arts-skills into an integral reality. For, in probing the presuppositions of the specialized knowledges and arts and further dicing them into autonomous and unrelated parts, philosophy would be indirectly disintegrating itself. As the solvent of the university, philosophy would be evaporating its own *raison d'être*, much as Sartre exhausted his existentialism with process decisions, or as Vahinger's "as if" philosophy dissolved reality and, thus, itself, and as Nietzsche's acid aphorisms vaporized reason so that blind will had to be invoked to unite humanity-society-universe. Full appreciation of what such insane atomization means should help a person to gladly admit that philosophy has a fundamental unity.

Furthermore, since philosophy recognizes values within the subject matter of the various specialized knowledges and arts, the dichotomizing of these specialized knowledges and arts would isolate values within each atomized knowledge and art. This would make priorities unintelligible, since a priority is the ranging of one value over other values because of its comparatively greater importance. To avoid injuring a child who has fallen from a bicycle, for example, a driver swerves even though this will mean mangled fenders and high repair bills. But once knowledges and their values have been isolated from each other, there is no way to compare relative values and to establish priorities. So, to continue with the preceding example, the driver might reason that the next time he or she is in a similar situation, it might be acceptable to mangle the child rather than the fender.

Besides the functional unity of philosophy, the fact of convergent pluralism is a second reason for asserting the fundamental unity of philosophy. Convergent pluralism implies an underlying flow of common convergent principles beneath the world order. Fundamental philosophy would actually be the recognition of these explanatory principles.

But what is really meant by fundamental philosophy? Does it mean perennial philosophy?—that mysterious philosophy to which every major philosopher contributes but which is owned only by the total community of philosophers. Dr. James Collins, in his *Three Paths in Philosophy*, has outlined the various unsuccessful historical attempts to define the exact meaning of this term—despite its crucial importance for understanding philosophy. Often the defining philosopher has preempted the term for his or her own personal philosophy or for some vague generalization distilled from his or her personal survey of all leading philosophies. Etienne Gilson, in his *Unity of Philosophical Experience*, has tried to document (as was noted in chapter 4) how philosophic ideas, once they have been conceived by a particular philosopher, have a life of their own.

For these ideas follow seven laws of development that are only modified, not controlled, by historical, economic, and sociological factors. This would be the perennial philosophy that is gradually accumulated over three thousand years by the ongoing tradition within the total community of philosophers.

Such a continuous tradition, or cumulative unity, which is always growing in complexity of content and articulation, would be what is meant here by fundamental philosophy. Thus, perennial philosophy could hardly be the exclusive possession of any particular philosopher or school of philosophy but, rather, would be the common holding of plural philosophies. Each philosophic school would more or less enjoy the fundamental philosophy in proportion to the openness, diligence, and acumen of its practitioners. What Gilson had imaged as an ongoing cumulative dialectical sweep between contraries down the river of history implies an underlying unity of philosophy; this is the fundamental philosophy that is meant here.

After all, philosophers—whether they be the more casual prescientific type or the more highly trained scientific variety—must use some common language and have some common reality to which they point with this language. Otherwise, how could they talk to each other when each sits within his or her own tightly unified system of thought, which may well contradict other systems of thought at their very centers? Thus philosophers must have, outside their systems, a common ground and a communicative language derivative from that common ground. This common holding is of necessity, it would seem, fundamental philosophy, that is to say, the unity of philosophy on which all philosophers depend for communication and according to which all universities are structured.

There is certainly a common reality or cosmos according to which each philosopher tailors his or her philosophy and against which he or she slams and breaks the ideas of those philosophers with whom he or she disagrees. When a philosopher is asked to provide evidence for his or her ideas or principles of explanation, he or she always refers to the objector's experience of this cosmos. In fact, as Josiah Royce has noted, every major philosopher thought of his or her own philosophy as the single ultimate explanation of mankind and the world, or, at the least, as the most plausible and livable explanation. Thus, the cosmos is single and appears to demand a single explanation called fundamental philosophy, which all philosophers aim to produce. This aim is present, even if a philosopher should admit that his or her achievement of the fundamental philosophy is merely partial, that all other philosophers have had the same aim, and that all of them together have only grasped a part of this fundamental philosophy. But the single cosmos is the single fact with which every prescientific thinker instinctively works as he or she observes the rhythm of night and day, of the seasons, and of the stars; it is the single fact that every scientific philosopher believes he or she has expressed well. Yet, the total ultimate explanation of this single cosmos eludes them all as they hand on to the philosophic community their plural sightings on this great single fact. This ever present, ever alluring fact of a single cosmos, a single world order, would seem to demand a final single explanation called fundamental philosophy, which is the basic unity supporting and directing the dialectical unity of the five functions of philosophy. For the single evolutionary tree of life on this planet earth—evolution with its singular ordered accumulation of differentiations—could not ultimately be explained without an underlying unity of philosophy, without a fundamental philosophy.

A fourth reason can be offered for supposing an underlying unity of philosophy: the remarkable correlation between the unifying human mind and the unifying world that this mind observes. To put this simply, the way the mind works seems to be the way the world works. Thus, the mind is unceasingly comparing events and things in order to distinguish them so that it can later unite them. One compares the changes of expression on a friend's face to know that events of sorrow, hope, anger, or humor are happening inside him or her; one then attempts to unite these several interpretations into a single impression, e.g., "Yes, she is taking rather well the diagnosis of cancer." One compares biological specimens in order to group them more accurately according to two new subspecies in the hope that this will better explain their genetic linkages. The mind also checks differences in order to establish *intercausality;* the youngster in the high school physics class watches how the iron filings on the sheet of white paper change formations as he or she moves the magnet underneath them. Thus, the mind is forever assuming that reality is unified in its intercausality, its origins, and its serial events. What would science or any knowledge become if it could not assume such unity of world events?

Ever since Plato's Cratylus lost confidence in the accuracy of his sensations and, therefore, of his thought and speech, philosophers have examined whether or not their understanding of a situation accurately matched the situation. Is it possible that the mind has been "built" to understand reality and that reality has been "built" to be understood by the human mind? Whether one notes the medieval definition of truth *(adaequatio intellectus et rei)*, or whether one agrees with Bernard Lonergan's contention that the serial activities of the mind perfectly parallel the serially related principles of reality, or whether one denies the phenomenologist's definition of intentionality (the active and modifying copresence of mind and thing to each other), or whether one wonders with Ricoeur how much the interpreting mind projects upon the reality known, one is nevertheless deeply aware of how the mind is always unifying what it has carefully dissected and how the mind assumes that the world is always unifying the disparate into a single higher type of being despite simultaneous steady disintegration.

In fact, survival can be defined as the steady ability to reintegrate what is disintegrating. Indeed, human beings understand that their own mature growth greatly depends on their ability to achieve higher and higher integrations of mind (specialized knowledges united in wisdom) and of heart (specialized virtues in disciplined liberty) so that they can integrate themselves more fully with their community (family, neighborhood, church, nation) and with the world (health, business, entertainment, government, education, and so on). This is why it can be said that human sanity, or "interior integration," depends on the exterior unity of things, events, and persons. Take away the world's unity, and one removes the possible unity of philosophy; take away the unity of philosophy, and one removes the possibility of a person integrating himself or herself interiorly. Thus, the individual person's ongoing unity proves, it would seem, the ongoing unity of philosophy itself, even though philosophy, because of its unbelievable complexity and depth, can be known only partially by way of multiple converging philosophies.

Because of this remarkable interdependence of human mind and world, because of this strange co-unifying between and in mind and world, major philosophers are convinced that a "superintelligence" (who is also a "superlover") is simultaneously illuminating the human mind for penetration into the interior of beings and giving dynamic existence to these beings for radiant intelligibility to the human mind. How else is one to explain the concurrence of activity in the understanding mind and in the thing understood? This "superbeing" is the "agent intellect" for Aristotle, the *Verbum's* illumination for Augustine, the "Divine Ideas" for Aquinas, the "divinely implanted innate ideas" for Descartes, the "categories and regulative ideas" for Kant, *Der Geist* for Hegel, the "primordial nature of God and the prehension of eternal objects" for Whitehead. The existence and operations of this superbeing ultimately explain why the human mind so successfully measures reality, why human speech can establish internal union between two separated minds, why the human mind is ravenous for total truth about everything, and why the human heart is dissatisfied with less than total loving embrace of the world.

It is not that this illumination must insert content or ideas into the human mind but that it offers assistance to a person's own perceptions and unifying thoughts and also lends hope and confidence to a person's courageous efforts to love. In the end, this "superbeing" is found to be the total object of all human striving to grasp the whole universe with mind and heart; this superbeing also turns out to be the total subject of all the truth and beauty lent to the universe. Thus, this superbeing becomes the final goal and unity of fundamental philosophy. Such a goal, of course, gives point to all the strivings of the university and its community (and incidentally, highlights Teilhard de Chardin's Omega Point).

And yet, even if one felt this superbeing to be merely the dream of a fevered philosophic mind that was willing to sacrifice its identity for the sake of unity, one must still admit that the relentless unifying activity of the mind, taken individually or communally, points toward what must be a real unity in philosophy, i.e., the fundamental philosophy underlying the dialectical unity of the five philosophic functions. For when philosophy evaluates the presuppositions of each and every specialized knowledge and art—the radical function of philosophy—it does so by way of its own unity, i.e., by way of its own presuppositions about knowledge itself and about the relation of knowledge to the known cosmos. Philosophy, then, can unite the differentiated knowledges and arts into a single understanding by way of this same unity, i.e., by way of its single understanding of all its own presuppositions. Since the very meaning and existence of human knowledge itself, and hence of the world itself, is being employed, could it be that the unity of philosophy is the very unity of the human mind—as well as the very unity of the cosmos, insofar as the cosmos is now partially understood by man? Could it also be that the human heart, in following the human mind, can thus desire and try to love the whole of reality? Is this fundamental unity of philosophy more than unity of the mind; is it the unity of human life itself?

The fifth reason for affirming a fundamental unity of philosophy—and, therefore, a fundamental unity for the university—is simply the unified life of mind and heart that results from assuming and living the unity of philosophy itself. This is a rather practical inductive approach to the fact of fundamental philosophy. Thus, when a group of people (e.g., the religious founding group—Baptist or Presbyterian or Buddhist or Catholic) unite to form a school that eventually grows into a university, they group according to a definite set of presently lived values and understandings and according to a set of hopes that form a vision of the future. This is actually a traditional communal lifestyle. It acts like a sifting device for finding the dominant philosophy and theology that best express and articulate the group's common understandings, values, and hopes; it is a vibrant lure for attracting and hiring colleagues who can more easily cooperate with the founding group toward these goals; it is a beacon for alluring students who will be susceptible to these common understandings, values, and goals.

But the lifestyle itself—even when joined to its founding group's understandings, values, and hopes—is not enough. A visionary statement is needed wherein the group compactly enunciates all this in imaginative terms. This statement has to accomplish for the university what Lucretius' *De Rerum Natura* did for atomist philosophy. Because this vision is a unified understanding of life-purpose and of priorities, it forces the dominant philosophy and theology of the university to articulate (to unify) themselves better. This, in turn, requires that the vision be made clearer. It is important to note that this never ceasing dialectic of mutual modification among vision and dominant philosophy and theology demands a unified reality because the mutual modification is heading toward unity according to evidence from daily living in the world. Further, unless philosophy (to say nothing of theology) has a fundamental unity to which the dominant philosophy can refer all the modifications demanded by the advancing vision of the university, then this dominant philosophy is merely adjusting to external demands and has lost its intrinsic autonomy. But what is this fundamental unity to which this particular dominant philosophy adjusts itself in order to reflect the demands of the university's vision of itself? Could it be the unity of the university community's philosophic wisdom, which, of course, includes more than one philosophy and, thus, enjoys a fuller grasp of fundamental philosophy than any single philosophy could offer? But being a wisdom, this unity is more than philosophic understanding, it is also philosophic values grasped as priorities in the university community's cooperation. And would this not be the disciplined liberty of the university community acting like a single life-force as it issues from the tradition of the founding group?

Thus, the university community has worked on three assumptions: (1) philosophy has a fundamental unity; (2) this fundamental unity underlies and directs the dialectical unity of the five proper functions of philosophy, especially the radical function of testing the presuppositions of each specialized knowledge and art; and (3) the university community can employ this fundamental philosophy as a wisdom to structure the university according to its dual aims—even though the university has a single dominant philosophy, which only partially reports the fundamental philosophy. Happily, these three assumptions have proved fruitful in the style of life of the university community: disciplined liberty. This practical unity points clearly to a basic speculative unity of philosophy that underlies its functional unity. This basic unity would be fundamental philosophy.

Perhaps the sixth reason for positing the fundamental unity of philosophy is the most striking: the philosophic process of integrating specialized knowledges and arts for unity of understanding (and, incidentally, for the

157

unity of the university). This unity of understanding, though present now in the university community, is not yet fully achieved; nor is it very likely that it will ever be finally achieved, since it is so vast, complex, and mysterious. But the integrating is occurring, and its process can be described. Could this possibly happen if philosophy lacked a fundamental unity that, in underlying all particular philosophies, enables those particular philosophies to communicate, to grow, and, so, to assist each other in this single integrative process?

But what is this process? It is composed of at least seven tightly and simultaneously cooperative dynamisms. The first is epistemology, the philosophic community's awareness of the presuppositions that unify philosophy itself. This "gnoseological integration" enables philosophy of science to become aware of the presuppositions of the specialized knowledges, philosophy of art to sound the presuppositions of the fine arts, philosophy of meaning (hermeneutics) to plumb the ultimates of literature. Meanwhile, each of these specialized knowledges and arts is reinterpreting its traditional truth by constantly moving toward deeper self-unity in awareness of the other academic disciplines. But philosophy of science-art-literature, the second dynamism in the integrative process, finds its context in a third dynamism, namely, in the triangular dialectic of humanity, cosmos, and God in metaphysics. For this triangular dialectic offers the structural integration of the ongoing world in which the more functional philosophy of science-art-literature occurs.

If this integrative process is to be living, however, it must be infused with the fourth dynamism of ethics, a moral (value) integration within a person's decisional life. This, again, is the disciplined liberty that, following a central life-purpose, fulfills both the individual's vocation and the community's destiny. But because this living of liberty is a unique focusing of all one's life-energies within each unique historical moment as it rises, common-sense knowledge, the origin and final testing ground for any integration, therefore, becomes the fifth dynamism in this integrative process. Again, because this uniqueness contains the ultimate mysteries of life (e.g., human destiny, matter, person, evil, God), the integrative process loses direction, challenge, and hope without the sixth dynamism—faith. For faith humbles the triumphalism of rationalism with the facts of Original Sin, personal and communal sin, God's rescuing love, the great community of the great tomorrow, and moments of sacrament. The utter realism of prophetic faith introduces the perspective that enables men and women first to laugh at themselves without disrespect, bitterness, or self-recrimination and, then, to shoulder the cross of disciplined liberty with some joy and hope. Thus, there is need of theology, the seventh dynamism in the integrative process, to reflect on faith data in terms of secular learning (the specialized knowledges and arts) so that, in this way, it can specify the faith perspective. It does this, with the guidance of philosophy of science-art-literature, in order to discover the intelligently patterned unity of mankind's road to destiny. This last dynamism gives point to all human purposes and to the university, since it shows the worthwhileness of all human work, sufferings, joys, and loves as these develop the person and assure men and women of their destiny.

Note that, within this integrative process, philosophy plays a central role as a mediator between theology, faith, and the specialized knowledges and arts. One may rightfully assert that philosophy is the knowledge least needed for survival and that faith and everyday, common-sense knowledge are enough for humans. But it must still be admitted that philosophy is the most strategic of all knowledges when it comes to living decently in a scientific culture where personal integration has to match the complexity of civilization to keep one's self-respect, one's basic liberty. Could philosophy be such a unifying mediator in this complex integrative process if it did not have within itself a fundamental unity?

Conclusion: Philosophy Serves

Philosophy, then, would seem to be more than an irrepressible urge driving men and women toward the understanding and the loving of ultimate reality in all its secular richness. Its five functions help men and women to be at home in their own developing culture-civilization, to discover the limits and potential of each specialized knowledge and art in its presuppositions, to stretch their minds and hearts to all reality as they correlate into one speculative wisdom all the specialized knowledges and arts, to find the unity of themselves and of the world in a supreme permeating presence, to use all these speculative findings practically to control their own destiny and the world's destiny. Since these five functions of philosophy are closely cooperative, always stimulating each other, constantly using each other's discoveries for advance, they have a dialectical, functional unity.

This operative unity points to a deeper fundamental unity—despite all the difficulties of determining precisely what this fundamental unity could be—since the alternative explanation atomizes humanity and the world. The fact, if not the clear structure, of this unity can be recognized in the fact of convergent philosophic pluralism, namely, in that continuous, cumulative tradition of philosophy, which serves, in the midst of much conflict, as the common ground and means of communication among philosophers. Furthermore, even the philosopher must use the single order of the cosmos when endeavoring, with evidence, to refute a colleague or to establish his or her own idea. Indeed, this same philosopher is implicitly exhibiting the remarkable way in which the human mind can enter into reality or into another's mind because the activities of the mind marvelously mirror the activities of the universe. As a result, the fundamental unity of philosophy would seem to be the very unity of the mind's dynamics. Consequently, it is no surprise to discover that the disciplined liberty of the human personality reveals, in its unity of life-purpose, the fundamental unity of philosophy.

The final demonstration of the fundamental unity of philosophy, then, is the integrative process mediated by philosophy. This process offers a pattern by which both the university person can integrate his or her personal life and the university can integrate itself by reformulating its structure. Clearly, the unity of the university is hardly to be achieved unless philosophy itself has a fundamental unity and unless this unity is recognized as not merely possible but operative now in the university community of wisdom.

The profound mediating of philosophy among all the knowledges-arts-skills can be described as an opportunity for the philosopher's triumphalism. However, this mediatorship is actually a servanthood, much like that of the university itself. It serves to unify the knowledges and arts into an understanding that is far greater than itself in concrete depth and benevolent embrace. It does this so unobtrusively that people may feel little need of philosophy—and even condemn it. Philosophy, nevertheless, remains an indispensable guide for the university as she structures herself to better serve her constituencies more beautifully.

Given this perspective of fundamental philosophy, one could well ask: Why bother with the added complexity of a Christian philosophy when the secular philosophy just described does so much already? What could Christian philosophy add to the university except unnecessary complications and perhaps a thin veneer of piety, which only brings deserved contempt upon the university? But, then, is a Christian university possible if it lacks a dominant Christian philosophy not only in its philosophy department but also in the minds and hearts of its administrators, faculty, and students?

8 Can a University Remain Christian Without a Christian Philosophy?

Let us suppose that the secular philosophy of which we have been speaking does distinguish and challenge the limits of the specialized skills-arts-knowledges; that it does demonstrate the need of speculative wisdom when one starts to integrate the specialized arts-skills-knowledges and their values within a university community; that it does develop a philosophy of education for reasonably structuring the university and for serving well the needs of student, professor, and administrator; that it does challenge theology to describe humanity and human destiny in terms more in keeping with the times; that it does incite the specialized knowledges-skills-arts to new awareness of what they are doing and why they are doing it (at the very moment when philosophy receives from them the concrete data-understandings-practices that give it life); that it does suggest (by extrapolation from its metaphysics and from common-sense knowledge) an alluring vision of the university's work and destiny; that it does defend the integrity (structure) and freedom (future development) of the university from false ideological approaches. If secular philosophy does all this, then what could be left for Christian philosophy to do?

Moreover, it could be argued that the very meaning of Christian philosophy is a mystery and would only mystify, not clarify, the meaning of university. Christian philosophy, for example, would be pluralistic not only by its philosophic nature but also by the influence of multiple Christian theologies. Would it be anything else than an artificial hybrid, neither philosophy nor theology? Evidently, the true cause of the Christian university's birth, growth, and unity is the one faith of its community. An *ersatz* Christian philosophy would only give grounds to those who accuse the Christian university of being ghetto-minded. Or it would merely offer false solace to those who thought to preserve their university from secularism by a pietistic philosophy. Secular philosophers, in turn, would have reason to suspect that Christian philosophers are full-time theologians who spend their spare time tailoring a pseudo-philosophy to fit over their previously developed theology. Thus, the supposed integra-

161

tion of Christian philosophy with Christian theology and revelation would simply be a cloak hiding the fact that, at best, pure theology is being offered under the confusing guise of philosophy. Far from being an indispensable guide to the Christian unity of a university, Christian philosophy would be a blind gypsy reading the palms of the faculty and administrators and offering them all the directions on the compass for their guidance. Such are the fears of some people who are diligently working in Christian universities.

To allay some of these misapprehensions, it will be necessary to clarify what is meant by Christian philosophy and how its pluralism paradoxically works for the unity of a university. Then, one can consider what advantages a Christian philosophy can offer to a university. In a third step, it will be important to show reasons for the modern failure of Christian philosophy, since this scandal undermines the credibility of any contemporary statement about Christian philosophy. We face here a problem that is monumental in both size and, possibly, rewarding insight. At stake is the very unity of the Christian university.

Christian Philosophy—Monster, Misnomer, or Mother of Learning?

Would it be shocking to hear that Christian philosophy is the previously described secular philosophy now stimulated, enriched, corrected, and guided by faith in Jesus Christ? In other words, when the Christian philosopher is working at secular philosophy, he or she finds the presence of the risen Christ personally illuminating and encouraging precisely in this philosophizing, so that it builds toward a fuller wisdom in service of God's people throughout the world. To see how this can happen, it would pay us to note how Christian philosophy began and what autonomy it enjoys.

A bit of history can be helpful in sorting out the relationships between philosophy, theology, and faith and in thus better defining the meaning of Christian philosophy. When the risen Christ instructed His apostles to "Go, therefore, and make disciples of all nations," He put them into the education business. If, at first, the apostles were mainly confronting Jewish theologians, the seond-century Christian apologists got involved in debates with philosophers, for the Christian community and its faith had to be defended from philosophical attacks. Consequently, Irenaeus and Justin Martyr, both trained in philosophy, would use their education to explain how Christian revelation contained all the worthwhile principles of pagan philosophy—and more. To do this, they had to show how Christian principles of faith were related to the insights of pagan wisdom.

This compatibility of secular learning and revelation was advanced further by the Alexandrines, Clement and Origen, who were more interested in explaining the faith to the faithful and to converts than in defending it against pagans and who, consequently, developed a full-scale "philosophical" synthesis of Christian truths. This compatibility between pagan wisdom and Christian faith happened to be what is now called "theology" and, of course, it included philosophical terms and understandings from the contemporary Neo-Platonic and Stoic schools. Yet secular learning was considered to be a helpful preparation for the Christian wisdom of revelation, a means of discovering the inner meanings of Christian revelation, rather than a knowledge that was worthwhile in itself. Thus, pragmatically, the early Christian community found that it could not get by with faith alone. A theology was needed, the resultant of the dialectic between faith and secular learning. Naturally, this theology had to contain, or at least to develop for itself, a philosophy.

This somewhat murky situation begins to light up with the fourth-century appearance of Augustine of Hippo. His hunger for life-purpose led him through Cicero's eclectic Stoicism and North Africa's Manichaean Gnosticism into Neo-Platonism. Later, his faith-conversion and his year of scriptural study before he received the priesthood, enwombed this philosophy and generated a Christian theology. Augustine called the resultant integration of mutually permeating faith, theology, and philosophy "Christian wisdom." Though Augustine carefully distinguished the powers of faith and reason, he saw no need to distinguish their respective products, theology and philosophy (secular learning). Thus, Augustine's faith, the received presence of the risen Christ, directly challenged his Plotinian view of the world. In modifying this view to meet the demands of faith and of his daily experience, Augustine developed a theology completely enwombing his philosophy. His *De Doctrina Christiana* and *De Magistro* illustrate this with their heavily philosophical theology of education.

Eight centuries later, Thomas Aquinas, employing Augustine's distinction between faith and reason, recognized within Christian wisdom two basic and distinct knowledges: theology and philosophy, i.e., sacred knowledge and secular learning. From this basic distinction would issue the process of secularization now so powerful in twentieth-century culture. For once philosophy (which then enwombed what would later be known as the physical and social sciences) was seen to have a separate method and life, she could assume her full autonomy from theology and faith and, in turn, give autonomy to her children, the sciences. For Aquinas, however, philosophy was the young daughter of theology and was always to remain in subordination to her. Their lives were too intertwined to be separated. In his view, theology, the faithful expression of God's presence in our lives, must always have priority over philosophy, a totally reasonable way of life that is compatible with faith. For Christian faith, while aided by reason, is the most precious of God's gifts, since it includes God's triune presence. Theology, therefore, must always have priority. Philosophy had been born from the womb of theology but was nevertheless under her tutelage.

Aquinas achieved this magnificent perspective because he had wrestled with the "pure" philosophy of Aristotle in his highly skillful commentaries on Aristotle's major works. Meanwhile, he received priceless insights from both the Arabian philosophers and the Jewish philosopher, Maimonides, when he witnessed their struggles to integrate, respectively, the Koranic and Old Testament faiths with Aristole and Platonism. The encounter with Aristotle could only indicate the actuality of secular learning that was living apart from revealed faith; the witnessed struggles to integrate the Stagirite with such different revealed faiths could only make evident how the same philosophy could undergo diverse interpretations under the influences of diverse faiths and yet retain a certain unity (again, perennial philosophy). Moreover, Aquinas was well aware of the diverse medieval European Christian theologies of Anselm, Bonaventure, and the school of St. Victor, all of which were developing diverse philosophies within themselves. He was aware of the struggle within himself between Augustine, Aristotle, and Neo-Platonism. This pluralism of the diverse Christian theologies, far from discouraging him, impelled him to seek a deeper unity underlying them, with the aid of diverse philosophies, since he did not despair of finding and using the fundamental unity that was underlying all these diverse philosophies. Out of his mammoth labors came a new method, *sacra doctrina*, outlined in the First Question of his *Summa Theologiae*. This method, by respecting the qualified autonomy of philosophy, enabled Aquinas to develop a theology that offered a new intellectual freedom to secular learning and, thus, spoke the Christian faith in the language of the autonomous European universities. In this way, Aquinas' *sacra doctrina* offered the intellectual life of Europe a fresh Christian *esprit*.

But the fully adult autonomy of philosophy can be best observed, after another eight centuries, in the Christian philosophy of Marcel or Blondel or Maréchal. All three philosophers were thoroughly influenced by a Christian faith; all three would subordinate their philosophic conclusions to the Christian faith; all three were aware of receiving stimulation and guidance from Christian theology. But all three were convinced that philosophy has its own distinct method and conclusions, which must be respected under pain of sinning against the human mind and God; and all three found that an autonomous philosophy is the best ally for stimulating theology to a deepened understanding and appreciation of the Christian faith.

But what precisely is this autonomy of philosophy with regard to theology and faith? For Augustine, it is the autonomy of a human reason always in dialectic with faith (*fides quaerens intellectum*). For reason and faith are two distinct approaches to the same reality of God, humanity, and world. Even though faith is more vital, necessary, and effective than reason (since faith is the acceptance of God's operative, revealed presence in one's life), nevertheless, one cannot work well without the other. And the joint product of these two autonomous activities is the one Christian wisdom issuing from the person's unique life within the community.

For Aquinas, this is not enough. Even though life is single, it is composed of two basic dynamisms that are not merely two approaches (reason and faith) toward life. Within a person's natural life, there is also operative the sheer gift of God's grace—a distinction between nature and the supernatural forged by Augustine himself. As a result, within a person's mental life, there are two complementary elements since the gift of faith-revelation merges into his or her life of reason-philosophy. Though these two elements form a single living process and, once given, are meant never again to be separated, they are nevertheless as distinct as the two sides of a coin. For this reason, sacred knowing cannot be confused with, nor reduced to, secular knowing without confusing or diminishing the life of a person. Because of their close relationship, faith-revelation and reason-philosophy (secular knowledge) influence each other deeply. The understanding of this reciprocal influence happens to be theology. Thus, the autonomy of philosophy as a knowledge, and not merely as the power of reason, is asserted.

But this is an interdependent autonomy, not the autonomy of sheer separateness or of complete independence. Moreover, it is an autonomy that is subordinated to the higher autonomy of Christian theology and to the still higher autonomy of Christian faith. Yet, Christian theology and faith operate awkwardly without the enriching challenge of secular learning or philosophy. Thus, Aquinas, the university man, considered the university's knowledges, skills, arts, and wisdom to be critically important to the development of Christian theology and to the enriching of mankind's faith-life. But he also felt that, without faith to point the destiny of secular learning and without theology to interpret this destiny, secular learning would inevitably deviate from its path and could possibly become, at the end, a trivial entertainment rather than a noble vision of world, humanity, and God.

Marcel, Blondel, and Maréchal were Christian philosophers who, acknowledging Aquinas' basic understanding of the autonomy of philosophy, nevertheless recognized a greater autonomy. For the very complexity of modern philosophy and its post-Cartesian history of independent development would indicate a lesser subordination to theology and faith. Its distinct method has made a distinctive contribution to society and to the university—indeed, a monumental contribution. It is much more a copartner, than the child, of theology. But, then, what precisely is this autonomy of philosophy and what is meant by "qualified" autonomy?

Study of the reciprocal dependence of philosophy and theology on each other can reveal what the qualified autonomy of each is. For example, if a person should take the extreme of totally denying the autonomy of either theology or philosophy, he or she is denying the very existence of one or the other. If philosophy is reduced to being a part of theology, then there is no mediating knowledge between theology and the specialized knowledges-skills-arts. As a result, either theology is completely cut off from secular learning or it is at the mercy of secular learning, because, as we have seen, philosophy is meant both to establish the limits of these knowledges and to determine the mode of communication allowed by their presuppositions. No exegete of scripture could operate without a philosophy of meaning or hermeneutics as a guide. Without some philosophy of community and history, no dogmatic theologian could go beyond the scriptural metaphors of the kingdom to say what the ecclesial community is or how it could be advanced.

If, on the other hand, theology were reduced to being a part of philosophy, à la Hegel, then faith would either be isolated from everyday living or reduced to what reason grasps. For, in the first instance, the living presence of the risen Christ as sheer mystery is beyond reason and, therefore, would not be livable in everyday affairs; in the second instance, this presence would be so totally livable that it would be indistinguishable from one's own presence. In both of these theoretical cases, faith really would have no effect on life; it would be completely neutralized. Practically, however, one ends up explicitly denying, in words, the existence of faith and theology yet implicitly affirming them, in actions, as when the atheist psychiatrist submits to the pantheon of Freud-Jung-Adler-Rank or when the Marxist submits life and mind to the "holy trinity" of Marx-Lenin-Mao.

But to go to the other extreme, and to give total autonomy to theology and philosophy, is impossible. For no knowledge is ever totally autonomous and separate from other knowledges. If one had ever thought that biology, physics, and chemistry were separate and totally autonomous knowledges, then the advent of biochemistry and biophysics should have cured this prejudice. If philosophy were totally autonomous, it would not have received the concretion of its principles from the social and physical sciences, as well as from history, literature, and the arts; likewise, these disciplines would not find their mutual relevancy, presuppositions, limits, and hopes because philosophy, isolated from them, could not aid them in these discoveries. As a matter of fact, Western philosophy has seldom been without the influence of faith and theology, starting with the religious experiences of Socrates and Plato, continuing with the Eleusinian mysteries of the Pythagoreans and with the Jewish religious influence on Philo, moving to the total religion of Plotinus and then to the Christian wisdom of the medievals. Further, Étienne Gilson has chronicled Descartes' futile attempt to shut off his mind and his philosophy from the influence of his theology and faith. The ecumenically minded Leibnitz, like Descartes, tried to find a common ground in reason upon which the religious sects and the skeptics could meet to heal the rifts in Christendom. Malebranche, the French priest, thought that his interpretation of Descartes was Augustine's Christian wisdom reborn. Kant had hoped that his philosophy could serve as a reasonable basis for German pietism, and it did become the philosophy for any Protestant wanting to express the primacy of the individual conscience for his theology. Hegel's life of Christ shows his earlier religious orientation; his employment of *Der Geist* to explain the evolutionary dialetic of world history is not detached from the tradition of the Holy Spirit as former of community.

Only in more recent philosophic history has an outright denial of faith and theology become a characteristic of some philosophic schools. But their very denial, insofar as they have attempted to support it, has turned into at least a negative theology, e.g., Vahanian's Death of God theology. But deep faith is operative within the Vienna Circle analysts—faith in the implicit atomistic philosophy of the early twentieth-century scientific community. The Marxist is doomed to accept the revelation according to Marx; the Maoist, the faith according to Mao. Thus, a new faith in divine humanity and a new theology of superman influence Marxist philosophy. Seemingly, because philosophy has become so vast and its history so interminable, the philosopher who refuses to accept the revealed faith of Koran or New Testament or Vedanta must accept this humanist faith and theology in order to understand his or her destiny and to conceive some hope of future community. Could it be said, then, that no one succeeds in isolating his or her philosophy from some type of faith (and theology) accepted as revealed?

Consequently, the Christian philosopher is not nearly so strange among other philosophers as he or she is honest in recognizing the true

167

influence of theology on philosophizing. Indeed, could it be that this awareness enables the Christian philosopher to be more autonomous in doing philosophy than is the secular humanist philosopher, who blindly thinks that he or she is free of all theology and revealed faith? This point becomes especially pertinent for those secular universities that may be under the influence of an implicit faith and theology working unobtrusively in their philosophy departments. Apparently, these universities have felt that they could not afford to have a theology faculty. As a result, there is no means to challenge this hidden theology. If philosophy is the indispensable guide for the university, then it behooves the university administrators, faculty, and students to know what particular theology and faith is helping to guide their philosophy department. Thus, Christian philosophy is not an exceptional monster, but an ordinary happening in philosophic and university living; it is precisely what you would expect of an honest Christian university.

Because every philosophy is under the influence of a theology and faith, however, Christian philosophy is not freed from giving an account of its ability to unify the university. For even if Christian philosophy is secular philosophy that has been permeated with the received presence of the risen Christ, it is still pluralistic by virtue of the various influences of multiple Christian theologies. How is this to be dealt with?

Do Plural Christian Philosophies Disrupt the Christian University?

Our response will be two-fold: (1) Christian philosophy enjoys the same underlying unity as does secular philosophy, namely, fundamental philosophy; (2) Christian philosophy like all the other types of philosophy also enjoys an extrinsic source of unification, namely, revealed faith influencing it.

First, it should be noted that the convergent pluralism of philosophy—and this would doubly apply to Christian philosophy—is necessary to the growth and liberty of philosophy and, consequently, of the university that is influenced by philosophy. Convergent pluralism is not a liability. Secondly, just as there is a fundamental unity underlying all particular secular philosophies, so there is a fundamental Christian philosophy underlying all particular Christian philosophies, such as those of Tillich or Newman or Rosmini or Marcel or Josiah Royce. This fundamental unity of Christian philosophy is precisely the fundamental unity of secular philosophy, insofar as the unity of secular philosophy is enriched by the single Christian faith in Christ Jesus risen, and insofar as it is grasped by the plural Christian philosophies. Thus, the pluralism of Christian philosophy, *as philosophy*, has the same source as the pluralism of secular philosophy. But the pluralism of Christian philosophy, *as Christian*, has its source in diverse Christian theologies, which are diverse approaches to the single faith, i.e., different ways of appreciating the presence of the risen Christ in the various Christian communities. Thus, Christian philosophy, in being doubly pluralistic, has two sources for its underlying unity: (1) the fundamental unity of secular philosophy as intrinsic source and (2) the single faith in Jesus Christ risen as extrinsic source. Christian philosophy, then, offers to the Christian university an especially strong source of unity.

Because contemporary Christian philosophers carefully distinguish philosophy from theology and faith by way of philosophy's unique method, principles of explanation, and content, and because they are especially alert to the fundamental unity of philosophy (which they call "perennial philosophy"), they are sharply aware of the intrinsic source for the unity of their Christian philosophy. But modern Christian philosophers are also aware of the extrinsic source, their Christian faith, because most frequently they are members of the Christian church, because they have inherited from this community a rich, unified tradition that has been purchased with much suffering, and because they have struggled intensely with the problems of their church. Blondel was deeply concerned with the religious indifferentism of France in 1893, particularly in the universities. Marcel was disturbed by the mechanistic or antipersonal attitudes of people toward themselves, their government, their families, and their church. Descartes wrestled with the skepticism that he saw corroding the faith of Catholic France. Newman felt that English university education was heading for a godless paganism and that a new Christian philosophy of education was the response needed at the time.

But unity of church residency, of received tradition, and of social intent does not fully assure us of contemporary unity of faith operating within Christian philosphers and their philosophies. What would assure us is doctrinal consistency. This we have. For Christian philosophers generally hold that God infinitely exists, that miracles are possible, that the human person has an immortal destiny which is achieved through free decisions, that matter is good, that personality evolves best through virtuous activity, that obedience (loyalty) to the legitimate authority which promotes the common good is necessary for human maturity, that the human mind can know more than material reality, that love is the highest form of human activity, and so on. Furthermore, Christian philosophers are agreed on the existence of some basic philosophic principles: the ongoing creation of the world by God's provident activity, the principle of noncon-

169

tradiction, the ability of the human mind to attain truth and certitude, the objectivity of various types of causality, and so on. These commonly held principles and doctrines express the fundamental unity of Christian philosophy.

However, the differing explanations of these commonly held doctrines and principles provide the reason why these Christian philosophies are diverse. For these explanations come out of diverse philosophic methods and different communal experiences. Consequently, the only way left to account for the underlying unity of these plural Christian philosophies, precisely as Christian, is their common extrinsic source—the faith-acceptance of their one risen Lord, Jesus Christ. Together with its intrinsic source of unity, namely, the fundamental unity of secular philosophy, Christian philosophy enjoys this extrinsic source, which makes it doubly able to provide unity for the university. Thus, Christian philosophy has a deep fundamental unity despite all its variations.

Practically speaking, however, how can this unity occur in a particular university? It can occur, basically, because every particular Christian philosophy (e.g., the personalism of Mounier or the transcendentalism of Lonergan) shares in the Christian fundamental unity just described. But more practically, it can occur when this Christian fundamental unity is represented by one dominant Christian philosophy within a faculty—along with other Christian and secular philosophies. This unity is stronger because there is a stronger affinity among Christian philosophies due to their double source of unity. The very pluralism of Christian philosophy restrains the particular dominant Christian philosophy from totalitarian ambitions. Yet the fundamental unity of general Christian philosophy also implies that, practically speaking, there must be a single dominant philosophy within the philosophy department and within the university if the university is to be aided in its quest for its own unity. Meanwhile, the extrinsic unity of faith will offer Christian philosophers some hope of escaping from the divergent pluralism of distracting, false, philosophic leads (e.g., trying to compose a Whiteheadean process-philosophy with the immortality of the human person). Such purification of philosophic unity can, then, be passed on to help unify university life.

In order to demonstrate how Christian philosophy, because of its double source of unity, is especially helpful toward unifying the university, it would be helpful to examine how Christian philosophy can enhance the five proper functions of philosophy. First since the intrinsic source of its unity is the fundamental unity of secular philosophy, it will, like any other philosophy, be operating out of that strength. But to this intrinsic unity it will add the extrinsic unity of faith to strengthen these proper functions and, thus, to provide a tighter unity for the university in all its operations. When, in its first proper function, Christian philosophy is searching out the direction of the national culture, it will be keenly aware that faith and common-sense knowledge precede, enroot, and test whatever intelligible patterns or trends it discovers. There will be, then, an earthiness about its discoveries that is enriched with a deep feeling for salvation history—a feeling that issues from the close contact of Christian philosophy with a warm Christian faith and theology. Christian philosophy will also underline the irreplaceable role of each nation and each individual as Providence calls them to make their unique contributions to history and, in this way, to experience the worthwhileness of their lives.

When, in its second proper function, Christian philosophy explores the presuppositions and limits of the specialized arts and sciences, its thirst for finding the ultimates of reality will be sharpened because each knowledge, skill, and art reveals a new facet of the world and of the human mind and heart so that the artistry of God and the fullness of Christ's humanity can be appreciated in ever more specific detail. This ignites the wonder that fuels the curiosity and ambition of the philosopher toward deeper penetration of the mystery of humanity and the world. Each deeper plunge into this mystery looks toward fuller appreciation of the unity of reality and, at the same time, becomes more reverent before the always growing mystery—two marks of genuine philosophizing.

The Christian philosopher is more ready for the correlation of the arts and knowledges into a speculative wisdom, the third proper function of Christian philosophy, because he or she has already struggled with the integration of theology and faith and has already assisted the theologian in his or her attempts to use the arts and knowledges in reflecting on faith data. The Christian philosopher can appreciate more fully the allegiance between philosophic speculative wisdom and the wisdom of theology and, consequently, should be just as anxious to use physics, biology, literature, history, and sociology to stimulate his or her philosophy as he or she is to employ theology and faith for this purpose. Just as the Christian philosopher would not think of simply transferring method, data, laws, and theories from the sciences and arts into his or her philosophy, but does use them to help himself or herself properly reconsider philosophic objects according to philosophic method, so, too, does the Christian philosopher act with theological method, data, and theory. Thus, he or she sees the correlation of the arts and knowledges as a highly intricate and technical philosophic procedure that does not lose its need for crucial deftness when dealing with theology and faith. For this reason, to be a Christian philosopher worthy of the name, one must be sharply aware of the need for integration of knowledges and arts, just as poignantly aware of the difficulties that are involved, and yet also aware of the unavoidability of this integration if one's philosophic life is to be wholesome.

The discovery of the structural unity of the cosmos in the triangular dialectic between humanity, world, and God (the fourth proper function of philosophy) unfolds within the philosopher the very unity of philosophy itself. Because Christian philosophers have struggled for centuries (ever since Augustine) with the unity of Christian philosophy, as distinct from theology and the Christian faith, they are especially sensitive to whatever threatens this unity. Thus, through the centuries they have struggled, using strictly philosophical principles, to compose (1) God's foreknowledge of the future with human freedom, (2) the seeming independence of physical laws with God's causality and capability to intervene with miracles, (3) God's transcendence with the human ability to understand and communicate with Him, (4) God's immanence with the world's distinct identity, and (5) mankind's ability to sin against others (and to suffer evil from the brute universe) with God's supposedly loving concern for all mankind. These dialectically related problems can torture the Christian philosopher because, through theology and faith, the Christian philosopher is particularly aware of the Christian God's mercy, the Christian person's dignity, the Christian world's destiny for greatness.

The fifth proper (and practical) function of philosophy—namely, the converging of the knowledges-skills-arts upon current civic problems with reflection upon ethical values—stimulates the Christian philosopher if he or she has experienced Christian brotherhood or Christian zeal for salvation of the *anawim*, the dispossessed of the world. Because of Christian faith and theology, as well as because of a distinct philosophic vision, the Christian philosopher is quite distrustful of any ideology that promises quick, efficient, long-lasting relief for the world's poor. The Christian philosopher's awareness of multiple theologies and philosophies, which all endeavor laboriously to understand the world's problems, makes him or her rightfully suspicious of the monomanic ideology.

These five proper functions of Christian philosophy find their extrinsic and final unity as they are guided toward the reality of the risen Jesus Christ in the Christian philosopher's faith-experience. For in the first and fifth functions, Christ is luring the Christian philosopher and his or her community to the eschatological kingdom where all cultures converge in ultimate serenity and joy. In the second and fourth functions, the risen Christ is unifying the individual person and his or her community in His providential, incarnational kingdom of sacrament, revelation, and common body of Christ. Finally, in the third function, Christ is educating men and women to Wisdom itself, the *Verbum*, through His illumination of human understanding and through His strengthening companionship in human love. This is the single Christian faith, the received presence of the risen Christ, which lends extrinsic unity to Christian philosophy so

172

that it can, in turn, lend unity to the university. For this reason, it can be truly said that the term "Christian philosophy" is not a self-contradictory misnomer. Christian philosophy is as truly philosophy as is secular philosophy. But, as truly and wholly philosophy, it is also extrinsically, yet influentially, challenged and unified by the living presence of the risen Christ within the Christian philosopher.

The Advantages of Christian Philosophy for the University

Has secular philosophy been enriched by Christian philosophy? In other words, if Christian philosophy is not a monster, nor a misnomer, is it truly a "mother of learning"? Actually, the enriching contributions of Christian philosophy to secular philosophy have eventually played an important part in the unifying of the university. These contributions are philosophic not only in content, but also in attitude. We look to philosophic content first.

According to Étienne Gilson, who was an expert in medieval philosophy, one of the main and early contributions of Christian philosophy was the concept of a transcendent God who, having once created the world out of nothing, continues this creation through activity immanent to this world. Here was a God who existed before the world, when there was nothing except Himself. Then, by efficient causality, He called this total world into existence. Because He was immanent to this world, which He had created, His oneness enabled the world to be a *uni*verse and not a *multi*verse. Because He was transcendent (i.e., because He preceded the world, lived in and far beyond it, and could nevertheless live without it, since He was not in any way dependent on it), this God made it clear to the world that He was "other" than the world, quite distinct from it, even though He permeated it with His presence. Thus, the creature feels itself both dependent on God because God's activity keeps it in existence, and also independent because this creature is not God and, therefore, has its own structure or autonomy.

Now this transcendent-immanent God of Christian philosophy, having created men and women, body and soul, must respect the totality of mankind. Further, through His divine activity, He must support everything that men and women do, both spiritual activities and material activities. Thus, the human body and its sensate life is as essential to men and women as is their soul and its intellectual life. Indeed, because the God of Christian philosophy is reasonable, human freedom is guided by natural laws or reasonable practices. The observance of these laws, then, tends to render men and women more unified in their personality and more identified with their world and their God. As God has married

Himself to the world with His immanent activity, men and women are encouraged to do the same through their understanding of, and practical dedication to, the world-God-humanity.

In fact, God's marriage to mankind is seen concretely in His personal providence for mankind, that is to say, in His directing the human race through history toward the one great community of the great tomorrow, which will be centered around this transcendent yet immanent God. This living hope of a magnificent destiny for each person is precisely God's friendship with humanity. This makes the universe friendly instead of hostile. Given this sense of a friendly, reasonable, and even lawful universe, which does not have to apologize for being physical or material, it is no wonder, then, as Whitehead suggests, that modern science would emerge in the Christian world and that controlled physical experimentation would be its special technique. Further, if the finishing of this creation is to be shared with mankind, then the universe will be molded by such understanding and control through science, the other knowledges, the arts, and the technological skills. In fact, this ascendancy of mankind over all creation illustrates Christian philosophy's great gift: the concept of person in contrast to nature. While attempting to help Christian theology discover the inner meaning of the Incarnate Christ and the Triune God, Christian philosophy found that all things were *natures* but that mankind was more than nature. Men and women were persons, reflective beings, whose ability to reflect on themselves described their spirituality and gave them the power to mercifully dominate all other creatures. Thus, mankind's domination was to serve the unity of both the human race and the universe by way of love. Men and women were to preserve the present unity of the human race and world, and put order into what was yet chaotic and unreasonable out of respect for their own dignity, for the intrinsic worth of the world, and for the beauty of God. And men and women were to do this in liberty; otherwise, there could be no true friendship between God and humanity. This, of course, meant that God was willing to gamble on human goodness and to take the consequences of massive sinning by men and women.

Thus, Christian philosophy has offered to secular philosophy a meaningful universe by way of a transcendent-immanent and creating God; a metaphysical causality; a natural law theory; a personal providence; an ultimate community; a human freedom; sin; a body-soul unity (intellection-sensation, emotion-will) in each person; a personal divine friendship with humanity; a basis for later development of sciences, knowledges, and arts; and a centrality of love in a friendly universe. But Christian philosophy had two more, large and intimately connected gifts for secular philosophy: (1) the basis for human liberation from communal domination

174

and (2) the basis for unifying all human understanding of the universe and humanity itself. First, because a person is totally dependent on the transcendent God, and because this God is totally dedicated to all the good that humanity does, a mutual friendship of gratitude arises. This friendship is person's highest value and most solid security and, consequently, enables person to gamble all else. This is a person's radical liberty from the oppression of the community and its routines; it is also the basic source of human pluralism. This God, as immanent within the community, can say, "Whatever you do to the least of these, you do to me," while, simultaneously, mankind's friendship with God demands sacrifice on behalf of the community. This is, of course, disciplined liberty and results in a practical, convergent pluralism within the community. Thus, the unities of unique individuality and community are preserved in a higher unity— divine friendship working toward the great community of the great tomorrow. The first and the second of the Gospel's two great commandments interpenetrate at this point.

Another great gift of Christian philosophy is a developed theory of analogical knowing. This highest form of philosophic judgmental cognition makes wisdom possible. It was noted, in the previous chapter, how the sciences work almost exclusively with univocal understandings that stress the sameness of objects and how, on the other hand, philosophy must also employ analogical understandings that simultaneously emphasize both the sameness and the difference, both the likeness and the uniqueness, of an event or a thing or a person. A univocal understanding groups things according to sameness and segregates them from other different beings; an analogical understanding, however, groups things in order to unite them. The power of univocal thinking is aimed at deeper and deeper *specialization*, but the power of analogical thinking is aimed at deeper and deeper *integration*. Thus, these two ways of knowing are reciprocal, just as the first aim of the institutional university (the reintepretation of traditional truth for deeper specialization), and the second aim of the communal university (the accumulative wisdom for deeper integration) are reciprocal and unify the university by their reciprocity. In fact, the reciprocity of univocal and analogical knowing are the basis for the dual intrinsic aims of the university.

Thus, it is readily observable that the content offered by Christian philosophy to secular philosophy is of critical importance not only for seeing and appreciating the unity of humanity, God, and universe, but also for understanding the unity of the university. This is to be expected if the university truly mirrors the problems, needs, and possible advances of the universe. But what may not be so expected is that the attitudes, or lived values, of Christian philosophy minister so well to the university

175

and to philosophy. For example, because Christian philosophy undergoes the continual influence of faith in the risen Christ, it is very sensitive to its own inadequacy in dealing with mystery and, consequently, it is wide open to the contribution of faith to university life. Christian philosophy recognizes that faith is a stabilizing and unifying influence, even as it challenges the specialized knowledges, the communal wisdom, and the civic service of the university people. For this reason, too, a Christian philosophy is willing and able to cooperate with any theology, though it is admittedly more sympathetic to Christian theologies and most sympathetic to the particular Christian theology of its genesis. Because Christian philosophy has developed out of a pilgrim people on their way to a definite destination, it has a sense of both tradition (absolutes are the threads of history) and linear movement (the world is evolving) that enables it to appreciate the need for the constant reinterpretation of traditional truth in all the specialized knowledges, according to the first aim of the university.

Further, the ability of Christian philosophy to distinguish univocal and analogical knowing, and, thus, to appreciate the difference and the reciprocity of both the specialized knowledges and wisdom, helps Christian philosophers to be at home with the dual aim of the university. University communal wisdom is not so distant from ecclesial wisdom that it is unaware of their common roots in Augustine's Christian wisdom. Augustine's Christian wisdom did serve as a model for the cathedral schools that eventually produced a number of early universities, most notably the University of Paris. Thus, the history of Christian philosophy would make it alert to university wisdom, in the event that it had not been previously prejudiced by the fact that the *Verbum*—Wisdom itself—is the risen Christ. Nor does this render Christian philosophy snobbish. The fact that Christianity, of its very nature, has special concern for the uneducated and for service of the *anawim* should bring it to respect the commonsense knowledge of people. Christian philosophy, over the centuries, has been schooled in the hard fact that the everyday knowledge of men and women is the origin and final practical test of all university wisdom. For this reason, Christian philosophy can be a competent mediator between university departments that might have been separated by specialization, between antagonistic segments of the university community (e.g., liberal, neutral, conservative), between the university and civic communities, and, finally, between faith, theology, specialized knowledges, the arts, and skills. In fact, Christian philosophy is well equipped to mediate between the various types of secular philosophy as they attempt to integrate their visions and their cooperative efforts for solving civic problems.

Thus, Christian philosophy is attuned to university service of the larger community when the university (a) speaks truth, like a prophet, to the needs of the city; (b) heals civic hurts, like a mediator, between the government and the governed; and (c) works, like a servant, at the physical, social, and religious needs of the nation. Because Christian philosophy is in touch with the risen savior, Christ, it can support these models of the university and, at the same time, recognize deeply the ever-present power of evil in the physical and psychological wounds of people. Its whole history sharpens its sensitivity to the inherited social drift of society toward chaotic violence (original sin), to the social injustices structured into society and into the university, and, finally, to the mystery of personal sin which enervates the disciplined liberty that is needed for growth. For these tragic reasons, Christian philosophy highly values the communal university wisdom put to the service of the civic society.

Lastly, Christian philosophy is deeply convinced of the fact of convergent pluralism—if only by its sense of destiny and of ultimate community. It has long experienced and benefited from its own pluralism (e.g., medieval Christian philosophies were notoriously numerous and mutually challenging) and from the multiple Christian theologies of the past and present. And yet, at the same time, it has been aware of the single risen Christ within its experience of philosophy. It is this firm hope in convergent pluralism that is the foundation of the Christian vision offered by Christian philosophy. For the convergent dynamics of the various Christian philosophies imply a single fundamental Christian philosophy (as we have already seen), and the convergent dynamics of the various Christian theologies also imply a single fundamental Christian theology. Out of these two disciplines, in accord with all other university disciplines, can arise a single Christian vision that can then help to unite the Christian community at the university so that the university is thoroughly Christian. These unifying attitudes and the centralized content of Christian philosophy evidently offer great advantages to any university, but especially to the Christian university.

There is one problem, however, running through all that has been thus far said about Christian philosophy: Where is this marvelous philosophy and why is it not more in evidence within our American universities? Clearly, this idealized portrait of Christian philosophy can only further undermine its credibility—unless one can partially account for the recent failure of Christian philosophy in the nineteenth and twentieth centuries.

The Puzzling Failure of Modern Christian Philosophy

If Christian philosophy is as rich in content and attitude as recently alleged, and if it is so beautifully adapted to the needs of the university, then why are Christian philosophers a small minority of the philosophical community, and why are their voices not heard in the university world? Six historical reasons can be offered, together with three psychological causes, and this assessment is, perhaps, still superficial.

The first historical cause for the decline of Christian philosophy from its medieval peak was the Reformation. The schism of the Lutheran church from Catholicism, and the later splintering of the Reformation into numerous Protestant sects, introduced a divergent pluralism into Christian philosophy; on all sides there were unnecessary and perduring misunderstandings of each other's pronouncements (as recent ecumenical discussions have rediscovered). Furthermore, among Protestants, Luther's distrust of philosophy became a way of life.

A second historical cause was cultural. Because of the close ties between religion and the state at this time of religious strife, the young national governments strove for unity (a) by oppressing all but the national church and (b) by encouraging the local universities to squeeze "troublesome churchmen" out of their faculties. Out of these snarled roots would later stem the nineteenth-century French laicism and the German *Kulturkampf* wherein the governments divorced the churches from education and succeeded in isolating Christian theologians and philosophers from both the advances of science and philosophy and the assimilation of the new technological-scientific culture. Again, one witnesses a divergent pluralism operating to unnecessarily and perduringly separate communities and knowledges from each other. This false pluralism did not develop out of philosophy itself but, rather, because of extrinsic forces— hostile theological mentalities, government pressures, even deliberate commercial oppression (e.g., in Poland and Spain).

Thus, in the late eighteenth century and during the whole nineteenth century, the Christian philosopher became politically and professionally suspect. Although Descartes had thought of himself as a Christian philosopher, despite his attempted methodic divorce of philosophy from theology, and Leibnitz had considered his philosophy a common ground for the reunion between the warring Christian churches, despite his own rationalism, Voltaire and Diderot despised Christianity and burlesqued its philosophy; Comte founded his own religion of reason in disdain for Christian thought; Fichte identified God with humanity's advancing moral order and set his philosophy as the measure for the truth of St. John's Gospel; and John Stuart Mill, though he was respectful of theism, nevertheless was convinced that the religion of mankind would inevitably officiate at the death of Christian theology and philosophy. In turn, an isolated Christian philosophy would naturally undergo stunting.

Indeed, the third historical reason for the decline of Christian philosophy was the power of secular philosophy in government and university circles. For example, in line with his predecessors' reliance on the French deists, Frederick William IV of Prussia secured Schelling, in 1841, for the chair of philosophy at Berlin, precisely to counteract Hegel's influence. Although John Stuart Mill could not match the ambassadorial and diplomatic work of Leibnitz, nor the long governmental service and politically influential writing of Locke, nor the more subtle governmental weight of Hume's position as secretary to important British officials, he still became head of India House, was a Member of Parliament, and wrote important applications of his utilitarianism to both political liberty and representative government.

But, more important, secular philosophy became powerful in university circles. Contrary to the outstanding sixteenth century and seventeenth century scientists and philosophers who seemed either to avoid the universities or to feel unwelcome there, the late eighteenth century and nineteenth century philosophers seemed to thrive in the university atmosphere. Fichte spent his most fruitful years, from 1794 to 1814, lecturing at the universities of Jena, Erlangen, and Berlin, at the last of which he was, for a brief time, the rector. Schelling spent his last thirty years in a similar way. During the last two years of Hegel's life, he crowned his years of university teaching with the rectorship of Berlin University. Bergson lived his most influential years holding the chair of philosophy at College de France where, during regular class lectures, the intellectual leaders of Paris took seats next to his students. Nothing comparable occurred for Christian philosophers in the great universities of Europe—except, on a decidedly much smaller scale, for Cardinal Mercier at Louvain University and, later, for Étienne Gilson and Jacques Maritain at the University of Paris.

A fourth historical reason for the decline of Christian philosophy was the failure of its practitioners to enter the scientific communities that formed twentieth century culture. It is a commonplace that the founders of secular philosophy were also important contributors to the development of science. Descartes and Leibnitz are almost as well known for their contributions to physics, mathematics, and psychology as they are for their remarkable work in philosophy of method and system. Even the scientists Newton and Galileo fancied themselves philosophers. Locke, who was a close associate of Robert Boyle and collaborated with him in the analysis of air, even took a degree in medicine. Kant was first known for his work in celestial physics and used his findings in this area as the model for his philosophizing. So, too, Hegel first set about to master the social sciences of history, politics, and economics before he wrote his major philosophical works on the dialectic. Meanwhile, Comte—and, later, Herbert Spencer—was working out the philosophic foundation for sociology, which was then an incipient science. Before John Stuart Mill attempted his influential *System of Logic* for the sciences, he immersed himself in the associationist psychology of Hartley, the economic theory of Ricardo, the social theories of Saint-Simon and Comte, and Whewell's historical studies of induction. A very competent student of mathematics, Bergson disappointed his science professors by choosing to devote his life to philosophy; his most lasting work in perception, however, is solidly based on the findings of psychology and biology.

On the other hand, among Christian philosophers, Newman's cultivated interest in mathematics and the physical sciences and Maritain's study of biology under Hans Driesch are the exceptions rather then the rule. Contrast this with the intense preoccupation with science that was exhibited by William James, Dewey, Wittgenstein, Peirce, Whitehead, Russell, Merleau-Ponty, Cassirer, and Nagel. It becomes clear why nineteenth century and twentieth century Christian philosophy has not very effectively contributed to secular philosophy and contemporary culture.

A fifth, connected reason for Christian philosophy's loss of influence was the decline of Christian theology that was matched by the simultaneous rise of classical physics. On the one side, theology (a) was distracted from creative work by the bitter wranglings of the Reformation, (b) in her exhaustion, caught the virus of a diluted faith, (c) was bled white by a literalistic nominalism and blinded by a defeatist fideism, and (d) under force and in frustration, finally withdrew from government, education, literary publications, and cultural institutions. Meanwhile, Newtonian physics was not merely performing prodigies with her new discoveries about mass, force, and light, but also offering her method as the model for the physical and social sciences. (Later, her power would become so imperial that her wide successes and public verifiability cast doubt on the validity of any other type of knowledge—even philosophy.) Naturally, Christian philosophy suffered the double jeopardy of being philosophy and of being associated with a supposedly dying theology.

The sixth and last historical cause for the decline of Christian philosophy is of comparatively recent origin: a systematic, widespread, and active atheism. In his *God in Modern Philosophy*, James Collins has noted that only in the post-Hegelian period could there emerge an organized, militant atheism, the aim of which is total elimination of God from the accepted convictions of contemporary society. Before this, atheism was rarely publicized as a position of important thinkers; atheism was generally considered destructive of society. In the nineteenth century, however, leading thinkers publicly espoused atheism and then linked it with major scientfic, cultural, and moral trends to give it a certain attractiveness. Public atheism is, then, a recent phenomenon that is hardly condoned by the classic modern philosophers.

In fact, Leibnitz was a pioneer ecumenist whose interest in philosophy was the result of his desire to provide divided Christianity with a common ground on which the Christian sects could stand and clasp hands in friendship. Descartes thought of his philosophy as a road to the Catholic Church—a road that, in its strictly rationalist smooth-paving, would prove congenial to the nonbelieving skeptic. Both Descartes and Wolff intended some of their books to be used by seminarians. In his early days, Hegel wrote a life of Christ. And the pietist Kant felt that his philosophy bridged the gulf between Leibnitzean-Cartesian rationalism and Humean-Newtonian empiricism and, thus, provided a rational basis for Lutheran pietism.

After Hegel had absorbed the Christian God into his absolute spirit, and had thus made Christianity (and its God) merely a phase of the development of the absolute spirit, Feuerbach went on to declare that the divisive *idea* of God should be plucked out of culture, Marx stressed the contradictory opposition between the *idea* of God and social progress (the liberation of humanity), Nietzsche declared the inhibiting *idea* of God to be immoral, Dewey asserted than the *idea* of God was a dangerous illusion, Comte (and modern logical positivism) considered the *idea* of God to be a relic of mankind's primitive attempt to find security from nature's overwhelming forces, Sartre felt certain that mankind's ultimate triumph was to recognize human essence as the contradictory desire to become a God who never had existed and never would exist, and Heidegger and Merleau-Ponty felt free to remove the problem of God's existence from the proper domain of philosophy.

Consequently, though the source of the tide against Christian philosophy may reach as far back as Descartes' dichotomizing of faith from philosophy, the sudden full wave of professedly non-Christian philosophy, and its overshadowing of Christian philosophers, is still comparatively recent in Western civilization.

We can point, then, to six causes for the eclipse of Christian philosophy: (1) the divisive effect of the Reformation, (2) the alliance of church and state in nationalism, (3) the power of secular philosophy in government and university, (4) the forced and willful withdrawal of Christian philosophers from the scientific community and its institutions, (5) the decline of Christian theology, and (6) the rise of public atheism.

But all these historical currents do not totally explain the engulfing of

Christian philosophy. There is one reason that is intrinsic to Christian philosophy itself. Over the centuries, Christian philosophy has successfully met such a vast array of problems that it has developed an unbelievably large body of principles, to say nothing of the immense field of literature in which these principles are embedded. In addition, the very success of meeting a wide range of problems necessitates that the philosopher mine his or her truths at a great depth and with the most delicate of instruments. To pick up such a trade, ambitious philosophers must have both extraordinary intellectual stamina and matching subtlety. Such philosophers are not common, especially when a scholarly tradition has been badly mauled by strong antipathy and cultural skepticism. Thus, because of its vastness and subtlety, the Christian philosophic synthesis is open to the most total of breakdowns.

Perhaps non-Christian philosophers would feel less scandal at the timidity, abstractness, seeming smugness, and apparent unconcern of Christian philosophers if they were aware of how difficult it is to acquire Christian philosophy. The timidity is often the result of suddenly viewing the vast and perilous landscape of Christian philosophy from the giddy heights of an acute modern problem. The abstractness is more understandable when one begins to appreciate the subtlety and depth of the principles involved in Christian philosophy. The smugness may, perhaps, be a cover up for a fear of exploring the philosophy far beyond one's depth or stamina; likewise, the smugness may also be the lazy and contemptible substitution of the certitude and content of faith for their philosophical counterparts. The seeming unconcern for modern problems such as technology, the theory of evolution, the arts, the philosophy of science, and so forth, may well be simply a bitter feeling of inadequacy to apply the breadth of Christian philosophy to these difficult areas. This scandal has made it easier for non-Christian philosophers to neglect the account of Christian philosophy and to give little credence to its claim of being an important part of fundamental philosophy.

A second intrinsic cause for the overshadowing of Christian philosophy is its emphasis on analogical knowing for understanding the universe as a unity. Analogical knowledge lacks the clarity of univocal knowing in which only sameness is seen, for in analogical knowing sameness is suffused with difference. For this reason, in philosophic contemplation by way of analogy, there is always the possibility of misleading error and of warped interpretation—a condition quite unlike that of a mathematically univocal physical science, whose univocism renders error much less prevalent and much more a matter of public observation and of common rejection. Yet the analogical knowledge of philosophy, in which sameness is suffused with difference to increase the human proneness to error, has the advantage of staying with the concrete experience and avoiding the abstraction of the univocal knowledge that is characteristic of the physical sciences. Consequently, philosophy is capable of mirroring reality more existentially and more ultimately than is physical science. Still, philosophy pays a price for this advantage, the price of precarious grasp on what reality is. This makes Christian philosophy a very delicate enterprise because of its steady emphasis on analogical knowing.

So far, the two reasons given for the decline of Christian philosophy exist within Christian philosophy's very structure. It may be, however, that another reason is present within the non-Christian philosophers. For, if fundamental philosophy, of which Christian philosophy is an outstanding analogue, has its foundation in the very structure of mankind, it would seem that non-Christian philosophers would be deeply persuaded toward Christian philosophy by their very nature—unless non-Christian philosophers place some obstacle in the way of this persuasion.

It is a matter of common observation that a philosopher can talk and write a particular type of scientific philosophy and yet live by what appears to be a very different prescientific philosophy. The purest idealist, such as Bishop Berkeley, has been known to eat food, raise families, and get violently angry at some gestured insult. On the other hand, the crassest materialist, such as Herbert Spencer, has been known to wax enthusiastic about a friend's loyalty, a certain group's unselfishness, and a second cousin's bravery.

There are at least two reasons why such an ambivalent lifestyle is possible. First mankind's prescientific, or humanistic, philosophy of life is distinct from a scientific philosophy of life, even though the latter grows out of the former and is continuous with it. Thus, if the scientific philosophy is not an open contradiction of the prescientific in a person's experience, that person can manage to live with both on the assumption that eventually he or she will develop a scientific philosophy that is congruent with his or her prescientific view.

Such ambivalence is also possible because even the modern atheist often lives in a Christian manner. For the remnants (and perhaps more than the remnants) of Christianity remain deeply embedded in contemporary culture, and the atheist cannot escape imbibing them from his or her earliest childhood. As a result, the atheist's prescientific philosophy may be deeply structured by both strictly Christian principles and the principles of fundamental philosophy. This realistic, prescientific philosophy will constantly challenge the principles and conclusions of his or her scientific philosophy, constantly enabling the atheist to live more realistically than his or her scientific philosophy would allow. Unless the atheist is a remarkably logical and committed person, this ambivalence will enable him or her to survive the scientific philosophy because the more realistic, prescientific philosophy will dominate, at the very least, his or her, daily living.

There are, then, three possible psychological reasons to account for the minority situation of Christian philosophers. They are evidently not reasons for cowardly complacency, yet they do serve to explain the present eclipse of Christian philosophy and, in this way, remove some of its scandal.

Conclusion

The chapter has asked the question, Can a university stay Christian without a Christian philosophy? The answer, drawn from the material that has been presented here, is that a Christian university which does not have a Christian philosophy only remains Christian with great difficulty and with eventual failure imminent. The grounds for this response follow. First, every philosophy, without exception, is influenced by some revealed faith and theology—even Marxist philosophy has these influences, despite its professed atheism. If the philosophy of a university is not Christian, this does not render the university neutral; rather, the university is assuredly under the influence of some implicit faith in, for example, the current scientific community, Marx-Lenin-Stalin, American humanism, Allah, Buddha, Tao, the agnostic community, and so on. This philosophy, with its definite content and attitudes, shapes the academic community and produces its own brand of wisdom. If Christian philosophy, the received tradition of the Christian university, is no longer operative, then the Christian university either runs along by an implicit prescientific philosophy or develops a non-Christian philosophy for its community. In the first instance, the Christian university is trying to achieve its highly sophisticated purposes with somewhat primitive and unprofessional means. In the second instance, the university must, in all honesty, dutifully announce to its constituencies that it is no longer the same university. Its mind (its way of integrating its specialized knowledges-arts-skills) and its heart (its attitudes or lived values) are those of a different collective person.

There is a second reason for predicting that the abandoning of Christian philosophy means the demise of the Christian university as Christian: Christian philosophy mediates between Christian theology and secular learning. If this particular mediator is removed and another substituted, the result for the university will be a different theology department and a new theology that will necessarily be compatible with the newly professed secular philosophy. A glance at the histories of the great American universities, once Protestant sponsored and now totally secular, should sufficiently demonstrate the point of the last statement.

A third reason for the dechristianizing of the Christian university is a purely secular philosophy. Philosophy, in performing its five proper functions, does much to structure the university in content and in spirit. Much is sacrificed when Christian philosophy is allowed to evaporate out of the university, for Christian philosophy can perform its five unifying functions for the university in a stronger, Christian way because of its content, attitudes, and double source of unity. It does this at the very time when the universities are exploding with pluralism.

It must be admitted, however, that Christian philosophy is presently under a cloud; it is poorly known and respected. Yet, it is alive in any philosopher whose work is permeated with the presence of the risen Christ. What is badly needed is the leadership of men and women who are convinced that Christian community at a university is very possible and that the Christian philosophy that animates this community can be made a powerful agent of both the university's balanced growth and its dedicated service to the civic community. This is possible because Christian philosophy has the richest of histories and has Jesus Christ pulsing its life.

But if Christian philosophy is to be fully formative of the Christian university, another element is needed, namely, a strong Christian theology. For Christian theology offers a wisdom that is less abstract than that offered by philosophy. It is more practical and down-to-earth, more passionate, more suited for day-to-day university living. If the university community is to be a disciplined liberty, then it needs an asceticism of felt spirituality; it needs to love passionately. Can Christian theology draw a Christian vision of such beauty that the university community will gladly unite to sacrifice for this vision?

9 Christian Theology: Promise of Destiny and Lived Unity for the University

Trying to define theology is akin to trying to make clear what motherhood is. It is a complicated process, with a long history, about which people seem to enjoy disagreeing. Part of the problem is the vast variety of theologies. Then again, if one says that theology is a scientific knowledge, the scientists may scoff; if one claims that it is a wisdom, the sophisticated may equate it with cracker-barrel aphorisms. Or another says: "Take your choice; it can't be both a science and a wisdom." Many find it hard to fathom that reason and faith could possibly cooperate to produce a child called theology, since these critics take it for granted that reason and faith live in two entirely different worlds. If one should daringly include tradition in one's definition of theology, one is accused of foisting a Roman Catholic or Anglo-Catholic definition on all theologies. Besides, even if there were some agreement on the definition, what could theology, a "pulpit tool," offer to the secularized university except reasons for passionate dispute about hiring practices? Is not theology simply a "knowledge of the heart" that is beautiful but not fitted for the rational university process? Can it be anything more than a vision without scientific basis? After all, is it not a benevolent passion that is wholly lacking scholarly intelligence?

Such an array of problems and opinions indicates the need to construct a cautious definition, first, of theology in general, and then, of Christian theology. Next, it would be good to highlight the elements that constitute the dynamic field of sophisticated forces that is Christian theology. Later, one should note Christian theology's direct, unique contributions to university scholarship and life. Lastly, the central role played by love in both Christian theology and the university community should be traced.

Everyone Has a Religion; Every Religion Has Its Theology

No person escapes having a religion because no one escapes being vitally interested in how to live cooperatively with the "ultimate." Even when the atheist decrees God's death, he or she still has to explain how

186

one manages to live with the "ungodly ultimate" of pure science or with the "nirvana" of Buddha or with the "triumph of the divine proletariat" in the more and more distant future. Nor can any religion escape having a theology since everyone must first learn all about who or what the ultimate reality is and, then, learn the method of contacting this ultimate and of living, day to day, in its presence. This is simply because men and women, as human beings, need religion to stay sane just as they need companionship to stay human and air to keep alive.

Now because humans are *reasonable* animals, it is impossible for men and women to confront the sacred writings or revealed events of their religion without reasoning about them. For, in addition to the fact that the word *revelation* itself has philosophic content, no revelations or sacred writings contain all of reality. One must *interpret* them in order to fill out a picture of reality that is applicable to everyday living. Moreover, the believer must further develop his or her religious vision in order to adapt it to the particular changing times, places, and cultures. Believers do this by means of that particular philosophy or particular secular learning that explains their culture. Philosophy (or secular learning), then, has an inner moment within the believer's faith and, together with that faith, produces theology, which is a cultural interpretation of this faith.

Such a procedure does not necessarily mean that the resultant theology is simply a disguised philosophy or that it is dominated by its helpmate, philosophy (secular learning). It does mean, however, that the theological judgment is always conditioned or stimulated by the type of philosophy or secular learning owned by the theologian. Thus, if a theologian's prized philosopher is Hegel, then his or her theology will inevitably have an Hegelian caste. Or, if a theologian has been specially trained in sociology or psychology, then his or her theology will have a sociological or psychological air about it. Consequently, just as no person lacks a religion since everyone constantly hungers for ultimate happiness, and just as no revealed religion escapes being completed with a theology (a reasonable explanation of a person's faith in the revealed events), so, too, this theology cannot escape being molded according to the believer's life-experience and knowledge of his or her culture.

With these points in mind, one discovers that theology is that knowledge of the ultimate, and of the ultimate's doings with men and women, which arises from reflection upon revealed sacred writings under the light of faith and in terms of cultural experience. Theology is not philosophy or secular learning, for it touches mysterious events and persons in a way that is beyond reason, even while it is using reason and secular learning to guide it. Nor is theology simply pious generalizations, or cracker-barrel wisdom, since it is a resultant of the best scientific knowledge available from one's culture and since it has its own method of procedure (its use of faith as its light), its own data (the sacred writings and events), and its own conclusions (principles of religious life affecting the believer's daily lifestyle). Nor is theology merely revealed writings and events, since it is the result of reflection on these revealed writings and events. Nor is it a particular specialized knowledge, such as the archaeology or anthropology used in the process of theologizing, for its subject matter is the ultimate and the ultimate's doings with mankind as these are perceived through faith and not simply through reason. Nor is theology a fond hope, a sheer poetic leap into the dark, since it is done with intelligent use of the ultimate's authority expressed in those sacred events that are revealing the unmistakable presence of the divinity. Nor is theology even the faith, the accepted presence of the enlightening and loving divinity in one's life. Instead, theology is the carefully made and collated reflections on this presence. Indeed, faith is the sunlight by which the plant of theology is generated, grown, and recognized.

Within each theology, one finds three elements that are particularly relevant to university life: (1) a promise of a particular destiny, (2) a source of lived unity, and (3) a center of power for enriching the local culture. The promised destiny, the ultimate, beautiful goal of one's life strivings, may be Buddha or Tao or Brahma or Christ or the liberated proletariat. Gradual union with this ultimate involves the fullest contentment. This gives a perspective on all of life's events—a perspective that is seemingly so fragile in the face of physical powers such as armies and economic pressures, yet so strong that, with its support, the believer finds himself or herself able to live through life's harshest tragedies. Each theology also is a source of lived unity insofar as it proposes a distinct way of life for reaching union with one's destiny. In the light of this theology, life's events are seen as a pathway to the Absolute, and one's actions are chosen to fit this pathway according to a disciplined liberty.

Furthermore, one does not proceed along this path alone but is joined by others who lend their strength to one's own endeavors. Thus, a pilgrim community takes shape, and its cumulative experience forms a religious culture out of the local secular culture. At the center of this religious culture is its power and ultimate meaning—the present Buddha or Tao or Brahma or Christ or liberated proletariat. At this stage in its development, the theology of this religious group becomes a unifying cultural force in proportion to the strength of this people's faith in its absolute. One can now glimpse a fundamental theology that is common to every religious group. Hence, it becomes clear why deep study of any particular theology will simultaneously enable one to enter into other theologies without denying their large individual differences.

188

Such a fundamental theology makes men and women aware of their dependence on the absolute for their salvation, for their wholesomeness. Men and women must cooperate—at least by accepting the self-revealing presence of the absolute into their everyday decisions so that these decisions lead toward the absolute, not away from it. If a man or a woman refuses to cooperate, then his or her manhood or womanhood becomes diminished as each injures the self, and those around him or her, with totally self-centered actions. On the other hand, cooperation renders a man or a woman wholesome and unifies the community. When such men and women constitute a university, they give it a destiny, a unified life of disciplined liberty, and a cultural centering.

Christian Theology as Scientific Wisdom and Way of Liberation

If one applies the previous definition of theology to Christian theology, one sees that the Christian theologian's job is to determine the inner meaning of salvation history. Somehow, within the unique linear evolution of Yahweh's self-revealing dealings with mankind as they are detailed in the Old and New Testaments, the Christian theologian seeks general patterns of intelligibility. These patterns enable a person to come to some understanding of God, of himself or herself, and of the Christian community. They also describe the way in which a man or a woman is expected to live with God in this community, so that, eventually, all God's people will finally be gathered, with deep joy, into the great community of the great tomorrow, which is centered around the Triune God.

Fortunately or unfortunately, as the centuries roll on, as the cultures surrounding the Christian communities become more dense, as the riches of God's being are gradually revealed within the Christian communities, and as humanity becomes more sophisticated about itself and the world, the resultant Christian theology becomes amazingly intricate. Fortunately or unfortunately, this complexity peaks at the very time when it is becoming more and more necessary for Christians to explain, both to themselves and to others, their destiny and their disciplined way of liberty toward that destiny. For Christian theology happens to be that ever-changing knowledge that (a) arises out of the confrontation between the Scriptures and cultural learning and (b) attempts, by the light of faith in Christ, to mediate, between the Scriptures and the culture, a common understanding of life.

What this growing complexity is, why it must be, and how it works can be best understood if a description of "process" theology is made according to the very disciplines found in a university. Thus, at one stroke, theology will be seen as a scientific endeavor, as a university knowledge, and as an autonomous discipline of unbelievable complexity. The following brief glance will also hint at the strategic importance of philosophy for theology and of Christian philosophy for Christian theology.

To chart Christian theology in process, one must note its three dynamic phases: the positive, the systematic, and the pastoral. The first phase, or *positive theology*, involves, as does any wisdom process, the gathering of all the data—in this case, the data of revelation. In collecting this data, the theologian must employ instruments and techniques. These instruments and techniques are the auxiliary secular disciplines such as archaeology, philology, comparative religion, and comparative literature. With the help of these disciplines, and under the light of faith contemplating Scripture, positive theology develops into at least four branches; (1) biblical theology, (2) history of dogma, (3) patristics (the study of the Church Fathers), and (4) history of liturgy and Christian practice. In positive theology, philosophy plays a hidden role, for the theologian estimates the value of the basic principles, techniques, and even data of anthropology, archaeology, philology, comparative religion, and comparative literature with the aid of philosophies of hermeneutics, esthetics, and history. With this protective certification, the theologian can feel free to use the auxiliary disciplines in order to challenge his or her contemplation of Scripture.

The second phase in the theological process is the discovery of general patterns or formal unities among the data of revelation that were previously illuminated by positive theology. This discovery phase occurs in what is called *dogmatic* or *speculative* or *systematic theology*. At this stage, the auxiliary discipline of philosophy plays a more evident role, since it furnishes the theologian with patterns and unities whose analogues may be used to unify (i.e., to understand) the data of positive theology. Thus, medieval and modern theologians have used the philosophic pattern of matter and form as an analogue to explain the material and spiritual elements in each sacrament. Again, theologians have used the philosophic unity of body and soul as an analogue to explain the relationship between the members of the Mystical Body and the Holy Spirit. Philosophy, in this way, does not enter into theology, but it does offer theology models according to which theology can fashion its own unities, or patterns of understanding. The indirect influence of a philosophy can, therefore, be considerable.

Furthermore, even if this philosophy is succeeded by a later, more adequate philosophy (the way in which, for example, the Neo-Platonism of the Fathers was "absorbed into" and succeeded by the Augustinianism and the Aristotelian-Thomism of the medieval theologians), nevertheless, the influence of this earlier philosophy never disappears insofar as theology, in developing out of the past, always recapitulates this past in its present growth. Thus, the Neo-Platonic elements of St. Augustine's theory of wisdom will be fermenting within Christian theology as long as Augustine and medieval theologians are read and loved. Once a philosophy influences the church's theology, this influence rolls on to the end of time. For this reason, the history of philosophy is especially relevant to students of theology, even when they think they are only working in modern systematic theology.

The third phase of the theological process consists of a scientific study of how to incarnate in the lives of the faithful both the revealed data of positive theology and the intelligible unities of systematic theology. This is *pastoral theology*. In this phase, the auxiliary disciplines of experimental psychology, sociology, metahistory (the philosophy of sociocultural change), and history are particularly helpful in developing ascetical and mystical theology for the individual as well as moral theology and liturgy for the community. Furthermore, they help to implement "specific pastoral theology" (as opposed to "generic pastoral theology," which includes ascetical and mystical theology), which takes the form of missiology, when it is applied to non-Christians, and theology of the apostolate, when it is used among Christians.

Insofar as these secular disciplines are positioned and evaluated by philosophy, the powerful influence of philosophy is also felt in pastoral theology. And insofar as speculative theology, already influenced by philosophy, guides pastoral theology by furnishing it with the content of its implementation, philosophy again enters into pastoral theology. In addition, pastoral theology, above all, must keep in the forefront of its consciousness the natural philosophically recognized structure of the human mind, heart, and body if it is to effectively persuade humanity to do God's will. Finally, philosophy of history re-enters the theological-pastoral process to give perspective and balance to the expressions (later to become clichés) and techniques (later to become routines) that are to move people within their religious experience. Consequently, on a third count, philosophy, which interprets mankind profoundly (though never so concretely as biology or theology or psychology), must play a large role in the work of pastoral theology.

Of course, these three phases of the theological process occur simultaneously and mutually develop and modify each other in a three-cornered dialectic that occurs not only in the individual theologian, but also within the collective awareness of both the community of theologians and the faithful. In addition, the three phases of theology are also constantly being related back to those secular disciplines that have first stimulated this three-phase theological contemplation of Scripture according to the light of Faith. Such relating is possible through the mediation of philosophy, since philosophy, alone of all the secular learnings, has a breadth and depth of contact that in some way matches those of theology and of the auxiliary disciplines taken collectively. Because of its mediated return through philosophy to the secular disciplines, theology retains its autonomy and distinctness, yet is, nevertheless, integral with these disciplines. In this way, theology reaches out into the world and assures Christian revelation of a fair hearing in modern culture. For, when a developing theology, by way of philosophic mediation to the various secular disciplines, is penetrating the world, then God's word is seen to be relevant to humanity's ongoing daily living. And this worldwide and "world-deep" penetration by theology is rendered possible through the mediation of a philosophy that is vitally contacting all the secular knowledges.

In focusing all secular learning on the data of revelation, Christian theology can rightfully be called a scientific endeavor—especially when she employs Christian philosophy to check out her use of the various university disciplines. Christian theology also demonstrates that she is the most complex of all knowledges—a matter documented with care by Bernard Lonergan in his *Method in Theology*. This, however, is merely a "vertical cut" of twentieth century Christian theology; if one takes a "horizontal view" of the history of Christian theology over the centuries, one sees her as a cumulative body of knowledge that has been carried along by tradition. Newman's *Development of Doctrine* aims to show how, through the centuries, a dogma constantly may be reinterpreted and yet not lose its central core of truth, even though new insights gather around and permeate this core. As a result, this evolving core discloses more and more of its latent meaning in new relations to freshly evolving history. Such reinterpretation of traditional truth, which renders theology relevant to contemporary society, is very familiar to the university because this is the first of its dual intrinsic aims. Since truth is alive in every discipline, it is expected to grow without denying its previous identity. This is most true of the central truth of Christian theology, for the understanding of the risen Christ's living presence naturally grows as Christian theologians and the faithful become more familiar, down through the centuries, with this presence. The light of faith would make this possible, of course, but secular learning focused by philosophy would also generously stimulate this growth of understanding.

If Christian theology as a scientific endeavor would be most characteristic of positive theology, then Christian theology as both a cumulative body of knowledge and a revealed wisdom would be most characteristic of dogmatic, or systematic, theology. That Christian theology is a wisdom becomes evident when one notes its total view of world, humanity, and God. It covers the history of the world, from creation to the present moment, in all the nobility of the prophets, in all the ignobility of sinners, in all the fecundity of animals and plants. It considers the total history of mankind, from the ecstasy of Eden, through the depressing fall, and along the long road back with Abraham, Moses, Elijah; through John the Baptist and Jesus Christ, and then through the two-thousand years of Christian church history up to the present moment. In each generation, men and women have proven to be both the beloved of Yahweh and the one rescued from their own betrayal of Yahweh. As God leads His people to their destiny, He also slowly reveals His many faces and His great depths through the events of His people's life with Him. This destiny, this ultimate view of life, is occurring now ("Whatever, you do to the least of these, you do to me"), and yet it is also in the distant future (the great gathering of all God's friends at the end of time).

Meanwhile, as the people of God move through the centuries, their living of biblical revealed wisdom enables them to increase the wisdom of secular philosophy, with the concepts of creation, person, a transcendent-immanent God, personal providence, and so on. So intimate is the relationship between this revealed wisdom and philosophic wisdom that Walter Kasper has written that any believer in the Incarnation of the Second Person of the Trinity must also be doing metaphysics. As a wisdom, Christian theology would be sensitive to the second dual aim of the university—the accumulation of wisdom.

Christian theology, then, as a revealed wisdom, naturally results in theology as a way of life; it is theology entering into practical, day-to-day decisions. The pastoral element of Christian theology is found, for example, in its explanation that the sacraments are moments of Christ's strengthening presence in all the critical events of human life, such as birth, adolescence, serious sin, eucharistic celebration, marriage choice, life-dedication, and death. At this juncture, Christian theology also provides (a) liturgy for celebrating joys and for comforting sorrows, (b) devotional practices for personal prayer, (c) spirituality for giving life to the ascetic demands of career and vocation, (d) guidance for virtuous living (with the help of the church's teaching authority), and (e) instruction and hope for the forming of a Christian community that is centered in Christ. These activities make Christian theology well attuned to the extrinsic aim of the university—service to the civic community.

Because Christian theology is aware of both a fundamental theology and its own pluralism, it has little tolerance for the narrow passion of ideology or for the imperialism of a monomaniacal, single theology, which claims to be absolutely true. It understands the need of having a dominant Christian theology within a Christian university faculty for that faculty's unity, yet it simultaneously sees the need for balancing this dominance with the presence of other theologies, especially Christian theologies, since this balance gives rich adaptability to the faculty so that it can better meet the needs of the faithful. Hence, fundamental Christian theology would be that common base present in all Christian theologies— a base that would guarantee the central core of the Christian message, yet supplely allow for variations in emphasis, explanation, and devotional practices. Thus, the basic theological content of divine Trinity, God-man, sacraments, structure of God's people, and the Scriptures—together with the basic attitudes of love for God and neighbor, mercy, and hope of future destiny—would all be present in each particular Christian theology, but with many differences of emphasis and explanation.

In this view, it is characteristic of Christian theology that it scientifically accumulate its revealed wisdom and, then, skillfully apply it to daily living in a way that is called disciplined freedom. Such a Christian theology would seem to be quite at home in a university setting—so much at home, in fact, that one wonders how it could be healthy outside such a setting. This becomes even clearer if one charts the dynamic relationships between the seven elements in the field of Christian theology: (1) individual faith-life, (2) revelation, (3) tradition, (4) communal faith experience, (5) philosophy, (6) secular learning, and (7) apostolic drive.

Christian Theology as a Dynamic Field of Influences

Earlier, we noted the unfairness of the accusation that Christian philosophy is a patent contradiction because it welcomes the influence of Christian theology. At the same time, we also noted that even Marxist and secularist philosophies were influenced by an implicit natural faith and theology. Should we now remind ourselves that no human act occurs without an implicit faith founding it? Sophisticated agnosticism has made it appear that some actions are purified of all faith, namely, those actions that are totally agnostic. More healthy minds have found that it is these so-called agnostic actions that are "diseased" in their faithlessness. For no one orders a meal in a restaurant without putting faith in the management's integrity; no one crosses the street under a red light without having faith in the approaching drivers. Even placing one's head on a pillow late at night includes an act of faith that the young child will not turn on a blaring stereo in the next room. In short, the average person's day is a network of actions that is tautly held together by the tension of faith. Remove faith, and all life unravels in a continual nightmare. The person is unable to trust others is headed for more than bitter loneliness.

194

Nor is this faithfulness in life without warrant. Because we cannot possibly know everything, we must have faith in the doctor's prescription, the auto mechanic's diagnosis, and the computer expert's program. We do not put faith in people, however, without some intelligent warrant such as the medical school's approval of the doctor, the friend's recommendation of the auto mechanic, and the reputation of the computer expert's employer. The demand for some form of warranty in these natural acts of faith is also present in acts of revealed faith. One does not believe in Christ or in Allah or in Brahma unless there is some experience of God in oneself and some faith in the community that is living the life of Christ or of Allah or of Brahma. The act of faith is intelligent insofar as it is based, first, on the evidence of the wholesome life of the community that is professing its belief in Christ, for example, and, then, on this community's interpretation of one's personal experience of Christ. Yet, with all its basis in intelligent evidence, the individual's act of faith is still made toward a mystery that far exceeds any evidence. This is why a deep type of trust is demanded within any act of faith.

As a believer's act of faith penetrates deeper into its object—into the living presence of the risen Christ, for example—the believer must have more knowledge to fully appreciate what is happening. Furthermore, as the culture in which this believer lives becomes more complicated, the believer must have more knowledge of this culture in order to apply his or her faith to day-to-day living. For example, because Christ has revealed Himself in the Scripture accounts of His life, insofar as the believer learns more about the Scriptures, he or she can better understand the Christ who is met in the prayer experience. Moreover, if this believer feels that Christ is calling him or her to a work of social justice—to start a business cooperative among the impoverished fishermen who live near a large city, for example—then his or her act of faith in this project must be guided by the economics, sociology, social psychology, anthropology, and history of the people.

Thus, the better educated this believer is in approaching the Scriptures and in guiding the business cooperative (i.e., the better his or her theology is), the more penetrating can be the act of faith into the risen Christ's life within himself or herself and within the business situation of the fishermen. Nor is there any bottom to the depth of this "faith penetration," just as there is no end to the development of the believer's theology. For it enters the total mystery of Christ's risen life and will always demand more and more intelligent information as the act of faith enters more deeply into the cultural situation. Thus, the faith within a person's theology is not merely aimed at a mystery, but is actually lured into greater fullness by this same mystery so that there is room for more and more theology, or, in other words, more and more intelligent interpretation of the events. For this reason, the university person who is endowed with strong Christian faith can well appreciate the university's preoccupation with the many mysteries of life and the inherent difficulty in reporting its findings to its constituencies. So, too, this same person will be well aware that the university community that operates with a weak faith in God risks eventually losing faith in its own processes. For all the mysteries that the university struggles to understand actually focus into this ultimate mystery of God. Were the university community to lose the light of faith in this central mystery, would she begin to lose hope and intelligence as she explores its satellite mysteries such as the human person, the atom, biological life, the constituents of light, the paths of stars, and the evils of disease, war, and sin?

The individual's Christian faith, however, would have no focal point if it were not aimed at the divine revelation of the Old and New Testaments, those living covenants of friendship between Yahweh and mankind. This is the second element of Christian theology. As it is, Yahweh the Father has spoken into history through chosen prophets and apostles and through the Christ. On account of the Father's unpopular message, which accused the people of sin and demanded of them more just actions toward their fellows, all of the messenger-prophets suffered much, and some were murdered. But strangely, around this fearsome message, a people reluctantly gathered because they experienced Yahweh living in their midst—an experience that was so powerful they had to express it in laboriously building the great temple, which contained the magnificent holy of holies.

As this people lived this life down through the centuries, Yahweh, by way of His prophets, told them more and more about Himself, in both word and symbolic deed. He became an intimate part of their history; in fact, He called the Jewish people His bride and the covenant their marriage bond. Because of Yahweh's fondness for His people, He imparted to them a wise way of life that would slowly introduce discipline into their living. Along with discipline would come liberty from foolishness, from destructive emotional outbursts, from cruelty for the sake of entertainment, and from merciless abandonment of the helpless. As a result, this people became not only somewhat ready to admit revelation, but also capable of embodying it in their prophets' actions and in the customs and liturgies of their daily living. Thus, their revelation gradually took on intelligence, ascetic sacrifice, and respect for mystery, as God molded them into a living expression of His word. We note, at this point, the parallel between this people that had gathered to express God's word and the university community that is structured to portray wisdom in service to the civic community.

We come, now, to the third element of theology, for this progressive revelation of God's word in His chosen people's history demands a tradition. This faithful way of life in Yahweh must be handed down from generation to generation (and later, from country to country) with a developing understanding and living. But, for such a tradition to be alive requires a constant reinterpretation of one's history, a constant recapitulation of it in terms of new problems, hopes, knowledges, and setbacks. Thus, the Jewish people were instructed by Yahweh to commemorate their great victories and defeats with ritual memorials of feastings and mournings, respectively. These commemorations allowed them to both reconsider their history by reenactment and incorporate within it the new victories and defeats. Not only did these people have room for new revelations through historical events interpreted by the prophets, but also they could integrate these new revealings of Yahweh with the older manifestations of His will. The Spirit of wisdom guided this unifying of the Jewish race so that their enactment of the divine Word would be clear and powerful.

Later in the New Testament, this tradition was totally focused into the human personality and divine person of Christ, who then commissioned His apostles to help Him form, with the Spirit, the community of the risen Christ. Then, this living communal message of Yahweh could be handed on to the following generations through the apostles' successors. And this new community would grow as the very *Body of Christ* through the organizing power of the Spirit, and it would come to the fullness of life-after-death in the great community of the great tomorrow.

Such communal faith experience of the Christian community is the fourth element of Christian theology. Each generation is the present focal point of a tradition that carries within itself the whole history of God's dealings with His people, ever since Sinai and Moses. Of course, each succeeding generation cannot possess this ever richer tradition of ultimate truth and value unless it reinterprets the tradition under the light of faith according to its own experience of its own recent victories and defeats. This is the way it appropriates the past as its own present and, then, is able to hand it on to the next generation. Nor can it do this without a relevant theology, for a theological understanding of the community's present experience, which takes into account the community's past tradition of revelation, is the further light by which the whole community appropriates the past tradition for the next generation.

One can now begin to appreciate how important the first dual aim of the university is for university theology, and how helpful scientific theology is to the university's self-understanding as it tries to fulfill this aim of reinterpreting traditional truth in all the other knowledges of the institution. Furthermore, the forming of a wisdom community out of a revealed wisdom has much to tell this ecclesial community about the university community of wisdom, just as it gives a model to the university community for fulfilling the second intrinsic aim of the university, namely, the accumulation of wisdom.

The fifth and sixth elements in the field of forces that constitute theology are so closely intertwined that they must be taken together. The fifth element is the philosophy that a theology uses to help discover intelligible patterns in salvation history (e.g., what prophesy is, how law and custom differ, what sacrament and ritual are, and so on). Philosophy also helps a theology to criticize its use of the various sciences in its hermeneutical pursuit of intelligible patterns. In this way, philosophy protects theology both from being captured by one or another of the currently dominant knowledges (such as sociology or psychology) and from being rationalized away from mystery. The sixth element is the ensemble of secular knowledges (especially the social sciences) that are employed by theology to give context to the data of revelation, e.g., the meaning of fellowship *(koinonia)* for St. Paul. To understand the dynamics of philosophy, and of these secular disciplines within Christian theology, a bit of history must be reviewed.

The history of revealed Christian faith is the story of complementarity among various kinds of human knowledges. When faith in Christ was first preached, the apostles tried to relay its message as simply as possible— without the complications of philosophy, contemporary science, and the humanistic learning of literature and art. An attempt was made to speak pure "faith-facts," lest added interpretation introduce the contamination of error. This, of course, was virtually impossible because, as soon as the audience responded to the gospel message with questions, the preacher found himself endeavoring to use the words, background, and knowledge of the questioner; in so doing, the preacher repeated the message with different words and, therefore, with different connotations. At once *interpretation* was operative. The only other alternative was simply to repeat the gospel message in the very same words as before, as though it were some magic incantation.

As a result, Christian preachers and writers quickly found themselves illustrating the Christian message with the materials, and in the style, of contemporary humanistic literature. As soon as they did this, they began to develop something other than the revealed faith, i.e., they were shaping a humanistic, or imaginative, theology in order to interpret the faith-message of Christ. For theology, as the knowledge that results when men and women focus their faith on the scriptural message in terms of another knowledge, such as humanistic learning, becomes the interpretative mediator between scriptural faith and the ambient culture. Theology, consequently, is always changing because the culture for which it is interpreting the faith is in constant flux. This is a danger to faith since, under these circumstances, its interpreter, theology, can be mistaken for the faith; yet, it is a necessary danger. For faith cannot be preached without some interpretation, and this interpretation, when done with true faith, is theology. Thus, the preaching—and, consequently, the living—of scriptural or revealed faith, necessarily involves a complex dance between three distinct partners: faith, humanistic learning, and theology. Each is modified or influenced by the other, yet each retains its own identity. (Because of his humanistic *logos* theory, John the Evangelist naturally interpreted the Christ of faith as Wisdom Itself and, in turn, considered the world of literature to mirror the Wisdom.) Yet, if each of the three dancers is to contribute understanding to the other two, each must preserve its distinct identity, or autonomy.

Though philosophy was always operative in the culture and, therefore, in Christian faith, not till the fourth century did philosophy, in the shape of Neo-Platonism, exercise an inescapably evident influence and reveal itself to be the fourth dancer. Imaginative, or humanistic, theology had not proved to be an adequate interpreter for the faith when the church began to reach out to the educated and ruling classes. Questions that went beyond humanistic learning into philosophy were asked. This produced a second level of theology that was beyond the humanistic; it gave us philosophic theology that was written, at first, in somewhat humanistic terms by Augustine and, later, in much more scientific conceptualizations by the medieval theologians.

Against the tendency to confuse philosophy with theology and theology with faith, Thomas Aquinas developed, as was noted earlier, his theory of *Sacra Doctrina*. Through this theory, Aquinas demonstrated how, without the loss of distinct autonomy, faith used philosophy to produce for the medieval culture that interpretation of Scripture which was called *medieval theology*. But this more philosophic theology arose out of the earlier, more imaginative theology of Augustine and of the Fathers and, as a result, was still closely in touch with the humanistic literature that had been preserved and used by the monastic culture as it developed its imaginative, humanistic theology. Thus, these four ways of knowing reality were carefully kept distinct, so that they could influence each other in the search for the ultimate within the medieval world.

Moreover, this distinctness of being and function also served to make medieval men and women aware that there were many levels of reality in each situation and that a distinct level of knowledge within a person corresponded to each level of reality outside the person. In this way, medieval men and women came to see how the knowledges, in complementing each other within the person, filled out the personality so that a person could meet, understand, and apply himself or herself to all the levels of mystery in the world, in the community, and in the individual person. With this insight, medieval men and women better fitted themselves to search out the ultimate within their world.

The Christian theologian was somewhat ready, then, when the physical and social sciences developed from the sixteenth century to the twentieth century. The usual mistakes were made; there were attempts to substitute physics for philosophy (Galileo and Newton), psychology and sociology for faith (Comte), philosophy of history and philosophy of anthropology for theology (Hegel and Schleiermacher). Modern Christian faith, however, has painfully learned how to employ philosophic hermeneutics so that the physical and social sciences, philosophy, and humanistic literature can illuminate the Scriptures without absorbing faith and theology. Faith's resultant understanding of itself then becomes the contemporary theology whose many levels mirror the contemporary humanistic, scientific, and philosophic culture and can, therefore, interpret scriptural faith to this culture.

For instance, Paul of Tarsus' letters stress *koinonia*, or fellowship, within the church. Christian faith, presently in intimate contact with that fellowship, can come to a better understanding of *koinonia*, (i.e., to a fuller theology of *koinonia* if it employs (a) philology for understanding the history of the word, *koinonia;* (b) economics and anthropology for appreciating the first century Mediterranean communities that received and interpreted the word, *koinonia;* (c) humanistic literature for comparing this usage with the first century poems and essays on community; (d) everyday spontaneous experience for an immediate and unique sense of community presence; and (e) philosophy for both reflections on the nature of human fellowship and methodic use of all these materials under the light of faith. Thus, all these knowledges are converged by philosophy upon the "faith-fact" of fellowship so that faith can understand itself. This self-understanding in terms of the contemporary culture is theology. As an interpretation of faith, theology clearly is not faith; yet, without theology, faith could not be preached and lived. This is the complementarity of faith with theology.

Theology, however, does not come into existence until the moment when humanistic literature is focused, under the light of faith, upon

Scripture to give birth to new and deeper scriptural understanding, or interpretation. Nor can this new understanding, or theology, keep itself distinct from humanistic literature unless philosophy stimulates reflective distinctions between the two. Nor can this theology advance to a second, more abstract level of understanding without employing philosophic data. Nor can theology employ the physical and social sciences for advance into a third, more precise level of understanding without the guidance of a philosophy of science and a philosophy of hermeneutics. Nor can theology dispense with these newly developed levels of understanding if she is to be the mediator between scriptural faith and the sophisticated contemporary culture, and if scriptural faith is to be preached and lived in this culture. This is the complementarity of faith and theology with all the other contemporary knowledges that are vital for an understanding of faith-facts. Since these other knowledges, when they are lumped together, are given the name of "reason," faith clearly cannot survive without reason. Evidently, too, complementarity is the source of faith's continuing vivacity. Complementarity is revealed as the dynamic process by which secular knowledges assist theology and faith to reach the ultimate in the secular world and by which theology and faith, in turn, help the secular knowledges to discover the context of their ultimate meaning.

The seventh dynamic element, which issues from the previous six elements, is an apostolic drive that results in pastoral theology. For the needs and problems of people, once they have been delineated by the secular knowledges and philosophy, call out to Christians for tending and healing. Theology, then, becomes equally enriched by its failures to save and by its successes. In both failure and success, Christian theology becomes more identified with the people and discovers within itself resources undreamed of in previous generations. For instance, because Christian theology looks to both believers and nonbelievers when it tries to bring salvation, its scope is as wide as that of the university. Because Christian theology tries to preach Christ's message according to the language and culture of the people, it must, like the university, be scientific and humanistic. Because Christian theology must dramatize its truth, it must, like the university, integrate the fine arts into its liturgical and cathechetical approaches to people's needs and problems. Because Christian theology must be inventive to deal with people's new problems, it must use the latest deliverances of the university's specialized knowledges and, later, it must imitate them in their search for new interpretations of traditional truth. And because Christian theology is a revealed wisdom, it must pool its resources, in the manner of a university community, in order to wisely deal with these problems.

Thus, it can be seen that all seven elements composing the field of influences that is theology render Christian theology a university knowledge. These elements also enable Christian theology to expand with the influences of all the secular knowledges and, in turn, to stimulate these secular knowledges according to the first intrinsic aim of the university. Furthermore, Christian theology, with its tradition of a lived experience that gradually builds into a community wisdom, can be a model for the university itself in its second intrinsic aim. Lastly, the apostolic thrust of Christian theology enables it to fit into, and to help generate, the fulfillment of the university's extrinsic aim, namely, service to the larger civic community. But, the fact that Christian theology makes use of the university in order to grow, raises the next question: What uses can the university make of Christian theology?

University Uses of Theology

Theology contributes to the university as both institution and community. On the institutional side, Christian theology calls attention to revealed values in the discoveries of the specialized knowledges so that these knowledges and Christian theology mutually reinforce each other. For example, Christian theology reaffirms the way in which literature and literary criticism move a person from prejudice to a just understanding of others (Shakespeare's Shylock: "If you prick me, do I not bleed, too?"). It also supports philosophic personalism's recent emphasis on the unique dignity of each person. Christian theology finds that the psychoanalytic stress on the human memory as the living source of both human values and human guilts is also found in Augustine's theology of decision and in the Old Testament use of feasts to reenact the Jewish people's past deeds and misdeeds.

A second contribution to the institutional side of the university is the way in which Christian theology, by using the specialized knowledges for its reflections on Scripture, calls attention to the intrinsic worth of each discipline. She then goes on to offer subsequent reflections on (a) the use of hermeneutics in textual analysis, (b) the illuminating effect of the biological evolutionary theory concerning God's ongoing creative act, and (c) the remarkable insights into God's power that result from considering the various cosmologists' theories concerning the beginnings of the universe. She may next warn that some scientific conclusions seem contradictory of revelation and, therefore, of truth (e.g., B.F. Skinner's absolutely deterministic conclusions about human behavior), and that some scientific practices appear immoral (e.g., the number of "mini-abortions" that are required to achieve one successful pregnancy following many in vitro fertilizations).

A third contribution to the institutional side of the university occurs when Christian theology, after focusing all the specialized knowledges for interpreting scriptural passages, provides a pastoral indication of how all the scientific pursuits can integrate into the great pursuit of God, of eternal happiness, and of fullest community. Perhaps, at times, this is merely a hint of the basic agreement of all the sciences, knowledges, and arts, but it can begin the forming of a magnificent vision. At the very least, Christian theology can give the ultimate practico-historical reasons behind the secularization process, according to which the human world is expanding and deepening.

Thus, the scientific enterprise and the literary enterprise—be it chemistry or biology or literary criticism or philosophy or economics—is assured of ultimate worth by, for example, a revealed Christian faith that asserts that the universe was created by the divine Logos and mirrors in itself, through its laws or consistencies, the reasonableness of its Creator. According to Christian faith, the reasonable person is the brother or sister of Christ, who is the perfect man-God. This person may, if he or she wishes, become a member of Christ's family and enjoy that family's enlivening and joyful presence no matter how ignorant or poor or disreputable he or she may be. Furthermore, each person's basic dignity may be increased through cooperative loving and working within the human community in order to complete the universe. A person does this with the provident help of Christ, the Lord of History, who makes sure that a person's work culminates in the immortal great community of the great tomorrow with God. In a culture in which the evolution of the universe is sometimes characterized as futile exuberance, in which men and women are occasionally appraised in terms of their salable chemical composition, in which a person's death is often considered final emptiness and one's work is frequently equated with a coolie's repeated digging and refilling of the same trench—in such a culture, it is crucial that a person's immortal worth and the lasting value of his or her work be believed with assurance. Otherwise, the willingness to undergo the suffering and discipline needed to support the unbelievably complicated culture of the twentieth century will disappear and, consequently, civilization will also disappear. At least for the present, then, a revealed faith that stresses these values and hopes is historically necessary to the survival of the human race as we now know it. This theological vision can be rendered more complete and more concrete than the philosophic view, since it reaches greater spiritual depth, opens its embrace wider to include the retarded and the handicapped, and makes fuller use of the specialized knowledges, skills, and arts to flesh out its meaning.

Christian theology, however, also contributes to the communal side of the university because it is an ultimate wisdom. One of the current, great needs of the university community is the stability that is necessary for the university to carefully do its reflective work. This stability is based on a confident hope in the future destiny of both the university community and its work and is expressed precisely in disciplined liberty. Christian theology assures the university community that both it and its work are moving toward the formation of the great community of the great tomorrow, as long as the work is honest and faithful. This gives the stability that is needed for both planning programs and developing a fuller understanding of the university's aims. Moreover, it gives a sense of unique vocation to the university itself so that the university is more sure of itself as a servant of the larger civic community.

Christian theology can also offer herself, as the ultimate revealed wisdom, to encourage the university community, first, as it pursues the speculative wisdom of integrating the specialized knowledges into a whole; second, as it acquires the practical wisdom for applying its speculative wisdom to the civic problems and needs; and, third, as it lets the revealed wisdom of Christian theology guide its sense of destiny and unique vocation. Christian theology also calls the university's attention to the common-sense wisdom of both its staff members and the people it serves through its scriptural wisdom literature and through its constant call to loving service of the uneducated, the forgotten, and the rootless.

Finally, Christian theology, as a revealed wisdom, is particularly competent to guide the spiritual (personal-social) living of the university community, to underline the vital importance of justice and charity in all human actions and thereby to elicit compassion for the oppressed and ignorant (especially at the university and in university work), to direct the worship of the community toward the burial of rivalries and hostilities in the one Christ, and, lastly, to heal the disunity that has been willfully prolonged throughout history by the desecularizing influences of original sin. Thus, Christian theology works toward the personal and social integrity of the university, that is to say, toward its wholesomeness.

Christian Theology Stresses the Heart in University Life

Perhaps the finest contribution of Christian theology to the university is its refusal to allow the university to forget the human heart. Christian theology valiantly fights against the hyperrationalism and heartless routinization of university living. Moreover, Christian theology is especially adept at this because it must constantly go beyond rational limitations, through faith, to mystery and beyond things, through routines, to persons. For faith, the light of theology, must include intelligence, but must also go beyond it to reach basic trust—the foundation of all loves.

There is a second reason why Christian theology continually empha-sizes the role of the heart in university activity: Christian theology is centered on the love of Christ for us and our love for Him. Thus, it demands that the university community not be satisfied solely with intel-ligence, but that this community go beyond sophisticated reason to enter family love, colleague love (friendship), student love (respect), and civic love (patriotism) of neighborhood, city, and nation. The university com-munity does this whenever it directs, by way of respectful love, its gen-eral routines and procedures to fulfill a particular concrete need of people. Hans Urs von Balthasar, in his *Love Alone,* has warned us that anthropological and cosmological rationalizations, which are so popular with university people, must be supplemented with a love-centered the-ology. Otherwise, faith itself becomes routinized, Christian theology be-comes paralyzed, and justice languishes. Then, when charity is dying, disciplined liberty tends to deteriorate. But Christian theology, if it is set on fire with love, projects a passionate vision that warms the heart of the university. Of course, this vision, if the Christian theology is scientific, will enlist all specialized knowledges in its formulation, will be constantly modified by reinterpretation of traditional truth at all levels, and will stimulate the growth of wisdom in the university community. When, and if, this vision becomes total, it will unite the various university processes, help the university recognize its own identity, enable the university com-munity to seize upon its unique vocation or destiny, and hasten the pursuit of both its dual intrinsic aims and its one extrinsic aim. Conse-quently, the university will be much more capable of reverently working within mystery. Ultimately, the Christian university, under the influence of Christian theology, will be distinguished for its intelligent work, yet will never be satisfied with this distinction unless this intelligent work is begun, carried through, and terminated with love.

Conclusion

The problem faced by a university community is not to decide whether to have a theology but, rather, to select which theology will have the dominant position among the community members and thereby give this community unity. Christian theology, as opposed to other types of the-ology, offers advantages to the university because it is a scientific, re-vealed wisdom that offers a liberating way of life. In fact, this Christian theology not only uses all the resources of the university's specialized knowledges and communal wisdom to stimulate and control its own growth, but also ends up being a model for the university community's wisdom and for implementation of the university's dual intrinsic aims and one extrinsic aim. Indeed, the university, always entering into mystery, could well use the guidance of a Christian theology, which forever surveys the ultimate of all mysteries—the risen presence of Jesus Christ in His community.

The seven elements of the theological field of forces clearly demonstrate that Christian theology is a university knowledge in all its aspects. But, in addition to this, the university finds herself receiving contributions from Christian theology when Christian theology evaluates the discoveries made by the specialized knowledges for human living, makes clear the intrinsic worth of each discipline for achieving human destiny, lends stability to the university community for its work, motivates a disciplined wholesome living for the university itself, and underlines the role of the heart for all the university personnel in their operations. For all these reasons, Christian theology acts as both the living promise of destiny and the living model of unity for the university.

In these nine chapters, we have tried (a) to describe the problems of the university, (b) to draw some lines of solution for these problems, and (c) to converge these lines toward a Christian vision of the university. But there is also a need for a more concrete assessment of the university, which will look to the undergraduate students, the graduate students, the faculty, and the administration and its staff. This assessment should assay the secularization and desecularization that is occurring in the university, reconsider the undergraduate curriculum (concerning the respective roles of the core curriculum, major study, and elective courses), ask about the wholesomeness of graduate students and graduate researchers, weigh the roles of prayer and worship at the university, test administrative decisions for the adequacy of their models, wonder about the unique vocation of each university, indicate the Christian university's unique contribution of Christian wisdom, and, finally, question the sponsorship of a university by a religious group. These areas will be treated in Part II of this Christian vision of the university.

Part II: The University Looks to Its Powers

10 The University as Prime Agent of Secularization

No Christian university or college has yet advertised to the parents of its prospective students that it is a prime agent for secularizing their sons and daughters. Secularization is a "naughty" word among Christians because it has been stolen by the secularists for their exclusive use. In the last ten years, however, the true meaning of secularization has been surfacing among Christian thinkers, and its vital role in world history is being recognized. For some understanding of this phenomenon, let us notice how a student becomes secularized through four years of undergraduate, liberal arts training.

How the Student Is Secularized

An eighteen-year-old woman, fresh from a successful stint at an excellent high school, enters the university with a rather global and undifferentiated understanding of all knowledge and all world problems. Counselors and others urge her to settle upon a major study as early as possible so that she will have a marketable career-skill and can get a job when she graduates. (She is being asked to specialize almost as soon as she becomes a sophomore, if not earlier.) If she is attending a strong liberal arts college, she will also be taking a core curriculum of mandated courses that are necessary for graduation. These courses will range over language, history, philosophy, theology, science, literature, and expressive arts and will be geared to give a broad, liberal understanding of the human being and the human situation. In addition, she will also be able to elect some courses purely according to her own needs and interests—either to support her major or to explore further some interests aroused by the core-curriculum or to have some fun with knowledges, arts, and skills about which she is curious and for which she may have latent talent. This is how she sees things before the undergraduate program actually begins.

But, a few months into this program, a basic fact dawns on her: university courses, though they have labels similar to those attached to high school courses, are much more intensely directed to the particular subject matter at hand and allow for little humanistic deviation; not much time is given to relating one subject to other subjects. The premed physiology class does not ordinarily begin with a prayer for wisdom and end with a panegyric about the fostering of life; nor does it include an explanation of how a knowledge of physiology will enhance one's understanding of psychology or physical anthropology. The business is physiology, and the complexity of the business does not allow much strolling off the main road to pick flowers, as it were.

If the woman in our example is also taking classes in the history of western civilization, calculus, American literature, and introductory philosophy, and if each course is deeply intent on its tightly circumscribed material, she will feel that her consciousness is being diced into neat compartments. Furthermore, each compartment is so complex that all her energeies will be expended in discovering and cataloging its intricate furniture and lighting fixtures, and there will be no time to look for doors that lead into the other compartments—though the professor-guide will, from time to time, vaguely mention other compartments.

In her sophomore year, she decides to become a nursing major and, consequently, she becomes more deeply committed to biology and biochemistry. But her mind is also opening up to sociology, psychology, Old Testament theology, philosophical ethics, American diplomatic history, and physical education (swimming). The dicing of her consciousness continues. She now feels a growing frustration at the seeming disconnectedness of these knowledges, at the use of the same words with different meanings (e.g., *life,* as used in biology, philosophy, and psychology, or *justice,* as employed in political science, sociology, and philosophy), at the unstated assumption of each specialist that his or her special knowledge is of more basic importance than others.

In her junior year, this nursing major is feeling new divisive pressures. She begins her *practicum* of assisting in hospitals and finds that the excitement of tending patients is not easily correlated with the quiet of concentrating on purely academic studies. Moreover, she is somewhat confused by the variety of ways to approach the same event. A two-week strike of the city's policemen and firemen, for example, aroused in each professor quite different comments: The *economist* noted the devastating effect on the city's business community; the *philosopher* wondered how to justly integrate the firemen's and policemen's need for increased pay, during a period of sudden inflation, with the city's need for protection against skyrocketing taxes during a period of unstable city government; the *sociologist* described how the city's recreational and business institutions were improved by a deeper understanding of their dependency on city government; the *urban anthropologist* noted the correlation between the higher education of city servants and the growing frequency of strikes. The nursing student then asks herself: how does the mayor of the city put all this together to get a single picture so that he can make a good decision? How can a student be expected to do this if the experts are puzzled? Has specialization of knowledges made it impossible to integrate them on a practical level? Where is the wisdom to untie and unify all these complications?

A more personal problem has also caused her uneasiness—the problem of free will. Once, free will was no problem for her, since free will seemed such an obvious fact; now, however, it becomes a problem because, in psychology, free will is denied, in philosophy, free will is treated with an ambivalent shrug, and, in theology, free will is strongly, even heatedly affirmed. There is no agreement, no universal opinion with which to guide one's life. What is more, justice seems to change colors according to the particular knowledge that is casting light on it: *Philosophy* defines it as rendering what is due to another person or to a community or to an institution; *political science* sees it as the balance of power among institutions for the protection of the individual; *sociology* reckons it according to the agreements of cooperation that have been fashioned by individuals and institutions; the *law* estimates it as the process that establishes, based on past precedents, what citizens can reasonably expect from each other and from civic institutions. Thus, the speculative wisdom of the university would seem to be a cracked mirror, when it is held up to reflect free will, and the fragments of a mirror, when it is faced with justice.

When the nursing major reaches her senior year, she has become somewhat belligerent about her education. She is being asked to simultaneously integrate (a) her practical life at the hospital and her academic life at the university, (b) all the liberal knowledges of the core curriculum and all the skill-knowledges of her profession, (c) her individual personality (as a twenty-one-year-old woman who likes to dance, play tennis, and pray), and her social life as daughter-nurse-fianceé-captain (of the tennis team). She wants to be wholesome but the demands of life seem to be breaking her into fragments. For the first time in her college career, she intelligently recognizes that her personal integration is going to come when she admits her need for authoritative advice and when, at the same time, she focuses all her knowledges, past experience, good attitudes, and authoritative advice upon a decision and makes it by herself, for herself. Integration, she finds, is a highly demanding, painful, and slow process that involves failure as well as success. Without integration, however, one literally comes apart at the physical-psychological seams or ricochets through life as a willful adolescent. She now knows that integration is a sheer necessity, not an option, if, ironically, one wishes to be free. At this point, the nurse-to-be has discovered the inner meaning of disciplined liberty. At this point, too, she is well aware that the integration of the present moment is quite provisional and must forever secede to later, more sophisticated integrations as new information comes from the specialized knowledges, as her own attitudes become deeper and yet more understandingly flexible, as the situation around her changes, as her own personality develops. Now the woman is secularized.

What does this mean? It means, first, that through the specialized knowledges, she is seeing more deeply into the mystery of self, world, and community. Secondly, it means that, for her, the integration of these knowledges into a single vision of the world (speculative wisdom) is necessary if she is to understand where she and the world are going. Thirdly, it means that the practical wisdom, which is acquired by applying this vision to the concrete problems of everyday living, lets her know how essential this vision and these specialized knowledges are as she makes decisions that will be helpful to her and to others. Lastly, this practical wisdom informs her about how much more she has yet to learn about this mysterious world into which her decision has just thrust her. When she had left high school, she had felt that she had known the world and its problems; now, however, she is certain that she has just begun to know these things and to be able to deal with them. In her freshman and sophomore years, the specialized knowledges induced skepticism and confusion as much as information; now, in her senior year, the fracturing of her earlier, naïve assurances has led her to begin a hestiant, provisional integration of the various knowledges she has been taught, and this integration has enabled her to use these knowledges somewhat effectively in making decisions.

Now that she has a sense of how fast the world is changing, she respects the various specialized knowledges for their constant reinterpretation of the traditional truth that is carried within them. She recognizes that this progress naturally results in the generation of new knowledges, which, of course, make new integrations more complex and, hence, more difficult to successfully accomplish. Yet integrations must be tried if the university process is not to fragment human beings and the world but, rather, to render them more wholesome in both understanding and practice. Thus, implicit to this woman's understanding of the secularization process within her is her assumption of a convergence of knowledges or of "plural truths."

The young nurse has experienced, then, both the specialization (differentiation) and the integration (socialization) of her consciousness. As a result, she can now distinguish the strata of the world as they correspond to the specialized knowledges and, then, reunite them into a single world that corresponds to her wisdom-vision (her own integration of these knowledges). Indeed, she has been secularized. The differentiated and integrated knowledge of the world around her now resides in her as an important part of her personality. Her very consciousness has been specialized and socialized. She has been humanized, made more conscious of herself and others.

There are hazards, of course, in the process of secularizing students. A young man may attempt to simplify his life down to a single specialized knowledge in order to make integration less necessary and to escape its pain. Instead of expanding his consciousness with other knowledges, this student may restrict it to biology or psychology, for example. He explicitly intends to judge everything from one viewpoint and to see only one aspect of reality. Consequently, he shrinks not only himself but everybody and everything to this one dimension. As a result, he risks becoming a narrow-minded counselor, a monomaniacal father, a manipulative friend, and a slightly boring companion. Thus, this young student of psychology or biology tends to become more and more individualistic, since his one-dimensional world and life tend to center on himself and reduce his ability to socialize. Of course, if he continues on this path, he will depersonalize himself into a functionary.

A second danger may be experienced by the secularized student. The painful difficulty of achieving integration—a difficulty that is lengthening in each decade due to the increasing complexity of contemporary culture—may lead the student into a prolonged adolescence as his or her years of education stretch into his or her late twenties. A third danger: If the student should ever give up on this taxing integration process, he or she may well leave his or her career for the sake of the "simple life" and, in angry alienation, drift away from the community, never to regain the same ambition. These are the risks of the secularization process in the four-year, undergraduate program.

These dark hazards, however, offer a contrasting background for the good effects of secularization at the undergraduate level. First, the painful integration that takes place during these years may well elicit a strong dedication to the world out of respect for its mystery and its beautiful potential for good. Second, a student may be transplanted from a purely individualistic life into community with those who are also studying the same specialized knowledge. This happens as he or she sends down roots into the art or knowledge shared with others. The integration of knowledges other than the student's major could impart confidence in other areas so that the student becomes open to new ideas, new attitudes, and new acquaintances. There could be a new wholeness about this person and his or her life as he or she opens up to truth and friendships from all directions. Yet, such wholeness would draw much of its integrity from the fact that this student would have become competent and mature in one specialized knowledge and, thus, could appreciate the strengths and relevance of the other specialized knowledges. This is the normal side of the secularization that is induced by the university's undergraduate program.

The Undergraduate Recapitulates Secularization of World and of University

The undergraduate nursing student's task of secularization had to be complexly difficult because she was recapitulating in herself, within four years, what the world has been rapidly doing for at least the last four thousand years and what the university has been busily accomplishing for the past eight hundred years. To understand this, it is necessary to take a brief glance at developing civilization. Note how the pre-Grecian cultures built their communities around particular skills. A priest-caste developed in order to protect a mysterious knowledge that was an amalgam of primitive theology, astronomy, mathematics, literature, and medicine. Gradually, other castes came into existence: government officials concerned themselves with military strategy and law; mechanics worked with tools, clothmaking, and pottery; farmers used age-old agricultural lore and techniques. All these skills could be passed on only by actually doing them, for there were no books that offered guiding principles of explanation; rather, each artisan or administrator passed on his or her skill to an apprentice by the "feel of things" rather than by conveying abstract ideas. Learning was somewhat akin to using a recipe book; everything was concrete, pragmatic, and highly individualistic. For this reason, skills developed slowly and could die quickly if a community of artisans lost its leadership or was decimated by a plague.

Then the Greeks changed the world by inventing a way of thinking and of expressing themselves that went beyond common-sense knowledge and the so-called recipe approach to cognition. This new type of learning was highly abstract and generalized since it got "behind" the common-sense experience and conceptualized principles of explanation. As a result, it could be passed on by books, not solely by doing. This "tree of learning" tended to expand by branching out into new methods, skills, and content. Socrates, living dangerously, distinguished philosophic ethics from civic religion and religious literature. Aristotle, in opposition to Plato, demonstrated that mathematics was not metaphysics and that metaphysics was not biology or cosmology. Later, as we have seen, Thomas Aquinas used Augustine's distinction between reason and faith to indicate how philosophy, theology, and faith were three different knowings. (Incidentally, for developing this distinction, he merited the accusa-

214

tion of heresy.) Consequently, when philosophy gave birth to Newton's physics and to Boyle's chemistry, these two new sciences escaped being mistaken for theology. Philosophy later spawned into their own distinct lives such sciences as psychology, sociology, political science, and anthropology. All these speculative sciences, in turn, gave new life to the distinctly practical sciences of engineering, medicine, social work, law, and psychiatry. Out of these practical sciences, cascaded numerous skills such as transport driving, electrical fitting, various types of construction work, military sciences, courtroom reporting, secretarial services, computer technology, and so on.

As a matter of course, each of these knowledges, skills, and arts is surrounded by its own distinct community of specialists who promote it, protect it, and hand it on. Among the speculative knowledges and arts, this process demands a constant reinterpretation, that is, a reintegration of new truths into the traditional body of principles, information, techniques, and method. Thus, every new discovery within a tightly organized knowledge demands that all parts of this knowledge adjust to accommodate it. Because each knowledge, art, and skill is so complex, only a highly specialized community of experts can hold all of its many facets in integrative tension. But a strange factor evolves, for, as a knowledge community becomes more specialized, it becomes more dependent on other specialized communities for guidance. Thus, specialization seems to demand the integration and socialization of communities that are seemingly separated by their intensely different interests. This occurs not only in city planning or in solving a gigantic problem such as pollution, where the planning and the problem cut across many disciplines, but also in the complex of interlocking knowledge communities that have formed to share knowledges and skills. The medical profession, for example, forms a tightly knit community around medical knowledge, but it is far from autonomous. The more specialized this community becomes, the more dependent it is upon the chemistry of drugs; upon subatomic or nuclear physics for the technology of radioisotopes and electron microscopes; upon psychology for psychosomatic medicine and for humane handling of patients in huge hospital complexes; upon philosophy for ethical clarifications of drug-use, human transplants, and extraordinary means for prolonging life; upon political science for securing national support for medical research; upon sociology for understanding the attitudes of health care providers and recipients; upon the communication arts for expressing the medical community's own ideals to itself and to its public.

From this, it can be seen that a whole knowledge community must face the problem of integrating its specialized knowledge or skill with other specialized knowledges, arts, and skills in a way that is remarkably like that of an undergraduate nursing student. Specialization without integration tends to dice the civic community into many uncommunicative subcommunities in the same way that it dices the consciousness of the undergraduate student into doorless, compartmentalized knowledges. What happens to the undergraduate student is a microcosm of what ocurs in the macrocosm of the nation. For this reason, the integrations or wisdoms that are offered by the university to both the civic society and the individual student, on both the speculative and the practical levels, are crucial to the survival of modern civilization. It is no wonder that every large government agency, every big business, every university, has a "committee on committees" lest integration be lost to hyperspecialization.

The student, then, recapitulates the last four thousand years of inculturation through recapitulating the last eight hundred years of university reflection. To prove this assertion, a person has only to page through a university catalog for 1928 and another for 1979; not only has a traditional field like biology burgeoned into new subsciences such as genetics, microbiology, and gerontology, but also there are whole new fields of science and art such as cybernetics, human engineering, electronics, and videocommunications. As noted earlier, the history of the American university for the last century-and-a-half demonstrates how the university has embraced more and more knowledges, skills, and arts within its program so that now there is literally something for everybody. Periodically, the university community has reintegrated all its acquisitions into a new unity, lest the university simply become an information warehouse or a wisdom supermarket. But the rapid acceleration of specialization during the last thirty years has made more imperative the need for integration. This is true not only on the speculative level of wisdom, so that one knows the context, the principles, and the cumulative direction of decisions, but also on the practical level of wisdom, so that the solutions offered to the civic community are down-to-earth and morally sound. If the universities and the United States are suffering from any disease, that disease is a directionless dispersal of ideas, energies, and hopes. Against this recklessness, only intellectual and moral integration will prevail. For this reason, the university community is under heavy duress to provide for both the individual student and the nation the various levels of wisdom that they both need to live wholesome lives.

But the university community is made up of individual professors, administrators, and students. Thus, the duty to provide these wisdoms eventually settles on the minds and hearts of individual persons— particularly on the minds and hearts of professors. Unless each professor is recapitulating, within himself or herself, the last eight hundred years of

216

university secularization, then he or she is not presenting to each student, to the university community, and to the civic community a balanced picture of specialization and integration. He or she is not really a university person. This is not to say that a single university professor is responsible for what only a community of professors can do; no one professor must hold in dynamic tension all the factors that make up speculative and practical wisdoms. This is to say, however, that, unless the professor is secularized, that is, unless he or she holds in balanced integration his or her specialized knowledge and the context of other knowledges and arts, he or she cannot contribute well to the university community's ongoing pursuit of wisdom, which is the university's second dual intrinsic aim of cumulative wisdom. Does this mean, then, that secularization is the wisdom process itself? Are not values excluded from the secularization process and is this not the disease of this process as well as the disease of the present university system? Exactly what is being asked of the university community and of the individual professor?

Secularization is Neither Secularity Nor Secularism

The secularists, in claiming the secularization process for themselves, have muddled the understanding of this process by implying that their practical atheism is a basic part of secularization. Actually, secularism is just one more secularity, or value system, among many that are found in the secularization process. Since a prime aim of the university is the advancement of secularization, the claim of the secularists to *own* secularization puts the university in the strange position of seeming to promote secularism and its eloquent indifference to God. Evidently some clarification of what secularization, secularity, and secularism are, and how they are related, is needed at this point.

Our previous exposition of how the undergraduate student becomes secularized by the university, in imitation of the university and world history, could bring us to the following definition of secularization: Secularization is the expansion of an individual's personality around a specialized skill or knowledge or art. This expansion of personality is vertical in the sense that the specialization roots the expert more deeply into his or her specialist community and, thus, enables him or her to grow more proficient in this special knowledge, art, or skill through communication with fellow specialists. This expansion of personality is also horizontal in the sense that this growing proficiency enables the expert to better serve the larger civic community and in the sense that, when his or her particular skill is linked with those of specialists in other knowledges, arts, and skills, he or she integrates into a grander community of cooperation for

217

service to the civic community. This horizontal aspect is precisely the *socialization* of the expert and constitutes, with specialization, the two basic dynamisms of the secularization process within the individual.

When this model of individual secularization is held up to compare it with the community, one notes how the specialized community—as, for example, the union of electricians—can become better specialized as it defines, with exceeding care, its special area of competence, its professional criteria for membership, and its controls for estimating and ensuring work quality. This would be the vertical, or specialist, dimension of the electrician community's expansion of its so-called collective personality. The horizontal, or socialized, dimension of this secularization would be the cooperative meshing of this communal electrical skill with the skills of other specialized communities to form a single creative force of great complexity such as occurs when a model city is planned, built, and set into motion.

Clearly, the vertical or specialized development of each university department and its horizontal linking with other departments in a convergent pooling of their resources in both speculative wisdom and practical wisdom (in order to offer wise advice for the solving of civic problems) is another example of how communal secularization and integration (socialization) is both a deeper and deeper penetration of reality and a wider and wider grasp of the fullness of reality. This may be taking place in the individual or in the individual's specialized community, or in the university as a totality or in the civic community as a whole. Each new depth of specialization requires a new reinterpretation of the traditional truth of a discipline, and each new integration of the specialized knowledges offers both a richer wisdom that embraces more of reality in greater depth and a consequent challenge that demands further specialization. In this way, each participant in this process has the opportunity to grow in wholeness of personality.

From this viewpoint, secularization is a natural, healthy process whose reversal would cause not only the ravages of unchecked diseases and starvation for millions, together with the attendant anarchy, but also the deterioration of human development. And yet, within this process there can also occur widely divergent moral attitudes (habitually lived values). When the development of knowledges and skills enables men and women to exercise masterful control over nature, then a person's sense of humanity (a person's creativity, autonomy, dignity, and responsibility for people and the world) arises against a previous feeling of the lonely human being cowering before the overwhelming natural forces of chance events. Indeed, the expansion of knowledges and skills allied with the discipline necessary to ply them, increases a person's self-awareness (and, thus, a person's awareness of others) and makes him or her more conscious of freedom of choice among all the new options that are offered by his or her own intelligence as well as by the latest technology and science. A person no longer needs to feel trapped in century-old routines and customs.

This creative automony or independence, which a person feels can, however, degenerate into a totalitarian drive to manipulate other people, into a fine *hubris* that declares God to be an unnecessary hypothesis, and into a dilettante curiosity that is divorced from wisdom. The secularization technique of constantly questioning one's presuppositions can be transformed from a marvelously fecund procedure that expects to discover beautiful truth into the enervating attitude that nothing is certain and that all of life's values are simply ambiguous. In addition, although the multiplication of specialized communities can result in an interlocking democratic system of checks and balances for the protection of liberty, it can also lead to a sense of loneliness in the face of the huge bureaucracy of modern society, the establishment.

Thus, it would appear that secularization is a neutral process that can be interpreted and run by divergent values. But from where do the values arise? How do they form a system, or a secularity, for directing the secularization process? Are the systematized values, or secularities, distinct from the secularization process itself? Are there many diverse secularities within the secularization process? How can they possibly cooperate with each other in the process? These vitally important questions must be faced, for the university structure is determined by value systems, and the university community cannot long survive without values, nor long escape from evaluating its work. Let us, then, turn to our first question about the origin of these values.

The sources of value in a person's life would seem to be four: (1) society, (2) religion or revelation, (3) the individual's reflective experience, and (4) the secularization process. By the time the child is five years old to eight years old, it has already built into itself a network of attitudes toward food and animals, family life and affection, hope in the future and reading books, storms and water, doctors and dentists, friends and strangers, punishment and reward. This network of attitudes, or habitually lived values, is the child's total attitude toward the world; it is the child's secularity. The family and the neighborhood, knowingly or unknowingly, have been busy molding this child to their image. The school and the communications media have also noticeably entered this molding of values. Nor is the church far behind, with its sense of God's providence for the individual and of His saving influence within weak, sometimes desperate, sinners—if, of course, the family and the neighborhood allow the church to enter into the child's life.

When the child becomes a young adult and wishes to survive decently in this world, he or she must learn a specialized skill or knowledge or art which is desirable in the job market. For a person to suffer, over a long period, the discipline necessary for the cultivation, maintenance, and growth of a skill-knowledge-art, he or she must learn to highly value the particular skill-knowledge-art. Furthermore, when this person cooperates with other skilled and knowledgeable people, he or she must learn to evaluate his or her own expertness by locating its position of relative importance within the cooperative project. In evaluating this work, the person cannot help evaluating himself or herself, at least partially, and also evaluating others and their work. If this person has tasted failure in his or her work, he or she may then be made more conscious of how much he or she values, and is valued by, family. If this person should ever feel temporarily rejected by his or her family, he or she then experiences more sharply the value of his or her work, of leisure-time friends, and of work-team companionship. This person may, in times of mortgage stress or of family wrangling, turn to his or her religion and its values and discover there a divine companionship, a peace beyond anything previously experienced. Indeed, there may come a time of sharp value-conflict in which he or she has to decide the priority of his or her values—who or what comes first, second, and last, for what values he or she would bleed, and for what great value he or she would be willing to die. Gradually, this person has moved into maturity, which means that he or she is explicitly aware of his or her values and has arranged them according to a hierarchy. This person has systematized his or her values into a total general attitude toward the world—in short, into a secularity.

This secularity, of course, is not totally individual. For within the specialist community, a collective sense of values, which centers around its principal unifying interest, rises out of the individual members' interaction and reinforces each person's set of values. There is a "tonal quality" not only in neighborhoods but also in communities of physicists and carpenters. These tonal qualities, in turn, harmonize or conflict to produce the national symphony of secularity. This does not mean that only the specialist community furnishes support for the person's values or that only these communities furnish the common national secularity. The individual often is also a member of a church community, an ethnic group, a neighborhood class (blue-collar, white-collar, etc.), a leisure group, or a business community. Thus, the individual's secularity is the sum total of many influences which personal experience has validated and appropriated according to his or her own inventiveness, and the national secularity is a compound of all these influential communities. Although there is constant burlesquing of the national type, still, the traveler through Germany, France, Italy, and Spain is well aware of the diverse lifestyles that issue from different secularities.

Out of all this interchange, there arises a great, single englobing value within each individual. It embraces all the skills, knowledges, techniques, and consequent valuations of every individual and community. This *Weltanschauung,* or worldview, is the total context of all the other values of a person; it is that from which all his or her goals in life get their value and meaning; it is the basic source of his or her joy or disgust at life's events. For Marx, it is the classless society in final peace of brotherhood; for Sartre, it is the brave acceptance of life's ultimate meaninglessness; for the American secularist, it is the perfectly democratic and satisfied society; for the Buddhist, it is the state of nirvana; for the Christian, it is union with the Triune God, amid the community of saints who surround the Christ. This is Peter Berger's "Sacred Canopy." Under it, everything makes sense; outside it, all is the chaos of meaningless activity, the dark night of despair and hopeless self-destruction.

Thus, a person's *Weltanschauung* explains why, ultimately, he or she should love or hate secularization, promote it or destroy it. This all-encompassing value influences a person's every action. It dramatically surges into view when it is challenged by death, unemployment, betrayal of a friend, rapid expansion of one's business, a new love of a lifetime. It explains to a person where his or her life is heading, why raising or not raising a family is worthwhile, how valuable his or her work is, why he or she should or should not sacrifice for friends, family, and country. Could it be suggested here that a positive *Weltanschauung* is itself a dedication to the world, that it is a love eager to discover and to embrace the whole of reality, that, as a secularity, it is a network of values, or habitual attitudes, which structures both the individual personality and the communal collective personality? This *Weltanschauung,* then, could be a reciprocal admission of intrinsic worth between man, God, and society, that is, each would recognize the autonomy of the other two, each would see the other two as worthwhile, simply on their own merits. This recognition would be more than a mere catalog of each one's extrinsic worth as an instrument for the others' achievement of some goal.

Given this description of what secularity is, could one say that it is not secularization, even though it can never be separated from secularization like a chemical in a compound? Could one say that the rationalization of reality (secularization) is not the valuing of reality (secularity), even though neither can be done without the other? There are reasons for affirming these statements. For secularization, with its emphasis on specialized knowledges-skills-arts and on their integration, certainly speaks from the mental side of human beings, while secularity, with its intense cultivation of values and motives, would describe the emotional-volitional side of human beings.

Furthermore, if secularization is not distinct from secularity, then human freedom becomes jeopardized. For the discovery of the various knowledges-arts-skills, and their subdivision into more and more circumscribed areas, occurs with a certain inevitability. The timing and the mode of discovery or subdivision can be by chance; but the development, once it has been made, fits in so well with previous developments that a type of natural necessity follows. This would make sense since these specialized disciplines are describing the developing structure of the world, which often proceeds according to necessary laws. Secularity, however, seems to be a more freely formed attitude or network of attitudes. Because evaluation involves, first, the mutual recognition of the intrinsic worth of things in themselves and then, only later, their extrinsic worth as means to an end, evaluation would seem to imply freedom to recognize or not to recognize, freedom to recognize as intrinsically or extrinsically worthwhile, freedom to recognize according to one's own understanding of the secularization process—one's own particular *Weltanschauung*. If freedom does not enter into the secularization process, then how can this process be controlled? Does not the secularization process become an army marching inevitably toward some single, unavoidable goal of Greek fate, or does it not seem a rabble stumbling blindly along to some chance destination? Does not humanity become the intelligent slave of the secularization to which it is contributing? Does not secularization become an omnipresent and always threatening Frankenstein? Lastly, if secularization and secularity are distinct dynamisms of world development, then they become distinct measuring rods of progress. One can truly say: "Perhaps we can do it (e.g., the cloning of human embryos), but should we?" or "I can understand it without liking it" or "Maybe it is possible, but is it worth the trouble or the danger?" In other words, if secularization and secularity are truly distinct, then the direction in which secularization moves is at least partially up to mankind's freedom. In fact, mankind's freely chosen values may impel men and women to attack the secularization process. One would think that the attacker should not be the victim also.

The real distinctness of secularization and secularity does not mean that they are separable or that one can exist without the other. Clearly, one cannot understand or do or promote something without having an attitude toward its worthwhileness. Besides, without secularization, humanity cannot control nature or itself, and men and women lose control over their situations and their lives; without secularity, humanity loses its free inventiveness in slavery to routinized technocracy. The two must develop together if either is to grow. It soon becomes clear, however, that a false secularity could do immeasurable harm to the secularization process, if, for example, the secularity involved hostility toward the world or if it condemned material things and the body as unworthy of acute and prolonged attention. These extreme examples indicate the possible variety of secularities working within secularization—a further manifestation that the single process of secularization is not the plural secularities occurring within it.

How Can the Secularization Process Survive Its Plural Secularities?

A problem arises, however: how can the secularization process maintain its unity if there are multiple secularities attempting to influence it? And since the university is the prime agent of secularization, this problem transfers to the very being of any institution of higher learning. We discussed, in an earlier chapter, how devastating divergent pluralism could be at the cognitional level of the university; now we can observe how fragmenting divergent secularities can be at the value level. The university is especially hard hit in its wisdom community.

Noting some examples of these contesting secularities indicates the dimensions of the problem. The Marxist secularity comes out of a historical determinism, centers all values around work, totally subordinates the individual to the communal, builds its strategy on the premise that conflict between classes is necessary, gives economics the imperial crown, and looks to a future classless society that is without even the idea of God. On the other hand, pantheist secularity offers union with God/nature right now, cannot allow for freedom lest it separate man from God/nature, centers all values on losing one's identity in God/nature, and implicitly affirms only one real mythic knowledge of which the sciences, arts, knowledges, and skills are shadows to be dissipated by the light of nature mystically revealing herself within humanity. Neopagan secularity practically tends to divinize humanity but theoretically pays respects to a vague God (the "man upstairs"); pursues sports, art, and entertainment with singular devotion so that the pleasurable appears to be the ultimate norm of morality; puts its emphasis on the individual, almost to the neglect of the social. Technological secularity measures all people, things, and events by their efficiency in getting something done; is primarily dedicated to the material control of nature and of human routines; makes the machine the mediator between human beings and universe, and yet, also the extension of human powers; considers nature principally for its plasticity to human uses, for its ability to image mankind; is rather indifferent to a God who seems so useless to men and women. Christian secularity considers the universe to be the ongoing exteriorization of the triune God's interior life, looks to human beings as free co-creators of the universe with the immanent God, sees human beings as deeply hampered in their good ambitions by their sins, yet also sees human beings as the living image of Christ, their rescuer; forsees human beings as joining, after death, the great community of men and women who have been found loyal to the triune God in their previous efforts at hominizing the universe. Scientific secularity is more than intrigued by the mystery of the universe, feels assured that this mystery will eventually be totally penetrated by the human intellect despite its unimaginable depth and diversity, offers scientific data as the ultimate base for all human decisions, tends to depreciate knowledges other than the sciences, extols a type of philosophy that is merely mythic generalizations of scientific hypotheses; thinks of God more as a universe-girdling hypothesis than as a personal reality.

Secularism is a special type of secularity since it claims to be the secularization process itself and, thus, attempts to exclude all other secularities as counterfeit. Its basic tenet, borrowed from scientism, is that the only true and certain knowledge is contained in the physical sciences (the social sciences are valid only insofar as they model themselves strictly on the methods of physics and chemistry); all other knowledges and arts—including even everyday common-sense knowledge—really reduce to genteel opinions; among these, theology is the least likely to touch truth. The universe, according to secularism, is self-explanatory in terms of merely physical science; God, if He exists, has negligible influence on the universe. Thus, the nobility of human beings is to be built by science alone; faith, at the best, is sheer poetic feeling detached from any basis in the world.

To propose such secularism as anything more than one secularity among many is to confuse it with its philosophic base, an exceedingly narrow scientism, or to muddle it with the total secularization process. At present, this is one of the most debilitating confusions with secularization. Thus, those universities that have no place or time for adequate theological faculties continue to induce this confusion into university education and into the secularized world. This confusion is bad enough; but the exclusion of important values, such as God, human freedom, myth, and mystery, from secularization by the attempted domination of one secularity is worse.

All these secularities evidently differ on basic values such as human freedom, the meaning of human work, future hope, the existence of a supreme being, the value of the specialized knowledges, arts, and skills. Thus, they can only produce conflict within secularization—unless they hold some basic values in common by which their communities can cooperate. Could it be that just as we have discovered a fundamental philosophy and theology on which men and women agree, so now, we may find an underlying fundamental secularity according to which all men and women can work together though they follow different secularities?

This would seem to be the case. For, *de facto*, though there are grave differences between Islamic secularity, scientific secularity, and Marxist secularity, technicians from these three secularities can work together on oil lines, on economic planning, on international diplomacy, on educational projects, and on facilities and programs for improving national health. There must be some basic agreements amid basic conflicts of principle. Earlier, the intrinsic worth of persons and things was stressed in the valuing process. This can also be seen as the autonomy of realities, namely, each having its own ontic order with its proper goals, means, and procedures. This is the independence of humanity from God, of the world from God and humanity, and of humanity and God and the world from society—a qualified independence, since every being (except God for the Christian) is dependent on other beings for its existence.

Is it not possible that, underlying all the diverse secularities, there is a common, fundamental secularity which would be constituted by four or five commonly admitted autonomies? There is, for example, the autonomy of the infrapersonal world of animals, plants, and minerals with its own proper laws and goals of existence, which are not to be squandered at mankind's whim but are to be respected, protected, and improved by mankind because of their intrinsic worth. Then there is the second autonomy of mankind itself in whom and for whom all these secularities operate in recognition of human freedom, inventiveness, willingness to sacrifice for others, and future potential for creating good for and in others. A third autonomy is that of a "superpresence" who is the ultimate, present-and-future hope of mankind, who establishes the universe in its expansive unity, who makes sure that all of mankind's individual actions have a final meaning. For the Marxist, this would be the triumph of the proletariat in the classless society; for the Christian, this is God; for the *laissez-faire* capitalist, this would be the success of the cultured rich class; for the pantheist, this is nature allowed to be herself in all her beauty. A fourth autonomy is the secularization process itself since its rationalization and institutionalization of human life is as inevitable, and yet as free for good or for evil, as is the development of the individual person's personality. A fifth autonomy is that of secularity itself, namely, the process by which the individual person freely forms his or her specialized values and integrates them with the community and with God. For no human can fail to undergo this process even though each does it in a unique way. Could these five autonomies, then, be the incipient description of a fundamental secularity that is the basis for unity in the running of secularization? Would this not partially explain how, in the Senate of the United States, a South Carolina Democrat, a Minnesota Populist, and Maine Republican could somewhat agree amid disagreements when all three vote affirmatively for the same bill?

This fundamental secularity underlying all the differing secularities is the source of unity not only for the world, but particularly for the university commmunity which attempts to mirror the world with accuracy. The way in which world secularization incubates and lives with multiple secularities gives some guidance to the university on how it can exist united while, at the same time, it incubates and lives with multiple systems of value. For the very causes of plural value systems are present in both the world and the university. First, if secularity is a system of recognized autonomies or intrinsic values, and if such a value system is internalized by each person according to his or her unique life experiences, the very uniqueness of each man's or woman's personality implies as many value systems as there are individual men and women. This is part of the fascinating mystery that each human being is. The eight-year-old child, heavily indoctrinated by family tradition, surprises his or her parents by holding to an embryonic worldview that slightly baffles them in its origin, its resistence to persuasion, and its novelty.

A second reason for multiple secularities is the free choice of a person. According to primary socialization principles, Democratic Polish-Catholic parents might expect their children to be Democratic Polish Catholics; the parents may discover, however, that their children are capable of crossing party lines, of disdaining Polish folk dancing, and of doing more than just politely visiting the Episcopalian church. To establish a unique personality, the young person may find it necessary to go against tradition in order to freely choose the elements of his or her secularity. Nor is this merely a negative reaction. A person's college experience and job-training as an economist or an insurance adjuster or a psychologist may give him or her a new look at the world that requires some adjustment of his or her own secularity.

The very complexity of the universe can be a third cause of plural systems of value. No single view of the world encompasses all of reality, so each approach to it must emphasize that aspect, or face, of the world toward which it advances and those values that are seen more clearly and felt more deeply from the particular angle of approach. The Polish-Catholic man or woman, for example, may see the world community from the viewpoint of the Polish struggle for liberty against Germany, England, and Russia; or from the stance of a Chicago ethnic neighborhood that is centered around Catholic parish life; or from the perspective of a young statistician who works for the Chicago City Planning Board. Because the world is obviously much more than Polish, Catholic, liberty-loving, Chicagoan, urban, and statistical, there are going to be other secularities. The very analogous nature of being of which the philospher continually reminds us, and the very limited capacities of the human heart and mind to which life's daily events call attention, both require a variety of secularities to express the richness of being and life in the universe.

Such variety is good because it makes possible a mutually enriching exchange among people and their secularities. Moreover, it can result in a purification or clarification of one's ultimate values. It is not rare that the Christian, in discussing prayer with the Hindu, finds himself or herself more deeply convinced of the worthwhileness of prayer, more aware of the wide dimensions of prayer, somewhat less "prissy" about the superiority of Christianity, somewhat less secure about his or her own goodness, and more humble before the changing world. Such variety, however, can also be the occasion for tragedy. More than a person's insights and genuine feelings enter into his or her secularity; errors of judgment, prejudices willingly retained, and misdirected emotions can warp a person's vision and his or her secularity. Variety of secularity has its source, then, not only in partial truth attained, but also in error entertained. The indomitable zealotry of Cromwell arose out of a vision and secularity in which the subjugation of Ireland appeared "beautiful." The Nazi terror arose partially out of an error in historical genetics and out of an unbalanced national pride dressed out as a metaphysics. A technological secularity that depreciates being and person for the sake of function and thing produces the nation that was satirized in George Orwell's *1984*, a nightmare of precise compartmentalized life, of dreadful routine without spontaneity, and of success without love and compassion.

Variety of secularities, then, is both good and bad. But to give up its goodness in order to escape its evil is to court a single value system. And what guarantee has one that such a monism would be true enough so that human beings could survive through the twentieth century? For reduction of the variety is also loss of good insight and value. And what guarantee does one have that, even if such a monism were adequately true, it could hold and develop its values without the challenge and enriching modification that are offered by competing secularities? As soon as a person or nation institutionalizes values so that they cannot be challenged, these values of the interested person or nation then take on *rigor mortis*. For this reason, it is important not to allow any secularity to capture the secularization process for itself either by imperial strategy, à la the medieval papacy, or by claim of *being* secularization, à la secularism. For not only is the stance of a person's autonomous freedom shaken, but the secularization process within him or her is weakened by impoverishment, by lack of nutrition. Plural secularity at least offers hope of betterment; a single secularity, to the exclusion of others, promises only senility.

But how does this understanding of plural secularities within secularization fit the university, especially when, as discussed earlier, a dominant theology and philosophy were advocated in their respective departments for the unity of the university? First, a university arises out of eight constituencies who continue to support this university because they like how it is growing. These constituencies who give sustenance and training to the university should be able to specify how the dual intrinsic aims and the additonal extrinsic aim of the university are to be fulfilled. As we have noted, at least at the beginning of the early American universities, these specifications, always modifiable, often included a dominant theology and a dominant philosophy. Second, this dominant theology or philosophy is always to be accompanied by representatives of other theologies or philosophies so that the dominant discipline is constantly challenged to fuller growth and to more accurate understanding. Third, undergraduate students, and even graduate students, need to see a single "picture," or wisdom, in order to begin their own incipient wisdom. A model wisdom must be seen, explored, and tested if any hope of wisdom, and not pure pessimism, is to be generated in the heart of the student. This wisdom will put the student in touch with fundamental philosophy, theology, and secularity so that he or she can begin to formulate a basic outlook on life by modifying this first wisdom and/or by later jettisoning it for something better. Fourth, philosophers and theologians are all too human; they need (like modern-language faculties) to carefully cultivate a unity that seems more naturally to come to faculties of other disciplines. For the analogical knowledge employed by both philosophy and theology does not offer the same unity as the univocal knowledges of the other disciplines. Its complexity more easily occasions conflicts. Furthermore, the ultimates of philosophy and theology do tend to run our lives and, therefore, do touch our emotions more strongly and lastingly.

Despite these difficulties, then, there would appear to be no contradiction between the advocacy of plural secularities in university secularization and the suggested need for a dominant theology and philosophy within the respective faculties in a university. For the Christian university, of course, these dominant disciplines would be of the Christian genre.

The University Promotes Secularization Amid Desecularization

It now becomes clearer that the university, as an institution, is the prime agent for promoting the specialization side of the secularization process. Through its various departments of knowledges, arts, and skills, the university, as an institution, is continually reinterpreting the traditional truths, art forms, and skill-techniques of these various disciplines. It is responsible for the development of almost all the new knowledges, arts, and skills conceived since the beginning of the twentieth century. Meanwhile, this same university, considered now as a wisdom community, is also constantly reaffirming the need for integration among these disciplines. In this way, too, it is a prime agent of secularization, for it attempts to provide that speculative and practical integration of the specialized knowledge, arts, and skills that is called wisdom. Thus, the communal side of the university integrates, or socializes, its products, its people, and, indirectly, the larger civic community; it provides a certain wholesomeness for the city and the nation.

In performing this critical task, the university community is also developing secularities, ways of systematically valuing the world. For this community has to evaluate the knowledges, arts, and skills, which it is developing, in order to discover their truth, beauty, and efficiency; it also has to evaluate the progress of the civic community that it serves if it is truly to serve it out of respect and trust; it even has to evaluate itself and its own wisdom in order to determine whether its wisdom is truly promoting the common good of both the university and the civic community. This evaluating must be systematic, that is, the values discovered and used must be ranked in priority, must be seen in their influences on each other, and must be watched for the direction that they are giving to all the communities using them. Such systematizing demands (a) expert knowledge, (b) selfless devotion to the truth, (c) much time for reflection, and (d) deep, patient hope in the future of the university, the nation, and the world. These are precisely the characteristics of a balanced university community as it endeavors to make the life of all people less fragmented and less distracted, more wholesome and more purposeful.

To achieve such wholesomeness, however, the university must struggle against a counterforce, which could be named *desecularization*. It is the reverse side of the tapestry of secularization. If secularization is constantly working toward a convergent wholesomeness, desecularization is a process that continually unravels, or randomly knots, the tapestry of secularized culture so that its civilization tends to fall apart. To put this less graphically, desecularization is any failure to properly specialize or integrate a knowledge, art, or skill and includes the resultant damage done to the community serving the knowledge, art, or skill and to the larger civic community that is served through this knowledge, art, or skill. Such desecularization naturally affects secularity because its failures depreciate, first, the value of the world in the minds of those who are suffering desecularization; second, the dignity of a person in his or her own estimate; and, third, the worth of God's providence in a person's hope for a decent future. Desecularization also produces distrust of one's culture and civilization so that a malaise seeps into a people's industries, businesses, schools, government, farming communities, and entertainment powers. This, in turn, affects physical and mental health in families and neighborhoods. If this malaise is not arrested, it can destroy a nation, a culture, a civilization. To see this more clearly, let us glance at some examples of desecularization among the knowledges, arts, and skills. By negation, these instances will also help to further define secularization as a human "wholing" process.

A prime example of destructive desecularization is the improper substitution of one knowledge or skill for another. Thus, there is a strong temptation now to substitute sociology for theology or to use the psychological skill of short-term group sensitivity training in place of long-term individual therapy. In the first instance, the practitioner theoretically seals himself or herself off from experience of the transcendent and opens himself or herself to a total relativism. In the second instance, the patient risks permanent disillusionment when he or she discovers that permanent personality growth is rarely achieved without long and careful perseverance in a guided day-to-day program of cumulative small triumphs in the face of discouragement.

A second example of desecularization is the domination of other knowledges by one knowledge. When physics is made to be the model for all other knowledges or the condition on which they are to be called, strictly speaking, knowledges, this imperialism forces biology into a rigorous determinism and turns the human subjects of psychology into things to be manipulated. When Augustine announced that any knowledge that was not usable for interpreting Scripture was idle curiosity, his theological imperialism imperiled the advance of the natural sciences—despite the fact that, in practice, Augustine excluded very little knowledge as irrelevant to Scripture. Such domination always involves a third type of desecularization, namely, the depreciation of a particular type of knowledge. This occurs when scientists, concentrating their attention mainly on the defects of common-sense knowing, depreciate the common-sense knowing because they have forgotten the fact that scientific knowledge not only arises out of common-sense knowing, but also must return to it in order to reduce itself to practical use or to further insights.

Socialization that is too quick and too easy is a fourth type of desecularization; it occurred, for example, when the nineteenth century Concordists attempted to link the discoveries of paleontology and archaeology with the seven days of creation that are "detailed" in the Book of Genesis. The resultant confusion not only made the Bible appear to be a poor scientific popularization, but also later cast doubt upon the use of modern scientific tools for exegesis. At the opposite extreme of secularization is the failure to socialize or integrate the various knowledges. Theology is not an apt interpreter of Scripture to its ambient culture unless its utterances show awareness of the mythic and the scientific. The biologist-theoretician who has failed to position his or her work in philosophy or theology, or who has failed to see the relevance of physical anthropology to anatomy, becomes less alert to other sources of biological insight, and is tempted to depreciate other knowledges (as well as other biological hypotheses) that do not fit his or her favorite viewpoint. The same may be said of the philosopher who is unaware of biological, psychological, anthropological, and political data as he or she works toward conclusions.

A sixth type of desecularization occurs, even though indirectly, when a particular secularity or value system is hostile to some element of the secularization process. Marx-Leninist secularity, for instance, insofar as it denies human freedom with its historical determinism, tends to inhibit human inventiveness in responsibly directing the secularization process and tends to twist other knowledges into subordination to an imperial determinist economics. This can lead to a seventh type of desecularization wherein a worldview is elaborated that is considered to be the only view that is tenable and, therefore, one that demands absolute allegiance—a typical ideological ending for any type of determinism. Thus, the Marxist vision of a classless society is characterized by a messianism that chokes off plural approaches to the betterment of society. This means the checking of specialization in the supposedly greater interest of integration.

Lastly, the balance and wholesomeness of secularization can be upset when the technological is allowed to determine what the theoretical may become. Only those ideas and skills are advanced, or even allowed to exist, that serve an immediate, pragmatic purpose: the artistic must be economic, the historical must be usable for propaganda, physics must be contributory to the military. At the other extreme, the balance of secularization is upset when the theoretical is left unchecked by the technological and the practical, when potentially destructive ideas are not made to answer for their practical consequences. Thus, utopian schemes that are based on unverified principles, such as the use of violence to attain just aims, would be desecularization.

What has been said about an imbalance or a fragmentation of knowledges in desecularization seems equally true concerning various skills. For skills follow from the knowledges and are equally capable of undergoing diviseness or unity, imbalance or balance. When the military skill is allowed to dominate the political, a strangulating dictatorship sets in. When business skill dictates to the artistic, then advertising replaces poetry. If sporting skill engrosses a person's attention, then theoretical skills appear more and more drab and the person's future shrinks to the present moment. Balance between skills evidently is the sign of secularization; imbalance is the mark of desecularization. For imbalance, or fragmentation, always closes off one or more of the secularization elements from its specialization: this, in turn, makes the integrative socialization process less and less successful since some elements are missing and since consequent frustration mounts in the communities serving specialized knowledges, arts, or skills. From the strife and community divisiveness comes a fracturing of the worldview and a growing lack of confidence in one's secularity. The crumbling of the worldview makes creative myth less believable and encourages ideologists whose use of power stifles the pluralism and the creativity necessary for good secularization. Human beings are forced back to primitive common-sense experience alone in their attempt to grasp the mystery of life. Wisdom is on the wane. Consequently, this picture of the dangers (even terror) of desecularization can sharpen our appreciation of convergent secularization.

Perhaps, out of this negative analysis, a tentative definition of secularization can be advanced: Secularization is the dynamic, balanced dialectic of all human knowledges and skills as they build toward individual and communal wisdom in the free, prudent, everyday decisions of men and women, according to a shared plurality of *Weltanschauungen* and their consequent secularities. Thus, desecularization is a failure of secularization, a fragmentation of, or a reduction of, secularization's "wholing" process. It is induced by strategic misunderstanding or by free decision to depreciate other knowledges-arts-skills. It becomes, first, a slow downward drift of culture, then, a gradual disintegration of civilization, and, finally, a thoroughly evil debacle. Desecularization turns the university into an arena of conflict when its community should be an agent of both wholesomeness and healing. The terrible irony here is that the university community is the best equipped group in society to warn against desecularization.

Christian Secularization and Christian Secularity—Again, Anomalies?

It jars the feelings of not a few Christians to hear the terms "Christian secularization" and "Christian secularity." Christian sensibilities have been tuned to another frequency because secularists have usurped the wavelength of these terms and Christian oratory has unwittingly broadcast secularist propaganda. The result is confusion in the mind of the average Christian who works six days a week promoting secularization in his or her specialization and then, on Sunday, hears the horrors of secularization and of secularity (love of the world). Like the little girl in the nursery rhyme, the average Christian is told: Yes, you may go swimming, but don't go near the water. Fortunately, when the translated works of Teilhard de Chardin became widely available in the 1960s, they offered another attractive alternative to the Christian, a much more real and wholesome one.

This book is an attempt to describe Christian secularization and Christian secularity within the Christian university. These processes, we have found, issue from the Christian *Weltanschauung* that has been received from tradition; but they are guided by the goal of exploring the central revealed mystery of the risen Christ's presence in the world process. Thus, Christian secularization is the use of all the knowledges-arts-skills to explore the ultimate meaning of mankind and of mankind's destiny by way of Christian theology. But Christian secularization is more than this, because Christian theology can only make use of these knowledges-arts-skills by the guidance of a Christian philosophy that is deeply in touch with them and their latest deliverances. The wisdom of Christian theology must be completed by the wisdom of Christian philosophy; faith and reason must develop each other. Yet, even this is not enough for Christian secularization, for it must also include a luring Christian vision of what the future can be. This vision looms out of and goes beyond the cooperating Christian theology and Christian philosophy insofar as it employs all the knowledges-arts-skills to glimpse the future potential of the Christian people as they become more aware of their risen Christ in the middle of their secularized lives. Finally, Christian secularization is the living of this vision in the Christian's everyday decisions.

Once this Christian secularization is grasped and found living in one's work, one's leisure, one's community relations, and one's future hopes, then the Christian feels that this is God's world, that this Lord knows where the world is going, that Yahweh is, in fact, directing and taking joy in its expansion, and that the individual Christian has a unique contribution to make to the world. Thus, Christian secularity takes shape within the person, within his or her work, and within his or her community—a Christian secularity briefly described a few pages earlier. It is a fundamental Christian secularity specified by the Christian's life experience as a French miner, an English Benedictine, a German farmer, a Hong Kong housewife, an American clothes designer, an Argentine secretary. It is a life of dedication to the world in its needs, hopes, fears, and loves; it is a life totally permeated with faith in the continuing presence of the risen Christ in each of life's events—a presence that lends its supreme value to everything by enhancing, rather than depreciating, the intrinsic value and dignity of each thing and each person.

In other words, Christian secularity and Christian secularization, taken together, are, at this moment, the total life of the Christian university. For the Christian university, they are the redemption process by which Christ is restoring wholesomeness to men and women and saving them from the fragmentation and diminishments of desecularization. To modify Augustine's phrasing, Christian secularity and Christian secularization are the "wholing" City of God within the City of Man that has been fragmented by desecularization.

The wholesomeness of Christian secularity and Christian secularization will be explored in more detail in its following six aspects: the academic, the liturgical, the decisional, the vocational, the religious, and the Christic.

11 The Pursuit of Wholeness: Balanced Specialization for Life

How can the undergraduate student, even the graduate student, possibly enjoy the wholeness or integration of the secularization process? Neither student has experienced enough of life to feel his or her provisional integrations deeply challenged by success and failure, by birth and death, by love and hate. Neither has had sucficient time to establish a solid integration within his or her speciality, much less a broader integration with other disciplines. What is more, such a synthesis demands close living with professors and others who have suffered the life-integrations that are essential to the secularization process and who, thus, can wisely guide students.

A quick response can be given to these objections. First, in a strongly academic college, the undergraduate will find a program that has been structured by experts precisely to enable the student to achieve a provisional integration if he or she is willing to work for it. The undergraduate's major study, the core curriculum of liberal studies, and the suggested electives give the average student excellent resources for discovering a wholesome way of living for the present and the future. Secondly, the gradaute student will pursue a specialized discipline in the context of some interdisciplinary studies, either by himself or herself (e.g., out of the needs of his or her thesis or other papers) or with professors from various disciplines in a university study of, for example, urban neighborhood improvement or colossal company farming. The interdisciplinary studies will help the graduate student to both develop an overall context for his or her specialized study and form his or her own provisional synthesis of the various knowledges-arts-skills for decisions in his or her own life.

This highly condensed response (later to be expanded) should be supplemented by the observation that no student, undergraduate or graduate, will form any integration of merit without the convergence of authority from his or her family, civic community, church, and university. The student has to start with a received authoritative integration (a wisdom) if he or she is later to develop one of his or her own. In other words, unless a tradition warranted by these four agents enters his or her life, the student is a primitive and will likely remain one. For the family establishes in a person's life (from toilet training to the sophistications of gestures of gratitude) a particular myth, a *Weltanschauung*, that explains the person's total world of self, other persons, school, sports, church, jobs, sorrows, and joys. This "englobing" explanation may be called Democratism, Marxism, Christianity, the spirit of Ireland, Black living. Whatever it is called, however, it is supported by society and sometimes even by one's government. Later, this myth is challenged by one's religion, through some faith-mystery that may have originally caused the myth to come into existence as its explanation. Finally, the university explores both the myth and the mystery by way of the secularization process—not simply to criticize them, but also to understand them and, at times, to corroborate them. Because these four convergent authorities closely cooperate in their support of the student's received *Weltanschauung* and accepted faith-mystery, any weakening of one authority is quickly felt by the others. Indeed, the university itself is enfeebled because these authorities are its constituencies.

Thus, it would seem that these supportive authorities must converge in the student if he or she is to begin well the pursuit of wholesomeness. Furthermore, this wholesomeness happens to be wisdom operating at three levels in the student, for, in the undergraduate program, the core curriculum of liberal studies and the electives are aimed at developing incipient speculative wisdom, the major study is more diected toward practical wisdom, and the resultant hunger for justice is focused on prudential, day-to-day decisions for self and for others. Because this triple process for wholesome living, that is, for fully secularized life, is fundamentally made up of myth and mystery, it would be convenient to clarify exactly what is meant by these terms.

Secularization Begins with Myth and Ends in Mystery

Let us grant that, within each person and within each specialized community, there operate, under all the knowledges-skills-arts, the two basic drives of specialization and integration toward individual and communal wisdom. One is still faced with a problem: How do these drives arrive at the wholeness of wisdom? Both the concentrated effort needed to reach the depths of specialization and the amazing complexity of any integration of knowledges-arts-skills would seem to block the journey to wholesome wisdom. Only a small answer can be given, at first, to this massive difficulty: when knowledges-arts-skills are carefully situated within a person's worldview or *Weltanschauung*, then, under its light, wisdom can begin to grow. This worldview arises when a person meets, by way of his or her common-sense experience, the mystery of the world. A poem expresses this mysterious world in the form of a myth and, then, builds within a person basic attitudes in accord with this myth. Let us now take each element of this brief response and expand it in order to see the meaning of myth and mystery for the secularization process and, hence, for the undergraduate and graduate students undergoing this process.

At the base of all value systems and of every scientific knowledge or skill is the nourishing ground of everyday, common-sense knowing. A person cannot value what he or she does not experience as somehow existent; and a person's scientific knowledge or skill cannot be understood or applied unless it is within common-sense knowing. Now, what a person most often and deeply meets in common-sense knowing is, ironically, mystery. In this case, mystery means a reality whose rich existence can be known by men and women, but can only be inadequately conceptualized into neat, maneuverable ideas. It might be the natural mystery of the atom, which is hardly encompassed by the two conceptual theories of wave and quantum—despite their marvelous intricacy that is based on vast surveys of empirical evidence. Again, it might be the natural mystery of one's wife or child or business acquaintance; years of reflective experience may yield more and more conceptual understanding but also many more new areas of ignorance concerning this person. In fact, the surest sign of deepening friendship is deepening appreciation of the other's mystery, of the impossibility of ever capturing the other's fullness in any set of intricate concepts. And yet, this fullness is recognized and somehow negatively known because the concepts, though they partially reveal the mystery, sharply draw the boundaries beyond which the mystery stretches on into the distance out of reach of the concepts. Mystery is everywhere—in embryonic growth, in weather changes, in the unlikely convergence of events, in religious experience, in the speed and constituents of light.

Nevertheless, men and women try to speak, in poetry, song, drama, and novel, this mysterious knowing of mystery that cannot yet be put in conceptual understanding. Men and women hint, through concepts, at this "more." They never give up their quest to better define "the more." In fact, before the Greeks entered intellectual history, men and women wrote ever more complicated myths in their attempts to explain the mystery of life, its beginnings, its present hopes, and its future. The myth is not some pretty fabrication of an individual's or a community's poetic fancy untrammeled by the harsh facts of life. Quite the opposite; myth is the community's very serious attempt to express in conceptual language its knowing of life's deepest moments. This is often a highly sophisticated try at describing an awesome experience of existential fact. The Book of Job is a prime example of such an attempt. Centuries after the Book of Job was written, Thomas Aquinas attempted to conceptualize Job's experience of evil in the face of a supposedly provident and merciful God according to scientific, rather than solely humanistic, terms. In other words, because of the previous mythic formulations of Job and of patristic commentaries on Job, Aquinas was able to use the highly specialized, or scientific, conceptual theologies of Augustine and of Aristotle in order to add to the humanistic insight of Job's myth an integrative scientific theory about God's providence and evil. For the Greeks, without denying the validity of myth (Plato was one of the most adept myth-makers), had meanwhile developed a new type of thinking in the evolution of Euclidean geometry, Archimedean physics, Ptolemaic astronomy, Socratic ethics, and Artistotelian nature-philosophy and logic. Out of their everyday, common-sense experience and out of myths, the Greeks developed the ability to derive concepts that gave causal explanations of their experience. These concepts were capable of being universalized beyond any particular place or time and then interrelated to form an explanatory network for plant growth, for human decision, for heavenly bodies, for governments, for drama, and even for the total universe.

Such specialization and integration, such secularization, did not mean the death of either everyday, common-sense knowledge or myth, which is the heightened expression of common-sense knowledge. In fact, among the Greeks, drama and poetry reached new heights as integral parts of the secularization process, for secularization is no more meant to supplant myth and common-sense knowledge than it is supposed to dissolve the mystery of reality that myth and common-sense knowledge describe. Instead, secularization supplements myth with the added dimension of specialization; the Book of Job, for example, was supplemented with Aquinas' scientific discussions. Thus, secularization offers a slightly better appreciation of the mystery of God's providence through Aquinas' efforts; or, to suggest another example, it offers a slightly better appreciation of the mystery of person through psychology when the psychology is employed, along with poetry and everyday experience, to explain friendship. Neither the mythic nor the scientific envelop the totality of a mystery, nor does either one, by itself, penetrate to the depths of a mystery. Nor do mythic, scientific, and everyday knowledges, taken together, accomplish this. Rather, just as myth offers additional understandings to the everyday experience of mystery, so does scientific knowledge advance a new understanding of mystery, clarify the myth, and, thus, reinforce human awareness of the factual existence of this mystery. As a matter of fact, secularization can be described as a knowledge process that, by using myth to focus on the reality of a mystery by way of everyday knowing, employs specialized knowledges and skills to render mystery more understandable, more appreciated, more acceptable, more deeply integrated within the community's common-sense experience, and, ironically, more mysterious, i.e., more deeply grasped as that which escapes total grasping.

But a further question surfaces: how does all this explain the rise of that worldview, or *Weltanschauung*, that is necessary for developing a wisdom? First, long before phenomenologists popularized the phrase "man-in-the-world" to signify that persons constitute the world and that the total world constitutes persons, men and women lived out this truth, whether the individual was Homer observing the doings of Olympus, or Lucretius watching the world and men and women take shape out of atoms, or Paracelsus expecting to find the macrocosm in the human microcosm. A person simply cannot long reflect about life without explaining the world's and his or her own beginning and without forecasting the future of each (often in terms of an indissoluble eternal marriage). In other words, men and women, of their nature, must discover or invent for themselves a worldview; nothing less than this will content them.

Second, men and women use any knowledge at hand to help them frame and paint their worldview. When men and women had only common-sense knowledge, they probably used that. But as soon as they developed mythic knowledge, they certainly used this in addition to common-sense knowledge—as any history of literature will demonstrate. After the covenant experience of the Hebrews, mankind had a revealed knowledge of the universe; after the Greeks, mankind began to have a scientific knowledge of the universe. In the case of Augustine of Hippo, one witnesses the focusing of all four knowledges upon the world's history in the magnificent *City of God*, and it can be said that the world has never been the same since. Augustine's accomplishment made him the father of medieval life, to say nothing of medieval thought. All the geniuses of the succeeding centuries could not help partially modeling themselves on him, whether it was Aquinas or Descartes or Hegel or Herbert Spencer or Whitehead or Toynbee or Weber or Freud or Darwin or Marx. Thus, any knowledge, since it is present in "man-in-the-world" and expresses itself most deeply in the twin drives toward specialization and socialization, inevitably leads to a worldview. The deeper one delves into reality through specialization, the greater is the need and drive to situate this new knowledge in a worldview through socializing integration and myth.

The everyday living of common-sense knowing demands that our work and our knowledge make some integrated, total sense.

There is a third reason why a worldview naturally evolves within human consciousness. Because human beings possess inventive freedom, men and women are always evaluating themselves, their companions, their present work, their past decisions, their future hopes. Men and women cannot escape this without abdicating their adulthood. But if persons are to compare their companions with themselves, their past and their present and future, their present work with other possibilities, then they must develop a system of values. But how should one do this well without eventually seeing these matters in the context of the whole universe? One of the reasons for the rapid and enthusiastic spread of Teilhard de Chardin's ideas is that he has offered a worldview molded out of a scientific matrix and painted in stylish, mythic colors—a worldview that gave meaning and value to the lives of both the scientist and the average person on the street. In a highly specialized world, the seeming fragmentation of reality and of self needs the healing wholesomeness of a worldview. Otherwise, the various functions of a person's life appear to be disconnected, not building to a recognizable future, distracting and distraught rather than full of intent. In other words, one's life is seen as worthless and directionless.

For these three reasons, then, a worldview naturally rises in every person's consciousness out of the everyday need to evaluate himself or herself and his or her actions. The worldview will be expressed in the various knowledges that he or she has at hand: revealed, common-sense, mythic, and scientific. The underlying intent of a person's nature toward specialization and socialization will drive him or her toward this valued worldview that, if it is lived out in prudent decisions, will generate a wisdom. Prudence, the ability to converge one's knowledges, values, feelings, and worldview into a practical decision benefitting self and community, is the last development on the path to wisdom. Professors who are so impractical that they cannot buy groceries at the local supermarket and zealots who cannot pursue their world vision without doing people to death through boredom, if not through bloodshed, are notoriously imprudent people, despite their highly intelligent worldviews. But these are examples of a very practical, lower level of prudence that has been taken for granted at this time. In this discussion, the concern is with a higher level of prudence that, of course, filters down to the lower level— sometimes at high intensity. This higher level of prudence is the level at which knowledges and skills and values may not always be kept balanced and in which, consequently, desecularization action can take place. For the secularization process, because of its complexity, requires the most balanced type of judgments and decisions if it is to produce good results. Thus, the worldview, or *Weltanschauung*, received simultaneously from one's parents, neighborhood, church, education, and even government is the myth with which one begins life. This "sacred canopy," to borrow Peter Berger's term, makes ultimate sense of life—until events that are seemingly irreconcilable with it happen. A person might then either turn to the mystery of his or her faith in God or bury these events deep into his or her unconscious. Or a person might start to weave another sacred canopy, if the first seems ripped beyond repair, by allowing the various knowledges-arts-skills free play within his or her life. Whichever strategy a person uses, he or she will never outgrow myth and mystery and will never stop using other knowledges to clarify both myth and mystery as he or she continues to move from day to day by means of common-sense knowledge of reality. In addition, as a person's worldview changes, so too, does the secularity and the secularization process within the worldview. For secularity reaches beyond knowledges and goes more deeply into myth and mystery; we do love and value more of reality than we conceptually judge to know. This is precisely the horror of secularism, the secularity that deliberately cuts men and women off from myth and mystery in the name of human reason.

If myth, then, is the start of secularization and of secularity, if mystery is their goal, and if secularization is constantly moving between myth and mystery to clarify them and to render them more beautiful, then men and women never leave these four principles of their life, nor can they live long without all four of them. Secularization, indeed, both reveals the meaning of life and offers the means to live as long as the mythic worldview is always "englobing" it; secularity, as long as it keeps in touch with mystery, gives hope and value to life's events. Finally, the forward thrust of secularization in the individual person and in his or her specialized communities requires constant service of the world's needs. For secularization offers the tools for solving the world's problems; and secularity, enlivened with faith-mystery, provides the love to ply these tools generously and loyally. With this understanding of how myth, mystery, secularity, and secularization generate the wholesomeness of wisdom, we are prepared to consider how the undergraduate pursues wisdom.

The Undergraduate Pursues a Provisional Wisdom in the Core Curriculum

In the first response to objections against the possibility of an undergraduate wisdom, it was noted that the structure of the undergraduate program made such wisdom possible because the core curriculum offered a contextual integration for the various knowledges-arts-skills. This integration, then, could root and concentrate the student's major area of study as well as help to organize his or her elective studies. The second response indicated that this program would not work unless it was supported by the four authorities of parents, society, church, and educational system and unless it used their worldview and their faith in mystery. Let us consider, one by one, the core curriculum, the major study, and the range of electives, and let us note their relationships to myth and mystery, to secularization and secularity.

Strong pressures from both faculty and students never cease trying to compress or to dismantle the core curriculum of liberal studies. Faculty members plead that their specialist accrediting societies (chemistry, engineering, premedical) are demanding more undergraduate hours to qualify students for graduate school and that the reputations of the university and of the particular department are at stake. They also urge that students should be allowed to freely pursue their major study with efficiency and without distraction. Such faculty members seem unafraid of narrowing the student's academic consciousness to one discipline, of breaking off his or her relationships with other knowledges, and, thus, of fragmenting individuals and society into compartmentalized, special-interest groups. They apparently have no fear that such a student might be bound by narrow routines and might live them without inventiveness and without the information to make informed decisions about affairs that are inside the discipline, as well as those that are outside the discipline. This diminishment of man and woman does not make certain faculty members hesitate in their pleading.

On the other hand, not a few students who transfer from junior colleges resent the "burden" of the core curriculum and threaten to go elsewhere so that they can finish, with "less sweat," in four years. They seem unaware that they are denying themselves a humanistic basis for their whole future life. They are abetted by some administrators who are willing to consider remedial work sufficient for college credit and to cheapen the undergraduate degree. A second group of students has only one goal in mind—a marketable knowledge or skill. Everything else comes close to being a waste of time. This total pragmatism assures them of narrow interests, small hopes, little inventiveness, relatively poor parenting for their children, and less ability to adapt when their functional skill becomes obsolete. In defeating the aims of the collegiate program, these pragmatic conservatives unwittingly inaugurate a Marxist theory of education that is centered on work as the supreme value of life.

These pressures against the core curriculum offer, ironically, the best reasons for keeping and strengthening it. The specialization of one's major study needs a rich integrative context in which to deepen its roots, draw up its nourishment, and prepare itself to bear fruit. If this integrative context is to be rich, however, the student must be deeply aware of the myth that animates his or her efforts, must learn to contemplatively integrate all relevant knowledges with all his or her powers, and, then, focus this synthesis upon mystery. This is the way of secularization to wisdom. In this context, American haste is quite inefficient, for the student needs much time to become aware of all his or her powers, of all the strata of reality that are revealed by these powers, of the liberty that is educed by good use of these powers with their resultant knowledges-arts-skills, and of all the values (especially justice) that are discovered in this liberty. Let us now consider how these four awarenesses, which constitute the liberally educated person, are achieved through the core curriculum.

If one surveys the disciplines that make up the core curriculum, one discovers that a student who is exposed to them can become aware of all his or her major powers and, thus, of his or her whole being, which underlies the interlocking cooperation of these various powers. In studying language and literature, for example, the student's imagination is stimulated and his or her feelings are analyzed for their powerful symbolization of the meanings and values that are central to his or her life. In studying history, the same student's individualistic memory, though it was once tied down to a particular neighborhood or twenty-year time span, is vertically stretched with new social relationships and horizontally stretched with old cultural traditions. Exposure to the study of theology enables the student to test faith experience, which is going beyond reason yet is partially living off reason; it also paints for the student a perspective on the ultimate, which opens up the meanings of both beatitude and play. When the undergraduate student tries to philosophize, he or she experientially knows what reflective reason is, how philosophy struggles to explore and integrate knowledges, and what goes into an integrative vision of the world. In studying the sciences, physical and social, the student does inquisitive, hypothetical thinking, under strict laws of evidence, to achieve inventive insights. In studying mathematics, the student experiences the pure joy of pure reason as he or she works with a god-like freedom in, and yet beyond, the imagination. A study of the arts gives the student the opportunity to embody his or her emotions in thoughtful, imaginative form so that his or her innermost life can be exteriorized, and he or she, as well as others, might see or hear or feel it. Communication arts thrill the student with the experience of seeing his or her own ideas and feelings take place in others. What human cognitional powers are left to be tested for validity, stretched for growth, and integrated for higher performance?

The student's awareness of all his or her powers cannot occur unless each power is touching a different stratum of reality in his or her own being and, at the same time, in those other outside beings that constitute his or her situation. In other words, the student's awareness of all his or her powers occurs only if each power is filled with experience of something other than the student. When the student unifies his or her powers, he or she is also unifying their deliverances; the student is in touch not only with all the levels of his or her own being, but also with all the levels of the situation. In other words, the student is truly informed about himself or herself *and* the situation. If other persons are present in this situation, then the student's self-awareness, at many levels of his or her being, makes him or her reciprocally aware of all these levels in the others. The sense of his or her own wholeness enables the student to understand the other's wholeness, dignity, and weaknesses. Sensitivity to the resonance of another person has become more "knowledgeful" and even more skillful. The fewer powers the student cultivates, the less he or she recognizes in the situation and in himself or herself.

When the student's consciousness has been thus differentiated, and yet not hermetically compartmentalized, he or she has become aware of a scientific consciousness that is distinct from his or her mythic consciousness (the *Weltanschauung* received from his or her four converging authorities). The student now knows that he or she is undergoing secularization. There will be wondering about his or her religious experience of mystery; the Christian, for example, will probe his or her experience of the risen Christ in sacrament, Scripture, and fellow-persons. Thus occurs the predictable faith-crisis of the collegian. If the student's faith-crisis resolves into a still deeper faith-penetration into divine mystery, then he or she sees his or her *Weltanschauung* in a new way. This spurs the student to reconsider his or her specialized knowledges and their integration. Meanwhile, at the level of common-sense knowledge, where the student must make his or her hour-to-hour decisions, there is a new sensitivity to the world, to his or her secularity, and to the mystery of God that was first grasped at this level.

Because of this four-cornered dialectic of knowledges, the student learns to value common-sense knowledge the more he or she realizes how myth and all the specialized knowledges are rooted in it and must finally be validated within it. Although all the other knowledges came into existence because of the limitations of common-sense knowledge, their strength is still drawn from common-sense knowledge. So, the truly educated person is not tempted to be a snob when confronting the man or woman who did not have the same educational opportunities. The educated person knows that the person who has had fewer educational opportunities has compensations of shrewdness and is far from ignorant. Moreover, this four-cornered dialectic makes possible another dialectic, namely, "contemplation in action" as the student moves from myth, through the secularization process, to mystery, and then back again into common-sense knowledge so that he or she can make wise, strong decisions. This practical contemplation in action will be further refined when the speculative contemplative integration of the core curriculum of liberal arts is challenged and deepened by the more practical major study in a specialized knowledge-skill-art.

Besides the awareness of all a person's powers and the consequent awareness of all the strata of reality in the situation, the core curriculum can engender a third awareness—the forsaking of adolescent freedom for adult liberty. Freedom is, as we recall, simply the child's ability to choose freely among a "cafeteria" of options without distinguishing whether they are good or bad, better or worse, helpful or destructive for the chooser and for his or her community. Liberty, on the other hand, is the adult ability to choose the better for self and for others because of a disciplined willingness to suffer for the good and the true. Thus, this awareness involves a fuller responsibility for self and the world; this is the reason such an education is called liberal.

If one looks to the aims of counseling, one can quickly see why the core curriculum contributes well to this third awareness. The counselor meets a client, for example, who is convinced that she is trapped into accepting a job as a waitress. The counselor's first step is to open up other options for the client; the counselor notes that she can type, is quick enough to learn shorthand, and has pleasant manners. Why not think of being a secretary or a receptionist or a filing clerk, he suggests. The counselor next encourages her to try one or another option. When she decides to be a filing clerk, the counselor then helps her follow out her decision by suggesting strategies for doing her job better and better. Her freedom became operative when her options were multiplied; her liberty rose within her when she followed through on her decision.

A similar process takes place within the liberal education of a core curriculum. The more knowledges-arts-skills a student possesses, the more ways he or she can converge on a situation to see its many strata and to note the need for caution in understanding and evaluating this situation. The more knowledges-arts-skills the student has, the more options he or she sees for dealing with the situation, the richer is his or her integration for a better decision, and the wider is his or her freedom. If

245

the student's discipline of virtues commensurately increases, then his or her liberty to pursue the better options also increases.

Again, the more knowledges-arts-skill the student uses, the more communities he or she can enter as a true member and not just as a visiting outsider, and the more entertaining he or she is for himself or herself and for others. Finally, the more knowledges-arts-skills the student operates, the more expansively he or she is creating himself or herself; the more he or she has to give to his or her various communities, the richer history he or she leaves to posterity, and the more liberty he or she enjoys. Thus, the student's liberty can naturally issue in the other-centeredness of love and service, for the liberally educated person's hunger for justice for all people is actually the desire to share with others the riches and joys that he or she has experienced from his or her liberal studies. The old Latin saying, *bonum est diffusivum sui,* can be personalized to "the good person feels a need to share his or her goods." So, the core curriculum may well induce a fourth level of awareness—that of justice. It is noteworthy that each of these four awarenesses aims, respectively, at wholeness of person, of situation, of liberty, and of justice. These four awarenesses, of course, interpenetrate and mutually modify each other to form a wholeness of cognitional awareness.

In addition to these four awarenesses at the cognitional level, the core curriculum also aims to help the student achieve a balanced, or wholesome, secularity. It "wholesomely" suggests (that is, it suggests in an organized manner) the importance of a wholesome secularity for one's life. Because of its wide range of specialized knowledges-arts-skills, the core curriculum shows a wide variety of diverse secularities. Both the core curriculum and the student also have time (no hurry, but *leisure*) to compare these secularities for their advantages and disadvantages. Furthermore, by contrast with the chaos of pure spontaneity, the core curriculum indicates the need for a system of values if one wants an orderly life that is lived with liberty and meaning, that is to say, if one prefers a civilized and cultured life for self and for others.

To be more definite, note that history (also anthropology) not only narrates how humans have lived by various secularities and *Weltanschauugen,* but also demonstrates how myth instills a sense of traditional value that must constantly be reinterpreted as people and times change. In fact, the history of cultures dramatizes how the values that are drawn from myth enter into and stimulate the secularization process as that process, first, explores the mysteries of life and, then, returns to reexamine the myth in terms of common-sense knowledge. Meanwhile, the study of literature and of language uncovers for the student expressions of humanity's highest values in the mythic language of poetry, drama, novel, and essay. The expressive arts and their communication skills help the student appreciate how human beings incarnate their cherished values in artistic forms and techniques in order to make these high hopes alluring and to make their opposite disvalues repulsive. All the values of these disciplines are very much humanity-centered. For example, the physical sciences focus in on the autonomies of the mineral, plant, and animal kingdoms by revealing the inner structures of these beings. Recognition of these inner values humanizes persons as they respectfully protect and enhance minerals, plants, and animals, and as they learn to feel grateful for the intriguing beauty of minerals, plants, and animals.

The social sciences, although they are not of themselves equipped to evaluate, display instances of how human beings have lived their professed values, or secularities, and of how human beings have built "institutions" such as museums, etiquette, assembly lines, business concerns, governments, and sports in order to structure society according to particular secularities. In fact, psychologist A. H. Maslow has joined with sociolgist Peter Berger and historian Arnold Toynbee to show how similar are the processive stages of building and dismantling values within both the human personality and society. But it is philosophy that specifically tests secularities for both validity in experience and inner contradiction of system. Philosophy is most interested in those ultimate values that are a person's powers and in the accomplishments of these powers, namely, the institutions of society. For this reason, philosophy explores the works of human beings: science, art, skills, technological expertise, the making of history. It weighs the influence of a person's myths as the person intelligently investigates the mysteries of life; and it wonders about the ingredients of human wholesomeness. Lastly, in studying theology, the student wonders at mystery itself, God, the source of all other mysteries, the supreme value of the believer. As the student studies theology, it slowly dawns on his or her consciousness that the two great commandments—love of God and love of neighbor—coalesce in Christ's saying: "Whatever you do to the least of these, you do to me." Thereupon the student has found the most intimate secret of life and of the universe, and wonders whether or not he or she can live in its presence.

Thus, the core-curriculum studies help a person focus his or her basic questions: What is life all about? Where is life going—my career, my family's future, my nation's destiny? Can we control the direction of our lives? If not, is life worth living? The core curriculum is dangerous because it forces the student to face the questions that so many men and women spend most of their lives dodging. Unfortunately, those who most need the core curiculum of liberal studies most resent it—and this includes the faculty.

How the Undergraduate's Major Study and Elective Courses Make Him or Her Whole

If these questions are answered positively, the student is confronted with a further question: How can I best contribute to my own happiness and to that of others? What can I do for myself and for the world that has been given to me? In this question, one recognizes the importance of the major study, or specialization, of the student. But first, to see how the core curriculum and the major study correlate, it is helpful to note their complementary differences.

In the core curriculum, the student contemplates the human person in his or her transcendent value (his or her dynamic powers and potential for good); the major study, on the other hand, considers the human person as chemist, nurse, engineer, lawyer, artist—the doer—in his or her utilitarian, or functional, value as both a helper of others and a satisfier of their needs. Thus, the core is more concerned with the absolutes of life, a person's inner stability, integrative wisdom; the major study centers on the relativities of life, a person's adaptability to his or her environs, a person's specialized knowledge-skill-art. Yet, like the core curriculum, the major study works out of a myth (e.g., the mystique of the medical profession, the *élan* of the artistic community, or the hardheaded and competent practicality of the engineering field) through a specialized knowledge-art-skill toward a particular mystery of life (for the doctor, it is the mysterious wholesomeness of health and the hell of disease; for the artist, it is the mysterious completion of a symphony or a sculpture or a dance theme and the frustration of fragmentation; for the engineer, it is the mysterious power of machine, of dam, of nuclear reactor and the hollowness of failure). In both failure and success, the harsh discipline of constantly reinterpreting the truth of one's specialized knowledge-art-skill is the secularization process as it moves into mystery and, then, flows back to myth and common-sense knowledge in order to regain the strength of value and of concrete experience that is necessary for one more chastened exploration of mystery. Thus, the core curriculum and the major study, with their complementary differences and their similar four-cornered dialectic inside secularization, are partners in the integration and specialization of the student.

This becomes clearer if one notes three basic reasons for pursuing a major study during the undergraduate years. First, in introducing the student to an in-depth study of one precise area of knowledge or art or skill, the major study displays the vastness of this supposedly highly specialized area (viz., the number of subareas within physics or biology). By extrapolation, the student gets some hint of how much more vast would be the area occupied by all the specialized knowledges-arts-skills if they were taken together. The result can be a humbling realism about the extent of any one person's knowledge, about the difficulties of holding on to a truth through its constant reinterpretation in terms of new data-hypotheses-problems, and about the mystery into which rationalization enters, only to discover new dimensions of its ignorance (e.g., astronomy exploring the heavens; cosmology searching out their beginnings). In attempting to master the method of clinical psychology, for example, the student first discovers the delicacy that is needed to estimate truth against the hypothesis and against the instrumentation that is employed and then finds the implications of other sciences, such as neurology, psychiatry, optics, and social anthropology, within his or her experiment. As a result, while grappling with the mystery of the human personality, the student simultaneously views the beauty of rationalization and its limping limitations.

Out of this experience comes a second reason for following out a major study—specialization done in depth dramatizes the need for integration, or wholesomeness. The student of social psychology who is working within an inner-city community finds his or her in-depth study leading him or her into the allied fields of family sociology, racial anthropology, pharmacology, political science, and theory of urban revolution. Unless one attempts some integration, the specialization becomes blurred and its findings become highly questionable. To achieve a whole picture, evidence must be converged from allied sciences.

Implicit in this second reason for following out a major study is the third—the major study roots a student into a community of fellow specialists and then, giving him or her the skill to serve other communities, enables him or her to also take root in these other communities. Thus, the specialist can be simply honing a skill to be marketed to the highest bidder, but he or she can also be using his or her competence for the support of a family, for alleviating misery and bringing joy to other families, and for advancing the competence of his or her specialist community. Such integration heals the fragmented society precisely through a specialization done in a disciplined and generous manner. In this integration, one views the tight cooperation between the specialization of the major study and the integration of the core curriculum of liberal studies.

But then, how do the elective courses of the undergraduate program fit into this close unity between core curriculum and major study? Since the electives are totally up to the choice of the student and since students are notorious for not seeking sufficient academic counseling, what is the rationale for electives? This question is vital at a time when the major studies are becoming more and more eloquent about their need for more courses to render the specialized student competent enough for graduate work. There are good reasons for saying that protection of electives from the marauding of specialist and core-curriculum advocates is a prime responsibility of faculty and administration. Elective courses, for example, balance the utilitarianism of the major study and the more structured experience of the core curriculum. Electives are, therefore, the third side of the wholeness that is a liberal education.

One reason for having elective courses in the undergraduate program is to give the student opportunity to take responsibility for his or her own intellectual growth, for academic wholesomeness. How else does one instill the principle that adult education is a lifelong work beginning in college, not ending there? Secondly, in addition to fostering initiative, elective courses stimulate curiosity at a new level of discipline and encourage inventiveness as they explore new fields, as they discover—perhaps unexpectedly—an underlying unity of experience with their major and some core-curriculum studies (e.g., a medical student is alerted to psychosomatic medicine by his anthropology course), as they find a new spontaneity in learning which is outside both the programmed routines of the major study and the core curriculum (e.g., in sculpting clay figurines during a plastic arts class). In all this, is not the student moving from freedom to adult liberty? Is it not possible that the insights and fun found in elective courses may seep into the major study and the core curriclum to give education a brighter coloring? Would this possibly be the play of contemplation and the joy of humane living?

A student may find among his or her elective courses one that makes him or her enthusiastic for the first time in his or her educational life. Could this be the student's true interest, one that personalizes his or her search for meaning and reveals his or her basic vocation? At least this course may reinforce the student's true interest and make his or her required core-curriculum studies less routine. But perhaps the strongest reason for elective courses is that the student can achieve enrichment according to his or her own unique needs—something that no program can promise, with much consistency, unless it includes elective courses. Electives can be dovetailed into the student's major or used to supplement the core curriculum in some area; but, more important, electives enrich a student precisely in areas in which he or she feels inadequate, unwholesome (e.g., in music, in the physical training of swimming, in writing poetry, in studying the history of Chicago, in learning Spanish for law practice, and in better understanding local or national politics). Electives are an attempt to assure wholesome education for and by the student. They impart to a relatively rigid program a pleasing adaptability to the student's unique needs and ambitions.

The three major elements of undergraduate education, namely, core curriculum, major study, and elective courses, are, then, aimed at building wholesomeness into the student's life. This is another way of saying that the university community would like to see the student graduate with a disciplined liberty. The student would then respect myth as the source of secularization, mystery as its goal, and common-sense living as its validation. He or she would have learned to balance specialization with integration, individual ambition with concern for the community's growth, contemplation with action, knowledge with values, present needs with future hopes, the traditional with the innovative. The student would be disciplined in the methodic approach to truth, that is, he or she would use all available knowledges-arts-skills to build an integrative context for his or her decisions so that this "wholing" process of secularization would lead him or her into wisdom. The student would be hungry for justice, for the beautiful society of wholesome people cooperating out of mutual respect and trust, and he or she would be willing to suffer for this just society. As with all ideals, this particular wisdom is impossibly perfect for now; but, without its guidance, how is it possible to justify the existence of current collegiate programs? After all, the wisdom promised to the undergraduate is only a provisional one. Although strategically it is of utmost value, still other programs will further challenge and develop it— programs such as graduate studies, family living, business life, and God's providence.

Graduate Specialization—Time for Neuroses?

Life presents us with more than one opportunity to develop neuroses, but the time of graduate study is the most fertile in aberrations. After all, it is highly artificial; the graduate student is expected to be totally preoccupied with one discipline. In addition, within that one discipline, the graduate student's major interest is to be the acquisition of a *proper method*. Content is never divorced from method, of course, yet the concentration on method tends to make the student as awkward as the aspiring ballroom dancer who had knobby knees and size 14 shoes. Then, too, the graduate student often must either postpone marriage or chance it with inadequate financing. In either case, demanding studies isolate the graduate student from his or her family and usual social rounds. Concepts and concept-juggling take up ten hours of the day; emotions become numb at times. If a term paper goes sour, the graduate student begins to have identity doubts ("maybe I'm just not cut out for history"), especially if the spouse is patiently supporting the family in anticipation of an advanced degree and a more stable financial future. The danger of losing one's perspective on life is highly probable. This is why the strong presence of myth, the constant lure of mystery, and the earthiness of common-sense knowledge are essential to the balance and wholeness of the graduate student's life and career.

Fortunately, there is a certain amount of wholeness built into the specialization process itself. If the graduate student has enjoyed a balanced undergraduate program, such as the one that has been described in this book, he or she has already acquired a wholesome perspective because he or she has experienced the "wholing" influence of the integrative core curriculum, of the specializing major study, and of the enriching elective courses. The graduate student has a provisional wisdom to warn him or her of imbalances and incipient neuroses. In addition, the specialized knowledge demands the use of other knowledges—if only to protect it from error, to check its findings, and to integrate them with other disciplines. Reality itself, once it is deeply penetrated, requires the integration of the specialized knowledge with other knowledges. How can the graduate student, as a sociologist, study the effect of the "redlining" of neighborhoods by banks and insurance companies without also studying economics, business administration of banks, political science of governmental regulation of banks, history of investment procedures, and so on.

Secondly, if the graduate student is psychologically normal, he or she naturally relieves his or her tension by practicing other skills, such as repairing household appliances, strumming the guitar, listening to music, playing tennis, taking a role in the summer theater, and so forth. Sanity, if it is anything, is wholeness; the graduate student's instinct for mental health demands wholeness of him or her.

Thirdly, the environment and community surrounding the graduate student, if it is wholesome, will draw him or her into wholesomeness by osmosis. The education that a graduate student's children receive can fill him or her with healthy wonder as well as headaches; the spouse's special interests in home furnishings or in art or in a law degree can keep widening the graduate student's narrowing perspective. The particular myth of his or her specialized knowledge-art-skill, together with the "englobing" myth of his or her own *Weltanschauung* (if he or she pays attention to them), will continually spur the graduate student's flagging energies and open wider his or her "mental" eyes. Lastly, the graduate student's faith in the mystery of God's providence can help him or her say: "This is God's world and He wants the best for us."

These three last elements contain the reasons why the graduate student began his or her pursuit of graduate study in the first place. Their values and perspective are meant to lend meaning to all that he or she does. Yet, even they are not enough if the graduate student has not yet touched the mystery of specialized truth in his or her discipline and the larger mysteries of life itself and of the divine. More than almost any other person— except, perhaps, the inhabitant of a psychiatric ward—the graduate student needs the feel of mystery to keep him or her from building a mighty empire of paper concepts or actually becoming a sack of dry concepts.

But the wholesomeness that is built into specialization (of its very nature) and into life itself is not enough. There is a *cultivated integration* that the graduate student must have. This is achieved when the graduate student works in interdisciplinary seminars with graduate students and professors from other specialized knowledges concerning a common problem, such as the educating of retarded children. It happens again when, in a more speculative atmosphere, the graduate student finds professors from diverse disciplines challenging each other's conclusions and assumptions as they work to develop a speculative integration. Perhaps the most effective spur and guide to the graduate student's integration is the living wisdom of his or her professors. Even the imperial arrogance of some of them can be a salutary lesson ("Only _____ goes to the heart of the problem" or "Who needs _____ or _____ to solve this problem?"). But if a professor has integrated his or her specialized knowledge, has recognized its dependency on other knowledges by investigating them, and has developed out of his or her speculative wisdom a wholesome lifestyle, then he or she is the graduate student's living hope and academic leader.

This last remark brings us to the second aspect of graduate school specialization—the graduate faculty itself. How does it bring wholeness out of its specialization? The greatest danger of our scientific culture and society is that it will become so specialized that specialists will be unable to significantly talk to each other. Then, when a potentially disastrous problem arises (e.g., genetic engineering, the destroyed environment, or rampant nuclear power), the integration that is needed to focus special knowledges-arts-skills will necessarily have to be forced, hasty, and inefficient. Some say that this contingency is purely imaginary. But lack of integration, or desecularization, is already causing fissures in society; the ethical dimension, for example, is frequently being left out of business, government, and scientific enterprise because, at times, ethicians cannot keep up with the mounting complexity of business, government, and science and because some businessmen, government officials, and scientists have not had the interest or time to consider the ethical dimension with sophistication. Another example of disintegration (i.e., desecularization) is the attitude that religion is the enemy of progress. The fissure occurs because many theologians have failed to integrate their faith and theology with the world of Einstein, Freud, Marx, and Darwin and because some scientists are amazingly näive not only about theology and faith, but also about philosophy of science and their own assumptions in both their work and themselves.

A third cause of failed integration are the precollege experimentations that, in the name of a particular psychological theory or sociological scheme or philosophic principle, have caused intense conflicts within children rather than helped them attain wholeness. Because the sources of these experiments had not been sufficiently integrated with other disciplines and with common-sense experience, fundamental mistakes have occurred, such as the neglect of rote in early schooling, the failure to cultivate basic reading and writing skills in the welter of new high school courses and techniques, information overload through speed-up programs precisely when the child needed leisure to contemplate, the loss of overall perspective when introducing collegiate studies such as philosophy to unready high-school students. The fourth cause of desecularization is the cultural deprivation sponsored by the American television and movie industries when they encourage ignorance by generally providing only one type of entertainment, such as, for example, a predominance of rock music, an overload of situation comedy and police tragedy, wide sports coverage in contrast to narrow documentary opportunity. Such lack of integration on these four fronts is beginning to cause vast fissures in our culture. Could this be partially due to the lack of integration in our graduate school faculties where the socialization of secularization is supposed to be generated, promoted, and directed?

Such a question should be dignified with at least a brief explanation of what is meant by "graduate faculty integration." Basically, one would hope that the graduate faculty could offer graduate students and the general public a certain wholesomeness of thought, action, and life. Let us look at the first of these three aspects—wholesome thought. The graduate faculty and graduate students, if they form a community, are the contemplative mind of the university as an institution, for they alone have the time, competence, and facilities to perform three tasks for promoting wholesome thought. First, only they can reinterpret the traditional truth of each discipline and reintegrate it according to the latest information. Because this graduate community holds all these specialized integrations in tension, it alone can move toward the general integration of all the specialized disciplines into a speculative wisdom; it alone can sponsor, umpire, and write up the interdisciplinary studies and seminars that express this wisdom; it alone can develop the integrated context within which the university professor can teach graduate and undergraduate students in a wholesome manner; finally, it alone can thoroughly explore both the specialized myth at the base of each specialized knowledge and the total, englobing myth, or *Weltanschauung,* for all the insights, values, and modifications contained with them. This is the wholeness of thought that the graduate community offers to the university and to the larger civic community.

Second, from this wholeness of thought, the graduate community of the university can draw a practical wisdom, for it alone has the competence, the leisure, the discipline, and, finally, the call of the community to implement the speculative wisdom in three important areas. The wholeness of thought implies wholeness of action (1) to restructure the university to finer competence through interdisciplinary cooperation, (2) to help restructure society without prejudice according to just institutions through the same interdisciplinary cooperation, and (3) to achieve the personal integration of each graduate person as well as the communal integration of scholars. Such cooperation is vital to the exploration of both the mystery of life and the mystery of God.

Third, within this wholeness of thought and action, there will be operating a wholeness of life *if* the graduate community has a secularity that can be called the true heart of the university community. In other words, does the *Weltanschauung* of this graduate community have a balanced and wise system of values? Is it other-centered and yearning for justice for all? On its way to mystery, does it direct, and yet submit to, that integration of disciplines called speculative wisdom? Then, as it descends back down to myth for validation in common-sense experience of life, does it direct and submit to that integration called practical wisdom? Are the *Weltanschauungen* and the secularization process of this faculty guided by Christian philosophy when the graduate community confronts the mystery described by Christian theology—the mystery, that is, of the risen Christ's death and resurrection rescuing all men and women of all times and places? In other words, is this graduate community enlivened by love (i.e., by respect, trust, and hope) in all its works for the university and for the larger civic community? If so, then this community offers wholeness of thought, action, and life because it is truly the heart of the university.

The Always Strained Relations between Undergraduate and Graduate Schools?

It would be dishonest not to paint some more somber colors into this portrait of undergraduate and graduate education. Unfortunately, graduate school professionalism, with its heavily concentrated emphasis on specialized disciplines and with its consequent heavy demands upon undergraduate preparation, has penetrated into the undergraduate program. It has fragmented the undergraduate program into separate departments that politely war with one another for the student's undergraduate hours, claiming that they are only trying to implement the demands made upon each department by each one's respective professional society. In turn, the undergraduate becomes more and more specialist-minded, more and more resentful of the demands of the core curriculum, more and more liable to use electives for the major study.

Subtle zealotry for a particular specialty and condescending snobbery toward other knowledges-arts-skills develop in those departments that are sealed off from other departments by the very intensity of their specialization efforts. If graduate professors have not integrated their specialized knowledge with other knowledges-arts-skills, and also with the needs of both the university and the civic community, then they will tend to disparage undergraduate teaching as something of a waste of time. This disparagement of undergraduate students naturally influences the attitudes of those graduate students who are so "unlucky" as to have to teach undergraduates—often for modest salaries. The resultant poor undergraduate teaching promotes poor preparation for graduate school, and the vicious circle is set spinning. Finally, it is becoming clear that the graduate school model has dominated university planning to the neglect of the undergraduate school. The criteria for hiring new professors, for example, is often heavily weighted in favor of the research-oriented person over the student-oriented teacher.

This situation is not easy to correct. Professors who are deeply attached to research and who significantly contribute to their discipline as well as to the civic community will hardly be lured to a university whose graduate program and students are mediocre. The loss of such professors can badly affect the undergraduate program, for these professors may well be stimulating to undergraduate students, highly effective in training graduate-student teachers (whose teaching will communicate this same stimulation to undergraduate students), and inspiring to those who, teaching mainly on the undergraduate level, do little publishable research. Such outstanding graduate professors also tend to be examples of integration and wholeness because they accept the spurring of their students, because they struggle for balance of a wisdom within and outside their specialized discipline, because they live their *Weltanschauung* and their faith in ultimate mystery. This is a powerful influence on the undergraduate students. Finally, the information that is gathered by such graduate scholars eventually percolates down to the undergraduates through other teachers and the graduate students. There is, then, no easy solution to the problem of integrating the undergraduate and graduate programs; yet, the price of not working at some betterment is desecularization on both levels of the university. The university, as a prime agent of secularization, can hardly afford this.

Conclusion

The secularization process, then, is the mediating factor between an individual's or a community's *Weltanschauung* and their touching of mystery. In proceeding out of common-sense experience and the myth, it generates a speculative wisdom; in proceeding back to myth from mystery, it develops a practical wisdom in conjunction, again, with common-sense experience. This wisdom is the "wholing" process of the core curriculum; the undergraduate student experiences it in his or her awareness of all his or her powers, of all strata of a situation, of liberty beyond freedom, and of hunger for justice. It also includes a balanced secularity, or system of values, that has been received from the authority of family, church, and local culture, but has been modified by the experience of the core curriculum of liberal studies.

This integration, ironically, can be deepened by the specialization of the student's major study when it makes him or her aware of the vastness of knowledge and the consequent need for integration, and when it roots him or her not only in the specialist community, but also in the other communities that the student serves through his or her expert knowledge-art-skill. Indeed, elective courses, sometimes dismissed as being frivolous, can also contribute to the integration, or the "wholing," of the student because they can arouse in him or her responsibility for his or her education, initiative for an inventive curiosity, spontaneous fun, and enrichment according to the student's unique needs. In these ways, the undergraduate program can help the student achieve the wholeness of disciplined liberty amid the fragmentation of cultural desecularization.

On the other hand, the graduate student, if he or she is to keep balanced amid the artificiality of his or her program, must always keep in view his or her mythic *Weltanschauung*, stay in touch with mystery (especially the mystery of God), and live deeply in his or her common-sense knowledge. Still, the graduate student will find that the very intensity of his or her specialization can impel him or her into integrating with other knowledges-arts-skills, with the interests of his or her family, with the interdisciplinary seminars and studies of the graduate school, and with the living wisdom of his or her favorite specialist professors.

What is particularly needed at this time, however, are the graduate faculty members who have attained, and can impart to others, that wholeness of thought which is called speculative wisdom, that wholeness of action which is called practical wisdom, and that wholeness of life which is called balanced secularity. Given these, the university may be better structured toward its aims, the personal and communal integration of university people may be more wholesome, and the civic community may enjoy more just institutions for that great community of the great tomorrow. But before this can happen, there must be a more fruitful integration of the undergraduate and graduate schools lest the graduate schools fragment the undergraduate schools in petty, enfeebling rivalries. Happily, there is within the university itself, a power for bettering this vital cooperation between the undergraduate and graduate segments of the university. It is the power of play and of worship, which will be studied in the following chapter.

12 Worship: The Balance of Work and Play, of Decisive Action and Contemplation

To put it circumspectly, the university community is not without its workaholics; in fact, it may specialize in them. It should be expected, no doubt, that hyper-specialization would be a constant temptation for the university person who has fallen in love with a particular knowledge or science or art or skill. A workaholic can be described as one who is *possessed* by his or her beloved profession. When the workaholic is separated from this domineering mistress, he or she finds little self-identity. There is the proverbial novelist, for example, who turns every event and person met into grist for his or her creative mill so that people become afraid to talk with him or her lest they and their intimate problems appear in the next short story or novel. In addition, workaholism is fostered by the professional demands that have overstimulated the overachiever ever since high-school days.

The university workaholic has a number of characteristics. First, he or she seldom thinks outside the categories of his or her specialized skill or art or knowledge. This variety of university workaholic might be the philosophy teacher who generalizes on all one's remarks and especially on those recounting poignant personal events, who continually switches the conversation to the philosophic problem of this month's interest, who refers only to philosophic writers, who closely observes his or her infant daughter for a new understanding of dawning reason, who is bored stiff by his or her spouse's friends when they talk about the theater or home furnishings, who sees history only as the march of ideas that confirm his or her philosophic conclusions, and so on.

As a second characteristic, the family life of the hyper-specialized student or professor is tightly subordinated to work so that the children never enter his or her workroom or work schedule. The spouse of a

259

hyper-specialized student or professor has learned to live a very quiet life and even to have friends seleted for him or her according to their ability to carry on intellectual conversation. As a third characteristic of the university workaholic, one notes that his or her hopes and ambitions are circumscribed by a definite area of specialization. The scholars in his or her field are great heroes, and imitation of their work is the sole idol. The sense of prowess in an athlete who receives his or her Olympic medal, the thrill of power in an army general or business executive who carries out a successful strategy that involves ten thousand people, the exuberance of an artist over a just completed sculpture—all these enthusiasms cannot begin to interest the workaholic. Not even a daughter's Girl Scout award for camping excellence elicits the workaholic's interest; he or she pats the youngster's head and quickly returns to his or her book.

The university workaholic in this last caricature has successfully specialized himself or herself out of his or her humanity, achieving something that looks like integration by excluding from his or her life everything that is not connected with work-interests. Ironically, in order to enrich a particular area of life, the university workaholic has suffered a crippling impoverishment. In some cases, only personal tragedy can break into the self-made prison to liberate this workaholic by forcing him or her to look at all the dimensions of life. Even colleagues within his or her university department find the workaholic's growing monomaniacal concentration a boring, if not unnerving, experience. If the university workaholic is working on a cooperative project with others (scholars, technicians, graduate students, and secretaries), he or she will find that his or her work-decisions meet more and more opposition because his or her narrowed view cannot encompass all the academic, emotional, and personal factors of the situation. A lack of humane wholesomeness now undermines his or her previously successful work. The university workaholic often becomes arrogant and autocratic out of desperation and brings his or her project to the edge of disaster.

Is it possible that the workaholic is suffering from a subtle careerism, a form of vanity or pride that desperately seeks attention and congratulatory support from colleagues? If so, then this ambition caters to a growing self-centeredness that, in turn, erects blockages against seeing or hearing anything that disagrees with the workaholic's viewpoint. This can only result in growing isolation from colleagues and from the reality of the situation. The workaholic has driven his or her amibition into a blind alley to a point where he or she cannot turn the vehicle around. The workaholic must climb out of the career-vehicle, humbly retrace his or her route, and walk onto the main concourse to join the rest of humanity. Many do just this when they rediscover play.

The Radical Remedy for Workaholism Is Play

Johan Huizinga has eloquently lamented how nineteenth century Europeans, unlike their Medieval and Renaissance predecessors, had let their ability to play wither. Walter Kerr, in *The Decline of Pleasure*, laid the blame for this on the single-minded utilitarianism of Jeremy Bentham and William Stanley Jevons who seemed to identify value and happiness with the useful and to make pleasure the profit of an experience. The practically profitable, therefore, became a matter of conscience and play became very dutiful. From this state of mind, it is not far to the style of life that has been called workaholic. Utilitarianism, if not Marxism, could next be made the philosophy justifying this lifestyle. It fits into the American grip on pragmatic efficiency like a strong hand into a snug glove. When this grip is put on the specialist, he or she is vulnerable to hyperspecialization, a vocational variety of workaholism that leaves no room for play. Consequently, the only way to break the grip of this utilitarianism is resolutely to play.

Naturally, the elements of such a prescription should be analyzed before one takes such a radical remedy. So, let us, first, describe various types of play, then, the characteristics of play, and finally, from these, the definition of play. Later, play can be compared to contemplation and to prayer in order to see how these ultimately fit together. This would enable us to appreciate how essential worship is to the university community and how essential campus ministers are to such worship, to university people, and to university work. This could well explain why the university feels a playful need to celebrate its work and its people.

Play is sometimes equated with games such as tennis or golf or basketball, or with instruments such as sandboxes, crossword puzzles, and watercolors. No one would deny that these are playful, but play can also be the reading of a novel or the watching of a drama or the observing of the Milky Way through a telescope. Play can happen when one cheers for a favorite football team or when one is swept away by a concert or when one forgets all else except the chess pieces on the checkered board or when one travels through Europe. Yet, because professional sports have been turned into a big business that can hurt more than heal and because people can be relentlessly serious about their play, we should describe the characteristics of *true* play so that some of this confusion is blown away.

First, play characteristically is timeless. In "getting away from it all" one does enter into another world where one concentrates on another flow of events, e.g., the action of a play, the varying theme of a symphony, the intense waiting for a marlin to hit the bait hard enough to hook. One does occasionally see a three-hour movie that was so engrossing it seemed to take only thirty minutes; one does get so involved with the sails and the wind that the hurly-burly reality of New York City has evaporated—even though realistically one is aware, far back in his or her mind, that this idyllic event will end and that one will find himself or herself back in the serious world of traffic jams, stock market reports, job-hunting, and insurance planning.

Secondly, in this "other" world of play, one experiences a joy that makes play worthwhile in itself. It does not need to be justified by the remark, "I play golf three times a week because my office work is better." Sheer fun is justification enough because all one's mind, heart, and body have been operating at a high level. This self-contained world of play seemingly frees a person to be totally himself or herself without fear of recrimination. Admittedly, one's work, when balanced by play, contains its own type of joy—at times a very great joy. Still, work tends to be caught in the demands of schedules, calibrated results, economics, peer pressures, and excessive ambition. When these demands become exorbitant, work becomes painful drudgery rather than enjoyable creativity.

This does not mean, however, that play is without suffering. But, compared to the joy of play, the suffering is negligible; even the skier on crutches or the amateur actor who is terrified at the first curtain will admit to this. The discipline that is required to play well (a third characteristic of play) does not dampen the joy; rather, the discipline coexists with, and even stimulates, the joy. Once a player begins to be paid for his or her efforts, however, play can gradually be turned into drudgery and the pains are resented, measured, and totted up against the salary. The play world has slipped back into the serious world where the means, which are strictly proportionate to the end, are carefully registered amid fierce competition. Clearly, those colleges that extensively subsidize college athletes carry a heavy moral burden for introducing a debilitating ambivalence into the lives of young, inexperienced people. Here, the fourth characteristic of play, spontaneity and inventiveness, has been lost. Play is supposed to lift us out of the serious, everyday world of routines, drudgery, and hyper-specialization into a fresh world where one creates ever new strategies, within clear rules, to meet unplanned events.

This is why celebration, the fifth characteristic, is part of playing. Play offers the delight of success, of understanding and managing a situation that is a greatly simplified imitation of the serious world and its success. Beating the local park's grand-champion chess player, for example, is somewhat akin to outthinking and outdaring a rival general or a competing executive. The joy of triumph has to be celebrated in some appropriate way. Play is a constant seeking for mastery or total control of a situation; it is the godlike quality of coaching a Little League team of awkward kids to a city championship; it is the bringing of unity out of chaos, and this is the sixth characteristic of play. It is also a creating of beauty, the seventh characteristic, as in the synchronized dance and music of ballet, for example, or in the exquisite deftness of a dance partner at the local bistro. All this does not deny that work, too, creates beauty, unity out of chaos, and something to be celebrated with joy. Rather, it affirms that play creates without the restrictions imposed by duty, ambition, and economic need.

A concrete earthiness is the eighth characteristic of play. If one is spectator or player, one focuses on each event of the game or watercolor or symphonic moment till the game is done or the object is made. The detective story aficionado or the amateur archaeologist or the bridge-playing fanatic can tell you each step of his or her story in minute detail because each one loves each moment of his or her respective play. Every move is precalculated, measured, and relished—sometimes with the laugh of great contentment.

As Peter Berger has noted in his *Rumor of Angels,* play contains a taste of another world, a future life, in which play, not work, will be the central pole of our lives. The created world of play puts heavy emphasis on teamwork, on playing before an applauding or booing audience, on bragging to others of one's successes, on accountability to the opposing team, (even in solitaire, one is playing against one's weaker self, the one that would cheat), and on celebrating a team triumph. In realizing this, one recognizes the communal and future-oriented aspects of play.

Besides this intrinsic orientation, there is also the fact that, extrinsically, play is purposeful or usable. Play does relax us for stepping back into the serious world. Its joy continues in us the next Monday morning and shows us where play can enter the routines of work ("Who can fold, stuff, and seal the most envelopes in one hour?"). Play makes us rethink our values and review the serious world; play sometimes even lures us into changing our perspective on life and our plans for the future. Thus, play is indirectly powerful; yet, play excludes no one from its embrace— anyone can feel the power of play by inventing a game or finger-painting a picture.

Perhaps these characteristics could be summed up in the following definition of play: Play is the lifting of the mind and heart out of the serious, seemingly uncontrollable, everyday world of time and complexity so that the player creates, by enthusiastic action, a new, orderly universe of great simplicity and of self-justifying joy—a universe that nevertheless demands inventiveness and always challenges one toward mastery (even with pain). Once this universe has been created, play enjoys its own earthy life of teamwork, even points toward a future life of play that lasts forever and, despite its very definite ending, keeps its joy sounding in one's body, mind, and heart in the later celebration of victory and in the still later return to the serious world. Such a concept of play makes it clear how important are intramural programs and decent sport facilities for the university's health of mind as well as for the individual's health of body. If play is later seen to make contemplation possible, it will be even clearer how play fits into the university needs and how anomalous is the paying of college athletes.

With this definition of play in mind, one readily sees that play can lift the hyper-specialized professor or student out of his or her self-imprisoned, yet imprisoning routines, can set him or her down into an atmosphere of meeting the unexpected, and, thus, can alert all of his or her expectancies for later transfer to the routines of his or her specialization. Play also sharpens the hyper-specialized person's inventiveness by its call for spontaneous response to unsuspected developments. Its sheer fun offers new types of both joy and hope and can open up new horizons of experience that are outside the specialization so that one feels a greater need for other knowledges and for new values. Furthermore, since play excludes no one, it checks the snobbishness of the clique that knows it all and does it all. Indeed, it is possible for the hyper-specialized individual to put his or her knowledge-art-skill into a larger perspective that would somewhat free him or her from the overly anxious need to excel. The hyper-specialized person might even learn to laugh, from time to time, at himself or herself and, while laughing, to reconsider his or her *Weltanschauung,* or basic attitude toward the world. Could it be that even this person's secularity would be reconsidered? And could this mean a more liberal attitude toward his or her own specialized knowledge-art-skill and toward all others? And could this lead to wisdom?

The Play of Contemplation

Because contemplation, as we shall see, can be the source of integration or wholesomeness in the university process, and because integration is the basic response to a fragmenting and divisive hyper-specialization, it would be advantageous to know how play and contemplation are related. A large obstacle results from a person narrowing the conception of contemplation to an artist's viewing of a landscape or to a mystic's sighting of God or to a physicist's enthrallment with the increasing size of the universe. True, contemplation is this; more than this, however, it is also one's fascinated gazing on the revealing face of the beloved; one's mulling and haunting question; "Where is my life going?"; one's wondering what is behind the magnificent variety of fish or beetles or monkeys; one's awe at a thunder and lightning storm over the mountains; one's puzzlement over how economic factors influence the building of culture on the Ivory Coast; one's being overwhelmed by another's description of his or her near-death in a boating accident; one's bafflement at what makes a university Christian. Contemplation, therefore, is a concrete, everyday experience. No one escapes it or remains undisturbed by the questions it raises.

Like play, contemplation is a "getting away from it all" in order to better "get into it all." At times, it is so powerful that one forgets himself or herself and loses all sense of time as he or she enters into a person or a scene. When one is searching for the single meaning or "person" behind the many changes in the beloved's expression and action during a party, one is surprised to realize that others at the party have begun to put on their coats and have started to go home. Research hours fly by for the historian who is attempting to find threads (absolutes) of meaning between the various Civil War battles and their connections with the economic blockades. In going behind the flood of appearances and events to find the underlying single current (the explanation of the whole), one is contemplating.

Such a search in itself distills a deep joy, for one is digging, (within a well-known specialized field of Civil War history, for example), for a treasure that has never before been discovered, namely, a total reinterpretation of traditional truth according to a new underlying unity. A strong sense of specialized mastery is nevertheless filled with the expectancy of surprise, with the challenging need for inventive insight, with the hope of sharing this discovery with others. Even if the insights are never published, the search and the discovery give a joy that needs no other justification as it turns the student into an enthusiastic historian—and this occurs in the midst of the tension and drudgery of the research. The enthusiasm of the scholar is a thing of beauty in itself and, thus, is worthwhile in itself even if it never produces beauty in the minds of students or in the pages of a specialized journal. This enthusiasm is a natural celebration, a joy in triumph, that does not need, but would be enhanced by, celebration with colleagues.

When contemplation finds the underlying unity of a face, of a series of historical events, of a person's life, of evolving species, of an opposing team's offense, of the economic factor that is crippling the cultural advance of a Third-World nation, it has found a real yet ideal world behind, and yet within, the serious everyday world of routines, infinite data, and complex duties. This ideal world provides the joyous, encouraging incentive to suffer for one's work. Its discovery unites all the parts into a whole, gives a joy of vision that is hard to match, and, with its absolutes, promises a future life wherein all factors will come together in wholeness, wherein secularization will finally triumph over the fragmentation of de-secularization, and wherein all members of the community will cooperate according to a commonly loved secularity. This is the great community of the great tomorrow—once again. It is also a baffling mystery since this contemplative vision of the ideal world can be clouded with the pain and tragedy of everyday living. Joy can change to despair of humanity and of the world's safety unless the contemplative can bring himself or herself to an ultimate trust that God's providence will finally unite humanity.

This communal goal is already present in the very beginnings of con-templation, since contemplation is a losing of oneself in the other. The engaged couple is so delighted because now the life of each one is a contemplation of the other; the historical novelist falls in love with Ren-aissance France and its people, whose lives he or she is now chronicling; the artist, studying flowers in preparing to paint a still life, tries to live "inside" them; the enthusiastic historian cannot wait to tell his or her colleagues about his or her Civil War insights. No one is excluded from the community of contemplatives; anyone can search out the hidden unities of life, if he or she can live with sorrow as well as joy, with dark mystery as well as splendid vision. Yet paradoxically, contemplation de-mands of lover, novelist, artist, and historian a willingness to live alone as he or she delves, with utter concentration, for deep truths.

Because these hidden unities are the source of all that happens in the world, contemplation is worthwhile in itself because of what it does in-trinsically within the contemplator, which is to render the contemplator more fully human, more wholesome. And yet, contemplation is very useful extrinsically, since it both makes one aware of the many factors that contribute to a situation and catches the underlying flow of the situation. Thus, the contemplative can make decisions that are rich in awareness and strong in directing a situation toward the fullness of being. This is why contemplation is so necessary for wholeness of mind, heart, and situation.

As soon as contemplation is used for making decisions, one becomes aware that it includes values that are to be rediscovered within the deci-sion. In fact, in laying bare the underlying unities of a situation, contem-plation uncovers the deepest values and beauties of life. In this way, contemplation leads into the wholeness of, first, contemplative wisdom and, then, of practiced wisdom. For this reason, contemplation is a "whol-ing " experience that always involves the integrative movement which is so essential to secularization.

All these characteristics of contemplation lead us to its definition: Con-templation is a knowing penetration to the underlying timeless unity of a definite person or concrete situation or series of historical events so that the knower is filled with (a) the celebrating joy of vision, (b) the hope of future living beyond pain and death, (c) a sense of mastery and also a feel of mystery, and (d) the readiness to make value judgments according to a wholesome secularity.

If a person compares the above characteristics and definitions of play and contemplation, he or she cannot help being struck by their similarities. A strong spirit of play is evident within contemplation. This explains why play is the radical remedy that is prescribed for the hyper-specialized person. Play would probably stimulate the contemplative integration that this person badly needs. Moreover, the close link between play and contemplation would indicate how the child learns to contemplate, and why contemplation gives so much joy amid the labors it demands.

But to more fully appreciate the relationship between play and contemplation, it is worthwhile to note their differences. For, whereas play emphasizes getting something to happen, contemplation aims at recognizing what has happened or is happening (or will happen *if* . . .). Although play creates another world that is outside the serious world, contemplation stays within the serious world to seek beneath it that underlying unity, or absolute world, which directs the serious world. In seeking this unity, contemplation is always aware of Unity itself—the ultimate mystery. Play, however, is not concerned with mystery (though its timelessness is an intimation of immortality) as it concentrates on the present moment of human creativity. Thus, the mystery of sudden tragedy on the playing field or the beach collapses the spirit of play as sorrow plunges us back into the serious world. Contemplation is more than play, even though it is learned through play and always includes play.

Another difference is that contemplation is sunk deeply into the historico-traditional to discover the underlying unity of mankind and of world because it finds that the serially cumulative action of mankind and of the world reveals absolutes or the threads of continuity. On the other hand, play, because it is essentially timeless, is oblivious to the historical tradition, except insofar as that tradition heightens the excitement of play; the ceremony at Wimbledon, for example, accents the drama of center-court tennis, and, similarly, the introductory Olympic pageantry sharpens the anticipation of the games ahead, and the final pageantry points interest to the next Olympic Games. It may be noted, at this point, that play involves a spontaneous cultivation of either rollicking joy or dismal dispair, when it focuses all the passions on a single, split-second event. It is no wonder, then, that play takes for granted all values, such as comradeship, honesty, patience, and so on, except itself. Contemplation, on the other hand, in seeking the underlying and all-pervading unity of humanity, world events, and God, is more interested in the values of this unity and their perdurance through time—although it is also quite conscious of the feelings attached to those values.

These differences indicate that, even though play is valuable in itself, it is only a preparation for contemplation. Yet, if play is ever shunted aside, the result will be a gradual loss of the power to contemplate, since it is always a preliminary stage of contemplation. Without the spontaneity, inventiveness, and emotional verve of play, contemplation goes dry and dead; without contemplation, play becomes valueless, trivial, and eventually boring in its lack of direction.

Play is clearly important to the sanity of the specialist and to contemplation; but how, exactly, is contemplation helpful to university life? If one looks first to contemplation's effects on speculative wisdom, one finds that contemplation, in seeking the underlying unity of events, must refer back to the unified and unifying *Weltanschauung* from which it issued. Thus, contemplation always demands that the *Weltanschauung* be constantly, and sometimes painfully, revised. Then, too, the fact that contemplation is constantly seeking the basic connections between events leads it to shape a "total picture." In other words, it tends to do its integration, first, within each specialized knowledge-art-skill and, secondly, between all the knowledges-arts-skills. It does this, however, not in some abstract realm of separated ideas but within the historico-traditional concreteness of everyday people and events, so that it is both cognizant of and promotive of the "wholing" process that is called secularization. In doing this, it inevitably looks beyond the present state of affairs to envision a better future situation, a scientifically rooted utopia, a place and time when ideal knowledges-arts-skills will be enjoyed and promoted by an ideal community of friends that is untroubled by the fragmentation of desecularization. Thus, it gives birth to a dynamic vision of the future. Its awareness of cumulative unity, meanwhile, keeps it unafraid of, and reverent toward, Mystery itself, to which all higher and higher integrations (to say nothing of hypotheses) lead and into which all eventually collapse. Thus, contemplation gives a sense of direction to the person's life and to the community's life while, at the same time, it humbles us before mystery and our own ignorances. Insofar as contemplation increasingly directs one's actions, and insofar as play increasingly energizes one's work and contemplation, wholeness enters one's life—a wholeness that is a knowing and a feeling of full manhood and full womanhood.

Contemplation is also leading into practical wisdom, since contemplation needs action to validate and enrich it with new understandings of data. For no integration lasts forever. To continue in life, it must always be growing since integration is always a reinterpretation, a reunifying of traditional truth with new truth. Sometimes this growth can mean drastic revision because of swiftly changing conditions in the self, in the world, and in perception of mystery. Thus, through its integrations, contemplation raises new questions that need to be sharpened and investigated in the specialized knowledges. In addition, it directs decisions out of the breadth of its detailed vision; these decisions, which are always inadequate to the situation, uncover new factors that had not previously been embraced by this integrative contemplation but now can be included for later decisions. In terms of beauty, contemplation delights us with its discoveries, but this pleasure is short-lived, since a restless contemplator always uncovers ugliness in the midst of beauty, as decay sets in or as times change or as new human needs arise. One has only to compare Orville Wright's winged bicycle with the present Boeing 747 to see how swiftly beauty changes—not infrequently for the better.

This restless factor in contemplation is not, however, simply the benevolent circling of ever increasing intellectual enrichment as one moves back and forth between deepening specialization and integration. Contemplation of beauty produces love, and, out of some divine dissatisfaction, the lover must ever be doing something for the beloved to increase his or her joy. In the university, this beloved might be the departmental community of scholars and students or it might be the total community of the university of it might be something in between these. Thus, contemplation, like the integration toward which it aims, is more characteristic of the communal side rather than the institutional side of the university. Contemplation is the sharing of power between individuals, between departments, between professors and students, between faculty and administration. It is the source of that wisdom with which they build their communities. That is, it makes friendships possible between academics so that the community of wisdom can be formed and the pursuit of truth can be warmed by the heart.

When such communities come into being, their heart and warmth make wisdom possible, since community friendship gives us the confidence both to risk mistakes in being inventively integrative and to make difficult decisions out of the "heart-values," as much as out of deep knowledge, of the situation. Play is extremely helpful at this point to promote such "contemplative friendship," namely, at the university's pageants for solemn functions, at its dinner dances and parties, at its great symposia, at its lunch conversations and dinner palavers, at its friendly exchanges after the business of classes and committee meetings. All these "playtimes" are, vital to the growth of the communal side of the university, but they are also important to the institutional side, since to be truly professional one needs to be radically and joyously human.

The friendship that is set in motion by contemplation has two other facets that are significant: First, contemplation shared with friends induces a "heart-warmth" that enables us to have, through love, connatural knowledge of unique beings as unique. This is a requisite for the wisdom that is the second intrinsic aim of the university. Secondly, the love that is provoked by contemplation is the source of that self-sacrifice and heroism which render civilizations vital and cultures beautiful. Obviously, without such love, civilizations and cultures—to say nothing of marriages and churches—tend to degenerate. Just as the university's institutional side, which is responsible for civilization, cannot long operate well without its communal side, which is responsible for culture, so, too, the degeneration of culture produces the disintegration of civilization, and vice versa, because culture and civilization also are opposite sides of the one process of secularization. Once again, it becomes clear how vital the university is to the total life of the nation.

To sum up our findings about play and contemplation, it is worthwhile to note how play vitalizes contemplation so that specialization is open to integration; how contemplation, in its search for underlying unity, must use and modify the basic myth or *Weltanschauung* of our lives; how contemplation must integratively focus knowledges to find this treasured underlying unity and, thus, must foster the secularization process; how contemplation also offers the basis for the values that are used in developing a practical wisdom and, then, presents them systematically as a secularity; how contemplation inevitably assumes a future great community of human beings and implicitly lives in the presence of the greatest unity of all, divine mystery. As a result, contemplation is recognized as essential to the secularization process. It is also essential to the building of the university wisdom community, since it promotes not only scholarship but also friendship, so that wisdom becomes both possible and rich, and so that both civilization and culture can continue to grow in a nation. Contemplation at its peak becomes prayer—either the specialized individual prayer of a person's private life or the integrative communal prayer of public worship in the community. Therefore, to understand the impact of prayer on university living is important to our endeavor.

Individual Prayer

Prayer is a communing with the ultimate mystery, God. It is the highest form of contemplation because it puts the individual person into contact with the source of all other unities in the universe. The praying

270

person touches the dynamic unity that is pulsing all things with existence, the personal lure that is living in all human knowledges, arts, skills, hopes, and ambitions. It is the root of each person's happiness, of his total manhood or of her total womanhood.

The praying person cannot touch Unity itself without feeling the need for integration within himself or herself, the need to make his or her actions better correspond with his or her thoughts, words, and expressed ideals. In this way, the praying person will find his or her true identity instead of a bogus front, since prayer carries a profound distaste for hypocrisy and double standards. Then, by uniting with Unity itself, the praying person becomes aware that he or she must unite with all his or her fellows ("Whoever says he loves God and yet hates his brother, is a liar"). Thus, contemplation of God leads to contemplation of one's fellow beings and to loving actions on behalf of them. Consequently, contemplation leads to the realization that "the more aware I am of the divine, the more aware I am of the human." From this type of contemplation can issue vibrant families, neighborhoods, nations, and university communities.

Naturally, this individual, specialized prayer fosters specialized service to the community, that is, it contributes particularly to the institutional side of the university. For, to be of service to either the specialized community of one's department or the whole university community or the larger civic community, one must be expert in his or her specialized knowledge-art-skill. This is equally true of those experts who work at museums, government agencies, industrial research centers, and various businesses. Thus, individual, specialized, private prayer fosters the integration of self, family, and society at the same time that it promotes the specialization which is necessary to competently serve these same communities.

Of course, this contemplative prayer will be no more powerful than the experienced image of God that allures it into existence. Thus, the personal *Weltanschauung* that one has received from one's family, neighborhood schooling, government, and church, will somewhat determine how the praying person approaches the ultimate mystery. A negative analysis dramatizes the importance to the contemplator of his or her image of God. Is God, for this person, a taskmaster (then the person is vulnerable to workaholism in seeking to please God), or a distant father (then the proper etiquette of dealing with God may be uppermost in one's mind), or an irresistible Spirit (then either stubborn resistance to divine takeover or casual indifference to freedom may enter one's life), or a sentimentalized Christ (then pious indifference to all but God may occur), or a rigidly stern Creator-Ruler (then subservience to the way things are now may be the "life-motif")? In any event, individual, private, contemplative prayer is very beholding to the family *Weltanschauung* and is very dependent on the way God's ultimate mystery is imaged. For this reason, the mediating secularization process in the world and in the university will be influenced by the specialized prayer experience of its members. Could it be that this private prayer might be raised up, protected, integrated, and advanced by public, communal worship in secular society and in the university?

Worship: Reinterpretation of All Life in Wisdom of the Word

Communal prayer, or public worship, shares a large number of characteristics with both play and contemplation. All three touch the eternal, the absolute, the One who is unrestricted by time and space. But in "getting away from it all to worship," the worshiper is specifically and consciously seeking the ultimate mystery of God. There is a direct touching of Wisdom Itself, which is at once the source and home of all being and striving. As a result, like play and contemplation, worship includes a self-contained joy that needs no other justification than itself because there is nothing better that men and women could do—no higher peak to climb. Yet worship always contains the suffering of discipline in mind, heart, and body. There are a thousand distractions to send the mind careening in all directions; there are some deep heartaches and bitternesses to haunt each prayer; and there is always the sometimes demanding, sometimes creaking body to take into account.

But this suffering, as we noted in discussing play and contemplation, often enough can coexist with a deep sense of peace, with a deep satisfaction in having found the center of one's self, one's life, and one's world. Salvation history, as revealed in the Sacred Scriptures and as lived today, is seen as a complex, but nevertheless wholesome unity. The world is going somewhere and not erratically spinning off to nowhere; the lives of all God's people do have direction and a final beatific meaning. Consequently, there is reason to celebrate, to take joy in the final and lasting triumph of God and His people. There is, in fact, a need for a great communal gathering with the Lord of History, Jesus Christ, at its center. And so, worship, like play and contemplation, creates beauty—the pageantry of the liturgy, the symbolization of both the great by the little (e.g., the body of Christ by bread, the blood of Christ by wine, the sinner's purification by water, the ascending prayer by incense) and the complex by the simple (e.g., civilization by a desk-top computer, culture by a book, art by a painting).

272

Such worship becomes fertile with invention. The seasonal variations of eternal themes, which are charted according to a liturgical calendar, enable us to recognize the richness and the profusion of God's self-revealing gifts to us. There is also the unique personality of the chief celebrant who, in attempting "to stand for Christ," simultaneously feels both the burden of the people's needs and the joy of serving them as the worship celebrates a wedding, a death, a new ministry to the poor, a birth, an adolescent trauma, a sorrow for sin, a thanksgiving for success. As it happens in play and in contemplation, all the great truths and events of life become concrete in worship. This happens in dramatic actions, as, for example, when the baby is washed clean of original sin and robed in the white garment of God's people, or when the bishop affectionately touches the adolescent on the shoulder to remind him or her that he or she is now an adult witness to Christ wherever he or she goes.

The total liturgy of worship is, in fact, an attempt to free men and women from the fragmenting desecularization of cultural and personal sin. It tries to heal any bitter wounds so that a person's future activity may be healthy and wholesome. Thus, like play and contemplation, worship, once the wounds are healed, constantly looks toward the future. For it encourages us to serve others in this world out of joyful charity (not merely out of routine or duty), and it promises us that, after death, we will join the great community of the great tomorrow with Christ, the Father, and the Spirit. In this way, worship blends today and tomorrow so that there is direction, joy, and hope in all one does in today's secularization process. For public worship is actually a communal reinterpretation of a person's entire past life, according to present needs-hopes-experiences, for future living. Indeed, it is the acme of the wisdom process as one climbs toward the Wisdom of the divine Word. Thus, public worship sums up the two intrinsic aims of the university and points them toward its extrinsic aim—the service of the community. This is why public worship on the university campus, when done with understanding and dignity, is essential to the university's life. It is the finest and most solemn means that the university has for dedicating itself, in accord with its intrinsic structure, to the nation and to God—again and again and again. For the university community, like any community, needs to be converted, over and over again, so that it can grow past its sins and beyond its current limitations into the wholesome community of wisdom.

Thus, public worship lifts to a higher intensity of intelligence, feeling, and purpose many characteristics that are shared with play and contemplation. It also has characteristics that are shared only with play or only with contemplation. Worship, for example, is like play in that it is more an action than merely a knowing. It happens to be the most significant action a person can perform, since it sums up all his or her actions and presents them in one act to the ultimate actual unity of God. Like play, worship is in a world of *ends* insofar as its one desire is final union with God almighty. Furthermore, like play, worship unconsciously and consciously cultivates all passions, from fear to joy, in order to focus them on the one event of the risen Christ.

In other respects worship is very similar to contemplation. It, too, remains in the serious, everyday world yet goes behind and beyond this world to another compenetrating world of the ideal—to the forming of the great community of the great tomorrow through the charity of today. For this reason, worship needs the sacred space of a church building, the sacred time of a Sabbath or Sunday, the sacred quiet of the recollected mind and heart and of the attentive body. In seeking ultimate unity, worship, like contemplation, of itself touches God, who is the ultimate actuating unity of all unities such as self, community, world. Like contemplation, worship centers its attention on mystery as it sums up all human knowledges-arts-skills and, then, uses them in its liturgy and fits them into the one salvation history described by the Scriptures and presently being lived by the assembled people of God. Therefore, like contemplation, worship is deeply involved in the historical and the traditional for themselves and also for their revelation of the creating and unifying Word, Wisdom itself, in the Scriptures and in the subsequent life of the church through twenty centuries. Public worship, insofar as it is public, tries to unite a whole people for present union with God. It is a single, communal action, a being in dynamic union, a Eucharistic receiving and cherishing of the Godhead into the body of the community. It freely allows God to possess the community as His own people, indeed as His bride.

This nuptial aspect reveals the intimacy of public and private worship as well as their consummate goal. This is why worship is a remarkable blending of play and contemplation; in fact, it is the play and contemplation characteristic of an engaged couple or a happily married couple. Specifically as Christian worship, it aims to introduce the worshiper into the family life of the Trinity, into the deep mutual trust and respect of Father, Son, and Holy Spirit for one another. Earlier, marriage was used as a metaphor to describe how secularization is a dedication to the world; here, one notes that worship celebrates such a marriage. God's immanence to the world is His faithful marriage to her; the incarnation of Christ, the trinitarian Son becoming a man, is a celebration of this divine marriage. Indeed, it simultaneously celebrates the marriage of each dedicated Christian to the world in service of the world's needs and hopes. In this way, secularization becomes more Christian through the liturgy of the Eucharist, through the other sacraments, through scriptural reading and praying, and through Christian service within the total secularization process.

For this reason, worship is an essential action within university life and, particularly, within Christian university life. Worship, because it is the highest form of prayer and of contemplation, adds much to university life. First, in individual, private worship, one gives himself or herself to God in grateful and praiseful return for God's giving of Himself and His Son to the world, for His giving us the world, for His giving each of us life and talents for university life. This worship becomes public, communal praise and gratitude when the members of the university community gather, first, to offer all their arts-skills-knowledges and, then, to focus them in homage on their ultimate source and goal, the Alpha and the Omega of life. This praise becomes greater as these arts-skills-knowledges become more specialized, because they actually penetrate or marry the world more deeply in the manner of God Himself.

This praise becomes even greater when these specialized knowledges-arts-skills are integrated into a great speculative wisdom, namely, the partial revelation of the mind of God by the collective mind of the academic community. There is yet another, fuller stage of praise that occurs when this speculative wisdom is made a practical wisdom which is applied to the needs and hopes of God's people in a selfless offering of the university community's gifts and energies. For, in this context, the heart of God is being revealed in the loving actions of the university community—in a love that is tender toward the feelings of the needy, that is filled with the intelligence of specialized and integrated learning, that is willing to suffer for one's oppressed brothers and sisters. Such love offers the highest of hopes and the warmest of homes for both civilization and culture in its blending of *logos* and *thumos*, reason and heart.

Such worshipful praise, making the love of God the pulse of university wisdom, can save the university community from heartless rationalism and can endow it with a connatural knowing of reality in uniqueness. This is a prudence of the highest order, one that will enable the university community to pursue the extrinsic aim of the university, the service of the civic community, with both a special deftness and a perduring warmth. For all these reasons, worship becomes the finest action of the university as community and sums up the characteristic powers and gifts of the university as institution. If the university community were to lose its power to worship, it would also lose its power to celebrate with gritty realism its greatest achievement, that is, a wisdom that supports and enlivens a continuing, benevolent civilization and culture. Ironically, worship keeps reminding the university of two basic facts of life: (1) func-

275

tions and processes are always for the sake of the person and, therefore, the person is never to be subordinated to them; and (2) work becomes meaningless if it is not subordinated to contemplation, if it does not lead to both play and prayer. For the person is always more important than his or her product and is never totally defined in his or her mystery by work, no matter how widely and grandly one defines work. Ultimately, men and women were made much more for play, contemplation, and worship; for men and women are, ultimately, living wisdom residing in Wisdom itself, the Word, the risen Christ.

Campus Ministry Is Essential, Not Merely Integral, to the University

If worship is vitally essential to the university, then those particularly responsible for this worship are just as vitally essential to university life. Campus ministers, therefore, play a crucial part in the growth of the university. If their ministry is not of university caliber, then any university will suffer—but especially the universities that call themselves Christian. What, exactly, is meant by ministry of university caliber or quality? This question can be partially answered only if we survey the usual activities of the campus ministers to calculate how they raise the quality of university communal activity.

One principle is clear: If worship is meant to produce ultimate wholeness in both individual and community, then campus ministers must be experts in wholeness. Paradoxically, their specialization is to make wholesomeness very possible for both individuals and community. If worship is the acme of contemplation, for example, then expert planning with full orchestration of all the university knowledges-arts-skills should go into the liturgical events of the university. Otherwise, the liturgy is not celebrating the works and gifts of the university in such a way that the university people can playfully and contemplatively give praise to God for His greatness and for His gifts to them. Such planning will increase in its validity as it is done by university people who have been trained to be sensitive toward all aspects of the university—not only its gifts, but also its irritations and its humor, its joys and its sorrows, its ecstasies and its anguishes. Such wholeness of university experience and sensitivity will be found only in campus ministers who have struggled with the problem of specialization and integration, who, consequently, have a sense of the riches and perils in the total university program of knowledges-arts-skills and of their administration, and who, therefore, know how to enlist university staff, professors, students, and administrators into shaping liturgical worship with them.

One way in which campus ministers may become more deeply aware of the wholeness of this university experience is to do "spiritual soundings" with faculty, students, and administrators, both individually and in groups. In these "soundings," the minister touches the central, focusing instrument of university wisdom, namely, prudence, because nothing is quite so delicate as "sounding." This sounding occurs, first, in spiritual-direction sessions in which the minister director and the person-to-be-directed share their common experiences of Christ in prayer, work, and human relations. Because of the delicacy of their work, faculty and administrators need someone who, if he or she is to advise them on their spiritual life, can appreciate the complexity and tensions of the obligations of faculty and administrators to departmental colleagues, students, fellow administrators, staff persons, and the larger civic community. Above all, these people need a spiritual director who has been humiliated from time to time as he or she has also tried to live university life. In fact, these specialists need a fellow specialist who has gone through the suffering, first, of integrating his or her life around a knowledge-art-skill and, then, of composing this with family life, civic duties, and church support. For this is where one's prayerlife is shaped and where prayerful decisions may be formed to improve these situations. If the "directee" is looking for wholeness of life, then the spiritual director must know what the wholing process is and be able to share with others how he or she has experienced it.

But the sounding is also communal. In other words, groups of faculty, staff, students, and administrators, along with campus ministers, need to form themselves into listeners so that the wholesomeness they experience is more than merely an individual experience. There is a marvelous spiritual direction that is received from the group by a type of spiritual osmosis; it is an *esprit* that rises among them as they discuss together, work together, suffer together, laugh together, pray together, party together, and brainstorm together in order to better the life of the university. It is a new dimension to individual spiritual direction because the Holy Spirit, working in the community, has new outlets for His inspirations. Communal prudence can operate to give more wholeness to the group and to each individual—a wholeness that is not achievable by any other means. It is a total Christian life experience that enables the campus minister, along with some academic people, to lead liturgies with a more wholesome realism and to do individual spiritual direction with a more informed delicacy. In turn, the community itself offers a center of great richness for each of its members insofar as each pours into the center his or her best expertise, fullest experience of life, and deepest faith commitment.

Because of its intensity, this "sounding center" is quite demanding. It is also very rewarding—especially for the campus ministers, since they can use its richness for their other pastoral duties. If the campus minister, for example, is going to administer the sacraments at critical periods in people's lives or assist at their administration, then he or she had better know what people's values and hopes are and how to identify with them. After all, the sacraments symbolize all the vital values and hopes of people who live Christian lives; they literally embody Christian secularity. If the campus minister and those who assist do not know their people's secularity or, knowing it, cannot identify with it, then the ministrations could become irrelevant or hypocritical or, at best, less effective in the decisive moments of people's lives.

In addition, since the campus ministers often set the tone for the sacramental moments with preaching, their explanation of the Word (Wisdom itself) should carry the latest scholarly findings of the exegetes and theologians if their instructions and homilies are to measure up to a university community's needs and expectations. It is, after all, a wisdom community and scriptural explanations are supposed to increase the community's wisdom, not confuse or deplete it. No one would deny that the dedicated lives of the campus ministers are the basis for respecting their presence in the groups. The basis for acting upon the campus ministers' preaching and instruction, however, is respect for both their careful study of the Scriptures (in the context of the converging results of modern scholarship) and their sensitive listening to the experiences of the wisdom community. In addition, this academic community needs to see its campus ministers walk beyond the confines of the particular university and confront the church's needs and the world's needs in order to call the university community to action on these needs. The community members need to have their eyes lifted and their hearts encouraged toward pastoral work among the needy. Such exhortation, however, requires the worldwide vision and preparation of a university person, since quixotic tendencies undermine confidence in a community that is dedicated to practical wisdom as well as speculative wisdom. Thus, the wholesomeness of the campus minister's education and life enables him or her not only to lead, but also to be united with the university community in worship and apostolic endeavor.

Finally, if campus ministry specializes in encouraging the university community to wholeness or integration, then its pastoral ministry needs to spur university people toward establishing Christian culture seminars on contemporary problems. So often, because of the traditional complexity of Christian culture, Christian universities lag behind in openly discussing complex cultural problems that are already harassing government officials or businessmen or journalists or parish pastors or average Christian families. Should not the speculative wisdom of the Christian university be constantly challenged by seminars that explore these problems? Should not its practical wisdom issue in decisive action for alleviating these problems?

The source of well-directed pastoral work, such as has been described here, is a lived pastoral theology. A lived pastoral theology will not happen, however, unless the theology department of the Christian university marshalls the aid of other university departments to help it reflect on the problems of the church and of society in terms of scriptural faith. For this reason, campus ministers need to be working intimately within this theology department, not just visiting it from time to time. Concretely, they should be teaching some of its pastoral theology courses, not simply to influence students but, what is more important, so that they themselves stay in immediate touch with the latest developments in the field of theology. Thus, the speculative wisdom of the university can more quickly filter down into the practical wisdom of pastoral theology to meet the needs and expectations of both the university community and the civic community. The provisional wisdom that is being gathered by the undergraduates, for example, requires the immediate support of campus ministers who are knowledgeable in pastoral theology. This provisional wisdom tends to set the tone for some years, if not for the whole life of the student.

Strategically, then, the campus minister who is doing spiritual "sounding" with such students needs better and better contemporary pastoral theology as the sounding goes more deeply. Moreover, if the campus minister is meeting graduate students who are living in the highly artificial atmosphere of graduate studies, his or her wholesome realism will be an oasis at which such students can draw much nourishment for their own provisional wisdom. The lopsidedness of graduate life, in which mature married life is walking hand in hand with adolescent apprenticeship in a specialized area of knowledge-art-skill, needs the balancing wholesomeness of a lived pastoral theology that is sophisticated enough to meet the needs of these graduate students.

All of this points to the fact that campus ministers cannot just drop in from the neighboring parish or high school to begin their ministry. For if campus ministry is essential to university life, then it better be as competent as the university people who need it and hope in it. In other words, if worship, prayer, and pastoral theology produce a final "wholing" or integration of all the university's specializations and wisdoms and secularities, then the campus ministers had better be well prepared for their paradoxical specialization in helping others to reach wholeness of life and action.

This means that the training of campus ministers should normally include graduate theological training, psychological internship in guidance and counseling, development in a specialized knowledge other than theology (e.g., sociology, philosophy, history, etc.), and an ascetical internship in spirituality. Moreover, there is a real need that they actively teach at least one course per year in pastoral theology; this is as much for their own sakes as for the sakes of their students and of interested faculty, staff, and administration. For continued interest in pastoral theology is critical to their spiritual and intellectual growth.

The Problematic of Campus Ministry

The complex training needed to develop the range of skills that are expected of a campus minister presents us with a seemingly insoluble problem: how could any one person cultivate so many skills and when would he or she ever rest? This is precisely the point. Only a *team* of campus ministers could both possess such an array of knowledges-arts-skills and employ them to meet the wide scope of university community needs. Even in the smallest college, a ministry team is required. For, although there may be only one full-time campus minister, this person must integrate part-time assistants and volunteers into a team so that Christian wisdom may be represented more broadly and deeply than would be possible for even the most talented person working alone. Only by acknowledging the humiliatingly difficult ideal of campus ministry that has been described here can the team be wisely organized and can the gaps in its range of skills be clearly recognized. The very complexity of the ideal convincingly demonstrates that teamwork is absolutely necessary for carrying out the Christian apostolate within the university and, thence, outside the university.

This need is further appreciated when one realizes that no ministerial team, no matter how richly talented and practically effective, can influence a whole college or university unless it successfully enlists the volunteer services of faculty, staff, administration, and student body and, then, integrates the efforts of these volunteers into teamwork. Thus, the one indispensable skill of every campus minister is the ability to imbue the members of the academic community with the desire to foster Christian wisdom and action both inside and outside the university community. Likewise, eliciting the cooperation of staff, faculty, administration, and student body should be the first priority of the campus ministry team. Perhaps the definition of an effective campus minister would be one who lures the academics into forming groups to minister to intra-university needs and extra-university needs, that is, to perform the corporal and spiritual works of mercy.

If campus ministers can successfully form such teams of academics, they will be developing embryonic Christian communities that will foster all the activities mentioned earlier: liturgy, spiritual direction, administering of sacraments and the Word, Christian culture seminars, prayer groups, apostolic works for the needy, a more sophisticated type of pastoral theology for parishes—all of university caliber, that is to say, all capable of touching the heartfelt needs of university people. Campus ministers, then, will truly be specialists at assisting university people toward wholeness, or integration, at all levels of life—precisely by their special skill for forming action teams and small Christian apostolic communities. The campus minister can do this not simply because he or she is intelligent and effectively practical, but rather because he or she is living intimately with the entire university community of wisdom as another member of the team, or apostolic community. On this basis, the campus minister is able to draw on the community's strengths and minister to its weaknesses.

No longer is it enough—if it ever was enough—to listen to the Spirit speaking within the individual self; one must listen to the Spirit speaking in the sophisticated terms of university wisdom within the university community. Here the Word convincingly speaks to the needs, wounds, hopes, and ambitions of the university community. This is demanding much of the campus ministers and their teams; but they are not walking alone. Everyone in the university community needs one another, and all march together as a community toward that great community of the great tomorrow. No one escapes being a member of the pilgrim church, which is lurching along, from side to side, on the path that has been blazed by the risen Christ.

This chapter admittedly paints a very high ideal of campus ministry. But then, the university is doing crucial work for culture and for civilization. Such work deserves the best ministry of Christian wisdom, of the Word Himself. From the Christian university issues the incarnate hope of Christianity: professional graduates who wish to serve God and the world well, Christian scholars who demonstrate in life and writing the presence of the risen Christ in culture, and Christian leaders who make possible a better future for both church and state. Without the best of Christian ministry, this hope might wither. Neither America nor the American Christian churches can afford such an event.

Indeed, this high ideal of campus ministry may serve very practical purposes. It might be used, for instance, as a profile with which candidates for campus ministry positions might be evaluated and job descriptions for them might be constructed. In addition, campus ministers might find the criteria of this ideal helpful in planning their future education and in describing the type of cooperation that they need from academics in order to form apostolic teams. Administrators will clearly find in this ideal reasons for mandating that campus ministers be allowed to teach pastoral theology within university programs. Yes, the ideal is very demanding, but it can also be very fruitful for the whole university enterprise. For the wholesomeness of knowledges, skills, and arts united within a university-wide Christian wisdom is fittingly celebrated in the Eucharistic liturgy when everyone present contributes to its unity of mind and to its love of heart through the integration of work, play, and contemplation.

Conclusion

It is a long road from hyper-specialization and workaholism to the essential role of campus ministry in the university. Yet it is a single road, for the basic remedy of workaholism is simply play. On the part of the workaholic, it takes no small act of faith (and some persistent practice) to set apart time for play and, then, (unbelievably) to enjoy the play. But once this happens, the workaholic begins to feel the exhilaration of liberty and the capability for contemplation. For play and contemplation do share many characteristics, even though play does create its own world and contemplation stays within the serious historico-traditional world to find its deeper unities. This continuity between play and contemplation enables play to vitalize contemplation so that specialization becomes more open to integration. For, in seeking the underlying unity of persons, things, and events, contemplation must modify the comprehensive *Weltanschauung* of a person or of a nation and, at the same time, foster the secularization process. Contemplation integrates not only knowledges, but also the understanding of secularities. Thus, the underlying aim in promoting contemplation is the future great human community of wholesome nobility surrounding divine mystery. In building toward wholesomeness, contemplation cannot help but inspire a community of wisdom.

For these reasons, contemplation leads to individual, private prayer, a communing with the ultimate single mystery of God. Such prayer makes the one who is praying aware of his or her own lack of integrity and of a personal need to unite with all other humans for the sake of wholeness—especially in the service of others through one's particular skill-art-knowledge and through cooperation with one's skill-art-knowledge community. Such private prayer becomes more powerful when it is lifted up in communal public worship that contains, of course, many of the elements that constitute play and contemplation. Indeed, public worship in the university is the highest wisdom act of the university community because it praises the ultimate mystery of God with all the talents and hopes of a wisdom community. In addition, it also beautifully unifies the university's two intrinsic aims and acutely focuses all its resources on the extrinsic aim of the university, namely, service of the larger civic community. This is why worship is essential to university life, not merely integral to it.

For this reason, too, campus ministry is essential to university life because its ministers facilitate the marriage between God and the university community. In this way, the secularization process becomes Christian in its secularity, in its hopes, and in its procedures because its heart carries a buoyant sacrificial love that animates the latest specializations and integrations for the building of a wisdom community and for the preserving of this community from sheer rationalism and rigid routinization. If this is the consummating work of campus ministry, then its members deserve professional training, full support, and the constant challenge of the university community's faith and needs. If these campus ministers ironically specialize in wholeness, then their training must be such that it both assures their own personal wholeness and induces a wholesome vision of the wide range of university activity. Furthermore, university structures should be wide open to the individual and group "soundings" that are offered by campus ministers and should lend themselves to opportunities for celebrating the Christian secularity of sacrament, word, liturgy, and sacrificial love.

Because all this may sound not merely ideal but *too* ideal, it would perhaps be of help at this point to take up the problem of every administrator: How does one implement these appealing ideals in definite plans that can enter into day-to-day life? Does not such implementation demand decisions that attempt to incarnate these ideals by way of certain models? What are the models for decisions, and what if they contradict these ideals? If the models are multiple, which one is to be the supreme model to which all other models bow? In the university decision-making process, all the rhetoric about speculative and practical wisdom will receive its final and decisive challenge.

13 Confused Models of the University Make for Shaky Decisions

Everyone would agree that clear insight into a situation and deep feeling about it promote a strong decision concerning it. The young woman who knows the law profession from clerking in her uncle's law office for three summers and who is thoroughly convinced that good lawyers are the guardians of civilization will normally make strong, perduring decisions on the way to her bar examination. Complicated as those decisions may have been, however, they are extremely simple when compared to those that face the university administrator. Because of the immense number of details to be assembled and because of the downright mystery of educating human beings for today's technico-scientific civilization, the university administrator faces the seemingly impossible task of making *good* decisions. Yet, surprisingly, the administrators and their universities survive these difficult decisions—in fact, they do better than merely survive. This in itself is a great mystery.

The reflective administrator is agonizingly aware both of how tentative he or she might feel about his or her most crucial decisions and of how surprised he or she might be by the success of a particularly shaky decision or by the unexpected factor that suddenly derails a steady decision. In the last instance, the administrator finds himself or herself saying: "I should have known that" or "No matter how careful the preparation, there is always some unforeseeable factor." The good administrator is nevertheless pragmatic; he or she knows that the human mind and heart have limited time, information, and patience for decisions of baffling complexity. He or she also knows that someone has to make the tough decisions and that, as the administrator, he or she has been carefully chosen by his or her peers to do just that.

This does not mean that the administrator is reduced to merely shrewd hunches because of the mammoth number of relevant details that routinely enter into his or her major decisions. The administrator, after all, has various staffs (e.g., budgetary, academic, personnel, planning, security, legal, public relations, and so on) who guide him or her with digested information, with relevant principles of decision, with alterna-

284

tive plans or potential outcomes, and with the collective wisdom of their specific area of competence. Nevertheless, the administrator must be able to correlate all this expert knowledge and advice that comes from the diverse and sometimes conflicting interests of the university. How does he or she correlate all of this so that "the buck *does* stop at his or her desk" and so that a truly informed and reflective decision is made with the strength of clear insight and of deeply felt values? The intelligent administrator clearly has more than some particular plan in mind; he or she has an overall view or a model, according to which he or she tailors decisions to fit the needs and hopes of a particular situation. This model acts as (a) the corrective for imbalances, (b) the inspirer of new plans and projects, and (c) the correlator for all the information and advice that is received from the various staffs. It must, therefore, be rather expansive yet definite, somewhat sophisticated yet simple. Evidently, the more conscious the administrator is of the influence of this model on his or her decisions and the more aware he or she is of its details, the stronger will be his or her decisions. After all, even when adapted to the pressures of the moment, this model is the last court of appeal.

It would pay us, then, to consider the following: (1) what such a model is, (2) how it is experientially developed, (3) what are the typical models used in university decisions, (4) how multiple models may be used within a single academic decision, and (5) whether there is a supermodel that controls all other models in such a decision. These questions not only outline this chapter, but also pose a further question: Can a Christian vision of the university act as this supermodel?

Decision Model: The Ultimate Control over One's Decisions

Let us begin by saying that a decision model is a constellation of rationally articulated values that control the application and intensity of a will act. It is not just one value and one understanding (e.g., "I am buying a dog because dogs are so companionable") but many values and understandings that are arranged with some priority in such a way as to be a unity. For example, the high-school teacher might say: "I'm satisfied with being an underpaid high-school teacher because (a) I find adolescents most open to intellectual growth, (b) I've got a knack for relating to them and their problems whether I'm teaching or counseling, (c) I find that their freshness keeps me from becoming too stodgy, and (d) I find a camaraderie among high-school teachers that I never felt at the elementary or college levels." If this same teacher is asked: "But what's the main reason why you teach high-school students?" he or she might respond: "Because this is the center of the arena, this is where the future of

America is decided—not in the elementary school where they don't know their own minds and hearts and not in college where they are already set in their prejudices." The more these various values and understandings are interrelated, weighed for validity, modified with other understandings and values, and, finally, unified more tightly with a reflective priority, the stronger this model is for influencing all the decisions of this high-school teacher and the more powerful will be his or her life.

This definition and example of a decision model is clarified if one notes how a model is gradually generated within an individual's life. The young boy, Joe, carefully watches his father when the father buys a car, corrects Joe's older sister, orders a meal at a restaurant, cheers Joe on in his swimming class, and has a tiff with the next-door neighbor over snow plowing. It slowly dawns on Joe that his father is considerate in his aggressiveness, intelligent in his earthiness of language-joke-work. Later, as young Joe tries to deal with the mystery of womankind, he notices how his sister neatly organizes everything she does from picnics to study programs, how she can somehow be affectionate with her father and at the same time resist his domination over her choice of dress, boy friend, and schooling. Joe begins to see how much she is like her mother, whom he admires for her quiet determination and sly humor when his father becomes a bit pompous in his opinions. His high-school baseball coach intrigues Joe by his nonchalance when everything seems to be going wrong in an important game and by his contrasting demand for discipline during practice sessions and for loyalty to the team at all costs. Joe also has a favorite teacher whose sardonic humor and occasional gruffness cover over an intense love of chemistry, mathematics, classical music, and students who quickly admit their ignorance and just as quickly get down to work to overcome it.

As Joe goes through his premedical program in college, he sketches a picture of his ideal future: he is a surgeon in Haiti working long hours in the slums and forming a clinic out of volunteer nurses and monthly doctor volunteers. He sees himself as competent, despite the stress caused by limiting conditions, independent of money and family ties (to more fully dedicate himself to the poor), very demanding of others but also, underneath his apparent harshness, very sensitive to their needs. Here, in the life of this young man, from early childhood to medical-school graduation, a collage of successive models gradually has become a single model for his life-decisions as his experience modifies and molds these models into a single constellation of articulated values. The uniqueness of his experiences and the unique mystery of his own being has made this model a unique picture of himself for his own viewing. Later, his wife or medical colleagues will help him see better within this picture the beautiful strokes of virtue, the shadows of ambiguity, and the ugly awkwardness of self-vaunting. As a result, he may well grow in realism and dedication. In any case, this young man has a definite model that will deeply influence all his personal, individual decisions.

This model for individual decisions is almost always supplemented by a model for social decisions—a community model that should correlate with the individual model. Here the same young man may have seen his family as loose-knit and mobile—each member seemed to have his or her own friends; the family members did not much center around each other. The young man liked this freedom and independence. On the other hand, his high-school baseball team and coach demanded total dedication of time and talent; they also blocked off the intrusion of others into their close camaraderie. The young man learned to resent this tightness once he got away from it at the end of the baseball season. Luckily, during his junior year of college, he studied in Rome and came to enjoy Italian warmth and spontaneity (so different from his own American family) because he lived with an Italian family and joined in their devotional parish life. The relaxed congeniality of this life strangely contrasted with the subsequent highly charged and ambitious office life in General Motors' Detroit Offices where he acted as medical advisor to the experimental division. He now wondered which life was more true and whether some compromise between their styles was not viable.

This wondering would lead him to change jobs and to become engaged to a woman who was more relaxed than the one he dated during his G.M. days. Now his community model for decisions was shaping into a single constellation and would have to be more closely integrated with his individual model if he wanted to escape unnecessary tension and even hypocrisy. He now sees himself as a man who prizes family life over medical success, yet who also highly honors medical competence and congenial intelligence. He finds that his liking for independence in family life has to be tempered by his wife's need for companionship; that their desire to give their three children a good education requires him to be more career-conscious, more dedicated to his medical advisory business. The very events of life are helping him to modify his individual and social models into a more integrated unity. His secularity is being defined more and more clearly.

Perhaps some tentative conclusions can be drawn from this experiential tracing of a decision model in its individual and social aspect. First, such a model is built out of one's memories of concrete events—key events that take on more and more significance as one compares them with subsequent similar experiences which reinforce their value. Values are actual faces, gestures of affection or disdain, unforgettably loyal or disloyal ac-

287

tions, supreme moments of sorrow at death or joy at marriage and birth. Consequently, not to know well the individual model for one's decisions is not to know oneself and one's life in much depth. Not to be well aware of one's social model for decisions is to stumble along one's career and to fumble one's family life away. Actually, if these models are only known vaguely, one's unconscious takes over in these decisions to make them sporadic and erratic. For the submerged memories are powerful in their individuality, yet they are not inhibited by recognition or by other memories which, rationally connected to them, modify them. Thus, the atomic memory works more by compulsion than by reasonable priority or by reasonable connection with previous memories of similar situations. One's life becomes a zig-zag and, occasionally, a circling back to adolescence and even to childhood; continuity and meaning disappear from it.

On the other hand, if one is familiar with the decision model behind one's decisive acts, one can be aware of its limitations, e.g., its prejudices, its narrow range of experience, its overindulged feelings, its unrealistic hopes. Then, too, one is able to consciously modify this model when events yield new insights that lead into new evaluations. The career executive, for example, whose wife suddenly dies at thirty-two and leaves him with four children must radically revamp his decision model as he faces the new values of life and death, of career and family, of leisure spent more with children than with adults. The better he knows his past model for decisions, the more quickly he can adjust it to a new situation without destroying it and without enduring a consequent period of ennui and paralysis.

Finally, if a person knows with some accuracy his or her decision model, he or she can occasionally go beyond it to trust in mystery—and, incidentally, to grow into a deeper and wider model. Thus, a domineering husband may employ an individual decision model that (a) never allows his wife to make a major decision, (b) is forever monitoring the lives of his college-age children, and (c) has never trusted the expansion of his small company to his associates. He must, at least for a time, abandon this highly conscious model when he sustains a devastating heart attack that necessitates six months of rest. He must put the reins of life into the hands of others and trust their decisions; he must abandon himself to the full mystery of life. If he knows his decision model well, then he will be immediately aware of what must be done to avoid the terrible frustration, depression, and anger that might prolong his recovery period. If he knows his decision model only vaguely, then he will feel frustration without knowing what to do about it, without being able to recognize the advent of new values, without being able to integrate the new values into the previous decision model so that his life has continuity as well as new depth of meaning. His implicit secularity, because it is so implicit, cannot grow intelligently but only haphazardly and dangerously, for himself and for those affected by his decisions.

The decision model, then, evidently plays a central part in one's life. It determines how one maps one's individual life and how one cooperates within his or her various communities. As a person is less conscious of his or her decision model, he or she proportionately loses control over life. Insofar as a person consciously possesses and employs the decision model, he or she knows himself or herself, is aware of the community, can modify the decision model to suit the changing circumstances, can retain the continuity of inner meaning of his or her life (especially during those "predictable crises of adult life"), and can prudently plan his or her future life in terms of past experience and present needs. If the decision model is so basic and crucial to the individual's life, what is its multiplied importance to the large organization, such as a government agency, a business concern, a church, a university? For, if a single person needs a decision model, must there not be a proportionately greater need for such a decision model in order to conceive, project, and test an organizational decision—especially since the organizational decision includes so much information and involves the futures of so many people?

Models for University Decisions and the Controls They Offer

There are, of course, more models for university decisions than the eight to be described below. But simply calling attention to the variety of models, to the advantages of each, and to the different ways in which they may be simultaneously used in one decision may prove profitable, if only to alert the university administrator to fuller consciousness of his or her decision-making process and to elicit the professor's sympathy for the complicated task of the administrator. It should be noted at once that each university employs more than one model. No single model stands for a particular American university.

Perhaps the most influential of all recent decision models among American universities of the twentieth century is the **graduate school model.** This model aims to promote technical skills and scientific knowledges out of concern for both the welfare of mankind and the progress of civilization. It emphasizes specialization of knowledges-arts-skills without a similar call for integration among these disciplines, stressing rather their distinction and autonomy. As a result, university departments become so highly specialized and autonomous that the university is hardly a unified entity. Although such a model often enough has places for philosophy and theology, they are still not looked upon as "wisdom knowledges," but simply as two more knowledges to be advanced.

It was earlier remarked that a distinct contribution of the American university to worldwide higher learning has been the ingenious blending of the German graduate school with the English college. Unfortunately, the prestige of Johns Hopkins or the University of Chicago, both principally founded for graduate work, has brought other universities to rigidly imitate them. This undoubtedly had the good effect of upgrading American university education to meet the standards of European universities by the late 1960s. Nevertheless, it also had the bad effect of penetrating deeply into the undergraduate college so as to fragment it into distinct, autonomous departments that gave little thought to integration until the recent burst of interdisciplinary courses and departments. For this reason, the liberal tradition of the college began to suffer from the disease of totally pragmatic specialism; liberal courses became premedical, prelaw, predental, preclinical, all of which were research oriented. Then followed the zealotry of the isolated department that developed superhuman requirements for undergraduates so that, upon graduating, the student might be accepted at the best graduate schools. Naturally, the core curriculum suffered constant attack, if not deterioration. The remedial prescription for such a situation is not abandonment of the graduate school model (without which the American university might slowly wither away) but rather the introduction of other, balancing models to the university decision-making process.

An important model for the university during times of either financial difficulty or great expansion is the **business model.** It naturally emphasizes efficiency and productivity. Its criteria for the achievement of these qualities are: (1) faculty-student ratio for economic viability, (2) number and diversity of degrees granted, (3) financial contributions to and from the civic community, (4) high-quality training and successful placement of students in jobs, (5) minimum course enrollments, (6) salary range and number of tenured faculty, (7) size of endowments for both developing departments and recruiting outstanding scholars, (8) increase of university investments, and (9) number of scholarships for securing students of high potential. A certain amount of consumerism is included in this model: students "buy into" sets of courses, public relations "sells" the students on the goodness of the "product" and its use for future economic advancement, faculty are expected to "please" the "buying public." Like ambitious executives, university personnel are expected to use the university as a step to higher positions in better schools or in industry.

Given the complex and huge annual budgets of even a small university, the administrator has no choice but to use the business model in his or her decisions. The temptation is to let this model be the final determinant (and not just the limiting determinant) of decisions. Expensive innovations can then be avoided, excellent programs that are not self-sustaining can be dropped—unless, of course, they might be significant for public image building. The business model, then, tends to be overly conservative in its laudable emphasis of fiscal responsibility. Thus, the university can begin to lose her character as a prime innovative force within the national culture. Instead of anticipating problems or of rushing to solve them, the business model tends to encourage the safer attitude of "wait and see."

A third model, more characteristic of the early American colleges before they became universities, is the **Christian wisdom model.** In this model, a Christian faith commitment permeates the entire life of the university and is expressed in a common understanding of culture, common goals of university endeavor, and corporate dedication to a Christian lifestyle. In this model, respect for *traditio* and a consequently thorough cultivation of history is stressed along with reflection on current cultural trends. Because of the wisdom context, philosophy and theology take on paramount importance and cooperate closely with the social and physical sciences—if only for their own vitality, to say nothing of the need for integration in the lives of the students and faculty. Insistence on values is a strength of this model.

Because this model aims both to achieve a vast synthesis of contemporary knowledges and to make this synthesis available to the whole university community, it tends to nourish skepticism in proportion to the increasing difficulty of integrating knowledges with the accumulation of culture. The vastness of the task also tends to consume all the energies of the faculty in work that is limited to the confines of the university. Thus, interest in service to the civic community can be lessened and result in a distancing from the needs of society; academic snobbery can shortly follow. At this point, wisdom's stress on values begins to sound hollow.

The **denominational college model,** despite its name, is different from the Christian wisdom type because it is totally dedicated to the preservation and advance of a single denominational faith (e.g., Mormon, Lutheran, Baptist, Roman Catholic, Fundamentalist-biblical, Buddhist, Islamic, and so on). This single faith dominates the religious, social, and academic life of the school because the overwhelming majority of students, faculty, administration, and staff are recruited from this one faith and strongly adhere to it. Usually, the continuity of this school is further guaranteed by the freewill offerings of the mother church. Since this single lived faith is the central dynamism of the school, academic life is subordinated to faith life. Moreover, the aim of the academic program is the integration of all knowledges within this faith. Pastoral ministry and theology would naturally play strong roles in this model.

The close unity achieved by this model is not without cost, however. Because the pluralism of theology would be narrowed (and, therefore, that of philosophy, if it is taught apart from theology), the type of integration that is accomplished in this model would not be comprehensive— especially if the dominant theology is somewhat ill at ease with the arts and sciences. Furthermore, the presence of a single lifestyle would appear so removed from the variety of American lifestyles (even from the variety of Christian lifestyles) that it could well isolate the university community from the mainstream of life. This could result in a smug narrowness of view and of life.

In contrast to this is the **community model** of university life. According to this model, best exemplified in expensive, four-year experimental colleges, the institutional side of the university is almost always to be subordinated to the community side, since the primary aim of this university is expansion of the person within the community. For this reason, small classes are prescribed to ensure close, individual attention to students. Both academic and psychological counseling are intensely pursued. Social problems receive much attention in both the formation of curricula and the day-to-day classwork. Although the autonomy of the distinct knowledges-arts-sciences and their respective departments is respected, nevertheless their integrative cooperation with each other in research, in cross-disciplinary courses, and in social life is expected. Final authority for major changes in university life is vested in a faculty-student senate; yet, the administration is given wide latitude in making daily decisions and in implementing major changes.

This personalist approach of enlarged freedom and experimentation can breed disorganization unless the administration is astute and the faculty persuasive of student opinion. The model seems to be better adapted to small student bodies of high intelligence and strong ambition, for interdisciplinary studies, especially those that straddle two or three disciplines, demand twice the amount of study and require a cultivated discernment of the distinct method and evidences of each knowledge-art-skill. Confusion here could mean lower quality performance and, eventually, rather poorly disciplined minds.

At the opposite end of the spectrum from the rather exclusive community model is the **servant model,** which, ironically, is best exemplified by the American two-year community colleges. For the aim of the servant model is to be totally integrated with the present needs of the surrounding community (agricultural or inner city or suburban) so that the university's courses, and even its departments of learning, are instituted or suppressed as soon as public needs arise or die out. As the surrounding society becomes more and more complex, so, too, do the offerings of this school as they range from sewing and plumbing to Latin and Calculus II. Professors are expected to band together to deal with local problems such as juvenile delinquency, care of the aged, recruitment of light industry, air pollution from the soft-coal burners, suicide prevention, assistance of local law enforcement and government agencies with computer technology, and so on.

Though this model stresses well the extrinsic end of the university, namely, service to the community, it risks depreciating the intrinsic ends of the university that ultimately make the extrinsic end effective. The student may never learn how to escape the purely pragmatic, with its often narrow horizon, or how to enjoy the liberty of an overview or how to discover where he or she is. The faculty, in turn, may become so caught up in local problems that they lose their taste for the grand view that could make them more creative in handling these problems. They might even begin to lose interest in their own specialized knowledge-art-skill, the taproot of their effectiveness and their integrity.

The seventh model is the **social activist** or **prophetic model.** It conceives of the university as an instrument of social change within civic society. Since the university, with its specialized knowledges, is usually ahead of civic society in its awareness of future developments and since, normally, university personnel have a freedom from close ties with business, government, the entertainment industry, the military organization, and the church, this model encourages the faculty (a) to warn civic society about cultural trends (e.g., amorality in government espionage, the breakup of the family, business monopolies, indoctrination by television programs, decline of church influence, and so forth); (b) to predict future events (e.g., growing consumption of rapidly diminishing oil reserves, peaceful use of nuclear power, pollution of the atmosphere, economic inflation, and so on); (c) to offer social solutions to these problems; and finally (d) to actively agitate for these solutions. This model sees the science of economics, for example, as an instrument not only for assessing current problems, but, more important, for agitating toward their pragmatic solution. Thus, the university, as critic of society and its culture, not only challenges popular error and destructive civic myth, but also is expected to offer alternative myths so that society can choose a better myth for directing its destiny.

The social activist, or prophetic, model of the university, a favorite conception of both the 1970 student riots and the Free University of Berlin, underlines in red ink the extrinsic aim of the university to such an extent that the intrinsic aims of specialized knowledges-art-skills and wisdom accumulation are obscured. The hot intensity of its efforts to promote needed social change tends to dry up the intrinsic sources of energy and inventiveness that are needed to fuel and direct beneficient social change. Furthermore, this intensity also tends to jeopardize the wisdom that is required to develop alternative civic myths, to challenge false myths, and to direct the energies of social reform for long-term persistence and success. Because of this, the social activist, or prophetic, model may tend toward supporting monolithic myth and secularity—a grand military dictatorship. Ideology may enter at this point to suppress truth and overpower liberty.

The eighth and last model to be presented here is the **techological institute model** prevalent in both Russia and France. Its aim is to produce highly trained technologists in abundance for the increasingly sophisticated machinery of modern civilization. In this model, the scientific is always kept in tight subordination to the technical, and the liberal is not allowed to distract from the vocational. For these reasons, although values are always operative in this model (how else could the above subordinations be decided?), they are not often subjected to close scrutiny. This model allows room for the less contemplative and more mechanical-minded student at the higher levels of education, teaches a disciplined attitude toward technical work, provides experts for a rapidly advancing technology, and quickly adapts to the needs of society.

While the technological institute model makes it possible to preserve our technological culture, its soft-pedaling of values leaves the student inadequately prepared for both personal life and social life. If such a technologist enters into a managerial position of power, what in his or her education will protect him or her from becoming a technocrat who is only interested in the "how" and is actually unable to formulate the "why" for himself or herself or others?

An alert administrator is, of course, well aware that all eight of these models (and others) may be present in his or her decision-making process and that they influence a decision from different directions with widely diverse presuppositions. What bothers him or her most, however, is how to orchestrate these varying notes into a single beautiful theme within his or her university decision. Failure to get unity here means a weaker decision and also a more chaotic university.

The Orchestration of Decision Models

The unifying of these models within a single administrative decision is not impossible because the models tend to complement one another's weaknesses with strengths. Although the Christian wisdom model, for example, emphasizes the intrinsic aim of cumulative wisdom, it needs to be balanced by the graduate school model, which stresses the other intrinsic aim of reinterpretation of specialized knowledge-skill-art; it also needs balance from the servant model, which aims at serving the civic community, the extrinsic aim of the university. On the other hand, the business model may well help the university survive because of its conservative stance about fiscal responsibility; this same university also needs the spur of the social activist model to keep it mindful of the problems of the surrounding civic community that has nurtured its existence. Thus, too, the community model of the university reminds the university that it is primarily meant for *persons* at the very time when this particular university is pursuing, with notable success, a far-reaching program of technological advance according to the technological institute model. Finally, the denominational college model points to the ultimate challenge that the faith commitment poses to all academic and civic achievements. There is, then, a complementarity among these models that allows the administrator to focus them together within a particular decision-making process.

But it is not enough to merely acknowledge this complementarity, for the impact of each model is different depending on the situation of the decision. How does one control this difference of impact within the complementarity? For example, the community model and the denominational model are the more difficult to apply as the university grows in size and complexity. Given the secularized state of American society, the university must be cautious in using the Christian wisdom model lest it arouse resentment rather than cooperation. Furthermore, if, as predicted, college enrollment steadily declines in the 1980s, competitive spirit will demand that the graduate school model be emphasized even on the undergraduate level and even if the danger of a narrow vocationalism must be courted.

On the other hand, a Christian revival would make the denominational college model more relevant since this model would ask for a strong theology program and a vigorous pastoral ministry to support the faith of the students. Indeed, the denominational college model would resist any attempt to substitute a religious studies program for theology because it would see in this action a reduction of theology from being a wisdom knowledge to being just another knowledge that must compete in the university cafeteria of courses for student attention. Again, should the cry against hyper-specialization be taken up, then the Christian wisdom model would be powerful, since its emphasis on integration of knowledges-arts-skills would require a strong undergraduate core curriculum, a theology program that is in close touch with all the other university

295

disciplines, and a philosophy program that demonstrates the possibility of all specializations converging into a wisdom unity. Lastly, when the nation becomes alarmed at the mechanization of life, university administrators will favor the community model because of its strong bias for the person—a bias which would insist on informal dialogs between faculty and students on a departmental basis, on interdisciplinary courses leading to overviews, on more leisure time for assimilating studies, and on less rigorous institutional demands that seem to lack trust in the students' sense of responsibility and initiative.

There might also occur a financial recession. The business model would then loom up dominant to restrain the very expensive emphasis on specialization and to put financial limits to team teaching, lowered teacher-pupil ratio, and expanded counseling services; it would also call attention to the financial opportunities inherent in providing trained personnel for industry and business. Recall how the appearance of the Russian sputnik in the skies of America got university administrators to take a good look at the technological institute model as the United States went into a semi-panic over its dilatory space program. Thus, it can be seen that the situation partially determines the type of emphasis which a particular model will receive within the decision-making process. It is the job of the strong administrator, then, to keep the other models in mind in order to balance the currently dominant model.

But what enables the administrator to manage this balance? Keeping the other models in mind is not enough because they must be given different "weights" in the act of balancing them. A snide observer might ask: "What determines the 'weights,' other than the administrator's personal penchants and the demands of the situation?" In response to this remark, a number of factors that are helpful to the administrator in weighing the various models may be cited. First, *traditio* (the history of the administrator's university, of his or her country, of educational changes over the centuries) gives a perspective for estimating the present and the future. Secondly, administrators from all the American universities may pool their experiences and their wisdom (if they are in close touch with their staffs, with their faculty, and with their students) through meetings, special reports, periodicals, and commissioned research groups. Thirdly, as we found earlier, there is a fundamental philosophy, theology, and secularity which underlie the pluralism of the many philosophies, theologies, and secularities. This fundamental unity in world process, though it is hard to describe accurately, is nevertheless present and operative; it is always available to be tapped when persons of good will join together to struggle with confusion and evil. These three factors give a "feel" for what is right and just and also enable the prudent administrator to make a good judgment even while he or she is struggling with the correct weight to give the various models that influence his or her judgment. For this reason, the multiple models do not necessarily fragment the administrator's decisions and atomize the university itself, though it is clear that their multiplicity and sometimes contrary tendencies could give more than a headache to the administrator and to the university operation.

There is yet another problem, however, that must be faced at this juncture. How does the administrator or the situation determine which model will be dominant among all the models that are to be used in a decision? It would appear, from the examples given earlier, that the situation of a sputnik or of a financial recession or of a cry against hyperspecialization will determine the dominant model. Yet administrators have, at times, strenuously fought against such panic thinking or fad promoting. Is it possible that the administrator not only lets the perspectives of history and of fundamental philosophy-theology-secularity influence him or her, but also uses a supermodel with which to arrange all the lesser models according to the needs of the situation? What would this supermodel be? It could not be one of the eight models earlier described since their very complementarity reveals their weaknesses. No one of them could be stretched to cover the breadth and depth of a university decision, nor does any combination of them cover all situations and novel developments. Besides, the supermodel has to advise when one model is more relevant than another, when a particular model is irrelevant, or when the priority or hierarchy of models has to be shifted to meet a new event.

Have we now come to the point where ideology must be invoked to explain how the administrator is to rise above both his or her models and the pressures of the situation? We have already noted how narrow-minded any ideology is, how singular its lifestyle is, how shallow its use of philosophy and science is, how prejudiced toward one class of society its liberation movement is, how power-hungry its users eventually become.

Rather, a vision such as we have previously described is needed. For a vision is an extrapolation. It arises, on the one side, out of and yet beyond a dominant philosophy and theology which are in close touch with all the other university disciplines, and, on the other side, out of the lived experience of university people whose lives are infused with dedication to each other, to the students, and to civic society. If this is a Christian vision, then the philosophy and theology are Christian and the university people are united in the charity of Christ. Moreover, this vision is colored by both the current resources of the university and the present needs and future hopes of the civic community that is served by the university community. Now this vision, although it is structured by theoretical elements, is aimed at enriching the practical principles that go into concrete university decisions about the goals, structures, and procedures of the university community as latter specializes knowledges-arts-skills and accumulates wisdom for the service of the civic community.

Because it is an extrapolation and is known as such, the vision is open to being modified or discarded since it is only one interpretation, among others, of the university's meaning. Because it arises out of university disciplines, the collective experience of university people, and the *traditio* of the American university, it carries a proportionate authority even though it is not considered "the single saving message for every university." Although it is open to being modified by the eight (or more) university models for decision making as they reveal its gaps or inconsistencies, it still is more comprehensive and deeper than they are because of its wider and more radical origins in the university disciplines, in university community experience, and in the American and European *traditio*. Because it is only one extrapolation out of other possible ones, it leaves its user free; yet it can elicit the user's enthusiasm because it comes from the experience of the university community—an experience filled with the strong feelings and memories of both great people and great accomplishments.

Thus, the vision can act as a supermodel to discover, challenge, develop, abandon, or gain insight into the eight (or more) university models. It can also unite them, weight them for influence, and direct them within the administrator's decision-making process. How else does one escape from being imprisoned within one or another university model except by using a vision to organize them into a unity—a vision that is, in fact, dispensable for another more comprehensive and more radical vision? How else could one orchestrate the eight (or more) models into a single beautiful theme, using the strengths of each to compensate for the weaknesses of the others? There must be a comprehensive and radical supermodel or vision. The measure of the administrator's conscious vision, then, becomes the measure of his or her decisions and even the measure of the person himself or herself, at least as an administrator. This vision is the final court of appeals before which the administrator brings all his or her decisions for final determination. Although dispensable and modifiable, this vision is nevertheless the mind and the heart of the university's future. This is all the more true of a Christian vision of the university because this vision more specifically addresses the needs and hopes of both the Christian university community and the civic community that it serves.

The Christian Vision Orchestrates the Christian University

Because a supermodel or vision is necessary to all the university administrator's decisions, if they are to be strong and illuminative, the question is not whether or not the administrator should have a vision, but what type of vision will he or she choose. Because the administrator of a Christian university receives the Christian *traditio,* in most cases, from his or her predecessors, he or she is expected to run this university according to a Christian vision. One such Christian vision, among others, is detailed in the nineteen chapters of this book. Because other Christian visions of the university are available, however, our present aim is to see how *any* Christian vision would, as a supermodel for decision making, orchestrate the Christian university.

Strong objections can be brought against the use of a Christian vision as a supermodel for university decisions. If it is, for example, only one vision among other Christian visions, would it not risk being as eccentric or narrow as the administrators who use it? Can the stability of the university be maintained by a dispensable vision, even if it is Christian? Are not visions highly passionate and idealistic, and do not university administrators need to work with cool reason and with earthy pragmatism? Does not the addition of the adjective *Christian* to the word *vision* narrow the supermodel enough to threaten the comprehensiveness of the university structure? If these objections can be met, perhaps a Christian vision of the university may be recognized as a most useful supermodel for university decision making.

To understand why a Christian vision would not necessarily be limited by the administration's grasp of it, it would be helpful to recall from chapter five that any dominant university vision must arise out of the university community itself. Its base, then, includes faculty, students, staff, and the other constituencies of the university. Otherwise, this vision will not be lived and, therefore, will not unite the university—no matter how often the administration exhorts to its fulfillment. Furthermore, any vision becomes dominant because it is more in touch with the evidences of the specialized knowledges (especially philosophy and theology) than are other visions. Indeed, a vision dominates because its imagery elicits passionate dedication to the university's ideals, because its suppleness is adaptable to the resources of the university and to the needs of the larger civic community, and because its strength is such that it can accept criticism. Lastly, it describes the university's singleness of purpose more accurately than other visions. Now all of these factors, when converged, are strong safeguards against eccentric use of this vision by administrators or by power-cliques among the faculty, for a vision is simply not a manipulable ideology. Indeed, these same convergent factors show that a vision can be a source of stability for the university rather than a dissolvent of its structure, and that a dominant vision can be as concretely pragmatic and yet as comprehensive as any university administrator could wish for.

These same factors, which are present in any dominant vision, are especially strong in the Christian vision of the university. Insofar as a Christian vision arises out of a Christian philosophy and a Christian theology whose very integrity demand that they be in touch with the evidences of all the specialized knowledges-arts-skills, then this Christian vision will be not only as comprehensive as these specialties, but also as supple as their constant reinterpretation of traditional truth requires. Creative criticism will be part of its life-force. At the same time, this Christian vision will have as its root system the stability of traditional Christian wisdom. For traditional Christian wisdom has always included plural Christian theologies and philosophies within its life-force; yet it has been able to maintain unity because these pluralities focus upon Christ, the living wisdom, at the center of the Christian community life— whether this life is liturgical, moral, academic, ascetic, or service-oriented. Personal loyalty to a risen Christ who is present throughout the universe, but particularly operative in human beings, elicits personal dedication as no other factor in the history of Western civilization. Because this Christ sees Himself as the Lord of History, because He excludes no knowledge, no skill, no art from His interest, because He feels at home in any culture, and because He considers Himself the brother of every human being, His accepted presence within the Christian community ensures strong unity and yet full comprehensiveness for the Christian community and its universities.

Furthermore, the presence of this Christ is a constant reminder of mystery, which it is the university's mission to enter, to explore, and to reverence. Here the Christian university also becomes aware of its destiny, its overriding single purpose: to develop out of the specialized knowledges-arts-skills a wisdom that is indispensable to the larger civic community as the latter makes its journey to the great community of the great tomorrow. For, as the Word, Christ makes clear to every Christian the worth of the intellectual life; then, as living Eucharist, He demonstrates how this intellectual life is the expression of love in the service of one's fellow human beings. At the same time, Christ's message, as it is expressed with common-sense wisdom in the Gospels, reminds human beings of the humble origins and destination of all human knowledge and technology; likewise, Christ's life of sacrifice unto death and resurrection reminds us at once of both temporal tragedy and eternal hope.

Thus, any Christian vision that centers itself in the risen Christ; that arises out of the Christian university community; that, by way of Christian philosophy and Christian theology, constantly reassesses itself in the light of the latest reinterpretations of the specialized knowledges-arts-skills; that elicits deep dedication to the intellectual life out of personal dedication to Christ and out of love for one's fellow men and women; that furnishes the university with strong singleness of purpose in its service of the civic community; and that reminds the university of its humble dependence on common-sense knowledge and on the day-to-day sacrifices of average people—such a Christian wisdom is of essential importance to the Christian university. No Christian university community would allow administrators to use this vision eccentrically. Nor could a Christian university, as Christian, maintain its stability without this vision. Furthermore, there need be no fear that such a Christian vision would cloud the administrator's reason with its passion and idealism. Rather, one problem of the Christian university may well be that its administrators have lost their fire and inventive daring by distractedly neglecting their Christian vision. Their reason may have become blurred as they began to lose a clear vision of Christ's face and their hearts may have faltered as the sounding of Christ's word within them began to grow weaker.

Thus, a Christian vision is a powerful supermodel for the administrator to employ within his or her decision-making processes as he or she attempts to coordinate the various models of a university into a unity that will preserve the integrity of the university's intrinsic aims and, at the same time, will direct these aims to the service of the larger civic community. If ever the administrator needed a vision as a supermodel for his or her decisions in complex and chaotic times, if ever the Christian administrator needed a Christian vision as his or her supermodel in these days of divergent pluralism, desecularization, and secularism, it is now.

But, again, the question arises: How does a particular university in its unique situation employ such a Christian vision? How is this vision to be rendered unique? Is it possible that each university has a unique destiny to fulfill, a unique service to offer its civic community and, for this reason, needs a unique vision? Indeed, is this uniqueness the source of the vision?

14 Can a University Afford to be Unique?

In its advertising literature, catalogs, and faculty handbooks, each university implies, sometimes rather coyly, its uniqueness. Let us consider a fictitious university. The brochures mentioning the charms of McBartlett University will assure us that it offers a "unique blend of urban and country living, of highly scientific and thoroughly liberal courses, of disciplined pursuit and leisurely contemplation in learning, of specialized skills and integrated outlook, of sports and serious study, of individual privacy and social cooperation." McBartlett University will also stress how its uniquely specialized resources (faculty, student body, traditions, and local customs) enable it to fit into the special needs of its local civic community and of its students. So, "If you yourself want to stand out as unique, join this unique adventure called McBartlett University."

Yet McBartlett University has to be careful about its uniqueness. If it becomes "too unique," will it be able to qualify, according to general criteria, for government funding of its projects? Will it meet the general criteria of accrediting agencies? Will its uniqueness allow it to prepare its students to live according to America's general norms for success? This last question can be translated rather pointedly to ask, will McBartlett's training assure its students of securing jobs? Will they truly be trained "to be at home in almost any situation?" In addition, will McBartlett's uniqueness render it incapable of cooperating with other universities, of imitating the successful programs and techniques of these universities, and of meeting national civic problems at the local level in the adjoining city of McBartlett, Oregon?

The problem of uniqueness is especially acute for the Christian university, since the Christian university usually warrants its existence solely because of its special claim to uniqueness. Frequently, the private Christian university will claim to be doing what the non-Christian and the secular university cannot do, that is, it will offer a Christian wisdom through the faith commitment of its faculty and administration. Otherwise, this Christian university has no reason to continue in existence; this is especially true if the neighboring non-Christian and secular universities are offering better academic training because of the large funding at their disposal for acquiring faculty and promoting inventive programs, and if the college-age population is dwindling so that competition for students is heightened. Why should the Christian universities busy themselves with producing somewhat blurred copies of what other universities etch sharply and beautifully?

Thus, the problem of uniqueness seems to narrow down to one important factor: how strong is the particular Christian vision (or supermodel) that animates a particular Christian university? But is the problem really as simple as that? What precisely is uniqueness? Could uniqueness be an illusion amid the evident homogenization of university systems? Can this mysterious uniqueness be known and then promoted or is it simply the indirect result of an isolating specialization of purpose? In other words, are the sources of a university's uniqueness merely its cumulative limitations? If uniqueness is a positive and knowable reality, who is responsible for its promotion and how is that promotion to be carried out? Could the uniqueness of a Christian university be more than its supermodel or Christian vision, that is to say, could it also be that Christian community which is animating this university and following out its mission? Or is this so-called uniqueness simply a blend of quaint eccentricities that is no longer economically feasible? These questions serve as an outline of intent for this chapter.

The Mystery of Uniqueness

The unique is all around us—in the prize rose or steer, in the unrepeatable event of a May snowstorm in Rome, in the fabulous Yankees of the Ruth-DiMaggio-Gehrig era, in the unforgettable personality of Ezra Pound or Robert Frost, and in the sudden death of someone dear to us. Because there is no escaping uniqueness, it can be taken for granted and even overlooked—except by the artist and the counselor. Even when uniqueness is recognized as fresh novelty that never again will be repeated, its full mystery can be missed, for one can be content with an explanation of only superficial novelty when what is needed is a knowledge of radical novelty. A scientist, for example, might explain to you that a unique event is merely the rearrangement of atoms in new bindings of a particular molecule. This is, as it were, a "closed universe" into which nothing new ever enters. It is as though the world were a great deck of cards and new hands were being dealt every second, but each new hand that is dealt always uses the same cards. The novelty would be the new hands (collocations of atoms) made up of new combinations of old cards. This would be superficial novelty, however, because only the combination is new, not the elements that make up the new combination.

There are other cosmologists who hypothesize that new energy packets are constantly being introduced into the universe from some mysterious source other than the universe itself. When these newly inserted energy packets enter into new combinations of atoms in this "open universe," it is called *radical novelty*. This type of uniqueness is not merely a reassembling of old elements but a modified reorganization that never before has been attempted and never again will be exactly reproduced because of the constant introduction of new modifying elements that never before had been present in the universe.

Such radical novelty, rather than its superficial imitation, seems to be the presupposition that underlies biological evolution. Biological evolution takes for granted a generally linear development of the tree of life, even though the branchings of this tree are occasionally broken off or appear to twine around each other. But only radical novelty can give truly linear development; superficial novelty implies circular development— even if it is a circle so mammoth that it appears, in places, to be a straight line. For the enclosed universe, with its definite number of elements that are constantly reshuffling, will eventually deal out the same hands as had been dealt out ten billion years ago, and the circle finally will have been closed. Evolution and history, however, take for granted a linear development of events that have never occurred before and will never occur again simply because it is impossible for them to be repeated. Furthermore, both evolution and history take for granted that events are cumulative, that is, that events grow out of and beyond previous events. In other words, evolution and history appear to suppose purposive cumulative growth rather than chance arrangements of atoms.

The mystery of uniqueness is recognizable in the methodology of the historian. The average historian is seeking trends that are made up of many events, each of which is very different in itself and yet, together they are similar enough to constitute a trend—such as a growing loss of confidence in a government or an increased expectancy for both higher wages and better working conditions or a growing willingness to support war against another nation or a growing understanding of abstract art. To trace the development of a trend, the historian must compare diverse segments of time and space as well as very diverse actions-people-events that constitute these segments. The comparison would be impossible if, despite the vast differences between the constituents of each segment and

304

between the segments themselves, some similarity did not link these segments and their constituents. For, without this similarity or continuity between constituents and their segments, there is no history, no recognizable, cumulative growth or decline.

In addition, the historian is asked to assign causes for this growing continuity or trend. As soon as the historian attempts this, he or she is taking for granted that events have cumulative effects on one another and that this accumulation produces the trend. The historian dreads the assigning of causes to trends because he or she is deeply aware that both the events that accumulate into a trend and the trend itself have never been observed before; nor will these events ever be exactly repeated again so that the historian might check out past estimates. Thus, historians can only shake their heads at those philosophers who attempt to judge history by rigidly deterministic universal laws. Historians are fascinated by the uniqueness of events and almost despair of setting up universal patterns of explanation like "trends." Some historians would even hold that the uniqueness of an era is such that comparing it with another era would be accurate only if the same person lived inside both eras and only if that person escaped total conditioning by one or another of the eras. Yet, as historians, they must compare diverse eras and plot out the cumulative development of trends if there is to be any understanding of human history and of human beings, those uniquely historical animals.

When one moves from public history to the private history of the individual, one glimpses new aspects of the mystery of uniqueness. The unbelievably swift development of the human embryo according to an unreduplicatable genetic pattern called deoxyribonucleic acid (DNA) is an example of uniqueness that is rendered even more unique by its interaction with the always changing environment of the embryo. In this development, the remarkably cumulative biological development from the zygote to the just-born infant not only is continued but is rendered subordinate to the cumulative (historical) psychological development of this child after its birth. Psychologists often speak of "growth phases" and of "predictable crises" and "subsequent conversions." The person is always reinterpreting his or her life to make new psychological growth possible and, as counselors soon discover, the person does this in a manner that is unique to himself or herself. When the person does this reinterpretation, he or she also formulates a new, more sophisticated model for the decisions with which he or she will express himself or herself in service of the various communities to which he or she belongs. The model also happens to be unique, for, if the person tries to use someone else's model, he or she horribly suffers through false expecta-

305

tions and consequent disappointments. One has to be true to oneself. This means that each person must fashion his or her own individual manner of life, which may be similar to that of others (how else would one ever find a marriage partner?) but is nevertheless always a unique expression of his or her own inner mystery.

What is said of the individual person has some legitimacy for the social entity of a team or a business or a nation or a university community. Each of these groups, somewhat like the individual person, has accumulated tradition (not genetic but historical), goes through a conversion process from time to time, and develops a new decision model after each conversion. Members of the New York Yankees baseball team speak of their pride. This is mainly their tradition of highly skilled baseball teams, frequent championships, good leadership, and decent relations with the owners. But each great Yankee team is the result of a conversion process during which the Yankee spirit is reassessed, revitalized, and relived in a fresh and novel way that fits the times, the personnel, and the rival teams. This new life, then, becomes part of the Yankee tradition, but not before it has developed a new vision, or supermodel, for all its organizational decisions.

Every business, every political party, and every nation (witness the United States of 1970) goes through the same process of accumulating a tradition, of converting itself through reassessment of its resources and goals, and of developing a new model for its future decisions. Thus, the uniqueness of each social entity (as well as of each individual person) seems to be rendered more intense by this three-step process because it (1) takes in new riches of experience, (2) modifies its structure in a more complex way, and (3) develops a new, more sophisticated model for decisions so that the individual or the social organization can take a new direction. (Recall from the last chapter the genesis of the decision model in the young doctor to see how this is verified in detail.)

It should be no surprise, then, that the university itself would enjoy a similar process and possess similar sources for its uniqueness. Even our brief survey of European and American universities could not fail to reveal the uniqueness of each university. Furthermore, our briefer comparison of their traditions brought to light not only the uniqueness that has structured each of the five major university models, but also the unique result that has occurred when these five models were simultaneously used to mold a Third-World university according to the particular needs of each country. There was definitely an homogenization process occurring, but the widely diverse needs of each country demanded a unique application of the five models to the planning of each country's university. It would pay us, then, to consider the meaning of uniqueness in the university. For, clearly, this mysterious uniqueness is a quality that is expensive in time, complexity, and effort. Yet it may well be indispensable to the existence of the Christian university.

What Is Good about Uniqueness for the University?

If one is strictly honest, would one not have to say that stress upon the uniqueness of a university is precisely the most expensive item in the university budget? Is this not the experimental aspect of the university that often gives the least return on one's investment, if one is lucky enough to escape losing a fortune? Moreover, in these times of the shrinking dollar, would not the various state legislatures appreciate an economical uniformity among universities? Likewise, would not the various accrediting agencies prefer a similar uniformity so that true comparisons of universities can be made and the better programs can be clearly singled out by comparative statistics. Such uniformity would be to the advantage of both faculty and students since it would make easier the migration from one school to another and result in a cross-fertilization of ideas and procedures. This, in turn, would make for a more unified nation. It would seem therefore, that uniqueness is a liability rather than a mysterious asset. In order not to rush too quickly to this conclusion, however, let us more carefully analyze what uniqueness is in the university—if only to better understand how to keep uniqueness from being a greater liability than it already seems to be.

At first glance, uniqueness would seem to be the sum of limitations within which a university is trying to grow. It would seem to be what the scholastic philosophers called *individuation,* the result of finiteness. One can point to at least seven major sources of limitation: (1) the weak constituencies of the university, (2) its fissioning specialization, (3) its failure to integrate knowledges-arts-skills, (4) its narrowing service to the civic community, (5) its tight finances, (6) its less than comprehensive supermodel, and finally (7) its original sin of anti-intellectualism, of individual laziness, and of unprofessional behavior. A quick survey of these seven factors will reveal this individuation aspect of a university's uniqueness.

Consider the eight constituencies of a university that resides in a hypothetical South American country and note how limiting they can be to this university. If the national government is controlled by a military dictatorship, the university will be constantly pressured to serve the immediate needs of the country and to become a propaganda instrument for the government. If the state or provincial government has been in conflict with the national government, it will be economically starved into submission and will not be able to give solid support to its local university. The national community of scholars will be divided when their respective universities maneuver as rivals for better funding, for more freedom, and for more influence within the national and provincial governments. Thus, this divided community finds it difficult to establish universally aceptable criteria of academic excellence and even more difficult to apply them.

The fourth constituency of this particular university, namely, its faculty, is likewise divided by political loyalties rather than united by common academic endeavor; so, too, is its student body divided. The level of trust between faculty and students is lowered as they divide up into hostile factions to promote better concentration of power rather than better understanding of knowledges-arts-skills in a cumulative wisdom. The divisions in faculty and student body render the consciousness of the administrators turbulent so that carefully orchestrated academic decisions become impossible because all actions are politicized. Meanwhile, the parents of the students—most of whom are from the business and professional communities—seriously think of sending their children abroad for university education and, thus, weaken personal allegiance and intellectual quality within the student body. At the same time, the religious founding group of this university, if it is considered deviant by the national government, renders every action of the university suspect and provides the occasion for suppression of much university activity and influence.

This overly dramatic and admittedly simplified example of the limiting influences of the university's eight constituencies can be rendered more complex by transposing the situation to an Alabama black university or to a New York Catholic university and by translating the South American dictatorship into racial prejudice or secularistic mentality. In each case, the university's individuation (the sum of its limitations) adds up to a cumulative tradition of throttled growth.

A second source of university limitation is specialization that, oddly enough, is also the cause of university growth. For, although specialization can inventively expand the university's knowledge, it can also atomize the university into competing departments of knowledge and turn the members of each department into anarchic competitors for attention and financial support. Ironically, at the same time that this anarchy is dissolving the communal unity which is necessary for the building of wisdom, it is seriously weakening the structure that is supportive of both the individual departments and their individual members. Such stunting of wisdom growth, the third source of limitation, renders superficial and slack the integration that is necessary for university life in committee work, in administrative decisions, and in cooperative academic research. This can only generate the withering hostility and violent power grabbing of hyperprofessionalism—"Set up your academic dukedom and protect it with the submachineguns of political maneuvering, economic self-sufficiency, and refusal to cooperate except on grounds of self-interest."

If the intrinsic aims of the university are effectively limiting it, one would suspect that a fourth source of limitation will be the university's extrinsic aim. Thus, service to the civic community will become less if the university's wisdom process is clogged by petty departmental rivalries, by the uncontrolled fissioning of knowledges-art-skills, and by strife among the constituencies. So, the university community may find both its sense of mission and its very abilities for solving the problems of the civic community enervated. This can only enhance the hoary tradition of "town vs. gown" hostility with new variations of harassing reactions from both sides. Naturally, such hostility limits the academic, psychological, and economic support that the university receives from the citizenry. In the resultant tightening of both the budget and the academic atmosphere, important new projects are abandoned and even the productive programs of the university are scaled down. Indeed, because of the heated rivalry for diminishing funds, misappropriation of monies is more possible. Behold the fifth and extremely potent source of limitation in the university.

The sixth source of individuation (the sum total of limitations) is certainly the supermodel, or vision, of the university. The vaguer it is, paradoxically, the more limited is the base of university decision making, since the vague vision or supermodel allows one principle of decision (e.g., economic expediency) to finally dominate all decisions. The more narrow this vision, or supermodel, is, the less specialization it allows and the shallower is its wisdom so that, consequently, its service to the civic community is weaker. To this must be added the seventh source of university limitations, a source shared with any human organization: the cumulative drift of one's inhumanity to one's fellows—original sin. In this limitation, one witnesses how anti-intellectualism can, ironically, be a paralyzing disease in a university. University personnel, for example, may resist the clear defining of aims for departments and programs lest such clarity reveal their self-serving styles of academic life and demand cooperative serving of others' needs. The anti-intellectualism shows itself, too, when any qualitative accounting that is required of department or individual is described as unnecessary "snooping" and unwarranted "distrust," or when smug self-satisfaction with past performance smothers experiments on new procedures and inventive ideas. A lazy and fearful preservation of the *status quo* becomes a strait jacket for the university.

Thus, the legacy of limitations from these seven sources becomes the cumulative individuation of the university. This certainly renders the university unique in a negative way; it is a chronicle of a university's failures. One naturally wonders how the university can still be alive and functioning under such a weight of strategic mistakes and moral failures. Could it be that uniqueness has another aspect to it, a positive element?

If one dares to look to the unique human person as a model for the uniqueness of the university, perhaps one could discover this positive element in uniqueness. For the human person is unique not merely by his or her individuation—the sum of his or her limitations—but also by his or her individuality—the sum of his or her positive powers and qualities. Is it possible, then, that uniqueness has a second side: an historical accumulation of good qualities within a human person, for example, and, by analogy, within the university? The human person who recognizes in himself or herself only limitations or individuation is neurotic and very likely suicidal. This person's return to wholesome living will be marked not by denial of his or her limitations through some illusory indoctrination, but by recognition of his or her powers and good qualities as they act within his or her acknowledged limitations. In this recognition, the person becomes more deeply aware of his or her cumulative successes in life. This new realistic awareness builds deeper confidence that, predictably, brings more and greater successes—as long as the person is realistically aware of his or her limitations, but does not let them crumple his or her hopes or cramp his or her actions.

Consequently, as the uniqueness of the person cumulatively builds by way of his or her historical actions, his or her individuality becomes dominant over his or her individuation. The person's uniqueness becomes richer because he or she learns to dominate unique situations through unique decisions that embody all his or her unique talents within his or her unique combination of limitations. Thus, the husband and wife who respect each other's growth become more and more aware of each other's richly growing uniqueness. In fact, this uniqueness is the source and sign of their growing respect, trust, and affection for each other. Both would be horrified at the prospect of the other becoming less unique. In a marriage, the spouses' growing uniqueness (principally his or her individuality) makes each one more interesting to the other, more inventive, more capable of cooperation (because of increasing richness of resources), more worthy of respect, more aware of the other's mystery, more willing to allow the other freedom for growth, more confident in each other's gifts, and, because of all this, more faithful to each other. This growing uniqueness keeps the couple from fixing on each other's limitations (though they are quite aware of them), from becoming bored with each

310

other, from stifling each other's initiatives, from underestimating each other, and from diminishing mutual trust. Could all this be applied analogically to the university's uniqueness?

First, if the eight constituencies of the university are operating to build the university rather than merely to inhibit it, then the university's individuality can develop. As we surveyed the history of American universities and the five national models for university development, it became clear how much they owed to the diverse traditions of each geographic area and of the national spirit. It became clear that even limitations were turned into advantageous qualities; recall, for example, how Russia developed the part-time student status and the technical institutes because of her need to catch up to Western industrialization. Also, recall how the American land-grant colleges, in endeavoring to achieve roots by serving all the needs of all their citizens, incorporated the professionsl schools into their later university development, introduced women to the full horizon of studies and to the full depth of graduate studies, and upgraded high school learning with two-year community colleges. Limitations did not strangle these colleges but rather challenged them to luxuriant growth.

A second example of cultivated individuality can be given. It took the constituency of the national government to pass the Justin S. Morrill Land-Grant College Act of 1862; the constituency of the individual states to exploit this bill to fulfill best the needs of its citizens (resulting in agricultural colleges); the constituency of scholars to recognize the fruitfulness of incorporating professional schools into the liberal arts colleges to form the university; the constituency of the faculty, both expand to the college curricula to the full range of citizen's needs and swing open the doors of the college to the farmers, to the lower classes, and to women. It then took the high ambitions and ingenuity of the students to make use of these opportunities while they also worked part-time to support themselves; it took the disciplined sacrifices of their parents to fuel and support those student ambitions; it took a remarkably supple administration to keep up with the gigantic growth of the universities during the last forty years and not stifle the unpredictable inventiveness of the American people. Furthermore, it was the original rooting of the religious founding groups that gave life to the first universities of the country and, as we saw, assured all universities of freedom from government interference.

Thus, the uniqueness of American university education is seen in its positive individuality: democratization of both curriculum and student body, the invention of the two-year community college, the extension of full educational opportunity to women, the reciprocity of freedom between public and private education that produced true autonomy for all the universities, the establishment of universal right to education that enabled the university to become a service agency for the whole community, and the remarkable synthesis of vocational and liberal arts education. This is the contribution of the constituencies to the uniqueness of each American university.

Although specialization, the second source of individuality, has certainly atomized and, thus, limited the university, it has contributed much more to the university's individuality. For specialization has enriched the curriculum of the university beyond the expectations of everyone. The retiring professor of 1979, looking over the catalog with which he began his educational career in 1928, can only chuckle in amazement—and satisfaction. It is not simply that the technology of our civilization is indebted to the discoveries of cybernetics, economics, engineering, agronomy, and biochemistry, but also that our culture has grown so vast with the exploitation of the social sciences and with the education of the business community to the support of art-music-drama through their respective university departments.

Though American universities are roundly criticized for overemphasizing specialization and the professions, they still have sufficiently integrated specialized faculties (1) to provide interdisciplinary studies and departments; (2) to furnish specialists for sagely advising the American government and, lately, for running it; (3) to democratize curricula and student opportunity; (4) to structure and run intricate universities of unique texture (e.g., the grafting of the German graduate school upon the English college and, then, the incorporation of the professional schools into this unity); and (5) to develop intellectually integrated programs so unique that European students have migrated to the United States and not a few Third-World students have preferred to enter American universities rather than European universities. All this takes a bit of wisdom, the third source of individuality.

To accomplish this, both faculty and administration had to exercise a disciplined liberty since all this was achieved, often enough, through faculty committees that cooperated closely with administrators according to a democratic process which also included the suggestions (and, sometimes, the votes) of students and staff. Such cooperation did lend itself to the forming of university communities of wisdom based on willing sacrifice for the common good. For this reason, labor unions have not generally been necessary at the universities. The same disciplined liberty (as the fourth source of individuality) has avoided wastage of economic resources and unfair distribution of university monies—though, as always, those in liberal studies will complain about the vast sums spent in the university laboratories. As a result, American universities have been able to quietly support, through long spans of education, large numbers of foreign students who have been attracted to them by their individuality.

All of these accomplishments have demanded that the university's vision of itself be expansible, inventive, supple, demanding of effort, concrete, wide in practicality, and well founded in the arts, sciences, and technologies. The effects of this vision were seen in the first chapter, which traced the growth of the American university and described its use as a model for Third-World universities. Here one notes the fifth source of the American university's individuality: a vision so promotive of individuality that the American university can serve as a preeminent international model.

Lastly, this individuality, or positive aspect of uniqueness, is richly elicited from the university when the university adapts to the unique needs of the civic community and when, in serving these needs, the university develops within herself new knowledges-arts-skills, new aspects of wisdom, and a more mature state of disciplined liberty. For, as we have seen, the university serves the civic community in a way that cannot be imitated by other institutions such as the government or industrial complexes or special scientific and technological institutes. Only the university cultivates the speculative wisdom that both controls all human knowledges-skills-arts and technology and opens up to men and women various paths of destiny for their choice. It does this not by its limitations (individuation)—except insofar as they stimulate the university person to seek the positive—but by its rich individuality, its cumulative tradition of qualitative successes. Thus, the uniqueness of the university, received from its constituencies and then richly developed by the university, is finally returned when the university offers its unique services to fill the current and future needs of the civic community.

For all these reasons, then, it should be noted that the uniqueness of the university is primarily its individuality and only secondarily its individuation. The historical accumulation of good qualities within the university is certainly limited so that the two elements of individuality and individuation do constitute the uniqueness of the university. But individuality, far and away, is the more important element and is even challenged to greater richness by the individuation of its limits, its cumulative negative history. Otherwise, the university, throttled by its limitations, would soon gasp its last breath.

When uniqueness is seen from this perspective, it becomes clear why the government and the various accrediting agencies, although they do set standards of minimum attainment, do not attempt to provide standards of conformity that would stifle uniqueness taken as the individuality of cumulative qualitative successes. The government rightly requests that the university use the uniqueness, received from its constituencies and developed by government support, to serve the pressing needs of the civic community—so long as this use does not attack the constitution of the university. Furthermore, the accrediting agencies are aware of a three-cornered dialectic of enrichment within the university. The university's resources are measured against its performance and its stated aims or ideals, and vice versa. The university is required, of course, to maintain the minimum standards that have been set by the national and local governments in teacher training, in financial responsibility, in quality of faculty, in number of class hours per credit, and so on, so that the nations's culture and civilization can survive. But beyond these minimum standards, the university has full freedom to set its own aims, to develop its own procedures for achieving the aims, and to gather its own resources needed to perform the procedures. It is the proportion between aims, performance, and resources that alone is studied by the accrediting agency. For the accrediting agency prizes uniqueness of individuality and tries to help the university adjust to its uniqueness of individuating limitations. Thus, standards do not undermine or smother uniqueness, as long as they are merely minimum-performance-criteria used to preserve the organized goodness of the community.

It should be noted that such a uniqueness, because it is constituted by the intrinsic aims of the university and because it is elicited to further richness by its extrinsic aim of assisting the civic community with its specialized knowledges and cumulative wisdom, contains within itself a sense of special mission to the larger society. No other civic institution can do what the university does for the civic community; no other university can do what this particular university can uniquely do for its constituencies. For this particular university has been given its unique genetic structure by its constituencies and has developed this structure by its uniquely cumulative decisions for positive growth. As a result, it can, in turn, serve the unique needs and hopes of the civic community (in which it was born and raised) by its history, its competencies, its hopes, and its destiny.

Uniqueness, then, is mysterious; yet it is not totally mysterious since its two elements of individuality and individuation seem recognizable, accountable, and relatable to each other. There are those who nonetheless dogmatically assert that uniqueness is unknowable and therefore unpromotable. Consequently, one must look directly at this assertion and test its validity, since it challenges all our previous conclusions about uniqueness and its value.

Uniqueness—Is It Knowable?

Clearly, if uniqueness is not knowable, then it is not controllable or promotable—whether this is the uniqueness of a person, a team, a prize bulldog, an historical trend, or a university. But if the immediately preceding investigation means anything, it means that uniqueness is at least recognizable and that it has two sides to it: (1) positive individuality of cumulative good qualities and (2) negative individuation of cumulative limitations. The first aspect seems to be reasonable and appreciable; the second aspect seems to be chancy and not appreciable—at least insofar as the uniqueness of a university is concerned.

Nonetheless, if one's understanding of the unique thing is by way of universal concepts, how could one ever claim to know the thing in its uniqueness? For the power of the concept is its ability to prescind from the singular and unique so that one can use the concept to group beings according to universal categories. It would seem, then, that the human mode of thinking perpetually condemns men and women to miss the meaning of the unique and, therefore, to be unable to control it. Though a person might somewhat grasp the unique by way of sensate percepts of the imagination, this grasp will not be conceptual and, therefore, will not be meaningful. The unique seems opaque to human understanding.

Yet this conclusion is not borne out by our discoveries, in chapter four, concerning convergent pluralism, in which the uniqueness in evolution, history, individual personality development, and personal salvation history pointed to the existence of absolutes by which unique items are compared and measured. For it was found in chapter four that the cumulative continuity that is necessary to explain these four phenomena could not exist except by means of absolutes, since these absolutes, acting as threads of continuity running through distinct eras, made comparison of unique eras possible. Without such comparison, there would be no way to recognize growth in evolution, historical trend, personality development, and personal salvation history. The fact that such absolutes not only made a convergent pluralism possible, but also denied the possibility of a divergent pluralism, was all that we needed to know at the time. But now, to understand how uniqueness can be known, some further exploration must be made of what Thomas Aquinas variously called the "absolute nature" or the "common nature." Understanding what Aquinas meant is crucial to the explanation of why uniqueness is not totally opaque to human understanding.

Working mainly out of Aquinas' logical compositions, some followers of St. Thomas have described his theory of judgment as a comparison be-

315

tween concepts. Unhappily, they missed his theory of perceptual judgment and found themselves in an arid desert of abstractionism. Thus, in the propositional form of the judgment, they mistakenly considered both predicate and subject to be representing concepts. Actually, for Aquinas, the subject of the proposition stands for the singular percept of the imagination; the predicate of the proposition represents the universal concept. The "is" of the proposition stands for the judgmental act that affirms that the common content of the percept and concept is to be found existent in the real being about which the proposition is being made.

Let us take a simple example to illustrate this. I observe eight-year-old Butch carrying a frog with which he is scaring little Ethel. I comment, "Butch is a real boy." To understand my meaning, I must note three important items. First of all, the word *boy* indicates a universal concept in my judging act—a concept that, because of its universality, is capable of truly representing Jerry, Peter, and Tommy, as well as Butch, even though at the moment it is referring primarily to Butch. But I do not mean to say in my judgment that Butch *is* the universal concept of *boy;* rather, I want to say that in Butch there is something that corresponds to this concept and is also to be found in Jerry or Peter or Tommy. This something (Aquinas' absolute nature) is, of course, not existing within each youngster in a universal or abstract state such as it exists in the concept. Nevertheless, although this something is in the singular being of each youngster, it is not absolutely individual; for it must be the same in each and all the youngsters if the term *boy* is to mean anything more than only Butch or only Jerry or only Peter, that is, if the proposition is not to be rendered meaningless by signifying simply that "Butch is Butch" or "Jerry is Jerry" or "Peter is Peter." Thus, the mysterious something in Butch (Aquinas' absolute nature) to which the term *boy* refers must be neither singular nor universal. The mysterious something, or Thomistic absolute nature, must prescind from both states.

Secondly, the word *Butch* in the proposition "Butch is a real boy" indicates the singular percept of the imagination representing Butch in his uniqueness. This image, united as it is with the external, or special, senses of the predicator, intentionally objectifies within the object, Butch himself, by the judgmental act of the knower. In other words, it totally identifies with the real Butch. Thus, the word *Butch* and the singular percept image representing him fuse into the singular unique reality of Butch playing with the frog.

Thirdly, the word *is* in the proposition, "Butch is a real boy," represents the act of predicating or of judging. This predicating is the act of judgment stating that the structure of *boy* is to be found within the singular being, Butch. This judgment, then, is a mental act whereby the knower, or predicator, simultaneously holds in dynamic tension both the universal concept of *boy* and the concrete singular percept of Butch—the percept being held in identity with Butch himself as just described above. This holding of meaning *between* the singular percept and the universal concept is precisely the judgment as a dynamic act of intelligence within the compenetrative union of singular percept and of universal concept. This judgmental holding, or grasping, is exactly the representing of the absolute nature of *boy* in Butch; it is the intending of that mysterious something in Butch that is neither singular nor universal. For this grasping, or holding, by the judgment is a dynamic holding *between* the singular and the universal; it is their common meaning or common content, which, because it is common to them both, cannot be either singular or universal. That is to say, the singularity of the percept-image and the universality of the concept are the distinctive mode of being of each one. This distinctive mode of each makes each one different from the other and from the judgmental act that unifies them. The judgmental act represents their common content but not their distinctive mode (i.e., singular or universal) of holding the common content.

In addition, this act of judging (represented by the propositional word *is*), in turn, represents the fact that the structure of *boy* is in Butch. In other words, the judgmental act intends the absolute nature in Butch. The judgment can so represent this fact because this judgmental act is an understanding (an "insighting") that occurs within the singular percept, which represents the unique Butch, and because the singular percept of Butch is objectified, or made identical, with the real Butch who is holding the frog. Acting, thus, within the dynamic singular percept by way of common content (the absolute nature) along with the concept, the intellect's act of judging can now terminate in the real Butch and can establish that Butch does really exist as a boy. The judgmental act, then, permeates Butch as a total being according to his structure of being a *boy*.

In attaining the absolute nature within Butch, the judgment grasps a "more"; the judger knows more than he or she had previously known in both the percept and the concept; he or she possesses more content in this judgment than he or she had before this act of judgment. If this were not the case, there would be no growth in knowledge; rather, the judger would be frozen forever within his or her percept and concept without the ability to attain more knowledge of the being represented by the percept and concept. Indeed, unless the judgment moves beyond its percept-image and concept to attain this "more" within the object to be known, the judger cannot be aware of new developments in the object, nor can he or she ever correct any previous mistaken judgments about this object, namely, Butch. Furthermore, the phenomenon of curiosity would be unexplainable if it were not that the judgment glimpses "more" than it holds in its concept and percept; thus, the judgment lures the knower into making additional judgments.

This "more," then, is the absolute nature of *boy* in Butch, which is represented by the judging act itself as it holds in tension the common content between the singular percept of Butch and the universal concept of *boy*. Because this "more," or absolute nature of *boy*, in Butch is not universal, it leads into the uniqueness of Butch. But because this "more" is not singular, the judgment does not grasp the uniqueness of Butch in its fullness. Thus, curiosity, the desire to know more about the *boy* in Butch, is enkindled and results in a series of judgments about this *boy*. The judgments gradually move around this uniqueness of the *boy* in Butch in a growing understanding of it. For each judgment renders the singular percept more precise and clarifies the universal concept of *boy* so that the series of judgments about the *boy* in Butch offers the sure experience of continuously intending and attaining the same real object and of continuously converging more knowledge of this object upon the absolute nature of *boy* found in Butch, even as Butch is himself growing.

In other words, the concrete singular percept of Butch that is contained in the judgment enables the knower to keep in contact with that which is historically contingent and relative in Butch, the *boy*; moreover, the universal concept of *boy* contained in the judgment enables the knower to know that each judgment is attaining the same boy and that, by comparison with the singular percept, a continuously growing knowledge of this absolute nature in Butch is being achieved with qualitative cumulation. Because of this two-sided continuity, the knower is able not only to experience the growth of his or her knowledge about the *boy* in Butch, but also to compare by means of this continuity, the sameness and difference of Butch's stages of growth. Such a process can, of course, be expanded to compare historical periods, diverse animal structures and systems, sociological situations, religions, business techniques, and artistic works. In other words, unless the judgment captures the "more," or the absolute nature, when it acts beyond the singular percept and the universal concept to enter its object, there can be no science, no history, no art, no development of skills and techniques, no exchange of religious experience, and no sense of another's uniqueness.

Although the series of judgments that are attaining the absolute nature (or the "more") asymptotically approach the uniqueness of Butch as a boy, for example, these judgments never quite adequately grasp that uniqueness unless they are supplemented by the connatural knowledge of *love*. For some reason, the judgmental asymptotic approach to the unique cannot achieve its aim well without an accompanying feeling of love for the unique object. If I want to know the uniqueness of Butch as a boy, I must make my judgments concerning him with love, that is, with appreciative respect and trust. Every scientist has experienced this. The more he or she learns to respect and cherish the plant or animal or person with whom he or she is working, the better and the more quickly he or she comes to know this object in its uniqueness. The fuller knowledge of the uniqueness in singular detailed images always contains more detailed scientific knowledge in universal conceptual understandings. Only when the counselor or doctor or friend allows the other person to be himself or herself, that is to say, when the other person is allowed to display his or her uniqueness in the confidence of being loved, only then does the professional person achieve a grasp of the other's uniqueness.

For this reason, as the secularity within the secularization process of the individual person or of the team or of the nation increases, so also does the grasp of the singular unique within this process increase and, hence, the specialization and integration of the secularization likewise increases. One can now grasp how important is disciplined liberty for recognizing the unique, since such liberty has a loving respect for others at its very core. As we noted in chapter six, the disciplined liberty of the individual person involves both a devotion to specialized knowledge of unique instances and a competence for truth within a particular discipline or art. But this liberty also includes a wisdom that employs the more speculative truth of the specialized disciplines to produce the practical truth of knowledge, which is then applied to bettering unique situations. In both aspects of disciplined liberty, love animated the justice of speculative truth-seeking and of practical truth-making within the unique situation. Clearly, when, from a person's judgmental side, he or she achieves a growing grasp of a being's absolute nature, and this grasp is strengthened by his or her love for that being, the person can attain some connatural knowledge of the unique person, animal, thing, or event precisely in its uniqueness.

To deny the possibility of knowing, in any way, the uniqueness of a being, is to fall into a formidable trap. This would mean, for example, that a person could not know his or her own self-identity, his or her own uniqueness. Would this not imply a diminished self-awareness, since one could not distinguish oneself from others with clarity? Does not diminished self-awareness cause confusion within the human personality, that is, does it not produce a diffused person? Does not personal confusion induce palsied decisions, even retrogression of confidence, if not of knowledge? If one applies this analogously to the university, it could mean that the university would have difficulty in accomplishing her intrinsic aims of specialized knowledges-arts-skills and of wisdom. Consequently, the university's services to the civic community would suffer from ignorance, faulty technique, and imprudence. Naturally, under these circumstances, the university would have less feeling for a "great cause," such as peace or for a "paramount ideal" of serving well one's country. It would then risk losing its sense of mission.

If the loss of a sense of uniqueness would necessarily involve the loss of the university's sense of identity, then the special quality of its education would be jeopardized. For, would this not dampen the university's enthusiasm for inventive knowledges-arts-skills? And would it not condemn this university to slavish imitation of other universities who may not have lost their sense of identity and their hope of knowing the unique in themselves and in others? Moreover, once a university's sense of identity is lost, would this not mean a diminished sense of its interior unity and, therefore, a need to emphasize extrinsic claims to unity, such as uniform procedures, rigid salary systems, sport supremacy, geographic placement, and economic power.

Once a whole university has begun to lose its sense of identity, the resultant drop of its *esprit de corps* usually affects the individual lives of its members by stripping them of pride in both their academic work and their university roles. Each person loses his or her sense of mission within the university and within his or her own person. As a result, each begins to look out only for himself or herself. Not so strangely, the lack of university *esprit de corps* produces the rank individualism of self-enhancement at the expense of the university. Hence, it is no small misadventure to doubt one's ability to know the unique.

Indeed, without knowledge of the unique, one may well risk losing even knowledge of the universal, for the dialectic between the singular percept and the universal concept in the perceptual judgment is the instrument for developing scientific knowledge at all levels of understanding. Consequently, to deny the goal of this judgmental dialectic (some knowledge of the unique by way of the absolute nature) is to necessarily weaken any knowledge produced by this dialectic.

On the other hand, if some knowledge of the unique is possible, then one may properly ask whether the university community can, first, achieve knowledge of its own uniqueness and, then, use this knowledge to promote this uniqueness. If this is the case, then the university has remarkable potential for controlled growth.

If Uniqueness Is Knowable, Is It Promotable?

Uniqueness is not to be underestimated; it is *mystery*. Two people who have enjoyed fifty years of creative and generally happy marriage will vouch for a constantly growing awareness of each other's mystery (translated: uniqueness). The ethologist who is concentrating on the group behavior of baboons learns to name each member of the troop for its uniqueness and to wonder at the complexity of each animal as he or she observes the animals adapting to each new situation. The trained eye of the horticulturalist marvels at the unique development of each cross-fertilized rose and wonders what are the missing elements in his or her knowledge of this process. Each of these experts wishes to promote uniqueness in some "other"; but each puzzles over the infinite complexity of unique development.

If the mother wondering how to help her family grow, the coach attempting to assemble a basketball team, the new executive pondering ways to re-enliven a discouraged sales force, are all mystified by the unique, then how much more sympathy is due the university president who tries to promote the uniqueness of his or her huge school? The president must ask himself or herself three questions: What precisely is the uniqueness of my university? How is it to be promoted? Who does the promotion? These three questions are so intimately entwined that they must be answered simultaneously, for each question involves the university's three aims, its constituencies, and its vision (supermodel for decision) insofar as they make up the content of uniqueness, establish its mode of promotion, and name those responsible for this promotion.

Thus, the first intrinsic goal of the university, its institutional specialization of knowledges-arts-skills, aims at exploring the object of each academic discipline at deeper and deeper levels and in greater and greater detail. Nuclear physics, for example, in discovering more and more subatomic particles, has moved away from a theoretically rigid determinism toward probability theory. It has met novelty—not simply the unexpected event, but the *unique* event. In this meeting, it has directly touched *mystery,* that is, the object as knowable but as inexhaustibly rich in further elements to be known. Ironically, even as the physicist is overwhelmed with both the immensity of detail in the unique event and the resultant complexity of interpreting it, he or she is struck by the need for more comprehensive universal principles in order to include this event within his or her general interpretation. Again, one witnesses the dialectic between the unique and the general, between the singular percept and the universal concept.

Consequently, the individual scholar or technician or artist is forever lured on by the unique event to wonder about deeper universal principles of explanation. In so observing and wondering, the individual university person is becoming more expert, that is, more unique in his or her specialization. Such uniqueness is, of course, contagious. It inspires the inventive enthusiasm that produces uniqueness of discovery in his or her department and, eventually, in the university community itself.

In this way, uniqueness is also communal—seemingly a contradiction. The mystery of uniqueness of the object peculiar to any discipline—the management of means of production in economics, for example—is so vast that this particular department of almost any university could specialize within this object in a unique way and could make a unique contribution to the particular field. The same is true of any well-developed discipline. This uniqueness can spread throughout the particular university if interdisciplinary study is done on a particular problem such as women's rights, urban poverty, proper financing of national health care, East-West spiritual influences, or interstellar travel. In pursuing the mysterious unique to its depths, the university community itself takes on a uniqueness of interest, procedure, knowledge, and action.

This is equally true of specialized skills and techniques that experts develop for the pursuit of specialized knowledges, e.g., fluorine for dating archaeological items, the electron microscope for delineating minute particles, hermeneutics for interpreting literary texts, and so on. First of all, these skills make possible the pursuit of specialized knowledge down to the mysterious unique event by inventing the technology and techniques intrinsic to this pursuit. Secondly, the experts who possess these finely honed skills and techniques are rendered unique by their very expertness, since any professional skill demands very finely tuned knowledge, sharply observed experience, and novel inventiveness.

Indeed, this expertness tends to render its environment more unique, as when the computer not only changes modes of scholarship but also the layperson's ways of thinking. Thus, the team of experts is rendered unique by the unique problem that they are solving and, at the same time, the community with whom and for whom they devise the novel solution undergoes a deepening uniqueness. The introduction of a windmill water pump into an African tribe that had been blighted by drought, for example, not only changed the team of university experts who inventively adapted this machinery to the economy, sociology, and religious attitudes of the tribe, but also uniquely transformed the tribe itself. Has the introduction of the computer into business by university personnel produced any less novel a change of mentality in the business community—to say nothing of the university community?

Consequently, it is not sufficient to merely trace the origin of uniqueness to the unique mystery of the object of a particular knowledge-art-skill. Rather, the uniqueness can also issue from the individual needs, interest, hopes, talents, and vocation of the particular student or faculty member. Or it may be demanded by a unique problem of the civic community that can be solved only by the unique pooling of the university faculty's resources. (In America, the early Agricultural and Mining colleges are an example of this unique pooling.) Then, too, there is always the unique spirit generated by the personal chemistry among members of a department of drama or history or sociology—a spirit that is enjoyed for a time and then disappears as mysteriously as it arose, leaving, however, its residue in all participants ("Will you ever forget those years when. . . ?").

Thus, specialization, as it moves deeply into the novel, the unique, the mysterious, generates a certain uniqueness in knowledge, in the individual expert, in the university faculty, and in the civic community. Specialization done outside the context of integrative wisdom, however, tends to narrow the minds of its experts, to render them unreally abstract, to make communication with others very difficult, to absolutize highly specialized university departments that are answerable to no one. These latter tendencies make it ever harder for such people to escape generalized routines in order to be able to recognize that which is novel and unique in mystery. Thus, specialization by itself will ironically tend to lose awareness of the unique in ever vaguer generalities that are untouched by inventiveness—precisely as it endeavors to explore the unique more deeply.

For this reason, from the communal side of the university, the second intrinsic aim of the university (the accumulation of an integrative wisdom) must be recognized for its contribution to the uniqueness of the university. Earlier, we noted how, within a particular discipline, its truth must be continually reinterpreted in terms of the latest discoveries. This means that the discipline is constantly undergoing new integrations, or syntheses, which attempt to incorporate the latest findings in higher unities. Each new synthesis clearly is unique insofar as it is a total reinterpretation of the previous truth by way of new items of truth. For, if the interpretation is truly total, it affects all the elements that constitute it. Such uniqueness occurs not only in the mind of the individual researcher, student, and technician, but also in the collective consciousness of the department members as they communicate with one another.

This sense of the unique within the individual department can spread to all the departments within a particular school of the university (e.g., education or medicine) if interdepartmental seminars are creative. Such a school can then challenge all the other schools of the university to achieve a synthesis that is unique to the university community. The school of education, for example, could assert that the linking of the term *Christian* with the term *university* is to mock both terms with a living contradiction. Or, the school of medicine could assert that biological evolution adequately accounts for psychological, moral, and historical evolution. The unique synthesis arising in the face of such challenging assertions would be a communal event inducing a fresh growth of uniqueness in the university community.

But the cumulative wisdom of the university community involves more than merely a unique synthesis of thought—a fact quickly observed if one explores all three levels of wisdom. Thus, at the highest, or speculative, level of wisdom, one finds the basic principles and values for structuring the university most beautifully (i.e., most uniquely) in accord with the positive resources of its individuality and within the negative limitations of its individuation. Out of the justice of equal rights and out of the realization of its need for women's full contribution to the university, for example, the university community could decide to include a program of women's studies within its curriculum. At the second, speculative-practical level of wisdom, in which middle principles operate most effectively between the individuality and the individuation of the university's uniqueness, the university community could construct a minor concentration in Women's Studies. This program could be designed to draw upon the most competent instructors, to be attractive to men as well as to women, to be an educative instrument for the whole university community, and to be attractively exportable to the large civic community for the raising of the community's consciousness. Not just a synthesis of ideas is involved in this example but an hierarchy of values. Again, at the third, practico-practical level of wisdom, the uniqueness of this program could be assured by its adaptation to the skills and knowledges of the available professors, to the needs of the particular student body (e.g., mainly dormitory students or mainly commuters, upper-middle class or lower-middle class, predominant ethos, secular or religious minded, and so on), to the university's economic resources for inventive experiments, and to the amount of interest generated by the announcement of the program.

Such a program would involve the total wisdom of the university community and would uniquely focus this wisdom upon a large problem in and outside the university. The program would not simply produce a speculative synthesis, but would include an articulated array of values, demand an attitudinal response, and gradually change the lifestyle of the university. But all this would not happen unless the administrators of the university acted within this wisdom to bring the Women's Studies program into unique existence; likewise, specialization would finally fail to reach the unique without the overall context and stimulative values of wisdom. Thus, a third source of the university's uniqueness must be taken into account, namely, the administration.

This makes good sense since the administrators are specifically charged by the other constituencies of the university with the orchestration of the dual intrinsic goals of the university. Their task is to carefully distinguish between the good qualities (individuality) and limitations (individuation) of the university's uniqueness in order to promote the individuality within the boundaries of the individuation. Their aim is to act as midwives in delivering the qualitative "more" into existence within the university community; this is the gradual approach to the "unique" development of the university; it is a constant bettering. This happens when the administrators work toward a *more* sound financial base for the university so that the university community is not continually distracted by worries over its future or, worse, held paralyzed by deep insecurity. In this way, administrators set up the conditions for full contemplation in the collective consciousness of the wisdom community.

Furthermore, administrators develop *better* physical facilities in library, classrooms, janitorial services, sports complexes, and campus landscaping, so that the university community experiences a sense of its own dignity amid the careful cultivation of cleanliness and beauty. Such administrators also provide *stronger* support for the specialization and accumulation of wisdom by the faculty through improved scientific facilities, strategically constituted committees, sabbaticals, convention attendance, secretarial services, and so on. Again, they stimulate continuing education through *fuller* use of faculty seminars, visiting professors, study institutes, career planning, and places and times for leisurely, spontaneous conversations. Indeed, these administrators try to attract a *more* academically ambitious student through scholarships, well-planned programs, and selective admission policies. Then even gamble *more* courageously when they set up a required core curriculum to assure their students of a liberal education as the students intensely pursue their vocational skill with a rather pure pragmatism.

Lastly, the administrators stimulate and use the supermodel, or vision, which arises out of the university community, to make *stronger, more* intelligent decisions according to the dual intrinsic aims of the university. Thus, they avoid the devastation of divided loyalties and the diffusion of energies that are consequent upon confused decisions about these aims. Because such administrators use well this supermodel, or vision, to better the university in all the above ways, they induce a unique collective consciousness in the university community—a consciousness that is nourished by contemplative action and animated by a disciplined liberty of devoted service to the community and its aims. Here one discovers fully developed individual persons and rich communal personality, for disciplined liberty allows the individual person to extend his or her personality into the communal enterprise of the university in a spirit of joyful sacrifice.

Such expansion of the individual enables the person to be more interested in the advance of the community than in the promotion of personal career. Ironically, this is the way that the academic person becomes more deeply aware of the university community's uniqueness and cultivates more fully his or her own uniqueness in one and the same act. Yet, of itself, this collective consciousness cannot assure the university community of continually cumulative uniqueness, since this consciousness can lose awareness of the extrinsic aim of the university, namely, service of the civic community. In order to keep conscious of its role as servant, the university community is very dependent on the constituencies of government, parents, alumni, founding group, local community, and the national community of scholars.

This brings us to the second responsibility of the university administrators, to direct the dialectic between the unique services of the university community and the unique needs of the civic community so that the university serves, in justice, the realistic hopes of its various constituencies. Just as the university has historically arisen out of the local community to fulfill that community's particular educational needs, and just as the university has been steadily nourished by this community, so, too, the university, in gratitude, wants to use her resources to respond to the unique needs of the local civic community. The community has lent its unique resources and support to form this unique university, which now uses its uniqueness to fulfill the community's needs. A university that arises out of Pennsylvania and West Virginia coal-digging communities will be glad to use its engineering expertise to ensure safety in mines, its geological competence to provide accurate estimates of future coal resources, its sociological guidance to help unions and management achieve peaceful work relations, and its economic foresight to protect pension plans. Nor does this dialectic proceed in one direction only. The constituencies of the university must be allowed to influence administrative decisions with their advice, to donate their resources (properties, historical lore, scholarships, and economic assistance) according to their desires, and to demand help in fulfilling their hopes and needs—provided these influences are not overly self-serving and prejudicial to the university's life.

Such a dialectic, as it builds the traditions of the university and of the local community, produces a rich uniqueness in both communities, since the mutual giving demands dynamic growth of both. To better serve the local community, the university community must specialize ever more competently and adapt ever more wisely to the needs of the local community. In turn, the civic community must use these resources ever more efficiently and prudently in order to be worthy of further university assistance. In this dialectic, the secularization process is beneficently operative to enhance the cumulative uniqueness of both communities with ever increasing awareness of their most distinct collective personalities. This means that each is becoming more aware of its mission. For this reason, the individuation (limitations) of historical town-gown rivalry is kept to a minimum by close cooperation in mutually beneficial work. Here, then, besides specialization, cumulative wisdom, and administrative leadership, is a fourth source of university uniqueness—service of the civic community.

The administration and its staff clearly are essential for developing the university's uniqueness as they call forth and support specialization of knowledges-arts-skills; as they form the wisdom community out of departmental, committee, and interdisciplinary actions; and as they point the intrinsic resources of the university to the service of civic community needs. Nevertheless, of themselves, they are not sufficient to assure growing uniqueness, since they lack a sufficient range of specialized knowledge-arts-skills, since they use but do not possess communal wisdom, and since they receive the vision, or supermodel, for their decisions in dialectic with the academic faculty. Something more is needed. A special knowledge like cybernetics, for example, may be uniquely discovered at the Massachusetts Institute of Technology, but another university might take this discovery and develop it far beyond the capacity of MIT. A special skill, such as that of social work, may be first formulated and rendered scientific by Columbia University, but it might then be imitated and developed more extensively at another university. An administrative program, such as Freshmen Learning Groups, may be uniquely invented at the University of Michigan, but can be duplicated more inventively at another university.

This ability to imitatively reproduce does not deny all the previous conclusions about the uniqueness of specialization, wisdom integration, administrative procedure, and mission service to the civic community; it does indicate, however, that there is at least one more element to be considered in the uniqueness of the university, namely, the value system or secularity that runs it. Knowledges, skills, and techniques arise and are employed in very different ways because of the very different secularities that direct them. Freshman Learning Groups, for example, may be run, in one university, by the value attitude which maintains that lived learning is crucial to the educational process and, in a second university, by the value attitude which maintains that peer pressure is the best way to assure intense study and that the camaraderie of small learning groups with their teachers is the best way to secure eventual influence over government and business, because the students will eventually become officials in government and business.

Secondly, by asserting the importance of secularity for the university's uniqueness, we do not deny that values arise from the university secularization process. It is clear that the development of a school of social work can put new emphasis on the value of corporal works of mercy that are described in the twenty-fifth chapter of Matthew's Gospel. Clearly, too, cybernetics calls attention to mankind's ability and consequent responsibility to provide for the future. Also, the administrative procedure of investment funding highlights social justice for the South African laborers and their dependents. And yet, it is the precise constellation of values that determines the content, the emphasis, and the orientation of academic programs and administrative procedures—no matter how autonomous is each knowledge, discipline, and institutional apparatus. Persons (who happen to be living value systems) teach and administrate according to values. Thus, the uniqueness of a university is very much determined by its value system. For this reason, the vision, or supermodel, which is used by administrators, faculty, staff, students, and other influential persons such as the university's board of trustees, becomes central to the discovery and promotion of the university's uniqueness.

Why is this the case? First, the supermodel or vision contains the radical source of the university's internal unity, since it expresses dramatically and attractively the commonly held values of the community. It does this with a unified constellation of ideals, that is, with a secularity or system of priorities. Second, since this vision, or supermodel, is open to much development, it lends a proper sense of mystery to both the dual intrinsic and the single extrinsic goals of the university. Third, at the same time, it suggests definite means to these goals and offers particular procedures in the use of the means. The vision, then, is at once indefinitely free by way of mystery and yet definitely committed by its goals and means. Fourth, the vision, not being abstract dogma, calls for constant readjustment to the uniquely changing situation of the university and of its civic communities in their dialectic of mutual support. This keeps both goals and means in a regular state of development.

Fifth, the vision is not an ideology, since it arises out of both the unique history of the university's various constituencies and the constant reinterpretation of traditional truth by the university community. Consequently, its values and secularity are pluralistic without necessarily being simply relative. Sixth, though the values enshrined in the vision are not to be confused with the larger vision itself (which includes procedures, techniques, and projections into the future), nevertheless the system of values is interpreted by the vision. The vision, therefore, suggests how this secularity should direct the secularization process, which is the living structure of the university. Seventh, the complexity of the university itself, the intricacy of its services to the civic community, and the acceleration of international events, accompanied by an attendant growing uncertainty about the future, clearly warn wise administrators that the marvelous ability of their vision or supermodel to mirror and direct the uniqueness of the university is matched only by its inadequacy. Faith in divine providence, then, would seem to be an equally important item in the life of the university administrator, for all the dynamic elements of the university must beautifully converge at one point of time, place, and quality if the university is to be a unique event rather than a chaotic mess.

The vision or supermodel for decisions is, then, crucial to the cumulative uniqueness of the university, even if it is only one of several sources of uniqueness and even if it is sometimes baffled by divine providence. For the vision appreciates the past, grasps the present in its amplitude, projects into the future, and then converges all this in a unified understanding and evaluation that will form the foundation of the faculty's planning and the administrator's decisions. It is the child of the wisdom community. In unifying all the complex processes of the university, the vision offers hope of a cumulative uniqueness and of a strong self-identity to both the individual member and the total university community. Such a vision cannot live with the pluralism of total relativism, which despairs of much internal agreement on values and, therefore, relies mainly on the external cooperation of neutral procedures such as erecting buildings, establishing salary scales, offering a vast cafeteria of academic courses, and providing a rigid set of services for the civic community. This vision, or supermodel, lives well only with a pluralism of analogous truth, a convergent pluralism toward a growing unity of meaning, value, and cooperation among members of a community.

Furthermore, this vision is dulled by a political pluralism that works on the chaotic expediency principle ("the only way to survive is to compromise and to avoid conflict at any cost") whereby all values are acceptable so long as they do not conflict with the expediency principle. At the other extreme, the vision or supermodel is blurred by a shifty common-denominator pluralism that allows many diverse approaches to the same problem in order to discover practically what is the better combination of approaches, since all approaches yield some truth and are somewhat compatible with each other. These last two pluralisms are ambivalent in that, sometimes, they are following divergent pluralism and, at other times, they are being guided by convergent pluralism. Thus, they can distort the vision one moment and restore it the next moment. Under these conditions, a cumulative uniqueness becomes erratic if it is not destroyed. Only a convergent pluralism, therefore, is ultimately reconcilable with the vision, or supermodel, and with the cumulative uniqueness which the vision promises. The vision or supermodel is, then, the crucial converging factor among all the elements that constitute the university's uniqueness, since the vision directs the promotion of this uniqueness by faculty, administrators, constituencies, and even God.

Conclusion: Uniqueness Is University Vocation

If it does nothing else, the density of this chapter will reinforce an early statement that uniqueness is a mystery that is faced in evolving plant or animal, developing personality, unifying team or family, cumulative historical trends, and growing university. But any attempt to explain uniqueness by the superficial novelty of shifting accidents and not by the radical novelty of newly issuing being is to depreciate evolution, history, cultural growth, and human conversion. For uniqueness is not merely a cumulative history of failures and limitations (individuation); much more importantly, it is also a cumulative convergence of good qualities (individuality) within, and because of, these challenging limitations. When one moves from the human being to the human being's grandest invention, the university, one finds that the seven sources of limitations or individuation (weakening constituencies, fissioning specialization, breakdown of integrative wisdom, narrowing service to civic community, tight finances, less than comprehensive supermodel, and original sin of unprofessional behavior), are more than matched by the six sources of cumulative quality or individuality (energetic and generous constituencies, enriching specialization, wise and wide growth of the American university, disciplined liberty, vision or supermodel for strongly intelligent decisions, and mission of adaptation to civic needs).

Hammered against these facts, the doctrinaire statement that uniqueness is simply unknowable, and thus unpromotable, sounds hollow. But the statement is cracked wide open to disclose its emptiness when analysis of the perceptual judgment reveals the absolute nature, or the-more-than-singular-percept-and-universal-concept, in the object intended by the judgment and when the love of disciplined liberty is seen to complement this knowledge with a respectful grasp of the singular unique. To deny such knowledge of the unique is to risk losing one's own sense of identity and to gamble with the university's sense of identity. It is also to lose the ability to measure difference or similarity between two similar things, persons, historical eras, or cultures. This undermines all cumulative knowledge, since it removes the possibility of recognizing any continuity in time, place, quality, or person.

But if one admits that the mystery of uniqueness is at least somewhat knowable, then one can recognize how uniqueness occurs in the university and how it can be promoted. Thus, the academic expert's total reinterpretation of traditional truth within his or her discipline, according to new discoveries, is itself a unique synthesis. This feat affects not only him or her, but also his or her departmental colleagues, school, and university as they appropriate the new synthesis. (This fact is equally true of a skill or an art.) But this uniqueness issues not merely from the object of discovery but also from the expert's own unique mission and from the unique problem which his or her reinterpretation illumines. Again, this uniqueness is lifted to a higher plane when wisdom offers it the context of a higher uniqueness, namely, that of the collective consciousness of the university community. Herein each reinterpretation is fitted into an overall synthesis, uniquely balanced for its particular contribution, and, then, applied, through three levels of wisdom, to a particular need of the university community and, eventually, to a need of the civic community. Uniqueness occurs, therefore, not only in the overall speculative synthesis but also within the system of values used to apply this synthesis to specific needs and, again, within the unique event issuing from this use of wisdom.

But because administrators are charged with the responsibility of orchestrating specialization, the accumulation of wisdom, and service to the civic community, they are prime agents of uniqueness when they try to bring the "more" into existence, when they try to better the university and civic communities. For they direct the dialectic of these three basic aims of the university toward the university's constituencies. In addition, they do this according to a secularity, or value system, that is contained in the vision, or decisional supermodel, which has been created by the university community. Of course, they are powerless without the tools given them by the faculty and students and without the energy provided them by the constituencies of government, local community, parents, founding group, and the national community of scholars. But once they have been given these tools and this energy, they exercise remarkable power to make the university unique. Indeed, could it not be said that the dynamics of uniqueness reveal the vocation of the university?

For these reasons, it is imperative that some study now be made of the uniqueness of the Christian university. Later, the influence of the religious founding group on this use of power by administrators to achieve uniqueness in the Christian university will be assayed. For, unless the uniqueness of the Christian university is something more than that of the non-Christian university, the Christian university may well have no reason to exist; and unless the religious founding group has, and continues to have, a strong influence on this Christian uniqueness, it should sever connections with the Christian university. These two problems will constitute the content of the next four chapters.

15 Christian Wisdom: Distinctive Characteristic of the Christian University?

Once the uniqueness of a university is found to be somewhat knowable and promotable, and once this uniqueness is positively recognized as the dynamic structure of a university's individuality and negatively diagnosed as the cumulative history of its failures and limitations, then one is ready to ask: What is the special uniqueness of the Christian university? If this question cannot be answered with some clarity and force, then there is good reason to doubt whether Christian universities, working in the same area as secular universities, can warrant the considerable sacrifices that they ask of their constituencies. An obscure answer to this question indicates that the Christian university is floundering in an identity crisis, which severely inhibits the pursuit of its aims. Under these circumstances, the Christian university would be giving a confused education in a world that is already thoroughly confused.

A defender of this confused state might remark that Christian education is dealing with ultimate mystery and, therefore, cannot be clearly expressed. But someone could reply that mystery is neither opaqueness nor confusion, but something to be lived and, therefore, something partially knowable and expressible. This reply would be especially acute, since the central dynamism of Christian education is claimed to be Christ, the intelligible Word descended from Wisdom itself. If the uniqueness of any university is now found to be knowable, then the uniqueness of the Christian university should be even more intelligible. Indeed, if uniqueness is the structured collective consciousness of the university community, then the Christian university community, if it is Christian and if it is truly a university community, should be able to give a somewhat clear account of its self-identity, mysterious though it may be.

Such a strident challenge forces us to review the total structure of the university, but with a critical eye to recognizing what special note "Christian" adds to the university's secular constitution and authority. Will

Christian wisdom be able to account for the *esprit* of the Christian university community? Will Christian wisdom strengthen the secular structure of the university and render its unity more decisive? Or is Christian wisdom, with all its complexity, a confusing factor which loosens a university's sinews and renders its actions palsied? In other words, is the so-called Christian vision of the university merely a public relations gimmick, which is added on from the outside, to warrant the founding and the control of universities by church groups? Or does this vision arise out of a qualitative difference called Christian wisdom that permeates the total being and all the operations of the Christian university? These questions will guide us through the following pages.

The Constitution and Authority of the Christian University

We saw earlier how the constitution and the intrinsic authority of the university are quite distinct from the eight constituencies that parent the university into existence. That is to say, the dual intrinsic aims and the single extrinsic aim of the university structure its life as autonomous. For this reason, the eight constituencies must respectfully allow this life to grow by its own inner laws, if the university is to be healthy. Moreover, we discovered that these aims (namely, the reinterpretation of traditional truth and the accumulation of wisdom for the university and, thence, for its constituencies) are achieved by means of various processes that are vital to the university: research in the graduate school, training for the professions, education for undergraduates (through major concentration, electives, and core curriculum), administrative procedures of leadership (department heads, deans, vice presidents, president, chancellor, Board of Trustees), seminars for faculty, expansion of library holdings, maintenance of grounds and buildings, structuring of finances, and so on. All this, we have said, is the university's complex exteriorization of its communal consciousness.

In the instance of the truly Christian university, this communal consciousness is centered on the risen Christ living in the university community's communal act of faith. Thus, the Christian university lives and operates, precisely as Christian, through its intrinsic authority insofar as this authority is suffused with the university community's act of faith in Christ. But the university's intrinsic authority has originated from the extrinsic authorization that it has received from its eight constituencies. Consequently, the Christian university, having received life from these constituencies, now gratefully serves them by means of an intrinsic authority that is powered by its community's act of Christian faith. This, of course, is merely an overview that demands more detailed scanning of the Christian university's authoritative communal consciousness.

Considered structurally, or formally, this intrinsic authority is the faculty's competent knowledge and teaching, its shared vision of and passion for the university's aims, its meticulous use of procedures to carry out these aims, and its *traditio*, or cumulative experience of past accomplishments. Considered efficiently, this same authority is the prudent decisiveness of the administration. Considered materially, or dispositively, it is the students' intelligent cooperation with faculty and administration. Considered purposefully, or finally, it is the university's striving to attain its own, and the civic community's, commonweal. All this is the university's constitution, or autonomy, in dynamic operation, its intrinsic authority in action. When the university exercises this authority well, according to its constitution, then it is a living justice, an incarnate balance of duties well done and of rights respected and enjoyed among all the members of the university community and toward all the members of the civic community which is served by the university.

But, historically, how does this intrinsic authority of the university become Christian? The university is Christian from its origin. The religious founding group usually participates in the university as administrators, teachers, trustees, and chaplains. From one angle, this constituency is merely an extrinsic authorizer. But insofar as its members also become members of the university community which strongly pursues specialized knowledges and accumulates wisdom, this group enters intrinsically into the full life of the university. Consequently, the Christian wisdom around which the religious group first formed itself makes entry into the university life through the group's individual members as they teach, administrate, and serve as trustees.

Secondly, because this original founding group is often a preponderant part of the new university community, its Christian vision, which is based on Christian wisdom, is presented with some fullness and concrete directness to the other faculty. The other faculty members are often individually attracted to the university by members of the religious founding group. They are naturally quite open to, perhaps even enthusiastic about, the religious group's wisdom and vision. For this reason, the founding religious group's own unifying Christian wisdom and vision becomes, with some modifications, the young Christian university's dynamic center of unity.

Thirdly, this Christian wisdom, in turn, is given endurance and fire by the university community's disciplined liberty, namely, the community's willingness to sacrifice and suffer intelligently for the commonweal of both the university and the local civic community. Such disciplined liberty is, for the Christian, *caritas*—God's gift whereby the Christian is able to simultaneously love God and neighbor within the same act, whether that act be prayer and liturgy or one's daily university procedures on behalf of students, faculty, administration, staff, and local citizens. Thus, the disciplined liberty of *caritas* blends the two great commandments into one act and calls the Christian, confident of final victory, to shoulder Christ's cross for the sake of others. In this way, Christian disciplined liberty frees one from narrow self-interests and encourages one to persevere toward one's goals despite formidable obstacles and long sufferings.

Fourthly, because of such disciplined liberty, the cooperation among faculty, students, administration, and staff can be close, for this type of liberty demands both additional respect for the university's constitution and just use of authority, precisely because constitution and authority are the work of Christian wisdom. Then, too, it strengthens the administrator's resistance to undue pressures that might be exercised by interested constituences against the university's constitution. Meanwhile, through baptism, the gifts of the Holy Spirit (particularly Christian prudence) are made available to Christian administrators and trustees so that their key decisions can be made according to the Spirit of Christ.

There are, then, at least four ways in which the intrinsic authority of the university can become suffused with a Christian spirit so that it becomes a Christian university capable of apostolic service to itself, to the church, and to the larger civic community: (1) through the religious founding group whose members carry Christian wisdom into the university community; (2) through the Christian vision that is shared with the university members who join the religious founding group in the university community; (3) through the disciplined liberty, or *caritas,* that forms the community in loving service to others; and (4) through the decisive Christian prudence that administrators and trustees exercise as they respect and protect the university's constitution.

Because this Christian wisdom is centered in Christ the Word, the communal consciousness of the university community is structured by a communal act of faith in this Christ and is animated by a strong desire to serve God's *anawim,* the dispossessed and abandoned poor. In this activity, lived justice, the very meaning and structure of any university, can now be permeated by *caritas* in the Christian university. This means that the Christian university cannot long remain Christian unless its Christian wisdom serves the *anawim* in its own midst and in the midst of the civic community. At this point, it becomes evident that Christian wisdom must be more thoroughly investigated if one is to more securely grasp the special uniqueness of the Christian university.

Christian Wisdom Is the Esprit de Corps *of the Christian University Community*

We have already discussed cumulative wisdom as the second of the dual intrinsic aims of the university. The first intrinsic aim, the reinterpretation of traditional truth within each of the specialized knowledges-skills-arts, was seen to demand an integration of its various reinterpretations through the spectrum of diverse disciplines to provide an overview of all the knowledges-skills-arts. With such an overview, the university person is able to position various recent discoveries and is, consequently, more competent to use these discoveries integratively for the better structuring of the university and for the better solving of civic problems. This integration at three diverse levels of operation is wisdom, the second intrinsic aim of the university. Such integration cannot occur without values being used and without new values arising, since the integration and use of knowledges for the structuring of the university and for the solution of civic problems forces the integrator to establish priorities. In other words, the integrator cannot escape from forming a hierarchy of values by which he or she decides what accomplishment is more important than other accomplishments.

Christian wisdom is simply this secular wisdom dynamically enriched with the life of Christian faith. In this faith, Yahweh, the divine Father, speaks through the Jewish lawgivers, poets, and prophets to tell the Jewish people how He has given existence distinct from Himself (autonomous existence) to the universe and to all human history as He guides the universe and the human race toward a great tomorrow. Thus, men and women have a magnificent destiny that they can, however, tragically refuse if they so wish. The Father also speaks through the gospel life of his Son, Jesus Christ, and through the letters and chronicles of the Apostles. This scriptural Word of the Father is not simply a writing on papyri, but a continuous inscribing by the Father on the human heart—an inscribing more easily recognizable with the help of the papyri writings and with the guidance of the Judaeo-Christian community to whom the papyri writings have been confided in the Spirit.

Thus, the scriptural Word is lived communal experience within each member of the Judaeo-Christian community. It is both a sense of being loved into full existential awareness of self-world-God and a sense of being guided toward a great future through comradeship with Christ. For this life of faith, described and inscribed by Scriptures within the heart of the Christian, is lived by means of the sacraments, which have been given to the Christian assembly by this same Christ. Through these sacraments, Christ is more intensely present at each decisive moment of a Christian's life: birth, adolescence, sin-tragedy, marriage, death, priesthood. In the daily Eucharist, Christ sums up His own risen life only to immerse it in the life of the Christian communicant so that the Christian can speak and live the Word in his or her hour-by-hour actions. Through the scriptural and sacramental Word, Christ (the living Wisdom of God) is meant to dwell and work vigorously within the members of the Christian community. Should this Wisdom work any less in the Christian university community as it accumulates secular wisdom?

Naturally, the Word, or personal Wisdom, is indwelling within the individual not only as an individual but also as a community member. For the Word is recognized not only within oneself but also within every other Christian. Since Christ the Word is one and personal, recognition of His presence forms a community whose inner meaning is wisdom and whose basic dynamism is devoted service to one's fellows. Such recognition is within and yet beyond the limits of any economic class, racial boundary, definite era or time, geographic position, and particular culture. It is *within* these limits, since a definite human community of wisdom is formed; but it is *beyond* these limits, since no one is excluded so long as he or she recognizes Christ as incarnate Wisdom itself, living forever, simultaneously dwelling within His people and within the creating Father and the gifting Spirit. Here is scriptural Wisdom operative within Christian wisdom.

Because of its constant quest for secular wisdom, the Christian university community is splendidly prepared to receive, to value, to honor, and to live Christ the Word as scriptural Wisdom itself. Christ can, thus, be the *esprit de corps* of this community, for the faith-presence of Christ in the university community does not lessen the members' pursuit of secular wisdom but intensifies it. And why not? To seriously pursue secular wisdom is to retrace the stages of the Father's creation of the world and to discover his continuing creative presence within all the new advances of the scientific world and of international society. In addition, the university member and his or her community are accompanied by the personal Word, Christ, in all His wisdom through every academic and personal action of the day as they try to serve the civic community and one another. In this way, the values of wisdom, secular and revealed, are discovered more richly because they rise during personal interchange.

Christian wisdom is filled with the scriptural Word and, therefore, affirms that the specialized disciplines should probe ever more deeply into all reality so that the autonomous values of things, processes, and persons might be discovered, clarified, and appreciated within the creative activity of the Father. By its own presence, scriptural wisdom encourages the further development of secular wisdom so that the

338

discoveries of the specialized disciplines can be interwoven to reveal the beauty of the world and mankind within the risen presence of the Word, within the careful providence of the Father, and within the strengthening guidance of the Spirit. Christian wisdom, far from discouraging the formation of secular wisdom, as though the latter were its rival, must arise within it. Consequently, Christian wisdom not only affirms the dual intrinsic aims of the university, but makes them more specific in orientation (toward the great community of the great tomorrow), in values (e.g., affirmation of the value of the immortal human person and of autonomous creation), and in importance for mankind's fuller happiness (the fuller the human wisdom—secular and scriptural—the fuller one's manhood or womanhood).

Furthermore, the single presence of the risen Christ as a brother of all cannot be acknowledged honestly unless in loving service to one another, the extrinsic aim of the university community. Clearly, then, Christian wisdom, considered to be the dynamic sense of the risen Christ's presence within the secular wisdom of the university community, must be the *esprit de corps* of the Christian university community. On this score, Christian wisdom can be a powerfully enriching experience for the university community when that community pursues specialized disciplines and cultivates wisdom for both itself and the civic community. After all, what better atmosphere is there for developing wisdom than brotherhood of Christians and friendship with all other human beings, in creativity rather than in rivalry.

Christian wisdom does more, however, than individually support and enrich the three aims of the university community. It also gives solid hope that they will reciprocally enrich each other; indeed, Christian wisdom tends to increase the unity of the university. It does this by implicitly affirming convergent pluralism over divergent pluralism. It has been noted earlier that the rapid diversification of the various knowledges-skills-arts was instilling an implicit cynicism about any attempts to integrate all these disciplines into a wisdom. This attitude is easily impelled toward a theory of divergent pluralism, which basically declares that the world is multiple and that the university, as a mirror of the world, can be only a multiversity. In this theory, neither the multiple worlds nor the multiple parts of the university have any deep relationship with one another. They only superficially affect one another by chance encounters of possibly latent destructiveness. Thus, according to divergent pluralism, the world and the university are inevitably moving toward chaos because of both the specialization of knowledges-arts-skills and the consequent subdividing of communities. Thus, the theory of divergent pluralism supports the fragmenting action of desecularization.

In contrast to this, Christian wisdom, centered in the single person of Christ, implicitly holds for a convergent pluralism, since convergent pluralism points to that unity of world and university that underlies their vast diversification of disciplines, values, and lifestyles. There are a number of reasons for this. First, in Christian wisdom there is a strong instinct for the unique event, the once-and-for-all unrepeatable happening to which all other previous events point and from which all other future events achieve their fuller meaning. This event is the birth of Jesus Christ, the God-man. All previous events have sharpened and specified more clearly the expectation of a universal messiah. Once He had arrived, this messiah developed in Himself the full range of human actions. Although His death was brought about by the forces of evil, His once crucified body was raised to new life—an immortal life that continues to absorb all the good and beauty of evolving human life, century after century, culture after culture, forever. Because of its unique richness, the event of Jesus' birth and, later, of His resurrection, could assume into itself all past events and offer the base for all future events, enriching each one rather than depreciating any of them. For this reason, Christian wisdom is at home with convergent uniqueness, cultivates it, does not feel itself lessened by it, and recognizes it in each historical event.

Christian wisdom, then, is fundamentally historical. Its innermost drive is to respect the uniqueness of each person, of each grouping of people, of each human project, and of each event, because it sees each one not as as independent atomic happening but as the end-result of an immensely rich accumulation of previous occurrences. This unique cumulative development is the second reason why Christian wisdom holds for convergent pluralism. How could there be such development unless diverse factors were contributing, in surprising and novel ways, to the gathering unity of an era or community or person or event or movement? Christian wisdom, thus, can feel at home with any theory of evolution that respects the transcendent in the world's history. So, too, it can expect the university to become more and more complex and yet not lose unity and uniqueness while evolving.

Thirdly, Christian wisdom is aware that neither uniqueness nor cumulative development can be recognized unless one discovers the absolute (Aquinas' *natura absoluta*), which dialectically points to the uniqueness, and, at the same time, acts as the continuity for universal comparison between unique eras, peoples, events, and cultures. These absolutes, derivative from the single underived divine Absolute, are the perduring understandings and values that enable the cultural anthropologist to make sense out of vastly different civilizations. They also help the historian to establish intelligible trends within the unique events of history and the moralist to ascertain perduring principles of decision. They even guide the philosopher of science as he or she describes the spectrum of knowledges-arts-skills with some continuity of meaning and value, the psychologist as he or she recognizes integrated systems of behavior, and the theologian as he or she plots the unique path of salvation history. Evidently, the sense of tradition in Christian wisdom could not exist without a convergent pluralism.

Given this sense of the absolute as continuity and of the unique as cumulative richness, Christian wisdom must, of its very nature, encourage the specialist to reinterpret the traditional truth within his or her discipline in a unique and new synthesis according to the most recent discoveries, for there is convergent synthesis within a discipline as well as between diverse disciplines. Then, too, each new facet, because of its cumulative quality, will also eventually reveal something new about the central events of the Father's world-creative act, of Christ the Son's salvific act, and of the Spirit's community-building presence. For these reasons, man and his life can take on new richness of meaning and value.

But Christian wisdom is, to cite a fourth reason, empathetic with convergent pluralism; it is sharply aware of analogical knowledge in contrast with univocal knowledge. Because the scriptural message within Christian wisdom is spoken in imaginative symbol, rather than in precise scientific language, its interpretation demands the use of analogical thinking. *Word*, for example, is used (a) for the Second Divine Person of the Trinity, (b) for the God-man (Jesus), (c) for the central scriptural message, (d) for any message delivered by an important person in the scriptural narrative, and (e) for a particular noun or verb. Each of these five usages refers to a similar reality, namely, *meaning*. But this reality is existent in vastly different ways, and the differences run throughout the similarity. As a result, the similarity cannot, therefore, be isolated as an identical, univocal element in each of the five instances. Thus, the Second Person of the Trinity is *meaning* because He totally mirrors the Father who has generatively spoken Him; while Jesus is called Word because He includes the Second Person of the Trinity as giving existence (i.e., ultimate meaning) to all that Jesus is. In turn, the scriptural message endeavors to mirror the life of Jesus, the messianic Word who is making God and God's message (meaning) visible by His actions. On this model, the word spoken by any person to another is an attempt to mirror the giver's inner thought and life (his or her true meaning), and any noun or verb in a written sentence represents the inner thought and life of the writer.

Meaning in these five usages ranges through divine substance, incarnate existence, meaningful action, true report of inner thought, and arbitrary written signs. Also, each use of *meaning* or *word* has, therefore, very great differences. Each difference exists throughout the totality of the instance, and yet leaves in the instance some similarity to the other instances; otherwise, the *Word*, referring to the Second Person of the Trinity, would be used for a pun or for a merely arbitrary, nonsensical expression.

Once one admits a real similarity between instances, even though each instance is shot through and through with profound differences, one has also admitted the existence of analogical knowing, thinking, and talking. One has allowed for a thread of continuity not merely between the various usages of the same word, but also between the things signified by this word. At this point, one recognizes an underlying unity that links these things in being as well as in meaning. For this reason, the analogical knowing contained in Christian wisdom enables this wisdom to recognize the unique (vast differences within the similarity between things) and yet prize the similarity uniting unique beings. In this way, Christian wisdom is ready for, and fully respects, the distinct specializations between knowledges-arts-skills as they proliferate at an alarming rate. At the same time, it is ready for a wisdom that will unify—even provisionally—all these disciplines within the individual, the specialized community, the university of scholars, and the larger civic community.

Consequently, Christian wisdom is more than compatible with convergent secularization but is scandalized by the divergencies of desecularization because desecularization dichotomizes the physical sciences from the social sciences, science from philosophy, common-sense knowledge from scientific knowledge, secular knowledge from theology, theology from faith, speculative knowledge from practical decisions. Christian wisdom and secularization work for the unification and expansion of mankind, whereas desecularization dices mankind's consciousness into compartments and belittles human beings by reducing them to one or another of these compartments. Christian wisdom believes in marriage more than divorce—marriage in which the partners develop the distinctness of their personalities precisely by their enriching union with each other. Consequently, Christian wisdom not only supports the dual intrinsic aims of the university, but also brings their reciprocity into closer union so that they can more readily provide the resources needed by the civic community. Once again, Christian wisdom can be justly called the *esprit de corps* of the Christian community. Not only does it support and enrich individually each of the three aims of the university, but also, by affirming convergent pluralism, it more tightly unifies the university through strengthening the dialectic of reciprocal enrichment that is operative among the aims.

Christian Wisdom—Basis for Christian Vision

Christian wisdom, however, does more than strongly support and then better unify the dual intrinsic aims and single extrinsic aim of the university; it also acts as the base for a Christian vision that is meant to both guide the university and invigorate its actions. We have earlier noted that any vision of the university is much more than an ideology, for, although it extrapolates beyond both the specialized knowledges and the accumulated wisdom, it nevertheless arises out of, and according to, the university community's synthetic grasp of all scientific disciplines. For this reason, it is not caught in one narrow, ideological thought system, but has room for a plurality of views and lifestyles. Since this vision has risen within a free community, it is not an instrument for acquiring power, but it is an attractive portrayal of future university goals that persuades to beauty.

This vision may well be messianic in its hopes to lead the world to a fuller life, but it does not have an ideological predilection for one segment of society, nor does it require of its adherents a singular way of life. Thus, a vision is a unique articulation of values according to the structure and history of a university as the university serves the needs of its members and of the larger civic community. But what does the Christian message add to such a vision used by every university?

Most importantly, the Christian vision is focused upon the ultimate divine mystery the rich and deep community of the Trinity. For the Christian vision uses Christian faith to give it ultimate perspective on all reality. Such perspective is the most prized element of any vision precisely because it is the most needed. Yet this perspective can be clarified only if it is interpreted by Christian wisdom, the source of the Christian vision, since even Christian faith is interpreted by Christian wisdom. Thus, by way of a faith that is interpreted by Christian wisdom, the mystery of the Trinity lends its richness to the Christian university's perspective. The richness of the divine mystery, for example, can be explored only by way of an analogical knowing, which implies diversity of knowledges-arts-skills, of secularities, and of lifestyles, so that the divine mystery can be adequately described from many angles. Yet this pluralism includes an underlying unity, since it can be converged upon the unity of the Divine Trinity only by an architectonic metaphysics (a fundamental philosophy) that is relevant to all possible philosophies and necessarily employed in all theologies to focus on this one God of three persons.

Since the mystery of the three divine persons in God is the ultimate value of all beings and of all their activities, it becomes clear that the personal is to be valued more highly than things, routines, processes, and accomplishments. As a result, the Christian vision of the university constantly reminds all the members of the university community that the institutional is finally to be subordinated to the community, that the sciential is secondary to the sapiential, that the means must serve the end and not vice versa. Here, too, the fact that the three persons of the Trinity form a community so tight-knit that it is one God focuses the Christian vision of the university upon the quality of university community life and upon that great community of the great tomorrow into which it will enter for the final fullness of life. This makes it piercingly clear that the university community, insofar as it allows Christian wisdom to possess it and direct its energies, is an important factor in the anticipatory building of this great community in this present world. Indeed, the Christian university becomes the servant of the civic community under this banner of building the great community of the great tomorrow which will center around the life of the Trinitarian community.

Because this ultimate mystery of the Trinity is so rich, so deep, so personal, and so communal, it renders the Christian vision a dominant vision within a university. All other visions can be only partial, no matter how noble and subtle they are. In addition, the infinitely rich status of this mystery opens the Christian vision, like Christian wisdom, to wide historical development. In other words, unlike the Marxist or determinist vision of the university, the Christian vision which arises out of Christian wisdom offers many historical paths, instead of one solitary way, by which men and women can walk into the great community of the great tomorrow. At the same time, however, these paths are sure to converge, since they must all meet in the one same community that is centered around the one same God of three persons. Thus, Christian wisdom gives its resultant Christian vision a strong sense of direction. Within the Christian vision, one feels a sense of destiny for one's work, for the United States of America, for the university, and for each member of the university. The Trinity is providing both the means and the alluring goal for the building of the great community of the great tomorrow, the communion of saints.

But because the totally free Trinity has made men and women free to cooperate or not to cooperate and because the creating Trinity has invited men and women to cocreate this universe with the three persons, this mystery instills a sense of deep responsibility for the world and for one's fellows. In fact, one might say that the Trinity's covenant with humanity to cocreate the world is a mandate for the university to exist and to help in building the community of mankind. Christian wisdom has thus enabled the Christian vision of the university to shed a bright light on the university's very *raison d'être*, its deepest existential root.

When Christian wisdom focuses the Christian vision of the university upon the mystery of the Trinity to reveal the important role of the university in salvation history, it cannot avoid what is at the center of this focus, namely, the risen Christ, the incarnately living Christian Wisdom. Experience, at least implicit experience, of this Christ is worldwide, including every single human being whom He illuminates and strengthens according to each person's situation and personality. As the risen Lord of history, Christ holds all past knowledge-art-skill, stands vibrantly aware of the present moment, and, in union with the eternal Father and the eternal Spirit, reviews the future course of events. But in this Christian vision and wisdom, He is also the Christ crucified by mankind; and so, He presents in His human wounds of body, mind, and heart both the cold shock of evil and the warm devotedness of His self-sacrifice for mankind. There is no attempt here to deny the deep sufferings that are involved in building this Christian university community destined to finally become part of the great community of the great tomorrow. Clearly, if Christ is at its living center, the Christian wisdom of the university must be realistic in its grand universal scope, thoroughly historical in its tradition, compassionate in its disciplined pursuits, and sacrificial in the stewardship of its resources. Are these not attitudes particularly fitting for the university living its dual intrinsic aims and attempting, thereby, to humanize the world?

In the Christian vision of Christ as incarnate Wisdom, we find Him humanizing God for mankind's sake and divinizing mankind for God's sake. Could the university possibly be a key factor in the recognition and even the pursuit of this remarkable transformation? This is what is meant by humanizing God. Christ's birth in flesh and blood made God recognizable by mankind, through faith; Christ's institution of the visible sacraments made God much more approachable by mankind; Christ's call to baptism made the companionship of the indwelling Trinity an acceptable fact of faith for mankind. But Christ also divinized mankind by liberating men and women from personal sin and original sinfulness and by endowing them with the powers of faith, hope, and *caritas*. Faith is meant to open up mankind's tunnel-vision of life; hope is meant to rescue mankind from the sense of despairing powerlessness; and *caritas* is meant to widen mankind's heart that has been narrowed by self-preoccupied concerns. Mankind could once again feel the tragedy of sin, experience personal dignity, and enjoy the humor of humbled love for fellow human beings.

When Christ humanized God by becoming a man in our world, He made it palpably evident that God loved the world and that the world was good. When Christ divinized mankind, He demonstrated to us how we could live a godly life and become part of God's family.

This Christian vision, which is illumined by Christian wisdom, helps the university community recognize that the mediator, Christ, intends to work through the community in producing this transformation of mankind. Insofar as the university community receives, develops, and offers Christian wisdom to others, it enables men and women to recognize their potential for divine living, to know the means of this transformation, and to contact the source of this life in liturgy, sacrament, holy women and men, and ecclesial community. Again, insofar as the university community is possessed by Christian wisdom, it is convinced that the goodness of the world guarantees the worthwhileness of all the community's endeavors to explore the world. Moreover, this community knows that the forming of a university community to master wisdom and to serve the needs of the civic community with this wisdom is among the grandest works of mankind. With these convictions instilled by Christian vision, a university community can endure heavy hardships and dare to make seemingly world-shattering discoveries for the sake of both Christian wisdom and mankind.

But when the Christian vision centers on the risen Christ, according to Christian wisdom, it is not limited to instilling convictions worthy of the university's most intense life or to raising hopes for energizing the university into highly creative action. It also reveals Christ as the *Verbum*, intelligence itself, or as St. Augustine's illuminating teacher, the light of the world. He is the dynamic plan according to which the world is being created even now. As incarnate, this Christ fosters common-sense knowledge, the base for the pyramiding of all knowledges-skills-arts, because He still lives and communicates according to everyday experience. The eye of the fully human, risen Christ now brightens at artistic invention, His ear now delights in the advance of music, and His imagination now thrills to the symbols of literature. Thus, for a person to know and enjoy these moments is to share the risen Christ's knowing and enjoying and to feel the worth of divine living. In the same way that He loved the world, which He married in His body, the risen Christ now fosters the physical sciences, which reveal the intricate beauty of this world; in the same way that He formed full community living in His Mystical Body, Christ now encourages the social sciences, which seek to promote such living; in the same way that He wished to serve the community better, Christ now exults in the finesse of technical skills. Finally, as the center of divine mystery, the risen Christ now stands beyond the grasp of all theologies, all philosophies, all poetry, and all cultures. Thus, He encourages their plural approaches to Him so that the ensemble of their very plurality can hint at the richness of His life. Yet, at the same time, He is their incarnate convergence point and unifies them in His single life-experience. So well do they converge in Him that each and all are needed to interpret Scripture, the presence of the *Verbum* among us.

Because the dynamic experience of the risen Christ is incarnate, it readily unifies the university community in contemplative appreciation of knowledges-arts-skills and in the active use of this contemplation for the neighbor. Because Christ is filled with the family life of the Trinity, He acts as the unifying mystery of the community, whether it be family or nation, parish or research team, church or university. Because He was strangely born of woman alone, His manliness enjoys a strong femininity, a special sensitivity to all sensual beauty, and a compassion for all that needs comforting. The masculine and the feminine attain full oneness in Him.

By reason of Christ's incarnate spirit, then, the Christian vision that arises out of Christian wisdom could never be an abstract blueprint; it must be as incarnate and as spirited as Christ, its center. Thus, it includes not only the individuality, the so-called risen life of the university community, but also its individuation, the sum of its crosses and hurts through the years. The Christian vision of a univeristy will be built out of its particular gifts and history and out of the unique needs of the constituencies it serves. But the uniqueness of the vision will also include the unique presence of Christ within the university community to instill convictions of its dignity, to raise its hopes for growth, and to unify itself and its efforts for better Christian community living. It will do this according to all the specialized knowledges-skills-arts, according to a full wisdom, and according to a balanced blending of the feminine and the masculine. Meanwhile, all this is occurring within the ultimate mystery of the Trinity, a mystery that opens out to include and to unify all pluralism, to stress the personal over all else, to span all time and all communities with the great community of the great tomorrow, and to offer men and women the opportunity to cocreate with the Father an ever evolving universe. Evidently, the Christian wisdom that produces such a vision must be the *esprit de corps* of the Christian university community.

Christian Wisdom—Source of Spirited Liberty and Justice

Even if the constitution of the university (its three aims) is permeated with Christian wisdom from its foundation, even if scriptural wisdom animates this university wisdom, even if there is strong insistence on convergent pluralism as the underlying unity of world development, and even if a Christian vision of the Trinity and of Christ is enthusing the university community, nothing will happen unless the disciplined liberty of *caritas* puts constitution, scriptural wisdom, conviction of convergent pluralism, and Christian vision to work in practical procedures and concrete accomplishments. Thus, this disciplined liberty becomes the final factor that Christian wisdom uses to enliven and unify the Christian university.

We have earlier defined discipline as the sustained willingness to suffer for the truth taken as a worthy good. In the eyes of Christian wisdom, this discipline would be the "folly" of the Cross, endured for the sake of justice and lived in union with the once crucified Christ who is now risen. From the contrasting viewpoint of merely secular wisdom, this action could hardly be more than a sign of contradiction.

We have also discovered that disciplined liberty is the power to rigorously pursue truth and vigorously seek the good. The exercise of such disciplined liberty requires remarkable balance in one's personality. But according to Thomas Aquinas, this balance becomes possible with the gift of *caritas*, since *caritas* is the unifying form, or control, within all the virtues. Such control manifests itself in professional attitude, in teamwork, in just actions, in the balanced pursuit of both personal and communal goods, in passionate life-purpose, and, finally, in devoted loyalty to the institution, to its personnel, and to those whom the institution, such as a university, serves. This is the beauty of *caritas*, the core of the Gospel message; it restores wholeness to the individual person and to the community that has been fragmented by sin. Indeed, secular wisdom is transformed into Christian wisdom principally through God's gift of *caritas*, for *caritas* leads men and women into the seventh phase of liberty (mentioned earlier). In this phase, loyalty to God arises out of loyalty to one's community because one trusts in God's providence for one's dear ones and hopes in God's great community of the great tomorrow for them.

Caritas is so powerful for forming community because, through faith, God is revealed as the ultimate source and home for all intelligence, all virtue, and all loving action. This *caritas*, at the heart of Christian wisdom, is a personal commitment to others—a commitment that finds its endurance and its tenderness in the companionship of God. *Caritas* is also a sacrificial love that is filled with joy in the good to be possessed by and with others. For this reason, the institutional side of the university can knowingly teach about the virtues and the values that are needed for personal and communal wholeness; likewise, on the communal side the university community can incarnate, through *caritas*, these very virtues and values. Consequently, because of the *caritas* in Christian wisdom, the disciplined liberty of the university community is seen to be an accumulated wisdom that has been structured by justice and then warmed, directed, and expanded by *caritas* so that a strong Christian community is formed. Since *caritas* is a love that is inspired by the Holy Spirit in the Trinity, it again becomes clear why Christian wisdom is undoubtedly the *esprit de corps* of the Christian university community when that community tries to live justly and evoke the wholeness of man and woman in and outside the university.

Because Christian wisdom, permeated by faith and hope, is made dynamic by *caritas* and because *caritas* incarnates values and attitudes through justice, Christian wisdom both requires and promotes justice. As we have seen, justice is the very order of the university itself, that is, justice is the very sharing of truth on research teams and in classrooms; justice is the very developing of secular wisdom within the university community, for the university's own sake and for the sake of its constituencies. On this account, Christian wisdom, of its very nature, demands and fosters justice within the university community. Indeed, this justice is enriched by the *caritas* that accompanies Christian wisdom, since *caritas* tempers the rigor of justice with a wise love. This justice is then rendered literally graceful, primarily personal, and highly motivated, since it is building a community that will later be integrated into the great community of the great tomorrow. Just as no community can long survive without the structuring of justice, so, too, no community can long avoid the divisiveness of harshness without the understanding warmth of a love that is operative within this justice. Thus, the wholesomeness (desired for every student, administrator, professor, and staff member for the sake of both university teamwork and the constituencies) arises out of a just living that is warmed by the *caritas* of Christian wisdom.

The *caritas* that is involved with Christian wisdom not only builds community for the present but also prolongs it beyond the grave into the great community of the great tomorrow. Ironically, the very future of any community is strengthening that community for present struggles and work. The sensitive warmth of Spirit-inspired *caritas*, for example, enables the university community to better discern and more concretely plan the future living of justice within its university decisions. This very planning enriches the university's existence and enables it to serve its constituencies more competently. Since well-developed universities are most distinguishable by their *esprit de corps*, that is, by their distinctive living of diverse value systems or secularities, it becomes clearer that Christian wisdom is truly the *esprit de corps* of the Christian university community as it promotes wholeness in the university's daily living.

But more precisely, how does Christian wisdom, through disciplined liberty and *caritas*-inspired justice, better serve the university's constituencies or the larger civic community? First, Christian wisdom is an integration of faith with justice through an intelligently exercised *caritas*. Such a wise integration is more and more needed as the commonweal (the organized goodness) of society becomes more and more complex. Professional Christian wisdom is needed—the type of wisdom achieved only in a university milieu and only by a university community that is deeply aware of Christian life. Secondly, Christian wisdom, because of its biblical basis, is specially sensitive to the needs of the *anawim*, those who are suffering unjustly without power of appeal, except to God. The *anawim* are the persecuted, the neglected, the refugees, the oppressed minorites— whether they be rich or poor, citizens or outcastes, young or old. Such a positive "prejudice" could keep the Christian university from becoming an instrument for exploitation as it attempts to fulfill its extrinsic aim of service.

Thirdly, because Christian wisdom is centered in experience of the risen Christ, the universal mediator, its influence is meant to reach beyond the parochial to the international. Fourthly, because its Christ has come to serve and not to be served and because its concern is to reach out to the *anawim*, Christian wisdom develops in the community a sense of stewardship and the attitude of a servant. These balance the pride of intellect and the arrogance of will that can, at times, blind and paralyze university people. Then, too, the attitudes of stewardship and service beautifully fit into the democratization that is so characteristic of American higher education; they also indicate why Christian wisdom is the *esprit de corps* of the Christian university.

As Christian wisdom incorporates the scriptural wisdom of the Word within its community; as it thereby strengthens the structure of secular wisdom in the university; as it adds intelligent thrust to the university community's service of its constituencies; as it thus intensifies the unity of the university according to a convergent pluralism of mind, heart, and will; as it grandly colors a rich Christian vision of the university through the mysteries of the Triune God and of the incarnate risen Christ; as it invigorates the disciplined liberty of the university with a *caritas* democratically open to all people and wholesomely forming all loves; as it renders the rigors of justice flexible and sensitive; as it builds community for now and for eternity, within both itself and its constituencies—as Christian wisdom does all this, it must simultaneously, generously, and strenuously absorb the vast *traditio* of past accomplishments. Christian wisdom, like secular wisdom, is a complex accumulation of intelligence and value, which has been distilled from the experience of past generations.

Christian wisdom must live gratefully in the past, for it not merely presents past accomplishments to us, but also stands for the best of these accomplishments when it is representing a fresh synthesis of past riches, present discoveries, and new communal needs. This *traditio*, however is not merely a receiving of past treasures; it is also a handing on of them. This simultaneous preserving and handing on of the past requires a new synthesis of wisdom—the most difficult and intricate of all feats. Since the risen Christ is the living *traditio* of the best in all cultures (He is in contact with all men and women of all eras and cultures), His presence at the dynamic center of Christian wisdom can make that wisdom more competent in performing this most perilous activity of the university: *traditio*. Here, again, one discovers how Christian wisdom is the *esprit de corps* of the Christian university and how it fits the Christian university for university living of remarkably high quality.

Thus, as Christian wisdom focuses all the riches of the past upon the present life of the Christian university, it simultaneously thrusts the university into the future. In doing so, it acts not only as the path, but also as the light for this path toward the future destiny of the human race: the beatific vision of God amid the great community of the great tomorrow. The scriptural wisdom within Christian wisdom sketches out the path. The secular wisdom within Christian wisdom offers the enlightening dynamisms for moving well along this path. The divine wisdom of the living Christ's experience within Christian wisdom suffuses these dynamisms with the faith-life, the hope, and the *caritas* that are necessary to recognize, pursue well, and achieve the full development of human beings as pilgrims within their present traveling community and any future communities.

It is this same Christian wisdom that renders the Christian university uniquely different from other types of university, even as it individually supports and enriches the dual intrinsic aims and one extrinsic aim of the university, even as it increases the reciprocity between these three aims to more deeply unify the university, even as it generates that Christian vision which invigorates and directs the growth of the university according to the living truth of the Triune God and the incarnate God-man Jesus, even as it enlivens university processes with the disciplined liberty that is the power to rigorously pursue truth and to vigorously seek good so that the Christian university community can be structured with justice and expanded with *caritas*.

Surprisingly, Christian wisdom is being defined at the very same time that its impact on university structure and life is being described. But this definition of Christian wisdom as the unique *esprit* of the Christian university needs further expansion. So far, this delineation of the *esprit* has been limited to discussion of the three aims of the university, the so-called superstructure of the university. The description must be extended, however, to the infrastructure, that is, the means to the attainment of these aims. In this way, Christian wisdom can be seen as unifying the university down to its roots. Even this will not be enough to fully define Christian wisdom in the university; one must finally see Christian wisdom affecting the operational unity of the university. One will then note with some clarity the distinctive characteristic that makes the Christian university unique among all types of universities. In this way, too, one may observe how Christian wisdom strengthens and clarifies, rather than weakens or confuses, both the secular constitution and the intrinsic authority of the university.

16 Christian Wisdom: Basic Unifier of the Christian University

To put it simply at the beginning, Christian wisdom is able to offer a basic unity to the university precisely because it has arisen out of the confluence of Christian philosophy, Christian theology, faith in the one Christ, and the Holy Spirit's gift of wisdom. Let us note how each of these four constituents of Christian wisdom serve to unify the university and, incidentally, more acutely define the meaning of Christian wisdom.

Christian Wisdom Gives Basic Structural Unity to the University

As we have noted, the Christian philosophy which contributes to Christian wisdom is itself a secular philosophy enriched by the guiding influence of Christian faith. This Christian philosophy is also a metaphysical wisdom that is in touch with all the other university disciplines. The other university disciplines render it concrete in detail, dynamic in growth, and congruent with advancing culture. Thus, through Christian philosophy, Christian wisdom can be vibrantly responsive to the new discoveries and values of the university community. In addition, because Christian philosophy is the pivotal point in the dialectic between the univocal specialized disciplines and the analogous wisdom knowledges, it can enable Christian wisdom to mediate between specialized departments whose univocal knowledges-arts-skills seem to isolate them from one another.

In other words, Christian philosophy enables Christian wisdom to appreciate the distinct contribution of each knowledge-skill-art, to insert each within a spectrum of knowledges-arts-skills, to see them all in a panoramic Christian vision, and to indicate their value for estimating mankind's future. At the same time, an intrinsic Christian respect for the *anawim* enables Christian wisdom, along with its informing Christian philosophy, to value common-sense knowledge as the radical beginning and the challenging terminus of all other knowledges. In this way, Christian wisdom enjoys a gritty realism that protects it from the arrogance of the sophisticate who is tempted to contemn the uneducated and to underestimate the compensating shrewdness that they have developed from "making the best of bad situations."

The earthiness of Christian wisdom is also revealed in its sharp awareness of the salvation process, as dramatized by Christian philosophy. For Christian philosophy, taking its clues from Plato or Nietzsche, has reflected long on the human penchant for self-destruction and on the strange inclination of cultures to disintegrate because of injustice. Christian philosophy balances this historical sense of divergent sin (amid. a person's persistent attempts to love others and to reverence God deeply) with a sense of destiny that has been inspired by the conviction that plural philosophies and lifestyles can be convergent. Thus, the Christian philosophy within Christian wisdom renders this wisdom open to much diversity of understanding and life, and yet establishes a reasonable confidence in the worthwhileness of the world and of the total university enterprise.

Once again, the diversity of disciplines and the plural approaches to truth within each discipline find a home and a hope within Christian wisdom and, thus, within the Christian university—without a loss of unity. This roomy Christian philosophy is triply unified by fundamental philosophy, by the Christian's single faith in the single person of the risen Christ, and by the consistency of doctrine that is guaranteed by both the single faith and the convergent analogical truth. Furthermore, this Christian philosophy is able to be dominant and, thus, to give unity to a university because it both enriches the five basic functions of secular philosophy and contributes new important content to the holdings of secular philosophy. This, in turn, furnishes Christian wisdom with a unified, dominating influence throughout the institutional university and within its community, for Christian wisdom can give more than it receives from secular philosophy.

On the other hand, if Christian wisdom is not dynamically structured by Christian philosophy, then it loses contact with the university structures of academic disciplines and departments and, thus, is shut out from the lives of the faculty, students, and administrators who form the university community. Under these circumstances Christian wisdom would quickly become a relic of the past, no longer growing, no longer adapting, no longer relevant to the lives of the university community. Thus, the Christian university cannot take a position of neutrality with respect to Christian philosophy and Christian wisdom. Without them, it either becomes a secular university or flounders neurotically in search of its identity; without them, its basic structure becomes ambivalent, then fluid, and finally, disintegrative.

The second element that contributes to the makeup of Christian wisdom is Christian theology. Because Christian theology contacts all the university disciplines through Christian philosophy, it is enabled to reach its full potential as a university knowledge. It is scientific and it is related to the first intrinsic aim of the university, both in itself and in its use of all the physical and social sciences; it is comprehensive and unitive insofar as it uses analogical knowledge to span all the univocal knowledges; it is sapiential and related to the second intrinsic aim of the university insofar as it deals radically with the whole of humanity and human history; it is pastoral and related to the single extrinsic aim of the university insofar as it aims to serve all people, but especially the neglected *anawim;* it is fundamental and constructive of the university's basic unity insofar as it contacts the base underlying all theologies and all philosophies.

Christian theology can lend these five characteristics to Christian wisdom so that wisdom can, in turn, reinforce the institutional and communal structures of the university and, then, point them toward a basic unity. Christian theology specifically adapts Christian wisdom to this reinforcing and unifying function when it focuses all knowledges upon the ultimate mystery of all life and history—the triune God revealed by the incarnate and risen second person of the Trinity, Jesus Christ. Unless Christian theology so focuses the Christian faith within Christian wisdom, Christian wisdom is helpless to give ultimate destiny, significance, and worth to the world and to the university enterprise. Without such ultimacy, the university tends to wander from its destiny into the more trivial, to wonder about its significance with consequent confusion, and to lose its sense of worth in resultant lassitude. For this reason, Christian wisdom, infused with Christian theology, is vital to the university, whether the latter is secular or Christian.

This leads us into the third element that constitutes Christian wisdom, namely, faith in that one Christ who gives life to fundamental Christian theology and hope to fundamental Christian philosophy. Because this Christ is God, because He is Lord of all history, even future history, and because He alone is the window into the ultimate mystery of Trinitarian life, faith in Him must be wide open to all encompassing mystery. This makes it clear that no single theology or philosophy, nor any set of theologies and philosophies (no matter how many, deep, and comprehensive they may be; no matter if they be Christian or non-Christian), will ever exhaust Christ's meaning. In fact, all of them will be needed in order that the convergence of fundamental philosophy and fundamental theology may yield some inkling of Christ's grandeur for mankind. Thus, Christian faith, of its very nature, demands an evolving *traditio,* a continuous reinterpretation of specialized traditional truth and lifestyle within the context of wisdom integration. This demand both requires a Christian wisdom and reveals its structure.

Furthermore, the Christian faith is for the so-called masses; no man or woman is ever to be excluded except by his or her own free choice. In fact, this faith is meant particularly for the uneducated, the poor, and the handicapped. When traditional Christian wisdom is suffused with such a Christian faith, then it relativizes all knowledges, all wisdoms, and all devoted services that are offered to the human race. This is to say that Christian wisdom puts all of them into the context of the single underived absolute, the triune God, so that the absoluteness of each one is seen to be derived and quite incomplete. In other words, each absolute is seen to be relative to other absolutes and then to the whole of God, man, and universe. Thus, all absolutes are seen to be derivative from the single underived absolute and, therefore, to be relative measures of other beings. In fact, Christian wisdom makes it clear how negligible each absolute would be in comparison to the triune God—unless He had loved it into existence and loyally kept loving it into continued existence.

Thus, faith in the one Christ frees a person from being imprisoned within narrow perspectives or derived absolutes and from turning these perspectives into absolute ideologies constrictive of both human freedom and the university's liberty. Here Christian faith intimately transforms Christian wisdom into the free and open *esprit de corps* of the Christian university. The Christian faith within Christian wisdom is, then, the light which discovers the fundamental unity underlying all knowledges and all styles of life and serving as the basic unity of the university itself. This basic unity is, of course, the vibrant life of the risen Christ and of the Trinity.

In order to contact this Trinitarian life in a quasi-immediate way, one requires the fourth constituent of Christian wisdom, namely, the Holy Spirit's gift of wisdom. This gift empowers its recipient not only to know God with existential affection as the sole source of all realities, but also to move, in partnership with God, from the sublime down to everyday decisions with an existential sense of how worthwhile, in God's eyes, is each person and each event. This intelligent concern for everyone and everything, when it is united in faith to Christian philosophy and theology, gives Christian wisdom the ability to render the extrinsic aim of the university pastorally powerful. Christian wisdom can now apply an existential personalism and a highly practical intent as it focuses the specialized disciplines on civic problems.

In addition, because the Holy Spirit's gift of wisdom heightens one's friendship with God, it reciprocally strengthens one's ability to cooperate, out of affectionate ties, with other members of the university. This union of the two great Commandments enters, then, into the university community's pursuit of the dual intrinsic aims of the university, which are reinterpretation of the specialized disciplines and accumulation of wisdom. Thus, this gift fires the ambition of the specialist to discover new truth about God's world, strengthens the university member's love for wisdom as existentially personal, deepens the interior unity of the university community membership, and makes the extrinsic aim of the university (that is, service of the eight constituencies) more powerful because it is more personal and practical. Here, in the ensemble of these four constituents of Christian wisdom (Christian theology, philosophy, faith, and the Holy Spirit's gift of wisdom), one can see how Christian wisdom unifies the very structure of the Christian university.

Christian Wisdom Gives Basic Operational Unity to the Christian University

It has gradually become clear to us that Christian wisdom is not a simple reality. We have noted that it is secular wisdom that has been transformed by scriptural wisdom, which in turn includes the growing presence of Divine Wisdom, the risen Christ. Moreover, this Christian wisdom embraces not only a Christian philosophy, which puts it into intimate contact with all the university disciplines, but also a Christian theology, which reinforces this contact and focuses it, through faith, upon the risen Christ, the revealer of the triune God. Furthermore, the Holy Spirit's gift of wisdom renders Christian wisdom particularly affectionate toward God and existentially personal and practical in decisions that relate to one's neighbor. This is the outline of the structure of Christian wisdom as it instills *esprit de corps* into the Christian university's secular constitution and intrinsic authority. But now it is necessary to see Christian wisdom in operation and to note how it organizes the *operational* unity of the Christian university.

An overview reveals Christian wisdom as a two-sided process, namely, an ongoing Christian secularization and Christian secularity. Christian secularization is the Christian community's persistent and consistent use of all knowledges-arts-skills to explore the ultimate meaning of humanity and of human destiny by way of Christian philosophy, Christian theology, Christian vision, and Christian faith. Operational Christian secularity, in turn, is the dedication of the Christian community's life to both the world and humankind; the motives for this dedication are the intrinsic value of world and humankind, and also community loyalty to the person of the risen Christ. This process, then, is the total life of the Christian university and its community; it includes redemption working within it and forms the City of God, which is composed of all those believers who sincerely seek God above all else. Thus, the Christian secularization-secularity process is aiming to bring wholesomeness to each student, faculty member, administrator, and staff officer of the university; to each citizen of the local community; and to each member of the university's constituencies.

An operational Christian wisdom, then, is an integrated secularization and secularity that works not only to restore, but to expand the wholesomeness of each man and woman and of the whole human race. Hence, it works within all the vagaries, all the tragedy and comedy, all the disasters and triumphs of salvation history. Christian wisdom in action is the total and never-ending education of the Christian toward the godly. It begins when a person's family, neighborhood, church, and school present him or her with a worldview (a *Weltanschauung*), an "englobing" explanation and value system for daily living. Through everyday, common-sense knowledge, the Christian soon meets mystery in death or in love or in economic tragedy or in self-doubt. This mystery is beyond the explanations of the person's worldview and threatens its reality. In such a time of confusion, the Christian looks to any, and to all of the secular disciplines for new explanations that, of course, must be checked against his or her everyday, common-sense experience and, then, related to Christian faith experience.

If this Christian is a university person, he or she can use Christian philosophy to guide the search among the secular disciplines for some answer to his or her life questions. University Christians can also employ Christian theology to help them interpret the partial answer offered by faith. In this way, the Christian runs a dialectic stretching between common-sense living of a worldview and a personal faith experience of Christ and of the triune God. The mediating road between these extremes is the secular wisdom of the university disciplines as they are interpreted and evaluated by Christian philosophy and focused by Christian theology. Thus, Christian wisdom is the dynamic process of Christian secularization-secularity. Naturally, such a wisdom can be powerful within any university in which people strive to live as Christians, but it is especially effective within the Christian university in which, with full awareness, a Christian community is cooperatively working out its salvation in service to others.

Of course, at the same time that Christian wisdom is working for wholesomeness in the Christian individual and in his or her community, there is a counter-process of desecularization and secularism working either toward fragmentation of the wholesome or toward paralysis of its growth. Any disruption of the Christian secularization-secularity process will serve this counter-process. Within the secularization side of Christian

358

wisdom, any fallacy introduced into the specialization of a particular knowledge, art, or skill through poor reintegration of traditional truth with new discoveries will disrupt the wisdom dialectic. Or any premature and misleading integration of diverse knowledges-skills-arts can fragment or paralyze the "wholing" process of this dialectic. If physicists, for example, were to deny the possibility of new energy entering the universe in order to avoid theoretical complications or if biologists, in the interests of a hard determinism, were to deny data pointing to the teleonomic or if economists for greater unity of action in international finance, were to reduce all theories to the Marxist, then reinterpretation of traditional truth would be vitiated by extrinsic factors. As a result, growth toward wholeness would be hampered in the secularization-secularity process. Of course, the exclusion of the possibility of ongoing creation or of provident purpose or of nondeterminist economics would affect the operations of Christian wisdom in the individual Christian and in his or her university community.

So, too, the second aspect of secularization, namely, the integration of various disciplines into a whole, is severely handicapped when one or another knowledge attempts to assume an imperial position from which to judge all other knowledges and their conclusions by its own limited criteria. Such was the imperialism of medieval theology, seventeenth-century philosophy, eighteenth-century physics, and nineteenth-century biology; such is the imperialism of twentieth-century psychology and sociology; such will be the imperialism of twenty-first century biochemistry or biophysics. In order to achieve a supersynthesis of all knowledges, this imperialism forces other knowledges to ape the predominant knowledge of the moment and, thus, to warp each discipline's autonomous method, theory, data, and practical conclusions. The result is an ideological constriction of the world rather than a truly scientific synthesis. It should not be surprising that such a constriction can blur Christian wisdom insofar as Christian wisdom is dependent on all secular disciplines by way of Christian philosophy and theology. This distortion of the individual Christian's wisdom can only blur the Christian vision of the whole Christian community, most especially that portion of the Christian community which is staffing a Christian university.

Naturally, the other side of Christian wisdom, namely secularity, can also derange the whole university process. Obviously, the denial of spiritual values, such as person, union with God, liberty, friendship, and justice, will change the whole meaning of the world and, in addition, cause the collapse of Christian wisdom. Less obviously dangerous, yet just as destructive, is the loss of contemplation or the denial of absolutes or the vaunting of career-success over personal integrity. The first undermines the overview, or speculative moment, in human thinking and in the university's pursuit of truth. The second reduces all events to chance convergences of influences. The third eventually makes manipulative power over others into the end of all life. Such upheavals of value can only fragment the individual person and his or her community. Under these conditions, Christian wisdom would take on the appearance of an impossible ideal or, at best, seem to be a process that overloads secular wisdom with too many demands. Under this misapprehension, which is widely held by not a few canny administrators, the Christian university administrator may well be tempted to forget the Christian wisdom process, to become supremely business-like, and to run his or her school on solely pragmatic principles. At this point, secularism has triumphed. To avoid this alternative, the administrator and the faculty must have a strong conviction that Christian wisdom is valid for running the day-to-day operations of the Christian university.

Such a conviction must have strong roots in some of the following groundings. In undergraduate education, for example, Christian wisdom can be the delicate balancing mechanism between the active vocationalism of the major course of concentration, the contemplative liberal intent of the core curriculum, and the ranging freedom of elective courses so that the undergraduate grows wholesomely in the use of all his or her humane powers. Furthermore, the undergraduate curriculum is meant to move the student from mere adolescent freedom of choice toward the mature liberty of disciplined pursuit of the good. As we noted earlier, these are precisely the aims of Christian wisdom. In addition, Christian wisdom offers both Christian philosophy and Christian theology in order to focus the Christian student's faith on living the full "Christ life" within a Christian community as this community heads for everlasting living with the triune God. The worldview that is thus offered is definite, historical, heart warming, and hopeful; men and women have a rich present moment because their future will be even richer. This is the wholesomeness of the fullest living of both present and future, which the Christian university can teach, exemplify, and support in its community.

The graduate school furnishes another example of how Christian wisdom can smoothly run the university. Christian wisdom offers an attractive way of life for graduate students and faculty. The hyper-specialization of the graduate school cries out for an integrating context so that its isolation may be balanced by communal understanding. Hyperspecialized persons also look, frantically at times, for the communal values that will make their sufferings seem worthwhile. Indeed, the graduate student needs wisdom to stay sane. He or she requires it to deal with family and friends, with the economic situation, and with his or her complicated doctoral program. By way of Christian philosophy and theology, Christian wisdom can place the graduate student's specialized knowledge or art or skill within the spectrum of all knowledges-arts-skills, can help him or her estimate a unique contribution within the scope of salvation history, can offer him or her the companionship of the pilgrim Christian community and of Christ on the lonely scholarly journey, can show him or her the worthwhileness of many personal sacrifices for his or her communities, and can promise him or her a life after death that is continuous with the present life and is even more abundant in friendships and in accomplishments.

Meanwhile, the graduate faculty is supposed to stand for wholeness of life when it reinterprets traditional truth in a new synthesis, when it works within the university to delineate an interdisciplinary wisdom, when it explores the basis of various mythic worldviews, and when it converges the riches of its discoveries upon a particular social problem. But every graduate professor is well aware how difficult, if not impossibly idealistic, is this concept of the graduate faculty. The graduate faculty is often fragmented by its studies, by its rivalries for funds and students, and by its heavy duties toward the civic community. If any group is undergoing the rigors of secularization and secularity, if any group needs the healing quality of Christian wisdom, it is the members of the university graduate faculty. They need Christian wisdom if only to remind them of their dependence upon common-sense knowledge—lest they become arrogant.

Christian wisdom can also help the members of the graduate faculty to deepen their awareness of the worldview that governs their decisions, lest they lose their sense of reality. It can also recall that God, too, is responsible for the universe, lest they sink down under their burdensome duties. Indeed, Christian wisdom can assure them, in moments of discouragement, that their sacrifices are worthwhile and that their work is imperishable in both God's eyes and His intent. It can even call them to generosity toward their fellow faculty members and fill them with confidence that, after death, they will have a lasting home with their colleagues, friends, family, and students—a home that is the very family of God. If the graduate faculty is the heart of the university, if it is the central factor in the Christian secularization-secularity process, if it can build the community's worldview with or without the risen Christ, then the dominant presence of Christian wisdom within this faculty is of critical importance. Otherwise, the Christian university cannot long remain worthy of its name.

But such striving for wholesomeness of life by way of Christian wisdom needs support. This is precisely the role that is filled by communal worship of the Lord, an essential part of Christian wisdom. Prayerful contemplation directly counters hyper-specialization as it searches out the underlying unity of face, event, life, and universe. In addition, unlike hyper-specialized action, prayerful contemplation is earthy more than abstract, spontaneous more than routinized, relaxing in joy more than suffering in tension, other-worldly more than enmeshed in time-constraints, leisured more than workaholic. Because of its wholeness, contemplative prayer paradoxically promotes the secularization-secularity process against hyper-specialization. Thus, the contemplation of Christian wisdom swings its attention from the common-sense knowledge of the Christian worldview to face the ultimate mystery into which all other mysteries flow in unity—namely, the risen Christ who reveals the triune God in Himself.

In such contemplation, however, the university person uses his or her Christian worldview as a context and the facing of ultimate mystery as a directive for all his or her decisions as they are being made according to the specialized knowledges-arts-skills that are offered by his or her university community. Thus, individual prayer, although it alerts the university person to his or her role in he world and to his or her own self-identity, nevertheless is not merely self-awareness. It is also a sensitivity to the community from which the university person has received so much and which he or she now seeks to serve, in gratefulness, through his or her wholesome decisions. This is the university person whose Christian wisdom has enabled him or her to live fully the Christian secularization-secularity process and, thus, to achieve full manhood or womanhood.

Such fullness of Christian wisdom could not be reached, of course, unless this individual prayer were correlative with communal worship, since the latter celebrates and enhances the ultimate wholeness (salvation) of a person precisely through his or her community. For Christian worship is a unifying reinterpretation of all life according to the wisdom of Christ the Word, since He is the vital absolute center of self-life-world within daily living. Furthermore, this Incarnate Wisdom points ahead along the path of salvation history to the final beatific gathering of all God's people. Then He pauses to strengthen the Christian university person with His sacramental presence at all the critical stages of this Christian's life journey along this path: birth, adolescence, tragic sin, marriage, community gatherings, death. This strengthening within the communal Christian life of the university is actually an increasing of *caritas* within each Christian. It is not, however, merely an individual's joyful healing and his felt sense of self-worth; it is also a concern for one's fellow men and women and a basis for forming friendship with Him.

In this spirit, the communal worship of Christian wisdom uses all the knowledges-arts-skills of the university to form its liturgy and, thus, celebrates the first intrinsic aim of the university. It also glories in God's marriage to the world: the incarnation of the Second Person of the Trinity as the historical Christ. This is a marriage of secular wisdom to sacred wisdom, the second intrinsic aim of the Christian university. Against a heartless rationalism and a despairing cynicism, this communal worship dares the Christian university person to spend all his or her energies as did Christ, that is, to bring more justice into the civic community so that love between people becomes more possible. In thus reminding the Christian that all the apparatus of government and university are for persons, not vice versa, and in thus setting all the Christian's works in a context of loving service, the liturgy of Christian wisdom both sacralizes and energizes the extrinsic aim of the university. This communal worship of the university community not only promotes deep sharing and friendship, but also cultivates the power to heal and challenges the participants to further growth in Christian wisdom. With Christian wisdom, the wholeness that is salvation thus becomes palpable. It is a wholeness that befits the university community, since it is a communal reinterpretation of all contemporary life in the wisdom of the Word, the risen Christ; it is a preaching of the Word in action so powerful that no one can fail to hear and, if he or she wishes, to be made whole.

In this way, with the essential guidance of a specialized campus ministry team, the whole university community of administrators, students, staff, and faculty members exercises the priesthood of the Body of Christ. Christian secularization-secularity within the university community is directed to the risen Christ who, in turn, lifts this community to the smiling face of the Father. Thus, Christian wisdom is seen to be truly the *esprit de corps* of the Christian university. One could ask: Is it also the manifestation of the Spirit, the Third Person of the Trinity, as He works quietly, because so deeply, within the Christian community of the university? And does this question point to the ultimate basis of hope in the Christian university's future?

Christian Wisdom Illuminates Administrative Decisions with Its Vision

So far, we have noted how Christian wisdom operationally unifies the Christian university, first of all, because it is the Christian process of secularization and secularity and, secondly, because it produces the human wholeness of ongoing salvation for the individual Christian and for his or her Christian university community. This has centered our attention on the present moment of the university. It is now time to glance at the Christian university's future, which is about to be enfleshed in the creative decisions of its administrators. How does Christian wisdom work within such decisions? Clearly, Christian vision (the supermodel for all decisions) will be operative here; so, too, will be the Christian university's uniqueness (later to be seen as her mission to the world). Let us look now to these two factors within our definition of that Christian wisdom which is the unique characteristic of the Christian university.

Already we have noted eight major models for university decisions (graduate school, business, wisdom, denominational college, community, servant of the community, social activist or prophetic, and training institute). We have also shown the advantages and disadvantages of each, and, then, we have demonstrated their potential for correlation and for contradiction. We have further observed these models acting together to form a constellation of values for directing and intensifying decisions. We have noted that these values can be well orchestrated only if the administrator enjoys a vision, or supermodel, that enables him or her to apply all these subordinate models reasonably (i.e., with different priorities according to the changing situations of the university). This supermodel can be called a university vision because it is grounded in the university's worldview and in the pooled common sense and everyday experience, of the university community. In addition, it is structured according to the university's *traditio* of specialized knowledges and integrative wisdom. For these reasons, it can enter into the great mysteries of life and, hence, promise to become a renewed and better vision. Thus, this vision, or supermodel, is at once authoritative as well as relatively comprehensive. And yet, it is adaptable, experimental, concrete, and, hence, nonideological.

Such a vision, or supermodel, becomes Christian when it touches all the university disciplines by way of Christian philosophy and, then, focuses its gaze upon the risen Christ by way of a faith-filled Christian theology. Of course, such a vision can arise only out of a Christian university community that is filled with historical Christian *traditio*, animated by personal loyalty to Christ and to His church, and missioned to teach the whole world by a risen Christ, who is Lord of history and Second Person of the Trinity. Because of the single Christ ruling the community and because of the single Spirit animating her, the Christian university community can be stable even though plural Christian philosophies, theologies, and potential visions are present within her *traditio*. Furthermore, historically, one Christian theology and philosophy usually dominates within a particular Christian university; so, one Christian vision will dominate temporarily—until a better one is found.

A Christian vision is essential to Christian wisdom because it stretches out far into the future. Such a vision enables the Christian university administrator to courageously and inventively plan according to the principles of Christian wisdom. Consequently, this wisdom is not diminished, but rather, it is enlivened and challenged by the administrator's decisions. Thus, Christian vision is protective of Christian wisdom. In addition, without Christian vision, it would be difficult for Christian wisdom to further explore the central mysteries of Christian faith, that is, to enter more deeply into the risen Christ's person, into the Trinitarian life, into the unfolding of divine providence, into the darkness of evil, into the brightness of human destiny. For this reason, Christian vision enables Christian wisdom to reveal to the Christian university some hints of the latter's unique mission of service. In turn, Christian vision must continually acknowledge its source in Christian wisdom if it is to remain prudently realistic.

Christian vision does more, however, than expand Christian wisdom. It also helps to develop the university structure by way of the expanded Christian wisdom. In other words, Christian vision has the potential to be dominant among all other types of university vision. Because it works through a Christian philosophy that is more deeply in contact with all university disciplines, it can be more in touch with these disciplines than can other visions. Because Christian vision works through Christian theology, which is of its nature deeply historical, it is more detailed about human destiny than are other visions. It can, therefore, more deftly and passionately motivate its viewers. For this reason, it can elicit from the university person a more disciplined liberty and a more devoted allegiance for the university and for its constituencies.

Because Christian vision is arising out of a Christian *traditio* that is basically "at home" with pluralism of philosophies, theologies, and lifestyles, it is less prone than other visions to succumbing to ideologies. It is also more supple for meeting the new needs of university, church, and civic community. Furthermore, because Christian vision is loyally centered on the incarnate person of the man-God, Christ, it is more personal and down-to-earth than other visions, and less liable to be abstractly idealistic or utopian. Indeed, because a Christian vision is occurring within Christian wisdom, its prognosis for the university's future will tend to be more realistic than other visions, and its descriptions of the university's perspective will tend to be better rooted in the university's unique history of failures and successes. Because of the gritty realism in Christian wisdom, a Christian vision, more than other visions, will enable the university to be prophetic not only in word, but also in deed, and to indulge in criticism that is not only more constructive, but even more creative. Finally, Christian vision rooted in Christian wisdom is better able to explore the university's unique mission of providing wisdom for everyman's and everywoman's long and tortuous journey to the great community of the great tomorrow. This, one would think, is a rather significant value for the Christian university community.

Because a Christian vision is the supermodel for the Christian administrator's decisions, it is central to preserving and to developing the uniqueness of the university—uniqueness taken in the positive sense of cumulative good qualities of life. It is also crucial to protecting the university from its cumulative history of mistakes and tragedies, its negative uniqueness of constricting limitations. A Christian vision, insofar as it is sharply focused by Christian wisdom and is, in turn, challenging this wisdom to grow in the university, will warn the administrator and faculty against an easy nineteenth-century progressivism, which looked only to the inevitable accumulation of good qualities. At the same time, it will lift them out of the despairing twentieth-century catastrophism, which looks only to the inevitable accumulation of tragedy and sin. This balance within a Christian vision enables the Christian university to rejoice in the specialization and integration of secularization process and, at the same time, to recognize the limitations and perilous delicacy of human wisdom as men and women strive to carry out their mission in the world.

Moreover, the historical awareness of original, personal, and social sin in a Christian vision will make the Christian administrator alert to his or her value system, his or her unique secularity, exactly at the time when the Christian vision is being used as a supermodel for making decisions about the university's future. The university's integrity of dual intrinsic aims must be protected, sustained, and advanced if the university is to survive as a university and as Christian. Yet, out of gratitude to its constituencies, the university must serve them well lest it lose its integrity and, hence, its Christian wisdom.

There is a further complication to be considered. As the administrator tries to balance out these aims of the university with decisions founded on Christian wisdom, he or she is both defining the uniqueness of the Christian university and more precisely determining its mission to the world. In other words, if the Christian university is being its unique self, it is also following out its unique mission. Thus, it is expensive for the administrator if he or she fails to know and to promote the uniqueness of his or her Christian university, for the administrator promotes this uniqueness insofar as he or she advances the university's three aims by virtue of Christian wisdom. In this way, Christian wisdom, through Christian vision, is uniquely specifying the university and its community and, at the same time, dramatically defining its mission. Would it, then, be taking seriously the command of Christ to go and teach all nations?

Because his or her decisions concretely define the university's mission, the administrator of the Christian university finds himself or herself acting as counselor, parent, and priest. He or she is the counselor when, out of a personal, unique Christian vision, he or she is directing the university in its unique contribution to the world and, thus, cooperating with God's historical providence. This last statement needs clarification: God did not create the world out of nothing and then walk away from it in disdain. Instead, He made it dependent upon His continuing immanent presence, that is, upon His compenetrative ongoing creation of novelty within world processes. Thus, God married the world, as it were, for better or for worse. Later, His covenant with the world, through the Jewish people, promised faithfulness to this marriage and asked cooperation of the world's people.

Of course, all this demanded a unique providence, that is, it required an historical, personal, free, cooperative planning of humanity's future in the world. Like a competent marriage counselor, the administrator is facilitating this unique marriage between God and the people when his or her wise decisions, made according to his or her particular Christian vision, providentially promote Christian secularization-secularity in the university community and, hence, in the civic community. This salvation process will finally bring these communities into that great community of the great tomorrow, which is centered around the triune God. The cooperative missions of the communities and of the administrator will then have been accomplished. In this way, the administrator is truly the wise counselor who is acting out of Christian wisdom, for his or her effective decisions are not only developing the *esprit de corps* of the university, but also revealing the First Person of the Trinity, Yahweh, since Yahweh provides for humans by way of the university's unique mission.

This administrator, however, may be more than a counselor; he or she may also be a parent for the university. This, too, needs explanation. When Yahweh sent His son into the world to become a man in the unique event of the incarnation, He made His wisdom and His love palpable to His people. The Christian university administrator, by competently using a particular Christian vision to guide his or her decisions, is making this crucified and risen Christ more palpable to modern men and women through the incarnate Christian university community. For this Christian university community, as the Body of Christ, does suffer the birth of wisdom, is at times bloodied for its intelligent convictions, and later takes

367

joy in its fulfillment of Christian wisdom. By participating in the Father's sending of His Son, the administrator exercises a parenthood. With this parental understanding of Christian wisdom, the administrator can help the university community discover and enjoy the basic unity of its life—the vibrant presence of the risen Christ. For this Christ is guiding, illuminating, and appreciating both the specialization of university knowledges-arts-skills and the consequent integration of them into a wisdom that is to be used for the university and for its constituencies. Thus, as the administrator's unique parenting decisively guides the Christian university toward the fulfillment of its three aims, his or her hope is to generate a family-like community of wisdom that would be an image of the Second Person of the Trinity, Wisdom Itself. Then, too, this unifying of the university would be, at the same time, the fulfilling of the university's unique mission.

The administrator's role, however, can go beyond that of counselor for mission and parent of unity to that of priest in sacrifice. For, with his or her understanding and appreciation of the university's particular Christian vision, the administrator can bring the university community to a fuller awareness of the *caritas* discipline within its life. In this experience, the university community discovers whether or not its *esprit de corps* is truly of God's Holy Spirit. Is a sacrificial love operating within the university's basic operations to liberate humanity? Herein the administrator focuses Christian theology and philosophy, in league with all university disciplines, to test the university community's mission and its unity for validity. In so doing, he or she also challenges them to new growth. Thus, as the administrator works to develop the *esprit de corps* of Christian wisdom within the university community, he or she is enabling the Third Person of the Trinity to more swiftly and warmly enhance the disciplined liberty of *caritas* within each community member. This means that a sacrifical love is being evoked within the university community in everyday living as well as in liturgical celebration. In this way, through Christ, who is both Wisdom Itself and high priest, the administrator helps the Christian university community to fashion itself and all its works according to the sacrifical love of disciplined liberty (or *caritas*). Thus, the university becomes a sacrificial gift to the Father. There is, then, a certain priestliness in the work of the administrator as he or she counsels the marriage between God and the people and as he or she is a parent to a family-like Christian community of wisdom. But the administrator is also revealing the presence of the Spirit in the *esprit de corps* of the university community precisely through this university community's mission of making Christian wisdom an incarnate reality.

In an earlier chapter, we wondered what could incline any person to accept the massive responsibilities of running a modern university. Now it is clearer that such an administrator is not alone in his or her shouldering of these backbreaking duties. He or she can have the companionship of the Trinity itself in making decisions. For, first, the administrator is counseling the university to a community life that can share the providential presence of the Father. Secondly, he or she is at the same time directing the university toward becoming the image of the Son as the Son is generated by the Father and offers Himself to be the pattern of Wisdom for the ongoing creation of the world. Thirdly, the administrator is courageously guiding the university in a crucial testing of its wisdom-unity, its unique mission, and its final destiny through the Spirit of *caritas,* or of disciplined liberty. As every administrator well knows, this last experience can literally be God-awful.

Conclusion

The assertion that Christian wisdom is the unique, distinguishing characteristic of the Christian university is just one more bloated, boring statement—unless it is validated by a detailed analysis that is scandalous enough to gain attention. Has it been shocking, then, to hear that university Christian wisdom is actually secular wisdom that has been animated by the university community's act of Christian faith? Has it been sufficiently heretical to state, first, that the scripture-Word and the sacrament-Word, which are contained within this communal act of faith in the risen Christ, form a divine wisdom and, secondly, that this wisdom not only affirms, but makes more specific the dual intrinsic aims and the single extrinsic aim of the university? Do we dare add that this divine wisdom thereby strengthens the university's autonomous constitution and intrinsic authority? Has it been even slightly astounding to note that this affirmation increases the reciprocal unity between these aims by advocating convergent pluralism, absolutes, *traditio,* analogical knowledge, and the wholesome effects of secularization? Could it be, therefore, that Christian wisdom is a powerful unifying agent within the university, that it is even the Christian university's *esprit de corps?* This could be the ultimate shock.

These questions become even more unsettling if one notes a few complex facts. First of all, the plural Christian philosophies and Christian theologies, which are contained within Christian wisdom, are worthy of the name only if they are in contact with all the secular disciplines of the university so that they can render Christian wisdom comprehensive, scientific, inventive, and pastoral. And yet, secondly, Christian wisdom is not simply the home of the convergent pluralism of knowledges-skills-arts and of diverse lifestyles; it is also the hope of unity, since it steadily contacts fundamental philosophy and fundamental theology, since it enjoys the consistency of analogical knowing, and since its faith is focused on the one risen Christ, Wisdom Itself, and on the triune God, both of whom are the single destiny of all knowledges-arts-skills, of all universities, and of all men and women. Moreover, this basic structure of the university throbs with life because Christian wisdom includes disciplined liberty, or *caritas*, so that the community can, as one spirited body, sensitively and courageously promote justice, the very order of the university. In this way, secular wisdom is rendered more wholesome and, then, transformed into Christian wisdom.

Is it an additional scandal to say that, operationally, Christian wisdom is simply the process of Christian secularization and secularity that is meant to bring wholeness (translated: salvation) to students, faculty members, administrators, staff officers, and local citizens? Here one observes the Christian dialectic swinging between its two poles: common-sense living of a Christian worldview and faith experience of Christ and the Trinity. This dialectic is, of course, mediated by the secular wisdom of university disciplines under the guiding light of Christian philosophy and theology. As a result, Christian wisdom, which is this total dialectic, can offer balance to the vocational and liberal aspects of undergraduate education. Through the liturgical life, Christian wisdom is able to sum up and dramatically challenge all that the university does in one priestly act of the whole university community; it is capable of marrying secular and sacred wisdom, the active and the contemplative, so that men and women may attain the ultimate wholeness of the great community of the great tomorrow in their present-day experience.

Finally, out of Christian wisdom arises a Christian vision, or supermodel, that focuses the administrator's decisions, by way of the triune God and of the incarnate Second Person of this Trinity, upon the mission of the university. The unified plurality of the three divine persons renders any Christian vision at home with the university's convergent pluralism, communal personalism, coresponsibility for the world, analogical wisdom, sense of destiny, spontaneous creativity, and hope for the future. On the other hand, the incarnate presence of the Christ, Wisdom Itself, in this Christian vision acts as a point of convergence for the university community, for all of its disciplines, for all the levels of its wisdom process, for the university's planning for the future, and for the transforming union of the human and the divine. Yet the Christ, as He stands beyond all theologies, philosophies, and human disciplines, preserves mystery in this vision even as He becomes more "experienceable" in action for the neighbor, in contemplation within the university disciplines, in the individuality of His risen life, and in the individuation of His sufferings and death. Because Christ is the window looking into the Trinitarian life, this Christian vision converges on Christ and, then, radiates out into the full mystery of the life of the triune God.

For all these reasons, a Christian vision can become dominant within the Christian wisdom of a university without turning into an ideology. It projects the university's future according to the strong historical lines of a Christian wisdom that is in touch with all the secular disciplines, that is structured by Christian philosophy and theology, that is energized by the disciplined liberty of *caritas*, that leads into the mysteries of Trinitarian life and of Christ's incarnation, and that, thus, precludes monistic knowledge and lifestyle. Consequently, the Christian university administrator can help to inventively define the university's unique mission to the world as he or she decisively develops the positive uniqueness of the university and carefully protects it from its negative individuation. Thus, Christian wisdom, the distinguishing characteristic of the Christian university, becomes the beautiful balance of Christian secularization and secularity as it builds the Christian university community for its future place and role within the great community of the great tomorrow.

Such emphasis upon Christian wisdom as the unique, distinguishing characteristic of the Christian university unquestionably makes one wonder more and more about the religious founding group that, out of its Christian wisdom, originated, developed, and preserved the university community in its *esprit de corps*. Is the religious founding group the principal source of this wisdom and, hence, of the university's historical uniqueness? Just how essential is the religious founding group to the continued presence of Christian wisdom and to the unique mission of the university? How dependent on this group can a university afford to be? These are questions that eventually must be faced by every Christian university. To recognize their urgency, one has only to look around at all the formerly Christian universities that are now rejoicing in being totally secular.

17 The Religious Founding Group: Patriarch, Umpire, Friend, or Dutch Uncle?

A new and more benevolent climate surrounds the American church-related college or university. The shocking discovery that Watergate corruption can also occur in Waterloo, Iowa, has humbled secular society into recognizing its need for religious values. The new heremeneutic of the physical and social sciences has revealed the fatuity of "pure objectivity" and "value-free methodology." Evidently, because knowledge is power, it must be tempered by the heart lest it become arrogantly inhuman, indeed, lest it play mankind falsely.

These are the hard lessons recently learned by secular society. Religious bodies, like secular society, have also learned to swallow their pride. The scandal of divisiveness among the Christian churches has brought them to a new awareness that they are, first of all, communities and, only secondarily institutions; that they must persistently seek the hidden unity which underlies their differences in doctrine and practice; that their religious faith can and should influence politics without being "political"; and that they must rediscover their heart. Secular society and religious community cannot afford to disdain each other. Both desperately need conversion, an intellectual-moral-religious reintegration, that neither one can achieve without the other. This is the new American climate in which church-related schools live.

Consequently, a new atmosphere permeates the questions that are asked about the role of the Religious Founding Group in its college or university. These questions truly express curiosity; they are not hostile statements framed with question marks for the sake of minimal politeness. Is the Religious Founding Group (henceforth RFG) a burden or a boon for the Christian university? Given the huge size of the university and the complexity of even a moderate size college, does not the RFG, whether it be a Catholic religious order or a Methodist Conference or a Presbyterian Synod or an Episcopal Board of Bishops, appear to be an anachronism? How can the relatively small religious grouping have any effect on the massive secular development of the university or college? How can it avoid becoming simply excess baggage, an embarrassing appendage?

If the RFG is not an anachronism, does it not appear to be an alien, even an oppressive, element within the body of the university or college? Is it not, of its very nature, paternalistic and, therefore, constrictive of academic growth? How can the RFG long abide the skeptical mood of academia without trying to suppress the freedom of the university or college community? Indeed, it would seem that the RFG, insofar as it is truly religious, would take a prophetic stance toward its university or college at critical moments. Would not this somewhat revolutionary attitude often disrupt peaceful academic pursuit of truth and wisdom and introduce an apostolic intent open to mischievous zealotry? If the RFG is neither an anachronism nor a mischief, then is it simply a neutralized factor, not even a catalyst, in the chemistry of university life? If so, then it hardly needs consideration at this juncture.

Suppose, however, that Christian wisdom is truly the distinguishing characteristic of the Christian university. And suppose, further, that this distinguishing element cannot long perdure unless an active RFG keeps it vital within the Christian university. These two suppositions are recognizable as more than fantasy when one studies the individual histories of Harvard, Yale, Brown, Princeton, Northwestern, and the University of Chicago. Once the RFG began to operate less effectively within these universities, they all began to lose their flavor of Christian wisdom. Could it be that the RFG sees to the development of Christian wisdom in the Christian university? Could the RFG also be a conservative element in protecting the university structures that arise out of faculty specializations? After all, the leading members of the RFG often enjoy multiple degrees. Furthermore, would the RFG generate the university's services to constituencies since the RFG, of itself, seeks to serve world needs? Lastly, would the prophetic factor in the RFG move the university toward a more liberal stance and would its strongly communal bent help the university to accentuate the personal in academic life? Evidently, then, it is not obvious that the RFG is either an embarrassing appendage or a disruptive influence for the university. It could be that the RFG would not only expand the Christian consciousness of the university community, but also build more strongly the institutional structure of the university itself.

For these reasons, we might well investigate (1) what the basic structure is behind the multiple forms of the RFG; (2) how the RFG fits into the university as institution and as community; (3) by what means the RFG attempts to preserve and promote Christian wisdom within the

Christian university; (4) what models are used for describing the RFG's sponsorship of a university or college; (5) what the unique contribution of the RFG could be for a Christian university; (6) how the RFG, in mediating between the church and the university, develops a mutually enriching *communio* between them; and, finally, (7) how such sponsorship can increase, rather than decrease, the academic freedom within a Christian university. By taking these seven sightings into the complex marriage between the RFG and its sponsored university, one may begin to see how each partner can contribute to the other's well-being and dynamic presence in the world.

One matter should be noted at the outset. The following survey of various types of union between the RFG and its sponsored university or college does not aim to give an historical updating of these unions. It seeks only to gather many inductive examples of them so that out of the examples a merely provisional scheme of diverse types of union can be sketched and, then, a preliminary model of sponsorship can be constructed. Our modest purpose is to achieve some understanding of religious sponsorship of a university or a college, not to suggest practical measures for improving such unions in the last two decades of the twentieth century.

A Survey of Various RFG Structures at the American University and / or College

When identifying the RFG of a college or university, one must operate at several different levels. The first level is quite generic, as when one speaks of the churches that support various colleges, for example, Baptist, Congregationalist, Presbyterian, Methodist, Lutheran, Episcopal, or Roman Catholic. At this level, one visualizes a national body of Christian believers that is spread out from coast to coast and united by a particular theology under some form of unifying leadership.

Each of these Christian groups, however, is structured rather differently so that the second, more specific level for defining the RFG suddenly becomes quite complex. In considering a Baptist RFG, for example, is one dealing with the local Baptist congregation or the Baptist Conference; similarly, regarding other denominations, is one dealing with the Congregationalist Association or Conference, with the Presbyterian Synod or General Assembly, with the Methodist Quadrennial Jurisdictional Conference or the Methodist Annual Conference, with the Episcopal Diocese or Province, with the Lutheran Synod or Council-in-the-USA or one of the three great Lutheran bodies (Lutheran Church in America, American Lutheran Church, Lutheran Church—Missouri

Synod), with a Catholic Religious Order or Catholic diocese or a group of cooperating Catholic laypersons and religious?

The specific level of defining the RFG becomes even more complicated when one notes that the RFG is integrated with the university or college according to the special impact of historical events. For example, after the 1816 Dartmouth Case, which assured the churches that the state could not arbitrarily take over church-sponsored educational institutions, great enthusiasm and a sense of unfettered freedom characterized the rapid founding of comparatively numerous church-related universities and/or colleges. Furthermore, the RFG also takes shape according to local traditions. Thus, the experience of the Congregationalists with the established Church of England brought them to the conclusion that each congregation must be autonomous; naturally, then, each Congregationalist congregation felt that each college that was founded should also be autonomous from its founding congregation. Also dictating the form of the RFG is its sociological locale. Unlike the relatively homogeneous, New England colonies, the Middle Atlantic colonies were marked by different languages, religions, ethnic groups, and environments, so that church affiliation had to be muted in the interest of unity. Rutgers and Columbia early proclaimed themselves to be *interdenominational* schools and the University of Virginia declared itself *nondenominational* and free of all theology.

In addition, how the RFG specifically initiates, supports, and develops a university or college is often determined by how the national church views itself and operates out of this theological viewpoint. Because of all these factors, the union between each specific RFG and its university or college is unique. Concrete examples must be given, therefore, if one is to appreciate the difficulty of defining the RFG and its role in the university or college.

Thus, among the Baptists, the local congregation as properly constituted becomes the church capable of ministering Christ; it need not derive its authority from any source other than Christ. This unity in Christ is made evident when the individual Baptist congregations form associations and conventions for counseled cooperation in dealing with common problems and hopes, even though these larger bodies have no control over any local congregation. Following the foundation of Baptist Hopewell Academy (1756), for example, the Baptist Association of Philadelphia founded Brown University (then known as the College of Rhode Island). The latter's charter (1764) affirmed freedom of religion for all denominations but nevertheless also established the college's close relationship with the Baptist church. It required that the President and twenty-two out of thirty-six trustees be Baptists and that eight out of twelve members of the board of fellows also be Baptists. Subscriptions from Baptists in England as well as in the colonies financially supported the college.

By 1825, eight more Baptist colleges had joined Brown. Between 1825 and 1900, over 130 more Baptist educational institutions were founded; these were crowned in 1891 by a national super university, the University of Chicago, which was supposed to unite all the smaller Baptist colleges. In the North, Baptist regional educational societies supported the colleges; in the South, state conventions or the Southern Baptist Convention. Meanwhile, Negro Baptist colleges were financed, at least partially, by the American Baptist Mission Society. Although a Baptist connection with the University of Chicago is now tenuous, at best, and Brown University severed all denominational ties in 1942, Southern and American Baptists still support several liberal arts colleges as do the National Baptist conventions. Expectably, given the autonomous structure of each Baptist congregation, each autonomously founded Baptist educational institution would have only tenuous ties with even the local Baptist church—especially in the North. This is particularly true when the college and/or university becomes large, complex, and self-sufficient. Again, note how the Baptist RFG was once as definite and detailed as the Charter of Brown University (1764) could make it, but how, later, the RFG became as distant as Baptist regional educational societies and Baptist conventions. No longer did the local Baptist organization, even if it were city-wide, have sufficient resources to intimately support the Baptist-founded university. Thus, the eighth constituency of the Christian university suffered eclipse in Baptist colleges and/or universities.

The Congregationalist experience of founding colleges and/or universities was similar to that of the Baptists. The Congregationalists had suffered some persecution under the hegemony of established churches. Consequently, much like the Quakers, they greatly emphasized the free discernment of the Spirit's movement within them and held strongly to the supreme authority of the Scriptures. Indeed, they felt that the free preaching of the Scriptures enabled the local church to be constituted as the total church. Not surprisingly, therefore, the Congregationalists extolled the full autonomy of the duly constituted local congregation. This democratic spirit, which prized common lifestyle much more than ecclesial organization, was then used as a model for constituting the civil government. When Congregationalists became more aware of their dependence upon learned preachers of the Word and upon prudent counselors in the Spirit, they founded schools for educating both their ministers and their layfolk. Of course, they firmly established these colleges as autonomous institutions according to the democratic model of their churches and their towns.

The list of early New England colleges founded by the Congregationalists is impressive in quality: Harvard (1636), Yale (1701), Dartmouth (1769), Williams (1785), Bowdoin (1794), Middlebury (1800), and Amherst (1821). But during the great Western Movement from 1846 to 1881, they developed colleges all over the United States: Beloit (Wisconsin, 1846), Carleton (Minnesota, 1866), Defiance (Ohio, 1850), Dillard (New Orleans, 1869), Fisk (Nashville, 1866), Grinnell (Iowa, 1846), Pacific (Stockton, California, 1851), Rocky Mountain (Billings, Montana, 1883), Westminster (Fulton, Missouri, 1851)—to name only some of their colleges.

Harvard and Yale illustrate the meaning of RFG for the early Congregationalists. Harvard is still working under the Charter of 1650, which then stipulated the forming of a corporation, a self-perpetuating body composed of the president, treasurer, and five fellows. Both major policy decisions and professional appointments made by the corporation were to be subject to the consent of the Board of Overseers. Originally, this board contained not only Congregational ministers from neighboring towns, but also the upper house of the Provincial legislature and the governor of the Commonwealth (who presided over the Board). When the state ceased all support for Harvard in 1823, the composition of the Board of Overseers naturally changed, and, by the 1860s, members of the Board were elected by the alumni. Thus, both state and church gradually lost direct influence on Harvard's future. However, from the time of its first president, Henry Dunster, Harvard has enjoyed a long line of scholarly administrators who were mostly Congregational ministers.

And yet, Yale was founded in 1701 by those who claimed to be fleeing Harvard's religious liberalism. These Congregationalists chose a unicameral college governing body composed of ten Congregational ministers who acted as trustees; in 1745, they finally allowed the rector, or chief administrative officer, to join their ranks. Presently, the Yale corporation includes the president of the university, the governor and lieutenant-governor of Connecticut, ten fellows who are the successors of the "original ten," and six alumni fellows.

Over the centuries, both the Congregational church and the universities it has founded have experienced much change. Though each local Congregational church was always considered autonomous and fully "church" in its own right, these churches still formed county associations, state conferences, and a national General Council (later, the United Church General Synod). Each local church, however, or any portion of the association, or conference, has always felt free to quietly secede from the larger group if it felt that the Holy Spirit required this. Such independence was, of course, given to each Congregational school if the latter felt inhibited by the sponsoring RFG. The democratic spirit within the Congregational church made it difficult for the RFG to preserve strong ties with its independent and rapidly growing colleges and/or universities. As a result, the influence of the Congregational church on institutions of higher learning has noticeably declined.

Presbyterians, and particularly the then recently established Presbyterian Synod of New York, were dominantly active in obtaining from George II, on October 22, 1746, a royal charter for the College of New Jersey (renamed Princeton University in 1896) so that the Middle Colonies would have a college and, incidentally, be able to educate persons for the ministry. Although this college had no official affiliation with the Presbyterian Synod, nevertheless its twenty-three member Board of Trustees, which nominated the president, appointed faculty, and controlled financing, contained twelve ministers and eleven laymen, including two Quakers and one Episcopalian. How strongly the Presbyterian influence worked within the RFG is clear from the fact that the first president (one of its founders) was the Rev. Jonathan Dickinson, pastor of the Presbyterian Church of Elizabeth, New Jersey, and the second president was Rev. Aaron Burr, pastor of the Newark Presbyterian Church. Indeed, every Princeton president has been a Presbyterian minister, with the exception of Woodrow Wilson and Harold W. Dodds (both sons of Presbyterian ministers), and also Robert F. Goheen (the son of Presbyterian medical missionaries). One notes a significant difference between the early New England type of RFG and the Middle Colonies' version of RFG. The Middle Colonies required a more ecumenical RFG, which also included more lay influence, because they lacked New England's remarkably homogeneous race, religion, culture, and environment.

Furthermore, the Presbyterian church is more tightly organized than are the Baptist and Congregationalist churches. The sessions, composed of a moderator-pastor and elected lay elders, rules the local congregation. The presbytery, formed out of ministers and elders, represents congregations of a district. In turn, regional synods are composed of presbyteries and these are represented in a national General Assembly. Presbyterian executives, though purely functional and not sacerdotal, exercise strong authority. Action boards (e.g., social action, education, and the missions) answer to the preceding groups. Because of this tighter organization, and because of its traditionally vigorous activity in founding colleges, the United Presbyterian Church, as late as 1963, maintained affiliations with forty-five colleges and staffed student centers (Westminster Foundations) on eighty other campuses. Of course, the affiliations vary widely in composition and student centers have diverse degrees of vibrancy; yet, Presbyterian influence in these colleges is evident.

Although the Methodist church was a comparative latecomer to the idea of church-sponsorship of colleges and/universities, she managed to establish colleges in thirteen U.S. territories before any of these had achieved statehood. The most recent of these was the Alaska Methodist University, founded in 1960. As late as 1962 the Methodist church sponsored eight universities, seventy-six senior colleges, and twenty-one junior colleges together with twelve graduate schools of theology, all of which had a total population of 214,428 students. Among the better known of these universities is Northwestern, whose charter requires that a majority of the Board of Trustees be members of the Methodist church, yet whose institution is to be considered entirely nonsectarian. Another well-known Methodist institution is American University of Washington, D.C., which was founded by the Methodist church in 1891, chartered by Congress in 1893, then put into instructional operation with graduate courses in 1914.

The highly organized Methodist support for education would be much less effective were it not for its centralized episcopal organization. Although the bishops who are elected by jurisdictional conferences are simply superintending presbyters and not prelates or diocesan officers, they do preside over the various conferences (General Jurisdictional, Central, and Annual), appoint preachers, district superintendents and deaconesses, and carry out the programs and policies developed by the conferences. Thus, Methodist leadership can be locally and nationally vigorous in supporting their colleges and/or universities with strong continuity.

The Episcopal church has had an influence within American life that is far beyond its numbers because of its traditional emphasis on educating its faithful. The following is an illustration: Between 1751 and 1753, the New York State legislature provided funds for a building and for faculty salaries so that King's College (later, Columbia University) could begin to operate. Its Board of Trustees was to be a civil institution comprised of the Colony counselor, the speaker of the General Assembly, the judges of the colony's Supreme Court, the treasurer of the Colony, the mayor of the City of New York, and three members chosen simply for their qualifications to appreciate good education. Actually, the college was interdenominational, not simply state supported. True, it had no direct ties with the Church of England, other than a covenant with Trinity Church (to which land had originally been deeded for the college site). In this covenant the college agreed to elect an Anglican as president and to conduct Anglican morning and evening services. Yet the fact that a majority of the board members were Anglicans aroused protests of discrimination by other denominations, particularly by the Presbyterians.

Again, when the College of Philadelphia (later to become the University of Pennsylvania) was chartered in 1755 as a nonsectarian institution, William Smith, an Anglican clergyman, was its provost and three-fourths of its Board of Trustees were Anglicans. Because the Middle Colonies, especially Pennsylvania, were too heterogeneous in race and religion to allow for a strictly confessional school, the Anglicans adapted to this factor by providing much of the personnel for the university. This is a risky procedure, as they would become well aware from their experience with the founding of the College of William and Mary in 1693.

In 1693, The Rev. James Blair obtained the charter for William and Mary, the second oldest college in the United States, and became its first president. He also had lands, tax funds, and other income assigned for the school's use so that, according to the college charter, the liberal arts and the Christian faith could be propagated and young men could be prepared for the Anglican pulpit. In 1779, however, the college became a university and, under the guidance of Thomas Jefferson, discontinued its grammer (classics) and divinity schools and established schools of law, medicine, and modern languages. Even with this pioneering effort and with state funds, William and Mary had to close from 1881-1888. The Virginia legislature later rescued her with annual appropriations and, in 1906, incardinated the university into the state's educational system.

With this case history in mind, it should not surprise us that during this era the University of the South at Sewanee, Tennessee, was owned and chiefly governed by the Southern Diocese of the Episcopal church. In this school, there are, of course, no religious restrictions placed on students or faculty, but all are expected to follow Christian precepts. Other important schools run by the Episcopal church are Trinity College of Hartford, Connecticut, Hobart College of Raleigh, North Carolina, and St. Paul's Polytechnic Institute of Lawrenceville, Virginia. Close ties with these schools became more possible because of the strong organization of the supporting RFG, namely the Southern Diocese. The local Episcopal congregations are organized into a diocese, which is governed by a local bishop. The local bishop is elected by the diocese, subject to the approval of both the majority of the bishops and the majority of the standing committees of the dioceses. The supreme governing body of the Episcopal church is the triennial General Convention, which is composed of the House of Bishops and the House of Deputies (the latter includes priests and lay persons). The General Convention created, in 1919, the National Council (with the presiding Bishop of the House of Bishops as its head) to deal with social work, Christian education, and the missions between sessions of the General Convention. Naturally, such an organization can focus national strength upon the college or university that it is sponsoring. Thus, the RFG can be as large as the National Council or as small as the diocese and its bishop.

Catholic colleges or universities present an even more complicated variety of supporting RFGs. There is, first of all, the so-called diocesan supported college or university. Gannon University, for example, is conducted by the diocese of Erie, Pennsylvania. In administration, its president is assisted by a Board of Directors, which includes the Archbishop of Erie as college chancellor and his auxiliary bishop as secretary of the board. Then, too, members of the Congregation of the Holy Spirit have filled some of the key secretarial positions in the college. Generally, about one-quarter of the faculty has been diocesan priests. This organizational structure is similar to that of Loras College in Dubuque, Iowa, a diocesan Catholic liberal arts institution whose chancellor is the Archbishop of Dubuque and whose faculty has been about one-third diocesan priests. Seton Hall University of South Orange, New Jersey, was founded by Newark's first Catholic Bishop, James Roosevelt Bayley, and is now conducted by the Archdiocese of Newark. Its Board of Trustees is made up of the bishops, priests, and laymen of the four Catholic dioceses in New Jersey.

Unlike the three preceding examples, Mount St. Mary's College and Seminary, founded by the Rev. John Dubois in 1808 (among American Catholic institutes of higher learning, only Georgetown University antedates it), is operated by a corporation of secular priests whose president, *ex officio*, is the Archbishop of Baltimore. The government of the college and seminary, however, is almost totally in the hands of the Council, which is made up of a body of secular priests. The latter have been elected from members of the faculty, half of whom have been lay professors and half have been diocesan priests coming from as many as twelve different dioceses. Consequently, though St. Mary's is in the Baltimore diocese, its RFG has roots in more than several other dioceses and in lay participation.

The Catholic University of America in Washington, DC, is also unique in its structure. Along with Harvard, Johns Hopkins, and Michigan, it helped to found, in 1900, the American Association of Universities, a union of primarily research universities. Pope Leo XIII in 1889 canonically gave it Pontifical status (it alone gives Pontifical degrees in all three fields of canon law, philosophy, and theology). It is governed by the bishops of the United States through a Board of Trustees that is composed, *de jure*, of a chancellor (the Archbishop of Washington), the rector, cardinals and bishops ruling metropolitan-size dioceses, and elected bishops, priests, and lay persons. Catholic University is partially supported by an annual collection made in all the Catholic parishes of the United States.

Another type of Catholic RFG is not so readily identifiable: the religious order that sponsors a university or college. Historically, a number of pioneer bishops turned over their fledgling diocesan colleges—at the time, some of them were nothing more than glorified high schools—to various religious orders of men such as the Jesuits or the Franciscans. Because these orders were "exempt orders," that is, they had been removed from the local bishop's jurisdiction and made directly answerable to the jurisdiction of the Holy See, the turnover produced a complex situation. The colleges were often teaching Catholics of the diocese for whose doctrinal welfare the bishop was directly responsible; the bishop, however, no longer had direct control of the college, since the religious order responsible for the college was exempt from his jurisdiction or power.

The situation was not quite so complicated when a women's religious order either founded a college or received one from the local bishop to staff and to govern. The women's order could well be a diocesan order under the local bishop's direct jurisdiction. Even if this order were international and had Pontifical status, that is to say, under the jurisdiction of a Roman congregation, it would still not be fully exempt from the local bishop's jurisdiction as were some men's religious orders. Thus, although it would have greater freedom than would the diocesan order of women, nevertheless it would be very dependent on the local diocese for its student body and alumni support.

In any case, the university or college run by a women's or men's religious order would see this RFG as a mediating body between it and the diocesan bishop who represented church authority. Although the Catholic church's highly organized monarchical authority would seem to give it an advantage in exercising doctrinal influence within the American Catholic university or college, this was simply not the case during the late nineteenth century and early twentieth century because of the intervening religious order—particularly when this order was an exempt one. In addition, the local bishop was usually completely occupied with other affairs and tended to trust the religious order. And yet such a university and/or college could not be fully autonomous for the simple reason that this school was responsible for the Christian influence it exercised among the local bishop's people. The Catholic university and/or college does not float above the commonweal of the Catholic people, but is rooted in the latter by as much as a century of mutual service and support.

If this is not a sufficiently complicated picture of the Catholic RFG as it works within the Catholic university or college, consider what happened when, in the early 1970s, several of the largest Catholic universities helped their sponsoring religious orders (their RFGs) to incorporate themselves separately from the university and yet announce a fuller dedication to the university. Prior to this, the religious order had been incorporated within the university and/or college. Incorporation usually meant that (1) whatever money the members of the order did not use to feed-clothe-house themselves and their dependents (e.g., the retired elderly and the younger members preparing for college teaching and administration) went back into the college and/or university funds—there was no separate financing for the RFG; (2) whenever administrative and teaching positions became open, the members of the order had privileged entree into them; (3) the order implicitly pledged to educate its members so that the university or college would never lack a fresh supply of teachers and administrators; (4) the order endeavored to make theology and philosophy important disciplines and tried to supply priest-teachers who were also pastorally oriented to the student body and the lay faculty.

During the late 1960s, however, colleges or universities swiftly grew so large that religious orders no longer could find among their members sufficient numbers of men and women who were talented enough to fill all the academic and administrative positions that had opened up. In addition, a critical number of their members began to express much less interest in college or university work. Moreover, religious orders found that their members were being extended beyond their human capacities by multiple, heavy responsibilities and that the resultant tension, in disrupting normal community life, was inducing people to leave religious life. Under these circumstances, it became clear that, in some cases, separate incorporation of the RFG from its college or university was necessary. Because of the diversity of state charters, however, separate incorporation would spell itself out in quite different contractual statements at the University of Note Dame or St. Louis University or Loyola University of Chicago.

Generally, however, in the larger Catholic universities or colleges, separate incorporation entailed the following: (1) the opening of the college or university's Board of Directors to a majority group composed of others than the religious order members; (2) the stipulation that only some university or college offices would always be held by a member of the religious order, e.g., the offices of president, dean of faculties, and chairman of the department of theology; (3) the separate financing of the university or college and of the religious order with some pledge of annual monies being given back to the university or college from the real salaries received by the religious order members; and (4) a pledge on the part of the university or college that the original Catholic aims of the university or college would be carefully carried out so that Christian wisdom would be generated and presented within the local and national Catholic communities. In this way, the original RFG would still be exercising its influence within the university or college but in a much less direct way, for the newly constituted Board of Directors would now be mediating between the diocesan church leaders and the university's faculty, administration, and student body. Indeed, the original RFG, the religious order, would be directly mediating only if it were represented on the Board of Directors; but in some instances (e.g., Loyola University of Chicago), members of the religious order who worked within the university were explicitly excluded from its Board while members of the same order who worked at other universities would be included.

Clearly, the Christian RFG is variously and complexly related to its university or college and to its church. It will not, then, be a simple matter to define how the RFG, the eighth constituency of the Christian university, is influencing the development of Christian wisdom within its university, even if this wisdom is the uniquely distinctive characteristic of the Christian university or college. Furthermore, it will not be easy to find some model with which to describe the Christian RFG in order to clarify and enhance its distinct contribution to the Christian university.

Causes of the Varying Degrees of Intimacy between the RFG and the University or College

It is noteworthy that the RFG itself, even within the same sponsoring church, can be structured differently from college to college because of the diverse historical and regional forces that are working within the church. Secondly, the type of union established between an RFG and its sponsored college or university varies widely because of the type and number of qualified personnel available to the RFG. Thirdly, a change in the university or college's growth or in the sponsoring church's intent or in the state's influence can drastically modify the support that the RFG is allowed to give. Lastly, even the way a particular church comes to consider itself theoretically can increase or decrease its support of the RFG.

Clearly, we have seen examples of how a particular Christian denomination can use the diverse structures of its RFGs for its colleges or universities. In the Baptist communion, for example, it might be the Association of Philadelphia that supports a college or it might be the Baptist regional educational society or the American Baptist Mission Society or the Southern Baptist Convention. In these instances, there are seemingly diverse support systems sponsored by different RFGs, even though all the Baptist RFGs are ultimately rooted in the Baptist faithful. So, too, the Presbyterian RFGs might be a Presbytery or a regional synod or a National General Assembly or an Action Board; and the Roman Catholic RFG might be a religious order (separately or not separately incorporated) or a diocese represented by its bishop or a corporation of priest-teachers partially elected by the laity.

But the variety of RFG structures is compounded by the varying degrees of involvement with which the RFG enters into the life of the college or university. The place of the RFG on the spectrum of intimacy is controlled by (1) the number of trustees and the strength with which they profess the same denominational faith, (2) the number of chief academic officers who strongly live this faith in their decisions, (3) the type of financial support promised and delivered by the sponsoring church, (4) the depth of presence exercised by the members of the RFG on the campus itself, and (5) the width of psychological and spiritual support offered by the church, that is, support might be merely local or it might also be regional and national.

The developing college or university itself forces the RFG to constantly adapt. The Seventh Day Adventist church, for example, uses its University of Loma-Linda principally to educate its lay ministers. This university is, then, a large seminary for the apostolic work of the church. But insofar as Loma-Linda trains its students in more and more specialized skills and knowledges (e.g., nursing, social work, psychology, and so forth) so that they can exercise their ministry with helping skills, its theological emphasis becomes less noticeable. Then, too, if this university should need to populate its classrooms in order to be able to support the growing array of faculties that teach these skills, it must risk accepting students and faculty members who do not profess the Seventh Day Adventist faith. As this type of secularization works through a church-related university or college, the administrators may find it more and more difficult to generate interest in the school at the local, district, and national levels of the supporting church. State intervention, in the form of required criteria to merit financial aid, can also weaken the influence of the RFG—especially if the RFG has been separately incorporated from its university and begins to doubt its mission within the university.

Lastly, the support given by the RFG can vary according to the type of church organization that the RFG represents. Because the Baptist and Congregational theologies of the church emphasize the local church's autonomy so much that the larger bodies of the church are loosely organized, this democratic ecclesial spirit translates into very loose ties between the RFG and its college or university. At the other end of the spectrum, the Episcopal and Catholic churches, with their strong bishoprics and national organizations, generally preserve close ties with the sponsored colleges or universities. In the middle range of the spectrum are the Presbyterians, with their National General Assembly and its action boards, and the Methodists, with their superintending bishops and their various conferences.

The structure of the RFG is, then, infinitely variable because of particular historical decisions, the sponsoring church's policy, the state's growing intervention, and the rapidly expanding structure of the university or college itself. Then, too, the intimacy of the RFG to its college or university life is, in turn, controlled by the five previously mentioned numerical and qualitative differences in its personnel. Such complexity makes it rather difficult to define church sponsorship of colleges or universities; indeed, it would seem to preclude the discovery of any model that would help to understand and develop the meaning of "religious founding group." Still, RFGs do exist. In fact, they currently initiate, preserve, and develop Christian wisdom within some six hundred American Christian colleges or universities. Perhaps studying how the RFG mediates the authority of Christian faith to the university and, thus, stimulates the university's development of Christian wisdom will give us some understanding of church sponsorship of universities or colleges. This, in turn, could enable us to find some flexible model for describing the functioning of the RFG within the university or college.

Sources of Christian Faith and Wisdom in the University or College

To better understand how the RFG mediates Christian faith into the life of its university or college for the development of Christian wisdom, one should note that the RFG is integrated with the Christian university or college at four levels. There is, first, *immediate* integration when members of the RFG are also administrators and teachers in the Christian university or college. There is, second, *mediate* integration when the local church (or sometimes, as in the Roman Catholic situation, the religious order) which surrounds the sponsored university or college, is considered to be the RFG. There is, third, *quasi-mediate* integration for the bishop, diocese, regional conference, action board, synod, or convention, when anyone of these organizations supports the mediate RFG, which surrounds the Christian university or college. And there is, fourth, the *more removed* integration when the mediate RFG and quasi-mediate RFG are being strengthened by national or international bodies of a particular denominational faith. In most instances, all four levels of incorporation are present and mutually influencing each other so that, through its immediate RFG, the Christian university or college is drawing upon the resources of its worldwide sponsoring church Thus, the immediate RFG is hardly alone when it initiates, preserves, and develops Christian wisdom by confronting secular knowledges-skills-arts with Christian faith. At this point, for sake of clarity, let us restrict the term RFG to *immediate integration* and use the more global term *church* for the other three levels of mediate, quasi-mediate, and more removed integration.

These four-level distinctions of the RFG, however, do no more than describe the mechanisms whereby Christian faith is induced into the university or college community and, hence, into the university or college as institution. These distinctions do not explain the sources of this Christian faith. Ultimately, the one source is the one risen Christ who is making His presence felt not only individually within each Christian but also communally, within each community that is united in His power. This Christ is, of course, present to all four levels of integration described above. He must be present in a special way, however, to the immediate level of the RFG whose correlative responsibility it is to initiate, preserve, and develop, by way of a confronting Christian faith, the Christian university wisdom that is the distinctive characteristic of the Christian university or college. Thus, it is the very authority of the risen Christ, His vibrant presence in each Christian, that both unites individuals into the immediate RFG and, then, specifically guides them so that, as a community, they can live the Christian faith vibrantly—so vibrantly that, in union with other university or college people, they develop a communal Christian wisdom.

But how does this risen Christ immediately work through the various levels of the sponsoring church and RFG? How does Christ incarnate the dynamics of Christian faith in the university culture so that the university or college not only is Christian, but also is growing as an academic institution? Let us begin at the broadest base of the church. Note how the Holy Spirit speaks within the individual Christian to elicit faith in the risen Christ as the living Word of God who is meant to bring men and women to the loving embrace of the Father. The Holy Spirit develops a sense of the church in the Christian that is simultaneous with the Christian's act of faith in Christ. For how can the Christian act in faith if he or she has not heard the word of Christ through the Christian community? And how can the contemporary Christian community preserve and pass on this word unless this community has received it from the previous generation of Christians? And how would previous generations have received it if not, ultimately, from the apostles and disciples of Christ?

Consequently, within the one church there is always the teaching church which speaks with the authority of Christ in His apostles. But this church requires the listening church, which accurately hears and tries to live fully this heard message. On both sides, the Spirit is operative because listening is never merely a passive recording and because teaching is never without some listening. Thus, the eight constituencies of the Christian university, since they are the listening part of the church, develop a *sensus fidelium*, a remarkable attunement to the Christian message and an inventive way of living the meaning of the message in everyday events. Also working within the Christian university is the teaching part of the church, for the Christian church is not just individuals who individually listen to the Spirit and to other individuals. Rather, the synod or diocese or local church or convention or bishops' committee or action board teach a communal, traditional faith in the risen Christ. Such teaching informs and stimulates the more passive *sensus fidelium* to a deeper commitment to Christ. Since the RFG immediately incorporated within the particular college or university is united to this teaching part of the church, it can make the Christian faith vibrant within the college or university and within its seven other constituencies. In this way, the authority, the dynamic presence of the risen Christ, is brought into contact with the university or college through the seven constituencies of the university (the *sensus fidelium*), through the teaching authority of the regional church and its administrators (the quasi-mediate level), and then through the local church (or religious order), which is acting at the mediate level as it surrounds the college or university.

At the immediate level, those members of the RFG who are also acting as teachers or administrators or trustees are usually the nucleus of the college or university taken as institution and as community. If these men and women are educated in diverse knowledges-skills-arts and if they communicate in some depth with each other, they form a mini-university or mini-college within the larger Christian university or college. Given these advantages, this RFG can immediately present the Christian faith strongly so that it can enter into secular wisdom to transform this wisdom into Christian wisdom. The word "strongly" can refer to both power and influence. The first, power, would be the direct control or exercise of university authority that is characteristic of administrators and teachers; influence would be the indirect use of power that is characteristic of university committees, moderators, and counselors. There is also a third way of "strongly" presenting the Christian faith: personal, or individual, presence as contrasted with the corporate presence of power and influence. Let us consider, in more detail, these three ways of making the Christian faith operative in the Christian university or college.

If members of the *immediate RFG* (henceforth simplified to RFG) are functioning as teachers, department heads, deans, vice presidents, trustees, and president, then they are directly exercising university authority or power. This "vertical" authority is dominative, no matter how democratic the atmosphere of the university or college might be; the administration and the faculty (acting as teachers) determine and police the goals of the institution, the means to these goals, and the criteria by which successful achievement of these goals is to be estimated. If the goals are competent specialization, secular wisdom, and service to the larger civic community according to the principles of Christian faith, hope, and charity, then the vertical authority exercised by the RFG in university or college life can bring into existence a strong Christian wisdom within the university or college community and, therefore, within the larger ecclesial and civic communities. This is the true power of the RFG, but it requires that members of the RFG be truly convinced of Christian wisdom and truly competent in university knowledges-skills-arts.

There is also the "horizontal" authority of influence, that is, indirect exercise of university authority, which can be employed immediately by the RFG when its members are active faculty. Influence is managerial or functional; it is the teamwork of university or college committees as they gather data, fashion criteria for specific decisions, develop courses and curricula, establish clear values for hiring and firing, note failures of means and of goal-setting. Such teamwork can build Christian wisdom into the structure and procedures of the university. This horizontal authority is also notable in the university member who represents the Christian university and its aims to the Chamber of Commerce, to the city's aldermen, to church groups, and so on. His or her aim is to offer the university's expertise for solving the problems of these other groups and to learn from them the practical wisdom that challenges university skills to new growth and to new areas. If the RFG member uses his or her expertise within the context of his or her own Christian wisdom, then this wisdom naturally enters into the audience like the air they breathe. (This is even more true of the RFG member who is an academic counselor or the moderator of a university student organization.) In this way, the horizontal authority of influence is a powerful agent for the casual introduction of Christian faith and wisdom into the university community and into all its constituencies. Ironically, the very indirectness and casualness of influence are the source of its strength.

Perhaps the strongest way of both eliciting Christian faith and inducing Christian wisdom, however, is personal presence in one-to-one conversation, service, and learning. The dominative power in the direct exercise of university authority and the insinuating influence in the indirect exercise of such authority are corporate mediations of Christian faith. Though they are certainly interpersonal and not solely functional, still their vertical and horizontal dimensions will be flat unless they are complemented with the third dimension—penetrating personal presence. All three aspects of authority dialectically develop one another; all three are dimensions of leadership. But Christian faith arises, first, in the one-to-one relationship of mother and child, of teacher and student, of apostle and disciple, and of spiritual director and directee.

Although university or college authority is present in these one-to-one encounters, since the university or college is the milieu and reason for the meeting, nevertheless more strongly operative is the personal authority of the faithful person's being, that is, his or her secular competence and accomplishments, his or her friendships and acquaintances, and, finally, his or her crowning and pervasive faith-experience. Such personal presence is not merely the necessary basis for all specialized learning; it is also the radical foundation for all university community and wisdom. The member of the RFG immediately exercises such presence among administrators, staff persons, faculty, and students when he or she is casually visiting in an office, enjoying a departmental party, doing pastoral counseling, informally discussing issues after a class, giving a prayer-retreat, assisting at a liturgy, sharing in a university carpool, and so on. In these one-to-one encounters, the Christian faith is seeded and takes root. Given this rooting, it can later enjoy fuller growth in the nourishing atmosphere of corporate presence, which is found in both vertical and horizontal authority, where Christian wisdom can flower more fully.

The member of the RFG, through his or her Christian faith and resultant Christian wisdom, can become more deeply aware of these three dimensions of authority and can learn to prize personal presence as the most penetrative of these dimensions. As a result, he or she will tend to put greater emphasis, even within the huge university apparatus, on faculty and staff over students, on individualized teaching over mass indoctrination, on student participation in university decisions over strictly vertical use of authority, on mediation between administrators and faculty over mediation between students and faculty, on individualized spiritual direction over large group retreats, and on casual reflective sessions with students over formal class proceedings. This does not mean that the member of the RFG underestimates the basic need and importance of formal classes, mediation between students and faculty, group retreats, mass indoctrination, vertical authority, and so on. But it does mean that he or she has a Christian bent toward the increase of personal presence in the university or college because this is the basis for Christian faith and wisdom.

Precisely for this reason, the RFG can become a major factor in initiating, preserving, and developing both Christian faith and Christian wisdom within the Christian university or college. The histories of all those outstanding universities and colleges that were once Christian but now glory in their secularism would each seem to point to the critical importance of the RFG in maintaining a strong Christian faith and wisdom within the very authority structure of the university or college. In this way, the risen Christ is constantly mediated on all levels of the university or college so that He and His people can enter the best of secular wisdom and transform this wisdom into its fullest growth as Christian wisdom.

It is important, at this point, to observe how indirectly the church works with the university or college and how greatly advantageous this indirectness is to both church and university or college. If we define "church" to include (a) those RFGs that are rather remote (the national and international church, for example), (b) the quasi-mediate RFG (bishop, diocese, convention, action board, and so forth), and (c) the mediate RFG (local church or religious community), all of which support the immediate RFG, then the "church" cooperates with the university or college only indirectly, that is, through the immediate RFG. The immediate RFG is immediate to the university or college, then, primarily because its members are competent administrators, faculty, and staff who are able to serve well the university and/or college precisely as institution. This competence gives the members of the RFG their "citizenship" within the university or college community. Only after they have thus established themselves can the members of the immediate RFG offer the Christian faith to others and, then, work to develop communal Christian wisdom as a means of bringing the university to its full growth both as institution and as community.

Thus, the faith-authority of the risen Christ arises only indirectly through the constituencies of the university itself and through the members of the immediate RFG. There is no direct influence coming from the more removed, the quasi-mediate, and the mediate RFGs—unless the bishop or members of a synod-convention-assembly are also present on the Board of Trustees or act as administrators by reason of their being bishops or synodal members of the church. But even in this latter, somewhat extreme case, the church officers must respect the autonomous structure of the university or college. They cannot deal with the university or college as though it were an ecclesial structure or community, that is, as though it were an arm of the church. Otherwise, they will gradually destroy the university or college by transforming it into a seminary.

This indirect influence of the church is to the advantage of the university, for the influence itself helps the university or college to maintain and develop that Christian wisdom which, in chapter fifteen, we saw as the crowning maturity of the Christian university or college. At the same time, the indirectness of this influence preserves the necessary independence of the university or college. In other words, the indirectness enables the university or college to operate according to its own distinct autonomous structure and not according to an ecclesial one while, at the same time, it enjoys the infusion of the risen Christ's life within its university or college community. In this way, the church and the university or college can be mutually corroborative against any unfair intrusions from government or from business interests or from revolutionary movements. For the risen Christ's faith-authority, when mediated into the university's or college's intrinsic authority by the RFG, promotes the university authority rather than hampers it.

Thus, as the intrinsic authority of the college or university arises out of the extrinsic authorization given by the eight constituencies, it finds within itself authoritative faith in the risen Christ—a faith urging it to (a) greater specialization so that it might discover the deepest secrets of His creation, (b) fuller wisdom so that it might make its own university community more capable of discovering and living Christian wisdom, and (c) greater service to the civic community so that it might help the civic world become more capable of a unifying and heart-warming *caritas*. This final, or purposeful, aspect of the university or college's intrinsic authority is made operative through formal structure, namely, the faculty's competent knowledge and teaching, its shared vision and passion for the university's aims and goals, its meticulous use of procedures to carry out these aims, and its *traditio* or cumulative experience of past accomplishments. For this reason, the authoritative faith in the risen Christ cannot grow well in the university unless it is stimulated and enriched precisely by this competence, passion, professionalism, and *traditio*. The incarnational faith of the Christian must take its flesh from the contemporary culture or remain a dead skeleton. Likewise Christian faith must promote university structures to ensure its own vigorous livelihood.

Let us take two more steps in our consideration of how Christian faith corroborates intrinsic university or college authority. Suppose one considers the administrators' prudent decisions to be the efficient aspect of the university's or college's authority; and suppose one sees Christian prudence (a gift of the Holy Spirit) as issuing from authoritative Christian faith and, further, as strengthening these university or college decisions of the administrators. One can then perceive how authoritative Christian faith enters the intelligent cooperation of the student body, which is the material, or dispositive, aspect of the university's intrinsic authority. The Christian prudence of the administrator provides procedures and structures, which the competence of the faculty fills with specialized learning and integral wisdom, so that the students are illumined and motivated as they both pursue specialized knowledges-skills-arts and cultivate that secular wisdom which is to be crowned by a Christian wisdom. In these ways, the authoritative faith in the risen Christ which is immediately offered to the university or college by the RFG enters into the intrinsic authority of the university or college to reinforce and enrich it in its three dimensions of power, influence, and personal presence. Thus, the indirect influence of the church on the university or college is beneficial not only in its protection of the university's or college's independence, but also in its support of the university's intrinsic authority.

It is noteworthy that the indirectness of this influence beautifully serves the church, which is represented by bishop or synod or convention or assembly. First, the indirectness frees the church to give full attention to its direct responsibilities of instrucing in the faith, administering the sacraments, celebrating the liturgy, conducting apostolic works for the distressed needy, and so on. Secondly, the church is free of accountability for any action of the university or college; in its office of prophecy, however, the church may well commend or reprehend a particular action of the university or college that appears to foster or attack Christian living. Thirdly, the independence of the university enables it to be an unbiased respondent on important church issues. Thus, the indirectness of the church's influences on the university or college ministers to the liberty of both institutions while, at the same time, the influence of the church renders the university or college more sensitive to the needs of the people of God.

Within these delicate relations between the church and the university, one can begin to discern how the authority of Christian faith works to enhance the intrinsic authority of the university or college and how the university, thus Christianized, can, in turn, develop a Christian wisdom that enables the church to live its faith more practically and profoundly. Such use of authoritative faith within the university or college, in order to develop a Christian wisdom that is beneficial to all God's children, is precisely what is meant by sponsorship of a university or college by the RFG. Once this definition is fashioned, it can be clarified and expanded—provided one can discover a model for sponsorship. With such a model, one can see how to enliven sponsorship and how to avoid crippling it. Let us now search for this model.

Model for RFG Sponsorship of University or College: The Dutch Uncle

At least four basic models are available for expressing the RFG's sponsorship of the university or college: (1) the patriarch, (2) the umpire, (3) the friend, and (4) the Dutch uncle. The patriarch model emphasizes dominative power, or vertical authority, in the sponsorship; the umpire model makes insinuating influence, or horizontal authority, predominant in the RFG sponsorship; the friend model allows personal presence to assume ascendancy over the vertical and horizontal authority; and, lastly, the Dutch uncle model works to establish balance between all three dimensions of authority in the university or college. Let us more fully describe and criticize each of these models.

When a university or college is small, the patriarch model of RFG sponsorship is often implicitly operative and, when it is rendered explicit, is found attractive. Its emphasis on directive power makes it efficient and provides the RFG with much control. With this model in mind, the RFG determines to fill strategic administrative jobs with its own members and to set goals and procedures that are more in terms of the RFG itself and less in terms of the college's or university's autonomous structure. Because the RFG members have already formed a faith community outside the university, they might attempt to reproduce much the same community within the university and, in so doing, restrict the university community to being something like a seminary community. This, in turn, restricts the specializations that are possible in the university. The dominant theology and philosophy of the RFG, for example, might well be the only theology and philosophy that is permitted in this model. This model provides a quick integration but one that is also narrow and sometimes incapable of growth. Creative mavericks who openly differ with the integration or with the heavy emphasis on vertical authority will tend to be eased out of the university or college and more docile (more routinized and less aggressive) personnel will be hired. The same restriction on freedom might close in on the students as the quickly integrated academic program tightens around them and as suspensions and expulsions put constrictive fear into them. Financial pressures, in the areas of salary raises and scholarships, might also be used to enforce university discipline. When the directive power, or vertical authority, is allowed to dominate in this model, then the RFG tends to operate in a paternalistic atmosphere and to arouse hostility. Such an environment might, at times, be academically lethal—especially when the faculty and students are cowed. Such a model appears to be unworkable in the large college or university as well as in a democratic milieu.

The second model for RFG sponsorship of a university or college is the umpire, the symbol of total neutralism and full functionalism. In this model, horizontal authority, or insinuating influence, predominates and takes a functional, managerial stance. The RFG decides against setting or influencing the goals of the university and/or college lest the RFG appear paternal and, thus, cause conflict. For this reason, it takes no controversial positions concerning university or college goals, nor does it strongly criticize misuse of procedures toward these goals. Rather, the RFG attempts to mediate between conflicting parties in the university or college community and to invent procedures toward goals that will please both sides. In this way, the RFG see itself as the constituency whose task is to maintain a delicate balance between power and truth, that is to say, between administration and faculty. Although this type of balancing tends to diminish the authority of Christian faith within the university or college, it nevertheless holds the university or college together in times of stress and assures it of growth at times when conflict might very likely tear the school apart. It is clear that this second model gradually sacrifices the authority of Christian faith, which is so needed to achieve the aims of the Christian university or college. It also tends to neutralize the Christian faith that is working in the RFG when its members find their faith privatized from public university or college activities. Such a model presents a "holding operation" that is inevitably destined to bring the RFG to the point where it finds itself grasping an empty bag lettered "Christian wisdom."

In the third model, that of friend, the third dimension of university or college authority—personal or individual presence—is heavily emphasized. The RFG puts most of its efforts into the endeavors of its individual members, since personal presence is usually exercised in one-to-one situations. The RFG as a community does not attempt to be corporately influential in the university or college; in fact, such influence would be considered almost traitorous to the university community. (Would it not be unfair bloc-action or power-mongering in the peaceful world of academe?) Rather, this model of RFG sponsorship of the college or university places its basic hope in fostering friendships and acquaintanceships between RFG members and other university personnel. It is hoped that these relationships will then provide the basis for solid committee work, for charismatic leadership in the college or university senate, for cooperative scholarship with colleagues, and for excellence in teaching and administration. Thus, in this model, the members of the RFG act solely as individuals and never as a corporate body within the university lest corporateness be interpreted as conspiracy. Each member relies totally on his or her solitary witness to university or college values and to the Christian faith.

One difficulty with this model is that it depreciates the use of teamwork among RFG members as a method of improving the university or college through corporate witness to Christian faith and wisdom. This attitude ensures that the RFG can never be a Christian mini-university or mini-college within the Christian university or college. The exclusive use of this third model would seem better adapted to Christian persons who are working in a secular university than to persons who are living communal Christian wisdom in a Christian university or college. The friend model of RFG sponsorship of a college or university, though beautiful, leaves little room for corporate leadership.

Consequently, we are left with the fourth model—the Dutch uncle. It claims to keep all three dimensions of university or college authority in a dynamic balance that cannot be achieved with the previous three models. It does not disparage the other models, so long as they are used in reciprocal balance; yet it asks: "How can this balance be attained without a supermodel—like the Dutch uncle?" According to this last model, neither power nor influence nor personal presence can be allowed to dominate over the other two dimensions of authority. Before this fourth model can be applied to the university or college for testing, however, it must be described in some detail, since it is not so evident as the patriarch, umpire, and friend models.

The Dutch uncle is a bachelor who lives in the family of his brother or sister and contributes much to the family life by way of a very indirect authority. He is a blood relation of one of the spouses, so, he is familial. He is present at all births and baptisms, partially supports the family with his earnings, sometimes quietly mediates in family disputes, lends the warmth of his affection to all the children and to the parents, occasionally instructs out of his particular skill and experience (if he is a carpenter, for example, he may teach the eldest son or the father of the family how to do house repairs), babysits not only children but also the house during the family vacation, offers support in time of tragedy and rejoices in family celebrations, teaches the children games and is usually around the house when not working at his business or job. He does not have the familial-political authority of the parents, but he does have the strange authority that bloodline, financial aid, love, concern, and dedication to the family give him. His is a disinterested authority, that is to say, one in which there is little to gain for himself, an indirect authority, yet nonetheless a true and sometimes strong authority.

There are seven important functions that the Dutch uncle performs for his "family." First, he offers the continuity of a distinct family spirit (a tradition) if the father or mother are absent, ill, or preoccupied, for he is always there and he reinforces the family spirit that is usually generated by the parent to whom he is a brother. Second, he lends psychological support to the family out of his knowledges-skills-arts when the parents do not have the time or the talent. So, the children and, perhaps, the parents learn to paint, to play sports, to keep a budget, to respect each other more deeply. Third, if he is pious, he may give religious support so that life's deepest values are seen and treasured through his own dedication to the local church, to the neighborhood poor, and to prayer. Fourth, he may pastorally educate the children not by sermons, but by his unobtrusive life of loyalty and concern and by his stories, which are often more powerful than any catechism lessons. Fifth, he may be able to give perspective to parents and children by a quiet criticism contained in his humor and gentle teasing. Sixth, in family emergencies, the Dutch uncle may act as a mediator by giving discreet leadership through hidden financial aid, competent advice, compassionate listening, or hopeful encouragement. Lastly, over the years his generosity beyond room and board may, become expected—so much has he become a part of the family. Strictly speaking, however, all he has done is sponsor this family.

Could this Dutch uncle possibly be a model for the RFG sponsoring a college or university? To evaluate this model, one could take the seven characteristics of the Dutch uncle and apply them, analogically, to the RFG to find out whether they illuminate the three dimensions of university or college authority as it is sponsored by the RFG. In his *Dimensions of the Church* (Newman Press, 1967, p. 15), Avery Dulles suggests that "the church exists to remind the world of its own nature and to help it achieve itself." Is it possible that the RFG exists to remind the university or college of its own nature and to help it achieve itself much as the Dutch uncle reminds the family of its goals and helps it achieve itself? The application of the Dutch uncle model to the RFG at the university or college may help us answer this question, for any model so implicit to thought and decision making controls our insights, sets goals for us, specifies means to the goals, and is built out of our most dear presuppositions.

First, like the Dutch uncle, the RFG does work for the continuity of the distinct spirit of a particular university or college when it strives to preserve the Christian wisdom that is within this Christian university or college community as its second intrinsic aim. Because the RFG is the founding community of the university or college, it is the expert on the university or college's unique *traditio* and acts as a thread linking the school's past with its present. Thus, the RFG gives discriminating support to trends, doctrines, hopes, procedures, and new insights into the university or college's goals. It also does this by literally being a mini-university or college within the university or college, since its members are specialists within various knowledges-arts-skills—specialists who are a community of faith endeavoring to live by the Christian wisdom that founded the university or college. Again, the RFG is the living *traditio* of the college or university because it is a community of traditional Christian faith that is corporately present within the university or college.

Secondly, as the Dutch uncle offers psychological support to the family structure, so the RFG, by furnishing the university or college with trained specialists in the various knowledges-arts-skills, structures the university or college according to its first intrinsic aim of specialization of truth. Thus, the RFG activates that detailed scientific pursuit of truth and art which is the base for all secular and Christian wisdom. In this way, the RFG not only leads the university into the future, but also helps it to exercise its horizontal authority of insinuating influence.

Thirdly, as the Dutch uncle gives religious support to the family, so the RFG monitors the university or college's pursuit of Christian wisdom. It does this by examining the university or college's planning for future development, its day-to-day implementation of past planning, and its daily procedures for bringing Christian values to awareness in the life-situations of faculty, students, and staff. This check is done against the school's panoramic Christian vision—a vision that arises out of a dominant theology and philosophy which are in touch with all the university disciplines. Consequently, this vision not only guides the university or college into the future but also serves to validate current decisions of administrators. The RFG works within the vertical authority of the university or college so that the university or college's power is as effective as the Christian vision is sharp and attractive.

Fourthly, just as the Dutch uncle may pastorally educate the children, so the RFG can, as individuals and as a community, offer their services for liturgy, preaching, healing, sacraments, retreats, work with the needy, academic guidance, spiritual direction, and so on. Furthermore, they can simply be open for friendships with other members of the faculty, staff, administration, and student body. Such activities naturally call attention to the extrinsic aim of the university: apostolic service to the larger civic and ecclesial communities. One recognizes in this service the third dimension of the university or college's intrinsic authority: personal presence on a one-to-one basis.

Thus, the first four characteristics of the Dutch uncle model show the RFG employing Christian wisdom and a Christian vision in order to foster, in a balanced way, the three dimensions of university authority: power, influence, and personal presence. The next three characteristics of the model reveal the RFG as a friendly critic of these three dimensions of authority as they operate within a particular university or college.

Like the Dutch uncle who, according to the fifth characteristic, sometimes gently criticizes the family, the RFG must exercise a prophetic office. Because the RFG is most in touch with the tradition of the particular university or college, it should be expected to remind the university or college of its distinct spirit as Baptist or Methodist or Catholic. True, all members of the university or college must remind the university of its nature; all Christian members must call the Christian university or college back to its Christian heritage. But the members of the RFG are especially obligated to remind the Christian university or college of its particular Christian heritage, be it Congregationalist, Episcopal, or Lutheran. Consequently, the RFG attempts, by its critiques, to make the university or college's horizontal authority of influence truer to itself and to the university or college.

Like the Dutch uncle who gives discreet leadership to the family by mediating between its members, so, too, in a sixth characteristic, the RFG may occasionally be called upon to be a power broker. Its discreet leadership may be exercised in finding a balance between the power-users (administration) and the truth-seekers (faculty), that is to say, between the practical and the ideal, between the active and the contemplative, between the institutional and the communal. The RFG is specially equipped for this type of mediation, for its members may be on both the administrative side and the faculty side of a debate and, consequently, might be able to appreciate the strengths of both positions; yet, these members are united in a community of faith and trust, and so greater openness to a just compromise should be expected of them. The RFG, of its very nature, must combine the contemplative element of prayer with the practical element of apostolic endeavor; as a result, the RFG can feel in its members both the struggle between the practical-ideal (the active-contemplative) and the reconciliation of these polar tensions. Thus the RFG, as a community, is specially fitted to deal with the constant push and pull between the institutional and communal demands of the university or college and to protect both the constitution and the community of the university or college.

The RFG, therefore, must necessarily be political in order to preserve the university or college. Politics always runs a university or college, and good politics is the prudent balancing of all the university or college elements so that they increase the commonweal of the university or college and improve the university or college's service to the larger civic and ecclesial communities. The RFG is qualified to do this not only because of its long-term contact with the tradition and distinctive spirit of a particular university or college, but also because it has additional means of support other than the university or college. That is to say, the RFG has its faith community to support it as it tries to be evenhanded in its mediation between competing elements in the university or college. In this way, the RFG helps the vertical authority of power to be truer to itself and to the university or college.

Lastly, like the Dutch uncle, whose dedication makes his generous actions expected, the RFG's services are usually taken for granted. Members of the RFG are expected to give extra financial support to the university or college, to take on extra committee work, to double-up and substitute for others during emergencies, and to live near or at the university or college so that they might always be available. It is scandalous if an RFG member "jumps" to another university or college and does not spend his or her whole life at the original school. Since the RFG members so often submit their own convenience, ambition, and hope to the needs of their church, they are expected to do the same for the Christian university or college simply because it is Christian. Of course, such generosity might possibly jeopardize the career and the future of the RFG member because Christian universities and colleges are not renowned for high salaries, frequent sabbaticals, or extensive clerical support for scholarly work. But this generosity is to be expected of RFG members, even though it may work hardships on their families. What such generosity does, however, for the university or college is to lend credibility to that personal presence which is the third dimension of university or college authority. This is no small gain for a university or college that calls itself Christian.

If the first four characteristics of the RFG are aimed at helping the university or college achieve its *full nature,* the last three characteristics of the RFG—namely, loyal criticism, delicate mediation, and expectable generous action—are meant to remind the university of its *true* nature. In exercising these characteristics, the RFG is, as it were, standing outside the university or college and objectively observing it in order to serve it better on re-entry. Hence, the last three characteristics of the RFG describe three functions by which it attempts to keep the university or college honest to itself and healthily growing.

Here, then, is the fourth model—the Dutch uncle. It describes how the RFG can sponsor a Christian university or college so that the latter's distinctive characteristic of Christian wisdom can be initiated, preserved, and developed. The advantage of this model is its explanation of how the church cooperates indirectly (that is, through the immediate RFG) with its sponsored university or college and, thus, influences the university or college in such a way as to strengthen, not weaken, its autonomy. This model also seems to show how the RFG promotes better balance among the three dimensions of university or college authority. In this way, it does not deny the valid emphases of the other three models but, rather, warns of their shortcomings. As a result, this fourth model—the Dutch uncle—is much more complex and difficult to use. Indeed, the very strangeness of this model could well point to the uniqueness of the RFG's contribution, and, reciprocally, exploration of this uniqueness may yield further insight into the model itself of RFG sponsorship of the university or college.

18 The Unique Contribution of the RFG to the Christian University or College

The homeliness of the Dutch uncle model is in vivid contrast with the following, high-flown (perhaps, even pompous) description of the unique contribution that the RFG can make to its Christian university or college. This contribution seems to be both incarnational and eschatological; it is enfleshed within the present operations of the university and/or college and, at the same time, it points to the university or college's future hopes. The incarnational moment deals with the RFG as a Christian faith community of great practical complexity and as a mini-university or college of speculative wisdom. Simultaneously, the eschatological moment reveals that the RFG is meant to ensure its university or college of unique identity, prophetic voice, full liberty, and wide ecumenical embrace. Let us examine these terms, one by one, to search for the fuller meaning of the RFG's unique contribution to its university or college. It is hoped that the ideal here described has its roots in the day-to-day grind of life, even if its full flowering seems to tower well above our present accomplishments.

The RFG: A Model of Faith and Wisdom Community

In a deeply incarnate way, the RFG enters the practical operations of university or college simply by being and by operating as a vigorous Christian community of faith. Thus, it tends, first, to counterbalance the powerful institutional side of the university or college because of its natural bias for the school's communal side. Naturally the RFG, taken simply as community, will be more likely to stress the personal element of the university or college—the friendships among faculty-staff-administration, for example, or the long-term remembrance of students, or the quality of academic and personal counseling, or the university or college socials, and so on. Second, the RFG, as a community of faith, will be alert to ways in which the university or college enhances the Kingdom of Christ; it will see that its university or college work is also apostolic and, therefore, of increased value. It would, as a matter of course, be anxious to foster within the university community those who sought to form an apostolic community of prayer and service. Since the RFG also considers its university or college work to be ministerial, it is ready to incarnate the extrinsic aim of the university or college—service to the larger civic and ecclesial communities.

Third, the RFG, as a Christian community of faith, finds itself composed of four realities that should radiate out from it into the whole of the university or college to enrich university or college life and to render it unified. The first of these realities is the RFG's commonly enjoyed Christian vision with which it founded the university or college and initially attracted people to work therein. The RFG had often adapted and developed this Christian vision, through the decades, as the university or college grew toward maturity. Consequently, the RFG, more than any other university group, truly appreciates the continuing need for this vision, and for its constant revision, so that the institutional specialization of the university or college and the wisdom integration of its community might be constantly advanced according to the needs of truth and of the university or college's constituencies. It should not be surprising, then, if the RFG came to the conviction that only in this way will Christian wisdom continue to grow in the Christian university or college.

The second reality that radiates out from the RFG to unify the university or college is its communal worship of the risen Christ. This worship should flow out of the prayer life of the individual members of the RFG as they converge all their works, hopes, thoughts, and plans toward Christ. With this powerful model central to their efforts, all the people who compose the university or college community can, in turn, sum up their individual lives within that single, unified university or college life that is celebrated by a university-wide liturgical worship.

This second unifying and energizing reality points to a third reality— the *caritas* of the RFG community. The *caritas* is a heart knowledge that is poured out in loyal self-sacrifice for the Christian community because of affection for Christ and for His people. It is the most powerful unifying agent known to mankind, as well as the most lasting and the most creative. Because the RFG, as a community of faith, cannot survive societal pressures without strong *caritas*, its very survival in good spiritual health offers the Christian university or college community solid hope that it, too, will survive well as a community in pursuit of specialized truth and Christian wisdom. This apostolic *caritas* can become, then, the heart of the liturgy at which the RFG and the university or college celebrate their unity in Christ. Thus, in these second and third realities, one witnesses the blending of contemplation and action into a powerful oneness.

Because of the three sources of unity (Christian vision, communal worship, and *caritas*) within the RFG, it can be a model for the unity of the university's or college's faith community. This is especially the case when the university or college community, along with the RFG, is embellishing the Christian vision that has been initially presented by the RFG. The RFG, therefore, can be the most cohesive force in the whole university or college precisely at a time when universities and colleges find themselves rapidly fissioning into autonomous, sometimes feuding, departments and schools and when educational leaders despair of ever again discovering a single vision with which to unite the vastly differentiated schools into a common effort.

For these reasons, the RFG turns out to be a very practical incarnation of university or college ideals and, thus, can make a unique contribution to their growth. The RFG, of its very being, stresses the precise elements that are now most needed in our Christian universities or colleges: (1) the personal, when the institutional appears to be throttling higher education with rigid routines and impersonal bureaucracy; (2) the apostolic, when the purely academic appears to be gaining total control; and (3) the unity of wisdom, worship, and *caritas* (care for the other), when the university or college seems to be fragmented with pluralist viewpoints, multiple theologies of worship, and divisive suspicions concerning creed, race, and ambition.

Not only as a practical incarnation of university or college ideals, but also as their speculative synthesis, the RFG becomes indispensable to the well-being of the Christian university or college. In other words, the RFG can be more than a model of faith community; it can also be a model of Christian wisdom community. That is to say, the RFG can be a mini-university or mini-college within its university or college sponsored. Three arguments support this seemingly grandiose statement.

First, the RFG is normally well acquainted with the university's specialized knowledges-arts-skills. Its own members are experts in these areas and can, by "conversational osmosis," share their findings with each other. In this way, the RFG members are not merely passively listening to each other as though they were interested amateurs, but are actively pursuing these disciplines within the developing departments that form the institutional side of the university or college. They are eagerly practicing the first intrinsic aim of the university or college—reinterpretation of specialized areas of truth. But they do this within the broader context of interdisciplinary interests.

The RFG can work like a mini-university or college community of wisdom in a second way. Underlying the RFG community of faith are Christian wisdom principles, that is, ultimate goals like the Trinitarian beatific vision and ultimate dynamisms like worship, *caritas*, continuing provident creation of the universe, and cumulative salvation history. Not surprisingly, then, the RFG is sympathetic to those secular wisdom principles which make a university possible and powerful and which are discovered by specialist scholars (some of whom are members of the RFG). Consequently, the RFG is appreciative of the secular wisdom that is generated by interdisciplinary studies and courses, especially since its members have multiple degrees that are frequently correlated with studies in the wisdom disciplines of theology and philosophy. Thus, the RFG can serve as a bridge that links individual departments of the university or college.

There is a third way in which the RFG makes a unique contribution to the Christian university or college—it can incarnate the highest speculative ideal of the Christian university or college by becoming a community of Christian wisdom. Since it is, of itself, a community of faith and since it is an integral part of the university or college community, the RFG tries to render explicit in the academic community a corporate synthesis of faith and culture. This would be a communal Christian wisdom. But the RFG cannot do this apart from the vast array of experts in the larger university or college community. To make such a synthesis possible, for itself and for the university or college, the RFG continually insists that the two most powerful wisdom knowledges, theology and philosophy, be vigorously present in the university or college community for the sake of both students and faculty-administration. Under the challenge of these two disciplines, individual university or college members are less likely to become narrowly imprisoned within one another's specialized areas and more likely to reach out across disciplines to contemplate the ultimate understandings and values that undergird western civilization. To make such a challenge unmistakable, the theology faculty must pursue a dominant theology among other theologies, and, likewise, the philosophy faculty must pursue a dominant Christian philosophy among other philosophies lest the challenge dwindle to a babble of clashing shouts.

The RFG, having such a dominant philosophy and theology to give its Christian vision some unity, will naturally promote its own dominant theology and philosophy so that the university or college can enjoy a single, though constantly modifiable, Christian vision. Without the RFG, the university or college community will be hard put to decide upon and to live a dominant philosophy and theology; without this university or college community, the RFG could never, of itself, develop the corporate synthesis of faith and culture that is Christian university wisdom.

Clearly, the university or college community will normally emphasize the search for secular wisdom as it works toward the Christian wisdom that is arising out of this secular wisdom; the RFG, on the other hand, will emphasize Christian wisdom within the same search. Clearly, too, such a dialectic works best when two distinct groups emphasize opposite poles. Thus, the unique contribution of the RFG to the university or college community is the RFG's insistence on Christian wisdom within this dialectic; at the same time, the RFG is working competently and eagerly on secular wisdom through its specialized experts. In this way, the RFG uniquely promotes the second intrinsic aim of the university, namely, cumulative wisdom.

Evidently, then, the RFG can be a university or college mini-community of wisdom, a model for the larger university or college community. But it can be this model only when it is, more fundamentally, already a model university or college mini-community of faith. In this way, the RFG incarnates, both speculatively and practically, its unique contributions to the Christian university or college.

The RFG: A Living Assurance of Four University Hopes

The incarnational is only one side of the RFG's unique contribution, it also has an eschatological side of distant, future hopes for the university or college—an assured uniqueness, a prophetic voice concerning the world's ills, a full liberty, and a wide ecumenical embrace. Is it possible for the RFG to call forth from its sponsored Christian university or college these four hopes? Let us check each hope for its possibility.

How can the RFG assure its sponsored university or college of its uniqueness? In chapter fourteen, we noted that uniqueness has two components: (1) negative individuation (cumulative historical limitations) and (2) positive individuality (cumulative beneficient qualities and powers). Because negative individuation yields to the domination of positive individuality, the RFG contributes best to the university's or college's uniqueness by developing the six sources of this positive individuality: (a) energetic constituencies, (b) integral specialization, (c) wiser wholeness of life, (d) disciplined liberty, (e) expansive Christian vision, and (f) more adaptive service to the larger civic and ecclesial communities.

First, insofar as the RFG shows singular dedication to its university or college—a dedication to excellent teaching, to well-balanced administrating, to personal rapport with students and their parents, to scholarly work, to loyal support of fellow faculty, to the university or college's spiritual life—the RFG will lead the other constituencies of the university or college to a more energetic academic life. Second, if the RFG is composed of academic specialists who also have degrees or at least strong interests in philosophy, theology, and one other academic area, then its expert scholars can direct their specializations beyond merely interdisciplinary studies and courses toward wholeness of life, rather than toward its fragmentation. Third, such wholeness of life is expressed as wisdom, the integration of one's knowledges, arts, skills, and virtues for a fuller life in community. Indeed, the Christian is convinced, from experience and from revelation, that this wholeness takes shape only when the inner wisdom of Christ permeates his or her secular wisdom. Consequently, as a Christian wisdom community, the RFG endeavors to incarnate such Christian wisdom in its daily university or college living. It thus tries to make this distinctive characteristic of the Christian university or college palpable for all.

Fourth, this type of living demands disciplined liberty, that is, the ability to consistently choose good over evil and, later, even to regularly choose the better over the simply good. In this matter, discipline is the power to rigorously pursue truth and to decisively choose the good; it is the willingness to suffer for what is true and good. If the RFG is truly a Christian community, then it sees discipline as Christ's cross and liberty as His resurrection. Thus, to retain its integrity as a Christian community of faith, the RFG has no alternative but to live a life of disciplined liberty. In no other way will Christian wisdom pulse in its life and, from it, into the life of its university or college. Therefore, so long as the RFG is wholesomely contributing to its university or college, it is promoting the individuality, the sense of identity, the uniqueness of its university or college.

Fifth, out of its constituency-leadership, its prowess at specialized disciplines, its palpable Christian wisdom, and its disciplined liberty, the RFG promotes the very Christian vision with which it first initiated the university or college and which it has been subsequently developing along with the faculty, administration, and student body. In some ways, then, the RFG is the first guardian of the Christian vision that, in its inventiveness and unifying power, renders the university or college "more unique." The Christian vision of this particular university or college is close to the very spirit of the RFG itself. Sixth, the unique service that is rendered by the particular university or college to the unique needs and hopes of the surrounding civic and ecclesial communities should come as a consequence of this unique vision. The RFG can be particularly influential, since its basic reason for initiating and preserving the university or college was to make apostolically incarnate the Christian kingdom of truth and goodness within the civic community.

These, then, are the six ways in which the RFG uniquely contributes to the identity of its university or college. But the RFG does more than make this unique identity possible. The RFG *assures* this uniqueness, since the RFG is nothing other than the continuity or tradition of the college or university. The RFG is a living embodiment of the university's or college's particular Christian wisdom, that distinctive characteristic which is the *raison d'être* of the Christian university or college. At this point, it becomes clearer how indispensable the RFG is to the unique mission of the Christian university or college in its unique historic-geographic-sociologic situation.

In addition to assuring the unique identity of the Christian university or college, however, the RFG uniquely stimulates the university or college's prophetic voice to speak sensitively, respectfully, and, above all, competently to the world's ills. Just as the prophetic voice of the church can be expected to admonish civic society according to revealed truth, so, too, the Christian university or college has the obligation to criticize positively both the civic community, by way of secular wisdom, and the ecclesial community, by way of Christian wisdom. It is the dialectic of competent criticism among free institutions that keeps them free to grow, true to themselves, and able to promote the commonweal.

The RFG plays a strong role in the university or college's prophetic chorale (1) because it is already filling such a role within the church, (2) because it tries to incarnate the university Christian wisdom that is used in the context of the critique, and (3) because its very spirit inspires the Christian vision whereby the university or college guides its own criticism. When the RFG uses the secular and Christian wisdom of the university to stretch its gaze into the distant future and to agitate the university or college into speaking out about the world's ills, it is simply continuing the tradition of Augustine, Benedict, Francis, Dominic, Luther, Calvin, Ignatius Loyola, Wesley, and Vincent de Paul—all of them deeply involved with university-type thought and living, all of them endeavoring to direct the Western secularization process toward more humane living by the secularity of a Christian vision.

Even on its own, the RFG is a prophetic voice, for within the university or college itself, the RFG speaks to the academic community with the tone of John the Baptist and Christ: "Repent; the kingdom is upon you." The university or college must be warned internally of its own weaknesses lest these weaknesses throttle its prophetic voice and keep it from warning the external civic and ecclesial societies of their illnesses. Indeed, if the university or college's prophetic word is to be spoken courageously and truthfully, it must rise out of a free ascetic heart, one that is willing to suffer for the true and the good. To avoid what John the Apostle called pride of body, eyes, and life, it must enjoy disciplined liberty. Somehow, Christian university or college life must express its firm belief that the Gospels require every Christian to strive to practice evangelical chastity, stewardship, and self-sacrifice. For pride of body, with its inordinate desire for the sensual, threatens to destroy the family, the basis of all community and culture; pride of eyes, with its avaricious desires, tends to undermine justice, the basis of all civilization; and pride of life, with its intense self-preoccupation, can reduce wholesome cooperation to a shambles of "everyone for himself or herself."

Thus, before the prophetic voice of the university or college can be heard, it must be amplified by the university's or college's credibility as a communal Christian witness. Such credibility will be composed of three factors. The first factor will be the spiritual ties (versus pride of body) of friendship and healthy family living among university or college community members, lest the university or college community, itself riven by prideful rivalries, fail to be an encouraging sign of vibrant unity for other communities. The second factor will be the university or college community's sense of stewardship (versus pride of eyes) toward the nation's resources, lest the poor suffer further deprivations at the hands of the "have-alls." The third factor will be the university or college's willingness to do self-sacrificing teamwork (versus pride of life) for the larger community's welfare, lest love of neighborhood, city, state, and nation be lost, and the country find itself hopelessly divided. In other words, the university or college community must already be doing what its prophetic voice implies must be done by the nation—if the nation is to be able to hear what it must do and must suffer to solve its problems.

If the RFG is truly living evangelical chastity, stewardship, and self-sacrifice, then it will have the necessary credibility to speak prophetically within the university or college community and challenge that community to speak out forcibly concerning the needs and the ills of the world. This office of prophecy demands eschatological commitment to the university or college community. This is a commitment that risks everything for the sake of a future good which, in this context, is the wholesome Christian life of the university or college community. As the history of prophesy eloquently paints in the colors of crimson blood and black defeat, such witness is a dangerous profession not simply for the individual prophet, but also for his or her community, be it the RFG or the university or college. Yet the university or college community, if its gratitude to its constituencies is genuine, and if its intrinsic university aims are to have any final meaning, must be willing to suffer for the true and the good. Since it will be speaking about radical needs and failures that demand costly response, it will need to summon up from its own ranks all possible strength of purpose and all possible competency for truth. It is at this juncture that the RFG's support will be of pivotal importance—a support that should be expectable because the RFG founded the university or college precisely for moments such as these and because the RFG loses its *raison d'être* in the university or college if it fails at these times to support the university or college.

In addition to reinforcing university or college uniqueness and raising its prophetic voice, the RFG can be forging a third eschatological hope, namely, full liberty, out of a flexible amalgam of Christian wisdom, vision, and discipline. This liberty can then be seen as the university's or college's autonomy, its full self-justification, its basic *raison d'être*. The RFG contributes uniquely to this autonomy of full liberty insofar as it contributes uniquely to all the elements that compose this mature liberty. But it also contributes in what appears to be a negative way; the RFG can be, *de facto*, incorporated separate and apart from the university or college or, lacking this, it can act in the spirit of separate incorporation. In this way, the RFG clearly signifies that, like the university or college, it has its own laws of growth. On this basis, its separate autonomy will enable it to more forcibly witness to the university or college and, in turn, the university or college's voice will be heard on its own and not as the ventriloquized voice of the RFG. Nor does such separate incorporation thereby reduce the RFG to becoming just one more pressure group in the university or college. Rather, this enables the RFG's unique contribution to be recognized as unique. Thus, the RFG does not simply escape the headaches that are incurred by trying to dominate a huge university or college according to a paternalistic model. Its separate incorporation positively enables the RFG to cooperate more freely with the university or college in their dialog with business, government, the communications industry, the church, and revolutionary movements.

This autonomy, or full liberty, of the university or college makes more possible the fourth eschatological—wide ecumenical embrace. The RFG is, in some ways, a paradoxical community when it is sponsoring its university or college. First, it separately incorporates itself so that it can dedicate itself with fuller liberty, that is to say, more strength, to its university or college. As a result, cooperation between the RFG and the university or college can become more efficient both within and outside the university or college. This means that the unique contribution of the RFG to the university or collge can be richer after the separate incorporation. In three distinct ways, ecumenical embrace is one clear example of this.

First, because the RFG is intensely sponsoring its university or college according to a particular faith—the Baptist faith, for example—the university or college community can know with clarity, if it wishes, how the Baptist faith is similar to the Congregational faith or Methodist faith or Roman Catholic faith and, therefore, how precisely these faiths differ from the Baptist. This enables the university or college community to recognize and prize the differences of its own Baptist heritage and, at the same time, be explicitly aware of its similarity to the other Christian communions and be encouraged by this fellowship in the face of a sometime hostile pagan world. This experience gives a solid basis for a true ecumenism, in contrast to an ambiguous indifferentism which may well undermine all Christian faith. The separate incorporation of the RFG removes any fear that the university or college cannot be free to exploit the similarity of Christian faiths and, yet, to stress the differences that ironically divide these communions.

Second, the ecumenical embrace is widened and strengthened by the Christian wisdom that exists in the university or college community. This community, from its privileged height of contemplation, not only delineates secular wisdom as the common base of all Christian wisdoms, but also points out the elements of Christian faith that are common to all the Christian confessions and communions. This technique can broaden the base of both understanding and practice among the various Christian communions. To strongly encourage such ecumenical study is the role of the RFG, as long as the RFG is working toward the one fold of the one Shepherd, Christ. As a paradoxical result, the RFG that is most deeply wedded to its particular Christian faith and most influential in its sponsored university or college would uniquely enable its university or college to extend an ecumenical embrace wider than other Christian universities or colleges lacking so strong an RFG. Moreover, the RFG's separate incorporation is, then, a clear signal of its desire to give the university or college full freedom of action for such ecumenism.

A third way in which the RFG can render its college or university more ecumenical is through its Christian vision. If the RFG and, hence, the sponsored university or college recognize that its prized vision, which gives so much strength and unity to the school, is only one alternative among others, even within the particular Christian faith (e.g., Lutheran or Episcopal), then both the RFG and the university or college are liberated from a narrow dogmatism, which blinds their intelligence, and from a restrictive parochialism, which paralyzes their actions toward other faith communities. Consequently, the separate incorporation of the RFG symbolizes that the Christian vision which the RFG has initiated and preserved in the university or college is negotiable because it is not the only possible Christian vision arising from the Christian faith of the RFG. This, of course, can widen the ecumenical embrace of the Christian university or college. In three paradoxical ways, then, the RFG strengthens the ecumenical stance of its university or college community to render this community unique in its wider embrace, which is the fourth eschatological hope for the university or college community.

In sum, the unique contribution of the RFG to its Christian university or college is not small. In a practical incarnational way, it offers the model of a faith community wherein the personal is stressed over the institutional, wherein the apostolic thrust toward Christ's kingdom is adapted to give power to the university's or college's extrinsic aim of serving the larger civic community, and wherein a common Christian vision-worship-*caritas* simultaneously unify and enrich the community with a priceless heart knowledge. On the other hand, in a speculative incarnational way, the RFG offers the university or college the model of a Christian wisdom community, the highest ideal of the Christian university or college. The RFG can do this because its members are specialists who share their findings not only among themselves, but also with colleagues in the sometimes isolated departments that form the university or college. This is possible because RFG members ordinarily have multiple degrees or have cultivated interests in areas outside their own specialized field—in areas such as the wisdom knowledges of philosophy and theology. Thus, they can appreciate both the need and the dangerous difficulties of synthesizing secular and Christian wisdoms. The RFG, then, blends the practical community of faith with the speculative community of wisdom. Thus, the RFG becomes both a model and an agent of these realities for its sponsored university or college.

But this is not all. The RFG can also make a unique eschatological contribution by assuring its sponsored university or college of four stabilizing hopes. First, because the RFG can take the lead (a) in sponsoring specialized studies that are open to wisdom, (b) in making Christian wisdom, vision, and disciplined liberty more palpable, and (c) in encouraging the university's or college's unique service to its constituencies, the RFG assures the unique identity of a particular university college. Second, the RFG's own prophetic voice within the university or college challenges the university or college to the witness of evangelic chastity, stewardship, and self-sacrifice; then, having established its credibility on this basis, it calls the university or college to speak out about the world's needs and problems. Third, the RFG attempts to foster the autonomy of full liberty in the university or college not only with all the above-mentioned positive contributions, but also with the seemingly negative one of separate incorporation, which symbolizes the freedom of both the RFG and the university or college to speak and act out of their own integrity. Fourth, as a result of this fuller liberty and separate incorporation, the now more autonomous RFG and university or college can stand side by side to widen their ecumenical embrace. Paradoxically, both the RFG and the university or college see more clearly the common basis, in secular wisdom and in commonly held elements of Christian faith, for more generous and free cooperation among various Christian communions; at the same time, both also recognize and, perhaps, prize the differences. Thus, if the full life of the RFG assures that these four hopes will be fulfilled, then the university or college can plan its future with the secure feeling that its unique identity will grow, that its prophetic voice will be heard, that its liberty will attain full stature, and that its ecumenical embrace will extend out to include many. At that point, the incarnational and eschatological contributions of the RFG become one unique gift to the Christian university or college.

The very grandness of this destiny makes it particularly vulnerable to the cynical observation: "But how is it even possible for church and university to cooperate without one dominating and, thus, crippling the other—especially because the RFG represents the church and its university or college represents the secular world?" This attack on the very possibility of cooperation between church and university, and its implicit questioning of academic freedom in the Christian university or college, must be faced.

Why the RFG Can Mediate between Church and University or College

Earlier, the question arose: Is it the proper task for the RFG to remind the university or college of its nature and, then, to help the university fulfill its nature? Though the previous section was meant to be a detailed "Yes" to this question, still the underlying reasons for this affirmation must be discovered lest the answer lack full credibility. These reasons are five: (1) the church and the university or college enjoy a community of aims and of models; (2) their differences of aim and structure are often reciprocally balancing; (3) the university or college can minister directly to the church and, vice versa, the church can contribute directly to the university or college; (4) of its very nature the RFG can mediate a mutual enrichment *(communio)* between church and university; and (5) this enrichment supports academic freedom for the university and religious freedom for the church. Here are five roots enlivening church sponsorship of universities or colleges. But are they set in the rich loam of fact?

In the first place, if the church and the university or college have a community of aims, then they have a basis for cooperation. That they do have such a community becomes clear when one notes how both the university or college and the church seek wisdom, the ultimate meaning and power of life. The university as university seeks secular wisdom; the church pursues the sacred wisdom of the Scriptures and the sacraments. Thus, both seek truth institutionally through a community of wisdom.

Each, then, heralds the newly discovered truth to its constituencies so that these constituencies might live fuller lives at the compenetrating levels of the secular (the university) and the sacred (the church). Because of this prophetic stance, both church and university or college are uncomfortable to live with, are usually suppressed simultaneously by the oppressors of truth, and challenge the present *status quo* (violently preserved by the "have alls") for the sake of a better future commonweal (for the "have nots"). Each one, of its very nature, is a mediating society. The church mediates between God and mankind and, therefore, between one person and another. For, as John the Evangelist reminds us, one cannot love God unless one loves one's neighbor, and vice versa. Because of this principle of life, the church often finds herself mediating between governments and the people, between the state and the university or college, between the worker and the owners. But the university or college, of its very nature, also mediates between past and future learning; between the disciplines that make up its structure; between the schools of thought within a single knowledge, skill, or art; between the theoretical and the practical; between the various wisdoms (secular, sacred, Christian, common sense, philosophic, and theologic); and between church and state (as in the late medieval period).

Perhaps the most striking similarity of aims is seen in the fact that church and university or college both endeavor to serve not only their constituencies, but also the larger civic community. For the university, service of the large civic community is an extrinsic aim; similarly, the missionary spirit of the church makes service to the non-Christian community an intrinsic aim ("Go and preach to all nations, making them disciples"). There is also diversity of aims-competencies-means, for the church's goal is to unite humanity with God and, thence, with the divine gift of the world; the university's goal is to unite humanity with the world and, thence, with God. The church is primarily responsible for the sanctity (wholesomeness) of her people; similarly, the university or college is responsible for the intelligence of this sanctity. It is the competency of the church to explore and preserve revealed truth about God and His world; it is the competency of the university or college to explore and preserve evidential and reasoned truth about the world and its God. Finally, the church's means to her goal are the sacraments and her communal authority to teach about God's revelation; the university's means are all the institutional (academic, financial, administrative, and so on) apparatus described in chapter three. Clearly, there is the possibility of cooperation between church and university or college, since their aims are complementary rather than conflicting. In fact, this similarity may indicate that these two community institutions may well need each other's help to

414

reach full maturity and to ward off common enemies such as oppressors of truth, the spirit of anti-intellectualism, and the blight of cynicism about humanity and God.

In addition to this remarkable similarity of aims, church and university or college also enjoy a community of models. Because models are used to help focus the mind on the structure of a reality, such as church or university, community of models means that these two structures are similar. In fact, it is the similarity of structure that makes similarity of aims possible. Indeed, similarity of structure makes cooperation between the university or college and the church basically possible and abundantly fruitful. But comparison of similarity between the two institutions is not simple, since each uses multiple models to understand itself and then focuses the multiple models on itself by means of a supermodel. In chapter thirteen, we observed the university through eight models and then offered a supermodel called a Christian vision to focus the eight models differently upon the diverse decisional situations that face the university administration. Avery Dulles has suggested, in *Models of the Church,* five basic ways of looking at the church: institution, mystical communion (community), sacrament, herald, and servant. When he endeavors to show how these models supplement each other according to the situation faced, he mentions two working principles and seven criteria for judging the manner of applying these multiple models to the single reality of the church. In this way, he is developing a supermodel, a Christian vision, for evaluating their use.

Let us illustrate what community of models may mean through Dulles' five major models of the church. The first is the *institutional* model, which is preferred by church officials. It describes the church as the perfect society that is subordinate to no other and lacks nothing for institutional totality. It naturally puts special emphasis on the structure of government as the central element of the church. The second model describes the church as *mystical communion,* or *community,* a model dear to the heart of ecumenists. The church is a communion of men and women with each other and with God—a communion that is primarily interior but, secondarily, has visible external bonds in its creed, worship service, and fellowship. In the third model, a favorite of speculative theologians, the church is more than a sign of God; it is seen as a *sacramentum* containing all sacraments. In other words, the church stands for and is what it contains and offers—the life-giving presence of the divine and human Christ. This is expressed tangibly in liturgy, in sacrament, and in holy and loving, individual and corporate, actions toward others (the institutional side of the church). The fourth model of the church, the *herald,* is the one extolled by preachers and Scripture scholars. For them, the church is a kerygmatic community that gathers around the preached Word to lift high for all to see the great acts of God in past history, especially His mighty deed in Christ. The fifth model, the church as *servant*, is stressed by social scientists and activists. It describes the church as following the Christ who came to serve, not to be served. Thus, it sees the church working within the total human family and its culture to develop brotherhood through the pursuit of peace, justice, racial harmony, and reconciliation of ecclesial groups.

These five models, when they are employed to understand the rich mystery of the church, have remarkable affinities with the eight models used in chapter thirteen to study that growing mystery called the university. The institutional model of the church, for example, which was so widely used in the nineteenth century to characterize the Roman Catholic communion, has emphasized specialized bureaucracy, efficiency, tight unity, and strong sense of identity—all of which fit the university models of graduate professional school and of business corporation. The intricate network of autonomous departments that constitute the graduate school resemble not a little the ecclesiastical bureaucracy of interlocking committees or action boards or associations or synods or assemblies or diocesan organizations or Roman congregations. On the other hand, the business model of the university, with its cost-accounting efficiencies, with its demands for close unity of purpose, and with its consequent need for finding strong self-identity is not unfamiliar to the churchpersons who struggle with budgeted activities, with clarification of program aims, and with dependence on loyal teamwork.

The second ecclesial model—mystical communion (community)—resembles the community model of the university wherein expansion of person is prized over the merely academic; small classes, much counseling for personal integration, and a democratic style of government prevail. The church of mystical communion also stresses the interior person over external organization, spontaneous communal intimacy over routine ritualized worship, and a sense of the mysterious union of its members in a divine destiny. Both models point to that fragile, momentary synthesis of much that is right and just which enables the church or university to reach a peak experience, to glimpse a breathtakingly beautiful vision of the future, and then to descend into the valley of ordinary grueling life.

The third model of church—sacrament—much resembles the picture of the university as a Christian wisdom community. Just as the church is seen as the sign of the Christ-life, which it contains, and as becoming this sacrament-sign by educing the Christ-life in its members, so, too, the university is seen as the communal sign of the wisdom-life, which it contains, and as becoming this sign precisely by educing wisdom in its members. In other words, just as the living unity of the church is the interior Word, the graceful Christ, spoken into the individual lives of its members for exterior expression, so, too, the vibrant unity of the university or college is that Christian wisdom of common faith, culture, goals, and corporate dedication which interiorly animates the university or college community and exteriorly expresses itself in the university institution.

There is also a striking resemblance between Dulles' herald model of the church and the activist-prophetic model of the university. In both instances, the ecclesial reality and the academic reality are seen more as *events* rather than as perduring organizations. The church is a momentarily sounding voice of the people proclaiming humanity's unending need of Christ's saving act, and the university is a chorale of scholarly voices singing not only the need for social change, but also the practical program for alleviating the evil—and all this according to a new mythic score. Both models are seen as dangerous because they seem to depreciate the very structures that make prophesy responsibly competent. Sometimes the herald model of the church is also related to the technological institute model of the university, since both models can be drastically pragmatic; the church is conceived as simply the megaphone of God, and the university or college is seen as merely the nation's machine for producing technologists to run its sophisticated civilization.

The fifth model of the church—the servant—correlates well, of course, with the model of the university as servant. If the church is seen as serving the human family by working within the latter's culture, problems, and hopes so that a universal brotherhood and sisterhood with Christ is discovered and lived, then the university can be described as that marvelously versatile service organization that meets the hungers and hopes of its surrounding civic community with a vast cafeteria of adaptive courses and a large staff of professors whose multiple skills can be applied to curing contemporary social ills so that the health of neighborhood, city, and nation is preserved and enriched. Both models dramatize the risk; both the church and the university are vulnerable to losing their respective souls to all this external activity, eventually finding themselves too exhausted to respond to the needs of their people.

This attempt to indicate the community of models between university and church leaves only the denomination college model uncompared with a church model. However, recall that this last university model focuses on a school's dedication to a single denominational faith that dominates religious, social, and academic life through recruiting an ecclesially homogeneous faculty and student body and through keeping the academic life subordinate to a particular faith life. Also, observe that this model is not unlike the medieval church model as it has been mistakenly conceived by some nostalgic Christians who are little aware that the historical reality of the medieval church was actually quite pluralistic and noticeably free-wheeling.

Because of this community of aims and models, it should not greatly surprise us that their very differences could be reciprocally supportive of each other. The university or college can minister as directly to the church as the church can contribute to the university or college—if one does not mind this cute, though accurate, reversal of the terms "minister" and "contribute" that underlines the close cooperation possible between university or college and church. Notice how the following structural differences actually compensate for each other. The church, for example, is basically a community of persons who find that they must institutionalize their communal living in order to enrich it. Note, in this context, (1) the gathering of the twelve apostles before they became functional, (2) the apostles' recognition of the need for deacons, and (3) the gradual differentiation of priest from bishop in the early church. On the other hand, the university or college cannot exist without its specialized knowledges-arts-skills and their differentiated departments. Only when the departments are assembled does it become clear that a community must be formed to distill the wisdom that gives embracing meaning and stimulating challenge to all the specializations. Only the community can render the university or college humane and personal so that the university becomes more than a knowledge factory and a technique shop. Because of this diverse priority in their structures, the church's community priority supports well the university community's pursuit of wisdom; similarly, the university or college's institution priority ministers well to the organizational needs of the church.

As a second example of their complementary differences, we find that the church is primarily faith oriented and that the university is primarily reason oriented. By way of this faith, the church intimately contacts the sacred wisdom of the Scriptures; likewise, by means of reason, the university enters deeply into secular wisdom. These two wisdoms neatly supplement each other. Sacred wisdom is concerned with the ultimate events of life, the final historical destiny of humanity and the practical, day-to-day life that leads to this destiny. Secular wisdom, on the other hand, deals with both the underlying ultimate principles according to which the world is evolving and the perduring routines that protect these principles from interference. Thus, soil-conservation, international prevention of atmospheric pollution, national protection of endangered species, and development of political organizations like the United Nations are examples of perduring routines that are used to ensure the beneficent evolving of the universe. Consequently, sacred wisdom furnishes ultimate goals for daily living and a final home, or destiny, for secular wisdom. Secular wisdom, in turn, offers to sacred wisdom refined tools for interpreting the Scriptures, the Fathers of the Church, and conciliar documents. These tools include anthropology, archaeology, linguistics, comparative literature, philosophic hermeneutics, and so on.

The previous two examples should make it more evident that the church exists primarily as a faith community whose way of life puts particular emphasis on disciplined virtue and heartening love—although doctrine and intelligent analysis are indispensable to the church's growth. In contrast, the university exists primarily as a community of reason whose principal intent is disciplined reason and clarifying insight—although values of the heart and loyal dedication make it possible for the university to survive. Clearly, these two organs of the body politic need each other's support so that the primary "strength" of one might minister to the secondary "weakness" of the other and vice versa.

But how do the community of aims and structures and the reciprocally supportive differences between church and university or college concretely induce beneficial cooperation between the church and the university or college? Let us note, first, how the university or college ministers directly to the church, and let us take for granted that the university or college indirectly serves the church well by enriching the larger civic community, which is partly made up of church members. Fundamentally, the university directly benefits the church by enriching her understanding of sacred wisdom with new secular findings and her living of the faith with explication of values. Thus, the university advances the faith practically when she converges all her knowledges-skills-arts upon the Scriptures to make exegesis more scientific. Later, out of this exegesis and out of the challenge of a philosophy that is in touch with the social and physical sciences, the faith of the university or college community will provide a university or college theology. In other words, the university or college will provide Christian theologians who teach strongly and relevantly, so that the church may keep abreast of university or college advances in all major cultural problems. In the university or college milieu, one can expect university philosophy to elaborate lasting values so that church members might rediscover their basic motives. Indeed, the university or college can offer to the church philosophers who are sensitively aware of other secular disciplines, who are not afraid to use Christian theology for themselves and for their work, who do not undermine the Christian faith of students when challenging it, and who provide bridges into the lives of non-Christian thinkers.

All of the above university or college services to the church have a particular effect within the university or college community itself and in the larger civic and ecclesial communities—namely, the fostering of an available Christian wisdom that speaks to the present hopes and problems of the church, that provides a strong doctrinal and communal context for modern Christian living, and that can run a truly liberal arts education of depth for students. Then, out of this Christian wisdom, the university or college and the church can project a Christian vision for now and for the future. This vision can encourage a fuller living of the faith, a greater dedication to secular pursuits, and a more generous service to the larger civic and ecclesial communities. It can, thus, generate a communal Christian atmosphere for student and faculty living.

The university social sciences also minister to the church when they help men and women to understand themselves, their community, their church, and their aspirations toward God; when they delineate societal problems for the church's better understanding; when they suggest how the church's apostolic ventures can alleviate problems; when, in union with the university arts and skills (painting, dance, communications, counseling, etc.), they stimulate the spiritual life of prayer and liturgy; and when, in union with the physical sciences, they explore the artistry of God's creative action and the mystery of persons and the world.

In these ways, the university or college is also (1) educating leaders for church and society, (2) developing administrators who are not afraid to treasure Christian values and are alert to employ these values in university or college procedures-criteria-roles, and (3) providing the ecumenical atmosphere of converging knowledges-arts-skills and differing viewpoints. In other words, the ministry of the university or college to the church offers the resources, facilities, and procedures by which students and faculty can develop their manhood and womanhood as God's greatest glory.

But how, then, can the church gratefully respond to the university or college? What will be her direct gifts to it? An answer: People who are ready to live the university life to the hilt. Such people will be committed to the pursuit of truth and wisdom by the hunger of their Christian faith for full understanding. They will be people who reverence the past because of their own sense of Christian tradition, and yet are inventive of the future because of the risen Christ who goes ahead of them. Insofar as these people are united by *caritas*, they will be ecumenically open to cooperate with all types of men and women in the university or college enterprise, and they will be apostolically interested in the poor and the abandoned among God's creatures. Much of their motivational strength will come from a lived scriptural wisdom that constantly keeps them aware of the worthwhile life and destiny that is meant for all human beings. Out of their sense of Christian stewardship, these people will be especially protective of the world's natural resources: its mineral, plant, and animal life. Their first priority, however, will be the fostering of family life as the greatest resource of all for the future. In other words, they will be community minded, since their final destiny is the family of God and the familial Trinitarian God. Such community-mindedness will acutely sharpen their desire to defend the university from any encroachments of the business community, from the pressures of government, from the hyperaesthesia of the communications media, and even from the tamperings of the churches. The people who have been contributed to the university by the churches may well be the university's closest friends.

The Mediating RFG: Visible Incarnation of Church-University Cooperation

The similarity of aims and structures and the reciprocally supporting differences between church and university, which underlie any and all cooperation between them, are the first source of the RFG's ability to mediate. At the center of their cooperation, the RFG can be a potent mediator of their mutually enriching intercourse, the *communio* between university and church. In fact, the RFG is the visible incarnation of this *communio;* its very life is the *communio* because, like the church and the university, the RFG is both institutional and communal. It is institutional since it is an ecclesial organization structured by the church precisely to found the university or college and to help that university or college develop. Yet the RFG is also communal, for it exists simply because the larger faith community authorizes it as a communal self-expression to mediate her prevailing interest in education and because the members of the RFG must form a mini-university community to do this mediating well. But despite its structural likeness to both church and university and despite the fact that its members are also simultaneously members of the church and the university, the RFG can still be distinct from both organizations by means of separate incorporation from the university and by means of specific exemption from church jurisdiction in matters of university affairs. Thus, the RFG has, at one and the same time, a structure that is strongly similar to both church and university, an authorization from church and university, and yet an independent distinctness from both that can make the RFG a suitable mediator between them.

A second source of the RFG's competence to mediate between church and university or college is the fact that its members are influential members in both the church community and university or college community. For this reason, RFG members tend to be extremely sensitive to the weaknesses and strengths of both communities because of contrasting communal experiences. Consequently, RFG members can mediate reciprocity between the differences that are inherent in university-and-church structures, programs, hopes, and fears. RFG members can also indicate how church and university can share each other's similar positive interests and qualities. But above all, the RFG members will know, deep in their bones, that church and university can serve each other well only as long as each respects and refurbishes the autonomy of the other. To try to turn the university into a seminary is to destroy the university's ability to serve the church; to depreciate the church's specific contribution to human destiny and to help an outside force shackle the church is to allow the university to starve itself of sacred wisdom and to mold the shackles for its own wrists.

The RFG's appreciative use of models to understand its own meaningful structure is a third source of its power to mediate. The RFG's own experience gives it intimate knowledge of the importance of using models for either stifling or stimulating growth in both university and church. The RFG also knows how to focus the multiple models according to a supermodel of Christian vision. In this way, the RFG's dual membership in church and university enriches both of these bodies with its dual experiences of them and with its experience of itself in the inventive and corrective use of models for self-understanding and self-promotion. For this reason, the RFG offers a mutual understanding to university and church as well as a resultant possibility for mutual ministry that no other source can offer them. This indicates the ultimate roots of the RFG's unique contribution to the university, to say nothing of its unique gift to the church.

Lastly, the RFG's fourth source of mediation is its ability to serve as a balancing mechanism between power and truth in both the church and the university. Though the authoritative power of administering the institution and the authoritative skill of gathering truth are indispensable to each other, still, like siblings, they seem to naturally squabble. The RFG can act as mediator amid conflicts in the church because its members are extremely busy gathering truth in the university and, therefore, are not so ambitious to grasp power in the ecclesial establishment. The RFG literally has nothing to gain when its members speak the truth in the church; the witness of RFG members, then, is less suspect to other church members, and the RFG members' freedom from church ambition enables them to speak objectively. Thus, they are able to mediate between church theologians and university or college administrators or between incomplete viewpoints on both sides. Note, however, that it is their university membership that enables them to achieve this status of recognizable mediator.

The RFG, however, can also mediate within the university in like manner, for it will have members on the administrative or power side as well as on the faculty or truth side. Because the RFG is a community in itself, its administrative members can hardly avoid enlightening, if not heated, conversation with its academic members. Their common faith, wisdom, and vision require a sharing of facts as well as ideals, a careful hearing of each side, and a collective responsibility to provide the best efforts for the university's future. Consequently, it is possible for one RFG member who is an administrator to provide an eloquent presentation of the faculty or truth side of a conflict and for another member who is a faculty person to do the same for the administrative or power side of the conflict. What other group can perform such unique services? Thus, because the RFG can mediate within either the church or the university, it is uniquely qualified to mediate between the church and the university. In this way, it is the living *communio*, or mutual enrichment, between the university and the church; it is truly a mediator.

The strength of this "mediatorship" is dramatically demonstrated when the RFG is seen to be a consistent promoter of academic freedom in the university or college. To glimpse this, recall that the university's liberty is much more than academic freedom; it is the university's or college's ability to do full justice to the student's hopes and needs through the individual professor's dedication and the department's dedication to a specialized knowledge-art-skill and through the community's cumulative wisdom, which is structured by justice and directed by *caritas*. As we have noted, the RFG is itself a wisdom community composed of members who are experts in specialized fields or who are administrators promoting both the specialization of disciplines and the accumulation of wisdom. Its reason for founding the university is to promote justice and to make *caritas* more possible for the larger civic community. The RFG is, then, deeply committed to university or college liberty, since this liberty is the living autonomy of the university by which it is different from and distinct from any other organ of the body politic.

Within such liberty occurs academic freedom, which, as we recall, is the university community's wise use of its intrinsic authority (1) to promote the aims of the university, (2) to resist pressures that are harmful both for the university's constitutional aims and for its exercise of intrinsic authority, and (3) to support its constituencies in such fulfillment of their needs and hopes as is compatible with the constitutional autonomy of the university. The liberty of the university and the academic freedom within this liberty express the distinct autonomy of the university. But neither liberty nor academic freedom can live long without the support of all other free national institutions, such as the government, the churches, business, communications industry, and so on. This mutual support is made more possible through the RFG, whose members are influential in both the church and the university, and whose very distinct autonomy from both church and university communities allows it to mediate more objectively and freely between them. Furthermore, because the RFG members are influential in these two powerful communities, they are heard more receptively by the other free national institutions whose own freedom may well depend on free churches and free universities.

Secondly, there is a reason why the RFG, for its own good, should promote academic freedom in the university. Christian wisdom, which is the distinct contribution of the Christian university or college and which is the primary intent of the RFG, cannot exist without academic freedom. Christian faith, the root of Christian wisdom, is an act of free commitment to Christ and to His people and is freely exercised only within a community that enjoys liberty. Furthermore, Christian wisdom contains an essential element of revolutionary prophecy that can be expressed only amid academic freedom. Again, if Christian wisdom is secular wisdom animated by scriptural faith, then secular wisdom must be allowed to freely develop its convergent knowledges-arts-skills and to elicit free commitment to this work. Otherwise, Christian wisdom cannot grow. Moreover, Christian wisdom is the base for plural Christian visions because its rich analogical intelligence requires more than one interpretation; thus, Christian wisdom, which itself is a convergent pluralism, offers a range of free choices to the Christian. As a result, wherever Christian wisdom is promoted, academic freedom must be its atmosphere, its salubrious weather.

Thirdly, the RFG itself needs academic freedom to exercise its fundamental option of living its Christian faith and of promoting Christian wisdom within the university. Therefore, the RFG tries to protect academic freedom through mediation with administrative power, with external organizations (government, business, church, communications media, and so forth), and with faculty extremists. For three strong reasons, then, the RFG works for the increase, not the decrease, of academic freedom: (1) academic freedom in the university protects the freedom of other social organs such as the church, (2) Christian wisdom cannot long survive if the academic freedom of the university is compromised, (3) the RFG cannot itself be a free mediator between university and church unless academic freedom thrives in the university and religious freedom is vigorous in the church.

Conclusion: The RFG Is Indispensable to the Christian University or College

There are a number of factors that have made the last two chapters a long and rough road. First of all, a brief historical survey of ways in which the churches have sponsored universities and colleges reveals so vast a variety of structures that one despairs of ever finding a model with which to understand them. The RFG itself, for example, has four levels of involvement with its university and/or college: (1) immediate (members of RFG who are teachers and administrators in the school), (2) mediate (local church or religious order), (3) quasi-mediate (a supporting synod, action board, diocese, etc.), and (4) more removed (national or international church). Furthermore, the strength of this sponsorship depends upon how many members of the RFG are trustees, chief academic officers, or influential teachers; how deeply the financial support of the church reaches; how wide the psychological support base of the church extends itself; and how rich is the faith life of the university and RFG.

A second complication is that the Christian wisdom, which is the distinctive characteristic of the Christian university or college, results from the introduction of Christian faith into the authority structure of the university or college. Somehow, the presence of the risen Christ must operate through all the university or college constituencies, which are understood to be the church receiving and preserving *traditio* in its daily living; then through the quasi-mediate and mediate RFG, which may be considered as the church explicitly formulating the received faith and applying it to newly developing life situations; and, finally, through the immediate RFG, which is present within all three dimensions of the university or college's intrinsic authority—namely, vertical power, horizontal influence, and personal presence. Thus, the RFG's sponsorship of the university or college is its ability to use faith-authority within the university or college to develop Christian wisdom without compromising in any way the autonomy of the university, but rather in many ways strengthening it.

A third complication is that this influence of the RFG within the university or college can be modeled on the patriarch, the neutral umpire, the friend, or the Dutch uncle. The last model seems preferable since it offers the best balanced enhancement of the university or college through the RFG's continuous *traditio*, its presence of trained specialists, its monitoring of development in Christian wisdom, its call to the service aim of the university, its loyal prophetic criticism of the university or college, its mediation between administration (power) and faculty (truth), and its expected self-sacrifice for the school.

Describing the unique contribution of the RFG to its sponsored university or college is a fourth complication, for the RFG itself is the unique contribution in that it offers itself as a palpable model of both a practical faith community and a speculative Christian wisdom community for the university or college community. This incarnational contribution of the RFG is matched by its eschatological contribution—namely, the assurance, by its operative presence, of four hopes of the university or college: unique identity, prophetic voice for the ecclesial and civic communities, full liberty, and wide ecumenical embrace. Such sponsorship of the university or college, such mediating between church and university or college, such *communio,* is possible on the grounds that the church and the university share a community of aims and models, that their differences can be reciprocally supportive of each other, and that the university can directly minister to church needs and the church can contribute its finest members to the university or college community.

In a reversal of popular prejudice, the RFG is found to be a potent mediator of reciprocal enrichment between church and university or college. The RFG represents the church in the university precisely by being a mini-university of specialized experts who are working toward a Christian wisdom; simultaneously, it represents the university to the church precisely by being both a community of faith and a community of Christian wisdom. Yet, by the spirit (at least) of separate incorporation, the RFG can be distinct from both the university and the church so that it can enjoy a qualified autonomy to speak to both church and university with great freedom and with adequate competency of experience.

Popular prejudice is further challenged by the fact that the RFG's sponsorship must increase academic freedom in the university rather than reduce it. The RFG can promote Christian wisdom well only if the university or college enjoys full liberty to follow out its own laws of development. Only on this condition can the university or college contribute that secular wisdom which, in convergence with a free act of faith and scriptural wisdom, eventuates in Christian wisdom. Furthermore, the RFG can hardly be a prophetic voice except in an atmosphere of academic freedom. Nor can its mediation between church and university or college enjoy the integrity of liberty unless the university has academic freedom and the church enjoys religious liberty.

At this point, it becomes clear how vital the RFG can be for any university or college and how absolutely necessary it is for the university or college that claims to be Christian. What is not quite so evident, perhaps, is the role of the risen Christ in such a university or college. Yet, because the risen Christ is the source and center of all Christian wisdom,

He must be the common basis of unity for all Christian universities or colleges. Indeed, within the particular Christian university or college, He is the common focus for all Christians who work there, and He is the heart of the RFG that uniquely sponsors this school.

Clearly, the RFG so idealistically described in this chapter has never fully existed and probably will never so exist. Just as clearly, though, this chapter could not have been written if particular RFGs did not exemplify beautifully, at one time or another, some of the characteristics previously sketched. The description is not merely fantasy. But perhaps this chapter should never have been written, or at least in so idealistic a form? Still, the ideal RFG has to be sketched out somewhere if only to let people know how far contemporary RFGs must travel to reach the ideal. Moreover, how are such RFGs going to achieve a higher qualify of life and influence unless they envision an ideal structure and performance to which they can compare their present status and toward which they can then advance? Does the ideal simply discourage those members of the RFG who are finding it a tough struggle as they swim against the present cultural current in the United States and Canada? Or is it possible that these very same people are the ones whose tough realism will eventually make this ideal more and more incarnate in some of the Christian universities and colleges of America? This is the challenge not only of this chapter (and this entire book) but of the whole enterprise that is called the Christian university or college.

19 Retrospect: Has a Christian Vision of the University Arisen?

In the face of predictions of the inherent impossibility of the task, this book has attempted to sketch out one particular vision of how an American university or college, by being thoroughly Christian, could make a unique contribution to academe and to the United States. The plan was to consider one large university problem in each chapter, to discover some elements of a solution, and, then, to note how these elements are envisioned by Christians. As we threaded our way through problem after problem, through possible response after possible response, and through Christian principle after Christian principle, we were hoping that our gaze would weave a Christian tapestry of the university. Then, as each chapter was woven into the total tapestry, it became clearer and clearer that alternate colored threads and organizing patterns could have been used—indeed, more than one tapestry or Christian vision of the university was possible. It became equally clear that a Christian university cannot long survive as Christian without a particular Christian vision directing its growth and animating its actions. Lastly, we learned that a Christian vision could strengthen the very structure of a university, give new sharpness to its understandings of the world, and offer additional reasons for passionate dedication to the university community and to the encompassing civic community.

At the outset of this book, an historical overview demonstrated not only the European roots of the American university but also the unique characteristics of the American university: (1) a tradition of self-autonomy (versus the highly centralized French and Russian models), (2) a blending of the vocational-professional models with the liberal model (versus the highly pragmatic Russian model), (3) a democratization of curriculum and student body through strong state support (versus the more selective British and French models), (4) a unifying of the British liberal arts college with the German professional graduate school, and (5) orientation to service of the civic community (versus the highly mobile German model). Would the Christian American university have anything more to add to these unique characteristics of the secular American university?

428

Are we ready, then, to state our basic thesis and to give our substantiating reasons for positing it? The thesis is simply that Christian wisdom will make any university a better university and, therefore, enable this university to better contribute to academic and civic life. This thesis is true because Christian wisdom bestows seven gifts on the university: this wisdom (1) gives clearer perspective and destiny to the specialized disciplines of the university; (2) provides richer wisdom for the academic community; (3) keeps the university better united and growing; (4) enables the university, out of justice and *caritas*, to better serve its eight constituencies; (5) requires a core of liberal studies for better Christian secularization of the students; (6) offers a stronger intelligence and heart to the administration and staff; and (7) furnishes a sponsoring religious founding group to foster greater continuity and stability for the Christian core of the university community. Let us consider these seven gifts of Christian wisdom as each gradually reveals, in miniature, the Christian vision of this book.

Secular Wisdom, the Esprit *of University or College*

Although the eight constituencies of the university (the nation, the local state, the international community of scholars, faculty, student body, parents-alumni, administrators-staff, and the religious founding group) establish or authorize the university, they are not its constitution, nor its intrinsic authority. Any university's autonomous authority comes from fulfilling well its dual intrinsic aims (its *raison d'être*), which are (1) to persistently reinterpret the truth of all the specialized knowledges-skills-arts within the university's various departments and (2) to continually develop secular wisdom within the university community. This is the superstructure of the university. These two aims can be fulfilled because (a) the faculty, building on the particular university's *traditio*, is competent in knowledge, teaching, curriculum planning, and university visioning; (b) the university administration prudently uses these resources; (c) the student body intelligently cooperates with the faculty and the administration; and (d) the university, in gratitude to its constituencies, is attaining these dual intrinsic aims, which have been set by the constituencies, and, thus, is serving the constituencies well. This is the infrastructure of the university.

But the university's reason for existing is fully actualized only if its wisdom community is building the institutional side of the university according to a strong secular wisdom. Such wisdom consists of the overview of all the specialized knowledges-skills-arts, the critical underview of their presuppositions and limits, and the implementation, in decisive actions and procedures, of the values discovered by philosophy, theology, and common-sense knowledge in the truths of the specialized disciplines. Within this framework, academic freedom is the liberty of the university to be itself, to grow according to its own constitutional aims (superstructure), and to perform its proper functions (infrastructure) without undue interference from any other institution, such as government, business, church, or labor union.

But how does the university strive to realize its dual intrinsic aims without becoming schizoid? Fortunately, these aims minister to each other. For the first, or institutional, aim is dominant when the specialized knowledges-skills-arts are used immediately to serve the civic community, when they offer values recognized by the wisdom community, and when the dialectic between the specialized knowledges yields the unity of a wisdom-insight. On the other hand, the communal (wisdom) aim is dominant when wisdom animates the pursuit of the specialized disciplines or unifies the findings of those disciplines or directs those disciplines in service to the civic community. This last function points to the extrinsic aim of the university, which is the competent service of the eight constituencies in their needs and hopes. The extrinsic aim, of course, can be well achieved only if the dual intrinsic aims are competently and vigorously pursued, even though the extrinsic aim does offer stimulation, practical insight, and opportunity for recognizing speculative principles. The basis for the reciprocity among all three aims of the university is that the same skilled persons are present in the institution's specialized departments, in the community of wisdom, and in the university's practical response to the needs of its constituencies. Thus, the university is really the exteriorization of the wisdom community's collective personality, or *esprit de corps*.

Again, however, the question rises: How does Christian wisdom enrich the university so that it can become a better university in the pursuit of its dual intrinsic aims and its single extrinsic aim? To understand this, let us first sketch the substance of that secular wisdom which Christian wisdom enlivens through the faith life of the university community.

At its highest or speculative level, secular wisdom is an integration of all the physical and social sciences along with literature, technical skills, and the fine arts, through the mediation of not only philosophies of science-technology-art, but also a metaphysics-epistemology and a theology. At a second or middle level, this speculative integration descends into middle intelligible principles and discovers a hierarchy of values (the continuities, or absolutes, of life) that are to be implemented with concrete decisions in order to change unique situations for the better. These middle principles require a moral integration—a wholesome living ac-

430

cording to justice, courage, and temperance—as well as a focusing of all the relevant first-level speculative knowledge upon the historical situation that is to be changed. Thus, at the third level, the level of the situation itself, the resultant disciplined liberty enables the knowledges-skills-arts, by way of common-sense experience, to decisively enter the historical events with commitment and hope, and to modify these events for better living.

Thus, just as all the specialized disciplines rose as distinct, out of a common-sense knowledge of unique situations according to myth or vision, they now return as integrated and as envalued to re-enter the situation so that it can be intelligently and lovingly changed. Secular wisdom, then, as it rises out of common-sense knowledge and the pursuit of the specialized disciplines, reaches a total vision, or overview, of the world. Then it descends, with this integrated view, through middle principles and values to the unique situation. These middle principles and rules first been discovered as distinct on the way up to a total vision, were redis-covered and hierarchically integrated as they were applied on the way back down to the unique situation. When secular wisdom is regularly employed, it directs and promotes the whole secularization-secularity process. Secular wisdom is, then, a concrete knowledge of the real situation by means of the highest knowledges-skills-arts. It also includes two other major factors: (a) an awareness, in a mature disciplined liberty, of the deepest values of life; and (2) an ability to preserve and use this knowledge and these values so as to skillfully and artfully bring some good into a particular historical event in accord with a grand vision of universe, humankind, and God. In this context, contemplation suffuses action and action enriches contemplation.

Such a secular wisdom could live only in a cooperating community like a university; no single person could come close to this performance and remain a human being. For this reason, secular wisdom could be only the interior *esprit*, the collective personality, of the university community as it daily builds its university. It is this wisdom that holds the university together as both an institution and a community. If secular wisdom disin-tegrates in a university, the university breaks up into rival duchies fighting against one another for power, funds, and recognition, and, within each duchy, individuals viciously grapple for the same three trea-sures. Besides, secular wisdom maintains continuity with the heritage of the past *(traditio)* and hands it on to the present generation precisely when this wisdom skillfully applies past knowledges-skills-arts and values to new situations. In this way, secular wisdom directs the building of the future. Secular wisdom, then, is a protector and a promoter of the com-monweal, the organized public good.

Christian Wisdom Enriches Secular Wisdom

Given this richness of secular wisdom, what could Christian wisdom possibly add so that any university that already possesses secular wisdom would be further enriched and strengthened? It is not enough to say that Christian wisdom is nothing but secular wisdom suffused with the Christian faith-life. Such a neat package must be unwrapped, and its contents must be spread out on the table and examined.

First, because faith is at the center of Christian wisdom and must be lived with *caritas* in the day-to-day experiences of an American scientific-technical-artistic culture having a rich destiny, the following conclusions can be drawn. (1) The Christian theology that, at the heart of Christian wisdom, is interpreting this culture in terms of faith, must be in constant touch with all the specialized knowledges-skills-arts through its Christian philosophy. (2) Common-sense experience must be the source and the term of this Christian wisdom if it is to be lived daily. (3) A concrete supermyth, or Christian vision, must be used to touch upon Christ and, hence, to peer into the Trinity's life by way of this more abstract Christian philosophy and theology, so that the Christian community's daily life can be practically Christ-like and Trinitarian. (4) If *caritas*, self-sacrificing love of God and of others, is the core of Christ's Gospel message, then Christian wisdom must promote this love through the wisdom-gift of the Holy Spirit and must, likewise, guide this love into building a better university and, hence, a better civilization—one that is more humane and thus more able to image Christ. (5) In all of this, Christian wisdom, being in steady contact with fundamental philosophy and theology, should be convinced of the convergence of truths, of the value of the unique event or person, and of the meaning of human history—three solid reasons for hoping in the future of humanity and in the future of the university.

Thus, given the first conclusion, one would say that Christian wisdom, by using a scientific Christian theology, reinforces the importance of each special discipline and also indicates the need for both the reinterpretation of each discipline and the integration of all disciplines into an overview called "secular wisdom at the highest level." In this way, Christian wisdom offers secular wisdom a final home in Trinitarian life and an ultimate appreciation in the risen Christ, who is Wisdom Itself and the Lord of History. Given the second conclusion, one would say that the stress of Christian wisdom on the pivotal importance of common-sense knowledge can keep the specialists humble in their knowledge and realistically wise in their applications of that knowledge. Besides, Christian wisdom breathes with scriptural truth, which is a divine wisdom incorporating many humble values that are operative in daily living. The risen Christ actually is this wisdom living within each believer and guiding his or her daily decisions. The third conclusion implies that the Christian vision, which rises within Christian wisdom, is living off previous historical Christian communities, since the *traditio* must be used even as Christian wisdom is being reinterpreted to meet the changing times and the daily needs of humankind. Furthermore, this conclusion implies that the rich mystery of the Trinity is luring us, through Christ the teacher, into a future that will reveal many more aspects of Trinitarian life, the life destined for all human beings.

The fourth conclusion means that, when Christian wisdom promotes and guides *caritas* in the university community, it provides "heart," that is, greater sensitivity to values and persons, warmer loyalty to friends, and stronger trust in the community and its work. Allied with *caritas*, Christian wisdom also furnishes additional motivation for serving the community's needs and hopes. Thus it strengthens the disciplined liberty of the university. As a result, the university's services are practical, despite tensions, energy depletion, and sufferings. Given the fifth conclusion, one can say that conscious contact with fundamental philosophy and theology can render Christian wisdom highly aware of history as directional, quite sensitive to truth as both converging and noncontradictory, and very alert to each unique person and event as invaluable. These three characteristics enable Christian wisdom to encourage the total university enterprise of reinterpreting each special discipline, integrating all disciplines into a secular wisdom, and applying the disciplines patiently and prudently to the singular events and situations of the moment. According to these five conclusions, then, one can see how Christian wisdom can enrich any university's secular wisdom with a clearer perspective and destiny for the specialized disciplines and with significant additions to secular wisdom in its totality. Thus, the dual intrinsic aims of the university are reinforced and enriched by Christian wisdom.

Earlier, however, we insisted that the third gift of Christian wisdom to any university is better unity and growth. What does this mean? First, Christian wisdom is at home with pluralism of doctrine and of value systems because its inner conviction is that all true doctrines and value systems, insofar as they do not contradict themselves or one another, will eventually converge into the one risen Christ, Wisdom Itself, just as the unique event of Christ's birth acts as the pivotal point of all time and space. Such a conviction is meant to offer the basis of peace for departmental factions or for rival schools within the university so that the university can truly be a university. Secondly, this conviction is also based, of course, on the steady contact of Christian wisdom with fundamental philosophy and theology as well as on Christian wisdom's firm grasp of those absolutes that give continuity to history, friendships, and academic conversations. In addition, Christian wisdom does not abandon analogical knowledge, which makes possible metaphysics, epistemology, and philosophy of science, and which, indeed, makes possible sharing among distinct disciplines, among academic committees, and between practical common-sense knowledge and theoretical knowledge. Lastly, Christian wisdom, insofar as it is in steady contact with all the specialized knowledges-skills-arts by way of Christian philosophy and theology, is present to the whole university, precisely in the university's structure as a community of truth-seekers. All of these sources of unity are precisely what make *traditio* possible for diverse generations within the university; likewise, they are exactly what makes possible a dominant, unified vision of the university to provide guidance to administrators and staff. For these reasons, Christian wisdom could well be the *esprit de corps* of a university and could well enhance the secular wisdom that is acting as the *esprit* of a university. Indeed, this *esprit de corps*, this dynamic unity of Christian wisdom, when it is focused according to the intrinsic aims of the university, becomes the very intrinsic justice of the university—still another source of unity.

These aspects of unity, of course, make for the better growth of the university. Other aspects of Christian wisdom, however, also promote growth. A Christian vision, the supermodel for administrative decisions, for example, not only can dominate other subordinate models to instill strong unity in this university, but also can do this without becoming a strife-provoking ideology. Why? First, because this Christian vision projects the university's future along the strong lines offered by a Christian philosophy and theology, both of which are in close touch with all the academic disciplines; second, because this vision works out of a Christian wisdom that is rooted in historic *traditio* and community; and, third, because, for these reasons, this vision can elicit passionate dedication and not, like an ideology, reduce freedom of decision and hamper truth. Hence, growth is stimulated and encouraged; in addition, other, more complete supermodels can be generated.

Christian wisdom also fosters in the university a disciplined liberty that, in turn, encourages cooperation. For disciplined liberty, being the power to rigorously pursue truth and to vigorously seek good, is a self-sacrificing attitude characterized by both joy (if it is genuine) and self-effacement. There are few attitudes more elicitive of cooperation than this one—elicitive of the cooperation that not only holds the university together, but also builds and crowns it with glory. At the center of this cooperation is the Christian wisdom-vision: Christ, the risen Lord of History who holds all past knowledges-skills-arts in His presence as He views the future; yet the compassionate Christ who knew well the cold

434

shock of evil in His crucifixion; the Christ whose birth was a marriage between God and mankind so that God became human and humanity was divinized; the Christ whose marriage to the world fosters the physical sciences, whose forming of the Mystical Body fosters the social sciences, whose serving of the community fosters the technical sciences, whose teaching role fosters theology, whose hidden life of day labor fosters respect for common-sense knowledge, and whose name (the Word) signifies that He embodies the dynamic plan according to which the world was and is being created. Thus, for Christian wisdom, Christ is present in all human activity. His living presence works through the community for the humanization of the world; His person cherishes, therefore, all the accomplishments of the university community and preserves them within His own being. Thus, in addition to all the secular factors that unify the university and help it to grow, there are the further elements of growth— namely, the inventive Christian vision, the disciplined liberty of selfless cooperation, called *caritas*, and the Christian wisdom-vision of Christ, the Lord of History.

Christian Wisdom Animates the University

From these first three gifts of Christian wisdom—namely, clearer perspective and destiny for the specialized disciplines, richer wisdom for the university community, and better unity and growth for the university— one recognizes how much Christian wisdom can do for the intrinsic unity, or autonomous constitution, of the university's dual intrinsic aims. As we now move to the fourth gift of Christian wisdom—the enablement of the university to better serve its constituencies out of justice—we touch on the extrinsic aim of the university. Clearly, the university has justice as its very internal structure insofar as it fulfills its dual intrinsic aims, that is, insofar as it is expert in all its specialized disciplines and insofar as it enjoys a wisdom that arises out of both the integration of these disciplines and the hierarchizing of values. (Of course, these values have been recognized in the disciplines by philosophy, theology, and common-sense knowledge.) But what of the justice of the university toward its eight constituencies? In other words, what of the university's single extrinsic aim? The fullness of Christian wisdom can certainly enable the university to have its knowledges-skills-arts and its secular wisdom in highly competent readiness. But will Christian wisdom ensure an equally competent and strong application of them to the needs of the constituencies?

In response, it can be said that the disciplined liberty that ensures the university of the intricate cooperation that is needed for the internal unity

435

and growth of the university can now, out of gratitude and justice, be turned to service of the constituencies. The scriptural wisdom, which is included in Christian wisdom, powerfully calls forth compassion for the world's *anawim*, the defenseless ones, and then points the Christian's attention to Christ's desire to give every human being a fair chance. Furthermore, the *caritas* of the gospels warms the Christian wisdom of the university and thus uses this wisdom to intelligently structure justice so that, while justice in turn structures the decisions that are coming out of Christian wisdom, *caritas* brings these decisions beyond justice to remarkable generosity. In doing this, *caritas*, the unifier of all human virtues, integrates the faith in Christian wisdom with justice so that the constituencies are well served. Thus, the sense of stewardship grows as *traditio* now occurs not only within the university community, but also between it and the civic community. Because Christian wisdom has structured and guided both *caritas* and justice, it now increases, within the extrinsic aim of the university, the dynamic force for good in the civic community. Reciprocally, this dynamizing of the extrinsic aim not only stimulates new insights in specialized disciplines, but also drives the university toward new wisdom syntheses. Thus, the shared influences among the three aims of the university become strikingly evident. In this way, the university community moves toward a deepened sense of all reality.

It is worth noting that Christian wisdom is also effective in eliciting interest in the service of the eight constituencies because the Christian theology within Christian wisdom will always have its third pastoral phase focusing this interest and motivating it. It has already been seen that when the administrator promotes the uniqueness of the university with his or her decisions, he or she may well be fulfilling the destined mission of the university according to both its dual intrinsic aims and its extrinsic aim, since all three aims reciprocally affect one another in action and in growth. It is, however, through the influence of campus ministry that Christian wisdom can most effectively promote the extrinsic aim of the university. For all the varied activities of campus ministry, as they try to elicit wholeness from each individual and from the total community, become the intense focusing of operative Christian wisdom. Such focusing reaches its highest intensity in the liturgy, wherein one witnesses the marriage of secular and sacred, of contemplative and active. In the liturgy, both the individual Christian and his or her university community can learn of their wholeness with the local and national civic communities and with the international communities of First, Second, Third, and Fourth Worlds. Thus, the liturgy funnels centuries of accumulated wisdom and contemplation-in-action into one moment of Godliness and, then, sends the community out to gather truth, to fashion wisdom, and to pass all this on to the next generation.

This whole process of the *traditio* of Christian wisdom is actually Christian secularization, that is to say, it is the development of distinct scientific disciplines out of common-sense knowledge and their subsequent integration according to a Christian vision. But the process of Christian wisdom also includes the concomitant evolving of new values and their integration in a secularity or value system. This fifth gift of Christian wisdom explains why Christian universities strongly emphasize, at the undergraduate level, the combination of a liberal arts curriculum with a major, or vocational, study so that the student has some grasp of the secularization-secularity process and, thus, some feel for what Christian wisdom is. It also accounts for the fact that Christian universities find graduate departments so important to the educational process; these departments foster the specialization of knowledges-skills-arts and, it is hoped, will form a community of wisdom rather than become hyperspecialized in the disciplines, parochialized in viewpoint, and fragmented in person.

Furthermore, Christian wisdom encompasses the whole secularizing dialectic that runs between the lower pole of the Christian's common-sense knowledge and the upper pole of his or her faith experience in Christ. Mediating between these two poles are the upward development of the specialized disciplines and the downward development of their integration as secular wisdom. This mediation works, of course, under the guiding light of Christian philosophy and theology and with the probing light of Christian vision. The process has one aim, namely, to render each person and each community more wholesome, that is, more human. This process is salvation history in the making. Consequently, operative Christian wisdom, in this guise of secularization and secularity, is a strong facilitator of the university life processes as well as an able builder of the university as institution and as community. Indeed, Christian wisdom turns out to be the total educating of the human person to the godly and the worldly and the human, versus the counterprocess of desecularization, the fragmentation of the person and the community. Within Christian wisdom, then, secularization is the persistent use of all knowledges-skills-arts to explore the ultimate mystery of the human and the divine; the secularity process is the dedication of the Christian community's life to God, world, and humankind because of the intrinsic value of each and out of loyalty to Christ. In this way, Christian wisdom is not only the *path*, but also the *light* for this path toward the future destiny of the human race—namely, union with God and with the great community of the saints.

437

From the previously discussed five gifts of Christian wisdom, it can readily be seen how Christian wisdom gifts the administration and the staff for their decisions concerning the running of the university. For Christian wisdom, insofar as it clarifies, reaffirms, and enriches the three aims of the university, illuminates and gives direction to the decision-making process of the administrator. In addition, Christian wisdom keeps the administrator aware of the *traditio* of the past, wherein the roots of the university gain their food for future growth, and it reassures the administrator that the university is truly a university. For, like a great tree, its growth is capable of controlled balance rather than wild sprawl.

There is more than this to the sixth gift of Christian wisdom. For the Christian vision that arises out of Christian wisdom enables the administrator to make sound decisions for the future. This occurs because this Christian vision comes out of a Christian philosophy and a Christian theology, both of which are in close touch with the specialized disciplines. Furthermore, this vision achieves its unity by way of the overview offered by a Christian wisdom which is suffused with secular wisdom. As a supermodel for controlling the use of subordinate decision-making models, this Christian wisdom frees the administrator from ideology because this vision is at home with the pluralism of doctrine and value system that is contained in all the subordinate models for decision. Yet, at the same time, Christian vision is dominant, that is to say, it offers a unified view for focusing administrative decisions. In other words, this Christian vision encourages the administrator to be inventive, and yet it furnishes him or her with the stability to take the criticism that is always invited by inventiveness.

Indeed, Christian vision is closely allied with the disciplined liberty of *caritas* so that it can elicit passionate allegiance for both the goals and the ventures of the university as these ventures are incarnated in administrative decisions. This is vitally needed by the administrator, since his or her decisions, if truly inventive, are rendering the university unique and enabling it to fulfill its unique mission among its eight constituencies. Christian vision, to be sure, is far from being an absolutely certain guide against all administrative mistakes and fiascoes; yet it is a trustworthy guide into the ever more complicated future of the twentieth century, and it is able to rally the university community to its Christian vocation. The administrator, then, by directing the Christian secularization-secularity process in the university, is like a trusted counselor who facilitates the marriage of God and His people. The administrator is also like a parent whose decisions make Christ's presence more palpable in people's lives; the administrator is even like a priest who encourages sacrificial *caritas* as expressive of the community's *esprit de corps*, namely, its Christian wisdom. This is the role of the administrator when he or she sees Christ, Wisdom Itself, as the convergence point for the university community, for all its specialized disciplines, for all the levels of the wisdom process, for the university's future planning, and for the service of the eight constituencies. Thus Christ, the focal point, becomes a window into the life of the Triune God. In this life, the unified plurality of the three divine persons makes the administrator at home with convergent pluralism or communal personalism or coresponsibility with God for the world or analogical wisdom or a sense of destiny in one's decisions or spontaneous creativity in building the university. Yet, in all this, the administrator is faced with the overwhelming mystery of Eternity in time, of the Absolute amid seemingly total relativity, of great Tranquillity within passionate concern. This mystery, which is at the summit of Christian wisdom, has paradoxical influence; the administrator can feel free to take the chance of making unforgettably huge mistakes and yet experience the strongest sense of responsibility. Here, he or she finds ultimate stability amid swirling events. This sixth gift is no small gift for the university community, to say nothing of its importance for the administrator.

The seventh and last gift is the religious founding group (RFG) whose importance looms larger when one considers that the RFG is the reason why the Christian university or college came into existence, why it came into existence rooted in Christian wisdom, and why it has remained a Christian university or college. For the RFG, with its four levels of participation in university life, does give continuity and richness to the Christian wisdom process. If its role is modeled on that of a Dutch uncle, then it subtly exerts influence on the growth of the university without the slightest tampering with the autonomous intrinsic authority or the constitution of the university or college; rather, the RFG strengthens the university's constitution with the wisdom and disciplined liberty that have their source in Christ. At the same time, the RFG can be for the university a model of both the practical faith community and the speculative Christian wisdom community. Such *communio* between RFG and university is possible because church and university share a similarity of aims and models and because their differences minister to each other's weaknesses. In addition, the RFG can be a wise mediator between church and university, since its copresence in the two institutions enables it to appreciate the wealth of intelligence and compassion in both communities and, at the same time, recognize the limitations of both.

Furthermore, the RFG can promote Christian wisdom within the university only on the condition that the institutional university is free to follow the truth wherever it leads. Only in this way can the university community accumulate that secular wisdom out of which rises Christian wisdom as faith life; only in this way can the RFG be a free, prophetic voice within the university community and toward the civic community. Would the Christ of Christian wisdom, the prophet of Judea and the Lord of History, want it any other way? For the RFG could be the incarnate proof that Christian wisdom is the unique contribution of the Christian university to academe and to the university's eight constituencies. The RFG's Christian vision, expressed in its communal life at the heart of the university, can be the basis for solid hope in the future of the Christian university. Truly, this is the seventh and last gift of Christian wisdom.

These, then, are the seven gifts of Christian wisdom to the university— (1) clearer perspective and destiny, (2) richer wisdom, (3) better union and growth, (4) fuller service of the eight constituencies, (5) better Christian secularization of students, (6) stronger intelligence and heart in administrative decisions, and (7) an RFG that fosters greater continuity and stability for the Christian university community. Is this really a Christian vision of the university? Is it one for living, enjoying, and suffering on behalf of the university and its constituencies? Never does one feel the certainty that is desired. Only talent, work, time, and Christ will, in unison, give us the answer.

Epilog

In part III of chapter 1, we asked many questions about the university and about the Christian spirit within a university. Have any of these questions been answered—even partially? If there were some partial answers and if they began to interweave within the reader's mind to form a Christian tapestry, a Christian vision, then this book has not been written in vain. It is acknowledged from the beginning that such a vision is only one among other possible visions. But if it helps the reader to sort out some of the major principles that structure the university and face the major problems confronting the Christian university, this book has attained its first aim.

Furthermore, if this analysis has brought the reader to see dynamic relations between the major principles and the major problems of the university, so that he or she recognizes the sources of his or her Christian vision, then the book has reached its second aim. If the reader can, then, so articulate his or her vision that it begins to affect his or her planning for reorganization of the Christian university or college, a third aim has been gained. Even if the reader comes away from this book with merely increased respect for the potential of the Christian university, a fourth hope for this book has been fulfilled. Or, if the reader feels more confidence in his or her heart for the next day's university work, then a fifth goal has been touched. Finally, if only one reader were stimulated, out of anger or any other noble motive, to write another book on the Christian university in order to correct or devastate this book, then the author could take deep satisfaction in being a gadfly in the Socratic tradition.

As this book ends and as any action affected by it begins in the university community, would the following prayer be out of place?

God, our Father,
You are the warm wisdom at the expanding center of the great
 universe
as well as at the radiating center of each person's heart.
And we, your daughters and sons, have gathered here to do
 university work

in the hope of increasing, at least slightly, the sense of personal
  dignity
and the awareness of freedom.
We hope to accomplish this with the help of your illuminating
and liberating wisdom.

And so, Father,
  May our effort in the university contribute that intelligence
  and that encouragement-to-confidence which is
    so necessary to free and wise discussion in classrooms and at
      seminar tables,
    so necessary to free and wise decisions at business and
      government meetings,
    so necessary to free and wise worship in our church assemblies.
Father,
  May our efforts not remove one set of handcuffs in order to
    substitute a second pair, more subtly contrived;
  may our efforts not replace the violence of twisted arm and
    barbwire
  with the quieter violence of indoctrination and carefully cultured
    prejudice.
  Instead, God our Father, please teach us the liberty of the sons
and
    daughters of God—
  You who let the sun shine and the rain fall on both the good and
    the wicked.
  Please teach us how to value deeply the people we meet in day-to-
    day living
  and how, consequently, to esteem the value of each person's work,
  and to respect the value of his or her values even when they differ
    from our own.

And yet, Lord,
  let us not change our values lightly;
  help us to struggle faithfully for their growth in ourselves and
  in those who likewise treasure these values.

But Lord,
  When all is said and done in our university lives,
  it will be your wisdom that will illumine our values and
  make clear whether they form the pearl of great price;
  it will be your freedom working through us

that will accomplish any liberation of man and of woman;
it will be your strength out of which will spring our purposeful
     energy
to help ourselves and others find meaning in our lives and in their
     lives.

Without the strong joy of your presence in our work and in our
     leisure,
we may well sink back into tired defeat and bondage.
But with your joy-giving presence, we can continue striving to
     enhance a bit
the values and liberties of our universities, of our peoples, and of
     our civilization.

Please be with us, Lord God, Emmanuel. Amen.

End Notes

Because this book is an extended essay, I have not used footnotes; the text is not the definitive result of much research covering vast fields of literature on the subject. I do feel indebted, however, to many people for their thoughtful work and I would like to acknowledge this debt in the following series of end notes.

Notes to the Introduction

"A Bibliography on Catholic/Church-Related Higher Education, 1968–1978" has been compiled by Sr. Marian Brady, S.P., for the Association of Catholic Colleges and Universities, Suite # 770, One Dupont Circle, Washington, DC, 20036, in June 1979. The brief descriptions of philosophy, Christian philosophy, and Christian theology are more fully developed in chapters 7, 8, and 9; the end notes for each chapter will offer indications of source materials. Concerning the "vision painted by Teilhard de Chardin," W. Henry Kenney's *A Path Through Teilhard's Phenomenon* (Dayton, Ohio: Pflaum, 1970, pp. 28–30) stresses the "seeing" of the vast past as it moves into the future. Teilhard de Chardin's preface to *The Phenomenon of Man* (New York: Harper and Row, 1961, pp. 28–31) expressly denies any attempt at metaphysics or theology; rather, it asserts that this work is a scientific treatise, a kind of hyperphysics, but that its *vision* can appear to be something else since science, philosophy, and religion do converge as they draw nearer to the totality of being, the whole. This sense of vision is strongly stressed by Perry LeFevre in "Teilhard's Vision of Man," *The Chicago Theological Seminary Register* 55 (December 1964, pp. 1–9).

Notes to Chapter 1

Information in this chapter comes mainly from encyclopedia articles that have enabled me to see seven basic patterns in the developing

American university and college. Section I, "A Short History of the American University," was derived principally from the *New Catholic Encyclopedia* article on "Higher Education (U.S.)," (Vol. VI, pp. 1103–1111); from the *Encyclopedia Americana* articles on "Colleges and Universities," International Edition (Vol. VII, pp. 240–262) and "Education, History of" (pp. 650–657); and, finally, from the *New Encyclopaedia Britannica Macropaedia* article, "Education, History of" 15th ed., (pp. 317–408). Section II, "Five Great University Models," came principally from the *Encyclopaedia Britannica Macropaedia* article on "Higher Education" (Vol. VIII, pp. 857–867). Not a few scholars hold to the importance of a sixth model, the Scottish University, especially for the United States. On this point, see Douglas Sloan's *The Scottish Enlightenment and the American College Ideal* (New York: Teachers College Press of Columbia University, 1971). The lively, practical remarks of Jacques Barzun in *The American University* (New York: Harper and Row, 1968) still carry a sting for present university living.

Notes to Chapter 2

Edward Shils, in three lectures entitled "Government and Universities in the United States: the Eighth Jefferson Lecture in the Humanities" (London: *Minerva* 17, Spring 1979, pp. 129–177), defends the autonomy and unique enterprise of the university as it struggles to maintain a balance between government interference in university hiring and its own obligations toward the citizenry and the government. The intricacies of obtaining financial support from all the constituencies of the university are clearly explained by the long-time president of St. Louis University, Paul Reinert, as he tries *To Turn the Tide* (Englewood Cliffs, NJ: Prentice-Hall, 1972). Steven Muller's "A New American University?" *Daedalus* 107 (Winter 1978, pp. 31–45) explores the need for a new relationship between the American research university and the federal government so that the university can preserve its autonomy and yet cooperate closely with the government, which, alone, can furnish sufficient funding for long-term, expensive, basic research. John O. Riedl, in his *The University in Process* (Milwaukee: Marquette University Press, 1965), sketches the discrepancies as one compares the current practices of the university with its historical functions when, for example, the university was the sole agency for the advancement of learning, the education of clerics, and the determination of professional education and standards.

Notes to Chapter 3

A delicate balance between science and wisdom, institutional and communal, disciplined responsibility and academic freedom, church and civic society, is achieved in the Vatican Council II document, *The Church in the Modern World* (*Gaudium et Spes*, no. 53–62). A specific implementation of this document, in one area, is witnessed in *The Catholic University in the Modern World*, a statement of the Congress of Delegates of the Catholic Universities of the World at Rome, November 20–29, 1972 (*College Newsletter* 35, of the National Catholic Educational Association, March 1973, pp. 1–10). The application of this to the United States is spelled out by the American Bishops in "Catholic Higher Education and the Church's Pastoral Mission," *Origins* 10 (National Catholic News Service, Washington, DC, November 27, 1980, pp. 378–384). Pope John Paul II's speech at Catholic University on October 6, 1979—"Excellence, Truth, and Freedom in Catholic Universities," *Origins* 9 (National Catholic News Service, Washington, DC, October 25, 1979, pp. 306–308) puts heavy emphasis on the Christian wisdom community of any Catholic university. The responsibility of Jesuit universities to their civic communities is delineated in terms of justice by William Byron's "Stewardship, Justice, and the Religious Purpose in Education" (*Review for Religious* 38, Jan.–Feb. 1979, pp. 3–12).

In *The Lure of Wisdom* (Milwaukee: Marquette University Press, 1962), James Collins outlines the Renaissance and Cartesian understandings of wisdom and then contrasts them with contemporary approaches to wisdom. The history of the concept of wisdom, taken as secular and as sacred, is neatly summed up by Eugene Biser in his article "Wisdom" in *Sacramentum Mundi*, vol. 6, (New York: Herder and Herder, 1970, pp. 359–362). The relationship between the societal (institutional) and communal is searched out by John Cowburn in *The Person and Love* (Staten Island, NY: Alba House, 1967, pp. 157–8, 187–8, 369–7). Josef Pieper's *Prudence* (New York: Pantheon, 1959) articulates how the ethical virtues of justice, temperance, and courage are directed by prudence so that concrete wisdom decisions can occur. James Gustafson's "The University as a Community of Moral Discourse," *Journal of Religion* 53 (1973, pp. 397–409), asks the following of the university community: (1) greater critical sophistication in exchanges about morality, (2) fuller cooperation among specialists from all disciplines in discussions, (3) greater awareness of the educative value of such discussion (greater wisdom?). The variations of Christian wisdom (Roman, Germanic, Celtic, Spanish Medieval, secular) are seen historically in Albert Mirgeler's *Mutations of Western Christianity* (London: Burns & Oates, 1961).

Notes to Chapter 4

A convergent pluralism presupposes that the universe is developing according to a single ultimate purpose. Because of his fear of F. H. Bradley's and Josiah Royce's absolute monism, William James calls convergent pluralism into question in his *Pragmatism* (Cleveland: World Publishing, 1968, pp. 89–108) and unwillingly ends up with a pluralistic theism (cf. James Collins, *God in Modern Philosophy*, Chicago: Regnery, 1959, pp. 298–314). Implicitly, Thomas Kuhn risks the same fate, since his *The Structure of Scientific Revolutions* (Chicago: University of Chicago Press, 1962) would seem to assert radical discontinuity between scientific paradigms. Such discontinuity is an example of divergent pluralism. But Ian Barbour's *Issues in Science and Religion* (Englewood Cliffs, NJ: Prentice-Hall, 1966, pp. 130–270) objectively describes a unifying spectrum of knowledge that stretches between physics and religion; subjectively, Viktor Frankl in his *Man's Search for Meaning* (New York: Washington Square Press, 1965, pp. 154–58) points to the dynamic unifying of the human personality and of its activities as it looks to the cause, the person, the God of its love. Indeed, a philosophy of secularization requires that pluralistic specialization be balanced by a subsequent integrative socialization (a convergent plurality) at all levels of society (cf. Frank Yartz, Allan Larson, David Hassel, *Progress and the Crisis of Man*, Chicago: Nelson-Hall, 1976, pp. 31–78). This convergence appears to be the underlying measure of Étienne Gilson's *Unity of Philosophical Experience* (New York: Scribner's, 1937, pp. 318–320) for calibrating that unity called *philosophia perennis*.

Peter Berger's *Rumor of Angels* (Garden City: Doubleday-Anchor, 1970) presents, from the standpoint of sociology of knowledge, a strong case for relativistic pluralism but then criticizes this divergent pluralism by establishing a framework of perduring values and understandings. In the classic *Christ and Culture* (New York: Harper and Row, 1951), H. Richard Niebuhr would converge his five models of explanation for the Christian's attitude toward culture upon the one absolute, God; but how could this be accomplished in day-to-day living unless the models themselves are convergent?

In the Catholic sphere, Robert Harvanek, in "Philosophical Pluralism and Catholic Orthodoxy," *Thought* 25 (March 1950, pp. 21–52), has analyzed the French Jesuit struggle with the Roman theologians over the meaning of historical pluralism for *philosophia perennis* and for theology. Then, he has evaluated whether or not the analogical nature of reality and of human judgment demands pluralism and yet points to a *philosophia perennis* ("The Unity of Metaphysics," *Thought* 28, Autumn, 1953, pp. 375–412), which, ultimately, may be accounted for by a Roycean communal dialectic of truth ("The Community of Truth," *International Philosophical Quarterly* 7, March 1967, pp. 68–85). Bernard Lonergan (in *Doctrinal Pluralism*. Milwaukee: Marquette University Press, 1971) distinguishes as many as sixteen differentiations of consciousness (e.g., stages of growth, common sense, science, religious, etc.) that naturally induce pluralism of understanding, even though reality is basically one.

Notes to Chapter 5

Karl Mannheim's *Ideology and Utopia* (New York: Harcourt, Brace and World, 1936) is a foundational work for sociology of knowledge and an historically important study of the role of ideology in society. The term *ideology* is meticulously traced through its ambiguous historical usages by John Plamenatz in *Ideology* (New York: Praeger, 1970). The work I used in this extended essay is Lewis Feuer's *Ideology and the Ideologists* (New York: Harper and Row, 1975). In *Ideologies* (London: Hutchinson, 1965, pp. 55–140), Patrick Corbett takes Christian faith to be simply an ideology used for power politics. Peter Berger and Thomas Luckmann, in the *Social Construction of Reality* (Garden City, NY: Doubleday-Anchor, 1967, pp. 15, 123–26), place common-sense "knowledge," rather than ideas, at the center of the sociology of knowledge and thus relegate ideology and utopian thinking to its periphery.

One's personal vision, or unified life-ideal, is the most powerful knowledge-factor in making decisions—such is the conclusion of Johannes Lindworsky in *The Training of the Will* (Milwaukee: Bruce, 1929). How Christian vision issues out of the analogical imagination (the realism of which is the source of all hope) is a central problem for William Lynch in *Christ and Apollo* (New York: Sheed and Ward, 1960) and in *Images of Hope* (Baltimore: Helicon Press, 1965).

Notes to Chapter 6

Though a person may disagree basically with John Rawl's *A Theory of Justice* (Cambridge: Harvard University Press, 1971), he or she must admit that Rawls has incisively drawn the reciprocal influences that are operative between justice, liberty, the good (love), and discipline (well ordered society). Étienne Gilson's *The Christian Philosophy of Saint Augustine* (New York: Random House, 1960, especially pp. 161–64 and footnote 85) shows us how the "schoolmaster of Europe" makes the careful distinction between freedom and liberty a basic strut in his theory of education. Meanwhile, Bernard Lonergan's *Insight* (New York: Philosophical Library, 1957, passim but especially p. 632) recalls how a lack of discipline, that is, the incapacity for sustained development within experience, understanding, judgment, and moral decision, is the source of individual and national collapse. Lonergan's treatise, *Grace and Freedom* (New York: Herder and Herder, 1971), describes the intricate theory by which Thomas Aquinas resolved, for his time, the problem of how the sinner retains his or her freedom while under the influence of grace.

It is the encyclical of Pope John XXIII, *Christianity and Social Progress (Mater et Magistra)*, together with the encyclical of Pope Paul VI, *On the Development of Peoples (Populorum Progressio)*, which underline the disciplined cooperation needed to redress social injustice—a cooperation impossible without the university community's intelligence and dedication. In *Teaching and Morality* (Chicago: Loyola University Press, 1963), Francis Wade demonstrates how the teaching act necessarily conveys values, how learning and moral virtue are simultaneous objectives of the one act of teaching. Robert Roth, in "Colleges Challenge 'Value-Free' Education" (*America*, April 9, 1977, pp. 324–326), has chronicled the surge of interest concerning moral issues among university leaders and has described Fordham University's undergraduate programs for focusing this interest. On the other hand, Gérard Gilleman demonstrates in *The Primacy of Charity in Moral Theology* (Westminster, MD: Newman, 1961, pp. 330–345) that justice, proceeding along the institutional side of life, is completed by *caritas*, or other-centered love, working along the communal side. Walter Kasper's *Jesus the Christ* (New York: Paulist, 1977, p. 87) reiterates this. In recounting the limits of justice, Josef Pieper's *Justice* (New York: Pantheon, 1955, pp. 95–107) describes how justice is completed, in Thomas Aquinas' view, by *religio, pietas, observantia* (respect), and *affabilitas* (friendliness).

Notes to Chapter 7

Although Jacques Maritain is convinced that philosophy is one and perennial, his *Range of Reason* (New York: Scribner's, 1952, pp. 3–50) acknowledges how difficult it is for philosophers to cooperate and for connatural knowledge to be explained according to a fundamental philosophy. In *Issues in Science and Religion* (Englewood Cliffs, NJ: Prentice-Hall, 1966), Ian Barbour spends four chapters establishing a continuous "spectrum of knowledges" as a unified way of understanding the universe. Bernard Lonergan's theory of isomorphism between a person's acts of knowing and the universe so known (*Insight*, New York: Philosophical Library, 1957) implies a single fundamental philosophy. A basis for such unity of knowledge is offered in George Klubertanz's *Saint Thomas Aquinas on Analogy* (Chicago: Loyola University Press, 1960).

The best exposition of historical evidence for *philosophia perennis*, or fundamental philosophy, is in Étienne Gilson's *The Unity of Philosophical Experience* (New York: Scribner's, 1965, pp. 299–320). Robert Harvanek's intriguing article, "Pluralism, Philosophical" in the *New Catholic Encyclopedia* (New York: McGraw-Hill, 1967, pp. 448–451) seems to imply that without the tradition of the universal *philosophia perennis* philosophers have a very difficult time explaining the vast variety of their works. For James Collins (*Three Paths of Philosophy*, Chicago: Regnery, 1962, pp. viii, 255–79, 376–97), a *philosophia perennis*, or fundamental philosophy, cannot be defined in content, but only in a perennial, methodic attitude of openness to truth. Bertrand Russell, with his atomized and severely limited philosophy of premiss-criticism—see, for example, *The Problems of Philosophy* (New York: Oxford University Press, 1959, pp. 141–161) and *Our Knowledge of the External World* (New York: New American Library, 1960)—renders a fundamental philosophy quite impossible.

Clearly, my understanding of what philosophy is comes not simply from Lonergan's *Insight*, but also from Jacques Maritain's *The Degrees of Knowledge* (New York: Scribner's, 1959, 4th ed., Gerald Phelan trans., pp. 35–99), which is fittingly entitled in the French *Distinguer pour Unir*, and from his *On the Use of Philosophy* (New York: Anthenaeum, 1965) in which latter he treats the unity of truth (amid its variety of expressions) as the basis for cooperation among philosophers and between philosophers and scientists. In *The Integrating Mind* (New York: Sheed and Ward, 1962), William Lynch shows the need to mediate patiently between the polarities of political right and left, freedom and law, culture and belief, private and public, transcendent and immanent; this is to be done by discovering that the reality of life is the puzzling and wounding compenetration of these polarities, not their separation by the choice of one over the other.

Richard Rorty makes a strong attack on philosophy as a foundational discipline in *Philosophy and the Mirror of Nature* (Princeton: Princeton University Press, 1979) and in "Pragmatism, Relativism and Irrationalism" (*Proceedings and Addresses of the American Philosophical Association* 53, August 1980, pp. 719–738). Robert Roth replies to this attack in

"Pragmatism and Foundationalism" (*Proceedings of the Forty-Third Annual Convention of the Jesuit Philosophical Association* 1981, pp. 12–39).

The various stages of Walter Lippmann's public philosophy are calibrated in Benjamin Wright's *Five Public Philosophies of Walter Lippmann* (Austin, TX: University of Texas Press, 1973); Clinton Rossiter and James Lare have devotedly made available Lippmann's important writings on public philosophy in *The Essential Lippmann* (New York: Random House, 1963). John Courtney Murray shared Lippmann's concern for the underlying philosophy of the United States in his *We Hold These Truths* (New York: Sheed and Ward, 1960, especially pp. 5–139).

Notes to Chapter 8

The historical development of Christian philosophy, from the Greek apologists to Nicholas of Cusa, is elegantly done by Étienne Gilson in his *History of Christian Philosophy in the Middle Ages* (New York: Random House, 1955). For a sample of the complexity of early Christian philosophy, consult Jean Daniélou's *Origen* (New York: Sheed and Ward, 1955). The educational scene within which Augustine developed his Christian wisdom is richly described by H. I. Marrou in *History of Education in Antiquity* (New York: Sheed and Ward, 1956, pp. 284–350) and *Saint Augustin et la Fin de la Culture Antique* (Paris: Boccard, 1958, Parts II and III). Étienne Gilson's *The Christian Philosophy of Saint Augustine* (New York: Random House, 1960) and *The Christian Philosophy of Saint Thomas* (New York: Random House, 1956) are classic accounts of how Christian philosophy occurs within Christian theology to the mutual enrichment of both. When James Collins considers *God in Modern Philosophy* (Chicago: Regnery, 1959), he delineates, from Nicholas Cusa to Alfred North Whitehead, the gradual distancing between secular and Christian philosophy.

Amid *Philosophical Trends in the Contemporary World* (Notre Dame, Indiana: University of Notre Dame Press, 1964), Michele Sciacca has positioned some modern Christian philosophers and schools, e.g., Maurice Blondel, Gabriel Marcel, and the Neo-Thomisms of Louvain, Milan, and Paris, together with the Neo-Augustinianisms of personalism and Christian philosophy of the spirit. In refutation of Émile Bréhier's charge that Christian philosophy is not an historically observable reality in "Y a-t-il une Philosophie Chrétienne?" (*Revue de Métaphysique et de Morale*, April-June, 1931), Étienne Gilson offers the stunning historical documentation of *The Spirit of Mediaeval Philosophy* (New York: Scribner's, 1936); Jacques *Maritain's An Essay on Christian Philosophy* (New York: Philosophical Library, 1955) refutes Bréhier by distinguishing between the nature and the state of philosophy, and then by demonstrating that moral philosophy is both distinct from and dependent upon Christian revelation and theology—a matter more fully developed in Maritain's *Science et Sagesse* (Paris: Labergerie, 1934).

Anton Pegis muses over the causes of the so-called collapse of Thomistic popularity among Catholic philosophers in his article "Who Reads Aquinas?" (*Thought* 42, December 1967, pp. 488–504). In *Catholic Theology in the Nineteenth Century* (New York: Seabury, 1977), subtitled "The Quest for a Unitary Method," Gerald McCool describes the Roman Catholic church's attempt to limit its theology to an Aristotelian Thomism only to see this attempt stimulate a variety of Thomisms and Augustinianisms. Otto Muck's *The Transcendental Method* (New York: Herder and Herder, 1968) recounts how Transcendental Thomism sprang from Maréchal's wedding of Kant and Aquinas to become the dominant Catholic philosophy. Among the outstanding contemporary Christian philosophers must be numbered James Collins who, from his first major work (*A History of Modern Philosophy*, Milwaukee: Bruce, 1956), has not only analyzed various systematic philosophers with sympathy and fairness, but also genially sketched their personalities and, with depth, criticized their structures in terms of the Thomistic judgment of existence—the dynamic core of the Neo-Thomist revival. This latter matter has been explored historically by Étienne Gilson in *Réalisme Thomiste et Critique de la Connaissance* (New York: Vrin, 1939), textually by Peter Hoenen in *Reality and Judgment According to Saint Thomas* (Chicago: Regnery, 1952), and systematically by Frederick Wilhelmsen in *Man's Knowledge of Reality* (Englewood Cliffs, NJ, Prentice-Hall, 1956).

Notes to Chapter 9

The description of theology in this chapter is much indebted to John Thornhill's "Towards an Integral Theology," *Theological Studies* 24, (June 1963, pp. 264–277) and to Bernard Lonergan's *Method in Theology* (New York: Herder and Herder, 1972); the latter, in describing the eight tasks or functions of theology, dramatically proves the dependence of theology on philosophy and on the social and physical sciences, as well as clearly indicates the remarkable synthesizing powers of theology. Theology and the gift of the Holy Spirit as the peak of wisdom are graphed by Kieran Conley in *A Theology of Wisdom* (Dubuque: Priory Press, 1963). Gerald Van Ackeren distinguishes Aquinas' *Sacra Doctrina* (Rome: Catholic

Book Agency, 1952) from Scripture, its source, and from the habit of sacred theology (supernatural wisdom), its term, in order to clarify how theological wisdom is generated. Against this philosophic-scholastic theology, Jean LeClercq's *The Love of Learning and the Desire for God* (New York: Fordham University Press, 1961, pp. 277–281) sharply contrasts the literary humanism and theology of the monastic culture.

Among Christopher Dawson's many books on Christian culture, *Religion and the Rise of Western Culture* (Garden City, NY: Image-Doubleday, 1957, especially pp. 18–19) shows how Western culture alone, because of the Christian religion, has a missionary character and how, as a result, the dual independence of cultural leadership and political power have provided an atmosphere of dynamic freedom for Western cities and universities. David Tracy endeavors to deal with the freedom of the new pluralism in theology according to five current models of theology, the fifth of these being his own revisionist model (*Blessed Rage for Order,* New York: Seabury, 1975).

On the other hand, Avery Dulles works with pluralism from the angle of *The Survival of Dogma* (Garden City, NY: Doubleday-Image, 1973) as he explores how faith, authority, and dogma are related in the development of dogma. In *Love Alone* (New York: Herder and Herder, 1969), Hans Urs von Balthasar contends that the cosmological and the anthropological approaches to theology are secondary to the approach of self-glorification given by divine love; he describes the contemplation intrinsic to theology in *Prayer* (New York: Paulist, 1961). The various meanings of "fundamental theology" are outlined in *The Development of Fundamental Theology* (Johannes Metz, ed., *Concilium* 46, New York: Paulist Press, 1969)—to which this chapter may have added one more meaning. Johannes Metz, in turn, speaks of his *Faith in History and Society* (New York: Seabury, 1980) as a step toward a practical fundamental theology by way of a political theology.

Notes to Chapter 10

My understanding of the Christian secularization process issues out of "The Church in the Modern World" *(Gaudium et Spes)*. The two underlying principles of Christian secularization found in this document are specialization and socialization (integration) under grace. Bernard Lonergan's *Insight* (New York: Philosophical Library, 1957), together with his later works *Collection* (New York: Herder and Herder, 1967) and *A Second Collection* (Philadelphia: Westminster Press, 1974), offer solid hope for the integration of the sciences with philosophy and theology; this is to be done within historical consciousness and according to the fourth level of intentional analysis (the level of evaluation and love).

My own brief attempt to sketch out a philosophy of secularization is contained in *Progress and the Crisis of Man* (Chicago: Nelson-Hall, 1976, pp. 31–78) and in *Working Papers on Problems in American Life* (Vol. 1, "Secularization, Secularity, and Secularism," Chicago: Argus Press, 1969, pp. 49–69). When I used the secularization of the individual human personality as an analogue of social secularization, I found Thomas Aquinas' elaborate philosophy of personality development in *Pars Secunda Secundae* of his *Summa Theologiae* (Ottawa: Piana edition, 1941) an accurate guide.

The following classic texts have been richly informative in tracing the secularization process as it evolves from the Greeks into modern times: *Before Philosophy* by Henri Frankfort et al.; (Baltimore: Penguin, 1967) *Greek Science in Antiquity* by Marshall Clagett (New York: Collier, 1963); *Medieval and Early Modern Science*, two volumes by A. C. Crombie (Garden City, NY: Doubleday-Anchor, 1959); *The Metaphysical Foundations of Modern Science* by E. A. Burtt (Garden City, NY: Doubleday-Anchor, 1954); *The Scientific Revolution, 1500–1800* by A. R. Hall (Boston: Beacon Press, 1954); *The Growth of Scientific Ideas* by W. P. D. Wightman (New Haven, CT: Yale University Press, 1964); and *Evolution: The Modern Synthesis* by Julian Huxley (New York: Wiley, 1964).

David Martin has written widely and deeply about secularization theory, both in a critical fashion (*The Religious and the Secular*, New York: Schocken, 1969) and in a more positive way (*A General Theory of Secularization*, New York: Harper and Row, 1978). Very important to my philosophic understanding of secularization has been *The Social Construction of Reality* (Garden City, NY: Doubleday-Anchor, 1967) by Peter Berger and Thomas Luckmann. Harry E. Smith's *Secularization and the University* (Richmond, VA: John Knox Press, 1968) gives a balanced study of the various theories of secularization, its history, and its gradual possession of the American university.

Notes to Chapter 11

The pivotal importance of common-sense experience is thoroughly demonstrated in Bernard Lonergan's *Insight* (New York: Philosophical Library, 1957, pp. 173–244). David Tracy's *The Achievement of Bernard Lonergan* (New York: Herder and Herder, 1970) brilliantly outlines the conversion method of Lonergan so that it is revealed as a remarkable philosophy of Christian secularization. Another overall view of Lonergan—this time merely his philosophy—is furnished by Hugo Meynell in *An Introduction to the Philosophy of Bernard Lonergan* (New York: Harper and Row, 1976). *The Sacred Canopy* by Peter Berger (Garden City, NY: Doubleday-Anchor, 1969) exposes the historical power of myth to unite. Of course, Mircea Eliade's *The Sacred and the Profane* (New York: Harper and Row, 1961) explains the roots and the necessity of myth for life. Larry Shiner's *The Secularization of History* (Nashville: Abingdon Press, 1966), an introduction to Friedrich Gogarten's theology, traces the roots of secularization in the rich loam of German thought. In two volumes by Johannes Metz, *Theology of the World* (New York: Herder and Herder, 1969) and *Faith in History and Society* (New York: Seabury, 1980), one finds within his political theology an underlying theory of Christian secularization and myth.

Attempts to define modern Christian secularity are not equally successful, as exemplified by *The Spirit and Power of Christian Secularity* (Notre Dame, Indiana: University of Notre Dame Press, 1969) and also by *Sacralization and Secularization* (Roger Aubert, ed., *Concilium* 47, New York: Paulist Press, 1969) in which interdisciplinary study is attempted. The more popular style of Gerald O'Collins, however, provides insight into *The Theology of Secularity* (Notre Dame, Indiana: Fides, 1974); Paul Hinnebusch's *Secular Holiness* (Danville, NJ: Dimension, 1971) delineates well, despite repetitiousness, the wholesome life of sacralization and humanization. I have tried to spell out this aspect of secularity in *Secularization and the Jesuits* (*Communications* 4, June 1975, pp. 1–67, St. Louis: Institute of Jesuit Sources).

The sewing which goes into a "sacred canopy," or Christian supermyth, is well illustrated by Jean Daniélou's magnificent *The Lord of History* (New York: Longmans, Green and Co., 1958) and by the volume Everett Morgan has edited, *Christian Witness in the Secular City* (Chicago: Loyola University Press, 1966). The place of myth in metaphysics, hermeneutics, history, subjectivity, and particular philosophers is sketched out in *Myth and Philosophy* (*Proceedings of the American Catholic Philosophical Association* 45, Washington, DC: The Catholic University of America, 1971). The seminal study of Ernst Cassirer, *Language and Myth* (New York: Dover, 1952) endeavors to find the forms of conception in the symbolic forms of myth.

In recognizing the impact of secularization in education, Jacques Maritain's *Education at the Crossroads* (New Haven, CT: Yale University

Press, 1943) is invaluable for its linking of basic philosophic principles of education with concrete suggestions for organizing the liberal arts curriculum. Jaime Castiello, in a *Humane Psychology of Education* (Chicago: Loyola University Press, 1962), shows how the human personality is molded by a liberal arts curriculum—a concrete way of seeing secularization in action.

Notes to Chapter 12

John W. Donohue surveys the educational philosophy of work in Marx, Dewey, and Babbitt-Adler-Hutchins, before moving toward a Christian philosophy of work in his *Work and Education* (Chicago: Loyola University Press, 1959). With contemplative power, Susanne K. Langer's *Philosophy in a New Key* (New York: Mentor, 1964) takes symbolic transformation theory into language, sacrament, music, and ritual to show the human person's hunger for wholeness. A terse history of the developing human understanding of the relationship between action and contemplation is available in Emerich Coreth's "Contemplation in Action" (*Theology Digest* 3, Winter 1955, pp. 37–45). Hans Urs von Balthasar's *Science Religion and Christianity* (Westminster, MD: Newman, 1958) maps the philosophic dialectic between contemplation and action as it connects science and religion. More than communication is needed between *The Two Cultures and a Second Look* of C. P. Snow (Cambridge: University Press, 1959), as Floyd W. Matson underscores in the expressively titled *The Broken Image* (Garden City, NY: Doubleday-Anchor, 1966), a study of how social science, by borrowing root metaphors and method-routines from classical mechanics, has dispelled the liberal vision of the whole person.

The personalist philosopher, Maurice Nédoncelle, in *God's Encounter with Man* (New York: Sheed and Ward, 1964), demonstrates that petitions and grantings between two persons image the meaning of prayer between person and God, and this, in turn, exposes the contemplative meaning of liturgy. Yves Raguin's comparison of eastern and western styles of contemplation in *Paths to Contemplation* and *The Depth of God* (St. Meinrad, Indiana: Abbey Press, 1974 and 1975, respectively) stresses the strength of the western type of contemplation when it is suffused with Christian living. In *Leisure the Basis of Culture* (New York: Pantheon, 1952) and in *In Time with the World* (New York: Harcourt, Brace and World, 1965), Josef Pieper beautifully choreographs the choral dance of leisure, work, worship, festivity, and philosophy.

Notes to Chapter 13

Gordon Lippitt's *Visualizing Change* (Fairfax, Virginia: NTL Learning Resources Corporation, 1973) offers numerous examples of behavioral models in their historical development. Marx Wartofsky develops an "historical epistemology" (a philosophy of models as basic representations) in *Models Representation and the Scientific Understanding* (Boston: Reidel, 1979, especially pp. 1–39). Wayne Lee's *Decision Theory and Human Behavior* (New York: Wiley, 1971) tries to bridge the gap between largely mathematical decision theories (those used in business and economics) and psychological decision theory in his studies of game theory, probability learning, subjective probability, utility, and so on. *Rational Decision* (Carl Friedrich, ed., New York: Atherton Press, 1967) presents a survey of decision theories and their application to concrete legal decisions. Paul Diesing refuses, in *Reason in Society* (Urbana: University of Illinois Press, 1962), to identify rationality of decision simply with technical and economic efficiency, but he opens it up to the political, legal, and social realms (in particular, to integrative decisions).

Mary B. Hesse describes how *Models and Analogies in Science* (Notre Dame, Indiana: University of Notre Dame Press, 1964) are used to grip the "natural" mysteries; Ian Ramsey explores their extended use in theology and Scripture with his *Models and Mystery* (London: Oxford University Press, 1964) and moves into the "supermodel" as he goes beyond the basic work of Max Black, *Models and Metaphors: Studies in Language and Philosophy* (Ithaca, NY: Cornell University Press, 1962) to speak of the objective referent to the model. In this same area, Ian Barbour's *Myths, Models and Paradigms* (New York: Harper and Row, 1974) painstakingly compares the scientific and religious uses of these explanatory models as they shed light on myth and mystery. The prudent use of models for making decisions is eminently the work of the practical intellect, and thus John Naus' *The Nature of the Practical Intellect According to Saint Thomas Aquinas* (Rome: Libreria Editrice dell' Università Gregoriana, 1959) provides principles for understanding how imaginative and intelligible models, employed by the practical intellect, could be used in making decisions.

Notes to Chapter 14

Knowledge of the unique is a problem that is particularly acute for the historian as Ian Barbour notes (*Issues in Science and Religion*, Englewood

Cliffs, NJ: Prentice-Hall, 1966, pp. 194–202). Martin D'Arcy immediately wrestles with this problem in *The Meaning and Matter of History* (New York: Meridian Books, 1961, pp. 14–57). John Henry Newman's *Grammar of Assent* (Garden City, NY: Doubleday-Image, 1955, pp. 86–92) makes knowledge of the unique singular thing not only essential to real assent, but also basic to his whole theory of knowing. In *Verbum—Word and Idea in Aquinas* (Notre Dame, Indiana: University of Notre Dame Press, 1967), Bernard Lonergan shows how basic to the discovery of meaning in the insight is the concrete, unique image of the thing being understood. To estimate the importance of knowing the unique person or event in the eyes of the theologian, consider Karl Rahner's early method-description, *Spirit in the World* (New York: Herder and Herder, 1968, especially pp. 65–67, 268–74). For Jacques Maritain, knowledge of the unique singular event-person-thing is crucially important for any advance *On the Philosophy of History* (New York: Scribner's, 1957, especially pp. 11–15).

The acute sensitivity of historians to the problem of knowing the unique is evident in Patrick Gardiner's *The Nature of Historical Explanation* (Oxford: Oxford University Press, 1961, especially pp. 40–46) and in William Dray's *Laws and Explanation in History* (Oxford: Oxford University Press, 1957, especially pp. 44–50) as they both struggle with Karl Popper's "covering law" model of historical explanation. R. G. Collingwood, in *The Idea of History* (Oxford: Clarendon Press, 1946, pp. 140–1, 162–3, 194–6), seems fascinated with "the unique" as object of historical judgment. In *Metaphysics and Historicity* (Milwaukee: Marquette University Press, 1961, pp. 78–99), Emil Fackenheim offers a metaphysics of the unique and finds that it demands the ultimate Other.

Notes to Chapters 15 and 16

In addition to the end notes for chapter 3 concerning wisdom, I would like to add the following. Étienne Gilson's *Wisdom and Love in Saint Thomas Aquinas* (Milwaukee: Marquette University Press, 1951) notes the role of love in promoting the life of wisdom. In *The Education of Man* (Garden City, NY: Doubleday, 1962), Jacques Maritain brings the Thomistic principles of Christian wisdom down to the pragmatic practices of the humanities, moral education, terminal freedom (mature liberty), and the education of women.

Walter Krolikowski's "The Protean Catholic University," *Thought* 48 (Fordham University Press, Winter 1973, pp. 465–73), in laying to rest some tired clichés about the unique contribution of the Catholic university, sees the Catholic university as an instrument of evolution and secularization because it helps preserve human creations when it grounds them in a faith that justifies them. Neil McCluskey has edited a volume of essays (*The Catholic University: A Modern Appraisal,* Notre Dame, Indiana: University of Notre Dame Press, 1970) that, from diverse angles, define the unique contribution of the Catholic (and Christian) university—along with at least one essay of demur. In *The Catholic University and the Faith* (Milwaukee: Marquette University Press, 1978), Francis Wade stresses the unique role of every Christian university in academe: an insistence on mystery—an insistence made definite with a strong theology department, with a unifying hierarchy of knowledges, with a reasonable order among values, and with a communal majority that professes the founding faith. *The Catholic Mind* (New York: America Press, January 1976, pp. 7–32) set two eminent practitioners of teaching and scholarship, James Hitchcock and Frederick Crosson, to the topic, "How is a College or University Catholic in Practice?" Both found that the answer is recruitment of Catholics who will educate the student comprehensively and traditionally with a sense of service to the community.

In the article, "What Catholic Colleges Are For" (Washington, DC: *The American Ecclesiastical Review* 163, September 1970, pp. 154–165), Raymond Schoder sees a specific role for them—to offer not only an illuminating context of supernatural truths but also a strengthening context of moral ideals—all issuing out of a tradition of Christian wisdom. James Schall finds that the Christian university exists to make intellectually possible both faith and virtue ("The Christian University," *Homiletic and Pastoral Review,* March 1979, pp. 17–24).

Since I have placed so much emphasis on the Trinity and the risen Christ at the center of the Christian university, it would be well to note three books that survey current thought on these subjects: *What Are They Saying about the Trinity?* by Joseph Bracken (New York: Paulist, 1979), *What Are They Saying about Jesus?* and *What Are They Saying about the Resurrection?* both by Gerald O'Collins (New York: Paulist, 1977 and 1978, respectively).

In a startling book *A Christian Critique of the University* (Intervarsity Press, Downers Grove, Ill, 1982), Charles Habib Malik, long-time university professor and influential member of the United Nations, calls all universities to face the revolutionary judgment of Jesus Christ upon their powerful works in science and the humanities, and then suggests that Christians establish an institute of world-wide membership "dedicated to monitoring the university from the standpoint of Jesus Christ."

Notes to Chapter 17

The materials describing the various modes of union between the sponsoring religious founding group (RFG) and the university or college are all drawn from the following encyclopedias and entries. Because multiple examples of union were needed in order to find some common characteristics and measurements of sponsoring situations, no need was felt to update the entries discovered in these encyclopedias; the aim was not historical up-to-dateness but only inductive examples for preliminary generalizations. The three encyclopedias used were: the *New Encyclopaedia Britannica Macropaedia* (15th ed., 1977), the *New Catholic Encyclopedia* (1967), and the *Encyclopedia Americana* (1973). Information was listed in entries for the various religious denominations (e.g., Baptists, Congregationalists, Prebyterians, Methodists, and so on) or according to educational titles (e.g., Higher Education, History of Higher Education in U.S., and so on) or according to particular schools (e.g., Gannon College, Loras College, Brown University, Georgetown University, and so on).

Church and Campus: Legal Issues in Religiously Affiliated Higher Education by Philip Moots and Edward Gaffney (Notre Dame, IN: University of Notre Dame Press, 1979) ranges through liability issues, public assistance financing, preference employment principles, academic freedom, student admissions and disciplining, and property relationships. Also of great use are the "Resources and Information Exchange—Index of Materials," "Background Material for Study Commissions on Church/ College Relationships," and "Supplementary Materials: Speeches, Additions to Study Commission Papers, and Denominational Statements," which were used for the June 21–23, 1979, meeting of the National Congress on Church-Related Colleges and Universities at the University of Notre Dame. Joseph Tetlow reported on this congress in "Churches and Colleges: Recapturing the Great Tradition," *America* (December 29, 1979, pp. 422–26).

Notes to Chapter 18

Jared Wick's introduction to *Communio: Church and Papacy in Early Christianity* by Ludwig Hertling (Chicago: Loyola University Press, 1972, esp. pp. 3–14) explains the modern uses of the term *communio* for ecumenism, episcopal collegiality, and papal authority; he thus opens the way for Ladislaus Orsy to stretch this term to include the union or unifying process between church and university.

Ladislaus Orsy, in his "Interaction between University and Church or How a University Can Be Catholic and Why the Church Must Support Universities," a speech given before the Delta Epsilon Sigma Honor Society at the January 1974, National Catholic Educational Association Convention, applied the early church's concept of *communio* between churches to the relationship between church and university; I have attempted to develop this concept further. *A Statement of the Lutheran Church in America* (New York: Division for Mission in North America, 1976) describes the partnership of church and college in their common concerns.

In "A College-Related Church," *America* (September 10, 1977, pp. 122–125), John Donohue narrates the difficulties of partnership when the Methodist-sponsored university or college has high expenses and a low population of Methodist believers. Similarly, in "Catholic Universities and the Vatican," *America* (April 9, 1977, pp. 315–322), Robert Henle warns that much tolerance and much creative imagination is needed in those who constitute the Vatican's Sacred Congregation for Education if they wish to avoid stifling Catholic educational institutions. In this matter, James Provost reviews what "canonical mission" means in Canon Law for the Catholic university in "Canonical Mission and Catholic Universities," *America* (June 7, 1980, pp. 475–6). J. J. McGrath's *Catholic Institutions in the United States: Canonical and Civil Law Status* (Washington, DC: Catholic University Press, 1968) was the basis upon which a number of Catholic universities became separately incorporated. C. H. Wilson's *Tilton vs. Richardson, The Search for Sectarianism in Education* (Washington, DC: Association of American Colleges, 1971) describes how the Supreme Court upheld the constitutionality of federal grants and loans for construction, yet warned that church-related colleges and universities must be very circumspect in their relations to sponsoring religious bodies.

The works of Avery Dulles—*Models of the Church* (Garden City, NY: Doubleday, 1974) and *The Dimensions of the Church* (Westminster, MD: Newman, 1967)—provide excellent materials for comparing church and university. A sixth model, or "supermodel," of the church is offered by Avery Dulles in his talk, "Imaging the Church for the 1980s," given as a background paper for the Jesuit New York Province Conference at Fordham University, NY, June 18–20, 1980.